"...You know that the opposite of love is hate; and as for day, it's night; for white, black. But could you tell me, what is the opposite of dream?" We think hard about that, searching for what it could be. "It doesn't have any. There is nothing nor nobody against a dream. All and everyone are in favor of dreams..."

...As I tape her, I am seeing the same eight year-old child that I met and fell in love with and with whom I fall in love over and over again today. I feel happiness and the formula is a mix of love with dreams...

...If you let your heart lead you, you will never go the wrong way. Listen to it always. Better than anyone it knows about dreams, of love. The cold mind thinks; instead, your warm heart feels. ...

Parksville, BC
Feb 2008

Andrea and Stephen

Thanks for being part

of this Dream.

Keep sparking your Dream!

Carole

SPARK YOUR DREAM

Candelaria & Herman Zapp

**A true life story
where dreams are fullfilled and
we are inspired to conquer ours**

Zapp, Herman
  Spark your Dream: A true life story where dreams are
fullfilled and we are inspired to conquer ours /
Herman Zapp & Candelaria Chovet.- 1 ed. – Buenos Aires:
el autor, 2007.
  424 p.; 22.5 x 15.5 cm.

ISBN: 978-987-23134-1-8

1. Autoayuda. I. Chovet, Candelaria. II. Titulo
CDD 158.1

A Dream within a Dream. As is the case with truly grand enterprises, the translation of the book is also the fruit of team work. They translated and edited the consolidated version of *Atrapa tu Sueño* that had been published in Argentina.
The spanish version became a best-seller in Argentina, following publication in 2005.

Translated by Christine Milakovic, *cjkovic@yahoo.com*
           Richard Skaggs

Edited by Maria Laura Terrone, mlauraterrone@yahoo.com.ar
           Miranda Plante, mirandawes925@yahoo.com
           Marta Garcen

Cover Design by Fernando Vela, *fernando@velacomunicacion.com.ar*
Chapters Design by Ezequiel Lopez, *ezequiel@adentrocomunicacion.com*
Book Design by Diego Bennett, *diego@tresdigitos.com.ar*

D.R. © 2007, Herman y Candelaria Zapp
Three_americas@argentinaalaska.com
www.argentinaalaska.com

Printed in Argentina
Printing Books
Mario Bravo 835
B1868BMQ Piñeyro
Pcia Buenos Aires
E-mail: printing_books@ciudad.com.ar

ISBN: 978-987-23134-1-8
Hecho el deposito que previene la ley 11.723

Index

Prologue

I write on paper. As I do, I only hear the sound of the pencil as it leaves its trail. Writing fills me with happiness, fears, and sadness. While, I return to those moments, those encounters with those people in those places in which I listen to their music, I inhale their perfumes, and savor their foods. Like this, the pages fill with these individuals who demonstrate the immense goodness that is humanity.

There were more than 800 families who received us in their homes, and thousands and thousands who extended their hands and encouraged us. I remember one young man working in the tollbooth who was so happy to tell us our passage was on him, the woman who made all those bookmarks with dried flowers so we could earn a little to keep going... Forgive us. A thousand times, we beg the pardon of those we omitted from the book; you are and always will remain in our hearts.

There were so many who added their own link to this chain that lengthened throughout the whole of America, and reaches all the way to Alaska! Thanks to them, we were able to accomplish our dream, thanks to them, today we are writing this new book. Not for us to be remembered, simply so you, the reader, feel that you are alive and know that your dreams, too, are reachable.

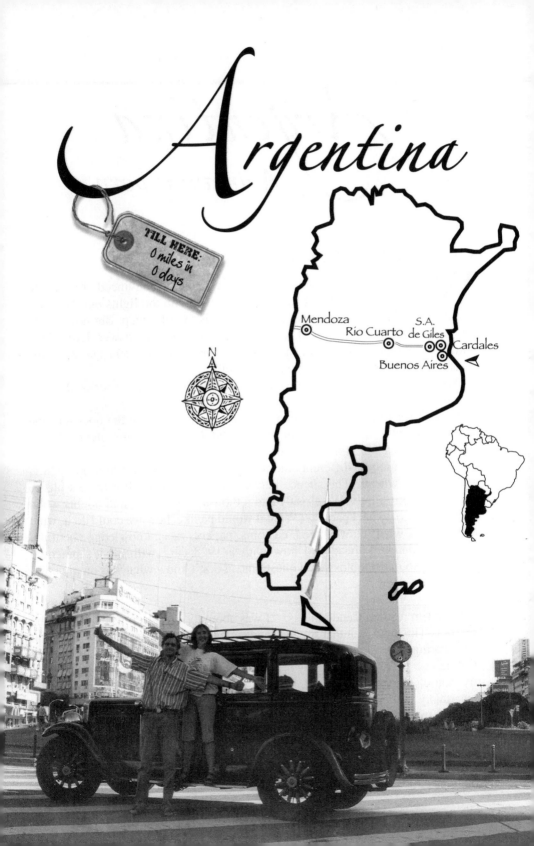

Argentina

TILL HERE:
0 miles in
0 days

N

Mendoza
Río Cuarto
S.A.
de Giles
Cardales
Buenos Aires

Argentina
A dream is born

Why Don't We Go by Car?

"Why don't we drive?" I ask her without yet being convinced of what I'm saying. It is night and we are lying down with the lights out. We have already shared a good night kiss; all that's left is to fall asleep. But now...who can sleep after this question? I remain quiet awaiting the answer. Everything remains motionless and silent in the room; the breeze is calm and even the crickets hush waiting for something to be said.

"You go in the car, and I...I'll walk!" Cande answers kind of seriously, a bit in jest.

"So wait for me," I reply, adding a touch of humor. As for the question, she says nothing else to me, I'd rather that she did, but she remains silent. At least she didn't give a "no" for an answer.

It would be unique, different, and unthinkable to go in a car built in 1928... with wooden wheels. The silence between us is complete. But there's plenty going on in our minds. We already had a thousand questions and doubts when the idea was to go backpacking. What it would be like, how we could do it, what will happen, what we will need, customs, papers, visas, knowledge about the roads, the dangers ahead and now with a 1928 car...with all it's potential problems. So many unanswered questions... I don't know what was on my mind when I fell asleep.

While I'm resting, Cande thinks: "I was about to fall asleep when I heard the question. This new idea that my husband suggest takes me by surprise. I remain here, staring at the stars I can see from my bed and lots of doubts pop up. I repeat the question over and over in my head and I visualize a 1928 car in the garage of my house, recently purchased, still unrestored, everything is old in it. The uncertainty is overwhelming. We are only two months away from the date we have set to fulfill our dream and now this new thing about taking the car sets in motion a chain of doubts. I think about them but I don't want to postpone once again my dream to travel, too many years have already gone by, yes, too many. We've been dating for ten years, dreaming about an adventure trip, ten years of planning telling each other that as soon as we got married we'd go, but now we've already been married for six years and due to fears, excuses, the house, work and other objections the only thing we've done is postpone it. No, I don't want to put it off once again. This last couple of years has passed more quickly than we could have ever imagined, without accomplishing our dreams, and without children, and we have really wanted to have them lately. When we started talking about having a child longingly and we felt prepared for that, we asked ourselves about the trip, our dream. If we go ahead and have a child now, it would be impossible to travel with a baby, let alone on an adventure trip... First let's go on our dream, and then we'll see about kids. We decided this together some months before. And now what? In a car? And such an old one..."

Questions without Answers

I wake up and keep on asking myself about my doubts. We get up as if no one had said anything the night before, I don't have the heart to ask again and while I fill my *mate* tea in the kitchen, it's Cande who breaks the silence.

"What about our departure date? If we go with the car, will the date still be the same?"

The question makes me overfill the mate. I grasp it with fear of getting burned, drink a sip to give myself a few seconds more to think of a reply.

"Yes, the date is set, we should have already left more than six years ago. The date remains January 25, 2000."

We have definitely set this date, we are leaving whether we're ready to or not because when it was flexible we never took advantage of the opportunity. Now, there are only two months before January and we feel something inside of us, a restlessness, a voice, I don't know if it's from the soul or the heart, that asks us to go on, no more postponements of any kind.

"And what about the repairs the car needs? What if it's not ready by then? How do you know the car is going to make it?" It seems that Cande had been thinking of many questions overnight, and although she hasn't said "Sure, let's go with the car," she is showing interest or at least curiosity.

"We have to get new tires, find a mechanic to look it over, fix the roof, reupholster the seats, put on a luggage rack..." I say as Cande's face express me how likely we are to get all this done by the set date, plus everything else we still have to do to get ready for the trip. In response to her expression, I cut

short my account of chores for the car, and give a list of the plus side to convince her. "You could take more clothes. We could sleep in the car and we would stop wherever we want, we could go to places that buses can't get to. We wouldn't have to carry our backpacks…"

"And what about the repair shops?" she interrupts me. I know what she's referring to, she knows I hate to go to the mechanic because I don't know anything about auto mechanics, absolutely nothing, and even worse, I don't understand why it's always so expensive to fix a car. I don't know how to answer her.

"Let's do a 500-mile test before we leave, we'll go around the surrounding area: if the car works, we go on it; if not, we go back to our original plan, to go backpacking." A comment that she likes, because now it's not up to her to deciding to go by car or not, now it's up to the car to decide if it comes with us or not.

The Test

On Sunday, two days before the beginning of the trip, we take the car out for its trial run and what a better place to start than mile zero of Argentina: the obelisk and the Congress in downtown Buenos Aires. Off to there we go from our home in the countryside, after asking Cande's sister, Ana, and her husband, Roberto, to come along with us just in case something happens.

On the way there, the questions begin, there are thousands, and many without answers.

"So what happened with the 500-mile test you were supposed to do?" asks Roberto.

"In fact, we kept working on our jobs during the week, and only had evenings and weekends to deal with the car. Beside, there was always something disassembled that the mechanic took with him to fix."

"But why don't you try it out, and then see?"

"That's precisely what we're doing right now."

"Yes, but today everything may go just fine and after a few days in the mountains, it may fall apart and your dream with it."

"No, don't worry, we're not going to fail," I say this as I do a very noisy gear shift. "Get in third, or I'm going to smash all your teeth!" I mutter to the car. The funny comment cuts off the conversation and I think to myself that it's much more successful to fail than to have never tried.

"Have you found out what's necessary to enter each country? And what about maps?" Ana asks.

"We only have a map of Argentina, I'm sure we'll find a map of Chile in Chile."

"But haven't you planned out a route, found out which way you're going and the mileage…?"

"I'm afraid of planning and finding out too much, I'm afraid of seeing all the drawbacks that may frighten us. I already have too many qualms as it is."

"But how are you going to achieve this dream? How are you going to find

everything you will need? How are you going to find help whenever you need it? What are you going to do when something happens, how are you going to make it?"

I think about his questions and he is quite right, we don't have any answers nor any idea of how we're going to solve future difficulties, but if we don't start, we'll never find out, if we don't start we'll never succeed, truly, I don't know how we're going to do it, I don't have any knowledge of mechanics, nor the roads, nor languages.

"It's true we don't know, Roberto, I have no idea…but I do have imagination, and that is more important."

"That's downright nonsense!"

"Yes? If it is, then Einstein was a moron, because those are his very own words!"

Let's Roll!

The 25th day of January has arrived. Two months didn't go by, two months flew by. The doorbell wakes us up when Carlos and Nieves, a neighboring couple on their way to work, come over to say goodbye; after them, Gustavo appears. Our plan was to leave in the morning, but there are still many things to arrange. My brother, Juanvla, arrives with his girlfriend and right away I send him to go buy more plastic boxes; also Ana and Roberto come over, and they help us to get things ready too. Then comes, Luis Berraz, one of our few "buddies" in this dream, one of the few who gave us a pat on the back when we needed them the most.

No one else comes to say good-bye, it's Tuesday and everyone is working. They all came over during the weekend and yesterday, but everyone said goodbye feeling pretty sure that they'd see us again very, very soon. Some even said, "See you tomorrow" and the optimistic ones gave us a week…at the very least, some offered to tow us back.

We load the car for the first time and what had seemed would never fit, goes in perfectly. The plastic boxes slide without a hitch into the luggage rack without rattling in extra space and the rest of the boxes fit as if they were tailor-made for across the back seat. Anyone would say we have calculated and practiced time and time again.

"Cande, say something for the camera…" Luis says while Juanvla films. "Say something now that you're about to start the dream of your life."

And Cande begins to speak, "We are beginning one of the projects of our lives…I won't say any more because…" her voice quivers. She's as happy as she is nervous. Because we're leaving without knowing exactly where we are going to, how to get there, or how we're going to do it.

We're at the point of actually leaving our place; our house, which we've just finishing building. We are leaving our friends, relatives, our jobs and our small triumphs. We're also leaving our dog, who for over a month has sensed that something was going on and wasn't happy about it at all. From the day she was born, she's been an excellent friend, a faithful companion all this time. However, at sixteen, with no teeth, poor eyesight and deaf, she just couldn't make this kind of trip. For this reason, with great anguish, we also say good-bye to her.

We say farewell to our home with a kiss and a pat on the wall. Now, all that's needed is that first step, the one to begin. I am so afraid and nervous; I don't know how I will be able to do it. Nevertheless, everything is loaded, all set, all I need is a bit of courage. I look at Cande, who is talking with my brother; she feels my gaze and looks at me. Then I ask her:

"Shall we go?"

"Let's go!" she responds. Her voice betrays she is feeling nervous, yet it sounds determined.

We approach the car, open the doors, get in and start the engine, which turns on immediately. We look at each other.

"Ready, honey?" I ask her, affectionately.

"Ready," she answer back in a confidence way.

For the first time, on the first day of the trip, I lay my hand on the gearshift, slip into first and we take off, feeling something very strong. On one hand, I feel fragile, on the other hand very powerful, because I'm going for my dream. My brother and Luis follow us in their cars while we drive away, waving to our neighbors who insist on calling us "nuts."

"All the way to Alaska!" yells our neighbor Arruti from his yard, at the same time waving his cap like a starting flag. Well, it seems like at least three people have faith in us: Luis, my brother and good old Arruti.

We leave the neighborhood, which makes some lose their bets that we'd never actually leave. Meanwhile, a back tire starts to make some funny noise. I go down to check but I don't see anything wrong so we drive on, but the racket continues, as if rivaling the clamor coming from the laughter of my brother and Luis. Cande drives and I stand on the running boards, watching, but I don't see anything. We stop and we meet with the person that I'd like least to see at this moment, Sergio, another guy from the neighborhood. He sees me lying on the ground, looking at the wheel.

"Didn't I tell you you'd never get anywhere with this heap? Do yourself a favor, go back home and stop kidding about Alaska!" As he is saying it is roaring with laughter, I feel smoke coming out of my ears.

We drive on very, very slowly and at the first gas station, we tell Juanvla and Luis not to follow us any further; from here on, we will go on by ourselves. I give a strong hug to my brother, I am breaks my heart to tell him good-bye, because although it will only be six months, I will feel like an eternity. They stand on the road, watching until we disappear from view and as soon as we can't see them anymore, we start looking for a shop where we can have the wheel checked. It is for this reason that we wanted to go on alone, so they wouldn't see us enter, on our very first day of the trip, on the first few miles, into a mechanic's shop!

"It's strange that on Sunday there were no problems and now this noise of the wheel," I am commenting to Cande as the mechanic tells the wooden spokes could be the problem.

The car seems noisier to me than when we went out for the test drive on Sunday, maybe it is because I'm paying attention to every sound. We are on the road, on the first day of our dream and for the first time driving an antique car. I want to listen to everything, to get to know our companion in the trip. Our feelings are a mixed bag; anxiety and nerves and adrenaline shake our hormones into a cocktail, the excitement is palpable, we laugh at every little thing.

"Pay attention to the gauges. The temperature can't go over 160 degrees, the water has to be around 140 and in this gauge, watch that the oil pressure doesn't go below 15. Make sure to check them because this car doesn't have any red lights that will come on."

"What about this one? What's this?" Cande asks.

"That one is for the gas, but it doesn't work, we have to watch and figure out how many miles to the gallon we get with each tank and count them on the map, how far that is and not go past it."

Now we are pilot and copilot, we two are partners in this and everything depends on both of us, just us. I look at Cande observing the gauges and then turning her gaze to the road. I cannot really believe what I am doing and more importantly with her, with whom I have been in love with since I was 10 years old…

"Cande, do you realize what we're doing. Can you believe where we are?"

"No, I can't believe it, and please say no more because I'm already incredibly nervous…" she says and then becomes very quiet. What could she be thinking of?

"Herman's question brought me back to the road again. No, I still can't believe it; I see the road and it seems incredible to be sitting here. I have dreamed of this moment for so long and here I am, doing what I have always wanted. I know that I am nervous about what we've left behind and about not knowing what to expect. We've disposed of almost every material thing, even our routine. I left my house that I love so much and where I felt comfortable. I've left my friends, close friends with whom I've shared my life, my family, whom I'm used to seeing everyday, my dog, Lucy, my constant companion who came happily looking for me at the train station when I came back home from work every day. Today, I have changed everything that was familiar in my life. From the time I opened the door of this car and sat down, it seems the world is mine and at the same time it seems it is also coming down on me. I am nervous, but this anxiety is full of freedom and of optimism that makes me believe that I can be free. Even if tomorrow we had to turn around and go back for some reason or another, I would feel free, free to have been able to leave everything behind, to go in pursuit of my dream. I feel anxious about everything. Gees, these nerves, are killing me! I am afraid of what the future will be from this moment."

"Do you realize, my love that we've left everything behind?"

"Yes, so much we've left behind and so little we've brought with us," I reply to her, feeling amazement with ourselves.

With her comment and her silence, Cande makes me think of many things. We haven't even driven 15 miles but I feel like a different person, now I am that person who I've always wanted to be, that person with a desire to hit the road and to see what's at the other end, to know different places, different towns and villages with different cultures. The one who wants to see what people do and how they live. Here I am, sitting in front of the controls of a car I don't even know, on a road that will carry me to a world I want to know.

"I Know About My Departure, God Knows About My Return"

We head west on National Route 7. We left from our house in Pilar county at 2:30 PM. A truck passes us without much effort, making us read the message written across the back end of it. At the most opportune moment we read the words: "I know about my departure God knows about my return."

We get to the village of San Andrés de Giles. Worried about the noise that the wheel keeps making, we stop at another tire shop.

"If the problem is the wooden spokes, go to Croce's, they are good people and know about this."

We have no idea where we're being sent, if it's a garage or tire shop or whatever…but if they say they are good people, that's enough for us to go.

We stop in front of an old handmade brick building that has mud for mortar built in the style they used in a by-gone era. It has only one door in the middle and two tiny windows, one to each side. I enter, blinded by the bright light outside and for a minute, I can see nothing. Inside, there's a fire burning at the bellows that provides part of the dim light. The first thing I distinguish is a huge mess; tools, wheels, woods, irons, things to repair, others waiting to be picked up, and a lot of cinders and ashes from the forge, all over the cool dirt floor making it uneven. When my eyes get used to the weak light, I can see that we

are in the best place in the world to fix these wheels; a blacksmith's shop from the turn of the last century that seems to be frozen in time, as if waiting for us to come in and repair our wooden spokes.

"This can be fixed very easily, come on, do it with me so you can learn how," Don Jose tells me as someone would teach a grandchild how to fix a bike.

I enter the ancient blacksmith shop that his immigrant father had built. The same one where now, he works with his brothers, where still today they are repairing wheels for carriages and sulkies, though only for collectors. Don Jose and his brothers Puli and Macarti, put their hands to work very enthusiastically.

"This wheel has seen many years of use, and many years out of use…those two things aren't good together," says Don Jose speaking from years of experience. "The wood has shrunk and we can't repair it just with water. But, don't worry, with a couple of shims, we'll fix it right up."

He has noticed my frightened face. I was already imagining that we would have to make completely new spokes…but, one wedge here, another over there will render the whining wheel completely silent.

This blacksmith shop functions as well as a kind of social club for the town, where the dues are one part friendship and a little of mate. It's a place to kill a bit of free time, drink some mate, watch work being done and gossip about some new topic. And the big news, in this summer afternoon, is us.

"Have you been on the road long?" I hear the question behind me as I am sharpening an edge of one of the shims on a stone.

"Well, you may not believe me, but today is the first day of our trip, we left more or less, three hours ago…"

"And you've already started having problems? Well, let me tell you, you won't get far like this."

I continue working on my wedges, the comment isn't very kind, but I'm getting used to them.

"Why are you doing it?" Don Jose asks me.

"It's our dream," my answer sounds strange even to me, not like something serious.

"A dream…in that case, don't listen to anyone but yourselves, don't listen to that dolt who doesn't know anything about dreams. If you ask opinions of others about your dreams, you will hear a speech from people who know how others should live their lives, but don't have any idea how to live their own. They will only mention the "buts," they'll tell you "that's nice, but…" he tells me while he positions the wedges in the wheels. "Only you, and no one but you, knows what you're capable of doing, those that do the least are the ones that criticize the most. So if you are criticized, it's because you're doing something," he continues as he fixes the wedge in place with only one blow. "Now this wheel is beefed up! This dream, whose idea was it?" continues Don Jose getting more interested.

"Both of us, It grew up from both of us, imagine, we've been together since we were children, we've been discovering everything together, with an enormous future ahead of us we began to imagine a trip that transformed into our dream," Cande explains.

"We read books about Marco Polo, James Cook, Magellan, travelers in boats, on horseback, on bicycles, in a jeep. Books about people climbing or diving and we always thought: 'Why not us? If they can have their adventures, why can't we?'" I tell him handing over the last filed shim, and I continue, "so, here we are. They say that life is a blank book and we are out to fill a few pages."

"Yes…life is a journey and you are beginning on the journey of your lives."

We finish adjusting the wooden spokes and the mate tea makes another round, encouraging us to stay and talk. Later, we follow Puli on his bicycle to the towns park where we can camp. It takes us some time to understand and figure out how to put up the tent since it's our first time with this borrowed tent. During the first dinner away from home, Puli is our first guest. He has to wait for us to find our stuff, see how to light the stove, and use a knife to open a can to finally share a delicious soup with us. We arrange ourselves in our new bed and new way of life.

"What a great day today! In the morning, I went to return a broken alternator and the man who sold it to me exchanged it for a better one. Plus, he gave me some inner tubes for a Model T Ford that we might be able to use. Ana and Roberto lent us their tent, their camp stove, a thermos and who knows what else. Now these people from the blacksmith shop got annoyed when we insisted on paying them…" I begin the conversation when we're already inside the tent, having no desire to go to sleep, at the same time Cande starts writing her first notes in the journal.

"Yes, everybody was wonderful. Do you know how many miles we covered on this "Great Day"? 35! We've almost made more friends than miles…"

"Don't worry, we have six months to get there"

We have worked out six months to travel from Argentina, in the south of South America, to the end of the road in the very distant North, a place on the map marked as Alaska. A word that sounds so beautiful. Between our house and

Alaska there are hundreds of places to know and 12,500 miles to cover. Six months for us, six months that seems like an eternity. We've never taken so much time for ourselves. I think, there was only one year since we were married that we left home for one whole month and that was for our honeymoon. I fall asleep, remembering about a particular moment of this honeymoon…

How Many Miles to the Gallon?

The car coughs, threatening to quit and instantly we look at the location of the needles on the gauges, they all read normal. We exchange a look that says "What was that?" And after other 20 seconds of silence, it does it again, and again, and again…and the car dies…with the impulse we coast over to the grassy shoulder.

"Do you think we might have run out of gas?" asks Cande. We are in the middle of the flattest pampa, a place where words have no echo.

"I hope so, I'd rather that than anything else in the engine." Opening the hood and trying to figure out what isn't working, beats me. Therefore, instead of heading for the motor, I go to the back, open the tank and as I do, I hear the sound of an empty tank. I look for a stick to measure the gas level, but in the pampas, there are no trees unless they have been planted, so I look around for a dry thistle and with its thorn, I measure a meager ½ inch of gasoline. "Yes, we have run out of gas," I give her my mechanical report.

"But…so then, how many miles are we getting per gallon? We should have easily been able to get to Chañar Ladeado."

"How much farther is it?"

"More or less fifteen miles, because we filled up the tank as soon as we got into Santa Fe province and we passed Firmat city 20 or 30 minutes ago…"

"Well, it seems something is off in our calculations, I'll go to this farm and see if they have any gas."

The car has come to rest a few yards from an open gate, the dogs come out to receive me in the sunny road. I continue walking till the shade of the eucalyptus without taking my eyes off the smallest pooch, I continue walking to the shade of a eucalyptus. The big ones don't worry me, as they are barking indifferently on this hot afternoon, but this small one that is eyeing my heels. A man calls off to the dogs and we greet each other as we are approaching. He looks over my shoulder and sees the car behind me on the road.

"Is the "old one" tired?"

"More than tired, he's very thirsty and won't go any farther without some of the precious juice," I reply while out of the corner of my eye, I watch the little cur who still seems very interested in my heels.

"I am on my way to town, I can't offer you any gas because all I have is diesel, I'm going to pick up a few things and come right back, so if you have the time, let's go."

"I do have time, and if you're willing to take me, I'd really appreciate it," we introduce ourselves as we climb into his pick up truck on our way head out to town. As any good country-man, his strikes up his conversation talking about the weather.

"Sure seems like the heat won't let up."

"Fortunately, while we're driving, we don't feel it, we keep fresh with the windshield open."

"With the windshield open, how's that?"

"The windshield opens to the front, it's our wind conditioner..." The man gives a short laugh.

"It opens to the front? And how fast does it go?"

"Since we've left, we've been doing about 25 miles an hour, we are loosening up a lot of arthritis and rust from sitting a long time, but after he gets warmed up a bit, then we'll go faster. For now, we're getting to know him."

"25 miles an hour...and how long did it take from your place to here?"

I realize that he repeats every word, as if he wanted to record what I'm saying. Surely tonight, we will be the topic of conversation with his family.

"This is our third day, but we're taking it easy."

"Third day? And...how far are you going?"

"All the way to Alaska, God willing."

"Ah..." This time he doesn't repeat my answer. Maybe he doesn't believe me, or he doesn't know where Alaska is, or thinks that I'm kidding him. So, the conversation about the car is cut short and we begin talking about good crops and bad crops. We get back to the car and I introduce Cande while I unload the jerry gas tank and the man walks around the car.

"If my calculations are right, we are getting 12 miles to the gallon," Cande shows me her notebook with sums and divisions of miles. I imagined we'd do more, 12 miles per gallon is nothing and this implies a lot more money for gasoline. I look at the man who repeats my thoughts.

"At 25 miles an hour, with a gallon of gas every 12 miles, all the way to Alaska..." the farmer thinks aloud as he shakes his head.

Asking Permission

We continue to cover more miles, but night will catch up on us before we can get to a town: we will have to sleep beside the road or try to camp in a farm. The road isn't our first choice: there are no trees nor water, but to ask to camp in some one's field, kind of embarrasses us. We see a thicket of trees, a signal that there's a house, and we try to find its entrance, something to give us a sign that we would be welcome, but our embarrassment stops us short and we keep on driving ahead as it is starts getting dark.

We have to decide because nighttime is not the right moment to ask. We go into a farm with an open gate and a shortly after we are back leaving a man that begs us to forgive him, because he is only a simple worker and recently hired. He's not sure his boss would like the idea. We try another place and from here we leave much more quickly when the person we encountered told us a flat out no in an unfriendly way.

We decide to try one more and if it's a no, it's beside the road we sleep. The third one settles it.

We pull up to a whitewashed house surrounded by a pine and cottonwood grove. The family is outside, hanging over the fence as if they were waiting just for us to drive by.

"Good Evening."

"Good Evening, welcome…" they tell us as they open the small gate of the fence surrounding their home. They are dressed in work clothes, something it seems they all do because none of them looks any cleaner than the others.

"My wife, Estela, our sons, Tato, Sebas and I, Hector Menna, at your service…" he introduces the family as he removes his cap to greet us. "I passed you on the road today, you were entering the farm on the hill."

The farm where they kicked us out. I would like to add.

"What a beautiful car, looks sturdy," comments Estela giving us an opportunity to tell and ask them.

"We're traveling to Alaska with this car and, since we don't know it too well, we don't want to drive it at night. It's already a bit late to get to the next town and we would like to ask if it would be all right with you if we camp here for the night."

"Of course, right over there is a cushy field, but if you'd rather stay in the house, we have space…" with tremendous enthusiasm, both of them gesture for us to come in to see and to pick the best piece of grass in the yard and also then into their home.

"Thank you, but, no, don't worry, we can make ourselves comfortable just fine right here in the yard," Cande tells them.

Along with the rabbit preserves, they give us other pickled animals followed by breaded cutlets and a mixed salad of greens from their own garden, for desert peaches from their own trees.

In the morning, as we say our good-byes, we don't know how to tell them that we in fact can't take so many vegetables, and beside a jar of each preserve is simply too generous. Once on the road, we think that if we had slept on the road, we would have missed out the chance to meet this family who opened their home to us.

Don Eduardo

We arrive in the city of Río Cuarto and continue to Picciani's house. We met in Buenos Aires and he also has a Graham Paige. Thought he's not home, his son welcomes us warmly and calls the members of the antique auto club who very shortly begin to show up. We comment to them that we need to check a noise from one of the rear wheels that sounds like metal on metal. It's Saturday and they don't know who can take a look at it before Monday.

"Eduardo Estibil would be the best. There's no one else like him, he's 76 years old, he ran auto races in this kind of car and then he prepared cars for racing, now he's a specialist in restoration," says one of the members.

"Let's go see him!" I accept with enthusiasm.

"I don't think it's going to be possible, this is his vacation time and everybody respects his schedule. No one dares disturb him during his down time."

Another member says: "But, you know, I think we ought to tell him. He might get annoyed, but not as much as if he hears about this trip, that they needed help and no one asked him."

Almost everyone thinks the same, so they decide to call him. While they're talking with him, I imagine that since he is so strict and professional, his prices might be as high as their esteem for him.

"He says to come to the house, he'll figure what the problem is and depending on what it is he'll see if he can fix it or not."

In a caravan of four cars, we go to his house. An old man comes out of the cool shade of his covered porch, without any gesture of happiness, climbs up on the running board asking me to drive forward as he looks at the wheel. He gives me a signal to stop after only a few yards, and gets down. The club members approach him and he says to them, shaking his head with his back to me.

"They can't go on like this." I overhear. The faces of the members show pain, as if they had been part of this dream from the beginning.

"Isn't there something that can be done?" asks one leaving the rest in silence and we all direct our gaze to the face of the expert.

Eduardo takes a look at the car, then to the troublesome wheel, lets out a deep sigh, then looks back to us and says to the group, "We need to pick up my assistant." That was enough, everyone offered to do it.

Opening the door of his shop reveals three magnificently restored autos, an impeccable shop, and a well dressed assistant with an apron and goggles. Everything inside me tells me that to open a shop during vacation, plus all the rest is going to cost a lot. Surely, he will fix the car but I'm not sure we'll be able to continue the journey with empty pockets. While his mechanic takes off the wheel, Mr. Eduardo cuts the side of a metal can to make a bushing, which he easily fits into place and the noise disappears. He also comes across other problems with the motor such as an oil leak, stripped threads on the axel and, a detail here, a detail there that I want to stop because if everything gets added up on one bill, we'll have to leave the car as part of the payment.

The club members go outside, to get out of the way. One takes Cande to buy film and for a moment, they leave me alone with Eduardo, who is adjusting the brakes sat on his knees. He takes advantage of this moment to tell me, "This is not the way to make a trip like this. You have to be prepared, with a rebuilt engine, new seals, new wheel bearings…" he speaks sincerely and with the wisdom of knowing what he's talking about, "not with a car in this condition. Furthermore, with a car of this make, you have to carry parts, you're not going to find them…" He is not giving me a very good diagnosis of the car.

What could I say? He is absolutely right, but I feel that my motives are much stronger than reason. I think and I feel that you shouldn't worry about parts for the car; you need to worry about life…because this doesn't have any replacement.

"Don Eduardo, thank you for your concern. Look, I don't know how to tell you, but this is all I have. If I do everything as I should, I would never do anything. How am I going to do it? I have no idea, but I have to at least give it a try. Alaska is a long way and perhaps this car may not be the right one, but if it were not the car, it would be the time, or the money wouldn't be enough or anything else. My grandfather drove livestock in Patagonia for thousands of miles crossing rivers, mountains, deserts, and snow. One time he told me that every time he started out, he didn't look at the miles left to do, but only at the next mile. I don't look at Alaska because it frightens me, I only look as far as the next town."

Eduardo doesn't reply, he continues with his work. He knows he's right but I'm intrigued by his opinion about what he heard me say. He calls his assistant and tells him to go buy a new bolt for the wheel. He leaves rapidly following orders. The elderly man walks to his worktable cleaning two washers with a rag, leaving them on the table, impeccably. He sighs deeply and tells me:

"The best memories I have about my racings are not from the ones that I won, but from the ones that I entered with a car put together and readied with what ever I could find or with whatever somebody gave me. Those are the races during at night, while all the other drivers were sleeping, I was under my car, fixing it. The other racers had teams that followed them with everything necessary; I only depended on the goodwill of the town mechanic. I lost many races but I still felt as if I had won them, I may not have gotten first to the finish line, but you don't know the triumph I felt just to complete it," his words quiver, mixed with emotion and memories, breaking his speech. He takes a deep breath, steeling himself against tears, and continues, "Even if when I got to the line, there was no one waiting for me anymore."

"Boss, look, I found the bolt, the exact same one," the assistant breaks the silence and the emotion, and we all come back to finish the job.

Along with the assistant, the rest of the club members come back in. They have plans for us; an interview on the radio, dinner at the club, the night at the

Picciani's and in the morning with everyone in their old cars we will all meet at the gas station on the way out of town to make a little good-bye parade for us.

Alaska is the goal, but every town is a triumph.

"How much do I owe you, Don Eduardo?" I ask fearfully.

"A post card from Alaska."

Among the Hills

We set out on another day on our trip and behind us trails a caravan of cars that bid us an emotional farewell. Little by little, it vanishes from sight. While we travel surrounded by some beautiful scenery thru valleys and over hills, we ford our first creek. As the wheels get wet, we hear a strange noise. We drive across and stop. I go back for water which I carry in my hand and throw it on the front wheel, I notice the water evaporates rapidly, the surface is hot, and evidently there is a problem. Maybe there is some wheel bearing that wants to quit the trip? We continue until we get to a house, listening to the complaining wheel the whole way. On the street we start to dismantle it. Right away the man of the house peeks over the fence and invites us to work in his yard. Incredibly, he has a '28 Model A Ford, the only antique car in town and, as an added bonus, he has mechanical knowledge.

I take apart the wheel under his direction and when he sees the bearing his opinion is, "It needs to be changed no matter what." He makes me take apart the other wheel, and gives the same advice for this one. He invites us to eat on the riverbank a picnic of gigantic sandwiches and to sleep in his home while we wait for Monday.

In his car, we go to the city of San Luis. As soon as we get inside the largest bearing store and put our worn out bearing on the counter, a salesman takes a look, frowns and tells us, "We don't have any of those…they don't even make those anymore." He even measures them and looks through all the catalogues, but comes up with nothing. "I have no idea where you're going to get those."

His colleague comes into the store and happens to hear his comment. He looks over the other man's shoulder at the bearings and asks: "Have you checked those old boxes that we got from that old man who closed his bearing shop years ago?"

A few minutes later, we leave the store with two new antique wheel bearings still in their original boxes. Furthermore, we didn't have to pay anything. We received them as a gift, just as the store had received them.

And so we head on for the mountains, with new wheel bearings, many repairs on the car and a strong desire to cross our first border of the trip.

"I'm worried. Is the whole trip going to be like this? Out of the five days we've been on the road, three of them have been spent fixing the car."

"Yes, I know but did you notice what happened? Everything worked out perfectly."

"Anyway, I'm still afraid, because if this keeps happening how can we manage in all those countries where we won't know anyone nor the place? What are we going to do if it happens in the mountains or in the desert, which we're going to cross in a few days?"

"We'll just have to wait and see. I know it wasn't a good start, but maybe this will be it."

Hello Aconcagua!

We are getting closer to a big test in the trip and our nerves show it. Through the windshield appear the mountains and the closer we get, the more insurmountable they look. The Andes are ahead of us and we must cross them. I ask the mountain for its permission and we begin the climb among very high peaks. The winding road is quite steep, and the car, which has been out of shape for so many years, goes up very slowly, passing through many tunnels following the road's lead. I am afraid that at any moment the car will quit. We both cheer. "Go, go, go!" as if encouraging a tired runner. Cande pulls herself up on the dashboard, off the seat wanting to help. Maybe she thinks she would weigh less that way. We are tense, there aren't many towns around here and we depend a lot on the push we get going down to help us back up.

The scenery is so beautiful that Cande wants to stop to take pictures at every corner, every hill. Though I prefer not to put more stress on the car. But no need to worry! We're climbing so slowly that she jumps out, runs ahead, takes her pictures, films, and hops back on board as I pass.

Among the huge mountains we make out a small hill of conical shape, and quite imposing despite its small size. On its summit, we see a cross which renders us silent. The hill contains something priceless, which is not a wealth of minerals nor gold nor silver but something much more valuable. Surrounding the cross are the graves of the mountaineers who, in their attempt to conquer the summit of the nearby peak Aconcagua, lost their lives.

They sacrificed their lives although they weren't soldiers, and they hadn't received any orders. They could have turned back whenever they wanted without being called traitors. Neither would they have been called heroes if they had reached their goal, but for me they are true heroes. They gave their lives for the sake of life itself, pursuing their dream. No one told them to go, nor would anyone have said anything if they hadn't gone, but they had a voice inside them telling them what they had to do. They had to take those risks, because it is when one risks the most that one feels the most alive. If they hadn't attempted to climb Aconcagua, they may still be alive today. But in what way? They weren't trying to conquer the mountain; they were striving to conquer themselves. Many men have set out to sea and were never seen again, many men have set off for distant lands, to a certain destination and never gotten there, and others have never even returned. I

feel a little afraid, but not as afraid as I would feel if I didn't try, just sitting there with my longing to live. I would rather die trying to live than to die without having lived.

Ambassadors

"No, without a permit, you may not take this car out."

"What permit?"

"You know very well what permit I'm talking about, the official permit to take a collectable car out of the country, since it's part of our national heritage. If you have any doubt, go and speak to the boss," says the employee, pointing in the direction of the office.

We do know what permit he's talking about, it's an authorization granted by Customs, necessary to take out any car built before 1940. It's a very bureaucratic and frustrating process due to the fact that the government wants to stop the export of antique automobiles. These papers include valuation, pictures of parts, information from the Ministry of Culture about the history of the car and many more papers…papers we never requested.

Cande wishes me luck, and gives me a sweet kiss, and I march off to the office. We are terribly afraid they tell us no. At our first border crossing we're already having problems. Yesterday, in the city of Mendoza, Tini and his brother, while giving us a super service to the car, told us about several instances of people who wanted to cross to Chile with their antique cars but had to turn around because they didn't have the necessary permit.

I knock on the door, I try not to lose faith in whatever has brought us this far, and strengthen my resolve to not leave with a "no" for an answer. Confident and calm, I go in, asking God for the right words to make my request. We've completed nine days of the trip, have driven 780 miles and so many things have already happened, they can't tell us "no" now.

"Are you the one with the old car? What make is it?" the boss asks me as soon as I enter.

"It's a 1928 Graham Paige..."

"I have two antique cars, a Model A Ford and a Chevrolet. Where did you say you're going to?"

"If God grants it and you allow me, to Alaska". The man drops his gaze as if he were thinking, which only takes five seconds.

"Go on then." I am left astonished standing there in front of him. Never had I imagined that it would be so easy to obtain a "yes."

"I appreciate this from the bottom of my heart, you have no idea how important this is for us. There are already many people behind this dream and now you have become one of them."

The man nods, he stands up and gives me a strong handshake. When I get to the door, he tells me something so important which feels like he just put two elephants on my shoulders.

"Go, but never forget, you two will be our ambassadors."

I don't know what to say. I walk out, I close the door while in my head I repeat this new designation. On one hand, I feel wonderful, but on the other hand I don't know if we can live up to this, its an enormous responsibility. From this moment on we will be representing our fellow countrymen in every act, movement, word, every thing we say or do.

Candelaria sees my "happy birthday" face, which I cannot disguise, she realizes we got permission to continue.

"We're going to Chile!" she begins shouting while she hugs me, "I knew we'd get permission, I just knew it!" she keeps yelling and then comes up with a little song. "When I'm on my way to Chile, over the snow-capped mountains..."

"Why were you so sure?" I interrupt her song.

"Because everything was working out, the people support us, wave at us on the road and the truckers honk at us. I feel like the queen of the carnival waving at everyone all the time."

"And me? I feel like the king."

We burst out laughing.

He Who Face the Unknown Discovers Treasures

"Now you follow us," two men dressed in green interrupt our happy conversation. One of the uniform labels reads: "Gendarmeria," they are the border patrol.

"Yes, we'll follow you but don't go faster than 75 miles an hour, in the mountains, because we go fairly slowly," Cande answers with a laugh and begins singing again while getting into the Graham. "When I'm on my way to Chile…"

Luis Gaitan and Marcelo Bustamante saw us at the Inca Bridge, where they invited us to sleep at the border post. They've been waiting for us at the customs house and now they lead us where we need to go. They give us the captain's quarters. Although it's tiny, we're treated like kings we take a warm shower and they cook a delicious soup for us, without accepting any help.

"OK,… ahhh, well, here we are in Las Cuevas, at 12,500 feet above sea level and we are sharing a very welcoming dinner with two friends," Marcelo made a toast:

"I would like to say that it is an honor for us to have you here, because you both, in some way or another, are going to represent us in distant parts of the world. Let me say that it is more than an honor to be the ones giving you the farewell from home," Luis tells us while looking us in the eyes.

We leave Argentina with a wonderful farewell and with memories of people whom we had never seen before but who gave us a hand to get our dream off the ground. Nine days ago, we left our house, now we're leaving our country, going into the unknown. But the one who faces the unknown will discover treasures, and we set off in search of those treasures.

Chile & Bolivia

Copacabana
Madidi
La Paz
Oruro
Sucre
Arica
Potosí
Iquique
S.Pedro de Atacama
Antofagasta
Copiapó
Concón
Santiago

TILL HERE:
874 miles
in 11 days

CHILE
VIAPANAM
I REGION
5

Bienvenidos a La Paz

Chile

Between the Ocean and the Mountains

Doorway into the Unknown

We made it to Chile!! It feels like a big achievement, it implies arriving in the first country apart from our own plus, having succeeded in getting over the crest of the Andes. Now it's time to go downhill so we take a road appropriately called "the Snail" because there's one curve after another on an extremely steep grade. We see a few cars on the shoulder of the road waiting for their engines to cool down. The view from the top of the mountains is majestic and Cande gets down to film, eager to capture the car among the giant peaks. I go down further and further while Cande is shooting me as I take curve after curve in the serpentine road. When I reach the bottom and look up at her, she is a diminutive speck, so going all the way back up to get her might just be the melting point for the engine, so I make a signal for her to come down.

"Is it *enpana*?" a man from a car with Chilean plate asks. I'm just 20 miles from Argentina, and I cannot get what people say already, I thought we all spoke the same language.

"I'm sorry, but I cannot understand what you are saying…"

"I asked if your *burrita* is broken. *Cachai po*?" what he said failed to clarify my doubts. Since I don't have a *donkey* with me, I suppose he's referring to the car.

"No, I'm just waiting for my wife. Thanks."

"Oh, is your *polola* walking down?

"Yes, she is," I respond without knowing whether 'polola' has a good connotation.

" *Tai po*" he replies and leaves.

The first encounter with someone outside my country reveals that we may speak the same language, but the words are different. How is it going to be with those who speak a completely different language?

While I'm thinking and getting more doubtful, Cande gets out of a car.

"This is Esteban and this is his girlfriend. They're going on vacation to Viña del Mar. They stopped to pick me up as I hitched a ride."

We get to the town of Los Andes where we stop for the first night. Then we reach Santiago de Chile; we visit museums, plazas, and parks, always on the lookout for a safe place to park the car since we don't know what might happen. Because of a noise in or near the gearbox, we look for an antique car collector whose name we were given in Mendoza. Right away he tells us he can help us, and even though his people are on vacation, he calls them and very quickly three enthusiastic mechanics start to make a bushing. I thought they would hate us for interrupting their vacation, but I was mistaken.

At night in Concon, we get some typical empanadas to eat on the beach. When we get there, we find ourselves barely illuminated by the faint light of a half moon. We have our "fanny pack" with us, and all our personal papers are in it, the documents for the car, and all the money we have with us about $2000. For fear that we might be robbed, we hide the bag under a fast food vending cart that is closed. We eat our empanadas in this beautiful night, listening to the waves crash against the shore. Some dogs come to keep us company and in the search of a few bites of an empanada. Later, we play with them on the soft sand.

In the morning, we get up a bit later than usual, at around nine. We are deciding what to buy for breakfast when Cande gives me some change to put with the rest of the money in the fanny pack…

"The fanny pack!! We forgot the bag!!" I shout at Cande desperately, as I take off to the beach. I run like crazy, thinking of everything at the same time, realizing what a stupid thing we did. How could we forget it with everything in it? How could we have made such a terrible mistake?

When I get to the beach completely out of breath, I don't find the desolate, spot we had left the night before, but one full of people. On top of that, the Navy is practicing maneuvers with a helicopter over a big boat, there are sailors on the beach and many curious observers. Exasperated, I go to the cart to look for the little bag, but I find nothing. I feel the whole world is coming down on me, I think that everything is lost. I am completely demoralized and at the same time, I am furious with myself, how could I have been so stupid!

Cande appears, she sees my long face, she is kind of nervous but tries to find a solution, so she says to me, "Let's look around, maybe someone just took the money and left the rest…"

We go in opposite directions; Cande heads to the only restaurant, maybe someone turned it in there. While walking among the people, I cannot believe that we put everything into one bag. Why didn't we leave something in the car? Now what are we going to do? Why this terrible start after only 15 days into the trip? Why does it have to end like this…and so soon? Does not God want us to do this? On second thought, this stroke of stupidity has nothing to do with God. The people don't look at me as I curse, they're concentrated on the helicopter and the sailors being lifted in and out of it; I ask around, but no one has seen anything.

I move a few more steps among them and see something blue in the yellow sand, it's only about nine feet behind a group of onlookers and I run to see what it is…Yes!!! It is! Our lost bag! I pick it up desperate, it looks like it's been chewed on, surely those dogs got a hold of it last night. I anxiously open it with shaking hands and it's intact, with everything inside! Everything!

My one thought was to thank God. How is it possible that no one saw it? How could it be safe and sound, with everything still in it so many hours after we left it? I run to Cande waving the bag in my hands. When she sees me, she jumps with a scream of joy, arising the curiosity of the crowd. To celebrate, we go to the best seafood restaurant right on the waterfront, blowing our budget for the day, but we don't care at all.

As we continue north, the scenery turns more and more arid. A very old well-worn truck in need of many repairs pulls up along side of us, and gives us some kind of signal. We wave and smile back. He stops behind us, then speeds up even with us again, showing us a melon through his window. Considering that he wants to sell it to us, we make signals to tell him we don't want it. The man accelerates and drives away, but we can see he has stopped ahead and is waiting for us beside the road, with the melon in hand. We stop to say "no, thank you, we don't want to buy a melon."

"Welcome! Please allow me to present you this melon as a welcome to my country," he says, and as we thank him, he asks, "Where are you going in this car?"

"To the end of the road."

"Where?"

"To Alaska," Cande clarifies.

"And where is that?"

"Where the horizon, the sky, the sea and the land all become one."

After we say goodbye and get back on the road, we realize that we didn't even introduce ourselves. It seems that for him, it was enough to know that we were not from his land, and for us he was an ambassador to his place.

We hug the Pacific coast which takes through villages with beaches and small fishing towns. We stop at their local markets to have that well-known seafood they can make, presented in such a variety of colors and flavors.

When the mountains meet the sea, the road undulates, we drive steep wave after wave. On one ascension, no steeper than any other, the car loses power until it just doesn't go any further. I start the engine again, but it fails, so we coast downhill backwards to a shop serendipitously situated right at the bottom. It caught my attention the large number of cars that there were around the small shed.

Immediately, the owner of the shop comes out from under a truck, informed of our arrival by a couple of chained dogs.

"What 's going on with the *burrita*?" he asks after saying hello, offering me his forearm so I don't get dirty as I shake his oily hand.

"She's very tired, doesn't want to go up the hills."

Right away he knows it's the carburetor and when he takes it apart, he removes so much muck that he looks at me astounded.

"I don't know how you ever left home without at least cleaning the carburetor, my friend...this has been filthy for years..." I don't know what to say, it simply never occurred to me.

Before leaving, much of the car service was done by Carlos Gil, a man who seemed to fall from heaven, like an angel. He is a mechanic and the owner of several Graham-Paige cars.

His grandfather was an official mechanic of the make, and after we told Carlos we were going to Alaska with the car, he began to come home every weekend just to help us get the car ready. However, due to the lack of time, we left many things unresolved; one of those, I can see now, was to clean the carburetor.

The man cleans it with a little gas from the tank and a bit of pressurized air, then he puts it back together. When the time comes to pay, he doesn't want to hear anything about it. When we get into the car, he says:

"Alaska...I don't know if you'll get there quickly in this car, but I know you'll be able to do it."

He spreads a bit of his faith to us. Sometimes it seems that other people have more confidence in us than we do in ourselves. With ease, we charge right back up that hill and the many more ahead of us.

We are inside the car, ready to go to sleep in Bahía Inglesa, a picturesque village right on a beach, I am more than concerned making notations and sums in our little book. So, I comment to Cande, "If we've only gone this far in 23 days, we'll never finish the trip in 6 months, we have to plan how many miles per day or number of days per country," I am nervous about this topic, and Cande, on the contrary, isn't and tells me very calmly, "But we have to relish the places...enjoy ourselves, we can make up the time later."

"We should be more strict; 13 days more in Chile, 15 days in Bolivia, 25 in Peru, another 20 in Ecuador...Central America 30 days, Mexico, the U.S. and Canada a month and a half...and stop counting because otherwise we won't have any more money to count...we must try to force ourselves to do more miles and fewer detours."

Cande lies down and closes her eyes.

"Or we do a certain number of miles each day, or spend a certain sum of money for the mile we make..." I continue talking to myself.

In the car, we are very comfortable. We can recline the front seat all the way back thanks to a hinge we installed before we left. We have the windows down, but no one can peep because Cande has adapted the curtains and mosquito nets. After a couple of nights on the road, we started putting the cloth cover over the car even if it was not raining, to reduce the attention. Without the cover, people come up to the car and talk about it until very late at night, and early in the morning, without knowing we're in the car trying to sleep.

At four in the morning, we hear some guys approaching.

"What's this?" we hear, as they curiously begin to lift the cover.

"It seems like a carriage, it has wooden wheels..." answers another while uncovering the wheels. Attempting to stop them from lifting the cover any further, without any warning, I blow the horn twice.

"Run! Run! Let's get out of here, this thing has an alarm!" We can hear them running away scared as we laugh.

It's the Silence Speaking

We enter the driest desert in the world; there are places where it hasn't rained in years, where we don't see any form of life, only the land markers announcing the passing away of miles and crucifixes announcing the passing away of lives in an accident. In spite of that, I feel really well behind the wheel: I am filled with the marvelous sensation of freedom, this feeling of really doing something for myself, for us.

Cande and I had good jobs, which is why we were able to build our own house, a home that means so much to me since it's something I never had with my mother, but always wished for. When I got it, there was still an enormous emptiness that wasn't filled with the house, I didn't want to complain nor seem dissatisfied, after all, I had the person I love most right beside me...but there was something else I wanted out of life...I believe now this is it...to be on the road, on an adventure, on our way to Alaska, to our dream.

Cande and I have much in common, and those things we don't, complement each other. We both grew up in the country. She grew up in the countryside near the city of Buenos Aires where the land is completely flat, in the famous pampas of Argentina. Her coming was a total surprise for her parents, big brother, and two sisters. She was the youngest and most spoiled member of the family. When she was a child, her family wasn't accustomed to going on vacation, but she had the good fortune of often being invited those three summer months to different places; to the sea, the mountains, other farms... Her parents never refused any kind of invitation, because they knew she always enjoyed herself and also because she had the opportunity to know, learn and grow in the best way possible, gaining a bit of knowledge of the rest of the world. Now, thanks to this, she feels completely free.

Cande often reminisces about being with her siblings, out in the country going to gather tadpoles in the pond, getting into mud up to her knees, riding horses, playing with the dogs, playing house, and knowing without a doubt that when her mom rang the dinner bell, the food was ready and waiting on the table. She and her brother and sisters had the freedom to disappear for hours without their parents knowing where they were. This way, they learned from the time they were very small to be responsible and to watch out for themselves, instead of being over protected.

When Cande was eight, her big brother died tragically, and the whole family moved to the city, but they were also in search of a better education. Her way of life changed greatly, but her vacations continued just the same.

I also grew up in the country. My mom separated from my father when I was a little more than a year old. She left me in the farm with my aunts and my grandpa so she could go to work in Buenos Aires.

"Old papa", as we the grandchildren called him, brought us up among ponies, horses, cows and dogs in a place with mountains, creeks, pampas and lakes. When I reached school age, my mom took me to the city; first we lived in the neighborhood of Chacarita in a borrowed garage of a house, where mom put two beds. We were very poor, but I didn't see it that way. I was simply happy to live with my mom, although she was already at work when I woke up to go to school and when I went to bed at night as well. However, when I woke up every morning, I knew she had been there because she always left me something by the pillow, a pencil, a piece of candy…something to tell me that even when I couldn't see her, she was there.

When her work began to get better, we rented an apartment in downtown. I remember with great joy the first vacation we took together when we went to the sea. I had the sea and my mother all to myself for the whole day.

When I was ten, my mother remarried. Now I had something I always asked for, siblings. However, the best thing was that when I came home from school, she was there.

With a new father and small siblings, everything changed. I was sent to a private school, we took vacations together, there were no more hand-me-down clothes from my older cousins. Now I had my own brand new clothes, and although I never had a great relationship with my new-father, I will always be grateful for my younger brother and sisters and most of all for having more time with my mother.

"Look, it seems there is something over there" Cande says calling me back to the present.

We stop after almost 200 miles of seeing nothing, in a small gas station that is the only thing for more than 300 miles, an oasis for autos. Night is coming and we go inland diving on the rigid desert floor, to get a fair distance off the road and set up camp. When we turn off the engine and we get out, there is complete silence and it surprises us. There is no wind, nor birds calling, just the sound of absolutely nothing. Since the sun is setting, we get out the chairs to enjoy it. We can perfectly hear the noise of the camera when the timer goes off and takes a picture, after that sound, silence returns. We start to listen to our own breathing, the whistle of the air as it enters our lungs. Searching for more sound, we find the beating of our own hearts.

As soon as the sun is gone, the stars begin to appear and as never before, we find ourselves under an incredibly starry sky. Hundreds of thousands of stars accompany us as we cook. We put on our music in the middle of nowhere, and very loudly begin to sing our favorite songs. This invites us to dance to the beat feeling immensely free. We only stop singing and laughing when our throats can't handle it anymore, and stop dancing when our bodies fall from exhaustion.

In this immensity there is nothing, only us and we want to feel ourselves. There is nothing to see, only us deep inside ourselves.

We climb to San Pedro de Atacama, a tiny village very close to the Bolivian border, in the shadow of the Andes Mountains.

The houses of the village are made of mud, built alongside unpaved streets. The place is magic and because of this, many tourists come here. In the area where there are many artists selling their goods, Cande slows down attracted by some handiwork.

"Are you the Argentineans in the old car?" an artist asks while he squats over the fabric to hand Cande a piece she wants to see.

"Yes, how do you know?"

"Because one of the girls you picked up in the road and let ride on the running boards is my sister."

"What a coincidence. Poor girls, bless their hearts, we found them hitching on a dirt road, where we saw only one other car."

"She had gone to sleep in the caves that have been in use for thousands of years by the aborigines as a meeting place and for ceremonies." This piques our interest. Cande continues to look and after a short silence, we hear more. "Have you ever watched the sunset and then waited up to see the daybreak?" he asks us.

We arrange to meet at eleven that night, the hour they cut the electricity in the village. The artist and his friend climb onto the running boards and his sister sits in the front with us. By the "old road" through stunning scenery, we go to the valley of the moon.

Good Day Sun, Good Night Moon

On foot, we climb some enormous dunes to arrive at the ridge of a hill, where everything around us is a lunarscape. We are not alone, there are others who have heard about the sunsets in this place and together on the same hilltop, we all wait to watch the end of another day.

Like us, there are many people taking photos of the once-in-a-lifetime setting of the sun. Even though we know there is no camera that can capture all of what we're seeing and enjoying, in time, the photos will help us recall a good memory. In the desert, when the sun goes down, it turns cold. In search of a shelter from it, we go back down to the small valley where the car is parked. Along with other young people, we build a fire with wood carried in because here there are only rocks and sand. The music and the pisco we drink, show up kicking out the cold. We share our music and for some short time they share theirs. Some of us break into dance. The artist, who is the first one to start dancing and the last one still standing with each song, takes a breath, comes over to us, and says, "Today you said to me, 'what a coincidence' when I told you it was my sister you picked up on the road. I call them signs, the sign of synchronization in alignment of everything in time and space for any given event to occur. Pay a lot of attention to the signs, they could lead you to live unimaginable things and point out the things you should avoid."

I don't really understand what he's telling me, who knows? maybe he's living a "mystical" moment and he wants to share it with us. I listen and take his words with a grain of salt. Of which, after a swig of pisco, there are more.

"Humanity in the XXI century still doesn't know what the nucleus of the earth is made of, and it's the same humanity that is almost totally unaware of what the nucleus of each one consists of. Perhaps you went out to look for your own core. Each frog lives in the pond of their choice. You left yours perhaps to find another one that suits you better. While you walk and travel this world, don't forget to greet each place when you arrive. Say: 'Hello, sea', 'Good afternoon, river'. Humans must learn again how to talk to everything that surrounds us. Even silence in this desert has something to tell you."

I did this when I was younger with my dogs and the ponies. But, I never greeted a place. I don't understand what he's saying to me or it could be that I'm not at the right level to be able to understand, or maybe it's the alcohol going to his head...

"I don't know how your life was, or why you made this decision to travel, to complete your dream, but go calmly. Because when you take life in your hands, when you give an opportunity to life, that same life gives itself so everything will come together for you."

Letting the hours pass the sun comes to us once again, Cande and I sit together in the sand while I think about what this young artist was trying to say, and why he was saying it to me. He doesn't know me, and I don't know him either, but I feel that he gave me some advice like he would to a brother. One thing that has me thinking is that when I tried to thank him for sharing his words, he said, "It's not me telling you this, it's the echo of my soul repeating the words that those along the road of life have taught me."

As we are about to leave Chile, we realize how misled we were before coming here. We thought that because we're Argentineans, we would be treated badly and ever since the first day we couldn't have been more wrong. Our governments have made us hate each other so much, we nearly went to war and we were willing to kill one another. Now, standing in the land of our former enemies, we don't see them nor feel them like that.

Bolivia

So Close to the Sky

As Happy As Children

W e enter Bolivia in Tambo Quemado. In the indigenous language of Quechua, *tambo* means a place for a traveler to rest. But not for us, on this border at 15,750 ft. above sea level, after making it through a terrible night, we feel totally bombed. The effect of the altitude makes our heads feel like they're going to explode. Fortunately, the formalities at the border are fast and simple to complete. When we leave the offices, there are four people sitting on the running boards on one side of the car and four sitting on the other side, as if they were park benches, plus there are some others hanging around too.

We ask for a map of Bolivia, but there isn't any. We will have to use our Chilean map that continues a bit into Bolivian territory. We see that in 20 miles there's a village and in 40 miles there's a city where there's sure to be a gas station. We leave as quickly as possible, anxious to get to a lower altitude. We drive past a gas station, but we pass without thinking twice, we're only interested in going down farther and farther.

This stretch of road is beautiful, the llamas and guanacos watch us curiously as we pass by. Snow capped peaks surround us and a desolate landscape is in front of us, but as for going down...we descend very little. We are in the Bolivian high plains, a highly elevated, gigantic flat expanse in the Andes, it seems our bodies have no option but to acclimate themselves.

We begin to see houses, built completely of mud, with thatched roofs, matching the corrals. We don't find any tree, we only feel cold and the altitude. The village marked on the map is a cluster of houses without roads. The buildings don't follow any set plan or direction; we don't see anyone, only one truck. The noise of our engine calls the attention, we see people open their doors to sneak as we go by. Many houses have no windows, the ones they do have are small. There is no gasoline.

As we go on, Cande looks at the flocks of sheep mixed with goats and some llamas. She is looking for black sheep, because black sheep means black wool and she needs some to finish a sweater she is knitting for me.

"There! Stop." She signals a flock that is at the base of the mountains, quite far away. The natives who are tending them are even farther away…

"You want to go all the way over there?" I ask with no desire to accompany her. The altitude makes me unwilling and the last thing I want to do is go for a long walk. At this time, I would like to be as strong as the Graham who laughs at this altitude and goes confidently, as if it's nothing.

Cande doesn't insist and she goes… Twenty minutes go by and she still hasn't even reached the *Cholita* woman, who doesn't move any closer either to Cande…I wish they'd get a move on. Finally, she gets there and other eternal twenty minutes pass. Surely, something

is happening because they are not moving yet. Maybe she doesn't understand Spanish? After a while, they begin to walk in my direction bringing the whole flock, which takes long but at the same time it is so beautiful to watch. I don't notice when from among the bushes a man, another woman and two kids appear, who, far from one another, round up the sheep. It frightens me to see Cande alone, so far away, what if there are more? I had better go to her.

After a long while, the shepherd makes it to where I am. He is very short. He has a loaded sling in his hands. It is hand made of woven yarn with two ropes a yard and a half long with a flat place in the middle where the stone rests. With one hand, he arranges the lengths of rope and swings it around over his head, at the moment of launching the stone he lets go of one of the ends of the rope.

"Could you teach me how to do it?"

With pure joy, he launches one stone after another. The sling hums in the wind, the stone whistles through the air, whacking the selected bush, breaking the branches. Happy to demonstrate his skill, he gives it to me to try. He selects a stone, places it as if there is only one way to put it in the sling and I give it a whirl, I do it, although it lands a long way from the bush battered by the man. Cande finally reaches me.

"She has some wool in her house, which is that one over there…"pointing out a small dot on a hill.

"Why did it take you so long to get back? What was going on?"

"The woman was very suspicious of me, she didn't want to talk to me, she spoke to me in Quechua and made gestures for me to go away, but I insisted that all I was after was some wool that I wanted to buy and suddenly she began to negotiate in Spanish. Very quickly, she learned how to speak it…"

The shepherd watches over the flock, every once in a while slings a rock close to a sheep who is wandering close to the road; and it runs back with the herd, knowing that the next one would hit her ribs.

He doesn't stop talking, but the woman is serious and doesn't say a word. He says she is his woman although she doesn't treat him very well. I want to buy his sling and he consults in Quechua with his wife. I can see she challenges him.

"You don't have one right now, come back another day, my wife is very distrustful…"

"What are you doing?" the shepherd asks us.

"We're traveling, we're getting to know things…"

"What are you seeking?"

What are we seeking? We never thought we were looking for anything. We're just traveling, but…what are we seeking? I don't know…

"We're seeking to discover," I answer him.

"Seeking to discover…" thinking he drops his gaze, "Discover what, every search of discovery has a purpose, a reason."

What will be the purpose of our search? Maybe we are trying to know ourselves, to learn who we are, maybe we want to know what we're capable of, how far we can get. How many of our fears we can overcome. The shepherd stares at me dead in the eyes and I believe he knows what I'm thinking…

The other woman takes about an hour to go and comeback with the hand spun yarn, with all the smell of a sheep and flecks of every plant in the zone twined into it. None of this matters to Cande, it's "rustic" just like she likes it and she continues to haggle a bit more about the price.

We ask them before we leave where we can find some gasoline. They don't answer us. Cande peers at the map and reads the name of the city, to which they respond with a signal down the road and a "just a bit."

We reach "just a bit" much later…we were more than just a bit worried about getting there because we are almost out of gas. I envision that we are stranded in this desolate place, no food, no gas, winding yarn into a ball.

The city is small; we stop at a shop, where they have a little of everything and even serve food. We ask about a gas station, but the shopkeeper only shakes her head. Great, now we really are in trouble.

On the road, we have only seen trucks. In this small city, we see no cars, nor paved roads, there are only two trucks and they use diesel.

"How can we find some gas, ma'am?

"In my other shop."

I never imagined this lady would have a branch and with gas service. Knowing that we will get fuel for the car, we get something to eat, rice with llama.

The woman comes with us in the car with her layered skirts and her hat which, she doesn't take off, although it touches the roof and looks quite uncomfortable. With her and her baby, who she carries on her back, plus another child in her lap who is six years old. In the back, Cande makes herself as comfortable as she can, among all our stuff. We go with the idea of paying whatever she asks as we have no other option, but when she finds the small tank it only costs slightly more than usual.

After only a few miles, in which we drop a little in altitude, Cande points out a little adobe house, next to the road surrounded by corrals in the back where two llamas and a donkey watch us curiously as we stop. Night comes. The little place turns out to be a grocery shop, bar, restaurant, lottery ticket outlet and general store, provisioned with everything even though it only measures about 9 by12 feet.

Later, a small, rickety looking bus full of passengers stops. The first one to enter the bar and ask for a "caña" -an uncured brandy- is the chauffer, who already seems tipsy. Outside, it is almost dark and very cold. Those that get out of the bus are wearing ponchos and wool caps that cover the ears. They are typical of this area with two cords that can be tied under the chin. Additionally, some put another hat over the cap to protect themselves more from the cold. But when I look at their feet, it makes me cold: They wear sandals made from old tires that leave the whole top of their feet exposed.

Many who don't go in gather around our car. We're getting things ready to sleep in it. We quickly stop what we're doing so as not to miss the opportunity to talk to them.

One of them is wearing a red poncho, which is the most striking; he is the first to respond to our greeting and he asks us, "Good evening, are those spokes made of wood?"

"Yes, they are," I take this opportunity to ask, "Excuse me but why are you wearing a red poncho?"

".We're on our way to a community meeting and I am the elected representative in ours, that's why I have this poncho."

"So are you the Chief?" the man looks at me in a way that makes me feel ignorant.

"A chief is another thing; in our communities we don't have them. We are elected for a certain term."

From the top of the bus I hear the bleat of a sheep and when look up, I see several as well as chickens in cages and dozens of bundles making the bus seem like a rolling tower.

"Is the community meeting for something special?" the chauffer continues to drink, giving us more time to talk.

"Yes, the natives in this area, before the whites arrived, had more than enough food and riches, now all we have left is a little of our land and our customs. Today they want to take from us the little we have, our coca leaf plantations. They say that far from here they use it in another way, different from our use and with another intention. Because of this, they want us to stop planting it. For thousands of years we have used it. It helps us in our work, against hunger, against cold, it is part of our tradition and we want to continue it. So we're going to the meeting with the idea to begin blocking the roads if it's necessary."

Everything was going along just fine until he got to the part about closing the roads...I was mentally supporting the movement of preserving his traditions until he mentioned blocking the roads...why now, just when we get to Bolivia. We shouldn't complain, we couldn't bring ourselves to be that selfish.

Since the driver continues asking for more drinks and ignores the call of the passengers to get back on the road, they seize him by the arms and taking him to the bus, they sit him in the driver's seat and they take off. When the bus pulls up to get onto the asphalt, it lurches almost tipping over, the chickens squawk while it wobbles from one side to the other. We are grateful not to be driving at this time of the night, although it might be more exciting because Cande instructs me to lift my arms, drapes them with yarn and begins to wind it into a ball. I'm sure that travelers like Marco Polo, Darwin, and Humboldt never had to do this!

While she inspects the yarn for thorns, twigs and anything else, I think about the shepherd's question, which I never would have expected from a sheep herder, and something I never even asked myself. What are we seeking? Are we looking to measure our capabilities? Drop the routine? What could it be? Who knows? The goal of the trip is to fulfil our dream but the shepherd made me see that we're also on the search for something else... What could it be?

Carnival

We get to the city of Oruro in time for carnival! We arrive the day before it started and are unable to find neither hotels nor motels with any empty rooms, not even one. It's been four days without taking a shower or sleeping between sheets and blankets. The altitude with its cold makes us very tired. We wish for a bath and a bed. We go to the town hall to ask about homes of families who are renting rooms. Just as we enter, there is a woman asking why they haven't sent anyone to her so she takes us to see her house.

Her 16-year-old daughter and 12-year-old brother accompany us like guides. The city is a whirlwind with thousands of street vendors preparing their posts; there are musicians in the stands with trumpets, drums, guitars, and charangos, a kind of small guitar, each group dressed in the same ponchos. The whole place is jumping with relentless joy, everyone is smiling, singing and dancing.

The rich smells of the food tempt us. We sit together sharing a bench with some others in front of a huge cooking pot, and we ask for two portions and two drinks. First, they serve us the food tied up in a small plastic bag, we need to have with our fingers. The next thing that we cannot believe is how they serve us the sodas, emptying the bottles into small bags, where they put a straw before being tied up.

The first day of carnival arrives and we are in the stands early. The participants in the parade keep filing by without stopping, one after another. Rows of the Diablada, the Tobas, the Morenada and many others dressed in strange disguises, the meaning of each of them is special. They are very picturesque, brightly colored. They are the same costumes they have been using since the very first carnival. This is a native fiesta. The goal of the participants isn't to win a prize but to honor the Virgin of Socavón, patron saint of the miners, and it's in the direction of the church that everyone is parading.

Between the ranks of parade entrants, there are lapses of time, which become an active war. Hundreds of water balloons start to fly along with foam and shots from water guns. It's a battle of one grandstand opposing the other across the street. In this onslaught, it's impossible not to get wet. A passage from a new parade division offers a little relief from this aquatic war.

Cande buys a can of foam, and in an act of bravery or craziness, walks calmly to the opposite stand and begins to spray the people while walking by. Revenge doesn't wait. There is a dousing from water balloons that burst on impact with her, plus there is foam and some guys that follow her with their water guns while she is running away. She comes back two minutes later unrecognizable. I can't see her face because of all the foam, only her unbridled laughter tells me it's her.

Under the stands there are local Cholitas girls filling balloons and selling them in bags. I get a couple of bags and during a lull in the parade, I go to the middle of the street where I start to attack a group of tourists who have been continuously lobbing balloons at our side. Between my throws, I have to dodge the ones they are throwing at me, they are all crowded together in one spot and I get several wet, but…they are many more and have all the provisions they need. Like this, as is any war, we all loose, we all end up drenched. I come back with more…only that this time I turn my back on my group of enemy tourists and commence to attack my own side that laughed uproariously

every time my enemies made a direct hit. In the end, I am completely saturated from being attacked from both sides. I am having a ball, everyone is laughing, celebrating with a particularly accurate balloon or a dodged one.

When I am out of balloons, I begin my retreat and everyone applauds my craziness. I lift my arms in a triumphant salute to the stands, and at that moment everyone roars with laughter as I receive a direct hit with a balloon right on my head.

We forget about the altitude and the cold because we are so happy and enjoying ourselves. Our inner child has been reborn, having broken the steel casing that had imprisoned it. The truth is we don't recognize ourselves; we are once again those childhood friends, laughing our heads off about being so wet, hearing how all the people are laughing at us, and us laughing at them. We had forgotten how to be children and today we are once again amusing ourselves greatly.

We follow the parade brigade in the street and see partying all around. The people stop us just to offer us a drink, a beer, or to throw a water balloon, until we end up at the church. Although outside everyone is dancing and festive, inside the church the faces show something else; gratefulness and petitioning. Our tears fall to see the parade entrants come into the church with emotion. They drop to their knees as they enter and advance to the altar, with their costumes and their musical instruments, tears in their eyes but also much joy. They kiss the Virgin of Socavón and they go back out to the plaza in front of the church where the groups disperse and join the people, and the party continues while the bands mix their music with the rest. We dance! The whole town dances for three straight, non-stop days of fiesta.

We leave the city, there are many drunks in the streets, the car is in a garage and we are on a bus bound for Potosí. It's a very long trip. We talk to each other many times about the carnival, about how great we feel after releasing our inner child. When we were kids we could do anything, but we lacked the strength, now we have it we think that we can't do it. At some point, life stops being guided by one's inner child and instead it is guided by an adult altered by the environment, where to be that adult means not doing childlike things and being responsible. When in reality our greatest responsibility is to be happy. We are responsible to be happy and if that means we have to act like children, let's welcome it.

A man seated almost at the back of the bus starts to sing a melody in Quechua, and I feel that if you want to sing, you have to sing like no one were listening, dance as you wish as if no one were watching. If we only do what is normal for others, we'll all end up doing the same, sitting around in silence, wearing the same, in a world without smiles or songs. If only those who know how to do things can do them, no one would do anything, because everyone at some time would have to learn. Don't miss the moment, laugh much, if it's big belly laugh all the better, be a child, without restricting your laughter, spontaneous, fresh. Don't tie yourself to your environment, forget your prejudice, laugh, dance, sing, and you will feel how fabulous it is to be a child once again.

Thankful to the Pachamama

We keep going in the bus, traveling this enormous distance over crumbling roads with over-loaded buses on a trip that has become like a test of endurance, especially how long one can "hold it". Six, seven, even eight hours could go by without stopping, bumping through holes that press even more the need for everyone to go to a toilet. When no one can take it another minute, the driver pulls over, but he stops in a place where there are no bathrooms…not even a bush.

"Men over there, women this side…" the driver organizes in the middle of the night and that's it.

The native women from the area don't have any problem, they are dressed in seven skirts, layered one over the other that touch the ground, all they need to do is squat and they're ready. However, it's not the same case for Cande and the other tourists dressed in pants…harder still because the locals don't want to miss the show. Among themselves, even though they don't know one another, they organize themselves as a screen for each other.

Beside Cande on the bus, there is a very old woman who doesn't stop talking to her for the whole trip. Cande doesn't understand a single word she says, because she's talking very enthusiastically in her own language, Aymaraic, to which Cande simply agrees by nodding her head occasionally.

We finally get off the bus in the market of Potosí at six in the morning. On the ground, we see about forty sheep and goat carcass split down the middle waiting for purchase. During the Spanish colonial time, the city grew so fast that there wasn't another one in Europe as grand and rich as this one. The wealthy Spaniards spent their money building churches; there is almost one per block. There is a hill, only one, conical: its ample veins of silver seem to have no end.

We go to the mines, which continue to be exploited, but the veins are almost exhausted. The miners working in them are barely surviving. Using mining tools from the era of the Spanish conquest, and lamps with an open flame, they carry the ore out of the mine on their backs. The miners, in exchange of gifts, let us visit their tunnels. The entrances are small drilled holes, and once inside the mountain, we get down sometimes on foot, other times on our knees, and sometimes crawling on our stomachs, down ancient wooden stairs, by ropes… There are holes in the floor, old wooden poles supporting walls or holding back the mountain from collapsing. Every once in a while we hear the rumble of dynamite. It's a strange sensation…shivery to be here. I feel like an ant in a ready to crumble anthill.

When we reach the spot where the miners are, we see they all have a cheek full of coca leaves they are chewing. We give them more, along with some dynamite and other gifts. One takes a pack of cigarettes and gives us a signal to follow him. He leads us to the "Uncle", for whom he lights a cigarette and places it in his mouth.

"The Uncle" is a representation of the devil. For them God is in the heaven above the earth, the devil reigns under it which is where we are. They venerate the devil with everything they consider vices, like cigarettes, alcohol, and coca leaves, and so he doesn't get mad for women entering the mines, they have to give him a kiss.

Potosí is also having a festival. It's the celebration of the Pachamama, people give thanks to Mother Earth for their harvests and the success of their business during the year. Everything is brightly colored, the street vendors set up all over the sidewalks offer petals of flowers, colored paper confetti, herbs to be burned which are also colorful. It's a feast for the eyes. Every place of work, if it's a garden, an office, or a truck, it's decorated with colored petals, garlands, confetti, and in all of them, they offer liquor and they burn incense. This is how they give thanks for what they have received and to ask for another fruitful year.

We go out to take a walk with a German guy and a Swiss girl and wherever we pass, we are invited to come in dance, and drink a "caña", liquor that is 90% alcohol. Before taking a sip though, we have to offer some to the earth, to the Pachamama, with which we take advantage to pour out almost the whole contents of our glass leaving only a few drops to drink.

With the celebration and the alcohol, the drunks are still in the street at sunrise. One, who comes walking up the narrow sidewalk as if following the zigzag path of a snake, falls face first to the ground and his head hits my shoe instead of the granite cobblestones of the street. I believe that man owes his life to my shoe.

"My Place is Special…"

We meet back up again with the car and drive to La Paz, one of the highest cities in the world. We go to the farmer's market where products from all over Bolivia are offered and you can eat typical foods of the country. We share a couple of portions of skinny chicken with fried bananas and a lot of fruit with a shoe shine boy.

We finally get a map of Bolivia, a little late, but like all travelers we are captivated by maps, so we're happy. On it, we mark the route we've covered, imagine where we might go next, and little by little the map converts into a companion that we grow to love. We always have it at hand, and it drops to pieces because of the number of times it is opened and closed. With tape, we help keep the country together. We preserve it like a diploma when we cross over to another country.

We want to get to the city of Copacabana which is on a lake and to get there we have to cross by ferry boat. A ferry I don't have much faith in…but this same ferry carries busses so it must be able to sustain us. After we get to the other side safe and sound, we can appreciate the road that follows the lake, it is gorgeous. The rains have caused a landslide and there are enormous rocks in the road, which the passengers of the busses help move so they can go on.

Here, no one can notice the passage of time. We see there are still roads of stone made by the Incas, farmers use the same terraces and irrigation systems that they constructed, and, as a means of transport, llamas are still in service.

We find a tiny hotel and park in the interior courtyard. It's very cold and the hotel has no heat, only a pile of ponchos over the beds. The showers, as in most places in Bolivia, have an electric heating apparatus attached right to the end of the shower pipe, but in reality, they merely keep the water from being absolutely freezing. We change rooms three times before we find a water heater that works. Now it's time for me to happily take a shower, and Cande's next while I write. I smell something burning, what could that be? Cande opens the bathroom door, almost asphyxiated; the hot water heater is on fire!

We go out to walk around Copacabana, where there is much to see. We follow a stone mountain path up to small plots, where we meet many people working the land. Happy to see us there, they invite us to watch how they farm. They work with the same tools the Incas used. The only change is the point, which is now made of metal instead of stone. They need two people to turn over the land. One strikes a tool which separates a clump of earth, and the other in front with another tool turns the grass under.

On the hillside of the mountain, there is a little old man, with a younger woman and a little girl of about six. The three of them are working together to turn the soil. They immediately invite us, the older man asks me to help and when he sees I've got the hang of it, he leaves…and I'm here working. "This is what I get for being curious," I think.

"And the man?" I ask.

"My uncle? He might come back…He is helping me because I'm a widow," in fact, he was helping, I think.

"And all this land needs to be tilled?" I wave my arm over part of the field to know how much there is to do.

"My part of land to work is only 36 feet by 24 feet, it's all the land I own. It's only a little but it's not bad because there are people who have nothing, plus we also have two pigs fattening up," as she speaks, her daughter hugs her legs.

"Are you going to cook them?"

"No, they're not for us, they're to sell."

Cande plays tag with the little girl and a baby llama. I work another hour without stopping, the earth is good, which is significant considering the hundreds of times seeds have been sown into it. In my eyes, the woman has nothing but still she's grateful for what she has…maybe because I grew up in a society that taught me to want more and more without seeing what you already have, without seeing what others don't have. It's around lunchtime and with the hike and the work, my appetite is more than fierce.

"I have something to eat if you would like some," she says as she lays out a piece of cloth.

We sit around it for the picnic. She shares with us a few small tubers, toasted seeds, and boiled white corn that with my appetite look delicious. She tells us about her place and her land which she deeply loves.

"If so many people visit my place, and if they look so happy to be here it's because it's special…it must be one of the most beautiful places. For me it is. And you, do you like it?"

"Yes, it is truly stunning," we respond as we look at the lake, the town of Copacabana, the thousands of colors of the crops all over the mountain.

With a dark sky we get back to the hotel, we didn't see the Inca museum, but we saw and lived a day as Incas. The country-woman gave us much to ponder and with our new thoughts, we write until very late into the night. We go to sleep but first, we say our prayers, this time not asking for more, this time to offer gratitude for all our blessings.

The Inca Empire began with Manco Cápac on the Island of the Sun situated in Lake Titicaca. This is where we are, in what used to be his house. Facing us, we see the Island of the Moon, gorgeous in the morning sunlight. We stay in a very tiny inn where a Colombian tourist shares her exquisite coffee with two Canadians, an Italian and us. We exchange names of places we've been to, and things we've done. But the Colombian woman with a sincere ache in her soul, doesn't recommend us to visit her country.

"In my country violence rules, there is no law, there is no one to believe in, without any doubt, they kill. We are about 40 million inhabitants destroyed by only a few hundred thousand of guerrillas, paramilitary, and corrupt governments."

"If 40 million are 100%, then 10% is 4 million, so 1% is 400,000, those 100,000 are one quarter of one percent of the total population," I calculate in an audible voice.

"It's always the same story. Why is it so that such a few can dominate the majority?" Cande questions.

No one recommended us to go to Colombia, but never had someone from Colombia spoken to us like this. On our part, we had already discarded the idea of going there before heading north. How difficult it must be to speak like this about one's own country, one always feels something very special about his own motherland…like we heard yesterday from the Bolivian woman who feels very loving toward her land, her place, and it makes her very happy to see people from other places coming to visit her place.

The Virgin Candelaria

In front of the church there is a kind of festival, there are many people with their cars parked.

"Which is better? "The Virgin" or insurance?" A man asks me while he decorates his truck with garlands, flowers, and colorful things.

He leaves me speechless, with all the faith in the world they come to ask for security for themselves and their vehicles. Car insurance isn't obligatory in Bolivia and for their own insurance against anything bad, the people gather with their cars to the Virgin of Candelaria, patron saint of the country, for a blessing from the parish priest. The man and other people spread this faith to us and we take our car, which is beginning to look beautiful under all the flowers, balloons and colored papers. People give us more decorations and even throw a glass of caña liquor on it.

A priest with many springs under his belt, with Nordic characteristics and accent, advances, dressed in his Franciscan vestments without slowing down, baptizing the cars on one side and the other with a rose he wets in blessed water. He stops mouth open in front of the Graham.

"I learned how to drive in one of these cars!!!" he tells us. First, he walks around it two times then begins to baptize it all over. He wets the rose time and again in his blessed water, making us open the doors to stick his nose in. Remembering something from his adolescence, he looks and looks wetting absolutely everything with his rose.

"Let's bless the motor. Open it..." he tells me waiting to satisfy his own curiosity.

We happily open it, and enchanted, he blesses everything, even Cande who is filming, dousing everything, camera and all.

"What's your name?" he asks her.

"Candelaria."

"The same as the virgin," he comments happily.

"Yes, but this one is not quite a virgin," is the comment that slips out of my mouth. This puts only a big grin on the priest's face while everybody else laughs.

A Border in the Way

We are on our way to Peru hugging the coast of Lake Titicaca. At the border we need a few photocopies, so I leave Cande while I go to a little town over the border of Peru in a "little motor taxi" which is a motorcycle with two wheel in the back and a seat for two passengers.

I realize I have crossed the border without completing any formalities, and I am not alone. There is a constant stream of people passing over and back carrying things here and there. Successfully, I get my copies. Nevertheless, the man in the customs office insists that we leave the originals of our papers and we keep the copies instead.

"How am I supposed to give you the title and the exit permit from Argentina?" I say but he doesn't want to hear it and detains us... We leave the office feigning some excuse and Cande and I go out to get some fresh air to relieve our jangling nerves.

"But what is he thinking? How can he ask us to leave the originals? How can he be so incompetent?" we say to each other, trying to blow off some steam.

People standing around the car are looking for some answers to their questions but the way we're feeling we don't have any desire to talk to them...

"Maybe it would do me good to answer a few questions," I tell Cande and I approach the car.

I immediately forget about part of my problem. A man with a short white beard asks me why we are waiting to go into Peru.

"Here, in the office there is a man who doesn't want to listen to reason and asks for something we can't give him."

"Did you try to speak to his supervisor?" No, we hadn't thought of that, we got involved in the problem with that person.

"It might be that the person who is asking you for those papers doesn't know much, maybe he's new, he doesn't know what you're trying to do...or who knows what's going through his head... Go, speak to the supervisor and tell him about your journey, your desire to enter Peru and he will surely be able to resolve this little nuisance."

It seems that the ones who didn't want to be reasonable was us, now this man with all the peace in the world shows us we were not looking for a solution, only for the problem.

"Obstacles, inconveniences and unforeseen circumstances don't look at them as problems, see them instead as a test. A test of strength, faith, of love and of desire. Problems don't exist; we create them. Every problem has a solution and if it has a solution, why is it a problem?"

We go back into the customs office.

"Excuse me sir, are you the head of customs at this border?" I ask putting emphasis in his work and his position.

"Yes, I am, what can I do for you?"

"My wife, Candelaria, and I are trying to accomplish an incredible journey in a 1928 car going all the way to Alaska." I also give importance to what we're doing and I continue, "We have come from Argentina with a great wish to enter and get to know Peru, but we've run into a small inconvenience that surely you will be able to resolve." I asked in the exact way suggested by the elderly gentleman, whose name I didn't even ask.

"I'll see what I can do."

In five minutes, we have everything ready to go into Peru.

Peru

TILL HERE:
3282 miles
in 2 months

Tumbes

Trujillo

Lima

Paracas

Cusco

Arequipa

Puno

N

REPÚBLICA DEL PERÚ
MINISTERIO DE AGRICULTURA
INSTITUTO NACIONAL DE RECURSOS NATURALES

SISTEMA NACIONAL DE AREAS NATURALES PROTEGIDAS

Reserva Nacional de Paraca

Turismo Convencio
Adulto : S/. 10
Válido por tres

INRENA
RUC 13136726

Peru

Empire of the Sun

Go light!

We drive to Puno, a town on the shore of Lake Titicaca. The scenery looks very similar to Bolivia. Mules moving people, people moving mules, animals piled up with sticks and sticks piled up on people. Sticks and grass… the load they carry on their backs is so vast, that anyone who sees it from behind would swear that grass walks. We also watch women tending the flocks while spinning wool…and on their backs they carry infants. There is movement and life wherever we look.

As soon as we get into Puno, a girl who searches out tourists begins to offer us things. She doesn't even wait for us to stop the car. When she realizes she has our attention, she climbs onto the running board while we are still driving and continues with her introduction about everything there is to see and do in the city.

"Do you know where we can sle…" before I can even finish my question she bombards me with a long list of hotel offers.

"Hotel Inti is economical and has very nice service and Manco Cápac…"

"Miss, excuse me, but we sleep in the car. What we need is a place to park and sleep."

"Ohhh!?!" exclaims the girl while looking at the interior of the car. Observing that we only have things and more things in here, she might be supposing that we sleep sitting up as we are now. So, Cande explains how we rearrange the stuff to be able to recline the seat.

Finally, the youngster guides us to a parking lot. If we pay for a night, we can stay in the car, but once they close the gate, we won't be able to get out at all. There are also the watchmen with their dogs, chickens and roosters sleeping in here. It's impossible to get to sleep because of so much barking, and when the dogs finally seem grow quiet, the roosters take over, even though it's still long before daybreak.

In the morning, we put aside our strong desire to make a big pot of chicken soup and decide to take a boat with some other tourists to the islands of the Uros Indians.

This place is quite unique. It's hard to believe but it's a floating island constructed and re-constructed frequently by the hands of the aborigines, with the same material that they use to make their boats and houses: reeds! They cut the plants that grow in the lake, which have many bubbles of air in the stalks and they layer them over the others until they form an island.

As this is something appealing, the Uros live off the tourists and there is one handicraft display after another. I prefer to walk among the houses, where the Uros really live. The few constructions are low and tiny, with only one room. Near one, something is smoking. I see they are cooking a couple of herons in two ceramic pots that are placed over a ceramic fire pit. Surprise! The fire is burning thanks to the bulrushes.

I try to see what they have inside their homes, when a man opens the curtain that functions as a door. He notices that I am curious and gives me a signal to look while he holds back the curtain. The bed is a mat made of woven reeds... I glimpse some clothes hanging on the walls, a bag with potatoes and onions, and a couple of tools...nothing else.

"Where do you keep the rest?" I ask curiously.

"There isn't anything else, this is it. If you have too much, you sink," he replies. I feel like what he's telling me is not only referring to this floating island. "The more you possess, the more problems you have. If you go lightly, you go freely," he comments while he stirs his food. "Everything you need in your temporal life, the world will offer you temporarily. Life is not eternal and nothing belongs to you eternally. All you have didn't belong to you, and all you have won't belong to you."

What could I say? I never expected a comment this incredibly clear and so contrary to the education of my society.

"Are you a traveler?"

"Yes," I answer.

"Life is a journey, where we're all travelers; we're all just passing through. Don't burden yourself, don't sink, lighten up."

"But there are some things I need to carry. I am traveling in a car."

"God made the world with all you might come to need and when this happens, it will be there for you, have faith. Now it would be better if you go or you'll miss your boat."

While we head back, with the words of the Uro still echoing inside of me, I tell Cande, "We're going to have to get rid of some things, we are carrying too much. I believe that it would be better for the car to travel lighter, and also for us."

Upon returning to Puno, we decide to get rid of some pots and plates, some books, some parts for the car…even placemats to set the table and in this way; little by little we end up surrendering a giant box of stuff.

Four Soles

Back in the city, we both need to take a good shower. We hear about places dedicated exclusively to renting showers that are not too close to us. We see a bike-taxi and ask the price for the trip.

"Up to there, two soles," the driver tells me.

After figuring out that's about 70 cents, we climb aboard. The bicycle taxis are quite charming and you can find them by the hundreds all over the city. They are bicycles with two wheels in the back and a seat, just big enough for a couple, sheltered by a gaudy awning. They are painted various colors with decorations attached and simultaneously function as roving publicity for mom and pop shops. The driver pedals and pedals…we get to the showers more quickly than we thought.

We revel in the glory. The water is hot and sprays out in abundance. There's nothing better than a hot shower after some days without one! But the good time is short lived…quickly the place starts to fill up with folks. The hot water disappears and even the cold water dries up.

I get out of my bath with goose bumps, without rinsing my hair, and of course, in a bad mood. Cande, with conditioner in her hair and ready to burst into fury, is on her way to complain. Shortly she comes back. "This explains why the attendant is behind bars, if they could reach her, they would throttle her!" she comments without hiding her anger.

In the end, we go with all our irritation still intact. We stop another bike-taxi driver. Just to make sure, I ask the driver again how much it would be.

"Four soles, sir."

"What?!? Four soles?" I shout, "To get here they charged half of that!"

The boy, with his eyes fixed on his feet and almost in a whisper tells us, "It's because now, chief, it's all up hill…"

I feel badly, very badly, because what he said is true. The street goes up and up. He pedals with great effort and sometimes he even gets out to push us. I feel worse and worse the whole time. When we get there, I give him five well-earned soles.

To the Empire of the Sun

We leave the city with the plan to sleep on the road; better that than being among singing dogs and roosters suffering from insomnia. We drive until the sun hides. We stop at a gas station. It's interesting to see that in Peru it's difficult to find multi-national gas stations. They're almost all family owned, something very nice, because each one is built according to the owner's taste. On the other hand, the gas isn't so wonderful, because it's mixed with additives, which stretch the product to the maximum, to the maximum profit of the owner.

We enjoy the sunrise while driving the road toward the Empire of the Sun, capital of the Inca world. We pass Mount La Raya, divider of the waters. From one side the water runs a short course to the Pacific; on the other, it's in for a long expedition all the way to the Atlantic. We are over 14,000 ft above sea level. Without much effort, we jump a small creek that little by little goes along its path growing until it ends up as the river with the greatest volume of water in the world: The Amazon. I whisper to the river: If I meet you again I can say to you, "I knew you when you were this small."

We get into Cusco in the evening finding it with its lights burning. We go directly to the central plaza, marveling at its beauty, despite the pain of knowing that the city was built on destroyed Inca temples, palaces and buildings. We leave the car parked and enjoy ourselves walking through the mixture of empires.

"Would you like me to guide you through the city?" asks a small voice that comes from far below. A boy of eight or nine insists, "If you wish I can guide you, and...at your will."

"At our will?"

"Yes, at your will," and without even waiting for us to say yes. He begins his speech and walking tour.

"When the Spanish, led by Pizarro, arrived they came across a city they had never dreamed of. They came seeking gold and treasures, and what did they pillage first?" questions the boy. Silently we think about what it was, but the lad answers himself immediately. "The Temple of the Sun, because its walls were covered with sheets of gold." We follow him getting closer to the remaining walls of the temple.

"Here you can appreciate the stone of the twelve angles. Why is it called this?" he interrogates rhetorically, letting a few seconds pass. "Because if we count, we can see, yes, it has them...one, two, three..." he counts each angle while pointing out each one with his finger.

The boy is amazing; he knows the whole speech by heart. Every time we ask him something, he answers and right away resumes his talk. He takes us to visit churches, the corner of vipers, and that of the lizards, all without ceasing to relate his stories and legends.

Quite unexpectedly, "Well, here we end our tour. I hope that our little walk was to your liking and I wish you a happy stay here in my city, I bid you farewell," he tells us completely naturally. The same way he extends his hand expecting our "will".

From a Frog to a Prince

We're looking for a parking lot where we can sleep. In the first one they don't let us sleep in the car; we don't like the second one because of the price and the treatment. Finally, we ask a woman walking along the street if she knows of any place. She points to a green gate, near the central plaza, although it doesn't say it's a parking lot. After knocking on the door for a good long while, an elderly woman opens it for us.

"I'm sorry, but it's for city residents. We don't take in tourists because we only rent by the month," she explains to us.

At that time a young girl approaches. Upon hearing our accent she asks us excitedly, "Are you from Argentina?"

"Yes, we've driven from there."

"Seriously? My boyfriend is Argentinean!" she comments very enthusiastically. Her face gives her away; she is in love!

"Terrific! Does he live here?" Cande asks her.

"No, in Argentina, we only see each other a couple of days a year," just saying this, she becomes sad.

"So, you have to marry him next time he comes, then he won't leave again," we answer.

She likes this comment, it brightens her up and she asks us, "What are you looking for?"

"A place to park the car, and, if it's possible, we'll sleep in it."

"Oh, let me go talk to my mom."

"Your mom?"

"Yes, she's the woman you were talking to. Wait a second, let me see what I can do."

She comes back and tells us with a smile, "No problem, you can stay here." And, this isn't the only surprise, "If you want to, you can use our bathroom and the kitchen." She adds while she directs us into the courtyard of her colonial house.

The next day, while we fix breakfast in her kitchen, the young girl keeps us company. She's very content, she's received a "ring-ring" from Argentina.

"My boyfriend and I can't afford to talk but we greet each other by phone every morning. I dial his number, let it ring twice and hang up. He does the same. This way we let each other know we're thinking about the other," she tells us, while she joins us in a round of mate. "And you, when did you meet?"

"We were very young. She was eight, and I was ten. Cande has always been the love of my life, since then she was so pretty but I never believed I had a chance. In our group of friends, there were lots of boys, some of them from the countryside, others from town as well as those from the city. For one reason or another, I felt like they all had the advantage over me. They had their families, their homes, their bikes… and I was always shuffled from the house of one aunt to another, with borrowed bicycles…"

"Concerning Cande, she was always sure, happy, always spreading her laughter, she was super easygoing and of course, she got along great with all the guys. Whoever was with her felt special. When we, guys, talked about the chicks, Candelaria was always the favorite. More than one of us was in love with her. Well, I didn't see myself in a very favorable position. Sometimes I imagined myself like a frog. 'If someday Cande kissed me...' I always adored her, I always wanted to be near her, and not only for who she is, but because of who I am when I am with her."

"So, what happened?" the young girl in love asks me.

"One time during vacations all the cousins went to my grandpa's farm. Each of us brought a friend; my cousin invited Cande, who had just turned fourteen. By that time, imagine how strong was my desire to tell her about my feelings towards her, but I still didn't have the courage. I was terrified of her rejection and losing her friendship. There were a thousand fears that held me back from telling her. Until one day everybody went out horse riding, we got to an entrance gate of a farm and the group was distracted greeting the neighbors; I felt Cande was looking at me. Without a sound, the words 'I love you' erupted from my mouth. The message was crystal clear; there was no doubt that my lips were expressing those words. Just the same, Cande looked puzzled and asked me also without uttering anything 'what?' It was as if we were having a secret conversation so no one could hear us. Once again, I plucked up enough courage and said in silence 'I love you' but by then, everyone was on the move. We took off at a gallop, like my heart. So, I had said it and I was sure she had understood me, but my fears were still there, because I would have to say it out loud and I didn't know what her feelings were. Finally, when on the way back we were herding the neighbor's horses, cleverly, I managed myself to be next to her. We started to talk about the animals and Cande got very close to tell me so as not to let the neighbor hear her 'These horses are very skinny'. It was my moment, and I took my chance: 'Yes, I love you'. And you know what? She just sat still in her saddle...and that was all!"

"Candelaria, you didn't say anything?" the young Peruvian girl turns to Cande without believing it.

"I was just frozen. At first, I couldn't believe that he had said 'I love you' silently, I thought I was dreaming. Later, when he told me clearly, I was caught off guard, I didn't expect it and I didn't know what I was supposed to say..."

"But, didn't you like him?"

"Yes, he was the love of my life. I had loved him, too, from the first time I saw him..."

"So, how did it end up?"

"At nightfall we were almost all playing in the yard around my grandpa's house. Cande, so tired from running, sat in the window of the living room, and when I saw her, I wiggled in next to her. We were both out of breath from so much running, and from nerves. I enjoy remembering that anxiety now, but at that time it was killing me. With the little breath I had, I asked her in a very low voice, 'Well?' She knew very well what I was referring to and she came right to the point, and said, 'No.'

"What?!" asks the Peruvian.

"Yes, just as I say, destroyed I asked her, 'Why not?' and she told me that if we ever broke up we wouldn't be friends anymore, and I said that I never thought of breaking up with her."

"Oh, well in that case, yes," says Cande repeating the words she pronounced that night seated on the window.

"Ohhhh, how beautiful!" exclaims our new friend as if she were watching a soap opera.

"And there we were, not knowing what to do or what to say, it was the first time we were dating and we didn't know how to act," I continue to tell the happy ending to the girl. "So we went back to playing with all the others as if nothing had happened, even though my running and shouting were for happiness, unrelated to the game."

"And there were no little kisses? No cuddling? Nothing?" asks the fascinated girl.

"When we said good-night, before going to bed, I got close to her. Cande offered me her cheek, I said 'No, not there' and with my hand, I turned her face so hers was in front of mine. I gave her my first kiss."

"Bravo!!" she shouts, pleased with the happy ending, toasting us taking a drink of mate. "And why do you want to go to Alaska?"

"Because you only live once, life is here today, gone tomorrow. It's very short and if you're not doing what you really want, you are wasting it."

"And we are out to live it." Adds Cande, while she caresses me. Meanwhile, the young girl drinks her mate in silence, as if she is reflecting on everything we've just said.

Coins for the Spirit

We look for a travel agency that organizes hikes to Machu Picchu over the Inca Trail. We go to the office of the Automobile Club of Peru, to get a recommendation with whom to go. The woman, delighted by our story, offers us a VIP company. "All the meals have meat, plus fruits and snacks served under a tent during the whole trip. They have tents and also tent bathrooms; you don't have to carry anything, not a sleeping bag, not even your jacket. The last night of the hike, you sleep in a first class hotel very close to the ruins and you come back in the sleeping car of a train. What I'm saying is that everything is at a five-star level and it will cost you the same price that any regular service would. The difference in price is usually enormous, but our Automobile Club would like to absorb it for you both," the lady points out, very happy with what she is doing for us.

Although the services she offers us are superb, we're not very enthusiastic. What she proposed sounds like those English in the movies crossing Africa, dressed spotlessly, carrying hats and umbrellas so the sun doesn't tan their skin and taking tea in porcelain under a tent. This isn't exactly the class of hiking adventure we are looking for.

"And how many people are in the group?" Cande asks.

"Oh, this is another really great thing for you. So far there is only one other couple, this means you'll have much more personalized service, with much more attention as well."

"Well, really, we are looking for a bigger group," we both reply at the same time, "we would like to enjoy this trip to such a special place with more people, who for sure will also be special." So, we say good-bye, leaving the marvelous woman with her mouth wide open.

Inside the Cross Keys Bar, there are no locals. Everything is decorated in the best London style. Cloudy with smoke, the place is full of dim lights, beer, and occasional loud laughter. An English guy we met on the way to Cusco invited us here, and now he is telling us about his life.

"My work brought me to Peru about 15 years ago to photograph the Madre de Dios jungle, and I felt my "mother" land was here. I got married, I have my house and my work. I will never make as much money as I did in England, I'll never possess the houses and cars that my brothers and my friends have over there, but there I would never enjoy the 'life' I have here," he takes a look at his surroundings and continues. "The differences are many, I've already lost three friends; one because of the guerrillas, another died in a very unpleasant way by contracting rabies, and the third got lost in the jungle...but I still feel that the life I want is in this place. Here with my camera I live in harmony, you have to live in the place you fall in love with. Not the one which serves your best interest. Just the same you do with your love, you don't live with him or her because it's in your best interest, you do it out of love" he pauses, then continues, "I am a photographer because it's what I long for, it's what I love to do and I get paid for it. Many times it's little, but if I do what I love there will always be enough coins to put in my pocket and many for my spirit."

"I am an electrician, but I was just drifting around until I fell into it, it's not what makes me happy, but with what I earned I built my house..." I tell him to excuse myself and give good reason for my work.

"First you work, even though you don't like it, because you need a house. Then it will be because you need a car and the rest of your life because you will need to maintain a family...and everything else you manage to have. And what about the work that you really wanted to do? What happened? Some wanted to be musicians, painters, actors, chefs, forest rangers, carpenters, firefighters, police officers...but the coins carried more weight and dragged them off the track. Now they only work waiting for the end of the day," answers the British guy while shifting his gaze to a group laughing very loudly. His eyes return to rest of us, "Don't work to have a brand new car, work to fill your spirit with miles, with life, with grand deeds, surmounted trials..." He serves himself the last of his beer, takes the last swig and adds, "With my heart full of these things I give you my advice: work at what you love doing, let the money earned be minor, even though it's very necessary."

He leaves us wishing us the best. Tomorrow he'll go back to the jungle to take pictures of Macaws.

Energy on Request

We have been awake more than two hours. At six, we get to the plaza, the pick up point from where a bus will take us to the place we'll begin the hike to Machu Picchu. Nobody knows anyone except his companion, if he came with one.

Spontaneously, we begin to introduce ourselves and say hello to those sitting closest to us, while on the bus, we hear languages from everywhere echoing around us. There is a Japanese guy, a Pole, a Bolivian, a Belgian, two French, two Germans, a Romanian, three from the States, five Argentineans and among the guide and the porters there are six Peruvians. All together, we form a group of twenty-two people.

We get off the bus behind some adobe houses situated at the end of the Sacred Valley. Here they sell the last snacks and drinks one can get. We brought salted, toasted corn, crackers with seeds, chocolate and water purification tablets, which we think is sufficient. We feel prepared.

This is the perfect moment. The sun shines as we begin the ascent full of aspirations and happiness. It will be three days of walking mostly uphill; on the fourth, we'll enter mystical Machu Picchu. At the time of the Empire, the trail we'll be following was reserved exclusively to be used by the sacred priests and nobility. We were told that there are tunnels, bridges and stairs, and we'll pass by three other cities in ruins.

We've already finished the first three hours of the hike when we stop to eat lunch. The guide takes advantage of this moment to introduce himself and tell us about the trip.

"We will make it, all of us will make it. No one in my group has ever given up. We are heading to Machu Picchu and none of you will quit. You have already come from so far away, now it is not the moment to quit. The first day is hard, because the climb is very steep, but don't worry, tomorrow it will be worse, it's even steeper. We'll leave the forest to enter a scrub land zone, then later another where only short grass grows. There, at that altitude, it will be windy and rainy, this is the place where many begin to wonder 'what am I doing here?' Thinking 'Why am I on this mountain?' 'Why didn't I take the train?' I am not going to tell you why. When you get to Machu Picchu, you will know the reason," the guide lets the silence reign while he looks at us one by one in the eyes. "If you feel like you can't go one more step, if you feel like you've used up all your energy and you don't have any more to go any farther, ask the mountain, the wind, the sky. This whole zone is loaded with energy and this energy will lead you on. All of us will make it up there, everyone at his own speed, but we'll get there."

"Machu Picchu here we come!" I yell, while I hear my companions express their own regional cheers.

We spot the first ruins. A round city that, from where we are, looks perfect, unique, impenetrable. When we're about to take off again one of the girls asks "Where are the restrooms?" this strikes us as very funny, 'the restrooms'! Evidently, the girl doesn't fully understand the class of excursion she's in for, but out of respect and because of her heavily built boyfriend, we refrain from laughing until she comes out with her next question. "And where can I buy some snacks?" Now we just can't help ourselves, and bust a gut, and once again hit the trail.

The first day is truly challenging. We advance with much difficulty until we get to the site where we will spend the night. The porters have gone on ahead of us, which seems incredible because they hike loaded down with 130 pound packs on their shoulders. When we get there, everything is prepared; the tents are up, dinner is fixed, and the fire is lit. We who have come up carrying only our small backpacks are the ones who don't even have the energy to chew.

Sitting around the fire gives us the chance to get to know one another better. We are more relaxed and there are numerous questions for the guide about the Incas. It's as if now that we're in their land, we want to know everything.

"Is it true that this zone is full of energy?" asks one of the French guys.

"There is energy in everything, even in just a few words there can be a lot of energy. In a look, in a smile, in everything that surrounds us. We are its center, energy comes in and goes out of us constantly," the guide opens his arms. "The place and the moment in which you are also spread out energy. A river, a cemetery, a ruin, a beach, a mountain all can give us a sensation of charging us with energy or consuming it. Just breathing deeply in a certain place can make us feel invigorated if it is positive or maybe we feel enclosed by an uncomfortable sensation with a desire to get away from when the energy is negative. Energy exists, it comes and goes, you feel it. It flows constantly from everything that surrounds us, from everything we eat, from those we love and hate, from the place and the climate. Energy can be felt but can't be measured, just the same as love and pain," the guide breaks for a few seconds, and concludes, "Even though everything has energy, we need to know how to be prepared to receive it or reject it, and also we need to know when to give it."

With these words, he leaves us. I feel what he said was powerful since it fortifies me in someway.

Who Governs You?

We've already eaten dinner and a few of us stay behind by the fire. The first human being who could make his own fire might have remained looking at it in the same way we are now. Our faces reflect the flames and our hypnotized eyes follow them.

A long silence persists for a long while. The night, the fatigue and something that I can't name, call for it. With a noise coming from the mountain in this small place in the world, the talk begins at a precise moment and with people from every continent. We talk about where we've come from, what we do at home and why we're here.

There are people that three days ago were at a desk in an office, where the biggest adventure of the day is to get there on time. One is an engineer who repeats time and again that he doesn't understand how the Incas could build such perfect cities without knowing how to write. Another is a builder, and seems to be happy about it... "I build homes for families, with my hands. I enjoy my work so much!" he speaks moving his hands as if he's holding tools. "You can't imagine how wonderful it is to go past the houses and see them full of life, painted and decorated, with children playing…"

"I am an electrician and I light up your work," I comment. Like this, the chat continues about everyone's jobs.

"I am a businessman, I sell clothes…" says someone who hasn't said anything up to this point. "Until this trip, I lived a routine. I always searched for ways to be busy and make the most money possible to have a well equipped home. I didn't want to get together with my buddies at a bar, for me this seemed like a waste of time. Until I realized that by filling myself up with work I was, in fact, smothering myself and avoiding the meaning of my life. I was one among many and I thought this was fine, but deep in my heart there was a little voice that repeated that I could do something different, that life doesn't rely on merely being occupied and acquiring more and more. This inner voice always found the right moment to remind me…and here I am, doing something I could tell my friends about and myself. I've started to adjust things and I realize that this is only the beginning of a change in me."

"I am still nothing," this from the young Belgian who's speaking, "so far I don't know what I want to do nor why I came, nor what I'm looking for…"

So then I observe, "Why is it that although we're all from distant places and we speak distinct languages, I don't feel big differences? The more I hear, the more I feel that we're all equal. How can governments separate us, send us to war and make us kill if in essence we're all the same?"

"I come from Poland, where there have been many wars with countries close to us and also within our own borders. For years we've suffered a communist government that wouldn't even let us pray, we couldn't travel or choose our own work, nor our own houses. As soon as the government fell, I left to travel the world and I'm still doing it. Nothing that I have been taught is true, they always taught me to believe that there was no better place on earth than the Soviet Union. They told us this is why everyone wanted to invade us and why we had to be prepared to defend ourselves and to attack the enemy. Today, after traversing many 'enemy' countries, all I see are humans, equal to me created by a marvelous God," the man fades to silence. While we listen, each of us thinks that's just what we've been taught. All of us arrive at the same conclusion as the Pole.

"Now, I ask you, what would you do in a war?" He continues looking in my eyes although he's talking to all of us, "That what the government tells you or that what your God tells you? If God teaches you to love your neighbor as you love yourself, could you kill another human if your nation ordered you to? Who governs you more? Your God or your government?

"My Faith," I reply, looking into his eyes illuminated by the fire.

"You're right, I have never thought about it like this," agrees the French man.

The fire and the silence are again with us in the dark night. We can't see anything behind us, but we can see ahead, into our future.

We two wake up feeling happy. We are hiking the Inca Trail, we're getting closer to Machu Picchu. It's time to leave again, we all depart together, save for the porters who remain behind to break camp. The farther we trek, the more the group spreads out, each one advancing at their own pace.

I move ahead with the guy from the United States. He is carrying a bag for trash and gathers what he finds along the way. I join him in his quest. Without realizing it, the climb becomes easier since we're more interested in a cigarette butt than seeing how much farther we still have to go. His gesture touches me, we aren't in his country and no one has asked him to do this. He's on vacation and contrary to the rest of us, who want to get rid of our backpacks, he's carrying an extra bag. Although the track is very steep and our fatigue increases, the young guy veers off the track to pick up some paper.

"Why are you doing this?" I ask him.

"Because doing this is very good for me, it makes me feel useful, and it gives me the possibility of demonstrating my respect to this incredible place."

"Excuse us, to your right please" announce the porters, who have caught up with us.

They ask us to let them pass because of their abundant cargo; they need the whole path. They are so well conditioned that the cold has no effect on them; they are in shorts and climb in sandals made of old tires.

"Do you need us to carry anything?" they ask us as they pass.

All is One

The panorama expands around us. The height of the trees lessens as we gain altitude, the lack of oxygen makes us crave for it, our feet feel heavy and our bodies beg for rest. I recall the words of the guide and I begin to ask for help from the mountain, the sun and from the water I drink. I observe their beauty; I concentrate on enjoying them. I feel better, with a stronger desire to continue. I am content to be here doing this.

I see the sun and I thank it for being there. The indigenous cultures that praise it and glorify it come to mind and I think, "How strange to worship the sun, I don't do it but I give thanks for its heat, for its light, for giving life to the plants which give life to the animals and them to me." I realize that I am extolling it myself. I feel the same way about mother earth, water, and the trees with their fruits and wood, the animals, the plants, the minerals…and it all begins to become a form of worship and a gratefulness for existing and being there for me. I feel part of them because I was part of everything before I came to the world, because now I take from them and they will take from me when I die to continue being part of it all. "Everything is one and one is everything," I whisper.

I reach the crest of the mountain with these thoughts, my lungs searching for air and overflowing with happiness for having reached the top. We still haven't made it the whole way, but the most difficult part has been conquered. Where could Cande be?

"And the others?" someone in the group asked me.

"They're coming along little by little, but they're coming…"

The sighs of our souls are highlighted in the icy morning. At a long distance, I can see a person who breathes deeply to fill himself with this scarce, magic air, and then he sighs long and warmly. I can also make out Cande who waves; she's three hundred feet below.

We spend two more nights on the trail, two nights with rain that wets our clothes and sleeping bags. Even though the climate is freezing it doesn't dampen our enthusiasm.

This morning is the last one of our expedition. Today we will conquer the mountain that stands sentinel between us and our goal. It's four in the morning and we are awake before the sun comes out, since we want to get to Machu Pichu before anyone else. After four days of traversing, we feel we have much more of a right than the tourists who come by helicopter or on the train.

Wet and cold we begin our last climb. As we hike on, the group starts to disperse. I have pulled out in front with the Pole, the Belgian, and now a Spaniard joins us.

The grueling climb wears out my companions, who sit down for a moment to take a breath. Wavering, not knowing if I would rather stay or go on, with screams my heart asks me to keep moving.

"Let's keep going, there's still a long way to walk…" the Spaniard tells me while I hesitate. He quickens his steps, as I follow him. "Why are you here?" Asks this man whose steps are longer than his fifty years.

"Because I have always wanted to know Machu Picchu, I've heard marvelous things about this place…"

"Yes, sure…but what truly attracted you to Machu Picchu?"

"It's one of the goals inside a dream that I'm completing with my wife. It's a big step and very important in our journey."

"So, how do you feel?"

"Full of life, of energy. I can't believe that after four exhausting days, in which we've eaten basically soups and seeds, in which we've slept badly, wet and cold, I am walking to this pace. Plus, I still have enough breath to talk with you…"

"It's your heart speaking. It doesn't need air, what it needs is this, what you're doing."

His Spanish accent, his deep voice in the silence of the misty morning that still doesn't want to break…everything seems to have deep meaning. This place, my feelings and his words are all mixed together somehow clarifying my thoughts.

"If you let your heart lead you, you will never go the wrong way. Listen to it always. Better than anyone it knows what is right and what is wrong, it knows about dreams, of love. Follow it, don't let your mind, influenced by the commands of others, reign over you. The cold mind thinks; instead, your warm heart feels.

Why is the Spaniard telling me these things? Has he been charged with an energy that he wants to share? Could it be that the words are coming out of his heart, a heart that has never been this happy before?

"I didn't begin this trip because I wanted to leave everything," I comment, "nor am I escaping from anything. I only left because I wanted to begin doing something that my heart asked for to feel happy. It was the same when It fell in love."

"What did It ask you then?"

"To do everything to conquer Cande, to love her, to let her know."

We take a few steps in silence until the Spaniard advises me, "Regard your dream as a very important part of your life and now that you're achieving it don't be too serious. Improvise, welcome the unpredictable, learn from your mistakes and laugh at yourself. When a heart pursues his dream, this is going to be fulfilled, but it takes you through places and does things that you never imagined when you decided to follow it. It's magic."

We've already walked an exhausting hour, and the light of the new day is approaching.

"When we get to the sun door, I will stop there…you go on," he tells me.

"It would be better to get there together," I propose.

"I told you, follow your heart."

"But…"

"Go, go for your dream. Be a conqueror yourself! Conquer Machu Picchu, Machu Picchu has to be all yours at least for an hour, all yours. Go, my dream has already been accomplished, now is the moment for you to go for yours…"

His strong words seem to infuse me with energy. I pick up my pace, accelerating and so does my heart.

"See you at the throne of the Inca!" I shout with a strong desire to see him again.

King for a Day

The sun appears behind me, as if it were trying not to blind me and at the same time wanting to illuminate everything for me. My shadow doesn't follow me; it goes ahead of me, blazing the trail. It's more anxious to get there than I am. It's my companion until I get to a rock jutting out over a steep drop off that seems more like a box seat. From here, I recognize the Huayna Picchu peak. I've seen it in thousands of photos as the backdrop of Machu Picchu. I am pained because of the white mist that covers the mystic ruins and with it my desires to see it. I sit and wait...the  stubborn clouds have to lift, but they don't, they hang on like they're waiting for something, someone...

"God, give me a day to reign over this place, make the mist open..." I ask out loud as I get to my feet. One minute later the rays of the sun fall over the whiteness inviting, granting movement, as if awakening it...the curtain lifts and Machu Picchu introduces itself-beautiful, just beautiful. It's not like I've been told, it's not like it appears in photos, nor like I imagined. It's much more beautiful, much more.

I run down the short distance I still need to cover to get there. I don't know anything about the site, but I get to an enormous boulder. I lean onto it and I cry tears of happiness. On a rock, perched on a mountain, in a small place on the earth I feel great, I feel that I can hug the whole world. It belongs to me. I feel I am a king. I wasn't born a prince, but a genuine king is not born, he's made. It happens when you realized that God made everything for you; the places with their persons, the mountains with their snow, the seas with their fish, the moon with its stars. Not for you to govern, simply for you to enjoy. Not for you to rearrange, simply for you to follow its equilibrium. Not for you to possess it, just for you to be a part of it. Today, with my arms, I encompass the whole world, I am its king, I am part of it, part of a world full of kings who don't need to fight for our kingdoms but to enjoy together the discovery of being a king.

The tourists begin to crowd the ruins. Cande arrives together with the group.

"Why didn't you wait for me?" She asks me annoyed.

"I don't know, I'm so sorry, but I had to be alone here with this place." She understands me, she knows my life long desires, and she knows this is one of them. I see in her smile that in fact, my action didn't bother her.

"How do you feel, Cande?"

"Excited. I feel fabulous. This is where I have always dreamed of being. I've waited a long time to get here and this is the precise moment for it. When climbing the mountain the splendor of the ruins fed my soul, now I can feel its strength. It's majestic. Immense rocks stacked up one on top of another and in this way, this city was constructed. It demonstrates perfection; its beauty is sublime. It motivates me to walk through it, to touch it, to feel it. The more I walk around here, the more I want to, I am moved simply by feeling its mysticism. With no doubt, the guide is right. You can feel the energy, you can't measure it but it's here, and I understand why I'm here."

Cande and I devote ourselves to get to know this place, surrounded by a special atmosphere. We want to take advantage of every minute. We sit up on a terrace, over Machu Picchu which we own and which owns us. We remain alone together for a long while, feeling something remarkable inside ourselves. We are part of the world, what happens to it happens to us and vice versa. We mutually influence one another.

"This is somewhere I want to come with our children." Cande comments leaving the ruins behind us.

The Eternal Crossing of the Andes

What is happening? We wake up with a jolt, Cande hits her head on the steering wheel. It must be three in the morning…or four. We can't see outside because of the cover, but the noise is deafening. It seems like the sky is falling. Hefty hunks of ice are bouncing on the car resounding thunderously. It's so loud it scares us. There's nowhere to take cover, we're trapped without being able to see anything. We remain awake until the hail changes to rain.

We wake up. It's the day of the presidential election in Peru and there is a lot of movement in town. We eat breakfast in a stable with mules and llamas, next to the market.

Today we want to cross the Andes once again. We know that there is a new entirely paved route, but not only does our map not indicate it, but also nobody knows about it, nor can they tell us how many miles it is to the next closest city. "It's about…a six-hour trip", "four", "seven." In view of the fact that no one agrees on quantity, we're better off filling up the tank, plus taking two extra jerry tanks with us in reserve.

The hail completely covers the whole road, so we follow some tracks from a truck. The crops that line the road look destroyed. I remember the Bolivian woman who has such a small crop and I suffer for her, and for everyone. I know how much work it is to sow, and how little they reap.

The road is steep. With the altitude, the car looses force and consumes more gasoline. We haven't even reached the halfway point and we've already added both extra tanks. We get higher and higher. We don't see any cars, much less any people. We've reached such a high level that the snow from the mountains comes right up to the road, the whole landscape is impressive.

We stop to take some pictures and to measure how much gas we have. A sign indicates "14,265 feet above sea level". I put a stick in the tank, it has less than half left! On a flat road, at sea level, we could get close to 60 miles with this much gas; now, in the mountains, and over 14,000 feet up it's not going to be enough to even go 45! Every 3000 feet a car loses 10% of power so how can we save gas? How are we going to get there? We'll have to turn off the engine on the downward slopes, and start it back up only on the ascension. But if this doesn't work? I'm really worried about being stranded here. We didn't buy any food for the trip because everything was closed for the election and we were confident that we'd be able to find something along the way. The few houses we've seen in the vicinity are uninhabited, they are summer shelters that the shepherds use when the snow is gone…and that's what there is in excess.

I get back in the car, I breathe, I don't want to get more nervous. We go over a few hills, turning the engine off and on until the road begins to descend very steeply. We're leaving the high plains, we're going down to sea level and we get to Moquegua with some gas still in the tank!

Since this is something to celebrate, we enter a restaurant and ask for a typical meal from the region. We receive fried guinea pig called cuy. That's what we get for being curious. But really, it isn't that bad…

It's the condor's time

In the "White City", Arequipa, we catch a bus that takes us to the Colca Canyon. It's the deepest in the world. We travel together with locals and tourists alike. One young foreigner feeling unwell asks the driver to stop and runs while unzipping her pants. She searches for a bush, a rock, or something to hide her emergency and her femininity from the curious public. She discovers a plant and right away in exchange for shielding her she "fertilizes" it. Inside the bus, we hear a little giggle…and when the chauffer revs the engine and moves the bus a bit, some emit a big laugh. The girl with her pants still down, gets up in a hurry.

In the area of the Colca, a large number of condors fly, so we go to the place where we can watch them. There are already people here anxiously waiting, among them I recognize a man whom I first saw in Cusco. Even though he doesn't know us, we approach him.

"Didn't I see you in Cusco?" I ask him.

"Yes, you entered the same agency as us."

"Do you know how long it will take before we'll see the condors?"

The park ranger standing behind us hears the question and looking at his watch answers, "There are only 45 minutes to wait, at 9:15 they'll begin to rise in flight." I can't believe how accurate he is…as if the condors had watches. "At 9:10 the sun will rise enough to illuminate the canyon floor, and the cold air will begin to warm up producing ascending currents that the condors take advantage of," explains the park ranger. Against such a scientific explanation of the punctuality of the condor I remain speechless.

The Argentinean introduces himself as Gula; he's with his girlfriend. My attention is captured by the fact that she is a head taller than he is; it's not that she is tall, the small one is him. Why does this make such an impression on me? Could I be so narrow-minded? Do I still believe in standards that hamper me from realizing that height has nothing to do with love? Submerged in these thoughts, I ask him, "How long have you been traveling?"

"We left about four months ago, and you?"

"Just two and a half months. Where are you going?"

"We want to do Latin America, the United States, and Europe…"

"How much time did you calculate for such a trip?"

"We don't know, however long is necessary. We are almost out of money and we have to think about how we're going to make it. We'll see," Gula replies to me with an admirable peace.

My life has always had a timetable. I never imagined myself doing something taking as many days as necessary for it. A schedule, a date or at least an estimated time, I always needed a guide or, better said, a limit. We were always limited by work; it decided for us, it was the owner of our time. Even when we said that we were leaving for six months, it sounded irresponsible.

Yet, here are Gula and his mate, who with great responsibility, give themselves the freedom to take all the necessary time to themselves:

"Until a few thousand years ago all humanity was nomadic. It was like this until it occurred to a man to remain in one place. To the others this man was crazy, how could he stop being a nomad, give up knowing new places, new horizons? Abandon the adventure of knowing other lands, eating different fruits and animals? In spite of the questions of the others, he stayed, choosing to wake up every morning of his life in the same place. He planted and harvested, his animals procreated and he didn't need to hunt anymore, he could easily feed himself," Gula pauses and then continues. "In time, other men joined him and when many did it, they didn't consider themselves crazy anymore. But, other difficulties arose. To begin with, not everyone had access to water and those that did, could have more animals and better harvests. This created the differences between the rich and the poor. So, the land was converted into a subject of dispute, and people went out, searching for others. In this way more settlements were formed. Those that had abundant harvests or storerooms expanded, and so this brought resentment and war. The wars called for soldiers and someone to direct them, in this way, from among the richest, the kings emerged. They dominated the people by defining themselves as their protectors. To them went the harvests and profits, because it was necessary to maintain the armies and construct their castles and walls. But why didn't the walls of the castle protect the homes of those who paid the taxes? Why, if the armies were there to defend the settlements, did the king use them to collect those taxes that were always rising? The years passed and more uncertainty arose. And here we are in the XXI century...nothing has changed, except that it occurs to a man to be a nomad. The others think he is crazy. How could you give up being in one place like everybody else, stop living in the same house to go somewhere unknown? How could you renounce seeing the same folks as always? Would you eat unusual fruits and food? In spite of the questions, just the same this crazy guy leaves and begins his life in a new world. What did your friends say when you left?"

"That we were crazy..."

"Could it be 'they' are the ones who are crazy? Think about it...who is crazy? The one who goes for his dream or the one who lets his dream pass away? Why is it that every time one distances himself from the masses he's considered crazy?" Gula implores me without expecting an answer. "Many ask us how so we keep going, and we start wondering the same about them. We live in a small sphere that doesn't allow us to see much outside. Each place we go we enter into a new sphere and we acclimate ourselves the best we can. We continue being ourselves, but with small differences. We live in constant change; we're neither strong nor weak, just flexible. If we were rigid, we'd stumble over the first rock, we'd fall in the first hole and there we'd stagnate..."

"Look, there are the condors, there are three...no, four," the voice of a tourist interrupts his thoughts.

"Here comes another one..." another person adds to the count.

In the end, we see seven condors. First, they fly inside the canyon, below us. Then they reach our altitude. Now they are over our heads and we can see their immense wingspan and incredible plumage.

"Gula, do you know why the condors can fly and we can't?" I ask him.

"Because they possess wings. We instead have hands that we want to fill with many things that don't let us fly."

We leave Arequipa feeling a bit more like nomads, with more wings and with a strong desire to fly.

We arrive in Nazca, a site that needs to be appreciated from the air. From that height, you can distinguish meticulously created designs made on the desert floor. It's not known who made them nor why. The view is magic like the lines.

A sign warns us we've reached the "Sand Zone". There are stretches where the road disappears completely under the dunes. It never stops moving and the wind carries a fine film of sand that obscures our view.

With the car filled with these particles, we pull into a gas station that is enormous in comparison to the typical family affairs here in Peru. We are starving and fortunately next door there is a lovely restaurant which offers breaded cutlets as the special. The cooks and servers are all family, and they're all curious about the Graham. Because of this, they begin to ask us who we are, what we are doing, where we sleep...

"Wherever we are when night comes," Cande explains.

"Well then, today you will sleep in an unimaginable place, unique in all America. It's the Huacachina oasis. Finish eating and follow us."

They escort us over a small road to reach the oasis. It really is; desert dunes, palms, and some houses surrounding the mirror of water. The family's home is right in front of the lake and it's marvelous, just as they are. They host us in the kids' room who happily move into the room next door.

Among the family members is a tiny baby; I take him in my arms saying, "What a beautiful *pendejo*!"

With this, the mother glares at me and takes the baby away from me saying, "Nobody calls my baby *pendejo*."

The same word with distinct regional uses now produces a diplomatic difficulty, which I remedy with an explanation. Where I come from, this means little boy. Here, as I see, like in the rest of Latin America it's very offensive.

"Well, whatever, nobody calls my baby a *pendejo*," states the mother more calmly.

After going up and down the dunes with something like a surfboard we leave the oasis. The next place we want to visit is the Bahia de Paracas, a reserve next to the ocean where we will be able to observe a hugely vast number of birds. We drive all day nonstop, but night falls before we get to our destination.

We pass through a valley with a river which brings water and with it life to the desert, next to the road there is a small settlement and we stop just in front of a house where a woman seated outside watches her kids and the traffic pass by.

"Ma'am, would you mind if we park in front of your house for the night?"

"No, please feel free. My husband is inside." I don't believe this is true; maybe in her kindness, she makes up this lie to make herself feel more secure.

"Do you have a little water?" Cande asks.

"I am waiting for the water boy right now, it won't be long until he gets here," she comments to us.

Water boy? I believed this was something only found in history, but I keep this comment to myself as not to offend her.

"Here he comes," she tells us signaling a barefooted youth of about 14 carrying a stick in his hand. With this he leads a skinny mule loaded with two plastic barrels full of water…tied to it there are about 10 more mules, each with their own buckets. The woman shares the dirty water she purchases with us. The children drink it as fast as she can pour it, while we, before drinking any, wait for our water purification tablets to work.

Paracas shines with colors and movement. The flight of the birds and the tides are a coming and going of life. We come across some backpacking girls from Lima who hop onto the running boards of the Graham. Together we search for a place to camp. We end up in front of the bay full of rosy flamingos. As the sun goes down, the wind picks up bringing the sand with it. All through our communal dinner, we hear the crunching of sand.

"It will remove the tartar," one of the girls comments.

"Yeah, and the enamel too," says another, laughing about our arid situation.

We want to put the cover over the car but the wind doesn't allow us, the girls' tents don't have any tent-like shape, they seem more like clothes hung on the line. We move the car so as to give shelter to them, but the sneaky wind looks for a way past and finds them again.

The whole night is like this. We wake up with stiff hair and completely dirty. The girls didn't sleep at all, they turned on their radio, lit their cigarettes, and bitterly they decided to wait for the calm. They leave with their backpacks filled with sand to look for better luck. Flamingos by the thousands are our only companions, but they also leave us, lifting in flight tinting the sky pink.

We heat a little water, wash and take off in the car for the other side of the bay. There is a tourist village here, this means, food without sand or wind. We have some mate. A young couple approaches. They ask us about the car, about the trip and they invite us.

"Come on over to the house, we have plenty of room. It's the third one down the beach, the one with a blue and white pier."

"Thanks so much, we'll finish our mate and come over."

It's a gigantic house. We wonder if we have the wrong place, we ring the bell and the door opens. A woman dressed in a domestic employee's uniform tells us, "Please come in, my bosses will return shortly, they told me to be at your service. May I offer you anything?"

"A shower," we reply simultaneously.

Blowing sand out of our noses, we plunge into a tub with endless hot water. Later we have a savory lunch with the couple and the mother of one of them.

Capital Lima

We enter Lima on a highway that empties directly into the center of the capital. We are heading to a shop, which was recommended to us many times throughout our travels, the one of the Nicolini brothers.

A huge gate with security leads us into a patio situated among three enormous garages each the size of about a city block. One is full of antique cars in need of restoration, another with already restored cars and the third has in its lower floor a fully equipped shop and the upper floor is full of spare parts.

I'm anxious to meet the brothers, we need to know how the car is, do a tune-up and maybe a service as well. I will help as much as I can, I don't know how to ask, or what they're like... Shortly a simply dressed man with curly hair approaches us. "Are you the *Che*?" he inquires.

"Yes, we are the *ches* ", we reply. I like the title, a little for coming from Argentina, but also because I feel a revolution inside myself like *Che* must have felt when beginning his trip around America.

"Is it true that you're going to Alaska?"

"If God accompanies us, it will be."

"Great, how can I help you?"

"We would like to talk to the Nicolini brothers to ask if they can do a service and a general check of the car."

"I am Jorge Nicolini. You can leave the car over there," he tells me without much enthusiasm. Maybe my request annoyed him. As he indicated, I moved the car. Cande and I start to take out the things we need to have with us.

Meanwhile, Jorge brings people and more people telling them, "Come here, meet these *ches*." He introduces us and yes, now he makes us realize he's delighted with our visit.

Although the next day I appear very early to begin the check, when I get to the shop, I find six people already working. I can't believe what I see, is it my car? What happened?! It has no wheels, nor hood...pieces are dispersed all over the place. The Graham has been dismantled by Julio Reyes, a smiling dark-skinned man and his assistants. Since he wants to check everything, he only leaves the engine and the transmission in one piece. I help him at the same time familiarizing myself with the car.

The same day they inform us that the "service" will take some time. They have to look for some parts and others need to be sent out to be remade. We had no idea that this would turn out like this, we begin to worry about the time we have left, but mostly about the money. We're already four months into the trip and we're still a long way from Alaska and very close to being out of money. We only have enough to continue two more months.

We can't just sit by idly, we have to do something or we won't be able to continue. We look for companies to sponsor us, we write letters to car clubs in Argentina...we knock on many doors, but the expected answer never appears...

We don't take it personally because we got ourselves into this, therefore we can't make someone else responsible for our trip. If we don't find some support in Peru, maybe we will in Ecuador.

We go down into the catacombs of the church of San Francisco. On display here there are more than twenty thousand skeletons. Never in my life have I ever seen so much death. In the cemeteries, I never saw a dead person and I didn't feel death as I now feel it and see it - by the thousands. Every one of these skeletons was a person, alive, with families, loves, dreams...now they are only bones. We come out of the catacombs into an internal patio of the monastery surrounded by galleries full of flowers and life. I breathe deeply to feel the life I have inside of me. The guide and the tourists leave us alone embracing on a bench with no backrest. A monk passes in front of us, he greets us and goes on, then retracing his steps seats himself next to us.

"Have you come from far away?"

"Yes, from Buenos Aires," Cande replies.

"So you are just passing through?"

"Yes...now, after seeing so much death, I feel like we are all just passing through," I answer him.

"Life is a loan, which some day will be collected. No one escapes, no one beats death," he tells us provoking a chill through our bones. "Life is a gift from God, what we do with life is our gift to Him," is his sentence, and after blessing us, he goes away.

"What we're doing now with our lives, might this be our gift to God?" thinks Cande aloud.

Leaving the place quietly, we take a walk beneath beautiful colonial balconies. We treat ourselves to something that we haven't done since we set out. Looking for a little of our inherited Buenos Aires tradition, we enter a café and seat in front of a window. The view is filled with the calm sea where only the waves and the gulls move the scenery.

"What would my mom think about this journey, about this time we're taking?" My mother died when I was twenty-one.

"You're not going to believe me, but I was just thinking about my brother and I see him overjoyed that we're doing this..."- her older brother died when he was fifteen.

It's evident we both feel a little bit guilty, we question ourselves about, "being here". Shouldn't we really be in Argentina working, finishing our house? We know the trip will be extended and paradoxically we are nearly without money. Are we careless with managing our time and our money? Suddenly Cande interrupts my rationality.

"I feel that God is very happy with what we're doing. And your mother and my brother too."

"My heart is happy, it's my mind that won't leave me in peace. It tells me that with the money we've spent we could have finished the house and with what we have left we couldn't even..."

"Herman, at least we tried," Cande tells me, "If instead we hadn't taken so many detours, if instead we had gotten this far in a straight line..."

"...we would have missed so much. So many people..." the faces crowd into my thoughts.

"What are we going to do when we run out of money? This dream is our life long dream, but without any money, what are we going to do?"

"Let's look for sponsors in Ecuador. I can't imagine turning around, can you?"

"No, me neither. It would be like a failure in my life, for my heart."

Cande's words remind me of the words of the Spaniard at Machu Picchu. "When a heart pursues his dream, this is going to be fulfilled, but it takes you through places and does things that you never imagined when you decided to follow it. It's magic."

It's Monday and I go to the shop. The Graham is almost ready. I put on my work clothes and help with the last details. Now only one part missing; the pinion gear that attaches to the differential.

I go to get it at the machinist's, a house transformed into a shop. The room in which they manufacture our part is very tiny, and they make it in an artisan way. The Peruvians' reputation is rightly earned, I have seen how they restore other antique cars and it's incredible. With very little they can make and copy everything. With the masterful piece in my hands, I go out to catch the bus that will take me back to the shop. This zone is not recommended for walking and in my hurry I turn off the avenue into a one-way street to shorten the walk. It's only two blocks over to the next avenue. When I'm about half way through the first block, a head appears and watches me from the corner. Behind it, two more appear. Should I go on? Seized with fear, I am unable to react. It's too late, the three surround me.

"Give me everything you have."

What I have is a lot of fear. I don't have anything they're looking for, only the dirty shop clothes and a few coins for the bus. I'm afraid they'll hurt me when they see what I have. God, please help me. I plead in silence.

The three gangsters take a few steps backwards at the same time as they say, in fear, "We didn't do anything to him! Take it easy!"

I don't understand what's going on, until someone grabs my arm from behind.

"Let's go," he orders me. I look at him. It's a man in his forties, dressed in a white apron tied at the waist, like a pharmacist. In one of his hands, he shows off a gun. Like this, without letting me go or saying another word to me, he removes me from that place. When we are at a wise distance from the thieves, they begin to shout threats.

"Why'd you get into it?! You better not come back here, you're a dead man! "

We get to the corner. The man releases me.

"Walk along the avenues, don't go around in these streets," he advises at the same time as he distances himself in a direction contrary to mine.

"Thank you, thank you so much," I tell him in my confusion, in my stress, in my admiration. And I let him go without asking either who he is or how I could thank him. He vanishes just as quickly as he appeared.

When I return I tell Cande what happened. She breaks into tears asking, "What would I have done if something had happened? How would I have known where you were? What would I do here, so far from home, if something happened to you?"

We leave Lima, with a strong will to complete our dream although the money is running out. We're making our life a gift to God and feeling that we are not alone, that there are guardian angels traveling with us.

We depart in a newly invigorated car, but a lot of vigor is not enough. We run out of gas on the way out of the city exactly where we've been told to watch out, not to stop, because there are many dangerous people. Moreover, they explained to us that if a rock breaks the window, or they ram us from behind, we have to keep going. And here we are: out of gas, at a standstill. More than a little worried, I set off walking in search of the valuable liquid; I can't stop thinking about Cande, parked in that place inside a very noticeable car.

When I come back with some fuel, I can't believe what I'm seeing. Many "dangerous" people surrounding Cande, all smiling and asking thousands of questions to a happy Candelaria who is responding.

We follow the road north, sometimes sticking to the coast, other times not, but always in the desert. We pass by small villages, and sporadically a city. Their sizes depend on the flow of the closest river. The silence of this highway is desert like. Until we hear a siren behind us accompanied by a patrolman's voice broadcast over a loudspeaker, "Pull over on the shoulder, please."

Since we've left Buenos Aires we've had many police stop us just to ask us what we're doing, how and most of all to see the car. It's like this so often that in Arequipa, when an official stopped us, I dared to signal that we couldn't stop because it was getting late. He made signs for us to continue.

"Good afternoon. Papers," a young officer with a serious expression asks us. I hand over my documents, he looks them over. "The last highway sentry informed me that you exceeded the speed limit."

"What?!?" we answer with an outburst of laughter. We can't believe what he's saying, surely this is a joke. Nevertheless, the officer stares at us without understanding, he's not laughing.

"Sir, did you see the car we're driving?" the man looks the car over once again. "As much as we'd love to, it's not possible to exceed any speed limit in this car!" the policeman scratches his head, knocking his hat askew...

"Could it be that the sentries at the last post are just playing a joke on you?" Cande poses.

Astounded, he goes to his truck. In the rearview mirror, I see him call on the radio. He returns.

"I believe they are, that they are pulling my leg, you may continue," he tells us as he returns our documents.

It's already getting late; it's time to look for somewhere to sleep. We stop in front of a little shop. As payment for the right to stay parked for the night we buy a few things. While we begin to get ready to go to sleep, a family approaches us. "This is not a good place to spend the night, come to our house."

Their home is small, only one room; the walls are made of flattened bamboo. During dinner, they serve us the only pieces of meat in the pot. After which they give us the only bed in the house to sleep in. They, along with their children, lie down on the floor.

In the morning, upon leaving they tell us with arms around their children, "Please forgive us that we couldn't give you more..."

They gave us everything and asked our forgiveness for not having more to give us. Never have we felt like we received so much. We see that no one has so little they're not able to give and no one has so much that they're not able to receive. After exchanging warm hugs, we say farewell.

We continue rumbling north, always hugging the sea and we're anxious to enjoy a swim in it. But the cold water always puts us off. We camp in front of it, with the view filled with water as far as I can see, but where we are standing there is not even one drop. The sea and the desert seem like water and oil that do not mix.

Cande starts to write in the diary, we take turns doing it. We imagine ourselves reading it when we're very old, maybe with our grandchildren surrounding us.

I put on a little music, which makes us feel so well, which moves us so much. I look around me and see so much: an ocean reflecting an enormous moon, a desert at peace, an old buddy with four wheels and a beautiful woman writing something so lovely, the diary of a dream, our dream, which together we're making into a reality. Ladies and gentlemen, in this moment there is no richer or happier person than me in the entire universe.

"Cande," I call her, she looks at me without putting down her pencil, "I am the richest man in the world," she makes a scowl, without understanding. "Everything I love the most, that which is more valuable than anything in the world, I have it" She puts down her pencil, sheds one tear and gives me an enormous hug.

The road takes us closer to Ecuador. We pass through fishing villages, where they make small, fragile boats out of reeds to take out to sea. In one village, with short wooden logs they make a small two-person raft and go on it out into the ocean. Far out at sea two fishermen struggle to get to the beach. They are getting closer, but there are many waves. The men wait to catch one that will carry them to shore, but it's the wave that catches them scattering everything; fishermen, fish, paddles and raft.

Finally, everything gets to dry land. The fatigue in their faces is noticeable; it's arduous, they don't have motors, and to paddle a raft requires a lot of effort. The women and their children are on the beach to help, they receive them with embraces and prepared food, which they devour. While the women clean the fish, they tell their children how the fishing was. I approach, very interested in talking to them. I admire that they risk their lives every day for a few fish and that the family waits for them with so much affection and concern.

"Hi, how's it going? Was the fishing any good?" I ask them.

"Yes, thanks to God. Would you like to buy one?"

"I would love to, but I don't have a way to cook it."

"You don't cook these, let me show you," interrupts one of the women, who immediately cleans a fish, mixing parsley with other ingredients, and after putting everything into an empty half of a coconut shell, gives it to me to try. "Just a second!" Before the first taste, the woman adds a little lemon juice. Simply delicious!

"Cande, try this."

"Raw?" she asks staring at me wide-eyed.

"Yes, try it, you will love it. It doesn't get any fresher than this," I'm right, she loves it and asks for more. "What do you call this food?"

"Ceviche" responds the proud chef. We pay and go to eat lunch in the only shade on the beach from a wooden boat under construction.

The bridge that joins Peru and Ecuador is a sea of people coming and going. After crossing a small river, we carry out the exit formalities with no problems. We leave behind a country that gave us more than we could have imagined. We take with us images we don't want to forget and lessons that we wish to put into practice.

Ecuador

TILL HERE:
5955 miles
in 4 months

N

Punta Pietra

Manta
Quito
Coca
Napo River

Salinas
Baños
Rocafuerte
Guayaquil

Cuenca

Machala

E

ECUADOR
LATITUD: 0°-0'-0"
LONG. OCC. 78°-27'-8"

10000
SERIE A.M.
11623963
DIEZ MIL SUCRES

Ecuador

Middle of the World

Enchanted Cuenca

We arrive in a magic city, Cuenca, built in the mountains with cobblestones, wood and clay and full of stairs.

We go into a bakery and the man in front of us asks, "Sir, would you be kind enough to sell me a pound of bread, please?"

"Of course, sir, I'll get that for you right now. Two thousand sucres, please."

"Thank you very much, here you are. I bid you a good day."

"Same to you, good sir."

This simple exchange over bread is all an expression of courtesy; they are effusively polite people. The use of the familiar terms doesn't exist here. Children address their parents and even their elder siblings formally and married couples use formal terms when speaking to one another.

Since our car generates curiosity, right away some people begin to gather around. In an orderly fashion, they surround us and in silence wait for someone to pose a question, this way everyone can hear the reply.

"It's not my intention to bother you, sir, but may I ask you a question? Could you tell us what kind of car this is?" asks somebody in a friendly way. Thus, the conversation begins.

They tell us that a fellow countryman of ours, a former-soccer player, has an Argentine style barbeque restaurant very close to here. We go straight there. The compatriot receives us very happily and lets us park right in the patio of his restaurant, so that we could be able to sleep in a little hotel right in the heart of this picturesque city.

Stars of Pain

It's time to continue traveling to the small towns in the mountains, so we go back for our companion of the road at the restaurant. When we get there, we detect that it has footprints on the running boards, on the fender and on the hood.

"I can not believe this! Who dares to climb on a car?!? What's the big idea?!" I shout with so much anger, and I call the first waiter I see. "Come here, show me the sole of your shoes."

He obeys my order with a puzzled expression, while asking me, "What's wrong?"

"One of you walked on my car and if I find out who it was, I'm going to break his face!" I continue calling over the waiters. I've already checked four of the five men and I still haven't found the matching footprint. There's only one more to check, but he doesn't want to approach.

"Come on over and let's take a picture," lies one of his companions acting now as my accomplice in this investigation.

"Show me your sole." I say as soon as he walks over.

"Why?"

"Show me and then I'll tell you."

It's him, the sole matches the footprint. Yelling, I demand,

"Why did you step on my car? What for? Did you want to break it? What?"

"I didn't do it," he answers, his lie increases my fury.

"What do you mean you didn't do it? This is your footprint" he looks at them, casting about while trying to invent something.

"I was just playing around," he says fanning the flames of the fire inside me. So I explode like a boiler and do something I've only done once in my life, in my adolescence. I punch him in the face, and then again.

My reaction shocks the people standing around, and a couple driving by in a car stop to ask me what's going on.

"This jerk walked all over the hood of my car," pointing out the man who is cradling his painful face in his hands.

"And...so?" they ask me showing me that I've caused more damage than I've received. The waiter begins to walk away and I feel quite bad. What did I do? Why? What changed? Nothing, I have only made matters worse. Now I am mad at myself. Moreover my hand hurts pretty badly. Cande wanted to stop me but I didn't listen. My heart told me to let it pass, but I didn't hear it either. I am terribly ashamed. So, we go away from the place and the farther we drive into the mountains, the greater is my regret.

We get to a small village. We're invited to stay on a small farm and we park in the corral. The owner accompanies me to see a shaman who will check my hand. I've never been to one, but my pain is so great, and there's no doctor in the area.

"They come from all over to see him," the farmer says to me on the way. I'm sure that now they'll add that "they" even come all the way from Argentina to see him, I think. "He cures everything and for ever," continues the promotion. Let's hope that in addition to my hand he cures this pain that I feel here, inside myself, a pain in my soul.

We stop in front of a house which is full of dogs and cats. We go in without knocking and wait in the only room there is. Behind a curtain, from where much smoke is rising, the healer assists someone.

"He's doing a cure. He's reversing a curse for a man that someone has cast or maybe he's curing lovesick or envy," explains my companion. I can't believe where I am, I want to leave but this pain is getting worse.

Finally, the witch doctor finishes with his patient. He is so big that it seems that his body is never going to stop coming out from behind the curtain. God willing he won't have to give me a massage…

"Let's see what we have here," he tells me while looking at the swelling that has formed on the knuckle of my index finger. I observe his heavy woolen poncho that only allows me to see his feet and his hands- when he pulls them out. At the same time he's moving my fingers, causing me more pain, he continues, "This is dislocated, one of your bones is out of place. There's nothing broken, with a massage I can put it back."

Then, he takes my right arm, passes it under his armpit and, turning his enormous back to me, he interposes his body between me and my arm. He knows that this is going to hurt. He grasps my fingers with his enormous hands and after rubbing on some oil, he begins the massage. I feel pain and heat that burns.

"Does your hand feel warmer?" he asks me.

"Yes…" I can barely speak, my face is so pinched that it's hard to enunciate.

"It's how it has to be, to make it softer…" while he finishes the phrase, I give a yell. The massage is stronger now and deeper into the zone of the pain. It hurts so bad that it seems I can see all the stars in the universe, "I only have a little more to go, hang on," he adds.

More? I want him to stop now. I feel his hand grasp my arm even stronger, and afterwards he grabs my index finger and pulls, as if he wants to pull it off. They could have heard my yell all the way to Cuenca, making the punched man feel happy about it. God has punished me and now I am suffering my condemnation. Not being satisfied with my pain and shouting, he pulls again… Gosh! How it hurts. In the end, the healer releases my hand, that doesn't look any better, it only looks greasy, injured and defeated.

He looks for a cigar made from a rolled leaf of tobacco; he lights it, inhales a big mouthful of smoke and exhales it over my hand. He repeats the operation three more times saying something between breaths but in an unintelligible mummer. And this is the culmination of the session of pain, which I pay for as if I were a masochist. We return to the farm over the same road we came on. It's a night without stars or perhaps it's me who doesn't want to see any more stars for today.

A Fork in the Road

We go from one marvelous mountain village to another; we visit the markets at mealtimes discovering that Sunday is the special day in which the people from the surrounding hills come down with their products for sale. They don't bring much, so little in fact. Some have a couple of chickens, others two guinea pigs, straw hats, a llama or some have leashed little pigs as if they were dogs. They all sell their own products and with what they earn they go shopping themselves, returning home with a few other things. So as not to break the custom of eating typical local foods, we eat roasted guinea pig, pierced through with a stick and manually turned over burning coal.

We begin to descend down the mountains toward the ocean; the ever-present fog is incessant. The rains have already caused many landslides, which carry away both houses and roads, and threaten to continue.

As I drive over the narrow, steep road I think about the dreamlike places we've left behind and the remembrance I bring along: my swollen hand that doesn't stop hurting.

We stop to eat, buying in the small shops that have little to offer and when night announces its arrival we stop near a house, which is also a small shop. It has only the basics: rice, potatoes, condiments and two avocados. We buy these last ones, because we already gave up our cooking implements in Peru.

An elderly man waits on us. His grandchildren are playing in our car. When he sees that our dinner will be just avocados, he invites us to eat in his home. First we go to the kitchen. In a big pot," mote", boiled hard white seed corn, is being cooked. On the floor there is hay where the guinea pigs live, only temporarily, since they will be a meal within the next few days. The kitchen

doesn't have any windows; the smoke looks for its way out through the door and we go with it. We go into the house and immediately the grandpa serves us boiled plantains. They don't have any taste at all and although we're hungry, it's not easy for us to get them down. The man realizes this and offers to cook us some scrambled eggs: "To improve the flavor," he tells us. And it does.

When we are about to finish dinner, a woman of our age comes and sits next to us. She's the two kids' mother. She is more at ease than the others and right away asks us where we're from.

"Argentina"

"Oh, really, I have a brother in Italy." As if Italy and Argentina were neighboring countries!

"Well, Italy is really a long way from Argentina," clarifies Cande.

"Ohhh, I'm going to Italy to work. Do you know anything about Italy? I have to leave my children because there's no work here. My brother left two months ago and told me that when he gets enough together, he'll send me money for the ticket. We still haven't heard from him, but…"

I go and get the map of South America, to show her where we come from. While walking to the car, I think about this woman's situation, having to leave her children and her land to go to a place she knows nothing about, not what it's like, or even where it is…merely for work. I unroll the map over the table.

" Is Ecuador that small?" she comments slightly disillusioned while Cande points out the smallest Latin country in South America. "And which one is Italy?" she asks searching with her eyes all over the map.

"Italy is separated from America by a big ocean, it's on another continent."

Cande and I continue looking at the map at all the land we've already covered. It's a lot! We've crossed the Andes three times; this is the fourth time that we over here. We traversed the driest desert in the world without the car being any problem at all. We feel very strong in our fifth covered country, capable of traversing many more.

I look with determination at a zigzag line on the map. It starts out very close to where we are and continues snaking all the way to the Atlantic. The line has a name: in Ecuador, it's called Napo, while in Peru and Brazil it's known as Amazon. The adventure calls to my heart, since I was a kid I've imagined going down the Amazon…but no, my mind calculates that it's impossible: we already have almost no money to continue, much less for such an adventure. Anyway, what would we do with the car? Apart from that, this is a land for those who know it and even so some of them don't survive. One has to know about navigation, have immunizations against certain diseases…what would happen if one little spider bit us in the middle of a hopeless position. Turning a deaf ear to all my fears and while following the long line with my finger I ask Cande, "What would you think about taking a detour to Brazil?"

"Along the Amazon? Sounds great, adventurous, pretty crazy…"I feel that I made her nervous, but her quick reply comes straight from her soul. She amazed me; I thought she'd throw the map at me.

"Is that why you have to go on an airplane?" interrupts the woman who is still thinking about Italy. We go to sleep fully aware that there is more than one way to get to Alaska.

On the way to Guayaquil, already on flat land, we come up to a cross roads with no signs at all. In doubt, we wait for someone to appear. My instinct tells me to keep going straight, but the first man we see tells us without hesitating, "Just a short way, that way," signaling to the right. Well, I still think it's straight ahead and this man tells us right, why don't we ask someone else? Another person passes by; we stop him and ask him. First he looks right as if his eyes were going along the road, as they could see the end of the line; then to the left, and lastly he turns his gaze straight ahead. He just stands there not responding until very hesitantly he comments, "It's that way, yeah, over there," signaling left. I don't know whether to laugh or curse. What I end up doing is telling him "thanks a lot."

Cande and I laugh. We'd better continue the vote. And we find it in the conductor of a jalopy of a truck. As if representing the vote of the populace, he does it and he does it wrongly. He sends us backwards, from the way we came! So, our vote came out null and void and in an act of tyranny, I drive straight on following my intuition, instead of the will of the people. We finally get to Guayaquil, via the longest road though.

Captain Forever

Roaming around the port of Salinas we meet a young European who is the captain of a boat. His small vessel is called Turtle and its crew is just his dream and his desire to get to know the seven seas.

"I crossed the Atlantic in sixteen days, I never thought it would be that fast. It took me more than fifteen years to make up my mind and in a little more than two weeks, I was already on the other side of the world. Do you realize how long I hesitated? And all the time I lost?"

"We felt the same when we began driving. When we looked back, we realized all that we needed was to begin," I tell him and Cande reaffirms my commentary with hers.

"The secret to fulfill a dream is starting," The mariner and I remain still after these simple words charged with so much truth.

"And where are you going?"

"My prow is headed first toward Galapagos, after a while a bit to starboard to Polynesia, and from there I'll tie up for a couple of years in Australia, to make a little money to be able to keep going," replies the captain.

How simple his trip sounds. It seems like ours, traveling to all these magical places and running out of money.

"I was almost attacked by pirates," he continues.

"Pirates?!"

"Yes, in the high sea, after passing through the Panama Canal, I began being followed by a motor boat about 90 feet long. Initially I checked them out doing unusual maneuvers, if I changed course, they changed theirs, and so on. In the end, they were getting closer all the time."

"Did you call for help over the radio?"

"Yes, but it was days of navigating away from the closest coast and on international waters. Every once in a while those on the radio contacted me to see how I was. I had told them to report me lost if I stopped replying. I even gave them my family address. It was horrible…"

"And what did you do?"

"The same thing as the first man who went around the world alone and in a similar situation. I made a doll with a hat and I put it in the door of the cabin, and I came in and out of it in different clothes to make them think there were more people than just me."

"And?"

"It seemed to work, because a short time later, they quit following me," he tells us proudly.

We are talking right in front of the Marine harbormaster's office, which makes me feel a huge desire to go in and ask about the Amazon River. Captain Espinoza assists us and we tell him about our idea, he never looks at us as if we were crazy. From the very first moment, he takes us seriously. He listens to us with attention. When we've completed our explanation, he tells us, "I need to speak to someone who knows the river. Come back and see me tonight "

At the port, there are many fish restaurants specializing in ceviche, so we make the most of them and stop to eat. An elderly man helps us park the car, he will be there to watch it. From inside the place, and while we wait to be served, I can't take my eyes off that old man. I observe how, under the sun, he helps the drivers park and guides them when they pull out...almost no one puts down their windows to say thank you nor to hand him a coin. I don't know why, but this man makes me feel so much respect that I walk out of the fish place and go to the car. As soon as he sees me, he prepares to help me back out of the parking lot.

"I only came out to look for something, thank you very much."

"It's nothing, sir. Shall I go on watching the car?"

"Only if you accept a refreshment."

"Excuse me?"

"If you agree to have a drink with us."

"If I don't inconvenience you..."

"Not at all," I tell him, and we both go into the fish restaurant. When he sits down, he seems to be a little uncomfortable, but Cande immediately cheers him up.

"How nice to have some company! We'd be delighted, that since you're already here with us, you would join us to a ceviche."

"No, no...thank you, I don't want to bother you," murmurs the elder.

"It's already ordered," Cande lies compassionately.

"Well, in that case, I don't want to be impolite."

The ceviche comes immediately, since it's already prepared. We savor every bite and the man enjoys his dish without caring that the people are leaving with the cars that he has helped to park. He has few teeth, an untidy white beard, a fisherman's cap that he doesn't take off and, although it's very hot, he also leaves his dark jacket on, which gives him a touch of importance.

"Why did the waitress call you Captain when she asked you what juice you would like?" I inquire curiously.

"Because I was a captain of my own boat for so many years that people forgot my name. When I lost my ship, there were those who asked me my name, but I never replied to them, I am the Captain, and my name...I think I've even forgotten it myself."

"What type of boat did you have?"

"A fishing boat, built with the best wood that one could get. There was no craft in the area that had withstood more storms. Whenever I rowed, I always arrived at the port, even if the wind and the tides were against me. One always has to keep rowing, because if you abate... "

"What does it feel like to sail?" I ask him.

"You've never sailed?" he replies astonished, as this is something elementary.

"No, never, but I would like to," I say not wishing to dissuade the conversation.

"Sailing is risking your life from the very moment you leave the port. It's entrusting yourself to God, the Virgin, the sea, the wind, the boat...your life no longer belongs to you, you become a sea game. You're floating on wood over hungry water, full of sharks. What happens doesn't depend on you. If the sea wishes, you come back with fish, you return to your family. Sailing is living on the verge of danger, but the rewards are many; you can feel alive with every beat of your heart."

"What's a fisherman's life like on land"

"On land, it's not worth much. When you get to the port you want to sell your fish as quickly as you can, even if it's at a bad price, just so you can go home to your loved ones. After a little while, you get bored and go out drinking in the bars until the money runs out. So, you prepare for another voyage, fixing the nets, the craft. On a boat, you feel alive, you know that everyone is as important as the captain, everyone depends on everyone else, you can't drink, nor sleep, nor be distracted, and in the face of a storm you must place yourself in God's hands but you have to keep fighting even though there's no way out. In the ocean one can never give up."

I order him another juice, I want this chat to continue; I don't want him to leave. "What's the best moment for a fisherman?"

"Being on the sea, where the horizon is only water, in his small and fragile boat in the middle of the sea, the fisherman feels the glory. He wants to catch the biggest fish and go back in the worst storm so then everyone in port will talk about him and his heroic deeds. The best moment for a fisherman is when he becomes a legend," I listen to him thinking that for me, he already is one.

"And, what is the worst moment for the fisherman?"

"To become a Captain and lose your boat."

"But, what happened with your boat?" he looks down, I don't know if it was appropriate to ask, I would like to tell him that he doesn't have to tell me, but my curiosity won't let me be courteous. After a brief silence, the Captain continues.

"The first and only time it went out to sea without me, it never came back. There was neither storm nor strong winds. Nothing happened, it just disappeared. It was the first time that it set out without me, it was the first time my son was the captain…" by saying this he allows us to know that he had lost it all; his son, his boat, and everything he had ever fought for now belongs to the sea.

"But why didn't you continue fishing in somebody else's boat?"

"When you get to be the Captain of your own boat, when you know the secrets of the sea and the storms, it's impossible to let another person tell you what to do. When you become a Captain, even though of a small boat, there is no way back. When you are a captain, you're a captain forever."

When we leave we see that the only car that's still parked in the lot is ours, we have spent hours talking. And although he has no reason to, the sea Captain helps us back out.

We go back to the Harbormaster. Espinoza is waiting for us. And as soon as we arrive he tells us to climb into the Marina pick up truck.

"I commented at the naval base about your plans and they want to meet you. They seem enthusiastic about the idea."

In the officer's club, Commander Jaramillo receives us together with various captains, who immediately begin to ask us questions.

" Where do you plan to set off from?"

"From the first navigable port," I answer not knowing where that is.

"That's Port Orellana," one of the mariner states.

"In what kind of craft are you thinking to undertake this trip?"

"We still don't know."

"How are you thinking you'll go about it?"

"In some way."

After the questions and our vague answers the captains begin to look at one another, perhaps supposing they are wasting their time on us, we only know that we want to do something that we don't have clear yet, neither how to do it or if it will even be possible. Commander Jaramillo has continued to listen to me attentively, with his look fixed, without uttering one word and without turning around to look at the captains behind him.

"Captain, you prepared maps of the Napo River, could you find a set for these guys?" the Commander breaks his silence holding off the skeptical questions of the captains.

"Yes, Commander, but I don't think they'll be much useful. The last survey was done five years ago and the depth and riverbeds change constantly."

"Just the same, bring them a copy. If these folks have come so far in such an old car, this new undertaking won't be impossible," he stands up while he continues talking. "It seems you've gotten here at the best time. Right now, we are signing a navigational agreement with Peru, as from 1950, the border in the jungle has been closed over boundary differences. If you manage to get down, you will be the first ones to do it and if you open this tourist route, it would be a big help for Ecuador. Then you can count on our help in everything you need," encourages Jaramillo and immediately he invites us to drink a glass of wine to celebrate our success. After toasts and a drink the Commander reiterates, "In any part of your journey, in any place in the world, if you need help, find a sailor. Every sailor is an adventurer and he'll help you. What you're doing is incredible. I admire you."

We cannot believe that a person with so much sea life and high rank would tell us this. In the morning we come in only to ask a question about an idea and in the evening, we leave from the naval base with total support of the Navy.

We go back to the harbormaster's office with Espinoza who has to contact Puerto Orellana to report our undertaking and also to gather information about the state of the roads, rivers and the possibilities of embarking with a destination to Peru or Brazil. He calls on the radio and captain Aldaz reports that the roads are in pretty bad conditions. There have been many landslides and some stretches of the route are closed, only trucks and 4x4 vehicles are able to pass. Because of the rains, the river flow is very high, but Aldaz believes there is a craft getting ready for a trip to Brazil. We leave it in his hands to investigate, we'll be in touch with him again in fifteen days, and meanwhile we continue getting to know Ecuador.

The Conquest

In the morning, we leave for Montanita. We're rather quiet, each one thinking on our own about the possibility of the new project. Going down the Amazon won't just be a risky adventure, but it will also divert us thousands of miles off the initial plan; adding Brazil, Venezuela and Colombia to our list. Before talking to Cande, I prefer to be sure myself of what I really want to do surely Cande is doing the same.

On the way, we see a hospital and we stop. The hand is still swollen and painful. They see me immediately, they find out the cause of so much pain; the X-ray reveals a fractured finger. After promising that I won't use my hand for a few days, the doctor decides not to plaster it. When I tell him about the massage by the quack, all he says is, "That must have really hurt, much more than when you broke it."

"Doctor, I saw all the stars in the galaxy." On our way out, I ask where to pay for the surgery fees.

"My friend, our hospitals are public, we are here to help and to cure, there is no charge for health," he says to me. We are in Ecuador in the worst economic moment and still the medical assistance to its people is not neglected, not even to foreigners.

We continue traveling until we get to Montañita, which is a small village inhabited by surfing fans. The simplicity of the place surprises us, there are only two streets, the constructions are made of bamboo and palm trees, and the prices, very economical. There are even places were you can hang a hammock for fifty cents a day. We're delighted, so we get a place in a guesthouse that has three rooms, a kitchen, and a playful puppy. We will stay here four or five days, to take a break, a vacation within our vacation, and since we're here, we'll celebrate my birthday.

Every morning, I go out to the beach with the puppy, returning with everything necessary for breakfast; octopus, oysters, and mussels that Manuel, a boy from town, teaches me how to find at low tide. I meet a Belgian surfer gathering corals and seashells. He's lived here for five months. He tells me he creates hand-crafted jewelry to subsist and get what he needs to go to other beaches with good waves when the sun vanishes.

"When the sun vanishes?"

"Yeah, pretty soon it's gonna get cloudy and we won't see the sun here again for a few months. Nobody hangs here then."

I go back with my breakfast, which I usually prepare for Cande adding some tropical fruit; I wake her up with a new and exquisite menu surprising her every morning.

The last day is incredibly sunny. Coming back from the beach with my papayas, I see a girl in a bikini. A beautiful one, lying on the beach, the sun all over her body. I stand there staring at her totally smitten; she is exceptionally stunning...I approach her slowly and sit down near her, I offer her some papaya. She cheerfully accepts.

"Will you marry me?" I ask not being able to take my eyes off her body.

"I've already been married for seven years, darlin'," she replies.

"So...will you marry me again?"

"Yes!"

She's told me yes, I've conquered her, she's mine, Cande is mine...!

When You Need it Most

We arrive in the city of Manta with only four dollars in our pockets, but with the possibility of getting some money out of our almost extinct savings account. We go from bank to bank, but we can't take out anything out of the ATM's with our card. We begin to get a little nervous; we don't understand what's wrong. Finally, we end up sitting on the running boards of the car thinking about what we're going to do with only four dollars. If we eat, we can't fill the tank, if we buy gas, we won't get far. What are we going to do?

"Good evening, excuse me for disturbing you, but who is the owner of this car?" asks a very well dressed man whose face shows he is astonished and shocked at what he sees.

"We are," we say as we stand up to shake his extended hand.

"My name is Bustos and I don't know if you're going to believe me," his glance going back and forth between the car and us, "This is incredible, today is my wedding anniversary, my wife and I have been married for fourteen years. And on a day like today, seventh of June, but fourteen years ago, we were taken to the church in an antique car just like this one...by two Argentine people... also on their way to Alaska."

"What?!" his story leaves us as perplexed as he is. So many coincidences are difficult to believe.

"Would you be willing to come and celebrate our anniversary with my wife and I? What a wonderful surprise for her."

"Yes, of course," we answer puzzled by what is happening.

"Perfect, so follow my car."

"How about leaving your car and ride with us?" Candy proposes, prompting the man to climb in joyfully.

"Keep following the waterfront until almost the end," he indicates. "I can not believe the incredible coincidence. All day at work I was thinking about my anniversary, but I had no idea what I could buy for my wife. And then, looking out of the window, I realized that I had the gift from heaven parked in front of my office!" continues the man without knowing that he was the one sent from heaven. "Why did you come to Manta? It's not tourist attraction…"

"We're looking for a ship to go to Panama, and that way avoid Colombia." We answer, without having decided yet whether to go down the Amazon River or not.

"Well, here in Manta there is only one shipping agent." He pauses and tells us, "And that one is me! Tomorrow we'll see what we can do."

We pull up in front of a very beautiful home. On seeing the car, his wife is overjoyed, she even thought it was the same one that took her to the church and that we are just here in Manta for her anniversary…in some way we are. In the evening they take us to a very nice restaurant to celebrate with them. The surprises don't stop here. In the middle of dinner, they offer us an apartment they have above their offices and a place to park the car.

When we're finally alone in the apartment, I ask Cande, "What is the reason for all this?" Have you realized about it?"

"I cannot believe it. It really is a miracle."

"But why is all this happening to us? Here we were not knowing what to do and this man appears…like the one who came from nowhere when I was about to be mugged in Lima."

"I don't know why, but it seems that there is someone else with us, somebody who wants this to continue," she says. I know who she is referring to, I also feel that God is traveling with us. I have always believed in Him, it's how I was brought up, but now my faith is different. Now I feel Him closer. Theory has given way to practice. God isn't an invention, He's a discovery.

In the morning, Mrs. Bustos wakes us up, with a packed agenda for us. She takes us to meet the mayor of the city, to the newspapers, to the radio and to every person she believes it's good for us to meet. In a moment, we get to have hundreds of people surrounding the car, because the woman seems like a pro at public relations in the city. She knows who everyone is very well and they know her. Later they invite us to lunch at the Yacht Club and to have a coffee in a five-star hotel…and with it all we still have only four dollars in our pockets; it wouldn't even be enough for the tip.

We go to Mr. Bustos's offices. All morning, he has been making calls on our behalf and he has some news for us, "May I introduce you to a traveler like you, Mr. Zambrano," he tells us indicating a man in his fifties. "As a kid, he was a shoeshine boy; in his youth, he was an adventurer like you and now he's the owner of a fishing company."

"Nice to meet you" we say while greeting him.

"Do you know?, I went on a trip with my friends in a car not as beautiful as yours all the way to Patagonia, Argentina. We didn't know anything about the place, we didn't have much money, and without doubt, many of my best memories are from your land."

"How nice to hear that," we tell him.

"And, now that I'm looking back, I remember that along the way we met another guy from Ecuador who was coming back here. So, I gave him some letters to give out to various girlfriends I had. The end of the story is that devilish man gave all the letters to one girl, the very one I loved the most. And of course, when I came back to see her, quite romantically, without knowing anything about this…she threw all the letters at my face and I could never see her again."

We all laugh at this tragic romantic story until Mr. Bustos comments, "I told him about you guys and your hope to go by boat to Panama. He, willing to help you, told me that he could take you in an empty boat that goes there to buy fuel." This leaves us speechless, free…to Panama?

"It would be a pleasure for me, from adventurer to adventurer, and also it would be a way for me to repay the kindnesses I received during my trip around your land" Zambrano explains so naturally. He doesn't have an exact date of departure. Neither do we want to leave Ecuador too quickly…besides, we're waiting for information about the Amazon River. Everything is coming to us at the same time.

Suspended in Air

After a few exhausting days in Manta, in which we attend many socials, we go toward our next stop, Portoviejo. An Argentine journalist has filled up our gas tank.

"Herman, do you remember the day we met the mayor of Manta and there were hundreds of people around us? A girl showed up and asked the value of the car. Remember, she said her brother might want to buy it," Cande tells me.

"Yes, I think I didn't pay much attention to her due to such a question"

"She told us her brother lives in Portoviejo and he's the only one who has an antique car."

"Well, let's ask around when we get there…if we can meet him, maybe he'll welcome us."

"How incredible, don't you think so?! We get to Manta with four dollars and we leave without having spent one penny."

"As well as an offer for a boat to Panama… Do you remember saying that the secret to make a dream come true is to begin? Certainly, it's as simple as that. Once you set your dream in motion, everything is given to you…it's an energy that flows and offers everything you need…"

"Yes, since we've set off we are constantly meeting people who teach us something, travelers or simply people who help us at the right moment, in the appropriate moment…"

"Cande, I believe we're being followed" I tell her after watching a jeep coming in the opposite direction, it stopped when it passed us and turned around and now without any effort it is close to us. It's next to us!

"STOP! Argentineans, stop!" shouts a young man with all his hair in his face because of driving without a roof nor a windshield. We pullover somewhat frightened. "Hi, nice to meet you, my name is Cordova, I am from Portoviejo."

"Nice to meet you too," we say without taking our eyes off him.

"Are you going to Portoviejo? Where are you going to sleep?"

"We really don't know yet, we're going to look for a man…" We're suspicious because of all the questions.

"My sister talked to you guys, I have an old car too. My name is Eduardo."

"No! It can't be so! We've been just talking about you…"

"Seriously? Do you want to come to my house? Do you want to stay a few days?"

"Great, but it would be for only one night, if you think that's alright."

"As long as you want. Follow me."

We go to his house to pick up his wife and his two kids. They take us out for some pizzas. The man is very funny, dynamic, and his batteries are charged up!

"Around here we only drink beer in the days with an 'R'," he tells us, "Mornday, Tuersday, Wednesday, Thursday, Friday, and Saturday. Except for Sunday, it doesn't have an 'R'." We laugh. "Tomorrow let's go around and see Portoviejo, if you want we can go on Harleys, I have two of them. Do you know how to ride?" he inquires.

"No, I barely know how to drive old cars…"

"Well, if you can drive this, you can drive anything. And, have you ever been paragliding?"

"No, but I'd love to."

"Great, tomorrow we'll go to Crucita. We'll go in tandem, I'm an instructor."

And that's the way it is. On the next day we go very fast, all around Portoviejo, on loud, old motorcycles cruising with Harley style and grace. We drive until we use the whole tank. Later, he takes us on a flight over the Pacific. Being in the air, in total silence, in direct contact with the breeze, with feet swinging, surrounded by gulls and cormorants is a magical sensation.

"We really enjoyed that, thanks a lot Eduardo," we say to him, before starting our trip again. We've been able to get money out of the bank; we took it all. It is not much, but we feel rich compared to these last days.

"I'm the grateful one, I see you and I realize that you woke me up. I was falling asleep with my life, with my dreams. By the way, yesterday, when we ate together and you told me about everything that's happening during this trip my wife and I thought that you had to go and visit a very special person. What's more, we ask you to go, please; he can teach you so much."

"Every time we go to see him we come back delighted. He has a way of being that fills you with energy," adds his wife.

"He's called Alonso Ordoñez. He lives on a spectacular cliff in front of the sea. He has three cottages that he rents only to special persons, he does no publicity, he doesn't even have a telephone, for sure he would gladly receive you. You have to go. Tell him that we sent you."

Magic Words

We drive along the sea, the coast getting greener all the time. We want to get to Alonso's early, before it gets dark, however hunger makes us stop in Jama. As we park, a truck pulls up next to us. There are a man and two women in it. He gets out, his look tells us he sees something he loves.

"Wow, are you guys traveling in this marvel? Would you give me the pleasure of receiving you in my home? It would be so nice for me to host you."

"Yes, of course, sir, the pleasure would be all ours," we tell him. In one second we decide to postpone our visit to Alonso Ordoñez for another day, there's no way we could refuse such a heartfelt invitation.

"Great! I'll drop off the ladies and come back for you."

And just as he promised, he comes back. He gives us the option of getting to his house the direct route paved road or by the longer way, a sand path, but more picturesque. We choose the second.

During the trip, we begin to doubt his friendliness. We're afraid. The road is attractive, but it's deserted. We're following a man we don't know, he's going in his truck and we in a car which we couldn't escape in if we wanted to. Suddenly, the man pulls over, gets out and approaches us, he stopped to point out a bird and a landscape; with much affection, he explains what he's showing us. So, we relax, if he wanted to do something bad, he surely wouldn't stop and waste his time being a tour guide for us, he seems a good person.

However, the long road has its compensation, we get to a cliff in front of the sea with a few beautiful cottages…there are three…Cande seeing all this, tells me that this could be just the man we were coming to see. No way! but he might be, this place is as beautiful as we've been told, there are the cabins, there's a cliff and this is a good man.

"Excuse me, but are you Alonso Ordoñez?" I ask him.

"How do you know my name? " he asks eagerly.

"We were on our way here! Mr. Cordova from Portoviejo sent us, he spoke very highly of you. We wanted to meet you!"

"It looks as if it had to happen, we were meant to come across each other…" he comments without showing much surprise while he leads us to a cottage in which he'll host us. The balcony juts out over the cliff. Through the bedroom window, we see half sea half sky. "When the person that I loved most in my life told me that we couldn't live together, I devoted myself to going around searching for my place, a place where I would sense myself in perfect harmony. It was after six years of travel that I found the edge of this cliff. I sat down and felt that my search was over. This cottage is in the same place I sat that day. It's where I feel the best. I hope you feel the same, well enough to stay here for a few days. Feel free to stay as long as you want and leave whenever you want. You are the ones I welcome. Now I will leave you alone, I'll be back at suppertime. Enjoy yourselves." We thank him as he leaves.

We feel very well here, the offer to stay for a few days tempts us. "But Herman, if we keep up like this, we won't even get to Alaska in a year," Cande tells me.

"Yes, but just look at this place. I think it would be fine waiting a few more days to go to Alaska."

"It's already taken us a few more months," she replies. Then she stands quietly looking at the horizon of the sea, and says, "What's a few more days?"

We eat baked plantains with rice and fish. Later, we go down to the shoreline. There, together with a couple of guys and girls who've come to visit Alonso, we light a bonfire; they play regional songs on their guitar while he prepares a surprise for us. It is a paper hot air balloon. Alonso asks us to write down three wishes each, he puts them into the balloon and lights a candle that fills it with hot air, lifting it.

"If we elevate our wishes very, very high, and we let them be taken by the wind to its place, these will be accomplished." and he releases the balloon which slowly drifts up and up as if following the rhythm of the guitar. The flame lights up the red paper, making it showy in the darkness. Then Alonso directs the conversation to our journey.

"What do you feel now that you are fulfilling your dream?"

"I feel full of life. I believe that I've spent thirty years without living, I feel I'm newly born since it's just now that I'm living.

"Have you learned anything on your trip up to this point?"

"So much, it seems like more than a trip, these are life long lessons. We learn something every day…it is a world that opens for us and shows itself."

"What do you remember most of all you've learned?"

"When we left we learned that to go forward you have to put your fears aside, because if you let them be ahead of you, they will never let you move on. We've learned that everything has a lot of energy and if we know how to use it, it will help us a lot to achieve many things, such as feeling very well, full of health and life." Alonso listens with attention. "Another super remarkable thing is that we are part of everything, a very important part, as important as being the king of the world, without disturbing the kingdoms of others."

"Wow, it seems that you have really learned. Anything else?"

"Yes, we've learned that we have to try to have less, instead of more. If not, the things tangle us up and make us sink."

"The conqueror conquered by his conquests…"

"Pardon?"

"No, nothing, go on, go on. Anything else?"

"Well, I believe that the most important thing we've learned is that we're not alone. There is someone else right next to us enjoying this trip, this dream. Someone who is helping us so much, because every time we need help, this turns up."

"You went out into the world and the world opened to you because you are open to it. You change, you've made yourself flexible like clay. Every moment, every lesson and every person that you meet molds you into a new shape of yourself. All this occurred because one day you decided to begin. Something so simple as to begin, but we never do. Every time that you live a special moment, don't forget to see the lesson out of it, because if it happens, it has a reason. Look for lessons. Every person can teach, but few learn. Many times right in front of your noses, there's something very important. You can see it and learn it, or let it pass by. From the same professor some will learn more than others. Learn with every thing that you see, with every thing that happens. Where some people don't see anything, you should see lessons. Keep being clay, remember that the more it is worked and mixed, the more perfect the final piece will be.

We look up to heaven searching for the porter of our desires; the wind has carried them away.

It's morning and we are on the balcony writing our diary when a woman comes to tell us that breakfast is ready. Alonso is waiting and has written a few things down for us and wants to devote a whole day of his life to us.

"You've told me that what you're doing is a dream. A dream that since you were very young has grown in your hearts. You told me, too, that you're very astonished about the incredible things that have been happening since starting out…things that have never before occurred in your life," he continues looking at us and goes on. "Well, how can I explain to you these things happen only when a dream is being chased…? You know that the opposite of love is hate…"

"Yes."

"And as for day, it's night; for white, black; for beauty, ugliness and so on."

"Certainly."

But could you please tell me, what is the opposite of dream?"

We think hard about that, searching for what it could be. "I don't know, I can't find any," I say.

"It doesn't have any. There is nothing nor nobody against a dream. We all dream, there is no one who doesn't. All and everyone are in favor of dreams. It is blissful happiness to achieve a dream, and also help one be accomplished is perhaps much happier. So, I'm going to give you some advice. When you need something, when you can't do it on your own, when you need help…ask for it. Say, 'We are Candelaria and Herman, we are chasing our dream. We need help. Can you help us?' No one will deny it, let others be part of your dream, share it, you can't do it all on your own. Many times you will need help and many people would love to help you, but if you don't ask, they won't know how." He pauses, drinks his coffee and continues. "Asking for help is saying I need you, I need your effort, I need your time, and your knowledge to do something that I cannot do alone, but it will be possible if I can count on your support. To ask for help is needing someone to do something together with you, and when someone needs our help, it makes us feel useful, necessary, that we are a part of something. Helping is a sweet feeling, as beautiful as accomplishing a dream.

"But how do we ask someone for help? How can I dare to ask? I would be ashamed, it is…embarrassing."

"None of the most important things you have learned by yourself. Think about your lives up to this moment, and you will see that you've always received help."

I remain silent, remembering. I have learned to walk with help, also to ride my bike and to swim that way. My teachers helped me learn to read and write. With help, I learned how to drive and do my work. I even needed help being born… since the very beginning, people have helped me. It's clear, others taught me everything that I know now and they were always so happy to have been a part.

So I wonder, why shouldn't I ask for help to go on with this dream, to fullfil it? Up to now I thought that if I got myself into this, I should finish it by myself. That I had to be self-sufficient in what ever I do, and if I wasn't I shouldn't do it. But who is completely self-sufficient? There is no such a man. Alonso is right, why do I have to do it alone? Why don't we share our dream with others and permit them to be a part of it? Then, our triumph will be the triumph of all. I'm going to put it into practice, if I need some help, I'm going to ask. If I can't do it alone, I will look for others with whom we can surely make it happen and at the same time make them happy.

After the conversation, Alonso takes us in his motorboat to see some shrimp fishermen. After we come up to one of them Alonso asks, "How's the fishing?"

"Its not going too well, but maybe it will get better," he comments while showing us a half full bucket that holds small shrimp mixed with crabs and mollusks that look really delicious. "You can have them, take them as a gift," he says to us.

"No, thank you," I say, thinking that we couldn't take all he has to sell. But my words wipe out the fisherman's smile.

"I'd love them," interrupts Cande to save the situation, and the man passes the bucket to Alonso happy for giving a gift.

As we leave him Cande and Alonso look at me. And before they can say anything, I explain to them, "I felt as if I was taking something he didn't have enough of, that his gift would hurt him economically…"

"Exactly, that's it, this is giving. Offering what you have too much of isn't an offering. Sharing is giving something that one wants and this fisherman has shared his catch with you. Doing this was the best way for him to tell you 'welcome to my land'." retorts Alonso. "Good thing Cande intervened so as not to reject the man's sacrifice and we showed that we appreciated his nice attitude!"

During the five days we spend with Alonso, we have been filled with something magic. Everything here is like this, only that we should say good-bye now. We are unhappy. We are realizing that everything is marvelous in this trip, except the constant farewells, as we leave people who have received us as if we were their children, their brothers, or their best friends, not knowing if we'll ever see them again.

Alonso has gone ahead of us to Pedernales; we'll meet up there for our final good byes. As we get to the entrance of the city we see that our friend is waiting for us…next to a fire truck, full of firefighters and sirens blaring, lights flashing, a fleet of taxis from town, many other cars and the mayor of Pedernales, who bids us welcome. Alonzo…what a man!

We're put right out in front of the caravan; the fire truck behind us announces our trip over the loud speakers. Honestly, we never imagined this. At first, so much attention, the sirens, the lights make us feel bashful…but while completing the tour around the city we get in the spirit and finally we are delighted. Finishing the tour, we get out of the Graham and loads of people gather around, many bring us gifts from their shops, others offer what ever we might need…I sneak away for a moment to make a call to the naval base in Salinas.

"They're waiting for you in Coca. There is a barge under construction that wants to take you without any charge to somewhere in Brazil, everything is ready." The answer I receive from Espinoza is the one I yearned for the most.

"When does this barge leave?"

"On July 15th."

"Great, this gives us time to continue visiting Ecuador."

Even though Cande is surrounded by people, I call her and tell her the news. "Cande, we're going to Brazil via the Amazon."

"What!?" Her voice expresses happiness and nervousness at the same time.

"There's a barge that will take us for free all the way to Manaos, it leaves on July 15th." I know that Cande loves the idea that we'll be taken and we won't have to navigate the river by ourselves. I am the one who's a bit disappointed, because I still want to experiment more. It's a call from my heart in search of more adventure and The Amazon presents itself as the ideal opportunity. But I can't let this possibility that has been offered pass on…I'd better to let it flow, there absolutely must be some reason for it.

Submerged in these thoughts I carry out a second call, this one to Manta, to thank them so much for the offer of shipping to Panama, but we're going to Alaska via The Amazon.

In the Middle of the World

Once again, we see the Andes range in front of us. We are pointed toward the capital, Quito, and to get there we have to climb these mountains again. The road is narrow and steep, there are no shoulders and so much traffic, which follows us as if we were religious gurus. It is on the curves where we see a long and slow line that goes up at less than 15 miles an hour, following the speed of our car. They can't overtake us, the traffic coming down, the curves, and the lack of shoulders, offer no chance. Surely those that follow us are calling us names and not in a nice way…we can relieve a bit from our nervousness when in some place or another we manage to pull over and the forced parade passes us. As soon as we get back onto the road, we start our car collection all over again.

When we get to Quito we're surprised by its beauty, before beginning our visit we want to make a check and quick service for the car.

"Are you going to Alaska in this car? Do you have everything? Maps, necessary papers…? Do you know how much money you're going to need? Do you have any idea of everything you need to have? Do you really know what you're doing?" All this from the owner of the garage.

"What I have is what you see, and because of my dream, I do everything I can. And you, what are you doing about your dream?" I answer. "I don't know if I'm going to get there with what I have, but I know I'll do my best."

The Huespe family, half Ecuadorian and half Argentinean, hosts us. It feels as if we've been friends forever. They live an hour outside the city, in a house built in the Swiss style by a Swiss owner. During the days we're with them, the family uses their free time to take us all around the area and its little villages. Regarding the city, our idea is to try to find a sponsor there, for which we have made elaborate beautiful folders with all the information about our trip.

We are looking for Argentine companies with offices in Ecuador as well as other national and international ones. We also writte to National Geographic and to several antique car clubs. We take our folders and introduce ourselves. Sometimes they receive us and many times not. Some, straight to the point, tell us immediately that they don't do this kind of promotion. Others ask us for a couple of weeks or even months to study our information and there are also the ones that inform us that their advertising budget is all tied up. They all have an answer, but none of them is the one we're looking for. Two weeks go by in this way. We spend the few bills we have in search of more, more money that doesn't appear and seems to be hiding from us. In the middle of these critical days, we receive an invitation to participate in La Television, a widely watched program in Ecuador on Sundays. Freddy Ellers, the host, will film our passage over line of the Equator by the monument of "The Middle of the World".

We're overexcited; crossing to the other hemisphere is very significant in our journey. So we arrange the car with its rear wheels at the southern hemisphere and the front ones in the north one. Then we position ourselves stepping in each hemisphere at the same time. Since this is a moment to celebrate, we open a bottle of champagne, we pour two glasses and Gramps Graham gets its serving in its radiator. This way all three of us can toast to getting to the Equator.

When we've finished taping the report, Freddy comments that he would also like us close his live program on Sunday. We present ourselves at the studio on Sunday. In the first segment, they show the interview we did at the monument. When they are back on, Freddy invites any company that would like to sponsor us to come aboard. Before going to another commercial break he comments enthusiastically about our trip. "And don't leave us because I have reserved for you a marvelous surprise at the end."

The idea is this; when the broadcast is about to finish, we'll drive into the studio bringing the other host of the show with us. The signal for our entrance is the word "Argentina". With everything all set, we wait inside the car for the clue.

"And now, the surprise I've promised you, the travelers from Argentina!" announces Freddy over the sound of the motor starting. "This is how they've come all the way from Argentina..." and without being able to finish his comment we hear the noise of something breaking, the car lifts its snout and drops its tail. Cande and I look at each other astonished at the same time the host with us says "push, push" completely forgetting that she has her microphone on. While Freddy continues, "Like this they are coming all the way from Argentina," this is the phrase that can be heard while the camera focuses on three guys pushing the car.

Still not knowing what happened, I accelerate, and with the three pushers, we eventually manage to get the whole car into the studio. With red faces, laughter from embarrassment and nervousness, we say good-bye to an audience that bursts into laughter over the way we got here from Argentina, violently jerking and three guys pushing. When the cameras are turned off, Freddy asks me what happened. I don't know, but it seems as if the earth was swallowing us. We go around to the rear part of the Graham and notice that one of the floor planks couldn't take the weight and the wheel fell into the hole.

The production receives a lot of calls. The public responds to Freddy's plea offering us many things, such as garages to fix whatever the car needs, places to sleep and even a gadget to reduce the gas consumption. The people back us up, but from the companies, no news. Even then, we're not feeling disenchanted, I don't know if its because we just don't want to face the problem or if it's because of this faith that has been growing inside us since the beginning of the trip. A faith that's telling us that it's all going to turn out.

The Huespe family is waiting for us at home; they've also been answering the calls. "You just don't know what beautiful messages we have for you. Can I read you one that brought tears to my eyes?" Leonor, the mother of the family asks us anxiously. "It says: 'You were great, you made us feel that with as little as we have in our hands our dreams can be achieved, that one can travel 30,000 miles in a car that it's not even sure will make a hundred. When the car appeared in the studio and then you couldn't go any farther, when we heard "push, push" and saw three men doing it while Freddy was saying 'and this is the way they come from Argentina', you seemed fragile, as fragile as we all are. But still, with this fragility you've made it from Argentina to the middle of the world. And do you know what I felt and for sure what so many others felt too? A huge wish to live our own lives, to complete our own dreams. You showed us that with our fragility and with the little we have, if we want to, we can go around the world'." Leonor lowers the paper and once again, she is on the verge of tears. "Isn't that beautiful?"

The Waiting

Again with empty hands, we leave another city where we have thought we would be able to find some economic support. For the present we're only counting on a little faith and on our hearts, which are full of affection and encourage us to keep going. We are headed to the Orient, to the Amazon jungle. As soon as we come down from the mountains to enter into the jungle everything changes. The road over the hills is very narrow, partially destroyed by landslides. There is so much mud; there has been three days of continuous drizzle. It's impossible to go over 10 miles an hour, there are so many holes, we only try to dodge the big ones and slide right through the little ones. This road is not for cars. Only a few trucks and busses pass this way. We even cross bridges in which we have to move the boards together to fit our narrow track. We feel the humidity in the atmosphere increasing. There are also some very steep uphill climbs. On one of these, Cande has to get out while we're still moving and push the car before it stops…it's a good thing that we followed the advise "if you have a lot, you sink", if not, there's no way we would have made it up.

We come across some Germans who have a 4x4 van, the latest model, totally kitted out, ready and adapted for the worst the jungle has to offer, it even has an international phone and a satellite tracking. However, so much technology has played against them, they are towing the van to Quito because they don't have a way to fix the computer in the engine. With enormous indignation, they watch us leave them behind, listening to the typical noise of an old car that goes slowly, but it goes.

We get to Coca. It's taken us three days to go 195 miles. After so much jostling the car rattles, all its screws are loose, but we are fascinated imagining what's ahead of us. Coca is a town developed by petroleum, there are many oil companies that have their oilrigs in the middle of the jungle and Coca is the closest settlement where petroleum services are provided. It grew up without any style, spread out, dirty, noisy, with basic constructions and where there's too much heat and rain.

Quite by chance we meet Rafael Galeth at the entrance of the town. He is the owner of the barge which is due to take us to Manaos and he is precisely the man who we need to find. He never imagined seeing us in this place and much less that our car would survive that road. After greeting him and introducing ourselves, he comments, "We won't be able to leave on the fifteenth of July, I think it will be around the end of the month or beginning of August, but I'm not sure about that either."

"Oh, well…thanks," we say not knowing neither what to do nor what to think. Looking for some solid ground, we decide to go and search for captain Aldaz, our contact. After receiving us with honors, we asked for his opinion about Galeth and his departure date. "He's building a barge. It's taking him longer than he thought. Also, he doesn't have enough cargo to cover the cost of the voyage, but if some cargo is confirmed, he'll leave in fifteen days."

"And if not?"

"You'll have to wait. It's the only option you have."

Watercolors

We wait for fifteen days until the end of July, then another two weeks and today, August 30, Rafael Galeth still doesn't have a fixed date. He always tells us that there will be a cargo ready, but at the last minute, it's not confirmed. We're living at a camp ground of a petroleum company, we've been here since the first day and we're now part of it, I even do electrical work in the jungle with the other laborers. In Coca, everyone knows us and the constant question is, "So, when are you leaving?" At this point, nobody here believes we'll actually set sail, they think it will be crazy to carry it out. We're already used to their jokes such as, "So, who are you spending Christmas with in town?"

Since we can see the barge will take longer than we expected, we have started looking around for some way to accomplish the trip on our own. But since the promise of leaving in ten or fifteen days with no cost and no danger always appears, we abandon our search until there's a new notice of the extension of the date. In relation to our spirits, the incertitude of the departure, not knowing what to do, and the scarcity of money because of having been traveling for six months, is starting to make us homesick, so much. This is creating a slight crisis, not only as a couple, but also in the state of mind of each of us. What are we doing?? Why? What for?? How nice it would be to be at home, with the family and friends, to eat a nice steak, sleep in my own bed, use my own bathroom…!

"I'm getting so bored, I've already been all over the place and there is nothing more to see. Here we are stuck in the middle of nowhere and our money is not enough. What are we going to do?" Cande tells me, worsening my worry.

"I don't know" is the laconic answer followed by silence.

Candelaria feels suffocated, it's too hot. In addition she's intolerant, because she just can't bear this situation anymore. She watches the cars go by, raising the dust that settles over us. Since the time we got to Coca, the days have become routine for her. Additionally, she knows that the action is in the jungle but although I go many times to the oilrigs with the workers, to get to know them, Cande can't come with me. No woman is allowed.

"Herman, is different from me, he has an idea floating around in his head. 'Build a raft, get the car onto it and leave.' What's worse, the more he thinks about it, the more enthusiastic he gets. On the other hand, I see danger. The car strapped to some tree trunks! I don't agree with this idea, I'm afraid. I know that neither he nor I know anything about navigation and less about a raft. Everything gets increasingly complicated." Cande thinks before breaking into.

"Dear, we have to decide what to do. We had enough money for a six-month trip, and instead of using that time to get to Alaska, we are in Ecuador. If we want to continue, we need money. A lot of it."

"Yes, but I'd rather not talk about that. I've thought a thousand times how we could get the point of no money and suddenly everything closes in on me. Everything was so easy while we had money! Now, I don't know, but everything seems more difficult. In Argentina I knew what to do and how to earn it, I had my work, but here...I am a little bit afraid, we are in a totally different place where every thing is strange to me, I even feel strange," I tell her with total frankness.

"We need money to get to Panama, for gas, for food...for everything. What are we going to do? Even if we wanted to go back we couldn't, not without any money. We can't go back nor forward, what-are-we-going-to-do?" Cande asks me. Why didn't we buy all those handicrafts in Peru before running out of money?"

"I don't know. But don't look back, keep looking forward. We have to be able to do something..."

"You mean work for some company or do something else? But I don't think we can do much here in Ecuador, not with their situation, we'd have to do so much. The salaries are of less than a hundred dollars a month."

"Yes, we'd only earn enough to live on, not enough to advance," I remain thinking, "Cande, why don't you paint?"

"Paint? Me? I have never painted. What am I going to paint?"

"Well, you painted the tiles in the kitchen, and the breadbox, and they came out beautifully. Something like that, but something like pictures."

"There's a world of difference between tiles and paintings. I've never painted and I don't think I'd be able to. What's more, pictures to be sold..."

"Come on... Let's give it a try. Let's buy some watercolor paints, they're cheap and they dry quickly. If you paint them...I'll frame them."

"And how are we going to sell them? To whom? Who would want to buy a painting from me?"

"If you paint them, I'll frame them and sell them…" With this, we form a partnership, a company is being set. Necessity forced us to do something completely new for both of us. Cande has never painted, I have never been a salesman, and we both must put in our best effort in this to work. From now on, to be able to advance, we're not only a married couple and a team, but also a company divided into two departments: production and sales.

Very enthusiastically, we go to buy materials. We go to a store that sells a few school supplies; a box of twelve paints, ($2), a school sketchpad ($2), and four brushes that don't look too good ($5) is our purchase. None of the elements is of the best quality, but we now have the materials and all for only $9. Since the investment is small, if we can get a good income, the cost-benefit ratio will be enormous. If it doesn't work, the loss will not be severe. But this has to work, we need to keep going and for this money is needed.

We return to the camp pretty anxious. We look around for a plate to use as a palette and a glass for some water. Then, we come to the biggest question. Cande, brush in her hand, asks me; "So now, what do I paint?" Right, what to paint? Houses? People? Towns? Animals? Plants? Flowers? What? We look through our photo album trying to find a solution, hoping that one of them would say "paint me" and we find a couple, but they are a bit difficult to start with. So, Cande chooses one that shows a little house in the beautiful countryside. "This one" she tells me and begins to draw it on the paper. I, her first spectator, keep my eyes on the line of the pencil, as one watches a portrait artist in the park. Then follows her first brush strokes and then a couple more. The drawing with the pencil came out beautifully, but now with the watercolors…I think that if I have to go out and sell this landscape, not even my mother-in-law would buy it.

Both of us, slightly disappointed, start to say to each other," Well, it's ok, it's not that bad, this happened because it's the first time with the watercolors, you need to get a hang of it," and this is the way we cheer each other up.

"Let's buy a technique book. And some other brushes, because these aren't much help," I propose. Our initial costs begin to mount and the sales are still a long way from coming, but we've already jumped into the pool, it's time to see if there is any water in it. We go to a bookstore on a trip to Quito and after spending three hours, we come out with not one only book but two, one of techniques the other of birds, one to learn how to paint, the other what to paint. We go back to our temporary home. Cande still needs to find her style. She begins painting a red macaw and when it's finished, it really looks like a macaw…maybe you could say an old one and attacked by cats, but obviously a macaw, feasibly saleable. Her second painting is a blue parakeet, which looks even more healthy.

Candy doesn't paint peacefully, she's a little stressed. While she's painting, I can hear her comments like, "What did I do?" "This wrecks the whole thing." "No, this color isn't the right one." She paints and suffers, but the sales department of the company doesn't take his eyes off her and demands something saleable. The parakeet is followed by a toucan, a sparrow and with the days the birds come to life. Cande has opted for a realistic style and the birds have improved noticeably. She's encouraged so much that in gratitude to Rafael Galeth for his intention to help us, she wants to give him a painting of his boats as a gift. With her papers, pencils and paints, she arranges herself in front of the two boats tied up in the man's armada and three days later the painting is ready.

This same day Rafael invites us to a hotel he owns, one that has a pool, a restaurant and a lot of green space. As soon as he picks us up, Cande takes the opportunity to give him her gift. Galeth, very surprised, starts to take off the wrapping until he comes to the painting, he looks at it, says "How nice…" and he continues looking at it. Cande is glad, but her happiness doesn't last long.

"And this…what is it?" questions the man, who doesn't see his boats. It seems more an impressionistic painting than a naval one.

"They are your boats," replies Cande while she points out first one then the other.

"Oh, yes, of course they are." comments Galeth without being able to hide his embarrassment.

The next day, after this setback, Cande continues painting, but focuses on birds. It's my guess that she won't go back to painting boats. Finally, we gather enough paintings to take to Quito to sell them in the central square. So, now the one who begins to feel nervous is me. It's my time, it's my turn to take action. We go to Quito with our paintings; Ruben Sanchez takes us. He's the son of the owner of the company that is hosting us. During our trip back, I make my first sale. Ruben, charmed by a toucan, buys it. We jump for joy, we now have our first $30 and we experience the feeling of richness, of triumph.

We go to the Huespe's house. They also buy a painting, one of a yellow parrot. This means that in only one day, we've accomplished the sale of two paintings, and during the following days, we manage to sell a few more. When we're at the point of going back to Coca, I tell Cande, "Cande, do you remember when we were out of money and we talked about what we could do? I said that I was feeling strange.

Today I think this place is different, just as I am, different but not strange. I believe that each place that we go to will be new and different and we will also change. Every time we get to a new site, we have to mold ourselves to it doing new and different things. But we will be able to do whatever is necessary to keep going forward. Now I don't feel like a stranger."

A Raft

By the time we get back to Coca we feel our faith in ourselves more strengthened…so fortified that we make another important decision: to go down the Amazon on our own. We go to search out Mr. Conteros. He is a supplier from Rocafuerte, a small village on the border with Peru further down river. He has two large canoes and at one time offered to take us there, provided that we should arrange some way to continue the trip from Rocafuerte to Manaos. On one occasion, we were very close to accept his invitation, but like many other times, the possibility of departing sooner with Galeth all the way to Manaos appeared and we refused Conteros'offer. Today we are looking for him again.

"Are you looking for Conteros? Don't wait. When we last saw him, he was trying to refloat one of his canoes. It sank. It's going to take him a few days to get back here," a man tells us.

"How did it sink!? He was going to take us on that trip…" I say totally surprised.

"Yes, it sometimes happens. The boat hits a hidden submerged log, it leans, gets flooded, then it goes down" he tells us as if it was nothing new, as though it happened every day. "If you want to see him, try again in a few days."

As soon as we go outside, Cande exclaims, "Do you realize that we could have lost the car?!"

"Yes." I don't want to say anything else. I am in shock, but I still want my idea to keep going.

We start to consider again the possibility of a raft. Tanguila is the Shaman of the Huataraco indigenous community and knows exactly what is possible on the river and what is not. His height doesn't exceed Cande's by much; he's short and plump. His facial features are indigenous, his cheekbones prominent, his hair dark, and his look could be defined as mysterious, penetrating, and analytical. He assures us that together with his community we could make a log raft that would be twice the length and width of the car. To power the raft, we'll use the motor of the car. We will lower the drive shaft and instead of rotating the wheels, we would put on a propeller.

"How much would it cost us to gather the logs? And to build it?"

"Don't worry, we'll do it with a 'Minga'."

"What's a 'Minga'?"

"When someone has to build a house, the whole community is invited to help. I will invite the community to come and help you."

"But what could we give you in exchange?"

"It isn't done to receive, it's done to give."

We conclude the conversation agreeing that three Huataraco villagers would accompany us on the trip to the border of Peru, after that we'd have to find a new crew. I have always thought that nobody does anything for nothing, but during these last months of traveling, I began to change my opinion about many things.

During this whole conversation with Tanguila, Cande has remained perfectly silent. "What fear, what incertitude. What is going to happen when we're on the river, drifting away from everything and toward the unknown? This unsettles me, very much. I have the chills in the middle of all this heat. I want to find an alternative that will permit me to escape from this daring idea, but I know we don't have many to pick from," she thinks. Nevertheless, she laughs.

"What are you laughing about?" I ask her intrigued.

"Because I'm nervous. All this frightens me. Will you hold me? I need a hug."

"Cande, it's the same for me." I approach her and embrace her in my arms for a long time.

The next day we tell Galeth our decision.

"We are in the dry season, at this time of the year you won't be able to do it, you're going to get stuck on the first sand bar and have to wait for the rains to make the river rise. Only then will you be able to continue. But if you're that decided, I have the hull of an abandoned big canoe; if the car fits into it, and you have the courage to fix it up, you can use it."

"It's a deal!!" I tell him, totally in favor of fixing it up, and immediately we go and see it.

We find it covered with weeds, full of water and with a few holes. We measure the width and the car will just fit, with only 2 inches to spare. We need to find; motor, rudder, propeller, batteries, floor, roof, welders, mechanics, machinists, paint, oh, and don't forget a crane, to move it…!

"How are we ever going to find all this?" Cande asks me.

"I don't know, but let's get started." And with an old paint bucket I begin to bail out. Cande stands there, staring at me with her hands on her waist and her mouth hanging open. She clearly wants to say something, but she only snorts and begins pulling the weeds that are around the hull.

"I pull out a handful after handful of weeds while I think about my admiration for Herman. He makes me fall more in love with him every day. His tenacity and vision that anything is possible passes on me. Where sometimes I don't see any possibilities, he can see them and with  his clarity, he erases my doubts. We've fought united since we were children, but these tests are different, they are about risks, they about danger and even so they unite us more than ever," writes Cande at night.

In town the magic of life shows itself in its entire splendor. I tell a couple of people that we now have a canoe and that we are fixing it up and soon the word spreads all over the town. Today, only one day later, there are a lot of people coming and going, some we know and others we meet for the first time. They approach us to give things they think might be of some service, and also offer themselves to weld, to paint, for the electrical tasks...

When the afternoon wears on we walk through town we're constantly stopped with offers for something, it's magic, it's marvelous.

A few days later, Captain Aldaz asks us to call on him.

"You had a boat going directly to Panama and you didn't take it, the barge you were supposed to take two months ago still isn't ready and who knows when it will be. Your idea to build a raft from logs is not possible, you almost went with Mr. Conteros on the voyage where his boat sank and now you're rebuilding one that has one problem after another. If it's not the motor that won't work it's the batteries or the oil cooler...and who knows what other problems are lying in wait...you don't have any maps of the river, and you don't know anything about navigation, but you want to try to learn on the longest, widest river with the greatest volume of water in the world. This is The Amazon; it's not a joke! Don't you realize that you are stumbling with every step...?" he reproaches me as soon as he sees me.

"Yes, you are right. But, you have no idea how many times I stumbled before I learned how to walk, or the number of times I fell off my bike and the water I swallowed learning how to swim, and here I am, walking. And if you want, I can show you how I swim...and I'm going to demonstrate that although I might swallow a bit of water, or stumble or fall, I am going to get to Manaos." I tell him.

"But we're talking about the Amazon jungle, there is nothing else but danger. You will not find any one to help you, there are only spiders, poisonous snakes, piranhas, crocodiles, malaria, electric eels...There are many indigenous who have valid reasons to hate white men and the Amazon is a river you have to know. It hides logs, sand banks, whirlpools, it's a river which in case of a small storm becomes worse than any sea, with waves that crash from every direction. Besides, you don't know anything about the motor that's taking you. It's been years without working... Listen to me, take my advice, forget about this idea. You have almost nothing in your favor."

"I'm not saying you're not right, but if I take heed of you or the others, who always told me that I wouldn't be able or that it would be very dangerous, right now I'd be in my house too afraid to go out into the street. Everything that you named as dangerous is what makes me feel more alive. When I risk my life for something I want the most, it is then that I feel most alive. I have the opportunity to navigate the Amazon River, a unique opportunity, as unique as the life I have. I can assure you I'm not going to let it go."

"Conteros has years of experience navigating this river, he still sank his canoe. How can you, who doesn't know anything..."

"Listen, roads are full of people that crashed after years of driving, so, what? Should I give up driving?"

"Are you taking some indigenous to steer the canoe?" half resigned, the captain changes his tone.

"Yes, they are the ones who know where to steer, hunt and fish, what to eat, the Quechua language and thousands of other things they could teach us."

"Have you found them yet?"

"No."

"And money to pay them?"

"Nor that."

"But, do you see what I am saying? What do you think you're going to do?" argues Aldaz once more.

"We still don't know, but it occurred to us that Cande could go to Quito and hang up notices, in the hotels, and cyber cafés, looking for tourists who want to share an adventure voyage…"

"Hold on a minute here, in addition to not having any idea how to steer a boat nor to handle a crew, no money, you want to include other people in something you have no idea how it's going to turn out?"

"That's why the sign will say: to share an ADVENTURE voyage down the Amazon…"

"Look, Herman, the permission to set sail has to be given by me. I really don't want to refuse, but neither can I disregard my responsibilities. So please start finding some solutions."

"You'll have them… Don't worry, nothing bad is going to happen: God is coming with us."

Yesterday Cande went to Quito and posted 12 signs. She only has four days to find travelers. It is dark and the phone rings, "Hello, love, I have good news. Two people have called me about the trip!"

"I can't believe it!"

"Yep, they're really enthusiastic and the price seems to be perfect for them, they want to come right away to Coca, because they also want to help with the preparations."

"Seriously? That is so great! Tell them to come right now! If we could just get the motor running, we don't have much more to do before we could leave."

Hold On, Breathe...

The next day, with great enthusiasm, I go to the turner to make some bushings. We finish about noon and as I leave to go find something to eat, I see Marcelo Chingo a pal from the campground. He's going by in a truck and I make a signal for him to pick me up.

"Hey, how's it going? Are you heading to the cafeteria?"

"No, my brother, Fidel is badly injured, he had an accident and I am going to get him. Do you want me to drop you off at the campground?"

"No, I'll go with you. Where is he?"

"In a police station. He crashed this morning, but we've just found out."

"How is he?"

"Sounds like he's in a lot of pain, he hit a bridge and the steering wheel hit him hard in his chest."

We are headed to Lago Agrio, which is a long way over a dirt road. Marcelo is serious, driving very fast with his gaze fixed on the road, but without really paying much attention. He and his brother work for the same company where Cande and I are lodged. We're good friends since we see each other almost every day and we do a lot of electrical work together in the jungle. I remember one night we told them that this journey was our dream and they told us theirs. Fidel's was that his kids would be able to study and find better jobs than his... But, what am I thinking? He is going to be fine.

"Your brother might be in pain, but don't worry, he's going to be fine."

"Thank you but I'm afraid."

We get to the police station; a paramedic is there with Fidel.

"How do you feel?" his brother asks. Fidel is seated, but doubled over. Recognizing the voice, he lifts his head, and strongly hugs Marcelo.

"It hurts, it hurts so much."

"Doctor, how is he?"

"He doesn't have any fractures nor cuts of any kind, but I'm worried about his pain in the chest and with this cough with a discharge that he started to have not too long ago. You must take him to a hospital."

We leave immediately and begin the trip back to Coca, where there is a military hospital.

We travel through virgin jungles and deforested land, the road is in very bad condition because it hasn't been repaired yet since the end of the rainy season. We go bouncing in a truck that seems as if it could career out of control at any moment. The bumping makes Fidel groan. His moans are the only thing heard inside the cabin, we don't know what to say or what to think.

"I'm not going to get through this." Fidel breaks the silence, after which he spits something pink.

"Don't talk nonsense," we tell him.

Time stands still, the miles stretch…it seems the truck doesn't advance. The journey is becoming eternal, matching the silence. It's as though we were in another dimension of space and time.

"Is there any water?" he asks. He takes a small sip. "What's going to happen to my children? Marcelo, will you take care of them?"

"Yes, brother, you know I will, but nothing is going to happen!"

Leaving the children, leaving a love, leaving a life, leaving everything…these are Fidel's thoughts, mine as well.

When we get to the hospital, Fidel spitting more and more foam, breathes strangely, as if he couldn't get enough air. When they take him into emergency, he says good-bye to his brother with a look.

From where we are, Marcelo and I can see everything that they're doing… everyone seems desperate; there is shouting and a lot of movement. Suddenly, a nurse comes running out and asks for an emergency airplane to Quito. We go to make the calls, but when everything is almost set, the same nurse gives us a signal that we don't need it anymore, it's too late. We look in the emergency room; the doctor leaves defeated. Death brought silence and now, nobody moves.

Marcelo falls to his knees in a wail, I can not believe it, I want this to be only a movie, not to be real. How can it be? So fast? He had nothing except a bump. How is it that death can just come like this, with no warning?

After a short while, in time to comfort a friend who needs more arms, some coworkers show up. Some help to complete the papers; Marcelo doesn't have the strength nor the desire to do it.

Regarding Fidel, his body, now covered by a sheet, is waiting in the hallway. A nurse comes up to him and attaches a tag to one of his toes, then she asks us, "What are you going to do with the body?"

"What? 'What are we going to do with the body'?" we are still trying to understand how he could have lost his life so rapidly and they ask us this. We look at each other searching for an answer, but we don't have one.

Just then, the foreman comes in and goes directly to speak to the doctor who attended Fidel. His bosses, in Quito, gave the order that an autopsy has to be performed very soon, because if more than two days pass, the insurance company won't pay off the policy. However, the Military hospital can't carry it out, so we're sent to a small hospital in town.

All of us together load Fidel into the back end of the truck, when we move him foam and blood come out of his mouth, and stain my hands. This creates a feeling of repugnance in me, but what would my friend think if I revealed this to him? What would I think if it were me who needed someone and he couldn't help me because of the impression…? I pluck up my courage and continue helping.

We get to a one-room building beside the hospital, with openings for a door and window, but they're missing. The cement table covered in tiles is filthy… dried blood from another autopsy. The floor is in the same state. Upon seeing this, out of respect for our friend, we begin to clean it in absolute silence, the only voice heard is that of the foreman who is outside debating the price of the autopsy with the doctor. Since it's Saturday and now quite late, he is demanding more money.

They send me to buy some blades for a scalpel, blades for a saw, formaldehyde, gloves, and thread and a needle for the closure. I come back and help put the body on the table, it's much colder and stiffer, his eyes don't want to close, they want to see what the Doctor is going to do. Everyone goes to wait outside, we still can't believe that Fidel went out to go to work this morning and now he's on this gloomy table. As I'm making my exit, the doctor asks me, "Would you have a problem helping me here a bit?"

Of course I do, I've never done anything like this and I don't want to experiment, but instead I answer, "No, Doctor. What would you like me to do?"

"Nothing right now. If you want to, you can wait outside and when I need you, I'll call for you."

I go out and breathe; I don't remember taking any deep breaths since I climbed into the truck to accompany Marcelo. I fill with fresh and humid night air, feeling life in me. The foreman continues with the organization, now he's sending someone to go buy a coffin, with clear specifications and margins of an acceptable price. How is this all happening so quickly? Why isn't it possible to stop death for a minute?

"Come in, che," the doctor calls me. He knows where I'm from, but not my name. I enter and see the abdomen open and so much blood. "Hold this, I have to cut. Put gloves on first." The doctor seizes his saw and begins to cut the sternum to get to the heart. I've never seen a human heart nor want to. The doctor finds the cause of death of my friend. "His lungs received the blow and filled with blood, he drowned. We also have to open the cranial cavity, I need you to hold the head." With his head in my hands, I see his face, still not being able to believe where Fidel is and neither where I am. When the doctor finishes, he merely says, "Clean him."

Marcelo comes into the room and comes across this horrifying scene; the blood and the sutures state too much. But he immediately grips a brush and begins to clean his brother; another man and I help him. After that, we dress him and we put him in the coffin. Marcelo, in total silence, takes him to the truck.

"Where to?" I ask the foreman.

"To his sister-in-law's house."

"Does she know yet?"

"No, she doesn't have a telephone, we didn't have anyway to reach her." I can't believe what is happening. Marcelo has to tell his brother's wife that he brought her husband home, but in a coffin. I hope this is all only a nightmare.

Before having a rest, I have a shower to remove the odor of blood and death that I feel in my whole body. I don't think I will be able to sleep, I only lay down.

I am awakened with the news that Cande is on the phone, calling from Quito,

"I'm coming back with the two English guys, they are very excited. Besides, we're on our way up, I sold five paintings!"

"Oh, that's good."

"Is something wrong?"

"No, it's nothing for you to worry about, but when you get here, I'll tell you."

The camp is in silence. I leave it to walk to where we're getting the big canoe ready. People have offered rides a couple of times, but it's only about a mile and a half and I want to walk it. I want to feel the wind in my face, breathe the warm air. Taking slow steps, I think about what I lived through the day before. I never felt, saw nor touched death, not so quickly. If for some reason I had to live this, there is absolutely something I have to learn…now I know that death is always there, ready for everything to end. It comes without being called or without asking us nor does it wait to take us. More than ever before in my life I give thanks to God for this new day he offers me. I believe that for me there will never be "just another day, "each day will be lived and remembered.

With a lot of energy, I dedicate myself to finishing my craft. I feel very well building something so important for our lives, for our dream. God has given us the miracle of life, and with it, we are doing miracles.

Cande finally arrives. She finds me at the river close to the canoe. We share an endless hug. We missed one another too much, they were the four longest days without her, and I needed her so much.

The Go Ahead

Today we manage to start the motor. In the end we'll travel with two Englishmen and two indigenous that we got at the last moment to steer the canoe.

Cande has taken charge, together with the Europeans, of buying all the provisions. The owner of the campground in which we have stayed for all these days has given the gift of two hundred and fifty gallons of diesel, enough to go to the Atlantic and come back…now all we need is the go ahead from the Navy.

"Captain Aldaz, I have come to say good-bye, we're leaving tomorrow."

"Did you finally find someone to crew the boat?"

"Yes, them," I reply indicating the natives.

"Let's see their papers," orders Aldaz, but I'm not worried because I know they have them.

"Herman, do you take the responsibility for what ever happens?"

"Yes."

"Aren't you afraid of death?"

"I have a fear of not living, of getting to death without having lived this life. I feel, now that we are following our dream, that I have resuscitated. I was alive but in a life without life. No, I am not afraid of death, death doesn't hurt. What hurts is life, the kind of life that is not lived."

"I wish you the best of journeys. Remember to introduce yourselves in Rocafuerte, on the border with Peru, at the Naval detachment."

As I leave the Marina I see a bronze plaque next to the river. It is at the point where in 1542, the conqueror Francisco de Orellana along with fifteen soldiers in a raft began an incredible voyage to the Atlantic. He was the first to navigate the whole of The Amazon and when they got to the ocean, with their hands and the little they had, built a tiny ship to get all the way to Spain. Orellana's courage pushes me to do it: surely, he had knowledge of the sea and armaments, but he didn't know where he was going, neither which monster of sea or land he would meet, nor whether he'd arrive at the end of the world. If Orellana could do it four hundred years ago, we can certainly do it tomorrow.

When we get to the campground we discover they have prepared a wonderful farewell dinner for us. We have lived together with the workers for three months, very closely, sharing many life experiences.

As soon as the festivities begin, Marcelo arrives, who came back a day early from his funeral leave to see us.

"I need to thank you for what you did for me and for my brother."

"I am the one who is grateful, for me your brother's death was not in vain. It might be slightly selfish to say so, but it taught me a lot. Now I know that life is so fragile, easy to be lost at any moment."

"Why don't you stay here a couple of years, make some money and then continue?" proposes Angel, the camp manager.

"No, we are in an incredible moment in our lives. It was so hard for us to start out and now that everything is working out little by little, it is not the time to stop, just the opposite we have to keep going."

"Yes, but your luck could run out and this is sure money."

"I don't think it's luck, I believe that everything is in our favor, but for an enormous reason."

"So, I see I can't keep you here even with this good offer…"

"Life doesn't stop, time waits for no one. Life flows like a river and I am with life, in its current. I don't want to restrain it. I thank you for your offer, it makes me feel very good, most of all useful, but I want to go on and be, above all, useful to myself. Your offer is a strong temptation, but these have always taken us a long way away from our road."

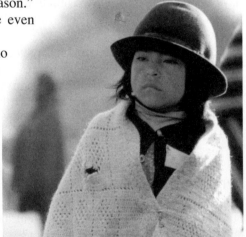

Amazon & Brazil

TILL HERE:
7312 miles
in 8 ½ months

N

Boa Vista

Amazon River

Coca

Letícia

Tabatinga

Manaus

Sta. Rosa

Iquitos

Amazon
Strong Word

All Aboard!

Today is the day we set sail. In a few hours, we'll cast off and begin navigating the Amazon. How powerful the word Amazon sounds! As mighty as Patagonia, Africa, Everest, Caribbean… This is a class of words that commands respect by just naming them. Cande and I both feel very strange, because we've never sailed and much less with a car onboard. I've never been a captain either, but I feel that if I can achieve this, I will be a captain for ever.

Before departing, Cande and I go around the town of Coca saying farewell to all the people, no one can really believe that the famous day finally has arrived. The greetings continue where the boat is moored, many villagers have come here to see us for the last time. Jaime, a man who has helped with the rebuilding of our new vessel, is operating the old crane to load the Graham. The car lifts from the ground and remains suspended from some ancient cables. I feel nervous; all the movements are brusque, the motor of the crane cuts out often and Jaime teases me by letting the car drop the final three feet stopping it just before it hits ground… I don't breathe until the Graham lands safely aboard.

Once again, we say good-bye, with strong bittersweet hugs mixed with tears, from women and men alike who have made us feel like part of their place, their families and their lives. When we're at the point of climbing aboard, a voice detains us.

"One more last good-bye," it's Captain Aldaz kitted out in his best dress whites. When he hugs me, he says in a low voice, "I'm bidding farewell to a future mariner. For if you make it to Manaus, you'll be one for always."

"And I'm gonna get me one of these!" I comment, signaling his Captain's hat.

Grown-Up Playmate

All of our friends keep waving until we can't see them any more. So, I do a half turn and breathe deeply while my gaze takes in our vessel, our crew, and our new step. The day is marvelous, but I think that even if it weren't, I would feel the same anyway. I only hope God and the Amazon want to give us a Bon Voyage!

Braulio, one of the natives, is in charge of the motor and the rudder. The other, Clever, is at the stern and indicates the course, dodging the hidden trunks and sand banks. Cande is organizing the cargo together with the English guys, James, Ben, and I check the motor which is running, hot. Without knowing how, we are a perfect crew. After two or three hours of traveling we see a helicopter that follows us for a while, at one point it gets close enough for us to see it belongs to the Ecuadorian Army. Very shortly, we see boats coming up behind us at a high speed, also occupied by soldiers and they speed up right next to us many times.

Three hours later, we stop in Pañacocha, a tiny settlement that we have visited previously. On the banks there are two moored boats from the army and many well armed soldiers with their faces painted.

"Are you practicing maneuvers?" I ask one of them without understanding what's going on.

"No, we're looking for Colombian guerrillas. They came into a petroleum camp and kidnapped ten people; eight Americans, a Belgian, and an Argentinean. They put everybody into a helicopter hired by a company and they took off for the border."

"Oh,…do you suppose there are more guerrillas?"

"We're looking for."

Cande and I translate for the British lads why there's so much commotion and we ask them if they'd rather return to Coca with the military. They say no, they'd rather keep going with us, so we spend a while walking around the village.

As soon as the indigenous children see us, they come running up, they are happy to have us around again in their village.

"Martin! Martin and Cande are here!!" shout the kids. Yes, they're talking about me. That's what they call me. On our first visit they weren't able to pronounce my name, so I told them my name was Martin. On that occasion we were in Pañacocha for three days, we came courtesy of a voyage that Galeth and Conteros made to the region.

I remember that during the first day we were striving hard to get close to the natives, who were very timid in the beginning. When we asked them something, they merely responded with a giggle, looking off to the side. The kids were the same, that is, if they approached us at all. So we decided to get closer to them with a game and we taught them how to play "Duck, Duck, Goose" a game we remembered from our childhood. They caught on immediately and their laughter was so compelling that it attracted the elders, curious to know why they were laughing so hard. They took great pleasure in watching the game and by the end of that day we were accepted into the community.

The next day, they invited us to participate in a wedding party. We attended and we had a blast. Their music, their dancing, their food…all of which had been hunted and immediately smoked during the last fifteen days and the menu included crocodile, monkey and venison. The person seated next to me got the arm of the monkey and watching him eat it, it looked like he was chewing an arm of a child…right down to the fingers it seemed so human! They offered us 'chicha' to drink, an alcoholic drink made from yucca. The women chew it; they spit into a jar they close tightly and the contents, mixed with the bacteria of the saliva, ferment producing the alcohol.

Another interesting thing about the celebration was that it wasn't centered on the couple. It was organized by the family of the groom to please the bride's family in gratitude for bestowing her to his family. Absolutely every member of the new family – parents, siblings, cousins, grandparents and distant relatives- had to come up, one by one, to the old family to receive advice on how to treat the new member.

The party finished with the guests scattered and asleep wherever they were, under the effects of the chicha. We took the food that we hadn't eaten wrapped up in palm leaves, since it is very poor manners to leave anything behind.

Today, during this visit, they invite us to eat fish. We stay with them a couple of hours and go back to the boat; we want to search for somewhere to spend the night.

The Beginning

We take a branch of the river and go upstream. From the 200 yard wide Napo River we get into a 45-feet wide open which little by little, continues to narrow. A log across the river prevents us from advancing farther, so we "decide" to stop. We are about to cut the motor when we hear a terrible noise coming from it…and it doesn't stop either! I am very close to it, but I don't know what it might be, or do I? Yes, with the engine running the starter has turned on even though we haven't pressed the button. Braulio waits for my signal indicating what to do, so I tell him to turn it off and I disconnect the auto starter. From now on, we will have to give a jump from the battery to the starter every time we want to turn on the motor.

We get ready to spend our first night in the jungle. Surrounded by thousands of noises, above the crowns of the trees, under them, and from the river there is hidden life. You don't see the danger; it's the danger that sees you.

"This day was a perfect adventurous start," James comments to me.

"Yes, for the first day of my life as a sailor, it wasn't bad." I reply to his perplexed face. It seems he didn't know that I have no experience navigating. But then again, he didn't ask either.

The next day we continue down river. We are seated observing the marvel of the surroundings. Since we set sail I have chosen to place myself in the very point of the prow with my feet dangling just touching the water and splashing in it. This way I can admire the environment. However, I have to interrupt my splendid moment to go and look at the motor. There are 60 feet between the stem and the stern and when I get there, the first thing I check is the temperature gauge. At this moment it's completely in the red. Without thinking twice, I cut the fuel feed line to turn off the motor and shout at absent minded Braulio.

"What do you want? Do you want us to get stuck in the middle of the jungle with a burned out motor? How do you want me to return the boat? Melted?" While I yell this to the whole great outdoors, Braulio stops looking at me and turns his eyes toward the front. "Braulio, we have to keep an eye on this motor because it's got to get us to…"

"It would be good if you watched out, indeed!" the native interrupts signaling a pile up of logs and branches stuck in the river, exactly where we're being carried by the current. Braulio moves the rudder, but without a motor, this action serves little purpose. "If we hit it, we tip over," he explains.

I realize that we don't have an anchor, perhaps I never thought of one. "Why would we need one if we were always going to tie up to the banks? But an anchor is essential!" I think while we continue to approach the log jam.

"Start the motor again!" I order. But the temperature got so high that it wouldn't. "Tie this line to the other one" I tell Clever diving into the water with one end of the rope and beginning to swim without caring about the current. We are not too far from the bank, I'm trying desperately to reach it. I am very afraid to lose the boat, the car and so many things. Also I am terrified thinking about what there might be between the branches and logs, I am heading right into them knowing there usually are crocs, electric eels…and worse, if a branch or something scratches me the piranhas will finish me! I touch something with my foot, it's slippery and smooth, with the other foot, I kick it and I realize that it is a log, because it's still there and now my foot really hurts. I tie up the boat just when it is ready to pull me with it and terrified, I shoot back to the boat like an arrow. We will wait until the motor cools down and then head towards Braulio and Clever's indigenous village. We'll spend the night there.

In the Jungle One is Born and One Dies

We thought that Braulio and Clever's families, would receive them affectionately upon their arrival, like sons they hadn't seen in a long time. However, this isn't the case, their families only greet them as if they hadn't even been missed. We saw the same in Pañacocha, where the parents are not very attached to their children, where demonstrations of love are scarce.

We walk along a path parallel to the riverside that unites house to house. Small bridges made of jungle materials cross the streams of calm waters. This is not a very big village and we stop to say hello in each home. We meet a cousin constructing a small coffin. Braulio talks with him in the language of Quechua and later tells us, "It's for his baby that's a year and a half, and last week he buried his six-year-old child."

"What did he die of?" James asks.

"Fever" responds Braulio, but they call dengue and malaria fever as well as any other malady that raises the temperature.

"I believe I understand now why they're not too attached to their children. At any moment they could lose them and if they love them too much, the suffering would be much worse," Cande says.

We get to Braulio's grandfather's house, who is a Shaman. He is examining a child with fever, but without knowing exactly what illness he has. In the Amazon, death is something natural, something as common as life. Here they don't deal with details. You're born; you die, if in the middle you can have life and love, all the better. They co-exist alongside with yellow fever, rabies, Chagas disease, dengue, malaria, spiders, snakes, piranhas, crocodiles, pumas, jaguars, ants, anacondas, sting rays, electric eels, leeches, mosquitoes, ticks, and thousands of parasites…all without any doctors or remedies.

Since we are one step from the jungle, we walk into it without hesitating. We ask Clever to accompany us. As soon as we enter, we feel alone in the shadows. Among so many trees we barely see the sky and it seems much later than it really is. The ground is muddy. Nevertheless, we don't care, the jungle is beckoning.

We just left the houses a few minutes ago, and already we are in virgin land, uncharted. The indigenous live near the river and they enter the jungle sporadically, to hunt. Here you can't walk straight nor follow a direct line because of the lavish vegetation. It's impossible to see more than a few yards ahead. Among the colorful plants, I recognize some sold in my neighborhood greenhouse as houseplants, the only difference is these don't have any price tags.

I'm beginning to feel that if I were left alone, I wouldn't know which way to go; I can't tell the position of the sun. Every now and again, we cross a stream… in reality I ignore if it is always the same one, because the water comes and goes winding all over. The only thing that keeps us calm is that Clever is native to this region and he knows the jungle. We see tracks, could it be a jaguar? And these from a tapir? There are many, but because of our noise, the beasts might already be far away from here.

We've spent only an hour walking and we are exhausted. Our shoes are full of sticky mud that makes them heavier; our clothes are wet from sweat and brushing against wet leaves; and our arms are begging for rest, worn out from swinging the machete. When we move silently we clearly hear the noises of the jungle. We listen to the monkeys moving the branches retreating from us, the birds alarm at our presence, the nervousness of the parrots.

We are immersed in the jungle, and it is marvelous; full of trees, plants, flowers and vines. We are near a Ceiba, a gigantic tree towering more than 180 feet and whose trunk is like a column that all of us together can't encircle. I feel an enormous pleasure touching it, hugging it.

An enormous butterfly shows its brilliant colors, poses on top of Cande's head. Everyone remains quiet so as not to startle it.

"So beautiful," comments Ben.

'Hold on there, bro, she's my wife," I tell him in jest.

"No, I'm talking about the butterfly," he says just in case.

"With such a tempting flower there's no butterfly that could resist," I answer lovingly earning a hug from her that startles the butterfly. Then we notice that Clever isn't relaxed, his eyes are darting around here and there.

"Do you think there's a dangerous animal?" Cande asks alarmed.

"No, no…it's that I'm not sure which way we came from," leaving all of us with our mouths wide open, shocked.

"How can you not know?" I exclaim.

"You don't know how to get back?" inquires Cande almost desperate.

"Yes, but I'm not sure…"

Clever's company made us feel confident. We let ourselves be led by him giving no attention to the trail, nor getting any bearings. We didn't even bring a compass. Now, in addition to being edgy, we're lost.

We decide to resolve it by following our own tracks left in the mud, but after a short time, they disappear, they vanish on top of the fallen leaves. So, we start to search out branches cut by the machete, but there aren't many because we don't know how to use it, and our ecological conscience wouldn't let us cut more than what was necessary. Looking for a way to relieve our anxiety, and out of the jungle, we organize ourselves. When we get to a cut branch or some foot print, one stays there and the others search for another sign close by, and we progress like this. It takes us a total three hours, which seem like much more, to get to the riverbank…and think that the walk in took us only an hour. When we see the river, we feel completely relaxed, as if we finally made it home.

Nothing to Report, My Captain

The next day we navigate down the river almost letting ourselves be carried by the current. We are going very slowly because if we accelerate, the motor begins to overheat. On one hand, this is better because we're traveling much more quietly, we can see more and the trip will take a couple of extra days.

"Don't you heat up, be cool," I tell the engine while giving it a pat. Then I head to the front of the boat and hear something almost like the crack of a whip. I look at Braulio with a "what was that?" expression.

"The fan belt broke," he tells me very calmly.

"But what's wrong with you, motor?? We had to postpone our departure because you didn't want to start. And now once you have, you put me to the test every day. I don't know anything about mechanics and I don't even like it, we're going at a speed that doesn't overheat you, what is wrong with you now?? A belt? Could you tell me where I am going to get a fan belt in the middle of the Amazon?!" I yell at the machine while Braulio watches me, thinking I'm crazy.

I check out what it is that works with this belt to see if we are able to continue or not. I see that the alternator and the water pump depend on it, so we're forced to stop, and if not the motor will definitely overheat. The Brits come to see why we've stopped and when they realize the condition of the belt, they just huff feeling all hope is lost.

It occurs to me to try the car's fan belt, but besides being too small it's a different shape. I go on staring at it, thinking that maybe I could repair it with my favorite tool, bailing wire. Let's see…no, no it won't work, the belt is dried out and cracked from many years out of service in the sun and the rain. I go back to the car searching for something that could be useful. "Think! Use your imagination…there has to be something we can do!" I tell myself.

The spare tire! It has an inner tube. What would happen if I cut it into rings and use one of them like an elastic band? Everybody watches me dismantle the wheel, take hold of a knife and cut the tube.

"I don't know if this will work, but we have nothing to lose." I comment to them.

"An inner tube," encourages Cande.

After a few minutes, I fit the new "belt" into place and we restart the motor. I check the water pump and yes! It works! Everyone shouts with joy at having passed this new test.

In the afternoon, we get to Rocafuerte, the last town in Ecuador. Many people are waiting for us on the pier. We present our papers to the captain.

"Anything to report?"

"Nothing, my captain" I respond.

"No difficulties or inconveniences?"

"Nothing, my captain," it's better to lie and keep going than to give him something to worry about and retain us. "The people that received us on the dock…is it like this with the arrival of every boat?"

"No, they came to see the car, almost none of the kids and many of the adults have never seen one," he explains making me remind myself of times gone by when the circus used to come to town.

We stop to sleep in the home of a marvelous family, who want to help us in every way. The daughter, Kerly, is in charge of Yasuni National Park; she doesn't have to say much to persuade us to go and see it. We restock our provisions on the boat and the next day we depart.

During the trip, she tells us it's a gigantic park, wholly virgin. It doesn't have any permanent park rangers because it's an incredibly difficult place to access. Almost no one visits, neither tourists, nor Ecuadorians. Everything sounds beautiful, except that it's in danger because beneath this marvelous jungle, there is oil and they are about to start drilling for it.

We go by an Ecuadorian military post that guards the border with Peru. We have to stop, show them our papers and state our intentions. Since everything is in order, they allow us to continue, but before we enter Peru, we detour to the river that takes us to the park. It's a small river that divides the two countries; one bank is Peru, the other is Ecuador. Every once in a while, the trees reach across, covering our advance and some dolphins begin to follow us, they are pink and they come with a baby. We stop in the last inhabited house to borrow a smaller canoe.

We continue traveling, aware that from this point onward we won't see anyone but ourselves. We continue on upstream and take another still smaller branch which carries us to an enormous lagoon turning the place into a paradise. There are macaws that cross the sky and birds of every color that come up to us curious to see what we are up to. Everything is so beautiful that we anchor in the middle of the lake. Well, we don't have an anchor, but there's no current nor wind so we won't move. The water is so perfect that we swim for hours not minding that it's the color of dirt and that as soon as we submerge our hands we can't see them. Caught in a fit of inspiration, Cande paints. The Brits take the little canoe exploring, Ben who preserves his English lineage even in the jungle, paddles it with a big black umbrella. We stay there until sunset; it's unique, one of a kind. The red sky glorifies us. We decide to go to sleep at the park ranger's house, which is abandoned, but it is still serviceable.

We turn on the motor but we can't move. The imperceptible current has carried us without us even realizing it. When you are stuck in the river, you have to wait for a rain, but in a lagoon, you must await a deluge. Braulio, with his experience begins to move the propeller and the rudder, thus managing to shift us a little to the front and back, side to side, stirring up a lot of mud which when it lifts, it allows us to move.

We arrive at the house, which is situated right at the confluence of two small rivers and offers us a captivating vista. Immediately Braulio and I start fishing for our dinner. He lands a bucketful of fish, on the other hand. I am only wetting my hook and feeding my bait to the fish. Yesterday I caught one little fish, which was horrible, blind, without scales and it was covered in gelatinous slime, so slippery and disgusting it was impossible for me to take the hook out of its mouth. Lucky me, I caught the only inedible fish.

Braulio, by merely throwing the hook in the water with a little hunk of bait manages to hook loads of piranhas while I keep pulling out a clean hook. He counsels me that if I do land one, to immediately cut the head off and then retrieve the hook. Otherwise, it could eat my finger. Now I've decided to stay out as long as necessary in the dark night until I catch something, even though Braulio has already gotten enough for everyone. At least, I want to land my own fish for breakfast. I hear the sound of the fish splashing and jumping. Every once in a while, there's a tug on my line, but when I pull it up, I find it bait-less.

"Any fish?" James ventures.

"Plenty but not one on my hook…" I tell him, annoyed.

"Give it 'er, let me give it a go." I pass him my line and not two minutes pass before he feels a strong pull. At the same time he tries to land it, he asks me for help and when I attempt it, I realize it has to be something big. We both pull. When we almost manage to pull the fish out of the water, we hear a huge splash that doesn't sound like a fish so we shout for Braulio to come to our aid and bring a flashlight. The three of us land a very large manta ray. James is thrilled with his catch and after everyone comes out to see it, we try to put it back in the water, but the animal has swallowed the hook and it is stuck in its stomach. The manta ray is making a big effort and gives birth to two babies that rapidly die…all of us remain sadly silent. James' happiness is transformed into pity and I am grateful that I don't have to feel the guilt for catching it. In the end, we leave the fish for breakfast and we have a delicious manta ray stew.

After dinner, Braulio, Cande and I go out paddling in the small canoe to go around the lake. We want to see crocodiles and this is the best place to do so. When we go up the small river that starts at the lake, we encounter a big floating island of aquatic plants that move down stream very slowly. Although they cover almost bank to bank, we discover a way to slip through and continue. When we get to the lake, it seems much larger. Everything is different in the darkness; the noises are distinct and the water seems to conceal life, we can hear the never-ending passage of animals. The moon, at intervals, illuminates intensely and at others hides behind the clouds shrouding us in total blackness. The small canoe looks fragile, it's only made from a hollowed out tree trunk, it's old and broken in places. Water leaks in, I bail it out in silence.

Braulio puts his hands to his mouth and blows, emitting a grave, strong sound, like a snort from a bull. When he stops, we can sense from around the whole lagoon similar sounds.

"What is that?"

"I made the sound of a female crocodile in heat and these sounds are the responses from the males."

"So many…?"

Braulio takes us to see them; we search for them using a flashlight. When we see a red dot, we go up closer. They are the reflection of the red eyes of a croc just sticking up out of the water. Slowly we move closer still to see the size of its head, we continue approaching him with admiration and fear until we notice there are several that are now submerging themselves. We manage to pick up a very small one, who must have been only a couple of days old and we put him right back in the water.

We coast along the shoreline searching for more life, the flashlight swings here and there, its spotlight is the only thing we can see. Knowing there are so many crocodiles makes us nervous. Cande and I feel uneasy. In the illuminated water, I perceive movement, and I focus the light in that direction at the same time Braulio shouts the name of the animal. "It's a venomous snake that is attracted to the light!" With his paddle, he picks it up and throws it a long way, on the other side of the boat. After a few seconds in silence, I tell Braulio may be it's time to go back. He asks me to turn off the light. In almost total silence, broken only by the sound of the paddle, we begin our return.

A short while, and not knowing how, we're suddenly back at the mouth of the small river. Braulio seems to have night vision, it's really very hard to see and still he recognizes the way. We all take a deep breath. We feel a bit more relaxed leaving the lagoon…when all of a sudden the canoe comes up out of the water, shakes, and we hear a huge splash. The canoe falls back down but now completely full of water. I turn on the flashlight and illuminate Braulio's face, which is no longer brown but white as a sheet. His eyes seem to have popped out of their sockets.

"What was that?" Cande asks scared to death.

"It could have been a crocodile, I don't know…" answers Braulio at the same time beginning to paddle more quickly than ever. While I bail out as much water as I can, and Cande instinctively grabs the knife. After a few yards, we can't go any further. The floating island obstructs the whole river from bank to bank. We search unsuccessfully for a way to get by. Braulio tries in a place where he thinks there are fewer plants, but the canoe gets stuck and we can't go any further. Making an effort, we back out. With the flashlight, we can see at the edge that it's a sea of plants and without a machete, it will be very difficult to cut them. Also, we're afraid to get close to them. We stay there a few minutes thinking about what to do. Trying to relax a little, we breathe deeply, filling our lungs with such pure air that oxygenates our blood. Calmer now, we look for a way to get around it.

"We have a knife. We can cut the tangle of plants of this island in front of us as we advance. To do this, we have to put our hands into the water, and as we know there are crocodiles, instead of us being afraid of them, let's make them afraid of us."

"How?" Cande questions nervously.

"You, Braulio, slap the water rhythmically with the paddle and Cande you do the same thing with the bailing bucket. At the same time, we need to make some sounds with our mouths. It must be in perfect rhythm. We have to avoid sounding like an animal trying desperately to get out of the water."

We go back to the same place Braulio tried to get through before and once Cande and Braulio find their rhythm in voice and with their instruments, I begin to cut the plants. Our fear dissipates giving rise to smiles and outbursts of laughter in seeing what we're doing.

"If the English guys come looking for us and hear these noises, they'll turn right around and run straight home!" Cande says.

"If the Huaoranis Indians find us, I'm sure they'd kill us believing we are possessed!" Braulio laughs.

So, with laughter and rhythmic noises, we happily cross through the island.

We wake up to the scent of fried fish that Kerly knows how to make perfectly. She overcooks the piranhas just a bit so spines and all can be eaten. The program for today is completely out of the water; we want to walk through the jungle with Braulio leading us.

"Going hunting in the Amazon, in search of food, can transform you from the hunter into the hunted one," he comments provoking a state of high alert in all of us. While we hike around, he teaches us the names of plants and their uses. He makes us try the sap of one. He cuts a kind of vine and a stream of tasty water flows out. Later, he slices a palm and offers us the heart, but the biggest surprise is when we get to a little tree which little branches form a special junction, like a knot. He opens it and we see a bunch of tiny, agitated ants running around.

"Try them," Braulio suggests.

"ANTS!?" we all say in unison.

"Yes, they're called lemon ants," he places his tongue on them. "Because they have the flavor of lemon," he explains while savoring them. So, we open our own knots and put our tongues on them. When we close our mouths we feel a little tickle with a lemon flavor. We eat the ants as well as the larvae.

Walking through the jungle, we're enchanted. We see monkeys, turtles, toucans, and a lot of different animal tracks that let us know that although we can't see them, they're there. However, Kerly needs to get back to Rocafuerte and we need to continue the trip, we head back to the big canoe, leaving behind this marvelous place of the jungle.

I Feel...

Now we're about to go down the river that we've already come up, but magically, instead of going down, the current is going up.

"How is it possible the water is coming the opposite direction it should?" I ask Braulio.

"It must be raining upriver on the Napo, so the level is raising and flowing into the tributaries," he explains to me.

I don't feel well, I have a stiff neck, and I'm weak, listless. As the hours pass, my condition gets worse, I only want to lie down, but I stay on my feet.

Night arrives and we can see almost nothing, but we have to make it at least to Napo River. We are close and there are fewer trunks submerged in the water, so I decide to relax a bit and lie down a while.

126

However, instead Braulio exclaims, "We lost the rudder! We lost the rudder!!" while moving the handle without any effort and without turning the boat.

"How can we not have a rudder? How are we supposed to maneuver the canoe without one? It's like driving a car on a mountainous road and suddenly holding the steering wheel in your hands."

"For sure we ran over a log and we lost the rudder," he answers.

"Fine, and we don't have an anchor either. How great it would be to have one!" I say thinking that when I get back to my house I am buying an enormous anchor that I'm going to carry with me even when I go on an airplane. Braulio begins to slow down.

"Full speed ahead!" I shout.

He accelerates as fast as he can and the motor gives a roar. Braulio looks at me without knowing the plan…and truthfully, I don't have a plan. I only want to avoid the current carrying us away and crashing us wherever it wants. Plus, it would be dangerous to pass the Peruvian military post without being able to maneuver, without stopping and at night, they could even shoot at us. Therefore, I prefer to go full out ahead and crash into the coastline, into the branches of the trees reaching out over the water searching out the sunlight. In a second, I think a thousand things; I imagine the impact into the branches, the car completely destroyed and how injured we could be…

"Get down!" I exclaim before we hit the shore. "As God wills it" I whisper.

We feel a thrust forward, the stop isn't too brusque nor do we hear the sound of branches breaking. When we finally stop, we all lift our heads and with the flashlight we see that the front of the boat is out of the water on a small and solitary beach about 18 feet wide. To the right and to the left we can see only trees and branches, but not where we are. We look at one another contently and astonished. I jump onto the beach with a line to tie up the canoe still not believing what happened. Yet another miracle.

After a few minutes to recover, with a machete, a board, and a few ropes we improvise a rudder. It doesn't allow us to maneuver much, but it will take us to Rocafuerte.

I wake up unwillingly to get up, because every time I do it I feel dizzy. Braulio and Clever, machete and bailing wire in hand, fashion a rudder easier to handle. The British are resting after such an adrenalin rush. And Cande is worried about me. She's afraid I have a "fever" or that some insect might have bitten me, but I don't have a temperature, only dizziness. I feel fine when I am totally horizontal, lying flat out, I can't even tolerate a pillow. I stare up, immobile. What would I feel in this same position if I were dead? If they put me in a coffin and buried me? There are still so many things I want to do; it's not time for me to go. I feel all the material things that I've gathered in my life I don't have anymore and that I've lost a lot of time trying to get them. Now all I have left is what's inside of me, I have to see the things I have there, because I know there are many. And still there are more things that I want to do. The dreams that I always wanted to complete and that I haven't realized yet because I let my life carry me to other paths. I feel there were few times that I've demonstrated affection to my loved ones, they weren't enough and that now it's too late. I feel…

"Should we go to the doctor?" Cande interrupts me.

"Yes, let's go," I reply waking from my thoughts.

The doctor simply tells me to take sodium, for dehydration. We go back to the boat and Braulio treats me with his own medicine. He gives me a cure with smoke and leaves on my back. Later he informs me that the rudder is ready and we go out together with him and Clever to try it. It's much heavier to move than the one we lost, but it will do.

We return to Rocafuerte and as we are tying up, a stick hidden among the leaves pierces Clever's foot making him cry out in pain. By nightfall, I feel much better and Braulio believes he's responsible for my improvement.

A new day for going to a new country, Peru. We're all ready except for Clever. He woke up with a very swollen foot, so it's back to the doctor we go.

"Only two days in town and you've come to visit me twice?" the doctor comments to us slightly surprised.

Clever doesn't have a fracture, but he needs to rest it. Feeling like he can be of no further use to us, with great anguish, he packs his bag and says good-bye. But Cande and I don't let him abandon us, and he very happily hops back to the boat on one foot.

Untitled Lands

Yes indeed, we are now navigating down the river. We pass the boundary to get into Pantoja, a Peruvian military and frontier post; they are waiting for us with a warm welcome. They facilitate everything for the entrance of the boat and the crew, so that we can continue. We were somewhat worried how it would be to do the paperwork for the car at a border without roads, but they tell us that the formalities need to be completed farther ahead because there is no customs office here.

We depart from the tiny village to advance a bit further. In the afternoon, we come across a boy in a tiny canoe, casting his net. As we pass close by, he greets us so I give Braulio a signal to cut the engine.

"Today we sleep in a family home," I tell Cande and the Brits.

The youth comes up to us in his canoe and offers us his fish; which we accept gratefully. Braulio and Clever make a remark in Quechua about our desire to sleep at his house. The youth nods, without caring about how many we are.

In his house, there are an older sister, and two younger brothers. His parents are travelling "down river", as the adolescent explains. The house, built completely out of natural materials found in the region and elevated on pilings to protect it from flooding, is very close to the river. It only consists of one big room and a kitchen; there are no bedrooms or living room, much less a dining room. Some of the walls are only waist-high. To sleep, they hang their hammocks, which are taken down in the morning. There are no decorations; they only possess the bare essentials.

On the floor of the kitchen, there is a box filled with soil, in which they build a fire and hanging over it from the ceiling there is meat and fish being smoked. Cande brings in rice to share, which we eat along with the fish. Dinner is delicious, served on squash skins. We eat sitting on our haunches. The locals use only their hands. If they had silverware, they'd need a plate; if they had plates, they'd need a table; if they had a table, they'd need chairs; if they had all of this, they'd need a dining room, but just as we are, in the tiny kitchen we feel very well and very close.

Braulio tells us there is no problem with staying to sleep, everyone does it because everyone has to travel and rest in the homes along the way. So we ask him if they are the owners of the land and he tells us, "The people construct their houses wherever they like and when they want. When the land doesn't produce anymore, they search for another place."

"And what happens with the abandoned house?"

"It quickly decays and becomes part of the soil, and in a few years, there's jungle."

"But whose land is it where you build?"

"The land doesn't belong to you, you belong to it. From it you came and to it you will go. Everything that you see in your body is a loan from the land and one day you'll return it back to it. The land existed before you were born and after you are gone, it will continue to exist. God gives you the Beauty of the land and the miracle of life to enjoy, not for you to take possession of it, nor to have a paper that says you own it," he pauses with a little smile on his face, "the land laughs at this paper."

"Who taught you this?"

"My Grandpa, who learned if from his grandfather...and so on."

Braulio gets up and looks for a place to hang his hammock. Before going to sleep, we all bathe in the river, it's getting later and the sun sinks into the wide river.

Innocently I ask myself if this might be the reason why water is so warm.

Cande and I walk hand in hand along the small beach. We sit down thinking that if we wanted to, we could stay to live here. We are pondering on what Braulio said about owning the land. Our families were farmers, in the places where we come from owning land is very important. Whoever is bigger is better and that person is more highly respected. This is why they devote their lives to caring for it and trying to accumulate more. My grandfather was only the second person to have the title of a property in the mountains, before him there was another man and before that it was "the land of the savages". But, who are the real "savages"? Those that crossed the land freely or those who fenced it into parcels, caging themselves in it? In this land where we are now, we are experiencing a huge cultural change. What a different point

of view about life and all that surrounds it! How many different roads we can take in our lives and with such freedom we can follow the one which we choose! Cande and I came out to see a world and it shows itself to us, showing us the personalities of each place, with their own way of life, with their different cultures and languages. Yes, they are different, but we have noticed that the most profound thoughts are common to everyone. Our bodies are of the earth, our souls of God and within every man in the world God has placed the same…dreams and love.

Not a single day goes by in which we miss the sunset and sunrise! We usually go to bed shortly after it gets dark and we wake before daybreak. Today we are awoken by the loud sound of the rain, which stops as quickly as it has started. When we put our heads out, we see that there is a gathering of many indigenous, who are seated here and there aboard the canoe. What are they doing there? They could rob us… Taken with these thoughts, I get up and head out to the boat. However, along the way I remember that there is no private property among these people and the canoe is just another place to be. As regards to stealing, everything they need they already have and they don't collect things just to have them.

Feeling calmer and attracted by the visitors, I climb aboard the canoe. They greet me with huge smiles and sweet words that I don't understand. I reply with a smile directed at each one of them and bowing my head. I really don't know why I nod, but I started it, so I keep on doing it. No one has touched anything, they were only sitting here looking at the car. Shortly, Cande comes out and also greets them one by one and they respond repeating my gesture, that is, bowing their heads. Cande imitates them. After finishing the presentation, she goes to the car to get her hairbrush. She is a little embarrassed to have messy hair; they all have neat hair with short cut bangs. When she opens the door of the Graham, everyone giggles, and when she accidentally hits the horn, they all laugh heartily and say things we wish we could understand. Enthusiastic about their happy reactions, I get into the car and start the engine, causing them to startle at first, a frightened look crosses their faces, but this quickly subsides into laughter.

The Crew

After a breakfast of bananas and papayas, we set sail. So far we haven't had any set hour to get under way nor a fixed point we have to reach every day, since we don't know where we're going. The maps they gave us in Ecuador are only of that country and we never understood them anyway. There was never a way to relate a place on the map to where we were.

Braulio and Clever have never navigated this part of the river, but in spite of this they don't seem nervous. The waters are becoming wider all the time and the farther we advance the more the river winds on in an endless succession of curves. There are islands too, and at some points, there are so many that the river branches off between them. This makes us lose our way and we are befuddled, we don't know which branch we should take. One could take us on a huge detour, taking another we could go more directly…but what does it matter if they all come back together to form the same wide river?

Perched in my seat, situated in the prow of the canoe, I break from looking at the scenery to concentrate on the crew; the English guys are marvellous, always ready to do whatever presents itself, they don't have any complaints about anything, they are just enjoying the trip. Ben continuously reads books, one after the other, moreover, he has brought a canvas chair with a cushion to be more comfortable. He is a proper "Sir", so much so that I don't understand much of his English and often I have to ask James to translate. Then Ben gets annoyed and says, "I am the one who speaks true English: the Queen's English." And my response is always the same, "Yes sure, but I don't understand you." Ben is a military man, just like his father and grandfather, he always sits properly or stands erect, he eats very meticulously and when we cook with water from the river he always monitors the boiling time with his stopwatch. He has everything he could possibly need in his two enormous backpacks: creams for the sun, for burns, for infections, repellents and many pills. He also brought his tent, his hammock, a mosquito net, and as an identity badge, he has brought along a British flag and a black umbrella. Additionally, he has music, which he is in the habit of turning on in the afternoons, according to the occasion.

Today he asked me, "Any type of special music?"

"Classical," I replied, only slightly because I'd like to hear this type of music but more to vex him.

"Any particular piece?" he asked surprising me.

"Yes, Tchaikovski's 6th Symphony," I responded to exasperate him, but it's him who kills me by fulfilling my request!

As regards James, he is completely different. He's streetwise, London's streets, works as a bartender. James, of course, is clearly not a "daily" diary, one day he writes, another does not. Besides, his sporadic writing is on loose sheets that he's borrowed from Cande. Regarding his backpack, it's not too big and could be even smaller if he arranged his things in an orderly fashion. Nothing he has with him is useful in the Amazon, because when he got to Ecuador his plans were to go to the cold mountains, so he brought jackets, hats, and socks.

James is with us because he read one of the signs Cande hung up in an Internet café and liked the phrase, "to share an adventure voyage down the Amazon..." So, he cut off his pant legs, bought a hammock and came to Coca, our point of departure.

Since he forgot to buy a mosquito net, he wakes up every morning full of new bites and Ben scares him by saying the net is good to avoid not only the insects, but also the many vampire bats, those that spread rabies. But the truth is that Ben, Cande and I, who all have nets, scratch ourselves until we bleed, because of the bite of a minuscule bug, which we are learning to dissipate by rubbing alcohol on our skins. With regards to Braulio and Clever, they have a better way to keep away insects and animals, something that works very well even though they don't sleep with mosquito nets. Everyday they cover their whole body with diesel. If this is the option, we prefer the mosquitoes.

We six each have a function, from the very first days, each one of us has been in charge of some task. For example, every time it rains, it's James who is in charge of bailing the water. Ben, for his part, has become the official "water boiler" to drink and to cook and he is the one who tidies up the deck, but it's Cande who's responsible for the sweeping. Which is exactly what she's doing right now, she's going around with the broom cleaning here and there and when she gets close to James, she puts on a serious face, a mad face, and while she bangs the broom on the floor, she says, "I am the bitch of the boat!"

"What!?" James asks her seriously, trying to act like he couldn't possibly have heard her right.

"I am the bitch of the boat!" she replies, with an evil expression, banging the broom once again on the deck.

"You...are?" James asks again, still astounded.

"Yes, I am," reaffirms Cande.

Ben is also looking on stunned, not understanding. Then I, having heard and seen everything, explain, "Love, it's not 'bitch', what you want to say is 'witch'. 'Bitch' means prostitute." I conclude while the Brits roar with laughter. Cande doesn't know where to hide herself, she wants to throw herself into the water and disappear. She was saying she was the prostitute of the boat and even affirmed it when James asked her twice!

The episode becomes a huge joke onboard. How much she charges, how they could pay, if she accepts credit cards, they ask and Cande picks up the broom and goes for their heads while they run for cover.

An Island in the River

The laughter and jokes are interrupted by a sharp screech coming from the engine. Since this is an everyday occurrence, I go to investigate it calmly, to verify what's wrong now. We've been travelling for months in a car that's more than 70 years old without any problems, but now in this boat floating in the middle of nowhere, there is something to resolve every day. The surprise now is that our improvised belts, which usually last six or eight hours, are so tight they've broken the alternator. So, we take it apart to see if we can do something, but this will be a waste of time. We have to continue travelling trying to turn on the motor only one time a day so as not to exhaust the battery since we can not recharge it anymore.

I return to my seat, in the front row, to see this river. At each curve, the jungle seems to be a different one. Once in a while, I can see aborigines in their canoes, enormous parrots crossing from shore to shore and trees falling into the river because of the change in the river bed. The panorama is always unique and in this part of Peru, the jungle is much more virgin, less explored.

At Ben's request, we stop to have a swim in the middle of the river and we throw over the anchor. Yes! Now, we have an anchor! We gathered together a few pieces of iron that we attached to a line. When we jump into the river, we're surprised that it only goes up to our waists, so the adventure of swimming in the middle of the river becomes a child's game.

We abandon the boat and swim to an island that is just emerging. It's of very fine sand and the plants are just beginning to grow.

Later, we take the rest of the day to play on the beach, eating sugar cane, pineapple, palm hearts, and avocados, all gifts from a family that had made signs for us to stop. We responded to their banquet by giving them some empty drums and others with diesel for their lamps at night. Still, I don't understand the reason for such kindness.

"Because we are travelling," Braulio reacts.

That night we move the boat to the shore, we feel more secure tying it up to a tree than relying on our anchor. Right away, it starts to rain heavily, but this isn't an impediment for three indigenous canoes that approach us. It is lovely watching them come toward us. The Amazon is beautiful even when it rains, the drops pierce the brown water, giving it a different color, the sky is enclosed in gray clouds, everything is refreshed for a moment and these three canoes are the crowning touch.

Some members of their crew are pregnant women and children. As soon as they tie up their dugouts to ours, they climb aboard without asking for permission, which now we consider normal. They speak with Braulio, but not too much, it seems they merely need the company rather conversation. We offer them crackers that they happily accept. One of the children has a tiny monkey in his small hands. Braulio tells me it's called a "pocket" monkey, but surely this is the name given by some foreigner, because the natives don't wear clothes with pockets, simply because they have no need of them.

Cande and the English begin playing cards and the native laugh at them while imitating their movements. They're also amused when Ben turns on the radio, this draws their attention and they even hum along to the music a little.

They are children, big children, innocent and simple. To dress, they only need something that covers their privates. To build their houses, they choose a place and with the materials they have around them, they erect them. To eat, they look at the river, the jungle and the land that offers them everything they need. They are always among relatives, always together, always happy.

"It's like they're from the Stone Age, they know nothing of the civilized world," Ben says to me.

"These uncivilized ones could survive in the city, but alone in the jungle we wouldn't be able to." I answer in total admiration for them.

We go to sleep inside the car, but before that, we put up the curtains and the mosquito nets, and then roll down the windows. We are very comfortable and the feeling is so nice. The movements of the water rock us; we hear animal noises, like those of the birds and sometimes, the whistle of a curious dolphin. By the next day, before the sun has gone up, we wake up with the sounds of laughter and giggles.

"I think we have some company outside," Cande tells me, and when I lift the curtain, I see many natives who, standing one next to the other, are staring at us from the riverbank.

When I open the door and lean out, they laugh even more. It seems that they spread the word that there are strange people with strange things in the area, so they've come to see us. From the shore, as if they were watching an opera, they

observe how we make our breakfast and preparations for a new day. The children's eyes are as wide open as those of the grown-ups. They don't want to miss a single movement.

They also fix their eyes on me when I get close to the car. It's occurred to me to put its alternator into the motor of the boat and even though they are different voltages, we figured out a way to make it work. Happy, I go up to the Graham and give it a pat.

"Not only don't you give me any problems, but you also give me a way to solve them," I tell it.

All is One

We continue downriver, almost at the slow speed of the current. When it begins to rain heavily, I see the drops falling and think about from how high they've fallen. Where did they come from before they were clouds? Now, in a journey farther than 3,700 miles, they'll get to the sea. But Cande, just now, with a pan ladled out some water and put it on the fire to heat…well, it looks like that's not going to happen for these drops, they'll all get to the sea. First they will be in our soup, after in our bodies mixing with our blood. They will be part of us until one of our kidneys removes it so in some way it will return to the river and will continue traveling to the sea. Also all these trees that surround us will some day fall and their bodies will become food for new trees, so its material will be part of another life. How many times has the same material been in different lives? And what about my body? How much of my body is formed with materials that were parts of other lives? How many thousands of times have they passed through other living beings? We are all connected in a cycle of life. The world existed without me and will exist without me. What can I do for it in this brief little bit of time that I have been given to live and enjoy it? What can I do? Maybe, live the present, because the only thing I know about the future is that one-day I will cease to exist. Today I am here and then I do what I am doing. I live my dreams, live my love. No, I am not afraid. It is when you live your life that you stop being afraid of death. When you have the knowledge that life has an end, it encourages you to start living it.

"Are you O.K.?" Cande asks me as she becomes aware of my tears.

"I am so happy," I tell her while extending my arms for her to come near and hold me. She hugs me tenderly. "I feel that I am in one of those best moments in my life, being with you, on this journey, chasing our dream…"

Today we stop in a family home. They have chickens fed on termite nests. More than 500 years have passed since the arrival of the white man here who after the conquest carried away so many things. The only useful thing the natives saw in the conqueror's arrival was his chicken.

Since we're very keen on a change in our menu of fish for some other meat,

we offer them a trade, potatoes and onions in exchange of a chicken. The family accepts the barter, and for more than half an hour we run after a very athletic chicken. We're very happy to have a new menu, but it hurts us to sacrifice it. When we finish plucking it, we find a rachitic animal, which we eat anyway. A few hours later, while we're moving along, James, without any kind of forewarning jumps up out of his hammock and hurls himself into the river. He manages to grab a hold of the side of the boat, it seems like he's gone crazy.

"What's wrong with you? Is your head filled with termites?" I ask him.

"No, I have diarrhea," he answers.

"I told you not to eat a chicken that eats termites!"

Permission to Circulate Number 001

We truly don't know where we are, we have no idea if we still have a long way to go or if we're close. For the first time in my life, I don't know exactly where I am. I can only say on the Napo River, in the Amazon, in Peru, but exactly where…I have no idea. Braulio asks the people of the area, but they respond with gestures and all the answers are different. In fact, it's really not that important, it's just that we don't want to pass Iquitos. It's on the Marañon River, which we have to travel on.

It takes us three more days, to get to Iquitos. The union of the Marañon and the Napo form the Amazon River. As soon as we reach it we all jump in the water to bless ourselves with 100% Amazonian water.

We begin to notice more movement of boats and people. It makes us all happy to be returning to civilization: that we've survived, that we have fixed up everything we needed on our own, that we've become such a marvelous human team, and to have learned so much together. However, we're also sad, it's the end of an adventure and that implies the group will have to break up.

"Stop, please," we've been requested via the speaker of a Peruvian Coast Guard vessel.

"With this car, they even stop us in the water," I comment to Cande.

"Welcome to Iquitos. Welcome to Peru," they say while climbing aboard our boat. Word of our voyage has reached them and all are pleased to see us well. They direct us to the port.

We see a few tugboats pushing enormous barges loaded with containers. We dock our small boat among the gigantic ones and we head to customs to complete the formalities before disembarking the car.

"Good morning, sir, we've come from Ecuador and we'd like to declare a car so we can continue our journey."

The man stares at us with a serious face and furrows his eyebrows. "Is this a joke?" he asks us.

"No, sir."

"We don't have tourist's cars here, there are no roads from Ecuador nor from here to any other place. You can only get here by boat or by plane, not by car."

"Yes, sir. It turns out we transported a 1928 car in a big canoe, from Ecuador."

"Hey, Ramirez, get a load of this! These folks brought a car from 19... What year did you say?"

"1928" Cande clarifies.

"Yes, of course. They brought a car from 1928, from Ecuador, in a dugout canoe."

"In a big canoe." Cande corrects.

"Whatever."

"I think they don't believe us," I whisper to Cande. So, she pulls out a picture of the car from among the documents.

"This is the car. And we need to complete the paperwork to disembark it so we can continue to Brazil," Cande tells the man, showing him the photo. Since he doesn't want to be the butt of a joke, he looks at it suspiciously.

"If this is the car, I'd love to see it up close."

"Of course, why not, follow us," we tell him, and he comes accompanied by two others. On seeing the car, the trio stands there, stupefied, scratching their heads without taking their eyes off it.

"I would have sworn this was a joke. Well, guys, you'll have to forgive us, we've never completed papers for a car, so we'll have to call Lima and find out how to do it. Come back this afternoon."

Together with our crew, we go on foot to get to know Iquitos. We stop to eat pizza! We're so happy to be here, but the farewell is looming closer all the time.

"With the army, I have been to Africa, to Belize, and to Greenland," Ben comments, "but this has been the best adventure of my life."

"Yeah, really it has, and I think for all of us. We're continuing with the adventure, we still need to get to Manaus and then we still need to get to Alaska."

"I don't want to say good-bye," James tells us, "I have had 15 marvelous days, I'd love to go all the way with you guys to Manaus, but I must be in Lima in a couple of days. I'm going to miss you."

"We'll miss you too. For sure, don't forget the "witch" and write often," Cande says laughing now about her mistake.

"Ben, if my government starts in a new war with yours, like the war in the Falkland / Malvinas Islands, would you come and kill me?" I ask.

"No, never."

"And what about my parents and my brothers, would you kill them?"

"No, never them either."

"Well, they are all my brothers. What would you do? Would you desert the army?" He doesn't answer; he knows he could never desert. "A country that uses war to resolve a situation only complicates matters. If between your country and ours there is a problem, they have to resolve it, without counting on us to kill each other. "When night falls, we say goodbye to the English who head out to Cusco with a promise to keep in touch and to see one another again. Farewells, sad farewells that end in tears.

The Gran Loretana

The next day, a crane disembarks the car free of charge and at customs they affix a sticker to the windshield that says "Transit Permit No. 001". Not only do we cause a sensation for the folks in customs, but also in the streets of the city. We drive around Iquitos surrounded by motor scooters, odd buses, and bicycle-taxis covered with curious awnings that carry people and things from one place to another.

We have to figure out how to continue to Manaus. We can keep going in the canoe, but the farther down river we travel, the farther it will be to return. If we've had so many problems going down, we suppose that Braulio and Clever alone will have many more going back up. For this reason, we start looking for another vessel.

After Iquitos the river hosts much more maritime movement. The site where we're docked is a well-built, new port, offering all types of services and commodities, but one has to pay and there are all types of regulations. Only the big companies disembark here. So, we head to Masusa Port, where there is more traffic of individually-owned boats. The car carries us over a muddy dirt road, full of hundreds of people carrying things on their heads. They hurry and scurry.

On reaching the river, we see the place humming and buzzing with activity. Some people are bringing things, others are waiting to sail with their belongings, and others are disembarking. Along the muddy, dirty, steep, gully-like river bank, there is one boat after another tied by the prow. Over this, there are boards the porters use to go up and back, loading and offloading. What they're carrying on their shoulders is heavier than they are, bending the narrow boards as they walk across.

The porters climb up on the running boards of our moving car to offer us their services. They yell at one another saying that they saw us first and we've already hired them. We continue advancing while others persist in keeping up with us running along side. When we stop, the offers from the porters are in the thousands, although we still don't know if there is a boat that can take us nor how they could do it, and much less if we'll need porters. In any case, they continue to offer themselves and we use the opportunity to ask about any boats to Brazil.

"The Gran Loretana sails today. It's the only one that goes to Brazil, if you don't get on, it will come back in about 15 days."

We walk aboard the Gran Loretana via narrow planks. The two owners of this ship are brothers who are looking, along with some others, at how the completely disassembled large motor is being fit together. "We'd like to go to Brazil, can you take us?" we ask them.

"We're almost full," answers one of the brothers.

"It's just us, with our things," pointing to the car on the top of the bank.

"What's that?" Since the bank is steep, it's hard to see the car shining in the sun.

"A very old car, which is taking us far away."

"Where are you from?"

"Also, from far away," I respond.

"We need your help. We are Candelaria and Herman, we come from Argentina and we are chasing our dream of traveling to Alaska. Could you help us?" inquires Cande using Alonso's magic words.

"Yes, of course. How?"

"We need help with the price, we ran out of money in Ecuador, later we made a little and with this we need to get to Manaus," Cande continues with her request.

"I've never taken a car, much less an antique one. It would be a real pleasure to see it on the deck. So much so that let's do it this way, I will only charge you for the two of you, the car will be my guest." Gratefully, we seal the deal with a hug with the brothers. Now all we need is to figure out where to put the car and how.

"Please excuse the indiscretion, but why are you doing this?" they ask us.

"For many reasons, among them, because we don't want our tombstones to say only the day we were born and the day we died, as if this is the only thing to say about our lives. We want to deserve stones that read, 'Here rests someone who has lived life.' "

On the banks, we take leave of Braulio and Clever, who we pay with the money our English friends paid us. Although they only asked to be paid two dollars a day, we give them four. We send them off as if they were our brothers. They have taught us so much, and without them, it would have been very difficult to complete the adventure of navigating the Amazon. We are very grateful to them.

All at Once

I don't believe we'll sail today, the motor of the Gran Loretana is completely disassembled. I see the heavy replacement parts arrive by truck and how they're carried on the porters' shoulders. The mechanics don't look like the part, they are men stained in oil, dressed only in shorts and sandals or barefoot. The boat is full of passengers, who, like us are snooping at the movements of the experts.

Amazingly, only three hours later the boat is ready to cast off. As soon as they finish assembling the motor, they start it to move the boat to a position that will permit the boarding of the car; they even need to move other ships to allow the Gran Loretana to maneuver. The Graham is on top of the cliff-like riverbank, some distance from the boat. It's night already and I still have no idea how it's going to be possible to load the car. So, here we are on top of this very steep bank; between the bottom of this and the water line there are some 60 feet of sticky, muddy earth. There are still about 20 porters hanging around the Graham, hoping to make some money.

We attach two long ropes to the back bumpers. We decide that 10 porters would hold the ropes so the car doesn't fall down the bank, while others will hold onto the car wherever they can. Two more have two big wooden wedges to put under the wheels to brake if necessary. Over the mud at the bottom, they lay planks that reach to the boat. I get in the car, put it in first and I approach the edge at the top of the bank. I feel like I'm driving off a cliff. I can't see anything below because the bank is really steep, and so I look at Cande. She is filming and gives me a thumbs-up.

I move forward, turn on the lights and start down. In the mirror, I can see the people holding the car with the ropes, and surrounding me there are more people holding onto the fenders. I feel like we're in the era of Ancient Egypt, doing something pharaonic. Everyone is talking at the same time, at the top of their lungs. Very slowly, we reach the bottom of the drop off, and I can breathe again.

We're still not finished, the Graham is not lined up perfectly on the boards and I can't maneuver it. Without any discussion or question, they all seize the car, shout in unison "ONE, TWO, THREE" and pick the car right up and move it. The car jiggles up and down with me inside as many times as it takes until they get us into position. Once it is straight on the boards, with no other problems, and with a little help, I manage to drive onto the deck of the boat.

The whole crowd gathered there breaks into spontaneous applause, which I thank them for when I get out of the car. The porters receive their pay that is an offering without a fixed rate nor demanded. For my part, I recover the color in my face and pat the car. Very quickly, we're under way.

A Sand Beach

The Gran Loretana has two levels. The upper deck is one big room without divisions and from the roof, almost touching one another there are hundreds of hanging hammocks. They are colorful and the floor, completely covered with luggage, creates a picturesque

ambiance. On the lower deck there is the kitchen, the bathrooms, the visible engine, two cabins, more hammocks and more baggage.

The car is in a privileged location, at the front out in the open. Surrounding it there are piglets and chickens, whole bunches of bananas, and people who come out to take some air and discover that the running boards of the Graham are very comfortable for sitting.

The boat goes and stops, at the request of the passengers in different places. Some get on, others disembark. We also tie up at some settlements and take advantage to go on short walks.

"Do you have any tools we could borrow?" I hear outside the car window. I am fast asleep and slow in responding. When I stick my head out, a man repeats the question. I show him the tools and he's disappointed there are such a few and they are so small.

"Why do you need them?" I inquire.

"We need to disassemble the boat's motor, something's wrong," the young mechanic tells me.

I go down to see what they're doing, how extensively they're taking it apart. We're still moving anyway. They've lowered the life boat with a 15-horse power outboard motor and incredibly, thanks to it and to the current, we are still progressing slowly downriver. Since we can't stop to pick up or drop off any passengers, the following takes place.

"Is anyone on land?!" they shout from the boat to the huts on shore.

"Yes!" we hear from the shores.

"So send out a boat; there are people who want to get off!"

Everything happens as if we were in another era. They yell to each village and give notice that they need a boat to discharge passengers and cargo. Some boats are rowed out, catching up with us along the way; they tie up to us, and are loaded while we continue downriver.

Later on the mechanic asks me for some sealing compound, and I give him rubber cement, the only thing I had. He figured out that they blew the head gasket and consequently the oil is mixing with the gas. To fix it, he finds a paint can, flattens it, cuts it and fits it into place, without necessary or adequate tools...

"You don't lose anything by trying" I say as I look around at where we are. They try to start it and as soon as they do, we start moving at full speed ahead.

"All or nothing!" one of the ship's owners tells me.

"If it goes, it has to go all out." The other brother agrees, seeing the look of disbelief on my face.

We've been traveling for five days now. We've used the time for painting, framing and a lot of writing. Looking back at what we've done, we're amazed at what we've been through in the last 15 days, actually, in the last six months. We can't believe how far we've gotten thanks to the day we dared to begin. It's the best decision we have ever made in our lives. At home, we never imagined we could do all this, and I don't want to even imagine all that we still need to do. I remember the phrase, "I know about my departure, God knows about my return", that makes me smile.

It is on this fifth day that we get to the border with Brazil. Cande and I celebrate what we've achieved, but our little party is interrupted by news of a little change of plans.

"We're not going to be able to go to Brazil."

"So...?" Cande inquires, somewhat puzzled.

"We can drop you off on the Peruvian side, in Santa Rosa."

"And where is this, exactly?" I ask.

"Right across from the shore of Brazil and Colombia, but on the other side of the river."

"And how do you suggest we get across? Swimming?" I say, slightly annoyed.

"I don't know, if you want, we can take you back to Iquitos."

We cannot believe it. They tell us right now they can't go to Brazil, instead of telling us before we set sail. And this is the moment they tell us they don't have papers and what's more, that they're carrying smuggled fuel.

Still reeling in shock we are deposited, via the same boards we used to embark, on a sand beach, in front of a settlement of six houses made of native materials. It is night. On the other side of the river, we can see a lot of lights. There is a nearby city, but we can't get to it. We are seated on the running boards of the

Graham; the beach is desolate, except for a dog that's come up to us to give us a welcome.

"What are we going to do?" Cande questions me.

"I don't know. There has to be something we can do. Let's sleep on it; tomorrow is another day. Tomorrow we'll see."

Triple Frontier

We wake up on the beach, which in reality isn't a beach, but a sandy bed where the river is low. We try to move the car, because the first rain could raise the river, but there are no streets or other vehicles, nor any possibilities to get off the sand. We are at the triple frontier between Peru, Brazil and Colombia. In a small canoe with a motor that serves as a taxi, I go to Tabatinga, Brazil, to look for someone to carry us to the other side.

This is a port of considerable size with a lot of movement. There is a docked boat that will set sail for Manaus in two days; if we miss it, we'll have to wait another fifteen or twenty days to take the next one. I need to find a way across urgently.

A businessman attends to me from across a cold desk. I tell him about our trip and our necessity to cross. He has a small barge and could easily do it, but he will charge us 300 dollars and this is more than we have. When I get up to leave, he tells me he'll be waiting for my call and not to look any further because he's the only possibility to get us across.

Another man who has a beautiful bar overlooking the river offers us the use of his raft made from enormous logs, which is on the side where the car is now. The problem is we have to return it to the same place, which is hard because of the size of the logs and the rival current. This is how the whole day goes by and night comes without any kind of arrangement. Before I go back to Cande, I walk over to Leticia, Colombia, to check my email.

I find a pile of messages which surprise me: people from South Africa, Uruguay, United States, Mexico, Canada and a load from new friends who in one way or another have heard about our trip. There are also reprimands. Since we left Ecuador, we haven't been able to communicate with our families and they are desperate for news. They don't even know we are on the Amazon, because we don't want to make them nervous, but apparently they already are. So, I send a message to Valeria, one of Cande's sisters, to spread the word: "We are very well, I am in Colombia and Cande is in Peru with the car. We're going to meet up in Brazil". About the time I leave the Internet café, I realize that with only this message, perhaps they all will get even more nervous. Tomorrow I'll send another message to clarify the situation.

I return to Peru. I find my love surrounded by children who are painting together with her. She tells me that when I left and she started to paint, the children came up to her timidly, but later they started easing up and ended up coloring a few sketches. In spite of enjoying this beautiful moment we go to sleep a little nervous, without knowing for sure how we're going to do it. Will it rain? Better to sleep, tomorrow we'll continue looking for a way out.

This time I ask Cande to accompany me. First, we go to Colombia, directly to the captain of the port to ask for help from the sailors. They respond that they can't help us much because the river left them high and dry: literally. Due to a change in its course, they now have a dry pier and immobile boats. However, they are still so enthusiastic about our journey, that they search for some way to help us. First, they accompany us again to Brazil, to the port, they ask around, looking for a solution but none appears. The only information they could have will be confirmed for tomorrow…but tomorrow at 2:00 in the afternoon the boat departs for Manaus.

We return to Peru a bit disheartened. Between all the coming and going I've never crossed so many countries in such a short time. Here at this border they don't bother with papers, there are no boundary controls. The most important issue is not getting further downriver to Manaus, but simply moving the car from here. If it starts to rain…we will feel a bit nervous, but if this were happening at the beginning of the trip we would be down right crazy and not just uneasy. To relax myself, I take a walk along the riverbank. While Cande, at the request of the children, gets out her supplies and begins to paint.

I see a man loading bags of potatoes into a canoe of about 15 or 20 feet long. I stand there watching him. The potatoes arrived on the same boat as we did and little by little they cross into Brazil to evade the taxes.

"How much does each bag weigh?" I ask.

"Oh, about a 100 pounds."

"How many bags can you handle at once?"

"Maybe 20, 25…more or less."

"This is between 2000 and 2500 pounds. What would happen if we put two canoes together, joined by some boards, and drive a car onto them?" it occurs to me to ask him. He remains silent, looking at the Graham. He, like everyone else in the place, knows about our problem.

"I don't know, it's not that I don't want to, but if something were to happen… this is my only boat, my way of making a living. Plus, we'd have to find another boat and see if they'd want to. I don't know, it could be very risky."

"Who can I talk to about finding another boat?"

I go to speak with his son, who very enthusiastically tells me that first thing tomorrow, when the river is calm, we'll try it. He also assures me that he'll take charge of convincing his father. Tonight it's a challenge to get to sleep; we aren't at all settled with the idea of crossing with the car strapped across two small canoes.

We wake up to the barking of the dogs that sleep beneath the car. The father-son team is already at the bank with what we hope is soon to be our ferry, both of their little boats. We begin to go house to house to ask for boards they could loan us, those necessary to join the boats and the ones to get into the boats.

Likewise, people from other houses come with ropes. When we're ready, the whole town shows up to say good-bye to the only car that ever touched down in Santa Rosa and the children say good-bye to Cande with sweetness. She will go in a different craft carrying our documents, the cameras, and the little money we have, just in case… Before I put the car up, I remember to ask how much this is going to cost.

"30 dollars, is this alright with you?"

"Perfect. Let's go."

We get the car up onto the boats easily. We are on a firm, flat beach and we have two boards we use as ramps. The people help us push the boats and just like that we're afloat, so we turn on the outboard motor and we start the crossing. It will only be a thirty or forty-minute trip, but the first few are tense. We relax little by little when we realize that everything is going just right. The river even helps us. The water is so smooth, very smooth.

I remember the words of a friend when we left Buenos Aires, "I don't wish you a journey without problems, but the strength to confront them". Gradually we are learning that every problem has a solution, there is always one. It's just that sometimes it's hard to find it. We shouldn't focus on the problem, instead on how to solve them. We don't have to look for problems, but if we don't have any, we are missing out on a great opportunity for self-improvement. A life without problems and risks is a dull life.

When we get to the Brazilian shore the people stare at us astounded, mouth open, to see an antique car arrive out of the jungle on two small boats, no idea where these came from. We don't get off at the main port because there's no way to do it with such small boats, so we go to where they load the canoes with products from the region. We are once again in the mud and front of a high bank to climb. Porters immediately appear who offer themselves in Portuguese, all at the same time. We understand little and less. Many of them together help us, laying out boards for the car to come down on. Everyone is directing everyone. Many jockeying for a position in front of the camera Cande is using to film the whole thing. Someone dares to say that she is from National Geographic and everyone wants to be in the limelight. The same folks who help us get the car off the boats also help us get it up the muddy embankment; they push and push. Another pharaonic performance.

Now on flat land and transient we go to give the good news to the captain of Port Leticia. They are thrilled to be of service and accompany us to the

port of Tabatinga to speak with the captain of the ship to try to get a better price. He succeeds.

"We are so grateful,"

"Don't worry, he owes me a lot of favors…"

Now they have to move the Coraçao de Mãe to be able to load the car. Just like in Iquitos, they have to reposition all the other boats to situate this one to get the Graham on. Once we're aboard, we set sail. We couldn't have picked a better time to arrive.

Coraçao de Mãe

Coraçao de Mãe is a three-level boat, constructed only of wood. It seems like a Spanish galleon. Since, we are on board and everything is resolved we can relax completely; now, we want to sit and watch the river, which is getting wider the farther downstream we go. We'll get to Manaus in five days. As soon as night falls, we fall exhausted out of sheer weariness and sleep very comfortably in the car.

When I wake up, I see that we are not moving, but docked along the side, among many broken tree branches scattered over the deck, which is soaked.

"What happened?" I ask.

"Didn't you hear anything? We were hit by a storm, with a lot of wind and strong waves. We had to make an emergency stop here at the bank. Don't tell me you don't know anything about it?" says one of the crew members with an astonished face to a passenger with a sleepy face. That would be me.

This boat, in contrast to the Gran Loretana, doesn't stop wherever people ask, but only in the small towns. We'd love to stop in these and spend a few days, but the boat doesn't wait.

At one of the stops, a young woman who has "fever" is carried on and they accommodate her

in one of the two cabins on board. Quite often, we hear a shriek she can't hold back. The poor woman is very ill, she is aching all over and her family has no idea how to alleviate her suffering. There are many matrons who propose different curative recipes but unfortunately, none has any effect.

Many vendors and children also come aboard when we stop in the small villages, the children use the high deck of the boat as a diving board to spring into the river. It's strange for the people to see a car on board, especially one like ours, and since the Brazilians are such extroverts, the questions are numerous. We answer so many that little by little, we pick up the local lingo.

The owner of the boat keeps building it as we move. He needs to finish the upper deck and the carpenters come and go. There are children everywhere who run and play without stopping, scattering both happiness and the bags of the passengers equally. In the kitchen of the boat, we hear the noises of pots and pans and the continuous singing of the cooks. They prepare three meals a day and one can help himself as much as he likes. And on the upper floor, where the majority of the people are hanging around in hammocks, there is music, chats and beer, and dancing tops off the night.

More than a boat for cargo and passengers, this seems like a pleasure cruise: we put on a few pounds, we learn new dance steps, songs and a lot of Portuguese. At first, we felt a bit like spectators, now they treat us as special guests and we, happily, enjoy the situation to the fullest.

We're still two days away from Manaus, when one of the ship's contractors tells us something in reference to the road ahead of us, "The route to Venezuela passes through a very dangerous indigenous reserve. No one can go through it at night and they had better not stop; some have been killed and others have disappeared. They are very dangerous aborigines, worse than any in the Amazon. Not even gold prospectors go in there, it doesn't matter how much gold there is…" I listen imagining what lies ahead of us is along the lines of the Wild West.

Suddenly, the boat brakes like it has been spiked in place. Many things, for example, us, hit the deck, while those in their hammocks all swing together vigorously, like they've been pushed.

"We've bottomed out on a sand bank," explains one of the crew while helping Cande to her feet. Then he goes to see to the rest of the passengers. There's no singing to be heard in the kitchen anymore, instead cursing. All the food along with all the pots is splattered all over the floor. For more than an hour with the motor roaring, vibrating and shuddering, little by little, they move the boat, until finally they clear it from the sand bar.

As if nothing has happened, the man continues his account about the indigenous. First they were indigenous, now they're savages and the tales of death are swelling. Other passengers add their comments to the conversation tripling the number of disappearances.

"But have you been there?" I ask to confirm the macabre tales.

"No, but I've heard all about it, which is why I don't want to go."

We always hear dangerous descriptions of the places we're going, but none of them from people who have been there, making the story lose their veracity. Stories are stories, they are always exaggerated from mouth to mouth. Even more if they're about something unknown of which people are afraid.

Arriving in Manaus is incredible. First, the sheer number of vessels there is impressive; the river is full of boats, cruise ships, barges, long boats, flat boats and galleons like ours. Second, the union of the colossal Rio Negro with the imposing Amazon creates a perfect line in the waters between the black and the brown colors, as if they were water and oil that won't mix.

In the port, there is nowhere to dock as every place is occupied, so we have to attach ours to another craft which is also attached to another and so on successively, until one is actually tied directly to the dock. Naturally the people take their things and begin to climb from boat to boat, over the planks placed over them all the way to the shore. But we can't just take our car and go, so we have to wait until tomorrow, until Coracao do Mãe has her turn to tie up to the dock.

We leave the Graham on the ship and we go out to look around the giant city. At one time, Manaus was the richest city in the world because of the rubber trade. The splendor from this bygone era still shines in many of the buildings like the port, the opera house, the churches and the municipal buildings. We walk around all these sites, totally enchanted.

Terra Firma

The next day we take the car off the galleon surrounded by tourists who are headed for a modern cruise ship. They look at us in amazement. One comments that only people with a lot of money could realize this type of trip. So, all of them are completely flabbergasted when we show them our last $40.

Before we can continue traveling, we have to make a little money. With what we have, we can't even buy 10 gallons of gas. We go out on the lookout for the perfect spot to sell. All the avenues are full of individual booths, all very close to one another. We situate ourselves among the artisans with our paintings. All for naught, in the whole afternoon we only sell a couple of indigenous crafts. The locals are impoverished and the paintings are a long way out of their reach.

That night we park in front of a restaurant visited by many tourists. We decide to go in even though we read a big sign posted on the door that says: "No sales allowed". We seat ourselves and order only a drink. We begin to look around, in search of the ideal client. Then Cande spies, two tables behind me, a couple who seem perfect.

We are so embarrassed that we can't stand up and go over to offer them, we've never done this in our lives. But out of necessity…

"Go on, go, they surely will buy something," Cande assures me.

"I can't. I'm embarrassed to death."

"What? Aren't you in charge of the sales department?"

" You go, please…" I plead.

After a short time of indecision, Cande plucks up her courage. I look at her astonished as she gets up with her paintings under her arm. She gets to the table and I can hear her conversation.

"Hi, how's it going? Would you mind if I sit with you for a minute?" she asks in shaky English to the surprised pair of tourists. They signal for her to sit down and she does. "My name is Candelaria and my husband is Herman, we are from Argentina. Where are you from?"

"Italy"

"We are passing through Manaus, we are traveling in this car," she recounts while she shows a photo.

"Is that the car outside?"

"Yes, that's the one, and to pay for our gas, we sell pictures that I paint and he frames. If you'd like, I can show you a couple."

"Why not?"

As they see them, they are fascinated and with our story as well. They invite me over to join their table. At the end of the conversation, they say farewell with two paintings under their arms and we, with the possibility of buying twenty gallons of gas. This was the first of the sales we continue to make with more tourists.

"You are an international painter now, one of a kind" I inform Cande, since her paintings are going to different countries and we are ready to go on.

"I feel so great! Not only because of the sales, but also and more importantly, I got over my shyness and embarrassment of going up to people and offering the pictures," she says.

The artists tell us that on Saturday and Sunday they close a whole avenue to set up craft booths. These are spaces you have to pay for, but there aren't any available anyway. Still Cande goes with a small table of crafts and tells the supervisor of the fair about our situation and about the trip. The man finds a small space for us to set up, and leaves Cande without charging anything. I didn't want to come, I'm dying of embarrassment and shyness. Nevertheless, Cande asked me to come with her anyway. After five minutes in the place, I tell her I'm going to go get something to drink. I make my reappearance in the afternoon just to go and get her. She's sad, she shows me the only two dollars she made, but at the same time she feels happy because she has overcome her timidity. With enough money to buy gas to the next city, we wave good-bye to Manaus.

Brazil

Vermillion. Ground

Land of Wild Savages

Once again, we begin our progress over dry land, over vermilion earth, after a month of navigating a river, a feat that has turned me into a captain. I still don't have the cap, but even without it, even without a boat, in my heart I will always be a captain.

I drive over a road opened through the jungle, tinted red from the blood spilled by the countless chopped down trees. Still the forest doesn't give up; the trees want to regain this stretch that has been torn away from them, so where man neglects the road, the jungle rapidly overgrows it.

After a few hours, we get to the entrance of a reserve of the savage indigenous. There is a barrier at the entrance, police buildings and various signs informing the visitor how to proceed: "Hours open", "No services", "Absolutely forbidden to stop for any reason", "No photography", "Do not remove anything from reserve", "Respect the inhabitants of the reserve", "Respect all forms of life in the reserve".

"Good Morning," an official tells us. We don't know if he's the police or a park ranger. "Do you have enough fuel?" We nod, "You may not stop, except in case of emergency, have no contact with the natives…"

"Are they that dangerous?"

"No," he replies a bit annoyed, "we must not maintain contact with them so we don't change their existence, their way of life."

"Please excuse me, but we were warned. We were told they were savages."

"There are savages, but that is not the aborigines," and he sends us on our way, giving us bags to put our rubbish in.

The extensive crossing of the enormous reserve takes forever. At one point, we encounter a small group of natives, torsos exposed, crossing the road; they stop and look at us. We mentally try to put ourselves in their shoes and think the way they do. Their land is crossed by a road invaded by strange metallic things that carry men inside. What must they be thinking? "Poor men locked up in these miniature objects! Where could they be taking them so quickly?"

As soon as we leave the reserve, we understand who the savages are. On both sides of the road, the jungle is burned, devastated. Yes, it's us, "civilized men".

The Engine of Our Dreams

We are in Roraima, a province in which 75% of land is indigenous reserve or national park and where there are abundant gold and diamonds. To enter the city of Boa Vista is to enter the world of the *garimpeiros*, those who search for gold; this site grew up overnight because of the discovery of many mines.

Speaking of riches, we need to make some money. The proceeds of our sales have evaporated because of the very high price of gas and with each painting we sell, we can only buy five or six gallons, which in turn allows us to continue not quite a hundred miles.

We were recommended to go and sell in the Park of Waters, the most visited place. In this plaza, there are several fountains, illuminated with various colors, whose waters "dance" following the rhythm of very pleasant music; there are also many vendors here. Fortunately, nobody offers the same merchandise like us. They don't want any competition, but if one sells something unique and also is just passing through, it doesn't bother them. We set up our table and cover it with arts and crafts from the Ecuadorian jungle and Cande's paintings framed by me.

The car, parked behind us, attracts so much attention that a television crew approaches us. They interview us in front of our post, while they're filming, a client appears and the camera crew doesn't miss the opportunity to show how we finance ourselves.

The lady asks, "How much is this painting?"

"Sixty reales," we answer. We're very enthusiastic to wait on her and thrilled she can't quit looking at the picture. The cameraman keeps filming. We all hope she'll buy it; it would be perfect both for us and for the ending of the interview.

"And how much without the painting, I mean, just for the frame? It occurs to me that I have a photo which would go perfectly in this frame." The TV crew laughs; Cande wants to throttle her.

"No, ma'am, we don't sell the frames without the paintings," I want to sell it to her, I am very proud of my frames, but if I did, my wife would kill me.

Many of the people who approach us have sparkling necklaces, bracelets, rings and even gold teeth. All around us is gold's presence, including the monument in the plaza, which is dedicated to a *garimpeiro*.

"How many grams is this?" Inquires a girl pointing to one of the crafts. While she waits for our response, instead of a wallet, she takes a tiny bag containing pieces of gold out of her purse. We have no idea what the value of gold is, neither can we weigh it or even know how to identify it. To avoid complications, we ask her to pay us in cash. Later, a man, who seems to have gone for a few days without a bath or a shave, tells us the price of gold and that it would be advisable for us to accept it. He explains that since we are traveling, we could sell it profitably in another place and that it would be best for us to sell everything we have, including the car, and later exchange it for gold. He assures us that our earnings would be enormous; he's desperate to infect us with his gold fever. Another man comes up and listens thoughtfully to the conversation. He interrupts us.

"Everything that I touch turns to gold or something even more valuable. I have friends that are treasures, a wife and a son that are worth all the gold in the world and more. I look at you two, with a priceless car, a dream that cannot be exchanged for any metal regardless of how precious it is. Why would you search for gold when you possess the most valuable things? Why would you lose them for something less valuable? Many people trade the values of their lives for the ambition to have gold. If you can exchange these for gold, it's because the gold has changed you, and when gold changes you, you are worthless, you're not even worth one gram of this metal."

The unshaven man stands there looking at us, sighs and he goes. The other, dressed in a volunteer firefighter's uniform, stays to keep us company.

"You don't know how many beautiful houses which were worth a lot of gold I have seen transformed into ashes. What you're doing is an unachieved dream for many of us. We watch the years and the opportunities slip away for no good reason. A fulfilled dream is the best fortune that a man could get, no matter what happens, it'll be safe within you, and nothing can take it from you, not even death, because you will carry it in your soul."

The firefighter appeared at the right moment, for the gold fever around us was beginning to prove quite contagious. His timely, heart-felt words are perfect for the moment, just like buckets of cold water the temperature of our heads begins to subside.

"What do you know about all these people you see here?"

"Nobody, they're all strangers."

"Yes, they are, but do you know what's in store for them?"

"No, we don't know. What?"

"All of them will die. Everyone. Still, they search for gold, believing that with it, they can achieve their dreams. Because they ignore that they can live by dreams, for dreams and through dreams. Their search for gold never ends, when they find it they look for more, it's never enough. And do you know what happens when they can't find more? It's the gold's fault they haven't fulfilled their dream." The fireman, who perceives in our faces our admiration for what he's saying, only interrupts his words to take a breath. "We have three incredibly valuable things in life; the first is life itself; the second, our dreams, and the third, death. Without the miracle of the first, we would never have the other two. Dreams are the treasure of life, without them nothing has any value and death, although it's the end of life, it is the drive for our dreams because it warns us not to lose one instant of life."

You Feel It but You Can't See It

We wake up in the home of a family we met last night in the plaza. While we have breakfast together, a young couple knocks on the door asking for us. They introduce themselves as Gerardo and Dorca. They are from Venezuela and are traveling around all the countries in South America, visiting the capitals in a very peculiar way: on foot, only walking.

"We saw the car with the decal and we realized that we're not the only nuts traveling around." Right away we find ourselves talking about thousands of things, we have many things in common, so much that we all decide to postpone departure for another day to have more time to continue talking. "The purpose of moving around on foot is to create a humanity that has a more careful attitude towards nature. We feel that we want to do something but all we have is ourselves, so we have made up our minds to visit each country on foot and with each step, show love for our nature."

We continue talking about the magic that you can only feel on the open road, about discovering it and discovering ourselves, and the things that present themselves along the journey, about the people who live nearby and above all, about the huge changes that we are going through.

"I don't know what it will be like on the road or how we'll get there, but it seems like someone has already prepared the whole way for us. Otherwise, how is it possible that every place we get to there is always someone waiting for us?" Gerardo asks me rhetorically.

"Maybe it is meant to be, that this is fate" I state.

"Maybe this is indeed meant to be, but I will have a say in deciding it is to happen. There is no value to it if you don't go for it." He responds.

"It has been the same for us, everything has worked out just right. How come that when we're searching for somewhere to sleep someone appears who invites us to his house? If we need something for the car, a mechanic and the parts show up. Why doesn't the car ever break down in a place where there's nobody? How come? Why do we always have fair weather? The few times the weather has been bad, what happens is that we stop and meet marvelous people. Why is it that when we need advice, a person appears with just the right words? Why has all this happened to us? Why are we so lucky?" I comment.

"One can be lucky once or twice, but not every day. I don't call that luck." He tells us, "I come from a very religious family who could never change my atheism, the more they wanted me to believe, the more I resisted. Then I set out to walk, and I changed. I was thirsty, and someone appeared on the road with water. I was hungry, and someone gave me food, I was tired and someone gave me a place to rest. Today, after living what I've been through, I believe there is someone who is very happy with what we're doing and to help us invited his angels. Now I believe in them, but they're not as I imagined, they're not dressed in white with wings, the angels that surround us take the form of people and there are hundreds of thousands. There are many more than I ever believed." The farther he proceeds in his dialogue, his voice becomes more animated. "Look at me now, I even sound like a priest saying all this. My family can't believe it, they almost fainted when we got married in a church before leaving Venezuela," he tells us.

"We feel like we have to be careful with what we ask for, because everything is granted."

"Yes, God always provides, but only if you strive hard. Don't try asking then sitting around to wait for it to happen", adds Dorca.

"If God exists, why can't we see Him?" Cande questions.

"You can see Him, you see Him in the landscape, in this butterfly passing by, in each person, in every thing…"

"OK, but why doesn't He show Himself?"

"Have you ever seen love or happiness? The soul exists, but you can't see it. When I feel well, I feel something very beautiful right here," raising both hands to her breast, "and when I am afraid, I feel it shrinking. What I feel isn't in anatomy books, but it's the part of my body with which I 'm most connected with. It's like God. What's essential is invisible to the eye."

Gerardo adds, "Have you ever seen the wind? Heat? Cold? No, you haven't, but you can feel it, like fear, love and life. We see the world that moves around the sun, in a universe that also moves although this movement we can't feel. Not everything you see exists, also not everything you can't see doesn't exist."

We bid them farewell, exchanging hugs and addresses. They give us their parents' and we give them ours, so they can have a home away from home. After we are alone, Cande and I spend hours together talking about our feelings, we are able to share this beautiful emotion we carry within us. Incredibly, our path has crossed with two people who are merely passing through here; they experience the same as us and with the same intensity. This encounter is not accidental, as Gerardo says, "There's someone who already has everything set for us".

Cowboys in the Savannah

Little by little, leaving the jungle behind us, we now continue through the endless savannah, it seems very much like Africa. We get off the road to see an enormous boulder lost here in this place without mountains, painted by ancestral cultures. To get to it we enter an enormous *fazenda*, as they call their cattle ranches. We ask for directions from some cowboys who are herding water buffalo. The road is amazingly beautiful; we fall in love with the panorama. A river with crystalline water passes near by and invites us to come and take a dip. On the other side of the river, we see a Governmental sign that reads: "NO trespassing", the whole area is an indigenous reserve.

We stay in the water for a while then we decide to go back to the cowboys' house without visiting the rock. We go back to the car to get ready to return. On the road, Cande insists, as usual, in taking a few shots. This involves stopping, turning around to wherever the track is a good angle for filming. As always, I drop her off where she wants and go back with the car until it disappears around a curve. After a few minutes, I return, passing in front of the camera and then coming back to pick her up. Now yes, I'm going to pick her up. I see her in the rearview mirror, she's jumping, shaking her pants and scratching her feet at the same time.

"What's wrong?"

"We have to do it all over, what I took was completely blurry, I stepped into an anthill!"

It always happens the same way, but if it weren't for Cande we wouldn't have many photos nor videos recording what we've lived.

When they see us once again, the cowboys, or as they call themselves, *vaqueiros* invite us to eat with them. We enjoy a delicious lamb stew together. The family is composed of the parents with two children and also another worker. All their conversation and gestures are accompanied by smiles. They invite us to go in the morning to another nearby *fazenda* to work with the other ranch hands. Delighted to go on horseback and live a day with them, we accept and arrange the car to sleep beneath the clear, cloudless night.

An enormous shake wakes us, we have no idea what is happening nor what it is, but the car is being jostled on one side and the other very abruptly, I put my head out the window and butt into an enormous zebu bull scratching his neck on the fenders. I yell at him to shoo him away and he stops scratching, turns his calm face with his enormous, long horns and stares at me as if asking, "What's your problem?"

I reply to his glare, "Excuse me, Mr. Bull, please continue, I didn't want to disturb you." Finally, he moves away parsimoniously.

After breakfast, we mount small sized horses. We follow a track that crosses the incredible savannah that lies ahead of us. It's early and it's already hot, the dogs follow us in a line and every once in a while they run ferociously in search of something or another, later they come back with their tongues hanging out trying to walk in the shade of the horses.

With a gesture, we all take off at a gallop, but very quickly, my horse changes into a bucking bronco. All the dogs begin barking, my beast lightens himself off my burden making me eat dirt, and when I land, the dogs come up to me and I'm licked all over. The vaqueros dismount a little worried, but when they see I'm ok, they all burst into laughter. We all remount and, at a gallop, I tell them this isn't the first time that a horse has thrown me over so quickly.

In the surrounding area trees are sparse, but they don't obscure the view of the undulating savannah: it looks infinite. It's abundant in diverse types of grasses and brush, occasionally we cross some water and once in a while we come across some animal, like this enormous anteater, who the dogs only dare to bark at.

After several long gallops and walks on sweaty horses, we reach a house where a smiling family invites us to dismount and refresh ourselves, offering us delicious natural fruit juice and cookies. They tell us that they already have fresh horses ready for us. The man of the house takes delight in showing us all that they do and among their farm animals is a litter of chubby piglets.

"They look delicious," I comment.

Decidedly, he grabs one and sacrifices it; I don't have time to stop him. He takes it to his wife to cook. My comment has cost the piglet his life, but it's given an enormous pleasure to the cowboy, who very shortly offers us his work turned into a delicious meal.

Afterwards, we remount and go in pairs into the bush to search for livestock. They are enormous zebus, taller than our mounts. Little by little, we all herd them together, then these gather with those of the others.

Later we round them all into a big makeshift timber corral. Here they work on foot, separating the jealous cows from their calves. Suddenly, the dust rises, one of the vaqueros takes off, running scared because an angry momma cow is chasing him. All the others laugh seeing him hanging from one of the posts of the corral. I ask him what happened.

"The ground is too hot, it burned the soles of my feet." He answers wanting to hide the true cause, making everyone laugh.

The afternoon continues with much activity; hot irons marking livestock, revolving lassoes, barking dogs, shouting cowboys, racing around, a little rodeo, falls, knocks, and laughs.

We feel so happy about this surprise on the road. Just a small detour has treated us to the opportunity to taste a day in the life of this place in which we're allowed to be one of them and savor their life shoulder to shoulder.

We go back, admiring a marvelous red dusk which changes the colors of the scenery. In single file on horses as tired as their riders, without saying a word we get back to the house, after a day in which we have helped others in their work, and in turn they have helped us live a day to remember.

After yesterday's mounted foray, we wake up aching all over. Now I am feeling my fall. During breakfast, they see us sitting down slowly, little by little arranging our painful butts on the bench. Our hosts scoff at our fragility and we catch their contagious laughter.

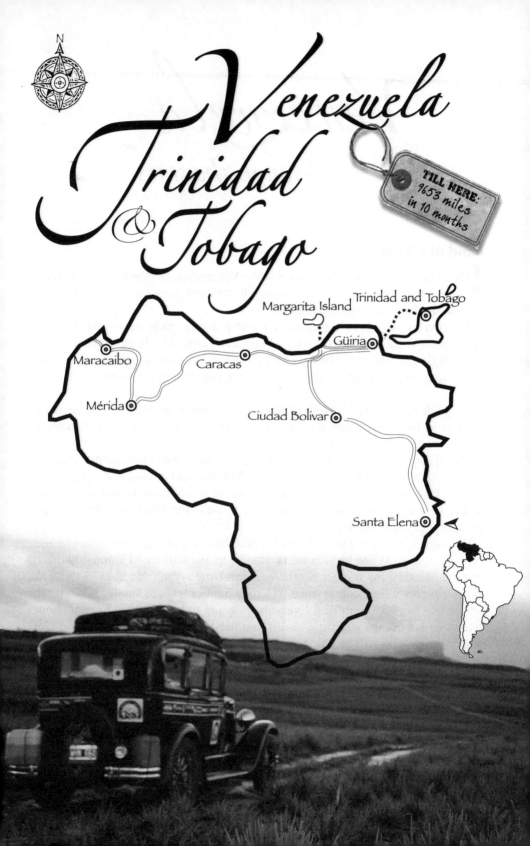

Venezuela
Trinidad & Tobago

TILL HERE: 9653 miles in 10 months

N

Margarita Island

Trinidad and Tobago

Maracaibo

Caracas

Güiria

Mérida

Ciudad Bolívar

Santa Elena

Venezuela

Through the stars

Land of Diamonds

It's six in the evening afternoon and the Venezuelan customhouse is already closed. However, they let us through all the same, they only ask us to come back to do the paperwork on Monday.

As soon as we begin traveling, we come across great news. We look in amazement at the pump, it shows $3.20 for a full tank. This is glorious, we have just left Brazil, where the fuel was more expensive than anywhere else we've traveled up to this point, and here we find the cheapest in the world.

We go directly to the city hall of Santa Elena, where the Venezuelan travelers we met in Brazil recommended us to go, and ask for Pedro. He immediately inquires what he can do for us.

"Word has it that you are a very good person," this seems to please him greatly. We explain that we need to stay here until Monday and it would be a great help to us if he could host us. He tells us to wait for just a moment and he goes in. When he returns he extends a diploma of welcome from the city with an invitation to spend three nights in a hotel.

We come away very pleased, and we find the car with a person seated on the running boards. When he sees us, he stands up and tells us, "I learned to drive in a car like this, my brother taught me. I am Uruguayan." He hugs us tight, as if we were his fellow countrymen. "Here in Santa Elena, as small as it is, there are people from 75 countries. Everyone is going to be delighted to hear about what you are doing. Welcome, and if you need anything, tell me because I'm sure to know who will be able to help you."

"Well, we need to have the car serviced, the last time was in Ecuador," I explain to him.

"I know just the right person, he's a 75 year-old Peruvian who knows more than twenty mechanics put together. If you don't have anywhere to go tonight for dinner, I'd love to invite you. What would you like to eat?"

"Something typical of the region," Cande replied.

"Arepas! Follow me."

Don't Believe You Know How to Live

We get up early. Cande will be devoted to selling her paintings today, and I will go to the mechanic, in the afternoon we'll meet up again.

In an open field, I see a small mobile home surrounded by a few abandoned cars, and a few others in different stages of repair. There are no constructions, not even a shed and this coincides with the directions given by the Uruguayan.

The man sees me coming long before I stop in front of him. His face is beaming. As soon as I get out of the car, he says, "I learned mechanics as a child in my father's shop, on cars like this," at the same time as he opens the hood of the Graham. "A Delco-Remy distributor as the starter, an Autolite generator…" the man knows everything at a glance. "We need to adjust the steering mechanism, some brake fluid is leaking here… As well as that, we're going to deep clean it to remove all the sand." He slides his hands all over the engine as if he were touching a work of art, watching every detail.

"Hi, I'm Herman," I tell him interrupting his ecstasy.

"Oh! Excuse me, I didn't even say hello." No, no he didn't say hello, because he is overwhelmed.

Immediately and before I can say a word, he jumped right in. I try to help him, but he only lets me clean the parts and fetch the tools. At one point, a man comes looking for his car, but he has to leave without it after the Peruvian responds that he's still waiting for a part. As soon as the client leaves, he comments, "I lied, I do have the part, but nothing is going to sidetrack me from the pleasure of working on a real car."

Under a strong sun, I spend the whole day together with this man, and although he's elderly, he seems like a child with a new toy. He tries to explain to me the function of each part of the Graham with such devotion that I learn while he disassembles every one of the parts.

"Everything is practical and very logical," I comment while I watch him work.

"No, not everything. It's the same as life, not everything is logical in it, not everything is practical, not everything is mathematical. You can't turn everything into a binary system. There are things such as love, mysticism, religion, talents, energy, forces, maybe thousands of things you feel, which are complicated to explain, although they're not difficult to experience. With cars, the same thing happens. Sometimes, with no logic, the car continues to go, and at other times, also sometimes inexplicably it stops. Have you had any problems with this car or with anything else?"

"I don't know if I'd call them problems, I prefer to say I've had complications or trials. For each one, a solution appears. Occasionally, they appear at the same moment and at other times it took a bit longer, but they never failed to appear. Furthermore, out of a complication a reason always follows. And I can assure you that every time we realize the motive we're grateful it happened. But you know what happens to us many times? It was hard to see the solution because we were concentrating only on the problem."

The man asks me and listens without taking his head out from under the hood.

"I feel like I'm learning things on this trip that will be useful for my whole life," I comment.

"Perhaps," now he lifts his head, looks at me and talking to me like a son he says, "Don't believe you know how to live because as a day changes into night, life changes, you learn day by day, it is a constant change. This day never existed, you are neither the one you were yesterday nor the one you will be tomorrow," He pauses, I remain silent, nodding my head with his words. "Did the car give you any trouble?"

"No, why?"

"The carburetor is clogged," he shows me while blowing a tube. "I don't know how you got this far," this is the last comment he makes before concentrating completely on the car. Without any extra movements, knowing what he's doing, he dismantles many pieces and puts them back together. Later, at his signal I start the Graham. It runs perfectly, nothing skipping and now it sounds much more harmonious.

"How much do I owe you?" I ask him contently.

"You should charge me for the pleasure it gave me to work on this car. Go on, just keep going."

When I get to the hotel, I find Candelaria brimming with joy. "You don't know how well I did. I sold so many! I went to the city hall and almost everyone bought something. And you?"

"We have a new car as well as a new friend."

Name Your Price

During the three days in Santa Elena, we go to eat in various family's homes. In all of them they make us try the typical food of the region: arepas! Cande copied the recipe and practiced how to make them in each home since they're so tasty. Now that she knows how to make a typical Venezuelan dish, it's time to go.

We are filling up gas when we see a Jeep pull up. It's a total jalopy, covered in mud everywhere you look. A man in the same condition climbs down from it; the only thing you can see is the white of his teeth.

"Well, I'll be damned! What the hell is this? What kind of car is this?" he yells while pounding the fender of our car. We are answering the same question just put to us by another man. The newcomer interrupts us. "I'll buy it, tell me how much, and I'll buy it." He has already more than decided.

"It's not for sale."

"Everything is for sale, you just have to name your price," he tells me while taking out a leather bag hung around his neck. "I'm just getting back from the mines, look how well I did." He extends his hand displaying a few little rocks that look like pieces of broken glass. "Diamonds! And this one, this one is an emerald. With this I could buy many cars like yours and more too. How much do you want? Tell me…"

"Excuse me, but I'm not selling the car, I want to have it as badly as you do."

"Damn! You lose," he looks around him and goes away very pissed off because instead of admiring him for his newly- found fortune all the people gathered around because of his yelling, and are now laughing because he can't buy everything he wants.

Finding Yourself in a Lost World

We leave the small village and enter one of the biggest national parks in the world: the Gran Sabana. It's fairly warm and to refresh ourselves a little, we open the windshield filling the car with the perfumes of the place, with its dust, its temperature and the occasional visit of some flying insect. We are in permanent contact with nature. We don't have air conditioning, but we have the wind conditioning which permits us to savor the breezes of the road and when it rains, to feel the drops that always find a way to sneak in through the cracks and crevices.

We trade the main road for a dirt one instead, which we feel is inviting us to follow it. We pass by an indigenous settlement; its houses all the same, grouped together forming a circle. The small children come running out to see us, while the parents and the youngsters work the jade. We say hello and continue.

Now the road forks off into two small tracks, we continue and drive through the undulating scenery. We turn off the engine on the downward slopes to hear the sounds in silence. We cross small creeks without bridges whose mud allows us to cross. We continue driving for a few hours, enjoying being immersed in this vastness.

When night approaches, we stop to set up camp. There is no one around us, only the infinite, glorious horizon. We roll out our sleeping bags in the grass and lie down looking at the sky. We're not in a five-star hotel, but instead in a thousand-star one, stars which shine all  around. We amuse ourselves searching for the ones that move.

When the moon peeks out, I watch it as I used to with my Grandpa on the farm, we used to go look for it, we knew when it was waning and when it wasn't, we also knew when to plant and when we had to reap. It's the same moon that inspires poets, invokes love. Moon, nocturnal display that makes us lift our gaze. The eyes of the first human must have gazed upon you as I do today. You are the common view to all of humanity; we can see you from anywhere. How can you be so beautiful that even the animals sing to you? Moon that moves seas, that moves me and touches me…submerged in these thoughts, we fall to sleep together in a cuddle, music of frogs and crickets as a background.

We get up at dawn because of the light of a new day, and because of the pecking of a bird fighting with his reflection in the car's windshield. We get up with stiff backs from the hard ground, but we feel happy looking around where we woke up.

We breakfast on delicious eggs with crackers and while enjoying this, it occurs to me that I don't have a clear idea which direction I came from. Last night we left the road to sleep near a creek…I continue chewing while I try to get a point of reference that would remind me of our location. They call this place "The lost world", and it seems that it is exactly where we are and how we are.

However, I feel that there is nothing bad in being disoriented and I believe that it's very good when one encounters oneself, whereas before I was so lost. At other times in my life I knew exactly where I was, but I was still lost. My work had no meaning, except for the salary. I lived in a place where I was close to everything, but I didn't like living; I dressed like my work demanded, even though those clothes didn't coincide with my style. I was lost, I didn't know who I was and I didn't know what I could do.

On the other hand now, I am disoriented but not lost. I know who I am and what I can do. At this very moment, I find meaning in the words of the English photographer we met in Cusco. From now on my work will be the one I love to do, even if it pays me only a little. I don't know where I'm coming from but I know where I'm going.

I leave my breakfast and go to the road. I see the tracks we made getting here last night. We stay the whole day close to this creek, surrounded by Tepuys, very big, tall, flat rock formations with straight walls and level tops, which host millions of trees and varied animal life. All the vegetation is strong, vigorous; the energy of the place fortifies it.

Cande dedicates to painting while I cut mats and wood for framing her work. The place is silent until dusk. As it happened in the Atacama Desert, in the Andes and in the Amazon. Serenity reigns in this immensity that makes one feel so small, as if we were only seeds. We sleep once again in the "thousand-star hotel".

When the new day begins to show, we move. We don't get too far, we are fascinated by the beauty of a waterfall over rocks as red as jade. Inspired we stop again and return to painting. We are in the middle of a lost world, but we still run into a family who coincidentally is passing by and who also by chance see their favorite bird painted by Cande and charmed, they buy it.

Christmas

The low price of gas tempts us; it makes us want to drive around, so that before we go toward Caracas we detour to Margarita island. We make plans to spend our first Christmas and New Year's holidays far from home. Getting to the island means we will step for the first time in the Caribbean, another of the many places in the world that we want to experience. We take the cheapest ferry that transports trucks and cargo and we disembark on an island of sun and beaches.

The first nights we pay for with a painting that is received in exchange by the very elated Italian owner of the place. The following, we are invited to a family home and we spend Christmas Eve celebrating with them.

It's our first Christmas away from home, and although we feel very well, we can't help feeling lonely. The festivities are a big reason for family reunions and we are a little nostalgic. We wait for midnight so Cande can call her family on Christmas. "Hi daddy, Merry Christmas!"

"Merry Christmas, honey. Where are you? We miss you so much!"

"Us too. We're on Margarita Island, in the home of a family," and after talking a minute he passes the phone to mom, who exchanges greetings, but with a strange tone of voice. Cande notices her nervousness and awkwardness. Her mother doesn't delay in giving the information she least wants to hear, they've detected liver cancer.

Cande's voice quivers a moment, she doesn't know what to say and she tries hard not to cry. "What's wrong?" I ask her but she continues to listen attentively on the phone.

"The spots are tiny and they are going to try to treat me with chemo. Don't worry, everything is going to turn out fine," her mother encourages. Cande remains astonished by her strength, her mother always puts up a good fight in all situations. She never surrenders and Cande feels she can do nothing. "Don't tremble," she repeats over and over to herself, "give her strength, give her what she needs, energy, positive energy." She wants to embrace her mother with her voice, so she pulls herself together and says, "Everything is going to be fine. And even though I'm not physically near you, I am surrounding you and protecting you. A couple of days ago, looking at the stars something occurred to me. Let's use them to communicate with each other, we can both see them, and among the stars we can wish one another good night, be together."

"I love it, that sounds great…because I miss you so much. I love you so much, dear!" and they say farewell, content with this new idea.

After this, Cande breaks down and falls into my arms and releases her sorrow. She is remembering her fears; those that she had before we left and still exist in her, but are hiding behind the marvelous occurrences of the road…fears of something happening to her loved ones without her being there, fears that get into the car with her. "What should I do? Should I go back? Should I wait and decide? Should I go on? Maybe they are hiding something from me and these spots aren't so small. What do I do? I can't believe what I'm going through." Cande's head is a whirlwind, and I tell her without pressuring her, with a calm voice.

"My love, she is going to be around for a long time. Your mom is going to be fine."

In some moments, my wife has a great deal of energy, she fills herself with faith, but in others, she gets weak and breaks down. She wants to go back, but she decides to wait for the first results and then see what she should do.

Look for the Calm, Not for the Storm

Margarita Island is marvelous and we move from one beach to the other. We've been recommended to visit a fellow countryman of ours, Charly, who receives us like family. He has a kind of beach club with parasols, tents, a restaurant and something more valuable, excellent attention that makes you feel like royalty.

I watch him work and he does so with such devotion, so contentedly that he spreads his enthusiasm and his cheer to all of his employees. He serves everyone equally, without taking into account who consumes more and who less, demonstrating a high regard for absolutely every one of his clients.

"Good day, sir. How can I serve you today?" he asks a man seated under a parasol.

"Nothing, when I want something I'll ask you," he answers curtly, without returning the greeting.

An hour later it seems he needs something and in a manner not courteous at all, he calls Charly.

"Hey, come 'er"

"Yes, sir, what can I do for you?"

"Bring me a Johnny Walker Black, neat."

"I'm sorry, but we're out of that right now. If you'd like, I have instead…"

"I want the drink I want, not what you want to give me," he interrupts in a way that if I had been his waiter I would have told him to go drink sea water, I wouldn't have brought him anything…

"Please accept my apologies sir, it's my mistake not having it. But at no charge I can offer you one of my best whiskies," Charly smoothes out the situation to my amazement. Then he serves him and the rude guy doesn't even thank him.

"Wait a minute, Charly," I say to him, "did you see how that guy treated you and how you treated him?"

"Just because he is rude doesn't mean that I have to be. I am the way I am, if someone comes in a bad mood or is disagreeable, they won't change my way of being. If I let myself get to their level, and get mad, I'm worse than they are. And what for? I am happy with the way I am, with my cheerfulness. Why should I lose it? Why would it depend on who I am with?

"Yes, right, but this guy was so rude to you…"

"If someone says something to you in a very inappropriate way, you reply in a nice way, don't put more fuel in the fire, because this will only make everything worse. Look for the calm, not for the storm."

"And what if he continues?"

"Very politely say that you'd be delighted to continue talking, but you have to take care of something else, nothing more."

During the rest of the day, Charly continues waiting on a world of people, always with an enormous natural smile. Once in a while I look at him in admiration. Every time someone wants to argue about something with me, I engage and don't let it go. When someone treats me badly I respond in the same way and sometimes worse; I can't let them win. However, now I understand that actually what happens is the opposite: they were beating me because I was going down to their level and I stopped being who I was, turning into someone worse than them.

When night comes, we get the cherry on the top, our new friend offers us his own room. It is over the restaurant, facing the Caribbean, it's a dream room, enhanced by the music of the waves and the sea, which cradles us and puts us to sleep

God's Will

New Year's Eve arrives and we celebrate it with the owners of an Internet café in which we had stopped a couple of days before. We're staying with them in their house tonight. A woman dressed in Hindu clothes accompanies us. She is very calm in everything; in her movements, in her voice, in her gestures, and she spreads a sensation of peace. Nothing perturbs her; she looks peaceful and contented and greets us with a warm affectionate hug. She tells us she's on vacation. She's from New York where she works in a church of her religion. I ask her if she misses her church, because there aren't any of them around here.

"God is where one is, you can find Him within yourself. He lets himself be seen in the sick or in the poor, in a child, in a baby… As you do on to others as you do to Him. For God, more than praying to Him, He likes that you pamper Him, take care of Him, love Him and He feels this when you do it to others. Every time that you get closer to your fellow man, you get closer to God. Do you know what is His biggest anguish, His greatest disappointment?"

"Wars," I respond surely.

"Although wars hurt Him very much, there is another thing, something He can not believe happens in His own human creation: the killing of thousands and thousands of babies, killed every single day. Killing of defenseless babies, who can't scream, who can't choose to live. They're children who never get to have dreams, although God loves them with all His heart, and to whom He granted the miracle of life."

"Who's killing children?!?" I ask enraged not being able to imagine anyone who could do that.

"The worst part is that they know they are assassins: it's their own parents, who out of convenience or for money or for some other inexcusable reason do it. When you kill a baby, you're killing God, because God is in everyone of these children and He loves them."

"You're referring to abortion?"

"Call it abortion, assassination, infanticide...whatever you call it, it's horrible."

Just then, the couple's three-year old son appears and interrupts our conversation to give good night kisses and big hugs with much delight. We watch him with the joy only a child spreads.

I lie down, close my eyes and meditate. I never thought about abortion in this way, part of society plants the idea as progress for the foundation of civilization, that it's better for the world not to have one who isn't wanted. And what about the desires of God? And the desires of babies? And those who desire to be parents but can't have a child? After talking to the New Yorker, I think that abortion isn't progress, but the biggest backward step in society. A child, even though he might not have been wished for, will be a human being who will surely fill us with happiness and love. I know many little ones who arrive unexpectedly and who come to be the best surprise in life. For example, I have Candelaria, her coming was completely unexpected to her family and I don't want to imagine what would have occurred if she had been aborted, if they had taken her life away. I also have a surprise little sister, we're 16 years apart. How much sweetness she brought to all of us! I remember they said there were many risks and dangers, both for my mom and for the baby, but my sister has only brought marvelous moments. I can't imagine what life would be like without her.

A Pleasure with Every Sale

We go to the beach everyday to take advantage of the high season and sell the necklaces and artisan crafts we brought from the Amazon. I recognize that it's very hard for me to go out and sell the paintings, making it nearly impossible to do so with the crafts.

"Go on Cande. They'll pay attention to you," I try to convince her.

"I'm not going by myself...I don't have the courage."

"Both of us together doesn't look good. Go on."

We go back and forth like this for an hour, without either of us really having the guts to set out. Until a girl comes up to us offering us rings and Cande says, "I sell things too, but my heart's not in it."

"Look, what you don't show, you don't sell. Just pluck up your courage and go, look at all those wallets on the beach," waving her arm, signaling all the people there.

Cande smiles at the comment, looks at the people for a little more courage, puts on her beach hat, hangs a lot of bracelets and necklaces over her arms and hits the beach. As she goes, I watch her and she looks like a real hippie.

Meanwhile, I stay near the car. A young guy approaches and just like all Venezuelans, begins talking to me. He tells me at length that he's a satellite TV door-to-door salesman. So, I tell him how embarrassed we are to go out and sell. This makes him laugh, and he explains that whoever doesn't want to buy, won't buy and he is happy to have given them the opportunity. His slogan is, "With every sale, a service; with every sale a pleasure" I tell him that Cande is selling crafts on the beach and it's up to me to sell her paintings. He asks me to show them to him, he looks at them, and likes them, and asks me about the price. I can't believe he's going to buy one without me having to go out and offer them, but no, he asks me to give him a few, he puts them under his arm and he walks to the nearby restaurant. I don't know what he's doing, so I don't let him out of my sight for a second. Incredible! He goes table to table offering them, until a man reaches for his wallet and keeps one. Shortly, the triumphant young man comes back telling me, "See that? I just made a man happy..."

"You made us happy."

"It's my pleasure. Now you try it, these paintings sell themselves."

Overjoyed, I go to look for Cande to tell her what just happened. I find her just as she is completing a sale.

"You ask me for a better price because you think I'm doing this as a business, but I'm not selling them to make money, only to accomplish a dream." I hear her say. Without further discussion, the guy pays what she asks.

All Mariners are Adventurers

We leave Margarita island and we come back to the continent with two possibilities: go to Caracas and follow the planned route or detour east to go to Trinidad and Tobago. We choose the detour.

We get to Guiria, a port in the extreme east of Venezuela, it's neither too big nor too small, but its heart is that of a town. The only company that regularly goes to Trinidad, Tobago and other islands in the Caribbean has just sold its boat and it will be a couple of months before the new ship arrives. We're sad because we were told that they have a boat and now we run into this surprise.

"There's a Dutchman, a man of the sea..." he begins to explain about another possibility of going, but he's not completely sure. We look at him hopefully and he continues. "He has a small boat that for sure is older than your car, it's from 1903.

It can only carry four small containers, but who knows, maybe he'll take you."

"Where can we find him?"

"Difficult, he lives in Trinidad and only comes this way when he has cargo, but ask for José. He's his shipping agent."

In these small towns, they don't tell you how to get there, they only say, "Ask for him" and you go asking on every corner. That's how we find José, who gives us good news.

"He's in port, let's go have a look…"

We see very colorful fishing boats, sailboats, and small ships. Anxiously, we look for our man. When we get to the boat, it looks like it's been out of service for years, it seems weak, very small, with patches welded all over the hull, some places painted recently, others corroded by the salt, with temporary fixes, eternal temporary fixes.

The agent calls the captain, a senior, with a disheveled white beard like his clothes and his boat, but with a young spirit. He invites us aboard and we enter what is or was his home. In his cabin made of artistic woodwork many parts are very organized, others are an absolute mess. Oceanographic maps, compasses, books, souvenirs from other ports, everything I always imagined of these old sea wolves, of these sea captains. The interior smells like salt, wood, and old things. It's our first time in a boat of the sea and the sensation is perfect.

"I can't take you now, I'm not sure if on the next trip I will be able to, this would be in about ten or fifteen days. If I'm not full, it could be…"

"How much would it cost us?"

"When the day arrives, we'll see," he answers. The man doesn't show much enthusiasm for our trip or for the car, but I would swear that he has as much of a desire as us to spend the time together talking about trips and dreams. I remember very well what the Commandant in Ecuador told us, "Every seaman is an adventurer and they will help you." With this thought, we watch the captain set sail for Trinidad.

The Kid's friend

We are coming out of shipping agent José's office when we're approached by a very well dressed man, too well dressed for this place. His broken Spanish establishes he's not originally from this region and when he tells us his name, it confirms that he's an Arab. We tell him about the trip and that we're going to be here ten or fifteen days waiting in Guiria.

"I have the perfect place for you two, it's a little weekend house very close to the sea, with many trees, lots of fruits, some animals and a watchman who can help you in whatever way you need. Come and see it and if you like it, you can use it."

"No need to see it, we say yes!" we respond excited by this surprise.

The house is exactly the same as those built by the natives of the area. And as

168

a bonus, in addition to hammocks, it even has a bed. As soon as we're settled, we set to work on our paintings, we want to get enough together to sell and pay for the boat and the expenses in Trinidad.

With fresh juice made from the trees in the yard and in the shade of the beautiful trees, we get to work painting and framing. Immediately children start to gather at the front gate, watching some strangers who came in a strange car. We invite them in and they happily begin to paint with Cande, to pick up leaves and glue them together in collages of a thousand shapes.

With the passing days, more and more kids come, and the little house is turned into an art school. So many kids come that we are obliged to organize visiting hours, so we can work on our pictures. The parents also come and bring us homemade foods. Delicious arepas we can eat for breakfast, lunch or dinner.

Every afternoon of those seven days, we go down to the beach with a group of the kids and play ball, swim, run and amuse ourselves. While I get ready to go, I can hear the kids asking Cande about me.

"Where is the Kid's friend?" the nickname warms my heart.

After a week we have enough paintings ready and with them we go to the square to sell them. We've been sitting here for four hours and only one person stops to look. Almost no one passes, and those that do aren't looking for paintings. Finally in the late afternoon, we retreat disillusioned for not having sold anything, we didn't even manage to attract any attention.

We drive back toward the cottage feeling sad, we pass in front of a beautiful home, then another and another. I brake, put it in reverse and return to them. Cande looks at me and asks, "What are you going to do?"

"Come with me. We're going to make someone happy," I tell her while I park in front of one of the picturesque homes where I ring the bell.

"Who is it?" a woman asks and opens the door before we answer her.

"Good afternoon, madam. We are Candelaria and Herman, we are traveling from Argentina to Alaska in this car," the woman stares at us, not understanding. "…and to finance our trip, we're selling these pictures we've painted. Would you like to see them…?" The lady stands there mute for an instant, while I move the painting closer and closer to her face of surprise.

"Yes, of course, please come in. Honey, there are some fellows here from… Where did you say?"

"From Argentina."

"Invite them in…"

We end up having dinner with them in addition to selling them two paintings. On their own, they call friends who buy more and they give us directions of other places to go. In this way the rest of the days, before the boat Nova Cura arrives, we devote to walking sales. We go to the banks, we ask for the manager whose very hesitant secretaries let us in. We introduce ourselves; we tell them about our dream and show them a picture of the car. In the end, only once did a manager try to evade us, saying that the red in the mat didn't match his walls, "If it were blue…"

"No problem," we reply and return the next day having changed the color. Now he can't refuse and buys the painting.

We feel great for having overcome our embarrassment and shyness to sell, which had really hindered us.

Nova Cura

Some kids come running in and tell us that the boat "Nova Cura" has arrived. Right on time, now we have enough money to pay for it.

"We'll head out tomorrow, guys, prepare to depart," we hear from the captain with the white beard.

"How much will the trip be?"

"Two hundred dollars, if you promise not to tell anybody."

"Round trip?"

"Yes, and that includes staying on the boat in Trinidad."

"Deal!"

"Bring the car now, this way we can take advantage of the rented crane to load it."

We set off that night with the car loaded in the empty cargo hold; the whole boat is for the car and for us. The sea is rough where the Caribbean and the Atlantic overlap in a war of currents; rocks and outcroppings stick up. The captain, in his cabin, calmly moves the wheel from one side to the other as if he could see something out there.

"Two years ago I would never have made this crossing at night, many boats have sunk. You can't go by the compass because the currents are so strong. But now, with this GPS gadget, I know exactly were every little rock is and where the boat is."

While he steers he narrates stories. His accounts of marine voyages are captivating. He tells us about ocean crossings, storms, ports…so many stories that any writer could write an excellent book with a dozen of them.

After a few hours, totally relaxed because of the "gadget" plus the experience of the captain, I go out to check out the little ship. I go to the noisy engine room, to its stern and to its stem. I sit at the prow, where I watch the waves crash. The warm Caribbean breeze brings me beach scents and

music from Trinidad which little by little is getting closer. A group of dolphins surprisingly appears swimming and jumping a little ahead of the boat. I yell calling Cande, but she doesn't answer. Maybe she is thinking about her mother.

"The night displays its stars, those through which I maintain communication with mom, united. But, this time they feel different to me, I feel something special, there is someone else taking part in this conversation, it's my brother. The breeze brought his smile and I breathe it into the deepest part of me. I remember that since he was a child, he was always smiling. I go to a highest point on the boat to be closer to the sky, closer to him. From there, I ask him to give mama strength but more than that, to cure her. I explain to him how to do it. I imagine everything, step by step all the time seeing it like it's real."

"I feel his calming caresses and his childhood advice. When I don't see him anymore I think about how intense this encounter was. Since his death, I've never felt him closer. I am transformed into another person, I am secure in my faith, mom will be cured, so I decide to wait, without guilt for the good news to arrive. I extend my arms and together with the breeze, I embrace her. 'Good night, mom."

I look for Cande to show her the dolphins, and I find her in the tower of the ship, I go to her, I see her looking at the stars, in a dialogue with her mother. Without dropping her gaze from the heavens, she comments, "Everyone has a star, which is yours?" expecting me to point one out.

"Mine is you." I respond wrapping my arms around her from behind.

Isla Trinidad

As we get to the port, the captain raises a yellow flag to communicate to immigration that we have to complete the formalities. It's not like an airport; in this case, it's the officials who come to the boat to give the newcomers here the ok to disembark.

While we complete the paperwork, I remain seated on the railing of the boat looking at the island wondering what surprises we'll be treated to. From the same pier we're tied to there is a platform jutting out. A man unfurls a little carpet on the ground; he kneels and begins to pray. He stands, then kneels, and bows his head to the ground. I believe that for the first time I am witnessing a Muslim pray, but to be sure I wait until he finishes to ask him. He responds that yes, he repeats this ritual five times every day and I tell him that now that I'm traveling I pray much more and at least five times a day I think about God.

"In one way, this is a prayer. And, how many Gods do you pray to?" he asks me

"I feel that there is only one God that we call by different names." I answer believing that a religious debate would surely follow or it would irritate him.

"Have you done any charity throughout your life?" he asks me.

"Yes, but not enough I think. I didn't give as much as I should have. And in this moment I feel that I am receiving much more than I've ever given…"

"How's that?"

"Because I am fulfilling the journey of my life, my great dream, and I am able to do it thanks to the people who are giving me so much."

He doesn't question me more, he looks at me quietly, he transforms into a very tender being and he tells me, "You are like a Muslim; we believe in only one God, we practice charity, we pray five times a day and during our lives we have to accomplish a journey, the dream of every Muslim is to go to Mecca." I feel an enormous joy to be included in a world that is completely foreign to me and a huge delight in not having been discriminated against. "And where are you going?"

"To Alaska."

"Ah…is that your holy land?"

"No, it's my dream."

Immigration officials don't let us disembark the car until the customs officials arrive. We wait for what feels like an eternity, and when they finally come two days later, they prohibit entrance to the Graham.

"But…why?"

"We don't have any regulations for tourist cars," they respond dryly, leaving us to understand that this is the first passing-through-tourist's-car arriving in Trinidad.

In search of solutions, we visit the Argentinean Embassy. All the people there try for three days to figure out a way to get the car off the boat. We meet with many people from the government of Trinidad who want to do something, but the captain of customs won't change his mind. We're only permitted to disembark if we do so at the official port and if we leave 30% of the value of the car as a guarantee. How much would this be? No one has an answer and anyway, we don't have any way to pay it. Furthermore, our captain informs us that the cost of docking up in the official port is unaffordable.

We decide to enjoy Trinidad anyway. It's very different from Latin America even though it's so close. There's music drifting everywhere with a population almost totally black and Indian who speak English, that only the Trinidadians understand. Their clothes are stylish and their hairstyles are very extravagant.

The captain and his wife drive us around in their car to visit all those beaches on the island, as well as other ports full of sailboats, many of which are searching for crew members with or without experience to help and navigate to Miami, Europe, Panama, or Australia. These sailboats arrive here with full crews, whose members then continue on by plane or change boats for a different direction. The offers are very tempting, traveling in a fully equipped sailboat to fascinating destinations. It takes a lot of will power to resist, but we must leave it for another time: one trip at a time.

During the ten days sojourn we sleep in the mansion of the boat, we have the captain's quarters, the galley, dining room and hundreds of uninvited guests: cockroaches. Coming in at night we see hundreds of them scurrying away to hide until later when they feel more confident and come out again. We don't even want to cook on the boat because they are everywhere, in the boxes of rice, in the spices… One night Cande wakes me up alarmed, "I feel something walking on my leg." Thinking of the worst, we open the sleeping bag and here is the big cockroach with his little antennas waving at us.

The Nova Cura has to return for cargo to Venezuela. So, to load a few containers, we take the car off the boat and leave it apart from the movement of the port. When the customs agents come to check the cargo and notice that the Graham isn't there, they start yelling to high heaven.

"Where is the car?!" shouts a man, angry for having been disobeyed and fearful of losing his job.

"My wife just went to buy a couple of things downtown." I answer and he stares at me with his mouth hanging open not knowing whether to yell at me or ask me pretty please on his knees to get it back here immediately.

"How is this possible?!" he says waving his arms around, but before he explodes, I point out the car which is right behind him. He calms down and I think that he's content, not for my joke, but for seeing the car in the port. "Who gave you permission to off load it?"

The captain, who heard the shouting, comes up to us and answers in a very soothing voice, "The car can't take the weight of a container, so I have to put it on one of them, for this reason it was necessary to remove it." After this response, the agent can say nothing more and he goes. We return to the continent once again escorted by dolphins.

Feeling At Home

I don't know why but we have always wanted to get to know Caracas. Getting into town requires us to take dozens of turnings, but we only get lost twice. We call the parents of Gerardo, the walker, and we tell them that we met him in Brazil and what we're doing. Without giving us time to ask, they invite us to their house. The whole family receives us like their own children returning after a long trip, they give us the affection they were saving up for Gerardo's return from completing his dream. They plan family reunions, prepare special foods and even organize an artist's fair for us to sell our things. They also take us to their beach house, where we eat as they say, "Something unique to Venezuela: arepas!" These are already beginning to come out our ears.

Also, at the Transportation Museum of Caracas we're received in a fashion very familiar among the collectors and lovers of cars. As soon as we arrive, everyone applauds our entrance. This warm reception touches us. It's not just men, but there are also their wives and children, complete families. Everyone has arrived in their cars and they are waiting for us with medals, gifts, offers of service and thousands of other things. On our part, we have also brought something: our paintings and crafts, the same ones a Peruvian girl puts her all into selling, nearly obliging every one of the participants into buying something.

In this type of gathering, it's usual to talk about what kind of car you have and about its quirks. One tells me that he has an MG model this and that, to which I can only remark: "Oh, how nice!" because in fact I have no idea what he's talking about. Everyone imagines that I am a fanatical car expert and mechanic. I, however, manage to discourage them, just the opposite I impress them when I tell them the truth, "If I had known about mechanics, I probably would never have left in this kind of car for a trip like this."

After dedicating a few beautiful words to us, they invite us to share an overview of the road thus far. When we finish our speech, the questions begin.

"Doesn't it seem a bit nuts to do this in this car? I see a very slim chance of you actually getting there…"

"If my possibility of completing this journey is only one percent and 99 percent against it, then for that one percent I would 100 percent go."

"Alright, but that's because you're an optimist." He answers.

"No. I am a realist. It's real that I am only going to live once, and that there is more benefit in trying than in not doing anything, that everything is possible."

Everyone remains silent until another question erupts, "How much does it consume?"

"Oh it goes 60 miles on about a gallon."

"No…really?"

"Yes, but of oil…" and the laughter starts.

"And it runs at?"

"Oh, about 90 or 100"

"What?!" they ask incredulously

"Yes, that's the temperature. In reality we go 25." And now the laughter is louder.

"It's better to walk and advance than to go fast and not last," agrees the club president.

This way we spend a splendid afternoon, in which we are made to feel like we've always belonged to the club. Once again they offer mechanical service for the car, but we explain that we don't think it will be necessary and we depart.

On the way back to the house, we hear a very ugly noise coming from the gearbox, the one that doesn't permit me any kind of movement. I can only continue in first, that's the only gear I can shift into with the car off.

When we get there, we call the club and we tell them what's happened. One hour later there are three cars ready to take us to a garage owned by two of the members. Very, very slowly they escort us through the whole city stopping traffic in each place we pass.

The next day the garage is converted into club headquarters, the number of visitors mounts; all preoccupied with the car, for us and for taking us to eat time and again the country's typical dish: arepas!

We depart from Caracas in a caravan with fifteen cars from the club. They escort us for more than 60 miles. As it is to be expected, one of the cars among the group quits, but what no one ever imagined is that it would be ours. The Graham runs out of gas, and the teasing we receive is merciless. Before setting out, we all met at a gas station in the country where gasoline is the cheapest in the world. We seem like cheap skates who don't want to squander coins on gas.

Upon reaching the point where we'll go our separate ways, we are treated to an excellent lunch with every type of…arepas! But we are also sent off with some very beautiful words of farewell and a collection that they don't let us open until we're once more on the road.

Whoever Dreams the Absurd Achieves the Impossible

We go to the mediterranean Merida among the mountains. Here we have to look up the recommended Alexis Montilla. He has three enormous amusement parks. In one of them, you leave the car, and take a trolley to enter a Venezuela of the 30's. The park recreates a complete town with all its buildings, shops, clothes and cars of the era. Another of his parks represents all the regions of Venezuela with its customs, music and typical foods: among them, Arepas!

When we get to the ticket booth, we ask to speak with him. A young woman calls him on the phone and without even asking who we are, she tells us he's on his way. Very shortly climbing out of a pick up truck we see a man of short stature, in his fifties, simply dressed, with the outline of a small smile in his cheeks, he greets us. It's him.

We tell him what we're doing and he asks us what he can do for us. We tell him we need a place to stay; with no hesitation, he says yes and asks what else. We respond that this is already so much.

We go on a tour of the park with one of its attendants. This place is pure excellent entertainment achieved. As we go around the site, we run into Alexis on one of the park benches. He doesn't have an office or a secretary. Wherever he is, there is management.

Alexis's right hand man tells us Alexis was born in the mountains, his family was very poor and lived in a one-room house, and that from the time he was young he dreamed of an amusement park for the young and the old alike. But everyone saw this as an absurd dream. He left the mountain and he worked as a kitchen helper, a traveling salesman, a teacher, a waiter and later owner of his own restaurant. After this followed a hotel and another...and later his first park. Today his dream has been achieved and a bronze plaque at the entrance of his third park reads, "Whoever dreams the absurd achieves the impossible."

We are near Alexis answering questions about our trip. In reality what we hear more than inquiries are dire predictions, they ask us about all the bad things that could happen to us. One after the other, "What would happen if you got sick?"; "Yeah, and what if the car broke down? Where would you get the parts?" "And what about if you were robbed?" And what about this and what about that...

"None of this is going to happen," interrupts Alexis totally calm and sincere, very sure of what he says from where he's seated. I look at him and notice he's right. Nothing bad has happened; nothing bad is going to happen.

"You heard him, nothing bad is going to happen," I reaffirm and comment to Alexis that it's common to hear questions of this type predicting we're not going to have a happy ending.

"There will always be prophets of failure, it's much easier to predict a ruin than a triumph. It's like a race where the safest bet is the failure of the majority than the triumph of only one. Don't listen to them, listen to yourselves. If you have faith in yourself, you're condemned to success."

Alexis takes us to a hotel that isn't his, because his are completely booked up. He pays for our stay out of his pocket, but we want to dissuade him, because we can arrange it in another way. He won't hear of it, he responds that it would be taking out the pleasure for him.

He stays with us a while conversing, as a dreamer who's achieved his dreams to dreamers who need his words.

"Listen, kids, through difficulties, one grows. With problems, one is fortified. Fears debilitate, doubts confuse, faith pushes, and with hope, you advance. Don't stop advancing. There in the park, you commented to my staff that the hardest part of the whole trip was to begin. There will be one more difficulty that will come up on the road before you finish. Don't see it as a difficulty, instead as the final test. Don't let up; don't make the mistake of the majority and give up at the last moment. Do not abandon your dream. If you pass this test, then you can say, 'Dream accomplished'."

"We have another dream," adds Cande brining another of our goals into the picture. "We want to have a small farm in the mountains where we can construct cabins and receive people…"

"Start it," he tells us as the only formula to complete it.

"But, how are we going to get the people to come?"

"Wherever you find a place you like, the people will come. Don't worry about this, the people will come."

Wheat Fields

We leave our car with Alexis to exhibit along with his other cars in the park and we go to Los Nevados, a small village on a barren plateau, very high in the mountains, so high even trees don't grow there.

You can only get there in a 4x4 jeep by a dirt road that is really scary, with its steep climbs, curves and abrupt drop-offs. It takes us four hours to get to the village which makes us feel like we're in a different world. There are no cars in the streets, only horses tied at the corners. The cobbled streets are steep; the houses are mud, stone and brick with tile roofs. The white church stands out in the background of the dark mountains behind it.

The next day we go out walking the trails that take us over the mountain. We traverse fields of wheat sewn by oxen, harvested and winnowed by hand.

Along the way, we come across its people, who greet us as we pass by. They dress differently. They are descendents of immigrants who have adapted to this place and to this style of life. The fastest way to get around is by horse or mule. The houses are scattered and very similar to one another. We pass a little school where the children are at recess and crowd together at the side of the path to watch us walk by. They make us feel as if we are different, strange. It's paradoxical that a few seconds before it was we who looked at this place and its people in that way. We continue walking for three hours, until the path fades on the cool mountaintop.

On the return, a family invites us to their home. They share their water and to ease our hunger they prepare some delicious flour tortillas. I've never had such great ones. They tell us with great affection about their ancestors, who came to this place. Later they show us their house. It's in a "U" shape and a veranda surrounds its internal patio. I only count three rooms, plus a kitchen. One is for the parents, the other for the kids, and in the third they store the tools, the harvest and it has an altar with its lit candle. We look with much curiosity at the simplicity of the place. Everything was made by them; the furniture, the walls, the decorated altar. When I lift my gaze to look at the ceiling, I get the chills. Resting on the rafters is an empty coffin.

"And this?" I ask astounded.

"Just in case I need it or for anyone else…," responds the man of the house as if this were something elemental.

I feel a shiver in my body; I never imagined having a casket in my house as if it were waiting for me to go. However, for them, since they live in the mountains, so far from everything, it would take a long time to find the wood and make one, so they have one ready. They have assumed death; they already assume that one day it will come. Seeing that box brings to mind the death of my friend Fidel in Ecuador and also reminds me how alive I am and how much I am doing to live my life.

When we go out into the sunny patio, we find the lady shooing a mule who took advantage of the open door to make himself at home. After closing it, she tells us, "Tomorrow we're going to make bread to sell in the village, if you'd like to watch, you're welcome."

"If you let us help, we'd love to!" Cande answers.

We wake up at six to get to the house early. After a fresh hour walking, they're waiting for us with a delicious coffee and a pile of wheat to grind. They are eight and everyone does something. Some come with mules loaded with sticks they've brought from far away, others cut it. And we grind the wheat, which others sift. During all this, the mother begins to mix the dough, and the father fills the oven with wood.

The day is passing with much joy; everyone dusted with flour. The flavorful lunch is small, mountain potatoes over flour tortillas accompanied by coffee made of beans ground after first being roasted in the fire on a ceramic plate. It's a simple meal, which because of being shared and for the warm family that surrounds us, is transformed into a banquette. In this place where the light goes with the sun and the cold begins to freeze the hands, where a cow, a donkey, and chickens are constantly kicked out of the patio that they hang around in search of something to eat, we are a part of something.

The day ends helping to load the bread fresh out of the oven onto the mules that will carry it to the village. And we say goodbye to our new family. We return over the trail that takes us back to the tiny hotel while happily recalling the day we have just lived.

Before starting our journey, we thought that our small world was all that existed and we felt very well in it. But while traveling we are realizing how wrong we were. We surrounded ourselves only with people of our same level, education, religion and culture. We shut out the rest, all the others, all the different ones. We used to reject people whose opinion was different from our own; we even mocked those dressed differently.

On the other hand, at the beginning of our trip we realized just how little we had grown up until then and how much we still have to learn. But one thing we know now: uniformity idiot-izes while diversity culture-izes. We are all together in this world to relate to each other, share with one another, live together and to help one another. Not for me to be interested only in my life, my family, my interests, my acquisitions, my needs, my feelings… It even sounds boring, so many "my's".

If we look past all of our "my's" we could be happy altogether and there is no greater happiness than when we can share it with an open heart, without any restrictions. It's wonderful to become joyful about another person's happiness, without envy, like it happened to us today. And one feels even more joy when one takes part of this happiness, when helping in some way, like for example, with right advice or dedicated time.

There are thousands of persons who didn't exist for us before; thousands of dreams yet to be completed, different types of cultures, fears, thoughts, lives, ways to have fun... One doesn't realize this diversity because we are surrounded by the people we pick to conform to our small world, a world that grows smaller as the years pass even though it's inserted in a gigantic universe that only keeps on getting bigger.

For this, we're taking advantage now and we sit with those we've never sat with, we talk, we enjoy and we learn from them without feeling superior nor inferior, only happy. There's so much to see and how blind we've been. Today we learn from the poorest, the richest, the artists, the mechanics...everyone.

Commandant Jaramillo

We leave behind Los Nevados taking much with us. We ride for four hours on some unhurried mules, until we finally arrive at the tallest, longest cable car in the world that quickly takes us down to the city of Merida.

We go get the car to participate in a carnival parade. As we go by, the people shout "There goes the car of dreams!" The Graham's been baptized with this nickname in a delightful report aired on television. Surrounding every car there are two or three couples who dance to the rhythm of the music which is blaring from speakers at full volume. The same occurs in the next car playing different music and so on. The city is all party matching the Venezuelans. Everything is cool and chevere.

Two days of driving brings us close to the border of Colombia. It's already getting late and we prefer to enter our next country in the morning. While approaching the border, we look for somewhere to spend the night. Then we spy a kind of fort, its sign indicates: "Military detachment".

"We've always had a fabulous send off from each country, why don't we try here?" Cande asks.

Thus, we ask the soldier on guard to speak to his superior. Very quickly, as we wait, many soldiers begin to gather around the car. Everyone is dressed in camouflage uniforms with enormous weapons on their shoulders, but looking at their faces we see the same expression that comes to any human when fulfilling a dream. They look at freedom in motion.

We know who the commander is because the soldiers make way for him to pass and he's the only one not carrying a weapon.

"Commander Jaramillo at your service," he presents himself. I never imagined having a commander at my service.

"Good evening we are Candelaria and Herman and we are leaving Venezuela. We would like to ask you permission to allow us to spend the night in your detachment." As soon as the request leaves my lips, I realize that I'm asking a lot. We are at a military detachment on a border ardently asking for hospitality as if this place were a campground for tourists.

The commander observes us. Then he directs his glance at the soldiers, every one asks him to accept with his expression. He smiles and with brisk nods of his head tells us yes.

"Sergeant, accommodate them in the club and have the kitchen take them something to eat."

"Yes, my commandant." responds the sergeant happy to complete this benevolent order.

"Thank you so much, sir," Candelaria says to the commander.

Even though he feels complimented for having been called "sir", clarifies, "The 'Sir' is in heaven, I am only His servant. I'll attend to a couple of things and see you in the club."

The sergeant takes us around the whole detachment showing us the barracks, the showers, and orders a few soldiers to look for cushions for us and the cook to prepare the best arepas!

"Have you eaten arepas?"

"Yes, we love them," Cande politely says. As for me, I don't want to taste another arepa for at least a year.

We spend a very lovely evening, talking about places in Venezuela many of which both, the soldiers and us, have seen. Finally, they get around to the million-dollar question, to which we reply, "We pay for the trip selling paintings. Cande paints birds that we see along the way and I frame them."

Consequently, the commandant asks to see them and to our surprise, he picks out two. Not only does he house us, but also gives us a push to keep going.

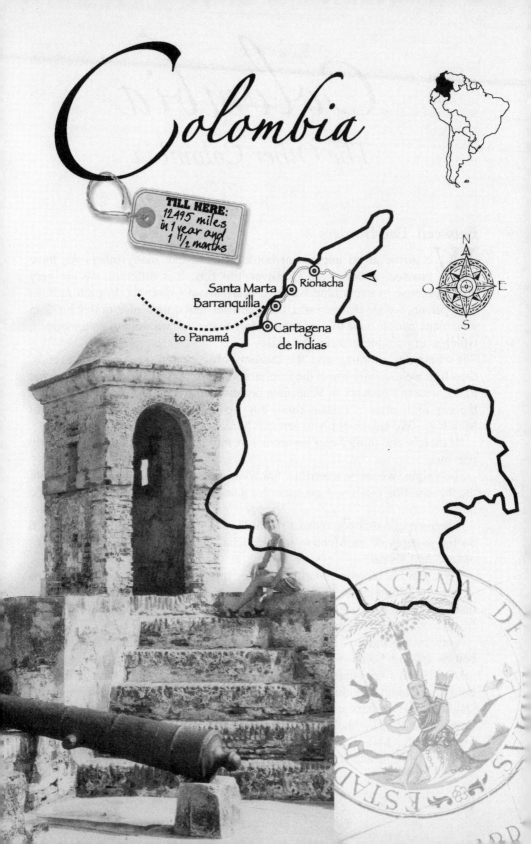

Colombia

TILL HERE:
12.495 miles
in 1 year and
1 ½ months

Santa Marta
Barranquilla
Riohacha

to Panamá

Cartagena
de Indias

N
O E
S

Colombia

The Other Colombia

Between Two Borders

We arrive at an unpleasant border which, like many others we have crossed, is not clean. However, this time it is different, we are very afraid because of everything we have heard about Colombia. In each face, in each person, we see that assassin, that guerrilla, that drug dealer, or that hit-man who many people have told us about. More than ever, we want to go unnoticed, which is impossible in a car like ours.

It's Saturday morning and the customs officers don't work on weekends, therefore we can only finish the immigration formalities. We don't know what to do: we can't go back to Venezuela because we're not allowed to return with the car until after a certain time, but we also can't enter Colombia until Monday… We are caught between two borders.

"If there's one thing I don't want it's to stay here," Cande tells me, slightly nervous.

She's right, we are in a terrible, hot zone. It's Colombia. I go back to talk to the immigration officers. I ask them for a suggestion about what we should do now.

"I recommend that you request permission to pass with a promise that you'll do the paperwork on Monday in Riohacha, where there is another customs office," he tells me.

We follow his recommendation and they immediately allow us to enter. Now we are on Colombian soil, a fact that we are reminded of when after a short time on the road, we come up to a well-armed military checkpoint. They don't signal for us to stop, so we keep driving.

A few meters past it, I stop to check the water and the oil, which I forgot to do before leaving because I was too nervous. While checking, I hear a loud "HALT!" Very frightened, I peer over my shoulder; an old man is running holding the hand of a child, his son or grandson, carrying a big bundle over his shoulder. The soldiers aim at him but maybe because I am watching, an official orders them to lower their rifles and pursue the slow moving fugitive. He drops his bundle, but his age and the child don't let him get far. We see how they throw him to the ground and frisk him for weapons. They don't find anything and they take him to their headquarters. I close the hood, open the door and as I climb in the car, I say to Cande, "Welcome to Colombia."

You either Have It or You Don't

Maicao is a frontier city that has thousands of street vendors and the main street is nearly blocked. A woman who is driving ahead of us in an incredible deluxe truck stops, gets out without caring about the traffic piling up behind her and walks up to us. She is supposedly ostentatious in the many gold bangles and bracelets she wears. It seems she is not afraid of this place, maybe she is the one whom people have to be afraid of... I don't know, maybe imaginations are running wild and we are mentally turning everyone around us into characters from some thriller movie.

"Let's trade. My truck for the car, exactly as it is, all loaded up..." she proposes very smoothly.

"No, thanks, we couldn't abandon our car in the middle of the trip."

"Where are you going?"

We hesitate to tell her, everyone has recommended us not to reveal our destination, but this is written all over the car. "To Alaska."

"Ah, well. The truck plus some money, then. How much will it take?" she insists.

"The truck is very beautiful and we don't have money, but we can't trade the car we're so attached to."

"I am a business woman, how much?"

"In this car you see business, we see a dream." She stares at us, as if unable to take it in.

"You lose." And she goes as she came, gaudy in gold.

We left Maicao. We drive through a very arid zone, surrounded by thick low growing, thorny brush. Many trucks overtake us, which are loaded with people who do their business at the border. As they go by, they shout "Welcome!" or they simply wave, giving us their best smile. Little by little, they dissolve the armor that had covered our hearts since we got into Colombia.

Finally, we get to Riohacha, and we register in a comfortable hotel that offers all their services at a very convenient price. The problems with the guerrillas and other subjects have chased off the tourists, and prices have collapsed.

After settling in, we go for a walk on the beach. Immediately a young guy comes up to us. He greets us, introduces himself, asks our names, what we're doing, where we're from...There are many questions in a short time that make us doubt his intentions. Our accent gives away our nationality. The guy comments that he has an Argentinean friend who is on the beach selling hand-crafted art and asks us to follow him. We do so suspiciously.

"Here's another "che!" he tells an artist who looks just like a hippie.

This situation frightens me, it could be he has drugs; perhaps this fellow-countryman has come to Colombia in search of them… What if the police are to come up and search while we're here? We would all be hauled off to jail together, I think we should leave,

"Would you like some mate?" he asks us.

"Of course!" Cande responds.

"Watch my stuff while I go get some hot water," and he leaves entrusting to us many pieces of quality hand-made art. I continue thinking what would happen if he's hiding drugs in his bags and right now the police were to come… we'd be in trouble.

"What beautiful things he makes," Cande comments to me, much calmer than she was this morning. "Are you nervous?" she asks me noticing my eyes darting here and there.

"Yes, my head is spinning, thinking the worst."

"Relax, today I remembered what many people along the way have told us, 'Nothing bad is going to happen, we have to have faith'…"

"Yes, but we are in Colombia…"

"Don't lose your faith just because you are in a different place. Either you have it or you don't," and with these words Cande shares her confidence and manages to relax me.

We drink some wonderful mate using the last of the artist's supply. He gladly shares it with us. Many curious people come up to us to see what we're drinking, and once again, my head begins to imagine that someone will turn us in to the police suspecting that we're druggies?. "Calm down," I tell myself, "nothing bad is going to happen."

Dangerous Roads

It's Monday and we present ourselves at the customs house. A very surprised woman completes our paperwork; she cannot believe that they let us pass without finalizing the customs procedures at the border.

After everything is square, we drive in the direction of Santa Marta, on roads full of dangers, full of guerrilla's checkpoints. The mountains come right up to the road and where there are mountains, there are guerrillas. While we move along, we notice that the little traffic ahead of us is slowing down, at the same time our hearts are accelerating. As we get closer, along the sides of the road we see machine guns aimed directly at the cars, the men dressed for war look very uneasy and we catch their nervousness. The sensation of being pointed at with a gun is horrible. We don't know if they are military or guerrillas.

The truck directly ahead of us is detained, causing us to stop. They indicate to the driver to open the back and while they are on their way to search it, they see us. Their eyes are glued on us and they say something to each other pointing to the Argentina plate. They smile to one another and with a nod of their heads, they greet us with a smile. We breathe again and continue.

After two more checkpoints en route, we get to Santa Marta. We were stopped at only one of them to ask what we are doing.

Once in the city, we see a museum that tempts us into visiting. We're surprised to see this is the place Simon Bolivar, "Hero of Latin America," died. The form of his expired body was cast in plaster. It reveals a thin, worn out general, very feeble, which in no way resembles the hero illustrated in the history books and in the monuments of the plazas. At the time of death, he was suffering from various illnesses: tuberculosis, syphilis, premature ageing, malaria, orchitis, malnutrition, and kidney stones. What is admirable is that he was suffering during his most glorious moments, in those when he most needed his health to complete his dreams.

A bit later, we go to a bay where the sea is an immense swimming pool and surrounded by buildings built for vacationing: Rodadero. The truth is we need to rest after months on the moving and these last stressful days. As we unwind, we enjoy listening to a simultaneous variety of vallenatos music from the beach. Various groups of five or six musicians offer to play and sing for whoever is sunbathing. The scene repeats itself time and again until at least midnight. The water is so calm that the visitors take their drinks and their conversations into the waist-deep sea.

Everything is very peaceful; the people are very nice. There is music, laughter, and families everywhere, none of the Colombia we've heard about. We are more relaxed and chat with the people, whose speech is accompanied by a sweet accent. They are very educated and cultured, well dressed and with smooth expressions invite one to feel at ease. The women are very beautiful and feminine; the men, real gentlemen.

A Hug From Here

Usually we work on the beach, Cande paints, and I build frames, but today she is writing to her mom.

"Dear Mom,

How far you are from me, nevertheless I feel you so close. You are always here, guiding my way and even in my dreams I meet you. Today, since it's a very special day, I want you to feel me as close to you as I do, to feel my strong hug and my face pressed to yours. But more than anything I want you to hear from me, a VERY HAPPY BIRTHDAY MOM, wishing you with all my heart everything you deserve, all the best you could ever hope for in life, because you are so beautiful inside and out. You are such a wonderful companion, a unique friend, and so admirable, that to wish you the best isn't enough for me.

I have learned so many things from you that reward me today. You always showed me the order of importance of the values in life and with them you guided me.

But the most beautiful thing of all is that today, on the day celebrating your birth I can tell you that I am still learning, that you continue to teach me many things. You can't imagine how satisfying it is to say that my mother continues to be my role model in life. How valuable it is that you always face adversities. I am happy to have you, and most of all I am happy to be able to tell you I LOVE YOU SO MUCH, MOM, so much it fills my soul.

I never thought we'd be separated for so long. I look at the stars every night and through them I send you my strength, and I know you are acquiring it. I MISS YOU, but I feel you close and that comforts me. Everything, absolutely everything which I am living I would love to share with you, I always think and even say "mom and daddy would be so thrilled to see this, or that." So, inside this dream, I have another one and it is that I want to see you and share a little of this adventure with you and daddy. So, whenever everything is better for you we will be waiting for both of you in any place you'd like. And you will get better; God has already granted it to me, so now it's only a matter of planning it.

Well, mom, I wish the best in the world on your birthday, for you to really enjoy yourself and have a great day. Have faith in your treatment and everything will turn out perfectly. I know it will.

I love you mom and I want to hug you… I do so from here.

A huge kiss from your "little one,"

Cande"

A Tairona Trail in the Sierra Nevadas

In a beautiful place called Tairona Park, we hear talk of a place called Lost City, the center of the Tairona culture. They are ruins of a city that are in the Sierras Nevadas mountains, immersed in a tropical jungle at 3300 feet above sea level. They tell us we could see ritual centers, dwellings, terraces, drainage systems, stairs and cobblestone roads constructed 1500 years ago, but they were only discovered in 1975. Also, they explain to us that only one group of tourists goes up in a week and they have to get there on foot, walking six days on paths through the jungle, crossing rivers without bridges. Facing this much adventure, without thinking twice we sign up for the next trip.

In three old and overloaded jeeps, so overloaded that some of us even have to travel on the roof racks, we leave Santa Marta to go to the Sierras Nevadas foothills. The road ends in a small settlement, in front of a bar/shop with no walls in which many men, almost all of whom are heavily armed, are hanging around a pool table.

I was filming the trip up to this point and now I capture how they unload the jeeps and load up the mules that will accompany us during part of the trek. I also capture the path we will follow…until a paramilitary man appears. He is furious and is shouting at me. The guide calms him down explaining I am merely a tourist and that I will delete the footage; after which the paramilitary man moves away looking at me with a face full of hatred. We already knew about guerrilla movements on the way to the ruins, but one thing is to hear about them and another thing is to come face to face with so many people prepared against them.

The mules are loaded and our group, consisting of twelve tourists (a German, a Belgian, a British girl, two French, five Israelis and us), five Colombian porters and a guide, head up into the very steep but beautiful jungle covered mountains. To get to the ruins and back we will walk for a week following a thin trail used by the Tairona Indians, who still inhabit the area.

Our guide knows the area very well, because he used to be a tomb raider before the government started to protect the area. The farther we climb, the more the humidity and the vegetation increase. There are parts in which we're covered in mud up to our knees, where we cross rivers getting wet to our waists, and sometimes we come into clearings where families raise animals. Our guide tells us few farming clans remain, since they run away from the guerrillas and the paramilitary because these recruit their sons, and if they refuse to comply, they are killed.

The first night we sleep under a hut with a palm frond roof, without walls, next to a boisterous river. We sleep in hammocks to escape the thousand and one bugs on the ground. Anyway, in the morning, I see something on Cande, near her ear, "Cande, you have a…a tick stuck to you…"

We continue the ascent and although it's difficult climbing, all of us explorers talk among ourselves.

"How are you going to go to Panama?" the Belgian asks us.

This is our biggest question. We still have no answer, but somehow we're going to do it. We know that we have to cross in a ship, but we don't even have a fraction of the money to ship the car, we'll just have to wait and see…

"Which place have you liked the most on your trip?" the Belgian continues.

"Every place we visited up to now was a kind of brother country and you never make comparisons between brothers. What I can tell you is what we like most in each place, as each country has something, each place is special. Many times, a place delights us not because of the beauty of the location, but because of its people. It does no good to be in a nice place if you're not received well," I reply and I ask, "Which would you prefer? A night alone in a five-star hotel or going camping with your friends?"

"No doubt, being with my friends…"

"In Venezuela we were in a small town called Temblador, a totally flat area, without rivers, without mountains or beaches, nothing interesting to see, but the people treated us so kindly that we would love to go back there. Truly, it's very nice to arrive in a place and hear people saying "Welcome to my country", the more they love their place, the better they will treat you, because they want to give you the best impression. The memories of each place remain in our minds, the people we remember in our hearts."

Passing by indigenous Kogi settlements, we see their round dwellings made of palm thatch. Women, men, and children use the same natural color in their vestments; a tunic to their knees and the men also wear pants underneath, made of the same fabric. They are barefoot and uncommunicative with our group. For the excursion, Cande has had her hair done in braids all over her head, with colorful eye-catching beads brought from Peru. The natives can't take their eyes off those beads until they finally dare to ask for a few of them. This is what breaks the ice for us to start having a long conversation with the settlers.

On the third day, on the other side of the river, we get to a stone stairway, hidden by the foliage, which our guide knows just where to locate. After a climb of 1100 steps, we reach what used to be a striking site.

"Both of you have seen Machu Picchu, which place seems more impressive? Machu Picchu or The Lost City?" the English girl asks.

"You want the truth?"

"Yes."

"The truth is that I have learned to travel without comparing, to get to a place and live it as it is, without looking for differences, without thinking about what's worse and what's better. Every site is as it is, and I enjoy it for this. Every spot is unique, without being better or worse, and it is precisely the uniqueness that attracts me to come see it. When I was comparing, I was not immersed in the place, but I was instead in two or three places at the same time and not enjoying any of them. Now I go and I mold myself to the climate, food and customs of the place where I am, I enjoy it in this way."

Machu Picchu is Machu Picchu; The Lost City is The Lost City. Comparisons are hateful and only look for something wrong, errors. I come for a short time and I don't want to waste it on this, I come to fill myself with its beauties. The one that searches for differences seeks to distance himself. The one that desires to get closer searches out similarities. And this is what I do for the two days we remain in the ruins, although it's not enough to see it all. Everything surrounding us is exquisitely beautiful, we hear the howler monkeys and worn out at the end of each day, we lie down to enjoy and to bathe in the energy of the site.

Tests of the Road

After we return and reunite with the car, we head for Cartagena to look for a shipping company to get to Panama. We are anxious to know how we're going to succeed in getting there, because we don't have any contacts, we don't know a single person there. This is a gigantic step and critical to our trip: crossing to Central America.

While I drive, Cande reads a small guide about places between here and there. She notices there is another city called Barranquilla and it has a small port. Off we go, considering we have nothing to lose by asking and we like the fact that it's a small port.

"Yes? What do you need?" we hear with difficulty through the window. It's already six in the evening and the cargo trucks pass on one side and the other, others are waiting for authorization to enter. We never thought it would be a port this big.

"We'd like to meet the director of the port. We are traveling in this car," we point it out, "fulfilling our dream of traveling from Argentina to Alaska, and we need to get it to Panama." The young woman looks at us with total indifference, without even glancing at the Graham.

"You have to have a shipping agent," she responds to us.

"Just the same, we'd like to speak with someone of the port, we need help and we're sure they will be able to help us," we insist.

"No, let me make myself clear: you have to see a shipping agent." She says while gesturing to the person behind us to come up to the window, dismissing us.

Why isn't there a road between South America and Central America? This forces many to desist from traveling as they have to look for a ship, which implies shipping agents, customs, port fees, containers, taxes, time and all this all over again on arrival at the other port. This turns these few miles into the most expensive ones in the whole trip, and the most difficult ones as well.

While we walk back to the car, I notice Cande silent, pondering, "If it were up to me, I would run away to the end of the land but I have to stay here if I want to continue. This isn't a difficulty, just a bump on the road. We can't give up now; being here is a big challenge for us and a very important step in the trip. I noticed that the secretary didn't understand about dreams, she didn't even want to see one right in front of her face. She seemed to be a person locked up in her own world, resigned to her work, one who looks at her watch every fifteen minutes just to see how soon she can go home. Our trip took her out of her well-ordered routine and for this she categorically refused our entry. Now what can we do? This is the question. Of course, we know that we need a shipping agent, but we don't have the money to pay for a container let alone an agent. We must figure out a way to get into this port."

Being Part

On Monday, we present ourselves at the Marine harbormaster's office. The captain promises to let us know as soon as he knows something. As we are leaving, a man comes up to us out of curiosity about the car and we comment to him about looking for help. He gives us the name of a man who works in the port.

We call him, but he tells us this is out of his area, and that we need a shipping agent to take charge of it. After all this, we finally go see an agent. We ask him for help and contrary to all our assumptions, the man passes from the business side of the situation to the human side, to the side of dreams.

"Suarez is the person to call, he's the one. Go to the port and ask for him," he advises.

"Let's do this, let's go to speak to him personally. If it doesn't work, we'll go to the port in Cartagena." Cande proposes knowing that, if need be, we could play our last card there. She is focused on asking for help, just as Alonso taught us in Ecuador.

Cande thinks to herself, "How many times have I asked for help in my life, maybe the fingers on one hand are enough to count. Why is it so difficult to ask for help? Why do I feel so ashamed in asking? I was taught not to ask, I could do it on my own…and if I couldn't then I was not to do it. Obviously during my lifetime, I have accepted various ways of help offered to me, but to ask? Almost never. And Herman? He drives serenely, but I know him very well and I perceive he is thinking the same thing I am. We both have Alonso's words swimming around and around in our heads. Magic words, that's what he called them. Will they truly be magic?"

"Yes, what do you need?" the secretary at the entrance of the port asks once again.

"We are here to see Mr. Suarez."

"Which Suarez? Mauricio?"

"Yes, him," we answer without knowing about whom we're talking.

"Do you have an appointment?

"Yes." We lie.

"One moment," she tells us, and automatically she picks up the phone to announce that we're here. We stand there frozen; she might discover our lie and kick us out again. All the while she's waiting for them to answer, more and more people are lining up behind us to get in. She tries once again, while other people hurry her.

"OK, go on in," she says with a sigh, "go down this road to the end, turn left to the pier. Go until you see a yellow building, Mr. Suarez is there."

We enter feeling an enormous triumph, even though we still don't have anything resolved. We walk toward the indicated office, it's quite a distance and in full sun; we can feel an intense heat radiating from the pavement and the containers surrounding us. Finally, we get there. A plaque on the door of the building announces: "Commercial Department." We squeeze each other's hand before entering hoping for the best.

We get into offices separated by glass walls. On our left, we see people immersed in their work. On the right, a very beautiful office with a round table where there are four men impeccably dressed, talking about work and drinking a "tinto," as they call coffee. We suppose one of them might be the boss, maybe it's Mauricio.

We introduce ourselves to the secretary. She picks up the phone and it rings inside. A person of forty something, with brownish black hair, tall and good looking picks up the phone. He immediately directs his gaze at us. Putting the phone down, he stands up and comes to meet us.

"Mauricio Suarez, how can I help you?" He introduces himself while stretching his hand.

He asked us how he could help us! With something we can't do alone, with something that costs $1500 when we only have $200. We feel slightly ashamed. But his offer gives us heart and using the magic words, we say, "We are Candelaria and Herman, we are accomplishing our dream to travel from Argentina to Alaska and we need your help. Can you help us?"

The man looks us in the eye while we make our request and without hesitating even a second, he answers us completely naturally, "Certainly, what can I do for you?"

"We have this car," I explain while Cande shows him a picture, "We're traveling in it and we need to ship it to Panama."

"Well, let's do it!" exclaims Mr. Suarez with great enthusiasm, "I have the ideal person, I'm sure she'd love to take part in this. Call Hortensia," he tells his secretary. "This car must leave from Barranquilla Port!" he almost shouts as if he were already part of this trip. As soon as a red-haired woman of about fifty appears in the door, Suarez joyfully begins telling her, "Horte, you have to find a boat! These guys are doing something incredible, we have to help them any way we can. Barranquilla Port has to be the port of departure from South America," the woman gapes at him.

"Ehemmm…Sir?…" calling his attention, the secretary signals with her head the men abandoned in the office.

"Oh! The meeting, I forgot…" he comments with a surprised face, "Horte, you're in charge, but count on me for anything you need and keep me posted about everything. This car must leave from Barranquilla!" he goes on proclaiming while striding back to his office.

We cannot believe what we're hearing; we are astonished.

"I have never seen him so enthusiastic. Now, what is it exactly I need to find for you?" inquires Hortensia still not understanding.

So, we tell her everything in detail. We perceive we are in the hands of a person with super positive energy. She does nothing less than tell us she will turn the port upside down to find a boat.

"And where are you staying?" she asks us.

"In a hotel that…" without letting us say anymore, she interrupts us.

"Let me see what I can do. I would love to have you stay at my house, but my husband Francisco works there. I'll ask him. He's an artist and he spends all his time there painting."

"Don't worry about it," we answer gratefully.

She leaves us with the people in the office. Everyone is thrilled with our story, happy because they will be part of it. Among them, they begin to list names of possible companies, ships…While Hortensia enthusiastically talks to her husband, at the same time she shouts out names of who might want to take us to Panama. After hanging up, she comes to us and informs us,

"You are invited to my home. My husband is happy about the idea of hosting you. He's a fellow countryman of yours."

We came here looking for the possibility of finding some help and we leave with the security of obtaining it, plus hospitality as long as the search lasts. We are totally blown away. We're surprised at how hard it was for us to ask for cooperation and now they offer it with enormous enthusiasm. Asking for help isn't bad, it's sharing, and it's inviting another to be part of it.

We remain in the office. Here there is no boss/employee relationship; there instead exists a team connection. Therefore, everyone outlines a strategy for finding a boat together. As soon as he finishes his meeting, Mauricio comes back wanting to know how everything is going.

"How great is this! Isn't what these kids are doing fascinating?"

"I'm going with them to Alaska!" responds Hortensia to which others in the office eagerly add their names on the list too.

An Open Nest

At the end of the workday, we follow Hortensia to her house. We're a bit nervous about causing them problems or difficulties, helping us cross to Panama is already so much, plus, we don't know how long the paperwork and finding a boat will take.

"Hello, Sweetheart. Here are the kids I was telling you about, Candelaria and Herman," Hortensia introduces us to her husband, whom we find in a room full of oils. His atelier has a view of the sea and feels very luminous and inspirational. We see canvases of all sizes on easels and on the walls, thousands of brushes in all shapes and squeezed tubes of paint here and there. Behind one of these easels, Francisco is adding strokes.

"Hello travelers." He extends his colorfully stained hand to us of a bearded man, with salt and pepper hair and the grin of an accomplice. Dressed in knee socks, Bermudas, and a white sleeveless T-shirt...he displays a lot of personality.

Immediately the wife shows us where we'll be sleeping. We will be surrounded by paintings and murals, many painted by the previous owner, another artist called Obregon. The house has a terrace garden on the cliff top. We are in a place called Puerto Colombia, in a site with an exceptional panorama of the movement of the sea that we hear crash and crash against the cliff. The whole picture inspires, we feel the very strong energy that is constantly renewed with positive ions charged by the sea and carried here on the breeze. Cande and I look at one another in disbelief that this is happening, what we're living. Hugging each other, we remain there beholding the Caribbean Sea.

Francisco comes up without us hearing him, giving us a welcome to his world. He offers us two glasses of cool, refreshing *panela* with lemon for a toast. We tell him again how grateful we are to be received in his house and he tells us, "My house is like an open nest, where birds from all over rest up as they pass by, bringing me different songs and stories, and leave me with a lot of color in my life from their feathers."

The next day, Hortensia and her team at the port organize a round of press meetings and in only one day we give interviews to twelve different media. A little press will help Hortensia explain who we are and solicit the favor we need from the companies. Other journalists come by the house in the afternoon, and in the evening we go see some other reporters. I don't believe that in the whole trip, up to this moment, we have had a day as stressful as this one.

The days begin to fall away, time passes without us knowing with certainty which company will take us, but it's not difficult to wait in this house where a world of new things appear before our eyes. The image we had of Colombia before we got here, is nothing like what we think now.

Hortensia devotes every day to our cause, always moving heaven and earth with the same tenacity. Finally, a week after we met her, she comes home with the first announcement.

"Well, I've found a company that wants to take you, its ships go to the island of San Andres, in the Caribbean, and from there an empty boat goes back to Costa Rica. All that's left is to talk to the owner of the boat that is headed to Costa Rica."

Dream Chaser

During the seven days we spend in the house, we rack our brains trying to come up with an idea for making some money. An artist we stayed with in Rodadero along with some other artisans taught us all their techniques. We were searching for something different we can make and, instead of keeping all their secrets of the trade, they show us everything. One gave us a recipe for modeling clay to make figures, another explained how to create art with magnets. Our plan was and is to make something more economical than the paintings because many people want to buy one to help us, but they can't afford a painting. The artisan who was our host, came up with the idea of making bronze key chains with our logo, and it didn't seem too difficult to do. That's why now, in Puerto Colombia, we buy bronze sheet metal, paints, acids and molds. We put our hands to work combined with all our effort...it's a total fiasco. I throw in the towel after the fourth attempt; I think it is a very difficult and delicate chore. Additionally, it takes a lot of time, first to make them, then to clean them. On the other hand, Candelaria, because she's invested "so much", and because of her incredible stubborn streak, keeps trying, angry with me for having given up.

Later on, a friend of Francisco's comes to visit. Mario Tarud watches my wife wrestle with the acids and asks me the most common question of the trip.

"How do you finance your trip?"

"With pictures Cande paints and I frame. But we're looking for something much more accessible and related to the trip."

"Let's see...give me a few photos, I'll go and see what I can come up with."

The next day, he comes back with the prototype of a postcard. On the front there is one of our photos and on the back a map with our route marked, the logo, and the name of our trip. Mario also shows us a notebook with the same picture on the cover and on the back, a map and something very beautiful he has written about our dream. He included the title "Chase Your Dream: Don't Let it pass you by". The idea is for people to write their own dream on the blank pages inside. Enthusiastically he prints 1000 postcards and 800 booklets that we want to pay for but we're not allowed to, neither by him nor by our host.

Holy Week arrives, and the best place to try to sell our postcards and booklets is Cartagena. We go there all together: Francisco, Hortensia, Mario, his girlfriend, and us and we stay in a fabulous house of a friend of Horte's.

In a triumphant way we enter the walled city of Cartagena de Indias. Cartagena is just like as it was in the year 1700: stunning everywhere you look and in any way you choose to experience it. It overlooks the Caribbean, in the surroundings there are castles that bring back memories of stories of pirates, buccaneers and ghosts. The weather always invites to the beach…and what beaches they are!

During the long weekend of our stay, every afternoon and even into the night, we park the Graham in the Santo Domingo Plaza, a very lively area. Bar tables on the sidewalks are full of people who enjoy the fresh air and the improvised spectacles whose performers are looking for a tip. Additionally, there are many artists and we add ourselves to their ranks with the car, the postcards and the notebooks.

The postcard is a big hit. Everyone is delighted to know that with the purchase of a card, we can buy a liter of gasoline. And the little books…we sell them, but the people are disappointed to find its pages blank, they thought they were going to read about how we're chasing our dream.

"Why not?" I wake up Cande the next day.
"Why not what?"
"Wake up, listen to me. Why do we have to wait until we finish the trip to write a book? Why don't we write about what we've lived up to here and now?"

The idea to write a book at the end of the trip has come to mind. And the booklet is the kick to get it off the ground.

Inspiration

As soon as we arrive in Puerto Colombia at the house of inspirations, I begin to write and write. Cande doesn't want to give up on the key rings and during the next few days she continues to struggle with the acids and the tars. In the meantime, I give her what I have written to read. So much, that she also begins to be enthusiastic, to write and correct what I have written. And finally she agrees to forget about those illegible key chains.

On her part, Horte continues to communicate with the shipping companies. She can't find the one that goes from San Andres to Costa Rica, but it doesn't matter, there have been two more offers.

One of them is a company that goes irregularly to many of the islands and the pacific coast of Colombia, passing through Panama. Its owner is delighted with the idea and that is the option we choose, but before long they tell us the ship is held up at one of the islands in the Caribbean and they don't know when it will come back.

The other possibility is Evergreen, an enormous Taiwanese shipping company that goes weekly to Panama. The only problem: they don't carry passengers. Therefore, now we have to figure out how we'll get there without believing that the car has offers to sail and we turn out to be the complication.

We have already been here for a month and a half. Francisco and Cande paint, I write. We are all inspired, transmitting inspiration one to another which is added to that from the place. We distract Francisco all the time, not because it's our intention, but because he wants to be distracted. Among other things, he cooks typical Argentinean dishes for us, that we all miss, and he always takes time to play cards with me, while Cande paints having the sea as company. Our friendship with Hortensia and Francisco and with their friends grows stronger. Almost every night there is a gathering in the house that keeps us up late. One of these evenings, we get to try enormous ants called "culonas" (big bumps) that they eat as a delicacy.

Every Fish Is In the Water He Wants

We are drinking *mate* on the balcony and watching the sea.

"Hey Francisco, when did you start to paint?" I ask him.

"Ooff! It's been a long time, and I didn't begin to paint because I wanted to. Every time my mother punished me for something, she sent me to the patio and as a penalty, she ordered me to paint the pots of her plants. I started to like this, to go and mix the colors and give life to what I imagined," he pauses momentarily and looks toward the seascape without seeing, like he had returned back to his childhood, to his homeland in Salta. "When I grew up a bit, I signed up to study painting and art, but they refused because I was too young and anyway they didn't have any more openings. I insisted until they let me take an exam, but when I looked at the results, I didn't make it to the cut off point. They told me I didn't know how to paint and I answered: 'this is exactly why I have come, I want you to teach me how to paint.' That year there was one extra over the capacity who entered. This is how I started to study." He caresses the mate with his colorful hands, "In time I got better and I signed up for an art contest. I won and got a scholarship to go to study in the capital, Buenos Aires, a city that was more than a dream for me. Since then, I have never stopped painting. This is what motivates me, what I like, what I want, and this is why I keep painting."

"Has it always permitted you to live and be well?"

"No, not always. Many times, it was bad. Many times, I couldn't sell my paintings, but I never stopped painting. At certain times, I subsisted on painting a mural, a fresco…and when I almost hit rock bottom, a possibility to travel and

exhibit in Mexico or Cuba or Spain appeared: so I started over again. Yes, various times I was in really bad shape, but it would have been worse if I had done something that I didn't like just to permit me to live. That's why I never gave up painting: Painting is my life.

"And what would have happened if you had failed?"

"I did fail, many times, according to the others, but few times in my own eyes…one way of failing in life is obtaining a lot of that which we don't need and none of our dreams. We reach death and once there see that we are not taking anything from this life, that every material thing remains here. Feeling unsuccessful is getting to know that you don't have much time left and that you haven't lived your life. Everyone searches for admiration, respect and social esteem, for this we try only to follow what society expects us to have and do, putting aside much of what we want and desire. Society rejects failures, but among those that are regarded as 'successful', there are many losers."

"Also what influences greatly your success or your failure is your education and your environment." I comment.

"The education of your parents and their treatment of you is very important, as is your own schooling and the society in which you grow up. That aside, you can't blame them for your way of life and your failures. You have the intelligence to change what is necessary, to be what you want to be. If you are a person who doesn't fit in the world that surrounds you, if you feel uncomfortable doing what you like, and everyone looks at you like a frog from another pond, that's how it is: that's not your place. Nevertheless, don't change, look for another pond, find your place, where the world that surrounds you is your world. Only you are responsible for yourself, don't look for excuses among others," are the words of Francisco, man of art and world wise.

I continue chatting with him, but Cande, who is next to us, is submerged in her own thoughts. "How wonderful would it be to never have pushed aside what I really liked to do! Why did I and why am I so weak against the system? Or I should say, why did I force myself? Doing what one really wants sounds marvelous. Why in the moment of decision, did I choose to do what I thought was necessary instead of what I wanted? I always gave priority to other things."

"Before I left on this trip, I worked with my father, who is an expert witness qualified doctor. I was in charge of a section of his office, as are my two sisters. My father is an enterprising man and very capable in his profession. And I liked working with my family."

"But If I have to talk about the work, it wasn't the work I always wanted for myself. I studied for six years for the career of Zoo technical engineering. I was interested in animal breeding and being in direct contact with the countryside, but two years after graduation, I was listening to patients' problems and astute attorneys in an office situated in the middle of the capital city. Of course I knew this wasn't for me, but there I was."

"Just the same, I worked with much firmness considering it was a family business. I was learning a lot, I felt comfortable with my sisters and my father, and I could even ask for a day off whenever I wanted. Except comfort is a double-edged sword: in my case, I was more content working with him than going out to look for my own. I tried to, but now I realize that I didn't try hard enough. My fear was stronger than me and I didn't encourage myself and to avoid running risks, I choose the easiest route: go for security. I took refuge in the typical phrases, 'I need to work', 'I'll work at this for now, but I'll devote the future to what I want.' It is true, it was necessary to live, pay the bills, build the house, and for that I devoted my time and my dedication…but, who knows if there will be a future?"

Cande looks at the sea with its infinite horizon; she can feel the salt in the hot breeze of the afternoon. Another day passes, leaving us with much to think about.

Smile Sketcher

Whenever we drive around the city of Barranquilla, people greet us. Almost everyone has heard something about our trip. "That's not the way to Alaska!" they shout when we're going in a direction contrary to our goal, or "There goes ' El Consentido'" meaning the Pampered one, referring to the car, which along the way has collected many nicknames. In Venezuela, "The Car of the Dream" and "the Gentleman Traveler"; in Peru, "The Smile Sketcher"; in Chile, "The Burrita of Hope"…but we still have not picked a name ourselves, we don't know which name fits him the best, so for the time being we call him "Gramps Graham."

"Gramps Graham" has already visited three mechanics shops in Barranquilla. Since everyone wants to do something we go from one to another. In the first, they chromed, in the next they fixed a dent courtesy of a post, and in the third, a complete check up. Even people who don't have shops want to do something, for example, a man copied the door handles and other missing bits.

During the whole trip the only one of the three of us who has been able to retain his elegance and style in every moment is the Graham. He has ridden along roads of gravel, made of dirt, mud, through jungles, over mountains, and passing rivers but still persists in his flawless blue frock, svelte, robust, and devouring hundreds of miles attached devotedly to his fine tractor tires.

His 25 miles an hour shows certain parsimony, letting us perceive the scenery, time and even ourselves in different way. On his part, Gramps feels he is totally ecological. His dossier is free of crimes against animals and insects, since his speed grants them all time to avoid him.

Gramps Graham's Party

We proceed in the direction of the port in a caravan organized by Alex, a new friend, with the Antique Auto Club of Barranquilla, where the good-bye party continues; the Graham will soon be on its way to Panama without our company. A tow truck precedes us with sirens and speakers that announce our trip and many other cars follow us. Many friends that we have made during our stay here have come, but also many unknown folks approach Gramps Graham.

At the port, Hortensia organizes a show and attracts everyone in Barranquilla. Even Aguila Beer Company is present with two promoters, tents and free beer for whoever wants it. Many people gather around, among them the journalists whom we thank once again for their support and warm reception.

And if that isn't enough, Horte has another surprise for us:

"Alright guys, you'd better sit down, because when I tell you this you will hit the floor: the owner of Coremar shipping, the one who couldn't take you in his boat, wants to pay for the air tickets to Panama!"

"No way! Are you serious? I can't believe it!" Cande and I both exclaim in unison.

The party continues well into the night. When they take the Graham to the container, we follow him. Then we stay a few moments alone. We like this moment. It brings to mind the first day we arrived at the port.

"Cande, do you remember? They wouldn't let us enter the port, we seemed pitiful. When we got inside, we asked for help and they gave us everything plus much more than we even asked for. We came to them and the people received us. We told them the dream and the people... joined us." I say.

"Not only this, but they loved doing it! I love them so much that I don't want to go, I am going to miss them." Cande confesses with her eyes bright with the tears she's trying to

hold back. "If we hadn't tried again, we would have missed so much…"

"We have to try and try again, knock on one door and another; there will always be one that opens."

When One Changes, the World Changes

The following night, we continue celebrating. Javier Redondo, general manager of the in-port movement company that didn't charge us, takes us to dance meringue at three different clubs. And the next day, he invites us to go diving to celebrate Cande's birthday.

When we are in the boat headed out to the coral, he asks us about Colombia and the Colombians.

"When we left Argentina, we didn't plan to come here. The farther we advanced, nothing made us want to change our opinion. But once we were in Venezuela, we decided to come, even though we were still very afraid."

"Why did you change your mind?"

"Because we had visited many cities which we had been recommended not to go to because of the potential dangers. Every one of them turned out to be completely different and we don't regret having gone to any of them. Also, our faith grew in ourselves and our belief that someone is watching over us to keep us safe. We learned that when you're following your dreams nothing bad is going to happen…"

"So what do you think of Colombia?"

"I don't know if it's because we had imagined everything terrible that it seems everything is absolutely great. I don't know if it's because of all the help or for the way we've been received, but we are delighted. It greatly pains us to see this war in which, as in every war, there are no winners." I tell him.

"He who uses violence, doesn't use intelligence." adds Cande.

"What would you change about Colombia?" Javier spits out.

"Listen, that's like asking me how I would change the world…" I keep thinking how I'd do that. How? I think my soul and my face brighten. I've got it! I just see it, but it's always been in front of us. "We don't have to change the world, the world is perfect. I look at this sea, remember those mountains and those people who always helped us, received us and gave us food. They were perfect, they are perfect, all of this, there's nothing to change."

"Yes…but, the wars? The tyranny?" Javier inquires.

"It's just as I said, the world is perfect, it is oneself who needs to change for the better. One needs to change and demand good, don't be manipulated by those who instill fear, pride and hatred. We have to say what needs to be said, demand what needs to be demanded, give what needs to be given and more. Don't try to change the world, let's change ourselves, we are the ones who need to change. When one changes, the world changes."

That night, still immersed in these ideas, I sit and write:

In my home, I don't want arms
because they are made to kill.
In my home, I don't want shouting
because he who shout doesn't listen.
In my home, everybody has a voice
because everybody has a vote.
In my home, I don't want any to feel hunger
because here there is food for all.
I want my home filled with peace and harmony.

There's no place

Like home

Everybody's dream

With tears, we bid a fond farewell to Francisco and Hortensia. During all this time, we have turned into a family, and now who knows if we are going to see one another again. Good-bye Colombia. It was so hard to get here. There were thousands of grounds for not coming, but it's even harder to leave. We fell in love with exactly that which we were warned to watch out for, its people. We started to lose the fear we came with little by little thanks to the Colombians, who stand out because of their solidarity, sweetness, and extreme friendliness. What a pity that this is only discovered after being here and that the media never shows this side!

Still moved by our good-byes, we get to the airport of Cartagena, where we're waiting to fly to Panama. The only thing not perfectly timed is that we get there Saturday in the morning and we can't pick up the car until Monday morning. Will we have to pay for two nights in a hotel in Panama City? We don't know where we're going to sleep, but "you don't look a gift horse in the mouth," so that's where we're going.

We take our seats in the plane; we buckle up and wait for takeoff. We hear over the speaker, "We're very sorry, but because of a slight technical difficulty, we will have a delay, for this reason, we ask you to exit the airplane. While we resolve the situation, we invite you to have lunch in the airport restaurant as our guests. We're very sorry for the inconvenience."

The passengers boo and curse the delay; some of them will now miss their connecting flights. On the other hand, we're happy and we look at one another guessing each other's thoughts: "Free Lunch!"

Over lunch, we get to know a couple and a guy called Martin, all from Argentina. He is a traveler who has spent his last cent in this country and now all he has in his pocket is enough to pay the exit taxes and the bus to get back to his house in Buenos Aires. He's with us; the free lunch came just in the nick of time. The three are fascinated by what we're doing.

"How did you have the guts? I couldn't have done it, there are so many risks," the woman asks us the question which a thousand times already we have been asked.

"Take heart, we're like ships, from the time we're born we are built and prepared for the high seas, we are constructed so we can face strong winds and storms. We have been taught that there is an enormous world made up of seven seas, and seven continents. And it is before we are ready that we want to go out, when we're still small and not prepared. By the time we are ready to set sail, when our hull and our sails are stronger than ever is when we don't lift the anchor... We feel that we're missing something, that still we're not ready, because there will be storms, because there will be... We are ships, in the port we are safe, but we're not built for this."

The engaging conversation is interrupted by a call to the passengers over the loudspeakers,"The trouble is bigger than we thought and we have to wait for a part from Panama. For the time being, we will put you up in a five-star hotel including dinner, until we have resolved the problem."

The passengers grumble about the company while we're jumping with joy. We love the idea of another night in Cartagena, and even better in a five-star hotel. They contract a bus for everyone and they take us in this to our luxury lodgings. After all the passengers get on, I notice that Martin is very anxious:

"Give me some postcards, those that you have printed here in Colombia," he orders me.

I give him a handful, still not understanding what for. He proceeds to the front of the bus where he stops. "Ladies and Gentlemen," he commences grabbing everyone's attention, "I have here for each of you some marvelous postcards." While he holds them high, displaying them to everyone, "...from the couple seated in the back," the whole bus turns to look at us. We don't know where to hide, we cannot believe what he is doing. "They are doing something that everyone dreams of at some time. I want to help them, and my way of doing this is for all of you to help them. They are traveling..." while he tells them about our trip, the brazen Martin, as if he were the best street hawker, passes out the postcards and in a little box gathers contributions from each passenger. The results turn out truly generous. When he finishes, he sits down next to us.

"What did you do, Martin?" asks Cande.

"I have no idea. But when I saw all those eyes looking at me, I felt I was burning up with embarrassment and I asked myself what am I doing here..." he lets out a breath and with a happy face adds, "I feel great! I wanted to do something for you. And I did! On board this car," he says signaling our cards, "you embody every dream of every person: dreams of adventure, travel, love and freedom. You loaded into a car everything we all want to load in a lifetime. I admire you, I can go as far as to say I love you, even though we just met, but I love you a lot."

The hotel is marvelous with a Caribbean beach view, two double beds, as if another couple were coming to sleep here too; piles of towels of different sizes, we have no idea what they're all for. There are pretty little bottles of soap and shampoos, perfumes, a folder with stationary, and many other "goodies" sure to make whoever pays the five-star hotel price feel like it's worth it.

After a spectacular dinner and the last lingering look at Cartagena by night, we lie down to sleep between starched white sheets with no patches. After a strong hug, we fall to sleep...

"Ring, Ring" Damn! The room in this kind of hotel comes with a phone too! How much more I would like this room if it didn't have a phone! It's the concierge. "I beg your pardon, but the plane is repaired and within twenty minutes, the bus will be here to pick you up." Deep in sleep, I manage only to ask the time. "Two a.m., sir."

We get up like children who are allowed to go to an amusement park who have to turn around and go back to the car because their parents "said so". While we get our things together, we look at the pillows that still beckon us, the television with many films to watch, the bathtub with hot water sure to last as long as we want to linger and...the telephone that ruined everything.

We finally get to Panama almost four in the morning. Everyone who has missed their connecting flights is given another room very close to the airport.

I look around from one side to the other, but I don't see Cande. I begin to look more determinedly and I see her in a place I hadn't thought to look: in the line of people waiting to receive rooms in a hotel. I look at her with a face that says: "What are you doing?" She replies with a gesture announcing: "I don't know, let's just see,"

She is the last in the line, and it's her turn. I back up toward the counter to listen without being recognized. The man of the company asks for the tickets, he looks at them not comprehending.

"Miss, your tickets are for Panama and you are in Panama..."

"Yes, but now what can I do? It's four in the morning, I have no idea how to get into the city, nor a hotel to go to. We were supposed to have gotten here at noon yesterday, broad daylight... Do you want me to go at this hour and try to find a hotel?"

"Yes, I understand. You're right, here's a room with breakfast. Take a taxi, we'll pay for it."

Hummm! How 'bout that little gal? Eh? She got us a room.

Drinking *mate*

Panama & Costa Rica

TILL HERE: 13156 miles in 1 year and 4 mo.

From Colombia

Pto. Limón
San Carlos
Pto. Viejo
Bocas del Toro
Colón
San José
Panamá
Montezuma
David
Manuel Antonio

5 BANCO CENTRAL DE COSTA RICA 5

PATRONATO PANAMA V·I·E·J·O

Panama

Union of the Seas

A New Leg

Central America is a new leg of the trip and sure to be full of surprises. We like not knowing what is in store for us in these small countries that we're beginning to travel through today.

The car is at the port and we feel strange without it. Why do we have to fly here and ship the car when the continent is connected? How come it was possible to connect two oceans for that gigantic ship to pass through and not possible to connect the continent with a small road? They have been able to unite what is separated and to separate what is already united. We hear some excuses but we think the truth is more along the line of "Divide and conquer". Next time I will go by land, no matter what!

We wake up in the hotel where the airline sent us and from there, we go to the Argentinean Embassy. As soon as we tell them about our situation, that we need to get the Graham off the ship, they get busy trying to find a customs agent to help us. They are very interested in helping us but they only find prices and timetables far beyond our budget. We go to the company that shipped the car for us to give them our thanks. Since we are there, we inquire about agents. Their prices frighten us.

Let Us Help You

We decide to go directly to the city of Colon where the car is waiting for us. We get a hotel there that is really dreadful. The noises of the drunks and women of the night doing their job, keep us awake. So, we decide to go out for a walk even though we are afraid. This isn't the Panama that we had imagined; advanced because of its canal and commerce.

With the first light of day, we show up at the company's port. It's nice to know that the Graham is inside one of those containers stacked on top of each other. We feel it close to us and what excites us most about seeing the car again is its air of freedom. We ask for the papers we will need to present to the agent whom we haven't yet found. We leave the terminal and two blocks from there we see the customs office.

"Why don't we just go in and ask for a quick and inexpensive agent?" suggests Cande.

The secretary informs us that they can't recommend anybody but she will give us a list of agents that we have to call ourselves. A man behind her who is looking at some files interrupts her. He wants to know what we are looking for. We tell him about the car, the trip and our dream. This is enough for him to invite us into his office where he explains, "You don't need an agent. You can do it yourselves. Let us help you. My name is Ramón," As our eyes grow wide in amazement; he begins to call his assistants.

"You write a letter of introduction for them, explaining what they have shipped and why." Pointing to the next person waiting for orders, "You, find the forms and fill them out and when you have them ready, tell me." He pauses briefly thinking of what else we will need. "Herman and Candelaria, you get me the title of the car and your passports and I will send someone to make copies and I will certify them myself," he informs us as we watch in disbelief all the action that is taking place just on our behalf. He is so enthusiastic that he talks and talks not giving us a chance to say anything.

"What size are you?" he indiscreetly asks Cande, looking at her waistline, "We have a lot of confiscated clothing that nobody has ever claimed and I am sure some of it would be right for you." He sends someone to bring some of the clothing to the office.

We try them on as we drink café latte while other people fill out all our papers. When everything is ready and we're all dressed up, they take us in a car to the bank. There we have to pay two dollars for some stamps.

"This is all you will need," the man from customs informs us, giving us a folder.

"What? You mean that everything is ready? The customs agents told us that it would take three days just to prepare the paperwork plus there would be expenses. All we've paid for were the stamps."

"Yes, I know. They make it look more difficult than it really is in order to justify the prices they charge. Please, Yarelis, take them to the Evergreen Port and wait there with them until they take the car out. I don't want anything to go wrong at the last minute. We give him a huge hug promising to come back to show him the car."

"That will be very nice. I'll be expecting you. Now go, I want you to get there before they close."

We get the Graham out without any problems, complications or searches. We thought that since it was coming from Colombia that they would practically dismantle it, but all they do is disinfect it.

Reuniting with our constant companion is emotional; seeing it again makes us so happy. I start the engine while it is still inside the container. It seems to be eager to go out into the light and to explore new roads. Cande gives it a kiss and I give it a pat; we're together again.

Once again on the road, we head for Panama City, crossing from the Atlantic to the Pacific in only an hour and a half. Once there, we find a place to park the car and to sleep. At a steak house, the Argentinean owner, makes some room for the car and treats us to a delicious steak meal, something that we really miss.

Out of Necessity, You Grow

The city is small. The prosperous buildings of the foreign companies stand out in contrast to the poor neighborhoods of the locals. The city was founded in three distinct locations. Pirates left the first in ruins; the second is the present day old Panama that is little by little regaining some of its previous grandeur; and the third is the modern Panama City.

In the old city park, we sell post cards as we wait for the Argentine ambassador and his Spanish wife who have invited us to dinner. They travel for their work and for pleasure, mostly for pleasure. Because of this common ground, we all have a pleasant conversation.

"What was the best thing that happened to you on the trip?" asks the wife.

"The best thing was to run out of money."

"Really?" says the ambassador, surprised.

"Yes, as incredible as that may sound, that's the way it is. Before that, while we had money, we were tourists who only passed through a place observing it. Now, as travelers we intensely live the customs of each place. Necessity made us open up to the people much more. They respond by opening their doors to us, sharing their traditions, cultures and food. Each person teaches us not only about his or her country but about life itself. For us, this is an ongoing learning experience that makes us grow and makes us want to continue learning more. You never stop growing if you open up to the world and its people," Cande says. I look at her in the same way as our new friends do.

"Every place we go we have to earn a little money," I explain to them. "Many times, something works in one place but doesn't in another place and we have to look for something new. For this reason we have to mingle, adapt and learn. We become one of the locals. Now we know what we are capable of thanks to necessity. We had never imagined ourselves making crafts, or painting or selling... much less becoming pros at public relations. We have also learned about other languages and religions, which has deepened our belief and taught us to become more sociable and humane. We have learned to become more organized, to observe, to write, to plan and to manage our finances. Today we are a better husband and wife, better companions, closer partners and a thousand things more. Our relationship is so much richer, it's hard to describe...there have been so many unexpected lessons we have learned from trying to find an immediate solution to every problem as it came."

"Everybody thinks that we are on a worry-free vacation," adds Cande.

"The street is the best school and the world, as you see, is the best university," I conclude.

Thank You for Letting Us Welcome You

We leave the city after visiting its canal, a titanic enterprise and which now turns out to be relatively small. It cost forty thousand human lives and with the earth they moved, sixty Egyptian pyramids could have been built. We cross the canal over the "Bridge of the Americas" heading south but after only a few miles the Pan American Highway ends, quite effectively separating North and South America, a continent that desires union. We take off, anxious to see Central America. We have decided to drive 125 miles to get ahead and make up some time and then we'll stop at different beaches or wherever people invite us to sleep over.

However, after only 18 miles, we stop for gasoline and a couple invites us, in broken Spanish, to their house. We would like to decline the invitation and continue. However, Cande and I are learning to get the message that "nothing happens by chance" and decide to accept the invitation.

They are Bob and Irene, pastors from the United States, who are on vacation here in Panama. They own a piece of land with a vacation house in which they pamper us and permit us only to rest. They prepare the bath with towels, soaps and perfumes. While we are bathing, they fix a delicious meal and after eating, they give us their own room. Although they want to ask a thousand questions about our trip, they hold back so that we can rest.

In the morning, after an elaborately prepared breakfast of fresh juice and pancakes with fruit they bid us farewell, thanking us for giving them the opportunity to welcome us. On the road again, we look at each other, wondering what that was all about.

"They treat us like kings plus they thank us," is Cande's comment.

For Whomever Needs to Chase His Dream

Only a few miles down the road it begins to sprinkle.

"I wonder if it will rain," Cande says.

"This cloud is only passing through," I say looking out the window. However, this "passing cloud" seems to have arrived too heavy to move on because it starts raining so hard we can't see the road ahead.

"It looks like the passing cloud likes this place," says Cande, laughing. Since the windshield wiper doesn't work, I have to clean the window myself. Each time I lean out to clear the window, I get all wet and it only stays dry for a few seconds. It's raining so hard that water is leaking into the car. Cande empties a plastic container and holds it under the leak.

"See if you can find a place we can stop," I ask Cande as I am only able to see a road mostly surrounded by jungle.

"There's a gate. It must go to a house," Cande says. It's open and we drive in. Following the narrow path, we come to a house surrounded by an enormous porch. The few steps from the car to the porch leave us soaking wet. The whole family comes out to see us. The woman who comes out of the kitchen wiping her hands on an apron asks us, "What can we do for you?"

"We don't want to drive in this rain. Could we wait here until it stops?"

"This rain isn't going to stop until the morning. If you'd like, put the car in the shed and come in to spend the night," says the husband who comes up to greet us with his hand extended.

"Yes, stay. I'm fixing a beef stew and it's almost ready. It will be delicious." The lady tries to convince us even though we're already convinced. To our surprise and without planning for it, we've stopped at the largest cattle ranch in Panama and we're at the house of the manager. The next day they take us to look over much of the property. We go all the way to the beach where they point out several islands, also part of the same property. He tells us that the person who founded the outfit, after a short time of managing the property, called his brother from Europe to help him with it. After his brother arrived, he died from yellow fever. So he called another brother who, after a short time, suffered the same fate. After that, he didn't call anyone else.

We pass the greater part of the day in the shade of trees, surrounded by dogs and chickens, editing our book, which is already taking shape. However, it is taking a lot longer than we thought and I am beginning to doubt whether we'll ever finish.

"Why are we writing a book?" I ask Cande.

"Because somewhere out there there is some person who needs a push in order to start to acomplish his dream," she responds without lifting her gaze from what she is writing renewing my desire to keep doing it too. "Are dreams alive?"

"Yes, each dream comes alive when we start pursuing it."

Links of the Dream

We stop in David, a city close to the cattle ranch. We're supposed to be on the local radio station. As soon as we arrive, the owner interrupts the regular program to put us on the air. He conducts the interview himself and invites the listeners to call in with questions.

"We have a call, go ahead."

"I would like to know what you think about Panama. How you like it?" This is a typical question from a person who loves his country.

"Panama is incredible. It unites two oceans. Now, I would like to see Panama unite all of America," I respond.

"What is the name of the country you come from?" comes the voice of another listener who missed the beginning of the interview.

"The name is Argentina, but we have discovered that it also has a last name, America, the same last name as your country. This makes us brothers. Anyway, we all have the same "mother" earth, so that makes us all brothers."

"It's true, being united gives strength," adds the interviewer. "There's another call, go ahead please."

"I only want to know if I could invite the travelers to my home," says a woman with a sweet voice. After the interview is over, we go to her home. The woman receives us as if we were her own beloved grandkids. As soon as we've had a snack with her, she takes us to meet her daughters and grandchildren. She is a person who enjoys her family. It is her treasure and she tells us details about the life of each one of the family members. She hugs Alexandra her grand daughter with admiration and love and says to us, "She is a swimmer, one of the best in Panama. She has won many competitions and in the most recent competition, she represented the province of Chiriqui. She won first place and received a medal."

Then Alexandra, who is thirteen or fourteen years old, runs to get it. She comes back with her medal around her neck and she and her grandmother show it to us with great satisfaction. They read the inscription on the medal very happily. It is so nice to see the emotion of the family so proud of that triumph.

The next day, little noises and giggles of all the grandchildren rouse us. They have come to wake us up before going to school, very early. They brought us a surprise that we consider one of the greatest treasures of our trip; the granddaughter who is the champion swimmer gives us a wrapped box. We open it and there is what she treasured the most, her medal, something that can't be bought. The medal is something that can only be won once, through effort and a lot of hard work can be won. She strokes it and tells us to remember her and her family. We show our appreciation for this with an enormous hug. Our hearts melt. We take leave of our Panamanian grandmother with many warm hugs.

"Thank you for such kindness," we say.

"I wanted to add my grain of sand toward this dream," she says.

"No grandma, it isn't a grain of sand, you added a link in the chain. Without it, the chain would be broken."

We Have Everything

We leave the Pacific Ocean and head toward the Atlantic crossing a low mountain range whose cool air refreshes us. Next to the road, we see next to the road a

little country style shop, without walls, constructed of materials from the region. It is attended by an elderly man sitting in the shade who gives a toothless grin. We see a big sign casually lettered that says, "Mr. Pimentel[s little country Market. WE`VE GOT IT ALL" We want to laugh because all we can see are some avocadoes and bananas. That's it, nothing more. We stop anyway as this is just what we need for lunch.

After our light meal, we continue traveling. While driving, we correct our notes for the book. Those which increase what Cande already has to write. And she thought that on the road she would have time to read books and knit…bless her heart.

"Have you written down the mileage for today?" I ask her.

"Yes."

"And the name of the woman and the granddaughter who gave us the medal?"

"Yes."

"Did you check where we are supposed to take the ferry to go to the islands?" Perhaps this was one question too many because…

"Do I have to take care of everything?!? I'm the one with the maps, the documents, the diary, the one who has to write down the names of new friends and places, and take photographs and film too. And what's your role?"

"I'm the love of your life, the one you forgive for everything," I answer, and she throws the papers at me tenderly.

The afternoon is hot and the road passes next to a river that looks inviting. So, we stop to refresh ourselves. Very soon five boys and girls show up to swim with us. At first, they are timid but after clowning around a little, they warm up to us. One of the girls can't swim very well. She can't move her right arm correctly because of a malformation. One of the kids keeps his hands under water and tries to hide from us the fact that he has six fingers on each hand.

We are in a banana-growing zone of enormous international companies. The workers live on the plantations with their families. Planes continually fumigate the zone, and pregnant women breathe the chemicals, which affect their babies. We see enormous injustice producing so much damage.

Profound America

We get to Almirante, a small coastal port town very near the border of Costa Rica. We want to go to Bocas del Toro Islands, described to us as a paradise. We find the only ferry service in town that can take us. It only travels twice weekly.

"You're in luck! What perfect timing! It leaves tomorrow," the captain tells us. He's a stocky man, whose body is as big as his heart. He immediately offers to let us use the boat as a hotel, use the kitchen and watch television.

"Go ahead, stay and use anything you want and tomorrow if anybody asks you about it, tell them you already paid me for the trip, for a round trip," he comments us, winking. "Some time ago some other travelers passed through here on an incredible trip, but I don't know if theirs was as good as yours..."

"Don't compare trips because if we do, Christopher Columbus will beat us all," I interrupt him.

The next day we disembark in a little town on the small island of Colon. It feels strange to drive on an island where we don't know exactly where we are. There are people of all colors. For example, black people aren't totally black. They were originally brought here to work the banana and coconut plantations. They don't speak perfect Spanish nor perfect English. There are also many people of Asian descent who mixed their blood, language and cuisine with the locals. As for the locals, they were the ones who put their stamp on this mixture of cultures.

We stop in front of a tiny place where a sign says, "Juices, Fruits and Sandwiches. Viva la Pepa! (Whatever!)" The owner comes running out to meet us, shouting,

"I am Argentinean too! My name is Ioca." Later she tells us that she came to the island four years before, in order to help protect the sea turtles and their eggs. She fell in love with this place and is still here. What little money her small business generates is enough for her to live on.

"It's that here you don't need anything...no heat nor refrigeration, clothing or car because everything is nearby. You don't even need electricity for light because you get up and go to bed when there is still daylight and if you stay up late, you can use candles. My house is built of boards and has a palm-thatched roof. If you want to you can fish and if do not you can eat bananas, avocadoes, or coconuts, which grow everywhere. And if you want to splurge you can buy a large lobster for two dollars."

Listening to Ioca, we understand how simple life can be. We have all dreamed at one time or another how it would be to live on an island but we imagined that the only ones who can do this are those who have a lot of money. How mistaken we are! Life on an island really requires very little money.

That same night she takes us to watch the sea turtles lay their eggs. It is fascinating to watch them come out of the water, lumber slowly over the sand, dig holes, lay their eggs and return to the water.

We end up staying several days more visiting beautiful beaches and staying longer than we had planned. Each beach is unique. Some of the beaches are calm and others are rough. The sands are different colors. Many are enormous and seem to exist only for us. We walk along some of them in our birthday suits.

It's remarkable that whenever we get near the ocean we feel a lot of anxiety as if it were the first time we were so close to such amazing power. The first thing we do when we get to any beach is go straight to the water and greet it as if extending a hand to a friend, saying, "Hello Atlantic Ocean, here we are again." Then we usually sit down on the sand next to the surf and silently listen to the voice of the water in the ebb and flow of the waves.

We go to Bastimentos Island by boat. Once there, we walk because it is the only way to get around. We pass houses where the people look very easy going. Some of the women leaning against the windows watch the people walking by; others are in their hammocks in the shade. The only movement is that of the children who run and that of a man who has to drag a pig that doesn't want to walk. We get to the beach on a rugged path. The waves and the surroundings enchant us and inspire us to write. We are close to finishing the first draft of our book.

Costa Rica

Pura Vida!

Happy Birthday

To enter Costa Rica we have to wait until a banana company train passes on a bridge that belongs to the banana company, and for this reason the train has priority of use. We drive along the same tracks as the train, following behind it. We get to the other side and observe a small hut. This is Customs and Immigration. Only one person is in attendance who, among other things, asks us for eleven dollars for the car and another twenty for us…I explain to him that we don't have much. The man looks at my passport and tells me:

"Because it's your birthday, and all of this is so cool, I'll pay the entrance fee for the car, you pay the rest."

Will he really pay part of it or is this just for show? Surely, he won't pay, and just let the car in without charging anything. Nevertheless, here he comes, and he gives us a receipt for thirty-one dollars showing that he did pay. With a great welcome and an unexpected birthday present, we enter Costa Rica! Pura vida!

This country has no military and just for this I consider it one of the most advanced in the world. A country that uses force becomes weak, those that don't get strengthened. Costa Rica is a perfect example. Besides, counting more than 25% of its territory as national parks and reserves, all the electricity in Costa Rica is generated by hydroelectric plants. They are environmentally-aware and with a very strong democracy. After we enter, the countryside is very beautiful. Unfortunately, we can't film anything: the camera is broken and we have no idea where we can get it fixed.

The Grahambulance

Our first stop is Puerto Viejo, a tiny town on the sands of the Caribbean, without banks, without gas stations, and without paved roads. All we see are bunch of surfers. We take a drive through what must be the center. We're looking for a place to spend the night. I see a bulletin board with offers and I stop to read them when a short man asks me very politely, "I don't want to bother you, but may I ask you a question?"

"By all means, please," I respond thinking surely there will be more than one.

"What model is this car?"

"It's a 1928, sir."

He thanks me and begins to move away. "Don't you have any more questions?" I ask, surprised.

"Yes, of course, but I don't want to disturb you…"

"Please, you're not bothering me."

So, he poses the typical questions, which are several. After which he inquires, "What are you looking for here?"

"A place to sleep, but it doesn't have to be a hotel. A place to park the car would be just fine."

"My name is Jaime. Would you care to park in my yard? If you'd like to, you may also use our bathroom."

We follow him. First, he takes us to a small restaurant, recently inaugurated by him and his family. There we eat together with his son and his pregnant daughter-in-law.

"When's your due date?" Cande questions, astonished at the great roundness of her belly.

"It's already past due, you might even be witnesses for the birth," explains the woman.

They are refugees from Colombia; they came to Costa Rica with a strong drive to advance and invested the little they had in a restaurant. The place was a bit slow because of the few people in the area, but they are happy to be beginning a new life.

"You can always begin again; it's not the first time we've started over. As long as we're all together, nothing else matters," Jaime comments to me.

"Did you have a restaurant in Colombia?"

"No, I fixed washing machines and appliances, but here there are almost none of these things. David, my son, fixes cameras and VCR's, and so…"

We open our eyes so wide that David interrupts his father to ask, "Do you have any break-downs?"

"Yes, our video camera," we respond. And in twenty minutes, situation resolved.

We stay another day, sheltered with this family. On these fabulous beaches, we walk for hours thinking out loud about ideas and memories for the book that is just about ready. It's almost midnight when there's a knock on the car that wakes us up.

"The baby's coming! Jadith is in labor!"

Immediately we're wide awake and we ask if there's something we can do. We are even ready to take her to the hospital.

"Don't worry, guys, I'm going by bicycle to get the pastor, he has a car and he already committed himself to taking us to the first aid station when the time came. From there, an ambulance will take us to the hospital in Puerto Limon," Jaime explains to us.

216

So, we stay there with the rest of the family until he gets back, along with the shouts and contractions. We film everybody who show their happiness and nervousness in front of the camera.

"The pastor isn't there," says Jaime as he runs into the house, with noticeable anxiety.

"Let's go in our car!" we exclaim.

The family looks at one another not knowing what to do it. However, as there is no other way, we empty out the car to make space. The six of us leave all together and it's the first time in the whole trip that we drive at night plus on a dirt road full of potholes.

"Where is the first-aid station?" I consult imagining that it would be near the small village.

"About 10 miles," responds David.

I am petrified. This makes me pretty nervous. I don't know if I have enough gas and in this village, there are no gas stations. In any case, I don't say anything, everyone is already sufficiently fidgety. Jadith complains about her pain; David, her husband, wants to relieve her, but he doesn't know how. He holds her hands, he gives her little kisses on her forehead as he speaks softly. Finally, after a long forty-minute trip, we get to the aid station. We all breathe a sigh of relief, except Jadith who continues to yell every once in awhile.

While I thank the Graham for pulling it off with so little gas and God for giving us the opportunity to be a part of a birth, I see the whole family coming back of the clinic in a hurry out.

"The doctor told us to take her to the hospital right away." David tells me.

"But, what about the ambulance?"

"There is no ambulance, it left about half an hour ago."

I am frozen. Everyone is climbing back into the car, I don't have any gas. And besides, I don't know anything about childbirth. On the road up to here, we haven't come across one single other car, what will the road be like to Puerto Limon?

"How many miles is it?" I ask.

"20 miles."

I sit stone still. I ask myself over and over if we will get there at this slow speed, over such a bad road, and with a woman in labor all the time more painful. No, not without fuel.

"Do you know of any gas stations?"

"Yes, about 6 or 7 miles from here, at the crossroad. We'll get there, won't we?"

"Sure," I respond without believing it could be possible. Why make them more nervous? "Only 6 or 7 miles more, I ask You, push me, God…only seven more." I plead in silence that is broken by a scream from Jadith.

The road is full of curves and we couldn't squeeze in anymore tightly than we are. We are three in the front, and three and a half in the back. I am trying to go as fast as possible, but each hole bumps everyone and that makes us afraid:

could this bumping push the baby out? On account of nerves, each comment causes a laugh followed by silence.

Cande, Jaime and I are concentrating on the road, six eyes searching for holes to avoid and the best way for us to go. Sometimes, one tells me right while the other left. We celebrate the discrepancy with big nervous laughs while we drive right through the hole we were trying to avoid. In back, the daughter-in-law is encouraged by her mother-in-law while her husband talks sweetly. She asks the baby to wait, not to hurry, that we're almost there.

"Why would he want to wait? He wants to see this trip, when else is he going to get another chance to go in a car like this?" the smiling future grandpa jokes.

When we see the gas station, we all give a cheer, as if the others were informed about my urgent necessity. Filling the tank, Jaime insists on paying:

"These will the best used gallons of the whole trip. Please don't take the pleasure of paying for them from me," I ask him with sincerity seeing that the pump indicates 10 gallons. It's all the tank can hold. I pat Macondo and say thank you looking up to the starry sky.

I am happy about this scene, about all that we are living. I remember the experience of the death of my friend in Ecuador, this is just the opposite. I was part of a death, and now I am part of a new life. Since everyone has gotten out of the car for a breath of necessary air and Jadith, in particular, walks to relieve her pains a bit, I call them to get back in to keep going.

I turn over the starter of the car, but no engine noise follows. We are all quiet in the silence.

"What's wrong?" asks the future grandma.

"Everybody push," I ask while I pray that it's just the starter. They all push and because of the speed they make me go, I pop the clutch and after a couple of shudders, the car starts.

We are driving for the first time at night and it seems that the lights consume more than the alternator can generate. The orange light slightly illuminates our path and the slower we go, the worse it gets. To animate the situation the jokes keep coming causing anxious laughter.

"Jaime, get on the hood and hold a flashlight!"

"What flashlight? We took everything out to make room!" adds Cande.

"At least get the matches!" exclaims David.

Everyone continues laughing, but abruptly we all stop when Jadith shouts out a request to stop the car. "God, I can be a chauffer for You but please don't ask me to be a midwife," I think while Jadith gets out with her mother-in-law. We all look at each other in silence without knowing what's going on. They come back in a few minutes, but it seemed like an eternity.

"The baby is getting lower and the pressure on the uterus makes her feel like she needs to go to the bathroom. It's just this, she needed to go."

She asks us to repeat this two more times, and two more times we wait with our hearts in our throats.

The dark sky can be perceived slightly illuminated. It's the reflection of the city we're wishing to reach. When we enter the city, we head straight to the hospital. We jump out of the car and create a commotion at the clinic. With surprising calm, they tell Jadith that she's not quite ready; she still needs to dilate and to go out for a walk. Now more at ease, we all breathe a huge sigh of relief.

The hours pass, the walking continues. The child that rushed us so much now doesn't want to make an appearance. I arrange the car for sleep and we take turns relaxing a bit. A doctor, who comes out after his rounds, sees us waiting and invites all of us to his house for breakfast, to shower and to relax. Jaime feels like this would be too much bother but the doctor convinces him adding that it's good for the future mama to bathe in lukewarm water.

When we enter the house, the doctor's wife receives us naturally, as if this happens every day. With an enormous smile, she takes the women to help give Jadith a bath. Afterwards she prepares breakfast for everyone.

I start to play with their five or six year old son and his puppy. After a half an hour, they tell something I hadn't noticed in him, he's deaf and mute. We were laughing the whole time and we didn't need other communication than happiness.

During the first hours of the afternoon of a marvelous sunny day, a new baby arrives in the world, a new tiny person. A boy is born whom we all surround with a beautiful sensation. This child is priceless. The fortune of Jaime, his wife, Jadith and David could only grow with the birth of another baby.

We take pictures of the new family, of which we feel and are made to feel a part of. When they give the baby to Cande and me, they say, "Now, a picture with the auntie and uncle."

We left as six and we return as seven. We left as friends, we return as a family.

A Book is Born

As soon as we arrive in San Jose, the capital of Costa Rica, we go to visit the Argentinean Ambassador.

"We have a book to be printed. Could you recommend where we could do that?" we ask him.

"I have no idea, but you absolutely have to print it. Find some way to do it. The International Book Fair in this city opens in four days and this year's country of honor is Argentina. So, I may find a place for your books, for your car and for both of you," he offers us.

We leave the embassy without knowing where to start. We have very little time and we don't even have the book designed yet. It occurs to us to ask at a used car lot about the Antique Auto Club. One of the salesmen begins to make some calls. And within five minutes, I am talking with the president of the club, Alan Rodriguez. I tell him about our trip and consult him about a printing shop. He gives me the number of a member who has a small one, I call him and he tells me to come on over.

This man recommends a graphic designer who drops what she's working on and doesn't stop until we finish designing the whole book. Immediately we begin printing, in an ambiance of camaraderie, with the three workers in the shop who are giving it their all. Among tints, letters, machines, smells and noises unknown, Cande and I play a role of assistants entering a new world completely foreign to us. Since we're allowed to stay inside the shop after hours, we can get ahead on the work putting the pages of the book in order, one by one. We arrive in time for the inauguration of the fair…still gluing on the covers.

The coordinator of the exhibition receives us very warmly and indicates to us where we can set up our stand, the location is excellent. However, we soon realize that we don't have anything to set up a stand with; no tables, or chairs, or anywhere to situate the books. We are only the car and us with the books in our hands.

The people of the nearby booths notice all this and they start coming up with a table, then another, with chairs, and someone even gives us a map of all of America where we draw our route and stick up some pictures from the trip.

The fair opens its doors to the public. The passersby visit our stand. It's a strange feeling, now we are authors and editors of our own history.

"I'm nervous to know how it's going to turn out. I never imagined I'd write a book and now I have a very special one in my hands," thinks Cande while handling one lovingly. "It tells part of my treasure, of my dream, of my growth and change. I reveal part of my life openly so the people can get to know me and can see that I'm like them. I'm not special because of what I'm doing. I am as normal as everyone, just doing something special with my life. I am chasing my dream. And, this is the title of the book, 'Dream Chaser'." Cande continues to caress the book, looking at it fondly. Then a boy of thirteen asks her to sign it. "I feel strange, signing my own book, I put my best effort into writing the dedication." She thinks while she writes, "Thank you for being part of this dream, follow and chase yours. With love, Cande".

After the dedication from Cande, the boy comes to me and asks for my autograph as well. Without taking her eyes off him, Cande thinks, "Just look at this kid. He's at the perfect age to think that dreams can be achieved, not to think about impossibility, only about possibility. I was fourteen when I dreamed about traveling and here, in front of his eyes, I demonstrate that dreams can come true. I don't have the heart to ask what he yearns to do. I send him off with a kiss, wishing him the best of his dreams and I send him on his way."

"Always remember, nothing is impossible." Cande sees her book go away in the small hands that hold it with love.

"When he reads it, will he like it?" Cande asks me without waiting for an answer.

Many of the people who approach us already know about our story because we were on the front page of the Sunday paper and on TV. This helps us a lot. We sign hundreds of books for people who bring us, encouragement, blessings and hugs. The people don't regard this as a trip but as the attainment of a dream, and a lot of energy flows as much in our direction as does toward them. I comment to a man who is studying the route on the map about the coincidence of having gotten here just in time for the fair, and that Argentina is the guest of honor and how everything worked out.

"Nothing is a coincidence, but causal," he corrects me. "There is no luck nor accidents, all is causal. Nothing is in vain, everything has a reason for being: Every thing that happens to us, every encounter, every movement that occurs has an enormous meaning, for us and for the universe. Not realizing this means losing a lot."

"Are you the two crazy ones who are traveling with this??" interrupts a young guy with a craving to ask a million questions.

"If they call you crazy, give thanks" continues the man who was explaining his concept of the universe, "this means that you're not like the majority," and with a wave he goes away. I would have liked to continue talking with the man, but the people are calling my attention. At the end of the exhibition, we all receive a great surprise. "Dream Chaser" was the best selling book.

Humane Treatment

Because of the book success we receive many invitations from the countryside people of Costa Rica, as well as another one from the Antique Auto Club, which we accept. They organize an outing with their cars along a picturesque drive to a restaurant out in the country. We all depart from a park, leaving us to bring up the rear of the caravan. Shortly after the beginning of the drive, the cars begin to disperse. They don't wait for us, so we keep driving, supposing we're going the right way, until a Jeep appears that has shown up late, which guides us.

As we get to the restaurant, while we park among the cars already here, we imagine that, as in all the previous gatherings, we would explain a bit about the trip and talk about the Graham, which is an unusual make among devoted car fans. However, when we get inside, they are all already seated at the tables and no one approaches us. We are the ones who approach them, but still not one at any table invites us to join their table. Finally, we sit alone.

It surprises us that there are almost no women or children, this seems more like a meeting of businessmen...and business is exactly about what they're talking about. At the end of the meal, the president of the Club stands up to speak. He talks about his institution and takes advantage of the moment to welcome us presenting us with a club umbrella and a letter. Everything wraps up as quickly as it started.

When we are leaving, a man called Carlos, with whom we have hardly spoken during the meeting, invites us to drop by his house to see his cars. He lived in a very exclusive, private neighborhood. We park in front of an enormous, beautiful home. With two of his friends he takes us into his garage and he shows us five cars while enumerating what he paid for each one. He encourages us to take pictures so we can show his collection to others.

On our part, seeing that he possesses many acquisitions, we offer framed paintings. He chooses one in front of his pals and asks us to come by the office on Monday for the payment, then he asks Cande to dedicate it for him. It doesn't go unnoticed that at no time does he invite us into the house. Nor does he offer any drinks to his friends or us.

The next day I introduce myself to another member of the Club that the president recommended as a very good mechanic. We're to have a tune-up, which is to be a gift from the club. This man owns a big house and a beautiful shop for restoring cars. Before we get to work, I ask about a place to change my clothes.

"Over there, between the cars," he indicates.

Later, I ask where I can wash my hands.

"There's a hose in the garden," he replies.

When he goes to buy some oil for the car, he closes up the shop with a key leaving me outside in the garden, to prevent anything from disappearing. When Cande gets here, I tell her about my indignation. Furthermore, even though his family is in the house, they don't say hello nor invite us to come in. I can't believe the treatment we are receiving! I pick up my things, and when the man comes back with his purchases in his hands, I bid him farewell saying:

"For us, humane treatment is more important than the service of the car."

On Monday, Cande calls Carlos, but his secretary answers that she should call tomorrow because he can't take her call. We persist, insisting for various days, calling and calling regarding the payment of our painting. The man never answers our calls and his secretary, ashamed of his actions, tells us she has given him every message and that there's nothing she can do. We never see the money nor our painting again.

Before we leave San Jose, we write a letter to the Club, addressing the president. In it we tell them how wonderful it's been so far, being received by other clubs, what lovely memories we have treasured by the time we leave, for example, the hugs, the encouragement and the blessings we receive for the rest of our trip. We also tell him how much we would have liked to leave this place feeling the same happiness.

Mandalas

We continue visiting beaches of the Pacific until we get to Montezuma, where we meet in front of his art display a Spaniard whom for many years has been traveling all over the world. To finance this, he makes *mandalas* out of wire. It takes the shape of an orange and its wires link forming various shapes. We watch how he shows his clients while he moves it and explains the significance of each movement.

"Atom: origin of life, foundation of all," he changes the shape of the mandala, from the atom to a ball, and continues, "No one knows how, nor why, nor what for it's the symbol of the energy to which we're all connected. When this blooms, the big cosmic explosion, scientifically known as the big bang theory..." he turns it into the shape of a drum, "...They say that all animal and vegetable life is connected with a cosmic vibration, known as the Om mantra..." and he continues to move the mandala in front of his clients, who are marveled, buy the object that has such significance.

The Spaniard, very happy about our trip, teaches me how to make them; he wants to help us and he does so by passing on what he knows how to do, what permits him to continue traveling. He also teaches us the story of the movements of the mandala, which Cande jots down onto paper.

With the materials he gives me, I construct my first mandalas. With practice, they are getting better. When I think they are ready for selling, I study the story and set up my post on the next beach, inclined to think that I will have as much success as the Spaniard. My first possible buyer picks one up; I with another in my hands begin to relate the story while I move it.

"The light blue dome, the foundation of the heavens, the dark blue, creation of the seas. Now it's an egg, origin of the earth..." and I forget what comes next, and I get totally confused.

My shopper puts it down and doesn't buy anything; Cande, meanwhile, is laughing her head off.

"I'll bet you a hundred kisses that I sell the next one," I challenge her before going to practice the story.

I am reviewing the story, when another customer comes, picking up a mandala. I try again. While I move the apparatus, I go on telling my story:

"...and it forms the yin-yang or equilibrium: good-bad, male-female. The flower of the allegory of the wisdom. A Hindu drum, symbol of the meditation..."

" Do you know about the mother Chakra... Kundalini, about the metaphor of the creation of the nine planets, nine orifices, nine senses...?" the woman interrupts me with one question. I have no idea what she's talking about.

"No, ma'am, I'm only trying to sell my mandalas..." I respond and she goes without completing the sale.

Another man comes up and asks me what they are:

"They're mandalas, they can change shape. It costs ten pesos. Do you want one?" is all I say.

This was my first and only day as a mandala vendor. Perhaps I had better say, first attempt at being one.

At a Sloth's Pace

Invited by the Spanish Embassy, we go to the Manuel Antonio National Park, where we sleep and eat with the park rangers, in a place where we once again meet the sea. There is no one on the beach; the only ones who accompany us are the monkeys with whom we try to keep their paws away from our lunch.

We are settled on the sand, Cande's head on my chest. We feel so well; everything is perfect, marvelous. Together we look back and see two years of travel. For the intensity with which we have lived them, it doesn't seem like that much time. Along the path we have changed so much as individuals and as a couple. A large part of the change is because others have altered us. The other big part of we've learned can not be taught, you can only learn it by living it.

In the park, the days pass very slowly. We are thoughtful and meditative. I've been here watching a sloth for nearly four hours. When I first saw him, he was moving and he looked at me with this face that inspired complete peace prompting from me one of my best smiles. Then he stopped moving, leaned his face on his arm and went to sleep. Since then, I have been sitting waiting for him to wake up, to see his slow movements, his gaze. So, one, two, three hours pass…then it starts pouring. With the drops, he must move, wake up, and seek refuge. However, the sloth doesn't think the same about the rain, he merely moves his head further under his arms. I remain out in the rain too: if he can, I can too. Neither, in all the hours that have passed, have I moved. I only shift my gaze to look at my surroundings, at how the drops fall from the sky dripping from one leaf to another creating small sounds. Drips of water add to the songs of frogs, the birds, monkeys and others creating a concert.

After the rain started there was some time before the drops land on me because of all the plants and trees. When the rain stopped, it continued raining from these same plants for a while. I see things while my sloth sleeps, things that make me think how can the wind, made of air, carry water or earth; how can water being so soft wear away a rock so hard with only its touch; how can a

Atacama Desert. Chile.

On a desert road, Peru.

Napo River, Ecuador.

To Almirante, Panama.

Amazon River, Peru-Brazil

handful of earth give life to a seed and make from this a tree. How can the sun so far away give me heat and how can this little animal sleep so much…maybe you didn't let me see you move, but you let me see things that I haven't seen before, with thankfulness, I bid him farewell.

The Door Is Open

In the city of San Carlos, we are hosted by a family that is "all heart". The father, a carpenter, constructed the house of his dream with the woman he loves along side the children he yearned for. They show us once again that to make a home all you need is love. We are welcomed us with a song they are all singing: "The Door is Open" giving us a warm reception. We are so comfortable here, Cande takes the time to paint.

One of the daughters who's 22 has a boyfriend, and she is very much in love. To our astonishment, her steady has to "clock in." This means he has to follow visiting hours to see her and only on designated days in a designated place of the house. With a lot of effort, she works on a gift for us. It's our logo of the trip, which she has recreated by gluing small seeds on a piece of wood. It takes her three days to make it, so we happily stay until she finishes it.

As we leave the city of San Carlos, after several days of such good company, the car stops dead in the road. Immediately a pickup pulls up. The owner offers himself for anything and everything, I mean everything, although it's not necessary, because the car starts right up again. All the same, he takes us to his house to have a drink, he offers his phone for us to call our families in Argentina and invites us to sleep there, but since we've only gone 3 miles and we want to continue, we decide to decline his offer. He asks us to make a note of his phone number and makes us promise with any inconvenience we would summon him.

After about three more miles, the car falters again and it stops. Since we are on a hill we decide to try to take advantage of the downward slope, to no avail, the Graham doesn't want to start. A farmer with a big machete in his hands appears. He asks us what we need and we tell him a telephone. I accompany him to a shop and from there we fulfill our promise: the man who offered us everything, thrilled, tells me that he's on his way to find us. When I go back to the car, the country-man brings us milk fresh from the cow, just for us, still warm and delicious. I don't know if it is because of the good milk or because of the good man, but the drink tastes very special.

Towed for the first time in the whole trip we are transported to a shop right across the street from the man's house, causing quite a commotion; everyone abandons their own work to try to help restart the car, which sometimes it does and other times doesn't. Other mechanics and electricians from other shops start to show up to analyze the problem. They try new batteries and cables, but when we see this doesn't solve the problem we give them back.

They say it can only be fixed by a crazy, a truly crazy man. He has a very small

shop which can only fit one car at a time, as he only repairs one car a day. He has on his agenda, two months worth of work reserved in advanced, on account of how good he is. We ask him why he left another car to work on ours.

"Because I can do it tomorrow along with another car. If I wanted to, I could fix three or four cars in a day, but I can make it doing one. I work to live, I don't live to work. I believe that if God had created us to work, heaven would be a big factory." He answers while taking apart the distributor. We towed the car here and he hasn't asked me to try to start it. He merely opens the hood and disassembles the distributor, piece by piece. "I don't take just anybody. And, just because they pay me doesn't give them the right to treat me anyway they see fit. Also, if a car isn't clean and tidy, I don't accept it." While he tells me this I think how fortunate I am I washed ours yesterday. "No one can demand good work for a car that isn't treated well."

I don't understand why they call him crazy, everything he says, although it's unusual to hear, makes perfect sense. I venture to take a picture of him while he is working. But when he sees the flash, he throws his tools yelling:

"Hey!! No one takes my picture! No one has a picture of me! Not even my own daughter has a picture of me…" now I understand about him and I don't know what to do. Bad luck is mine, it's one of the few times I've taken a photo without asking permission. I ask his forgiveness.

"Promise me that as soon as the roll is developed, you'll destroy it," he orders me. I am only grateful that since he considers me a little crazy too for making this trip he forgives me. When he's finished putting the distributor back together, he tells me.

"Fine, now it's time to start it," and it does like the car never had a problem in the first place. Although I try several times, he doesn't accept any payment. He tells us that he is the thankful one.

Vacation from the System

Guided by the smoke of Arenal Volcano we reach Fortuna, a small town. During the night, we can hear the explosions and see the red light over the crater. Our wish to see a lava-flow hasn't been fulfilled yet. While we wait, we meet an Argentinean who is traveling on a motorcycle from his town to Mexico. He's been on the road for two and a half years and he transformed himself into an artisan when he ran out of money. He looks exactly like "Che" only without the beret. We tell him how we crossed from Colombia into Panama. He also has a story to tell to us.

"In Bogotá I worked for a foreign trade magazine as an ad salesman. In one of the companies I called on, an air cargo company, I met with the manager. He noticed I was Argentinean, he asked me what I was doing there, I told him about my trip on the bike, and that I was working to try to pay for transport to Panama. You know what he said to me? 'You and your bike can fly for free. I traveled all over Europe in a motorcycle and you have no idea the thousands of times I was helped on the road. Now with you I can give back a little of the help I received.'" This touches us. Our fellow citizen asks us, "What do the people say when they see you in this car?"

"All kinds of comments and some of them are very funny. They can't believe the wooden spokes of the wheels, they ask us if the tires are solid rubber, if we're the owners of the car, if the car is rented...can you imagine driving a rented car for two years? Another funny question is when they ask us how many hours it's taken us to get here," we tell him. "There is one question that breaks my heart, because it makes me feel very old: 'Have you had it since it rolled off the showroom floor?' imagine how this makes me feel..." Cande confesses to a chorus of our laughter.

"And don't they tell you that what you're doing is crazy?"

"Sure, thousand of times. Now every time they say it, we thank them. They can't imagine how good this craziness makes us feel."

"It's the same for me. I feel that each one is a unique and special person, but when you let yourself go with the current, you become mediocre. Only dead fish go with the current. We only stand out if we go against the system. Look at me; according to society, I am a hippie. There's nothing wrong with this, as long as I don't hang out with their kids, because for society I'm worthless since I don't have a house or material things. This turns me into a wretch, and because I have a beard and long hair they consider me a rebel, even the ugly duckling. This hippie image is like a shield, a filter; the only ones who approach me are the ones who are interested in what's inside. Those who care about the image don't approach me. I am an arti-sane: my whole being is sane and with it I do my art. I know many things that they don't know."

"And what is it you know?" I inquire of him.

"I know that school, high school and university churns out mediocre people who don't learn what they want to know, but only what the teachers want to teach them. From the best universities have come presidents who took their homeland to war, engineers who constructed gas chambers, physicists who built atomic bombs and doctors who practice abortions. The schools and universities aren't turning out smart people who go on to use tools, but tools to go on to be used by smart people. Look at me; under these summer clothes, under this "hippie clothing," there is a person who studied dentistry because the system required him to study. I had to do it, because if not, in the future, I wouldn't be able to support my family. My future was painted very bleak. In it, there was no room for people without a degree and who didn't know at least, two languages. They told me I had to be prepared, although I didn't feel prepared for the present. I even grew to dread the future. I finished my course and opened my practice and... I felt empty. One day, a patient of the kind that one preferred not to have, complained that I was hurting him. He told me a thing or two, including that I was no dentist...I realized he was right. So I went home thinking about what I really was, what I wanted for sure, what I could do and why I even came to this world. I felt I woke up within myself," he continues his story as we watch him with attention. "Just imagine my parents, so happy to have a son well established in the system, they didn't like my new appraisal of life. They told me that I had studied and worked too hard, that I was stressed out, and that all I needed was a vacation. And here you see me, still on my vacation. A vacation from the system. I don't have a place or a fixed income. Neither do I have any money in the bank," he comments with irony, "...but I have a freedom, happiness and wisdom about things they don't teach in any university..."

"Such as?"

"For example, now I possess more knowledge about people, love, friendship, God and dreams. But I'm still learning, I still haven't graduated: Only my friends, my love, my children, who will be my teachers, may give me the degree."

Nicaragua

Time Waits for No Man

Be careful

After a few more days of continuing up and down the beautiful mountains covered in marvelous green, we leave Costa Rica to enter into "dangerous" Nicaragua as everyone assures us.

It's already late when we enter Nicaragua. This is something strange for us, as we always try to cross the borders early. Here in Central America, it's different, since everything is close and we get places more quickly than what we thought. The countries are smaller and driving long distances without seeing people or some kind of constructions isn't common, as was our experience in South America. Here we pass through countries as quickly as we could cross from one state to another.

Shortly after we enter, it starts getting dark. We see an open gate on our right and we follow the path until we get to a country outpost, with a very simple house, sheltering a large family. All the members come out one after the other at our arrival. They ask us if we have already eaten, while offering us rice and beans and happily show us where we can sleep. This is our welcome to Nicaragua.

Barefooted

We have been recommended to visit Isla de Ometepe, situated in Lake Nicaragua. We take a ferry to get there. The island is beautiful, big, with several beaches and right away, we find a family style hostel in which to stay. In the morning, while Cande paints, I go out for a walk along the dark sand. I come across a man tossing little stones in the water making them skip several times before they go under. I introduce myself and I start a conversation by asking if it's true there are fresh water sharks in this lake.

"There were some time ago. It's been a long time since anybody saw any though, a foreign company fished them all out," the accent of his voice establishes that he isn't Latino, but Spanish. He tells me that he's taking a few days vacation with his girlfriend from his work in El Salvador. "I've been there about two years. In Spain, I worked for a consulting firm. For almost three years, I worked to bring a company back from the brink of bankruptcy. And when I managed to do it was well-stabilized, they cooked up a conspiracy to frame me so they could fire me without having to pay what we had agreed to. Needless to say, I was outraged, then I packed my bag, went to the airport, and bought a ticket. Why to El Salvador? I don't know, I believe it was the first plane out. I came escaping from the law of the jungle, where only the strongest reign. I was looking for some peace. I arrived in El Salvador shortly after an earthquake. Everything was demolished, and walking through the mountains I found destroyed coffee plantations. The small amount the country folks could harvest was paid for in coins," he skips a few more stones and continues, "even so the people invited me into their homes and shared their food. I stayed a few days with them savoring such delicious coffee I've never tasted before. It is a special coffee that grows high in the mountains, in the shade of trees, and is harvested by hand, each bean chosen at the perfect time. Now I have spent two years working with these people; we formed cooperatives, we have our own brand and packaging, we sell to the public directly and now we're even delivering internationally. It changed my life; I'm no longer among people with whom I have to watch out for, now I'm among families who watch out for me."

"Is your girlfriend Salvadorian?"

"No, she's not. She's a woman who came with the 'Doctors without Borders' organization to help after the earthquake. It's her pleasure to give herself to the people and I caught the bug from her, she does it all the time, so much that now we both find ourselves doing it and it's turned into our dream."

"And now? Are you going back to the mountains with your friends?" I ask him marveled at the fact that many people are helping others only for the pleasure that it makes them feel, not because they are filling their pockets, but only their hearts.

"I'm saying good bye to them, the idea is they can go on alone. We will maintain contact and I will continue to help them any way possible. Now I want to be a part of 'Doctors Without Borders'."

"Are you a Doctor?"

"No, and my girlfriend isn't either, but they don't just need doctors. Anyone who has the willingness to help can join them. It doesn't matter where you come from, because it's an international organization. The group my girlfriend is with is building latrines for the schools in the mountains and thousands of other things. They also teach hygiene awareness to the people, as well as how to prevent the spread of a disease." The man continues telling me about marvelous things that make humanity marvelous. It strikes me to thank him and he says it's his pleasure to do it.

The packed ferry sets off on the return trip, jammed with vans and trucks, and many people on foot. It's small. One particularly eye catching vehicle is the latest model of a luxury make, whose owners richly dressed, come to us to ask us about our car and the trip. They are not Nicaraguans and after answering the typical question we all stand silently, until they break it with a commentary.

"How poor this country is! How hard life must be for these people."

It disturbs me a little the way in which he said this and the definition that many have of poverty.

"You see poverty, I see vast riches," I remark, "I see families with many children, which are their greatest fortune. I see families united, numerous; whose grandparents and grand children live together under a roof built by their own hands. You see poverty because you only see what your eyes permit you to see, but you don't live what you see. I lived in these homes, where they don't have guest rooms but there's still a place for one more. Homes where you can always join them for a meal, where you don't have to tell them you're coming in advance. They are homes where there is always life, laughter, tears, noise, games, and children running. Everyone feels useful because everyone contributes some how and they need each other."

"Yes, but...they go around barefooted."

"You're right, they don't have shoes, but I can assure you that these kids run and play more than those that have them. You see a few toys, perhaps broken, but it's because of the use and so much sharing. If they don't have any, they use their imaginations and create a new game out of anything. You see poverty because they don't teach their children to gather, horde, or make money. When they grow up, they will behave the same way they lived when they were children in their houses. The little money they will earn in their work, they will share, opening the doors to whoever passes by. They will give everything to whoever needs it, they will feed their parents, children, cousins, and whoever else is hungry. You see poor houses, I see rich homes. A house is made of bricks, wood, rocks or mud, but a home is made only with love. I measure the richness not by what you can show, but instead by what you have achieved in your life with the things you can't sell or buy," the man has no reply, he merely listens. "If I ask you which three most treasured moments of your life are, what would you tell me?"

"Well..." the man begins thinking. I can see when he remembers something wonderful by the happy expression on his face, then it looks like he remembers another one, and even though it takes a bit more time, he finds a third. "...among the best moments that I remember right now are: the birth of my children, my wedding day and the reconciliation with my father."

"As you see, the best moments in your life are centered around human beings, none of them are about anything material. So why do we try so hard to have more material things? Why don't we go for more of these human moments? This is what makes us rich."

No Armaments or Cells Can Restrain the Human Will

We reach firm ground and Macondo spins to a marvelous city. Granada, founded in 1524, is the oldest city in all of Central America. In its color and style, wholly Colonial, its churches and houses are well preserved. Women in long, flaring skirts with baskets full of fruits on their heads decorate this picturesque city still more. We stay for three days, and at night, we sleep in the garden of a kindly woman who allows us to park there.

Afterward, we continue traveling to the village of San Juan de Oriente. The beauty of its ceramic vases, which we see everywhere, draws our attention and we stop to look at them more thoroughly.

The whole town is dedicated to ceramics and as we walk the place, we observe the way in which they work on them. We are tempted by the price and the excellent quality of handwork, so we think of buying some to sell up the road. We stop at the display of a family that has arranged the stand in front of their house. We pick out only a few pots. We'd like to take more, but we just don't have the money. They are so beautiful, that surely, they would sell very well, we think over an over again.

The lady attending the shop seems to guess our idea and asks us to show her the things we've picked up in other places. So, we begin to trade. Later she calls her nieces and children from other houses to see and exchange their artwork for other handicrafts. I have faith that I can trade one of my *mandalas*, and it's the first thing I show to each one who comes, but none of them is interested.

Shortly afterwards her husband arrives, he's come from the cooperative formed by all the artists. While we have some *panela*, a sugar cane juice, and salted mango slices, he invites us to see how they make the pots. The vases are created in each house, where there is a potter's wheel, a kiln, and drying shelves. In the area there is very special clay that has been used since before the Spanish arrival. Each vessel involves many hands working very delicately and patiently. Each member of the family carries out his own specialty: One throws the pots, one is the designer, another paints on the distinct glazes, another adds the details and another fires them in the kiln. The whole process from throwing to firing takes each piece fifteen days, during which each day they run the risk of breaking, cracking, burning too much or too little, etcetera.

After the man explains the whole process, we understand all the work that is involved. We cannot believe the prices are so low and all the labor so much. Everyone is enthusiastic with our visit and each one wants to teach us his job, we even tried throwing pots!

The man, with his arm around his wife, tells us:

"In my house there is always a little nook for one more, please, stay with us tonight. It would be our pleasure to show you around, if you'd like to."

We happily accept, even though we don't know where we'll sleep, we don't see any space for us. The house has two rooms, one is the shop and the other, is the dormitory where the whole family sleeps together. Outside there is a kitchen and the workshop.

They take us to overlook a spot named "Caterina", from where we can see Lake Nicaragua and the big city of Granada. While we talk about the country, its civil wars and the guerrillas, the man tells us horrors that come with every war, for example, relatives being slain. Nevertheless, he speaks without anger or hatred; he speaks with forgiveness, with the idea of constructing a new Nicaragua:

"Tomorrow doesn't exist, because when we believe that tomorrow has arrived we are still in the present. It's like the horizon that you never reach. The past is gone, and it's only an experience to live the present. It serves no purpose to hope for a better tomorrow or to live in the past, the only thing we have in our hands is today and we have to live it with all of our being," his words capture us, we want to hear more.

"I've heard they have expropriated many large land holdings," I comment.

"It isn't expropriating the land, but restoring it to the natives," he looks at me in the face and says with a calm voice, "it's only a drop of justice in a sea of injustice. Now that the war has ended, we are achieving a lot, but it has to be remembered that neither armaments nor cells can restrain the human will. It is possible to kill the flesh, but not an ideal. The truth can be distorted, but it can never be suppressed…" with these few words he said it all, and his short speech isn't just for Nicaragua.

When we get back to the house, they create a space for us in the shop. Everybody helps put cardboard and newspapers on the floor to protect us from the humidity. Over these, we lay our sleeping bags knowing that it will be a hard night and that we could sleep much better in the car, but we are at home.

We wake up to the shouts of some young kids walking around selling plantains, pulling behind them a little cart while dogs announce their presence. Although the sun still hasn't come up, there is enough light in front of it for them to be preparing us a breakfast of *gallo pinto* a mixture of beans with eggs. After savoring meal all together, like a family, we say good-bye with tight hugs and receiving blessings for the rest of our journey.

We load the car with bulky ceramic jugs that need to wait a while to be sold. We travel toward the sunset, the summit, the horizon. On the way, we see the washerwomen beneath the bridges, scrubbing in the rivers, their legs immersed up to their knees. Spreading out the clothes over the branches, fences, grass and rocks, they cover everything in beautiful colors. The boys are playing around, the girls, for their part, help their moms with the washing.

Managua

We get to Managua, the capital. We enter the city via one of the main avenues choosing to drive in the slow lane. We cross an important street and within a half a block, we're stopped by a police officer.

He asks for my driver's license and after I give it to him, the official tells me:

"At the last corner, you were in the turn lane and you didn't turn, you continued on straight. For this reason, I am going to keep your driver's license…"

In a quick snatch I take it back, leaving him with his eyes wide open.

"Nobody keeps my documents. If you want to, we can go to the headquarters and talk about it there." I confront him.

The exasperated patrolman, tells me he has the authority and a thousand other things. I insist on going to the headquarters without handing over anything. His partner approaches him, calms him down and after a few words they let us go.

We happen to have gotten to Managua during a citywide celebration. Through its streets parade costumed groups and thousand of horses from all over Nicaragua. We amuse ourselves watching them pass by. Cande is invited to ride on an ox cart. She launches herself up in a single bound; when it comes to having fun, she's ready! Immediately a monkey up there grabs onto her and won't let her move, the same with a man disguised as death and another dressed as a skeleton. The whole crowd laughs with the farewell gestures they make toward me from the cart.

I am among the multitude waving at Cande, when three young guys take advantage of my distraction. I feel something in my pocket, and with a quick movement, I capture the intruding hand and I say to one of the boys, "You're in the wrong pocket, this one is mine."

The boy looks at me astonished, then he smiles and goes away together with his friends.

Time Doesn't Wait

After Managua, we head towards Leon, from where we depart for the beaches in Poneloya. On the way, a car stops us and the family invites us to their house, which is in Leon.

Their home is a colonial construction, like almost the whole city, with its inner patio surrounded by a gallery. In the afternoon, they invite us to sit out, on the narrow sidewalk, in the rocking chairs, as all the neighbors in the city do. Those who walk must constantly dodge the seated folks and greet them as well. We talk while we rock.

"I also had my dream and I wanted to accomplish it, to go to Europe. During my youth, I worked very hard towards this end. And when I had gathered the necessary money, I was doing so well that I kept working to save even more. Later came a financial crisis and I found myself with no work and no money. So I began to work again until there was another crisis. In the end I never made it there: either because I had a lot of work or because I didn't have any..."

"And now, why not?" interrupted Cande.

"I don't know, maybe I'm old, maybe I have idealized it too much...and now I am afraid it won't turn out to be that way. Who knows, perhaps it's only a dream and maybe the dream is more important than going. I don't know but maybe I prefer imagining walking the streets of Europe than remembering having walked along them. Sincerely, I don't know, maybe I'll go, maybe not. I'm not sure what I want, I don't even know what I want out of my life. It seems that you do know what you want, God willing, you'll never forget."

"Forget what?" I ask him.

"What you want out of life, the dreams you'd like to fulfill during it."

The man remains silent, rocking his chair. He knows I'm observing him. I look in his eyes and in silence, I wish him God's blessings and that he may accomplish his dream. I wish this for him with all of my being, because I know the huge difference between accomplishing what is yearned for and imagining it.

Anyway, his look tells me that he knows nothing in his life is going to change, but even so he appreciates it. We remain like this for a long while. Maybe it's dreaming that keeps him alive. Perhaps he thinks his dream can wait a while longer, but time waits for no one. The days don't have extensions, nor does death accept deferral.

Everything Is there and it Exists for You

We go to the central plaza to see how the people amuse themselves on a Sunday. We are talking with the artists when another family invites us to go tomorrow to their residence in Poneloya.

This place is so attractive and the house has an extraordinary panoramic view of the sea. The woman tells us that in years gone by, they were great land holders, with many properties, but due to some government, they lost everything. Some lose, many gain: many lose, few gain…from some they expropriate, to others they restore.

We watch the sea and we want so much to touch it, so Cande and I go out for a walk along the beach. We are almost the only ones. It's cloudy and it's a weekday, we only see one other person walking up ahead of us.

Suddenly it starts to rain interrupting our romantic hand-in-hand walk. We start to run and when we pass the man, who is still walking, we hear him say, "Why are you running if it is also raining up ahead?"

We continue to trot thinking about what he said. He's right, it's still raining, we are already wet and there is nothing wrong with that. We stand still and wait for him to catch up. He arrives with a smile, "Don't you love to feel the blessed drops coming from the sky?"

"Yes, we love it, but whenever it rains, we run. Since our first memories we've been doing this."

"You can change, one is always led to the change, and one has to change the way of looking at things. One is in a place and at the same time the place is in one."

"I believe I have felt this, that I am a part and that everything is there for me." I stammer remembering Machu Picchu and that unforgettable moment when I felt I was a king.

"Is the sky the stars', or are the stars the sky's? The tree forest or the forest trees? Humanity of man or the man of humanity? Which is your point of view? Which is more important?" he inquires. "Both are at the same level. Because, what's the point of one without the other and vice versa? Never feel that you are not important nor that if you're not here, nothing changes. Everything is there and it exists for you. In the whole humanity there is no one who is more or less important than you."

"Excuse me, but have you been thinking about all of this while you were walking or do you say this to everyone running past you on a rainy day?" I ask him. He looks me in the eyes:

"Do you believe in coincidences?"

"No, not any more."

"So why are you asking?" his interrogation leaves me absorbed. The three of us remain in silence for a few minutes, the rain continuing to refresh us. Then he asks Cande, "Which has been the best moment of your life?"

"Right now," she responds.

"What do you mean? Haven't you had any better ones?"

"The best thing I have is what I have right now, what I have in my hands, it is the present," responds Cande, surely.

"You know that you have a treasure in this young lady?"

"Yes, I know. I feel I am the richest man on earth."

La Griteria

The next day we come back to Leon, because it's a fiesta day. Today they are celebrating *La Griteria*, which means the shouting. The whole town fills the streets with their presence. The people go from house to house, knocking on the doors or the windows and whoever opens asks in a loud voice, "What causes such happiness?" to which those outside respond shouting, "The assumption of the Virgin Mary!". So, those in the houses hand out gifts, they can be food, tasty tidbits, pencils, or things to use around the house, anything goes.

Very excitedly, we take part in the party and go around shouting from door to door. The villagers have set up flowered alters in their homes for the Virgin Mary. Everything is festively decorated, in harmony with their faces full of happiness. The whole town is one giant party.

We knock on the door of the family who hosted us the first time we arrived here, that of the man who postponed his dream. We go in and change roles. Now, from inside, we are giving away the gifts we received before to everyone who passes by shouting. We are delighted by seeing the faces illuminated through the windows, while we are told that this celebration originated when the city was destroyed after the eruption of a volcano and an earthquake. They say it was the Virgin who managed to stop the destruction and that therefore all the people shared the little they still had offering to others what they needed to be able to survive.

A New Graham

Before we get to the border with Honduras, next to a family house we see a cart pulled by oxen. We stop to take some pictures next to it, so we could prove that vehicles slower than ours exist. All the family comes out to meet us. I ask them if we could attach the bull to the car and haul it like a cart. Its owner, delighted with the idea, unhooks the cart and exchanges it for our car.

For a stretch we abandon the fifty horsepower engine to experience two oxen power. Everyone enjoys the ride, even the animals seem pleased. After we take some photos, Cande writes the names of the people and asks the names of each animal:

"This one is called Joaquin," comments the wife, "but this one is new and he doesn't have a name yet."

"Yes, he does, from now on he'll be called 'Graham'," I interrupt while baptizing the ox with a pat on its head.

Honduras

Gateway to the Mayan World

When You Grow, Humanity Grows

We enter Honduras and getting close to Choluteca town, we stop at a little family restaurant. The mom is cooking, the eldest son serves, the daughter does the cleaning, the little siblings play and the husband works outside.

We are the only ones in the place, it could be because it is late, or merely because we are their only customers for today. They serve us the menu of the day; which is a little portion of chicken, white rice and beans. We ask if they will let us sleep in the car next to their restaurant. The woman asks us to wait, and goes out to consult her husband and comes back in with him:

"No way, I can 't let you do that. We will put you up in a little place we have," the husband tells us.

No matter how many times we tell them it's not necessary, we can sleep in the car very comfortably; they don't want to hear anything about it. They start to get a room ready for us separate from their home. It's a quite simple construction, adobe walls, thatched roof and a door of wood planks full of holes. We have a candle for light and sleep on a bed stuffed with who-knows-what that's very comfortable, surrounded by bags of seeds, a wheelbarrow and tools. We're charmed by our surroundings, by the atmosphere but mostly by the welcome to Honduras.

We shower very early in a small bath that is next to the house that consists of only three sides, no roof and a curtain that doesn't cover much. We bathe with well water, cold, that we provide for one another with a hand pump.

After the fresh shower, we go into the restaurant greeting the whole family, who don't allow us to pay for breakfast arguing that we have brought them blessings. The car parked in front of the restaurant attracted many passers by, who then decided to eat.

We begin to hear questions from the tables near ours. The first comes from a man who, trying to use very broken English, asks us where we're from:

"We're Argentinean, we speak Spanish."

"Ah, bueno, meester, me be your friend. Gwelcom to Honduras."

"Many thanks for the welcome, but we are from Argentina," I explain again as he continues to try to speak to me in English.

"He speaks quite well, 'the Meester'," he comments to his table companion.

"Are you trying to break a record to be in the 'Guinness' book?" we hear from another table.

"No, that's not the goal. We don't want to beat anybody, only gain a bit of life out of this life. Anyway, the book of records doesn't include everyone, nor the most important ones."

"Who has the world record of loving the most? Of helping the most? Who has fulfilled the most dreams? These are the records that matter," adds the lady of the house, happy to be the hostess, while directing her gaze over all the tables.

"Doesn't that nice old car break down?" we hear from the front.

"So far, it has not. But if it does, we'll fix it, it's very simple. The people help us a lot, the mechanics and antique auto clubs always give us a hand and make sure everything is in working order."

"What would happen if something broke inside the engine?" they ask from another table.

"God and Virgin Mary wouldn't allow it," says the owner as she quickly makes the sign of the cross.

"Listen, I believe that we need to worry about a breakdown the day we breakdown. I'm not going to worry about something that hasn't happened and may never happen."

"But you must be prepared..."

"I am prepared. First, because I don't make up problems, second, because I know that every problem comes with a solution, and third, because I have faith in myself and also in God, I know we will find a solution. Meanwhile, I am enjoying the present without having problems and without imagining them."

"But you should know..." he insists.

"Hey, don't be such a pessimist, O.K.?" someone shouts from another table. It's as if we're all in a coffee club chat.

"That guy's right. Let everything flow; make room for some positive energy," shouts another.

"How do you cook? How do you wash your clothes? Where do you sleep?"

"We eat and sleep, many times, in the homes of families who invite us. As it happens, I want you to give a hand to the owners of this place, who invited us to spend the night, giving us a wonderful welcome to Honduras," I request.

The lady blushes and bows to her public who is applauding. When the room calms, the questions return.

"But, how do you know the people? Are they friends? Have you contacted them beforehand? How?"

"We get to a place and people come to us, because of the car. But also because of the inscriptions that are written all over the car. Their questions start: 'Where are you from, where are you going?' 'What are you doing, how and where do you usually sleep?' To this last question we respond 'Wherever they invite us,' and immediately someone does. Nevertheless, there are many times when they offer their hospitality spontaneously. At other times, we ask ourselves."

"Yes, but…" the pessimist interrupts again, all eyes in the place on him, "how do you know they won't rob you? Not everyone in the world is good."

"And how do they know that we won't rob them?" I counter-argue. "The people open the doors of their homes with their hearts and we take with us the most valuable thing they have, their affection."

"Excuse me for being indiscreet, but where do you bathe?"

"Why are you asking so many questions? This is something personal," shouts a guy suddenly getting to his feet.

"Although you might not believe it, during this trip, we bathe more than at home," responds Cande, "it might be in a river, in a house or at the side of the car, with a bucket."

"What's your final destination?"

"In this trip, Alaska. In the journey of life, the horizon. It will be until I get to it."

"So, why are you doing it?"

"Just to accomplish our dream. Because life becomes a dream when you go for it and with all the help we receive little by little it becomes everyone's dream."

"When you complete your dream, you're not only fulfilling yourself, but also everyone who ever helped you; your parents, your life, the Creator and the world. Accomplishing your dream you grow as all humanity does," states a man leaving everyone perplexed.

We get to our feet and the lady covers us with grateful kisses for having stopped at her restaurant. We dedicate a book to her and leave it as a gift. Everyone comes outside to watch us start the car, to wave and shout farewell blessings.

A Reason to Be

We cross Honduras almost coast to coast to visit a coral reef in the Caribbean. We board a ferry to get to Utila, a very tiny island consisting basically of one main road traveled only by quadricycles and electric carts. This island is full of people of every nationality who come specifically to dive, it's one of the most beautiful and economical places in the world to do it.

We find a very inexpensive room with a veranda situated right over the turquoise sea. We stay a week celebrating another mini honeymoon during those days. In addition to diving and the snorkeling, we also cover the whole island on foot and discover although it's great for diving, it has very few beaches.

There is a small one, next to the miniature-unpaved airport. The colors of its corals and the fish invite one to spend hours and hours there. Every day we go and see the same faces as always and others that vary.

A group of six Italians, here for the first time, ask us about the best place for snorkeling. We explain that first, they need to swim about 45 feet, then walk across a huge sand bar and past that, in the sea, they will find a marvelous reef, with thousands of fish to watch.

Five leave on the expedition, but one of the girls of the group lags behind, it seems as if she doesn't really want to go. When she sees Cande getting ready to go back into the water, the slightly timid girl asks if she could go with her. Cande agrees with no problem.

The young woman puts on her mask and begins to follow Cande, until they get to the part where they have to swim. Cande swims away submerged under the water while the Italian begins swimming without going anywhere. She stays in that spot moving her arms and her head in a haphazard way, not moving forward. Cande calls her to follow. She can't see the young woman's terrorized face, but she senses something is wrong because the girl is going under and coming back up to the surface without taking off her snorkel. Cande swims back to her as fast as she can and when she is close enough, the girl, in her desperation, pulls Cande down. She is having a panic attack. She isn't swimming, she's only making rough movements, and when she raises her head, she swallows more water through her snorkel. Cande is able to snatch the girl's mask off permitting her to inhale a huge mouthful of air. She coughs repeatedly, while Cande calms her and slowly, little by little, brings her back to the beach.

The young woman thanks her for something Cande still doesn't quite realize. "*Tante grazie, tante grazie,*" she says many times, crying in fright.

Cande doesn't react until that evening, when we meet the girl again in the little street and she repeats: "*Molto Grazie*. Thank you so much, I can't tell you how much I appreciate what you did today," she says while she opens her arms to embrace Cande.

"I never thought I'd have the opportunity to save a life, to be responsible for one. I acted without realizing what I was doing, but now I get it. To live, how beautiful it is to live! Nowadays for me, every breath, laugh or cry is always a precious gift. Every moment of my life counts and it's the best thing I have. I can't imagine losing it in a minute, but she was at the point of drowning. Fortunately, I realized about it and now she has another chance," thinks Cande while we walk down the main street, "everything has a reason for being, what will hers be?"

We continue walking; Cande meditates a bit more about what happened. "Today I saved a life, Herman experienced death very intimately in Ecuador and we both were part of a new life in Costa Rica." These events are very intense and all happened within a very short time…they make us think and learn a thousand different things all at once.

Mayan Route

We begin the Mayan route in Copan. They are our first Mayan ruins and we are stunned by the quality and beauty of the construction. We walk among pyramids and temples seeing with each step unusual things for our eyes. We lie down in its central plaza filling ourselves with its energy.

Our next stop is Gracias, a village forgotten in time, lost in the mountains, and surrounded by coffee plantations. We walk its cobblestone streets lined with houses. All doors and windows are covered with grillwork that starts at the ground and goes all the way up to the roof.

In the afternoon, everybody opens their windows so the fresh air can come in with the scarce breeze. We stop when we see through an open door a painter who is working seated in front of a huge canvas.

"What an ideal place to paint!" Cande comments initiating a conversation.

The painter, a young guy with a dark beard, invites us in, to see his paintings and go round his enormous colonial house. He tells us his great grandfather built it to conquer his love. He had promised her to build a house with the biggest interior courtyard in the village where she could grow flowers from all over Central America. No one believed his words because he wasn't a wealthy man, nevertheless he finished the house and married his love.

"How do you paint? Do you have a particular style or method?" Cande asks the man admiring his paintings with an eye on perfecting her own style.

"It's relative, like everything else. I don't know. One day I use one technique; the next day I change it. In school I learned: my abc's, the order of factors doesn't alter the product, gravity is proportional to the mass of the object and inversely proportional to the distance, Pi is 3.14, water is H_2O, all objects expand with heat, every movement uses energy… They taught me that this is the way it is, the only way."

"However, when I was almost finished with my studies, they taught me there is a law which says that everything is relative, even this law. So, if someone tells you this is like this or if not, it is not. It's because he didn't study to the end. Otherwise he would know that everything he has learned is relative."

"Therefore, I don't have one certain way of doing things, I paint relatively. I carry this knowledge along my life; I've learned that nothing is for sure or forever. All we are and know can belong to history tomorrow."

"Would you like to buy some apples?" interrupts a little girl who is peeking in the window with a basket full of the red fruits. We buy three and she goes away as happy as the colors of her beautiful dress.

Two tourists we met told us that to enter El Salvador, they had to pay a lot of money for their vehicle. Therefore, we go and introduce ourselves at the embassy before entering the country and asked them to write a letter of recommendation for us, mostly to see if we could avoid paying the tax.

We leave for El Salvador with the letter that they wrote for us without any problems. But they did clarify we weren't exempt from any fines or charges. Off we go to El Salvador…

El Salvador

It Looks Small, but It Feels Big

Occupation: Globe Trotter

The comments people have made us about El Salvador are similar to the alerts we have received about Colombia and Nicaragua. With these thoughts we get to the border with El Salvador and just as every time when we leave one country for another we experience a mixed sensation of nervousness and peace.

As soon as we leave Honduras behind, we park to do the formalities. But before we even roll to a stop we are invaded by many children who offer to complete the paperwork for us. Also, the money changers appear with hundreds of bills in their hands, police, military, the curious, travelers and opportunists of carelessness. Several ask questions at the same time, a group tells anecdotes about others who have passed this way and some speak about their own trips… It's difficult to concentrate on the forms.

"In four hours, you'll get to Guatemala," a boy informs me, "It's less than a hundred and twenty five miles away."

"I buy your *Lempiras*, I sell you *Colones*," insists a money changer whom I avoid to present myself at the window of immigration while Cande waits in the car.

They hand me a form to fill out: "Full Name:" Herman Zapp. "Place of Residence:" Argentina (I really want to write "earth dweller", but that might cause a problem). "Occupation:" Globe Trotter, I respond and go on to fill in the rest of the form. When the official reads my paper, he asks without understanding:

"Occupation, 'globe trotter'? Explain this."

"I've been going from one place to another for more than two years," I tell him, "this is why I consider myself a traveler, a 'globe trotter'."

"Are you a millionaire?"

"Yes, everything that I want most, I have."

"Watch out what you say around here," he advises me.

"You say that because I might get robbed? My fortune doesn't consist of bills, most of it is intangible."

"Great, very nice, but what do you do for a living??" he pushes me.

"I chase dreams."

Relentlessly, the official exhales and stamps my passport signaling me to the customs window, where I have to do the paper for the car. The children intercept me again on the way, they all keep offering at the same time as the change sellers continue insisting on selling *colones*. Unfortunately, experience has taught us that they are the worst ones with whom to change money and also some children are used to blackmail tourists.

"Good afternoon, I'd like to speak to the Head Customs Officer. I have a letter for him," I ask the employee at the window, who immediately calls his boss, who comes out to see me. I show him the car, he is well pleased, then I hand over the letter. After reading it, he asks me:

"What do you need from us?"

"If you would please help us with the entry tax for the car, every bit saved helps us go farther."

"You know, it's not that much, it's only…"

"Just the same, it would really help us a lot," I insist.

"But, I'm telling you that…"

"Please, every coin counts, every penny helps."

The man takes our papers and in fifteen minutes comes back with everything ready and stamped. He comments that one of the agents paid the tax. I thank him for the gesture and take the papers, I say goodbye and return in the direction of the car. I see Cande surrounded by many people. We take pictures, as is our custom at every border and we pull away joyfully.

"So, how did the tax payments go?" she asks me intrigued.

"I showed him the letter and I asked him not to charge me as a favor and I got it!" telling her very happy for saving some colones.

"Genius, honey! You deserve a kiss!" She takes my cheeks in her hands and gives me a smooch. "How much would it have been?" I give her the papers to look over. Out loud she reads the tax, "Payment for vehicular entrance: One Dollar."

"A dollar?!? You've got to be kidding me!" Cande must be pulling my leg! So I stop to look at the papers with my own eyes. "Did I go through all that fuss for a dollar?"

We laugh our heads off, but at the same time, we're dying of embarrassment. All that clamor and agitation that I did just to look like a miser. Shame on me! Thinking about it again, surely those tourists that told us there was a high tax were cheated.

The Circus World

The first little village to visit is Santa Rosa de Lima as we were told this is festival time. Covering the main street there are hundreds of stands with all types of games, music and foods. There are families everywhere laughing and celebrating. It's party time!

At the end of the street there are two small circuses, whose patched canvas, faded signs, and dim lights don't promise a grand spectacle. Even still there are shouts of clowns in sad costumes and women in fishnet stockings with some holes at the entrance inviting everyone to come in.

We choose to go into the "Emperor" circus. We sit on one of the few benches in front of the diminutive stage. The master of ceremonies is also the light man and disc jockey and at the end of the show, he also appears dressed as a clown. The same occurs with the cashier and other members of the circus, who come on to the stage dressed up as differing characters.

The clowns that appear at the end of each act play up to Cande and me, and include us as part of the show. We participate shamelessly, being the laughing stock of the whole show. We have to do pirouettes, juggling, throwing up balls and catching them along with plenty of other gags, until the arrival of the knife thrower.

Now, the cashier, dressed as the assistant, leans against a wooden door while music of suspense begins. Around her, the thrower hurls the knives one by one. Some of them pierce the door too close to the woman, leaving everyone breathless and silent. For the following act, he asks for a volunteer from the audience while eyeing Cande and extending his hand to her to come onstage, but she's not crazy enough to accept. The knife thrower insists until a drunk, who can hardly keep to his feet, saves us. He can't stand still in front of the plank and everyone laughs, but more out of uneasiness than amusement. However, the thrower isn't fazed by the drunken movements and lobs the blades masterfully one at a time. At the end, he receives a well-deserved, long, loud round of applause.

That night, we sleep in the Graham. All the drunken people milling around worry me a bit, but in the car, I feel more protected than ever. I hear the rabble-rousers pass beside this small and delicate car, in a strange street in a remote village in this side of the world unknown to us. Despite how fragile I'm feeling. I close my eyes to sleep as a child sleeps with his parents. This is because I can see in each corner of the car a guardian angel in a sentinel position watching over us. There are four and they are able to deter anyone, even though they carry no weapons. These angels never rest nor stop, exactly like my willingness to achieve this dream.

You Can't Do It Alone

The next day we take the coastal road, on the way, many Salvadorans stop us to greet us and bid us welcome. They invite us to stop for a drink with them or eat pupusas. We accept only on with the condition that they let us keep going as soon as we're finished. We want to move along a bit faster, but due to the number of invitations we can progress very slowly. There were countless offers.

Why is it that when a country suffers or has suffered excessively its people are more prepared to open their homes and to help? Those who have lost everything

including their loved ones, because of a war or an earthquake, like those in Colombia, Nicaragua, and El Salvador, want to share what little they have left.

We talk about this with a family who is our host and who that has too many heartbreaking stories about the war. "During a catastrophe or a war, you can't do it alone. You need others and they need you. One helps another and that one helps someone else simply to survive. It's a lesson you learn that sticks to you. A society that doesn't need others becomes isolated. There are cities with millions of inhabitants in which everyone feels lonelier than on a desert island. Riches isolate, adversity unites. Many people in the world who come to help tell us that in the short time they stay here they make more friends than they've ever had in their whole lives. They tell us we looked like the poor ones, but now they realize it is them who are poor."

Conquering Distances and Borders

In the beach town of Libertad, we stay at an economical hotel frequented by surfers and travelers. There are people from all over. As soon as we get there, a group of young tourists invites us to their bonfire. Among the members of the group there are two Colombian brothers who have been here for about a month. They have come overland from Colombia and their destination is Miami where their parents are. One is 19 years old. The younger one is 16.

"Because of the ominous situation in Colombia, our parents wanted to take us to live in Miami. They had heard that we were on a list of potential people to be kidnapped, to be held for ransom. Therefore, they sold everything and we moved to Bogotá to request visas for the United States. But they ran into the big snag that if they had asked for visas for all of us we would have all been turned down, so what they had to do was to request tourist visas only for themselves. They traveled and as soon as they got to the airport, they applied for political asylum, because then they could ask for us and we could all be together again.

However, it was not granted. My brother and I didn't know what to do. We didn't want our parents to come back to Colombia for us, so we wrote them a letter telling them, 'We're on the way', we picked up the few things we had and hit the road," the older brother tells us.

"How did you get so far?" we ask the younger one.

"We crossed the Darien on foot, where we were robbed of several things including our passports and documents. But because we're Colombians, they really didn't serve us well anyway. In almost every country, we have to apply for visas and almost always, we're rejected merely for being Colombians. In any case, you can't imagine how terrible it is not to have anything that says who you are and where you're from. Being undocumented is the same as being nothing. From Panama, we have tried to cross at jungle borders or with the help of truck drivers and some good Samaritans. In Nicaragua, we had to give our camera to a guard who was going to deport us," the younger one tells us. We are very intrigued about the rest of the story of these brothers and listen attentively. "On the way we slept in the rain, freezing to death, we ate whatever we could find in the trash. Although, there were always those who wanted to help us and lodge us. Even though we could have been thieves or assassins, they opened their doors and gave us a place to stay, work, some kind of help…many mothers who already had various mouths to feed told us they were doing it because they are mothers and because they wished if someday some of their own children needed help, they would get it."

"Do your parents know where you are?" inquires Cande.

"Yes, shortly after we got to El Salvador we let them know, they were desperate. But we didn't want to go through big cities, only the small towns. We are afraid of being deported or locked up, we don't have any documents and because of this, they can do anything they want to us."

"What are you doing now?"

"We've been received marvelously here, we even gained back the weight we lost. Maybe it's because the people here have a lot of relatives in exile and they know how terrible it is. I work fixing surf boards," the elder tells us. "I'm even learning how to surf. I never imagined how exciting it is!"

"Now we need to raise/collect enough money to cross Mexico," the other brother explains, "Guatemala will be no problem, but Mexico, will. That is where they search the hardest for people like us. Later, we'll need to enter the United States. We know that will be difficult, but you have no idea the desire we have to be with mom and dad. That's where we're going, hopefully before Christmas."

We're talking to two guys who although they are still in their teens, are already men. They struggle but are committed, running thousands of risks, devoted to accomplish their dream. This discrimination for the sake of borders hurts so much. How many families remain separated just because of it! It's painful, it hurts deeply in the soul.

The two following days that we stay in Libertad, we hang out with those brothers and we mutually encourage to keep on living. At our parting, we give them a couple of postcards, a book and between its pages, a few dollars to continue their long journey.

Plucking the Heart Strings

When we arrive in San Salvador we go to the Argentinean Embassy to ask about somewhere to stay. The ambassador personally makes a few calls and tells us "You have two options. Option A: A house on the coast that we rent among four families, or Option B: The residence of the Embassy." We choose "B" to be in the city and get to know it.

The next day, the ambassador and his wife invite us to eat in a restaurant that also sells books. They read a lot and are enchanted by our written work. The parts they most admire are the narratives about the people we meet on the road. They ask us about this and we reveal that people we meet usually tell us incredible things about their lives and their dreams. We are amazed but don't understand why the people say what they say, why they're so sincere with us, why they show us their open hearts so frankly. They don't know us yet they confess their truths.

"Because you are unexpected visitors," the wife responds, "a breath of fresh air for the soul, a pluck at the heart strings, a wake-up call. You make us remember our dream, you make us question ourselves what we're doing for our lives, for our dream, for our love... Many of us have to make an effort to even remember what our dream was, which is so tucked away in our heart and we don't even remember it. Now that I know you, I can tell you that those who cross paths with you experience this feeling again. In some way, we confess to you because you show the truth of life and inspire us to achieve our own dreams. You're doing something that we've always wanted to do. We are frustrated adventurers, we are frustrated dreamers…but now we see a light at the end of the tunnel."

Helping, a Marvelous Sensation

In Suchitoto, a beautiful little town surrounded by coffee plantations. We take the opportunity to continue selling our books, as we have been doing in all the countries of Central America.

As usual, we also check our emails and that makes us feel so happy. Today we read a very special message from a girl from Costa Rica whom we've met on our journey, writing from Spain. She had always wanted to go there to study and work, but many senseless fears and excuses impeded her, until she met us. She's completing her dream thanks to our book. She dropped everything and left. Although still without a job, she's happy to be there. As we read we become happy for her, because we know that she will do well, because whoever takes the gamble for what he or she wants, can't go wrong. Thanks to her, we experienced what the people feel when they help us in this dream, because now it's our turn to be part of someone else's dream. In some way, we have helped her and it's a marvelous sensation.

Happy for this event, we continue the Mayan route in the direction of Guatemala. As we pass by the ruins of San Andrés, we stop to take some shots. This place is full of mosquitoes and worse than that, Cande steps on an anthill. The itching makes all the photos to come out blurry.

"Another mosquito bit me, I can't keep taping…" she comments annoyed.

'My love, if I were a mosquito, I'd eat you up and if I were an ant, I'd carry you back to my nest…" this way I get another kiss.

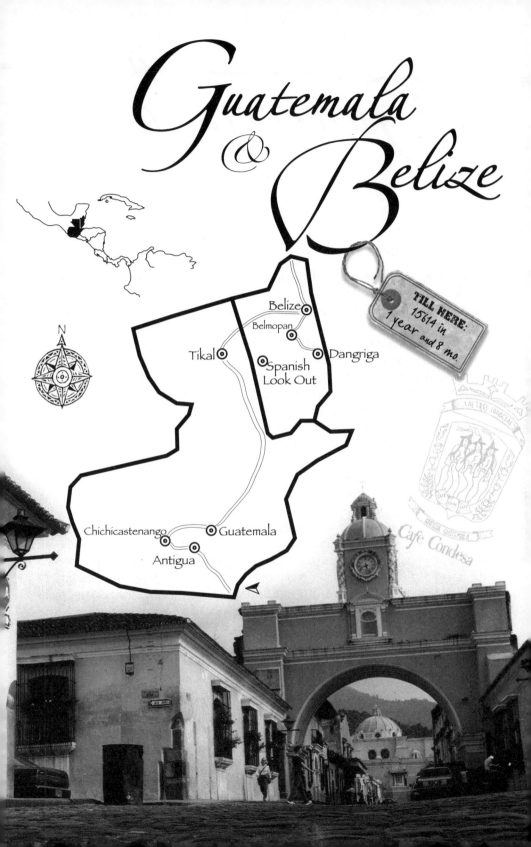

Guatemala & Belize

TILL HERE:
15614 in
1 year and 8 mo.

Belize
Belmopan
Tikal
Spanish
Look Out
Dangriga

N

Chichicastenango — Guatemala
Antigua

Café Condesa

Guatemala

A Colorful Land

Clowns Without Borders

Among volcanoes and coffee plantations we find the tiny town of Antigua, wich is completely colonial. Our idea is to walk its streets, spend the night and continue the trip, but as we get to know it, we discover it will be hard to leave so quickly.

After negotiating the price a bit, we get a room in a hostel, and room for the car in the inside patio. It causes a stir among the backpackers who originate from many corners of the world. We introduce ourselves to more than thirty who surround the Graham while we tell them about the trip. One at a time, they tell us of their own incredible experiences.

During the conversation, we all sit in a circle and share our mate tea. When they try it, some make a face of disgust but others really like it. Two guys introduce themselves as "Clowns Without Borders" an organization that goes around making children happy. Town-to-town and country-to-country, their aim is simply to spread happiness. Everyone is captivated by their story, and we ask them to tell us more.

"We go into some village, put up our puppet tent and right away the children start to gather. Their happiness attracts the parents. In this way, we start to break the ice and little by little, we become a part of the society. Once we're part of it, we can teach them how to plant a garden, build bathrooms, or other things that improve the quality of life for children. But, above all, we're dedicated to be with the kids, teaching them games, songs, doing art…" As we listen we explode into a joyful ovation.

"How much do they pay you?" inquires one who thinks that now-a-days nothing is for nothing, that money moves the world and controls everything.

The clown takes his time to answer, then says "At this moment someone is writing a love song, another is taking care of someone who's sick or visiting a stranger in a hospital because no one has gone to see him in awhile. In this minute, there's a teacher, who earns very little, instructing a child to read. Right now there is someone defending a nearly extinct animal and another, a tree. There are millions of people not generating any money, for them its all about love, and they are, in reality, what moves the world. Have you ever loved someone?"

"Yes, of course, my wife, my kids, my par...."

"Have you made money off them?"

"Certainly not, but...."

"Just like you felt the call from love to do things for your wife and kids, surely some day you will receive the call to help others in exchange for a smile, a hug, or simply for a feeling of enormous peace inside yourself. I don't know what will make you do it, and who knows, maybe you won't know either, but that call will come; it comes to everyone. I hope you will listen," the clown without borders says to him. He continues, "The same question was also put to me by a friend from my old job in Europe, where I was doing very well." He pauses to finish his mate and gives it back to Cande thanking her, "This is what I told him: 'Juancho is a nine year old boy whose parents are already in the fields working by the time he gets up. He wakes his brothers up, makes them breakfast and then they all go to school together. Later, when they get home, he fixes lunch for them and walks 3 miles to get to where I am to help me set up the puppet show. When we're done with that, he accompanies me in the task of inviting the kids to come and play. One day I asked him who is his favorite hero, because I wanted to make a puppet out of it. He told me that it was me and that when he gets big he wants to be just like me." We all remain tenderly hushed, "What better payment could one have!? What could be better than knowing you're a child's hero?"

"Do you know what you are doing? You are changing the world," comments Cande, her eyes bright with emotion.

A Mutual Desire

Later, alone in our small room, Cande and I start talking about a marvelous topic that we talked about a short ago. One day we touched on the subject and discovered that both of us independently have been thinking about the same thing at the same time...about having a child.

Neither of us brought up this idea before because we thought it would be crazy for Cande to travel while pregnant, giving birth along the way, far from home and continuing the trip with a baby, considering all the care a baby means. Plus, we're a long way from our families and have almost no money.

However, we opened the floodgates and unleashed our enormous desire to be a family. We are captivated by this conversation and we don't want it to end.

We've been married for about eight years and now we're both feeling a huge desire to be parents. We are experiencing the best time of our lives and we feel more prepared than ever. Yes, we have fears, but above all, we have a lot of faith. We know it will be marvelous.

We have been together for eighteen years, almost two decades of imagining our future surrounded by children who will bring immense joy to our lives, company, happiness and many other things. Now the future is present: we want to be parents.

On the other hand, something worries us: Will we be able to? We 're afraid it might not be possible, because during the years we've been married, we've only practiced natural birth control and besides, Cande isn't regular. Her sister has tried every treatment possible to conceive, without any positive results. Obviously, we're scared, and we need to talk about it some more, so we put the conversation aside until tomorrow.

Humanity Attacked

We are having breakfast on the patio with some Israelis, Cande is painting, very inspired. Suddenly some kids run into the hostel screaming like crazy. Everyone gathers around them to find out what is wrong; they clutch their heads, in anguish and pain. There is a young woman who explodes into tears, screaming, "A plane crashed into one of the twin towers in New York!"

Immediately one of the Israelis, Cande and I go out to find a television. We find one in a very old convent converted into a hotel. The images are horrible. A few minutes later, we don't understand what's happening, it seems like they are broadcasting a repeat of the airplane crashing into the tower, but no…now it's the other tower in flames, and shortly after the Pentagon and another plane… They're talking about thousands of deaths, without truly knowing how many there are. The images don't cease: people running, towers collapsing, wreckage. We are disturbed to our souls, without comprehending what is happening. Cande is crying from the images she is watching.

The three of us put our arms around eachother and look around. It seems like a lie: we're standing in an interior courtyard with a beautiful fountain where the water is trickling, surrounded by a poetic building, a view inundated with peace. Peace that is shattered by the frantic calls of a girl desperately trying to reach her family in New York. How can man make things so beautiful and at the same time so horrible?

We go out into the street and everyone is grief-stricken, silent. The faces of the people show sorrow and mourning. For today, we prefer not to continue talking about children, we simply hold one another, loving eachotherr more than ever before, feeling alive.

In the afternoons, for the rest of the days we stay in Antigua, we get together in the small hostel with the backpackers. Between us, we represent more than fifteen nationalities, and everyone feels pain about what has happened. It helps us to be together, to talk and think about it together. Everyone has the same wish; we all pray this crime against humanity doesn't trigger vengeance, hatred and more wars!

Special Kids

We depart from Antigua to visit indigenous villages full of colors: in their clothes, in their arts and crafts, in their mini busses, in everything, there is color. Over their heads, women and girls carry baskets full of beautiful woven objects.

When we get to Guatemala City, there are already people waiting for us. They have heard about our visit from someone in El Salvador and they receive us warmly, with dinner, a home and even a service for the car.

The woman of one of the families who hosts us directs a school for children with mental problems whom she prefers to call "special children". She asks us to go give a talk, and we accept. We get into a world of children unknown to us who immediately hug us and welcome us with smiles.

I have never thought about these "special" children as happy children, only as small ones with problems. Nevertheless, now we see them free, spontaneous, happy, demonstrating their feelings. We tell them about the trip and places we've been and where we're going. They applaud or laugh at each of our comments.

Later we open the front doors of the car. They climb in one side and out the other. They love to touch everything, feeling the traveling car. When one of the youngsters discovers the horn, everyone wants to get back in the Graham to honk it. Those that are waiting their turns hug us and the car or laugh contagious giggles at each honk of the horn or for the headlights they're now turning on.

I had always been afraid of being the father of a "special" child, but now I understand that God doesn't condemn a family when giving them a child like this. Instead, He chooses them because surely it's they who have more love to give to these small ones who need it so much.

On the Way to the Decision

The natural beauty of Semuc-Champey completely blows us away: In the mountain forest, for more than three hundred yards across the top of a torrential river, a natural bridge has formed and it continues to grow. This bridge consists of a series of terraced pools full of spring water in varying blues from deep midnight to a light turquoise. While we enjoy ourselves swimming from pool to pool, a tourist who's laying in the sun on one of the rocks comments: "They say because of its beauty, this place is the eighth wonder of the world."

"It must be the ninth, because the eighth is my wife," I reply, which earns me an enormous kiss from my love.

After a beautiful day, we follow on the route heading to the ruins of the largest city in the Mayan world: Tikal. On the way, we stop in El Remate, a small village next to a beautiful lake. We sleep in a cabin that is 100% Mayan. Built into the side of a mountain without doors, windows nor front wall, it has a spectacular view of the lake.

To get into Tikal, the tourists have to pay twenty dollars per person, while the locals only two.

"Cande, would you to go ask them if we can pay only what the locals pay."

When she is getting out of the car to ask, the folks from the ticket booth start to shout as they get closer.

"It's them with the antique car...the Argentineans!"

We stay there, looking at each other, not understanding what's happening.

"We've been waiting for you, the park director is anxious to meet you. Please come in, come in, we'll let him know that you've arrived."

"Thank you very much," we say still not knowing what's going on.

When we get to the offices, we are received marvelously; they show us a letter they have received from the Ministry of Culture where they ask that we be given free access to the site and preferential treatment. We are shown to a bungalow where we can sleep and they introduce us to two guides: One to accompany us during the day and the other for night-time outings.

We put together what's happened: Lorena Mendoza, a Guatemalan journalist, arranged all this just because we told her it would be beautiful to take some pictures with the car near the pyramids.

After we're all settled in, one of the guides shows us all around the immense Mayan city. This is inside a dense virgin jungle, full of animals, monkeys, toucans, and parrots who are not afraid of humans. The explanation of the guide made us imagine the place during another era: it was a city of hundreds of thousands of people in movement, with their noises, their trades, religious ceremonies, artists, builders, and their ball games.

In the afternoon, before our guide for the evening arrived, we climbed up to the pinnacle of one of the pyramids from where we could see the immense covering of green jungle plants and appearing above the green, three other Mayan pyramids.

Here we are: alone, arm in arm, captivated with this mystical, unique site, full of energy and power. The sonorous song of the frogs accompanies us, while the sun gives the end to another day. I break the silence in a voice very low and deep.

SECUOIA N.P.,
USA.

PAMPA ZAPP,
N.Y. USA

UTAH, USA.

BRITISH COLUMBIA, CANADÁ.

ALASKA, USA.

"Cande, I want to be a father."
"And I a mother, if God wills it."

In all we stay in magical Tikal four days, instead of three. A hurricane that hit Belize obliged us to stay. In Tikal, we only got rain and strong winds; we were protected. Instead, if we had been on the road to Belize, we would have had a very bad time. Over there, a whole city disappeared when the hurricane hit.

Belize

Pirate Treasure

A Dream Inside Another

We enter into a tiny country, with less than 200,000 inhabitants and only two paved roads that cross it. And in its mere twenty years of independence, it has made admirable advances, including having no army.

Crossing into this little country is to leave Latin America, mostly because even though it's situated among Latin countries, the language is English and the constructions are typically Anglo-Saxon.

In front of the sea, in one of the few buildings in Belize City, we stay with a Colombian, a businessman who is an advisor for the central bank and the privatization of the port. He happily shows us around the tiny city, the port, and inland the capital of Belize, which in no way seems like a capital city. Following the road to the sea, we go to meet the Garifunas. They, according to what the Colombian tells us, are descendents of slaves who survived a storm, escaping from the boat they were on and mixed with the natives of the area. We share some beers with the Garifunas in their small huts, recently constructed on the white sand in front of the blue, tempting sea.

A few days ago, because of a hurricane, they lost almost everything. With us are two of them who were left with only a bag in their hands; the only things they could manage to rescue. They don't seem depressed, as we would be if it had happened to us.

"It wasn't the first hurricane that's flattened my house with everything I had, nor will it be the last. As long as it didn't get us, we'll be back to start again," one of the guys explains to me.

"Why don't you look for somewhere else to live?"

He looks at me as if my question is beyond dumb and replies, "Nah, man, look at this place, this sea, this sky...it's marvelous, and it's what we have. It's like our life, which is

marvelous. We're not going to leave it for a few days of storm, right?"

This Garifuna is right, everyone has days in life that are horrible, but after the suffering there are glorious days that always get us to begin again. With every misfortune or sadness there is a lesson that comes out of it that helps us to start again.

Cande and I are enjoying ourselves, but we are a bit nervous. Not because of the place or the company, because there's nothing to fear here, but because she's a couple of weeks late. This is almost a habit for Cande, but this time I sense something unusual.

She tells me not to be excited about it because she doesn't feel any different. As soon as we're back to Belize City, motivated by my anxiety, I buy a pregnancy test.

When we're in the apartment as she goes into the bathroom to do the test, she gives me a "you wasted your money" face, but her look tells me that she's nervous...maybe because it's a test and tests make everyone nervous.

She shuts the door and everything is silent. I wait anxiously. I hear nothing, everything is very quiet. I put my ear to the door trying to hear something. Suddenly I am quietly deaf from a scream from Cande, which provokes enormous intrigue on me.

"What happened?" I ask, desperate to know.

Cande opens the door while with nervousness and happiness she shows me the results.

"It's positive!!! It is so positive!!"

We hold each other super tightly, with tears and with a strange feeling, one totally new for us. The feeling that we're going to be parents, and in a fragment of a second, thousands of thoughts flash through our minds, mixing happiness, responsibilities, fears and a great mystery: "And now, what do we do?"

We only interrupt our hug for a question or a comment, and then we come together again; fusing each to the other feeling between the two of us a new love.

"What are you going to do when your child is born?" Cande asks me tenderly.

"I'm gonna play! I'm going to play again."

I believe just like all first time parents the first thing we do is to plan, perhaps too much. To quit or end the trip is out of the question. If he comes on the road, it's because he wants to be part of it. So, in that case, one dream will be born within another. Two dreams at the same time.

Where should he be born? Mexico is too close, so it is the United States. Maybe Canada or no, better yet, Alaska, at the end of the journey! Traveling with a baby seems like it would be so hard, because of him or her and because of the limited funds. Additionally, the trip would change so much with a baby! Who would want to receive the three of us?

"It would be better to get to Alaska before we have the baby," I suggest.

"Let's look at the calendar, there are nine months and maybe we've already completed one," Cande comments looking at her tummy, "so we have eight to go. Let's see…let's stay in Belize another week, in Mexico, a month and a half; United States, three, Canada, one and a half, and a month in Alaska. To look for a place, a doctor and get used to the place a while…"

"Sounds good, but will it actually be like that? Nothing has ever come out the way we planned it. It was always different but actually better."

"This time it is different: we have to get to Alaska before the baby."

In the afternoon, we go to the hospital of Belize, which is public. Right away, a couple of Cuban doctors attend us and tell us, while we continue holding one another: "In nine moons you will have someone else to hold. Candelaria has a little traveler."

It will be born around the 10th or 11th of June, this means that we got pregnant that same September 11th, in which we loved each other so intensely. Without any doubt that there is an upcoming member in the family, we feel sure enough to celebrate, we tell our host, who just can't believe it. He thinks it was an accident; that we will never be able to realize the rest of our trip. He asks us how we're going to get back home, what we are going to do with the car…

"We're going to continue," we tell him.

"Continue? With a pregnant wife? No, no, you can't. She needs to settle down and rest, there may be complications, she will feel bad and you have to do medical checkups. It's not a very good idea…" counsels the Colombian.

"Right now I feel fabulous, I don't have any nausea; I've just been very sleepy and tired," Cande explains.

"Yes, but a pregnancy is something delicate, there will be difficulties…" our friend continues, whom we leave, talking to himself.

What For?

In a shared taxi boat, we pay a visit to the keys. We stop in San Pedro There we find a little hotel with a sea view for a reasonable price.

On the only street fit for traffic, we promptly meet a couple of artisans whom during their trip around the world choose this island to spend a couple of years. The lifestyle, the climate, and the ease at which one finds whatever is necessary to live makes everything go in a very slow rhythm. They take their time speaking, their movements are slow, and they don't have much organization nor many plans.

"I don't have anything, but at the same time I have everything," a painter tells us who is showing his work to a couple of tourists. "On this island, where I now live, tourists save all year to come here for only fifteen days. I used to live in Houston, and in any job I did, I couldn't make enough money to live, and now selling a few of my paintings, I make what I need. Plus, it's what I like to do." The couple pretends to be looking at the work of the painter, but their attention is on his words. "And it might be difficult to believe, but almost everyone is afraid of freedom, to do what they want and how they want. We are always striving to fit in, to be within the 'normal' parameters and do things like everyone else. Looking for ways to be busy, to have some obligation, to be an employee with a schedule, to receive orders when we could be our own bosses," the tourists have stopped pretending, they are now openly and closely attending to the painter. He continues talking, but now he's speaking to all of us, "You are a completely free being, don't tie yourself, do those things which can be actually begun and finished in a period of time, don't make them eternal, don't buy on credit, because this only enslaves you. Don't accumulate valuable belongings that always make you take care of them or watch out for, because your possessions should be at your service. Remember the richest one is not the one who has the most, but the one who needs the least."

"Do you know the story of the fisherman and the tourist?" the man who is listening asks.

"Yes, I know it. In a few words, it's the story of my life."

"I don't know it," I tell the tourist, curious to hear it.

"On a very beautiful beach," he begins to narrate, "a fisherman is unloading his fish. A curious tourist approaches the little boat and noticing there aren't very many fish, asks why he doesn't go out and fish more. 'What for?' replies the fisherman. 'If you fish more, you'd have a higher income and could buy a bigger boat.' 'What for?' 'To fish more, so you could make more money and buy a big fishing boat.' 'What for?' questions the fisherman while continuing calmly to unload his fish. 'With a big fishing boat, you could begin to buy others, and you could have your own fishing company.'" reels off the tourist, excitedly, "'You could grow and have your own processing plant, export it and this way you could have lots of money and...' 'What for?' the fisherman interrupts again. 'What do you mean, 'what for?!' Don't you see? It's obvious, you would be a millionaire! You could go on vacations to places like this and go fishing...' The fisherman raises his eyes to look at the man, shrugs his shoulders and answers: 'That's what I'm doing'."

The story is excellent; it makes me think about how simple life can be. One can do what he wants without complicating everything. To live simply is to live freely. The engaging conversation invites us to sit down. We are delighted to and while I listen, I see that our treatment of people has changed. Before we never talked to strangers and now we feel the necessity to. We need to enjoy unique personalities and opinions that may be correct or debatable, ideas we can use or not. What's important is that each one paints for us a world with different ways to live.

Before the journey, in front of others, we always were on the defensive, we introduced ourselves like clad in armor, portraying ourselves stronger than we really were, more serious and even more important, trying to make the tone of voice haughtier. Almost all of us defend ourselves; some standing firm in their name, mentioning their position in a company or maybe looking firmly into the eyes.

We have learned that if we introduce ourselves with only our first name, shaking hands, neither forcefully nor weakly, and looking at the other in the eye expressing that we are delighted to meet him or her and are at his or her service for whatever is necessary, we show ourselves as what we are: humans, and as marvelous as they are. It's a win-win situation. No victors or vanquished, just new friends.

Pondering on my thoughts, I don't realize the moment when the conversation is over; I take my leave and gathering Cande's hand we return to the hotel. She asks me what I was thinking about. I comment to her about the changes that are so obvious in me as they are in her regarding people and she responds:

"Do you know why I believe we've changed like this? Because at this moment we don't have anything that identifies us. We don't have a house, we don't have a specific job, and we aren't with only one type of people. We show ourselves as we are because the only thing we carry on this trip is ourselves. We don't have anything nor do things the people can "study." I don't feel, like before, pigeonholed into one specific kind of pre-determined society, because now we live in all of them at the same time. Being transparent helps us enjoy this. One day at noon, we dine in a luxury restaurant and in the evening, we eat in the market. One day we sleep in a double bed, with television, and a bathroom with hot water, and another day an improvised bed on the floor of a humble home. We do as well in one place as another. If you portray yourself as something you are not, it's impossible to enjoy the essence of the moment. I remember that before the trip, sometimes I showed myself differently from who I really was, just to please others. So what was happening was that I created a situation that in the end I didn't enjoy because I wasn't myself. One's value is in who one is, not in what one appears to be. Now that we are more transparent, I can verify that the relationships are stronger and clearer.

On the third day in San Pedro we are already part of the island. While we are on the beach, a boy offers us coconuts, even though he didn't have any. We answer "We'd love some." He climbs a palm as if it is nothing and drops a couple of fruits. Here everything looks so simple.

Despite the following two days of nausea, we celebrate our first time being pregnant like we're newly in love. The nerves have eased a bit, happiness spills naturally from our faces; we are not able to disguise it. We feel an enormous desire to share it with whomever we come across, and even more with our families and friends. When we return to the mainland, we have our first ultrasound. We pay for it with one of Cande's paintings. Just seeing the baby's heart beating fills us with joy.

Peace is the Way

Content we leave for the border with Mexico, following our new plan to stay in Belize only one week. Once we reach immigration, Cande makes the papers to exit the country while I answer questions about the trip and the car for many curious folks. Among them, I am surprised there is a Mennonite; a quite tall man, with a large beard and a high hat. His three daughters are dressed in clothes that seem right out of the "Little House on the Prairie" and the son has pants with suspenders. The two first questions the elder asks me are what we are doing and why. The next one amazes me. "Would you like to spend a week with us in our Amish-Mennonite community?"

I would love to, but Cande has finished the exit papers and we have proposed a schedule for getting to Alaska. To accept is to get off on the wrong foot with the plan. I go to ask her anyway while signaling who invited us.

"Yes, of course, this is something I've always wanted to do!" she enthusiastically exclaims, "But what are we going to do now about the passports?"

"We'll just do them again."

We leave the car near the border, in the farm of a friend of the Mennonite. From there, we climb into our host's pick-up truck to go all together to the community. It's far away; we have to cross a big section of Belize, almost to the border with Guatemala. In the late hours of the night, we get to the community that is in Spanish Lookout.

We stay in a small house, and in the morning, we go to the home of the man, whose family is quite numerous. As soon as we enter, we greet them Good Morning with hugs and kisses that induce a timid laughter in the women: it seems we've done something they're not used to here.

After having breakfast with delicious warm baked bread and fresh milk they take us to see the community, and the progress achieved by all of them. On meticulously maintained dirt roads, we see women and men walking who greet us warmly every time we come across them.

"The community owns the property, but each family has its own part." teaches the Mennonite, who now points out a small police post. "The government of Belize put that here. As soon as the police arrived, things started disappearing. Then, we caught them red-handed and sent them right back. Since then, they haven't sent any more police here."

We visit the milk factory, the school, and the church. We speak with the preacher, the teacher, his parents, his nephews and nieces, who all receive us with such contagious happiness that it spills over to us. We can feel the peace and calm in the air. It's our first day and we have already received many invitations to eat in different family's homes, to go swimming, to spend a day in the country, among many other offers. Our host asks us what we'd like to do, we tell him: "go horseback riding"

He has only one, but the same afternoon his family finds two others on the nearby farms. We go to see the community from a new perspective, which continually surprises us. Our two guides greet with great respect each one who passes mentioning his name. Everyone knows everyone.

After dinner, they take us to see an outdoor hockey game. We enjoy the spectacle in which the players really have fun, with no profane language or aggression. They astonish us because we thought the Mennonites didn't participate in games nor drive cars, nor listen to any music. I tell them and they explain that certainly, hockey and music are something new the Mennonites have adopted, not so the Amish, who we're going to visit tomorrow.

We arrive at a small wooden house; the door has no knob, only a wooden latch. An elderly man dressed in blue and black invites us in. We take a seat in very simple but beautiful chairs. We can tell from the small differences among them that they are hand-crafted, as is the table and everything surrounding us. There is no electricity nor refrigerator. The interior of the house is very simple; it only has what's essential. On the table rests a Bible.

Happy about our visit, the man offers us a glass of water. He begins to ask many questions although we feel like we are the ones who have thousands of queries. The gentleman asks from where we hail, what we do in Argentina, what we are doing here, how the visit is going, what we have learned, what we are going to do… Little by little, we answer his questions interrupting now and again with our own questions:

"How did you get to Belize?" is my first query.

"We go where they give us freedom, where they won't harass us. If after a while, they start to, we simply leave. We never fight, because there is always some place in the world where we can live in freedom, live a simple life in harmony with God."

"If we are a creation of God and He is perfect, why are there storms, tornados, and volcanoes in the world? Why did He create a human who is not perfect, a man who makes wars, has illnesses, and sometime inflicts a lot of damage to himself?" I ask with the intention of clearing my doubts.

"God created life; this begins with His creation because life can not come from nothing. And for life to have meaning, it has to be finite. How or when this life is lost, I don't know. The earth also has a life, and life has its changes searching

for its equilibrium and with this search for balance come the storms, hurricanes, floods… Man also has life and seeks his own balance."

"But can we reach balance with wars and deaths?"

"No, keep in mind Humanity never initiates war. It is those few, who by mixing fears, honor, pride and heroism move an enormous mass of people, convincing them to do something for the benefit of those few. This way they succeed in provoking people into doing something they would never voluntarily do: kill another human being. God always says, 'Love one another' without identifying races, nor religions, nor anything. Simply 'Love one another'. But without fail, there is always someone who makes us forget these words, who manages to generate hatred between neighbors, creating a war which includes many times fighting in the name of God. Peoples at war ask Him for glory over the enemy. But for God there are no enemies, only brothers. There is no way to peace, peace is the way."

"So, how do we search balance?"

"Humanity has existed for only 100,000 years, and since man started to think he's believed in a Superior Being, in a Creator. A few thousand years ago, Messiahs appeared, prophets giving a little peace and equilibrium, joining those who were killing one another, fighting for different gods. Now, even though there is war in the world, an enormous change is emerging. As incredible as it seems, in a world full of bombs capable of destroying everything, there is an outcry from the depths of each human soul screaming 'no more, I want more humanity.' More and more people are starting to think and say "More weapons? What for?" There are already too many. Why more war since nothing is achieved by it? Everyone can live here; everyone can help one another and be in harmony. The power to do something is growing in the people, to be heard on the other side of the world, to ask for help from very far way and also from very far away, to help. All are in direct contact. A greater spirituality is growing in everyone, where there is more value in living with others instead of against others."

"Yes, but there are some places where the war has been going on for over fifty years and the victims are always the civilians. I just can't see where it's going to end."

"Do you know where it's going to end? With a 'Gandhi' who repeats: 'I am free and because I am free, I choose non violence' demonstrating that much more can be achieved without weapons and with the use of reasoning. There are many 'Gandhis', 'Mother Teresas', 'Mohammads', 'Buddhas' and 'Jesuses' in the world who are doing a lot to this end. And many more will come to this planet," he pauses in his explanation to return a greeting of folks passing on the road in a buggy. "Humanity is reaching its equilibrium, it's becoming more intelligent, stronger, and all the time it becomes harder for 'the few' to dominate the masses. Humanity grows in information and history and knows that violence breeds more violence, hatred and desires for vengeance while at the same time on the opposing side it generates the same hatred without end. It's exactly this that the same humanity wants to cease, regardless of pride or honor or heroes, simply because we live much better without them. Today after a war, they don't count the dead from each troop, they count how many humans have fallen and they question why and for what. Today people think about who to follow: whether a ruler who incites hatred of other people in order to kill them, or a God who teaches us to love them." He takes a gulp of fresh water and concludes: "Harmony is very close although it may not seem like it."

The same day, we visit more Amish folks, who show us although they know about our modern world, they choose their own style of life: the direct contact with the earth, with what they produce and eat, with their children, their neighbors and their community. We had believed we were more evolved, but the road is teaching us how much more civilized in their thoughts and ideals they are than us. The way that Amish man in his dark clothes, seated in his hand made chair and drinking his glass of water showed us a clear interpretation of the world they have here, another resident of this place now tells us, while his horse powers the wood saws, "Seek to live a simple life, decelerated and plain. Live only with what's necessary. Every time you possess something new, you lose something. As much as you have is as much as you stand to lose. If you have almost nothing, you have it all."

Many people believe they are richer because they have more things to show, but in fact, a fortune is measured with happiness. Greater happiness, greater riches, where is my heart is my fortune.

In this place, we feel like we have grown so much although all in all, we have shared only one marvelous week. When the moment arrives to bid farewell, our Mennonite family and a few others now hug and kiss us without being timid. With each goodbye goes some part of myself. The more I travel, the stronger I grow within myself but on the other hand, more sensitive.

Mexico & Cuba

TILL HERE: 16832 miles in 1 year and 9 1/2 mo.

N. Laredo
Monterrey
Zacatecas
León
Querétaro
Mexico D. F.
Puebla
Veracruz
Mérida
Cancún
Tulúm
La Habana

Mexico & Cuba

Among the Mayan and the Aztec World

Together Again

W e never imagined we'd meet again so soon, much less during the rest of our journey, it's our friend, to whom we said goodbye in Iquitos more than a year ago, after boating down the Amazon together. Nevertheless, here is James, the Englishman, and we three unite in a tight hug.

"What are you doing here in Cancun?" he asks us as surprised as we are, "Are you still on your trip?!? Wasn't it going to be only six more months to get to Alaska?"

"Man arranges and God changes," I respond. "When we left our house, we left for what we thought would be a six month trip…that was twenty-two months ago."

"What are you doing in beautiful and beloved Mexico?"

"It's very beautiful and we feel very loved. If we told you, you wouldn't believe it…"

"Knowing you two I would believe anything, I spent one of the best months of my life with you guys."

"First, we went to the beaches inTulum. We thought that since the Mayans had chosen that place to build a temple, it must be somewhere special. We were not mistaken. In the same area, we visited the Cenotes, natural underground reservoirs full of crystal clear fresh water. It's incredible; you can dive in and swim through underground passages until you get to the surface in some other pool. Then we went to Playa del Carmen, where we stopped on the boardwalk to sell postcards and books. Until we sold out!!" Cande says.

"I guess you'll have to send me one when you get them reprinted," James says.

"A young man," Cande continues, "owner of a restaurant, invited us to eat. Another man, one who owns a canteen, offered us to sleep at his place once he closed to the public. So, for a couple of days we put together the tables, and seat cushions and felt like we were sleeping in the jungle, because the canteen was decorated with a rain forest theme. The Mexicans are receiving us very well."

"And you haven't heard about Cancun..." I tell our English friend, "When we got to town, we stayed with the owner of the restaurant in Playa del Carmen. The next day, we were stopped in the street by a woman who tells us that she's a member of the small Antique Auto Club of Cancun and there was a meeting that night. We went to five family auto club meetings and realized their cars were merely an excuse to have a good time. They immediately organized our whole stay. First, Jaime, one of the members, gave us an apartment which is in a tourist complex on the best stretch of beach in Cancun. Then they gave the car a complete service including chroming the bumpers, work done by a friend of theirs. Another member of the club arranged a medical check up for Cande and two passes for a visit to an excellent Mayan theme park. Plus then they invited us to eat and made contact with the newspapers..."

"But, it's hasn't been all just fun and games, we have also been working..." Cande interrupts me, "We introduced ourselves at the Forum Shopping center and we told the managers that if they permitted us to park the car inside the mall, we would be an attraction for the tourists. We could tell about our trip and at the same time sell our postcards."

"So, what did they say?"

"Very enthusiastic with the idea, they placed notices in all the local newspapers; they literally rolled out a red carpet and had special lighting as well as gave us invitations to eat at restaurants in the shopping center. During that week, we talked with tourists from all over the world who happy to see a dream being achieved, supported us by buying our postcards. Additionally, the folks from the stores of the mall invited us to dance and eat. At the Argentine grill house 'Cambalache' we ate some wonderful steaks," Cande comments.

"I can assure you it's been like this since the last time we saw you," I comment to our English friend, "We always meet hospitable people who desire to help, this is why it's taken us so long to get this far."

"I'm sure of that," James tells us.

"Ah, but there's more, and for this one, you have to come along with us," we propose.

"Where to?"

"How about Cuba, all expenses paid?" We can see the surprise on James's face. "Here's how it works. There are many exiled Cubans who cannot return to their country. But they want to provide things for their family who can't leave, essential everyday things, like clothes and soap, shampoo, and other healthcare stuff and medicines. So, they look for tourists who want to deliver them in exchange for paying for the whole trip including all the airport taxes. What do you think?"

"Let's go!"

Rumba Music

We arrive to the Havana airport where the family of the Cuban who sent us receives us.

When we get to the home of "our family," they open the bags we brought with so much excitement, it seems like Christmas. They find things inside them that one could buy at any supermarket. This way, in only a couple of minutes, we have our first glimpse into what real life is like for the citizens of Cuba.

Later, they show us to our room in a loft over the kitchen, the roof is so low we have to duck our heads. The house is small but; it's very clean and orderly. However, the paint is peeling from the walls, the furniture and other things show signs of years of use without any maintenance or modernization. The only really modern item that receives meticulous care is the color television. It is covered everyday to protect it.

"We saved for four years, plus a little money they sent us from Miami to be able to buy it," explains the father while uncovering the object with the care one would exhibit an extremely valuable piece of art.

We want to experience how it is to live like a Cuban and adapt ourselves to the place. In the afternoon, we accompany one of the sons of the family to the market. It has very little merchandise, almost all the shelves are empty, there are still many people shopping, even though they can get almost nothing. We greet the butcher, and as we are buying some pork from him he recognizes our accent: "Hey, Argentineans! Look!" he shouts at us while taking off his shirt to show us a tattoo of Che Guevara that covers his entire back.

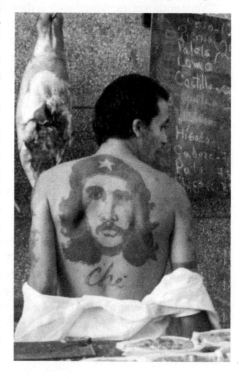

Once the shopping is done, we walk the streets of broken pavement, full of people, lined with houses that seem to be on the point of crumbling, many held up with wood posts. There are no publicity posters of any kind. The cars that pass us are so old and beat up we're surprised they are still running. Later we go into other shops we notice the same situation as in the market: empty shelves.

Considering all this, the people in this place, who are smiling all the time, amaze us. The Cubans are happy, their cheerful countenance is contagious and they greet us in passing like we're neighbors from the block.

There is music everywhere. Some play in the streets, others dance and those who aren't listen to the radio. Additionally, on almost every corner some group forms: some guys play handball against the church wall with a tennis ball, others discuss soccer, others talk about politics, the guys talk about the chicks, and the girls talk about the guys. It is like this on almost every block.

We go to the bus stop, where there are many people, but not in any kind of line. Our guide asks who's last. Someone responds: "I am." Then we know whom we follow. Another person comes up and asks the same thing. Now it's our companion who says: "We are." This continues until the arrival of "the camel," a truck with a trailer adapted to carry passengers. We get in for a ride after buying the cheapest ticket in the world.

During the whole day, we mix in the Cuban streets with its people. Our guide takes us to visit many tourist places as well as places typical in the life of the locals. We play dominoes in the park, we order drinks in "La Bodeguita del Medio" and dance Cuban salsa on the sea wall. While there, two women come to us and ask us for something. They don't ask for money, but for aspirin and toothpaste.

"Taxi, to the fort, please," says our guide to the chauffer. He asked us not to say one word inside the taxi, because there are those for tourists and others for Cubans. The difference in price is gigantic from one to the other. We're riding in this one not only for this reason, but also because we want to know a real Cuban taxi. They are prohibited to take foreign passengers and if the government discovers them doing it, they will take it away. The one we're in is from the 50's; it's painted by hand with house paint and decorated with objects and pendants that you can only find here. We ride on bags and fabric, which function as seats, feeling part of the Cuban fiesta, we listen to music accompanied by the mechanical noises from the car.

We are headed to the fort to see the cannon firing. Everyday, they revive the closing of the city doors, just as in the colonial time. On the way, the driver picks up more Cubans. Exclusivity doesn't exist here, if the driver sees a passenger who is going in the same direction, they pile in too whoever is already inside. In our case, we're now seven.

A police officer, one of three in the street, signals us to stop. The driver goes pale: although we've kept quiet, he's not stupid and has figured out we're not Cuban. He doesn't know what to do, but he slows down. The officer comes up to us, looking inside the car checking the passengers, but just when he's about to see us he's called by one of the other officers. So, the driver takes this chance to accelerate while shouting curses in the best Cuban style.

We get back at the crack of dawn after carousing in the center of the city, living the party that is Havana at night. We return walking the very dark streets, cutting through alleys. We see women alone and groups of guys on the corners, but nothing bad happens, here there is nothing to fear.

Freedom, What a Beautiful Treasure

It's a lovely day and we go to the beach. The splendor of the place is incredible, with a white beach and a marvelous turquoise sea. Everything stained by the presence of military control towers that turn the place into a jail. The armed uniform men search with their binoculars for people with intentions of escaping from their country.

My attention is on two Cubans who are in the water with goggles and a snorkel, but there are no fish nor coral to see only white sand, so I ask them, "What are you looking for?"

"Gold, earrings, bracelets…when the foreign tourists come, we always find something," explains one while I observe their hands and feet as wrinkled as prunes, and the goose bumps, from so many hours of being in the water.

"Last week, we found a gold ring which we sold for $20!!" adds the other happily, and not for nothing: $30 here is the average monthly salary.

Shortly, three musicians come up to Cande, offering to play. She happily accepts. They sing with much energy, the music is joyful and the lyrics are amusing…but the show is interrupted by three uniformed men who call them over and begin to take them away one by one.

"Excuse me, but what's wrong? We asked them to sing, they are friends of ours," I tell the officials.

"Don't get in the middle of this, don't complicate the matter…" one of them replies to me.

"Don't worry, it's routine." one of the musicians comments, with a resigned expression.

On our way back, we see a Russian motorcycle with a sidecar and a bit further on, a car with its hood open; being repaired for one of thousands of times it has been fixed. There are people watching all the alley action from their balconies and, on one patio, surrounded by hundreds of shoes and with a cigar in his mouth, a shoe repair man. After we greet him through the gate, he happily answers and invites us to come in. He asks his chum who is seated in front of him to go and find a couple of chairs for us. "And tell Mirta to bring some juice out to refresh our guests," he shouts. "What are you guys doing here? On vacation?" He asks us without taking the cigar from his mouth, his hands busy with his work.

"Well, how can I tell you? We can't call it a vacation, we are on a kind of trip that turn into a discovery journey…"

"So, what have you discovered about Cuba?"

"I don't think we can say anything yet, we've only been here five days…"

"I have something to teach you about Cuba. This place is an island, where everything that happens is a perfect example for the whole world. We are isolated, we don't have any countries bordering us to influence us nor can we influence. Cuba had a revolution that was very necessary, because the wealth was for few and the poverty was for many." He now takes the Cuban cigar out of his mouth to say clearly what follows, "Now we can say that poverty is for everybody. Now we all suffer equally. Before the revolution, I had my profession and now I'm a shoemaker, because if I had continued with my occupation, I would make less. I would be like the doctors, who don't have enough to pay me for fixing their shoes. Nevertheless, like them, now everyone can smoke these cigars, the best tobacco in the world..." he inhales deeply, delighting in the flavor of the smoke in his mouth. "This cigar cost one peso: With a dollar today I could buy thirty, but before I would have needed thirty dollars..."

"Yes, we saw a bum in the plaza smoking a cigar..." we recall.

"You see, even a bum can, and this bum always has enough to eat and the best medical attention too. It's true that many things got better, but also many things got worse for us...because of the government, because of the gringos. We've always been a rock in their shoe..." Mirta bring the refreshments and his buddy takes a seat. The shoe man takes another drag and continues, "But even if we were very well, even if we had everything we need: health, work, house, money, what good does it do me without freedom, freedom to go wherever I want, to read, write, and see. Freedom to choose my house, my car, my work... Freedom, how great it sounds! Such a beautiful and marvelous word and how far this is from Cuba. How I would love to have it, even if only for a moment!"

Vacant Bodies

"Kids, what would you like for dinner?" asks the lady of the house of the family hosting us.

"Whatever you'll be having..."

"Well, you should know it will be the same as yesterday and the day before yesterday, rice with beans, if not, beans with rice."

"If you'd like, buy chicken and something else for breakfast," I tell her putting money on the table. She is thrilled and takes it before bustling off to the market. Guests coming to dinner tonight are the oldest daughter and her husband who live with an aunt who could give them a room after they got married. The young couple has many questions; they want to know about the world outside. To start, we tell them that we are traveling over the whole of America.

"From Argentina to Alaska? And your government gave you permission? How much time do you have before you should be back?"

"We don't have any time limits, we didn't have to ask for permission either…"

"And the other countries let you go in and drive through just like that?"

"Yes, up to now."

"And how many countries are you traveling through?"

"More than twenty…"

"More than twenty countries!" they repeat with the eyes of children who are listening to a story of fairies and dragons, like an incredible, impossible story.

"Why are you doing it?"

"To accomplish a dream,"

Upon hearing this they remain silent without any expression on their faces, except in their eyes they show an enormous pain.

"Dreams don't exist here. Here one is born and tries to survive every day," says the son-in-law of the lady of the house.

"You don't have any dreams?"

"What kind of dreams? Of what? What for? If there is absolutely nothing we can do about them anyway. Why should we dream and be disillusioned?" he answers, totally convinced, and hopeless.

"But seriously, don't you have any dreams?" I insist, feeling that in front of me is an empty man, a mass of living flesh and nothing more. I've never felt anything like this before. We are nothing if we don't have any dreams, if we don't have faith. Nothing…

"Dreams…you have a passport that can get you off this island, you are the ones who don't have to stay, you are the ones who can choose tomorrow where you want to go, you are the ones who can dream…"

Freedom, you surface again, hidden treasure. Freedom, we possess you yet we don't value you. Freedom, just like the painter in Belize said, many don't enjoy you in spite of having you. We limit you tying ourselves to things, work, credit… Freedom, if the shoemaker and this young couple would possess you, they could complete their dreams too.

"What would you do if you were Cuban?" James asks me when we go out on the sidewalk to drink some coffee.

"Build a raft." We would prefer to sink than to live without freedom.

LA BODEGUITA DEL MEDIO

The next day, we fly back to Cancun, Mexico. Before going back to our apartment, we go to do some shopping at the supermarket. I stand there at the entrance, stunned to see the boatloads of products.

Aztec Roads

Our friends from the Antique Auto Club send us off from Cancun with a big Mexican breakfast. Jaime, who let his use his apartment, takes me by the arm and pulls me outside the courtyard, near his car.

"Herman, although I haven't told you this before, your trip is also my dream. Looking at you and Cande with this car, a couple and pregnant, inspires me to go after mine and I would like you to tell me everything I'm going to need," while saying this he takes out a pencil and paper, ready to make a list.

"Faith."

"Fine, faith and what else?" Jaime demonstrates he's ready to go buy whatever he needs.

"If you have faith, you have it all. If you have faith, you are destined to succeed. For this trip or for whatever you do, what you have or don't have is not what's important. All that matters is to have faith."

We depart Cancun. Cande now has something else to do while I drive. She pats her tummy, which is now showing, as she sings cradle songs and other childhood songs we're beginning to remember.

On the way, we pass Chichén Itzá, Mérida, Veracruz and Palenque, where our Mayan route ends. We are now entering Aztec land.

In very beautiful Puebla, city of churches, it seems, the first serious breakdown of the car occurs. We are a block from the center of the city. We want to go but the Graham emits an ugly grumble and refuses to start. I open the hood, only as a reflexive action, because I don't have any idea of what to look for.

"Is something wrong, sir? Because if so, about four blocks from here there is a museum of antique cars…" says a man right behind me, as if he fell from heaven.

At the museum, they call the owner, Fernando Garcia Limon, who drops what he's doing to come and see how he can help. What they do is disassemble a car on display, take out the piece and put it in the Graham that then starts right up. The next day, Fernando has organized a fiesta for us with many guests, food and even musicians. With a marvelous use of words, he dedicates a beautiful toast to us that leaves everyone in tears.

"A dream is a reason to live and for a dream one would risk even death. Here are two young folks, who being just that, two kids, two people just like us, who dare to risk their lives and lose everything. They hit the road and only reap triumph. They love one another thanks to their dreams, this is the reason one falls in love with another. Today with them we all journey, in them our dreams are embodied, so for them let's toast to their arrival, for the arrival of all of us!!"

We say thank you without knowing what to say after such beautiful words with so much affection. We simply stand up and shout "Mexico lindo y querido, let's all go to Alaska!"

"Let's go!" shouts every one of the guests in unison.

"I would like to request one small thing of everyone, including the musicians. Could we sing 'El Rey'?" As soon as the words are out of my mouth, the musicians begin playing while everyone joins in a loud voice. We ask Fernando about a print shop, we have our book ready for reprinting after having added a few anecdotes of Central America. He immediately takes us to the print shop of a friend of his, who gives us a great price plus we can work together.

While the book is printing, Fernando is already selling them among the members of the museum and his friends. One of them is the owner of the newspaper Sintesis, who sends one of his journalists to interview us. When this is concluded, the owner of the paper gives us a call to go and see him. After a few minutes of chatting, he asks us, "What can I do for you?"

"If you liked to buy some books..." we say a bit astounded by his question.

"No, something better than that... How about this, let's print calendars!'

"Calendars?" Cande and I look at each other puzzled.

"Yes, calendars. it's the best time of the year to make them and sell them. Let's print two thousand calendars, no, better, two thousand in Spanish, and two thousand in English, that way you can sell them in the States," the man, while

thinking gets louder and louder with enthusiasm almost greater than ours. "We will use two letter size sheets, printed on both sides, complete color. Bring some photos of the trip, use my designers, and come back to get them in ten days.

"Calendars?" we leave asking ourselves.

The books are ready and now it's the moment to pay for the printing. We don't have quite enough, but Mr. Lamas, a member of the museum, buys some ceramics we have from Nicaragua. He buys so much that we have no idea where he'll put them! All the same, he is happy to help us and when he pays us, he also gives us a book. It's about two Argentineans, Angel and Nestor, who got to Alaska in a Model T Ford, and to our surprise, we realize that they were the ones who passed by Manta, Ecuador and took that couple to the church. With great pleasure, we read about them arriving in Alaska, and to their credit, in the middle of winter.

On the Way to the Biggest City in the World

We depart from Puebla carrying a thousand books in the car and only $40 in our pockets. Now we are heading to Mexico City. We have heard many stories about it, many terrific, many terrifying.

"Cande, do you realize all the great things that have happened because the starter motor broke?"

"Yeah, if it hadn't broken, we wouldn't have had that party at the museum, the books, the calendars, all the new friends..."

"It's a good thing it broke!"

"It's like everything has a reason to happen. Like when we ran out of money, and everything got so much better. In Panama when it started raining so hard we had to stop; and, we woke up in an incredible place. In Colombia, we didn't have money to pay for the boat and thanks to that, we were able to enjoy the people more."

"Every problem has its solution, it arises for a reason, there's always a good one."

We both flinch with surprise when suddenly we hear police sirens following behind us, and while we stop, the thousands of comments we heard about the Mexican police come into my head. Many have recommended that we should simply offer them a bribe and keep going, but we promised ourselves before we started the journey not to pay one red cent. So, we are inclined to spend the whole day arguing with the police... I can see in the mirror that it's only one and he is approaching us with something in his left hand. Is it the ticket book?

"Excuse me for pulling you over, but I can't let you go on without taking the opportunity to take your picture." He takes one.

"Would you like me to take one of you with the car?"

"You bet, take one of me as if I am giving you a ticket..."

On telling us goodbye, he pulls the insignia of the Federal Police off his shirt and gives it to us, a gift.

The City and the Solitude

We enter the enormous city on a highway crammed with cars and trucks. A pickup from the 60's gets closer until he's right next to us.

"Are you going to the Auto Expo?" the guy shouts while driving.

"Where is it?" we ask and we go. We are looking for a place to sell our books and this seems like the ideal place.

Effectively the Auto expo is a car show, but only for brand new ones. There are all the marks in the world displayed in incredible booths to attract the public: they show prototypes, cars of the first generation, beautiful girls under a light show. They haven't forgotten the music and dancers either. And here we are at the door, us and our little old car trying to figure out how to get in. Asking around we find out that in fact the exposition just opened a couple of hours before, not for the general public yet but strictly for the exhibitors and invited guests. We happen to run into Fernando Garcia Limon, the manager of the museum in Puebla, who immediately takes us inside. He introduces us to the secretary of the show's organizer; she's very happy to hear our story and tells us as soon as she can, she will talk to her boss. She believes, because of what she knows of him, that he will have no problem doing something for us.

While we wait for a response, we go to see if everything is all right with the car. When going down the escalators, through the huge plate glass window we see the street and the Graham being towed away by the police! We jump down the stairs, pushing people out of the way, running like thieves rushing out of a bank, trying to get to the car. The security personnel at the door don't understand anything, but when they see us pushing to get out, they start following after us.

"STOP! STOP!" I shout running up to the police with the tow truck.

"This is a 'No Parking' zone, so we have to tow it away. Sorry"

"No, you can't! We're here to get into the fair," I lie because I don't know anything yet, desperate at the thought of them taking the car and knowing I don't have enough money to get it back out.

"Please, unhook this car and treat these people as they deserve to be," asks Fernando who has followed us.

"I'm just doing my job, there's nothing I can do. They should have thought about this before," respond the police.

The guards of the show don't know what they're doing here, but their presence gives us a touch of importance. In addition, a photographer from the newspaper, who's here to cover the fair, is already taking photos. Using the scene to his advantage, Fernando takes out his press credentials and shows them to the police:

"Fine, you do your job, I'll do mine. I've already have your picture, now I want your name, because it will come out in the papers as the worst Mexican in the nation. You have no idea whose car you're towing, no idea!"

The official pales, he adjusts his cap, hitches up his pants, and looks at us like we're the offspring of the king of Spain. Immediately, he begins unhooking our car, he begs our pardon citing he was only doing his job, if he had only known, if someone would have said something…and thousands of other excuses. While we're listening to this, we look at Fernando, who gives us a wink.

To avoid another scene like this, we park the car in the parking lot under the expo center, even though the by-the-hour rate is outrageous. We don't want to park it farther away because we have to show it to the director of the fair as soon as we can.

After safely reparking the Graham, Fernando departs leaving us a sensation of being completely by ourselves: being near him everything was much easier, but now we have to manage everything alone.

We go back to see the assistant of the director of the show, who tells us regrettably her boss will be unable to meet us today. It's the show's inauguration and he's going from one booth to another for a cocktail. This makes us a little

bit nervous. We could leave the car parked below until tomorrow, but we will not have the money to pay for it. If we do get it out, maybe, tomorrow when the fair opens to the public, there may not be any more spaces. Fine, better to leave it. But, where do we go?

Mi Casa es Su Casa

It is already dark, it might be around 9 p.m. We phone someone whose name we were given in Cancun. The man who answers the phone had never heard of us, so we tell him the story. After listening to everything, the man asks us, "What do you want from me?"

"We need a place to spend the night..."I reply, and I hear nothing else, the line is completely silent. Did he hang up on me? "Hello?"

"Yes, I'm here, I am just thinking..." the man doesn't know us, so he could very easily tell us there's nothing he can do to help us. He says, "Can you call me back in half an hour?"

Waiting for the agreed time to go by, and to not spend any of the few pesos we have, we slip into the cocktail party and eat some very tasty foods accompanied by the best champagne. I call him back, right on time.

"Can you call me back again, in another half hour? Right now I'm trying to find someone to put you up, because it's not possible in my house..."

We return to the party, and at a different booth mix among men in suits and women in party dresses. I call him back again.

"Where are you? My daughter is able to receive you, and I will go pick you up and take you to her."

We go back to the party, this time to celebrate since we have somewhere to go. It seems very peculiar that the daughter of the man is going to take us in, when we're not friends of her father, merely a couple of strangers coming to her at 10:30 at night. In any case, we don't have any other option. Our phone calls have reduced our already meager money supply.

In exactly forty minutes, the man is there to take us to his daughter's house. Upon arrival, she, her husband, and their three children receive us. They offer us a bed, among the toys and games, in the room of one of the children, who gives his space up happily because now he gets to sleep with his parents. While showing us around the whole house, they say: "Your house has a television downstairs, use it whenever you want to. The kitchen of your house is over there, eat whatever you want. Here are the keys to your house…"

We cannot believe they are so open with us, they entrust us with everything and we don't even have anything to introduce ourselves to them. Additionally, the car, which usually is our card of presentation and confidence, is parked at the fair. More than one time during our trip we have heard that we can not be bad people, because in a car so slow and showy we would never be able to escape too far.

Unexpected Kindnesses

Very early the next day, we return to the fair, which is already open to the public. People pour in by the thousands as we wait to be received by its organizer. It's been three hours and we suppose that we wouldn't have had to wait for so long for something bad.

"Nice to meet you, I'm William," a man introduces himself who comes directly to us. "Absolutely, I want you here, in my expo. I also organize others in LA and Chicago, and I want you there too." We are astonished.

"Rebecca, please, look for a spot, I want them where everyone can see them. I want all the people to see what is possible, that everything is possible!" he orders his secretary.

"We're very grateful but, could we ask you for one more little thing? Do you have a way to get the car out of the parking lot? We don't have enough to pay for it…"

Rebeca explains to us that the expo will last eight days and it is open from 11:00 am until 11:00 pm. She gives the car a place next to a door connecting two huge showrooms. Everyone who comes will have to pass this spot!

In this excellent location, we begin to tell our story once and again until we've repeated it at least a thousand times. The response of the public is marvelous, not only for book sales we are close to running out of, as the days pass, but also for the unexpected kind gestures.

One young man along with his brother, a friend and girlfriend come together to the expo after having read the book, all dressed in jackets; all new, all the same imprinted with designs which when we see them leave us with our mouths hanging open. It's our logo printed on the back and on the front our message. When they come up, they say, "We've made 100 t-shirts for you to sell." The guy hands me a black bag full of something soft.

In disbelief, I say laughing "Sure! They're t-shirts, I'll take them…" before taking a look in the bag. They really are T-shirt's with our logo and our slogan: "The secret to realizing a dream is: starting it…Start yours!!!

"Keep looking, go ahead," Cande and I take out all the shirts and among the jerseys we discover a very special one, hugely tiny, for our soon to be arriving baby. We are dumbfounded. When they leave us with big hugs and many thanks, they also give us their jackets.

"I read your book and came back," said a man who while shaking my hand slips me something, "Take this, it's for your trip, but don't consider it a gift, it's a loan. It's a help that you have to give back to me by giving it to someone else that needs it as you do today. That's how it was given to me. Today, that's how I'm passing it to you."

One curious guy asks: "The world record in Guinness is 25 days from Tierra del Fuego to Alaska. How long have you been at it?"

"If the record is 25 days, the record will stand, I don't believe we can break it."

"What a pity! Are you sure? How long has it been?"

"Let's say two years and twenty-five days."

Resuscitate From Life

After experiencing so many beautiful things, we are preparing to take down our stand when a man visits us who is in a booth of cars of a very exclusive make. He has the appearance and statue of a successful businessman.

"I have been working for this company for 20 years. Twenty years have flown. I got into it just to make some money, then do what I want to. However, 20 years have passed at the speed of light and now I don't know what to do. I'm not sure that I like this. I would love to do other things, but everyone tells me that I must be thankful for what I am doing, for what I have, for my work; and that there are people in worse situations than me," he pauses and continues as if he would like to unburden himself. "20 of my years have gone away and only to fit in the system, but it doesn't fit me. Still, I'm missing a lot, I crave to feel love for what I do; I want to feel that it's useful for me and for many. Now it's been twenty years and I only feel like a piece of another's engine. I keep my own motor turned off because of fears, fears of not knowing how to turn it on, fear of breaking down, and fear of not knowing how to fix it. Twenty years have passed. But now my fears have grown on par with my desires to change and to see what I can do for what I want to do."

He looks defeated, defeated by fear, comfort, conformities, and deficient value of his freedom. All this combined is against his dream. "Awaken and come forth", Jesus said to his dead friend. Here for this man, the same words will have the same result. Resuscitation isn't only for death, it's also to revive a life not lived, from a lost existence with no meaning.

"Do you know what a Chinese philosopher said? 'A walk of a thousand miles begins with the first step'. Why don't you rise and go forth...?" after my words he didn't say anything, he merely stares at me. So I ask him, "If you were given a pass to an amusement park, what would you do?"

"Hummm, I think I'd get up very early to be the first one in and be among the last to leave.

"Would you try to go on all the rides?"

"Yes, sure, I'd ride all the roller coasters, including those I'm afraid of, I'd wait in all the lines and go back to ride again the ones I really like, even if those lines are the longest. I'd try the rides that don't exactly pique my interest and if there were time, I'd do it all over again. I'd try to suck the morrow out of the day."

"What if instead of a pass to an amusement park, someone give you the pass for a life, what would you do with that life?" I give him a few seconds to think about it. "I believe this world in which we live is paradise, and we're here to enjoy it, not to live a life of sacrifices, on the promise of the reward of an afterlife full of pleasure. If God has granted us the miracle of a life and we still don't enjoy it, why would he give us a better one?"

We remain in silence, one standing in front of the other. He gives me his best smile with a hug and he goes. I remain standing in the same place thinking about what I said and noticed how much I've changed. Maybe dreams are contagious...

One thing that is contagious is "Montezuma's revenge," an infection that almost all the tourists to this city get and it's given me quite a fever. It could have been the burritos, or the enchilada or maybe the goat barbeque, or...any one of the delicious foods we've been trying. There is nowhere in the expo I can lay down, and inside the car people would feel sorry for me, so I lie down beneath the car and exhausted, I fall asleep. From here I can see hundreds of feet going around, listening to Cande talk about the trip... At one point, a little one dropped his little car and saw me when he bent to pick it up.

"Daddy, there's a dead man under the car!"

I wake up with this comment and numerous pairs of eyes looking at me...

Xochimilco

At the end of the auto expo, we move to another house, which is very hard for us, as hard as when we left our own home. Although we have hundreds of invitations, we can't accept them all, we can choose only one.

We decide to go with Miguel, a member of the Renault Club. He wants to install a heater in our car for the weather awaiting us in Alaska and do some other small necessary repairs. For more than a week, we stay with him and his wife. Together we visit Aztec pyramids, Xochimilco, and they even organize a procession of cars around the city.

Just before we leave, his wife tells Cande, "When my husband told me he brought you home, I went crazy, I was so angry. I asked him how can you trust strange people in the house, he didn't know anything about you...and now you're leaving, I don't want you to, I will miss you so much. I bought this to accompany you and your baby during the trip."

In a tiny wrapped box, which Cande opens enthusiastically, there is a medal of the Virgin of Guadalupe, the patron saint of Mexico, the patron of all of America. Sincerely touched, Cande thanks her graciously.

A Stumbling Block

At the auto expo, a Mexican told us that they don't need a visa to visit Canada. And what about us? Yes, the Argentineans do. At first, we were nervous and afraid about what would happen if they turned us down. However, thinking it all through, that seems impossible. During our stay here, we have been putting together a complete folder explaining about our trip; now it's stuffed full of newspaper articles, photos, our book, and letters of recommendation including those from embassies.

We drive there in the car with the intention of presenting it too, but we see it's impossible for them to see it. It's excruciating to pay the non-refundable $100 fee to ask for the visa. We are a bit indignant. Why do we have to pay so much for a transaction that takes so few minutes to such a rich country?

We stand in line mixed with people from all over the world. Finally, we reach a bulletproof window attended by a Mexican girl with whom we can only communicate through a microphone.

"Nationality?"

"Argentinean."

The young woman studies a form and fits us into a category. Next she continues with the questionnaire:

"How much money do you have?"

"Enough."

"Do you have a bank account?"

"No, but if you want, we can show you what we have," Cande get out our folder.

She looks surprised at everything we gave her. She tries to conceal her excitement about the journey, the adventure, but her face gives her away. However, she continues:

"Profession?"

"Electrician and secretary," her excitement is erased by an apprehensive expression.

"Is something wrong?"

"No, no…I'll go give everything to the consul. Please have a seat until we call you."

We take a seat as directed, very anxious and even more nervous. They begin to call back other people who are waiting too. Very quickly, from a distance and by only looking at the expression on their faces it's obvious to whom they've granted the visa and whom not. Who has been approved or rejected. Who has been admitted or segregated.

While I wait, I think about many things. The first thing they ask is where you are from, this says that depending on whether you were born in one place or another, you have more or fewer possibilities. From what I can see it also looks like it matters how you are dressed. It's total discrimination: if you belong to one of the lucky countries you can get in, whoever you are. Say you are not in one of these countries, a teacher with a low income and you just want to travel to teach about what you learned, you are not welcome. We heard our names, we squeezed each other's hands, we stand up and we approach the horrible bulletproof window. The girl doesn't look at us in the eye, maybe she doesn't want to. She looks at everything she is returning to us, the folder, the papers, and lastly the passport.

"So, can we go to Canada?" Cande asks.

"No, the consul has denied your visa."

"But why?" we ask her with quivering voices. We feel like dying.

"He doesn't have to tell you why, you just were denied."

"But we need to go through Canada to get to Alaska, to accomplish our dream. It cannot be. Did the consul look at everything we gave him to prove what we are doing?"

"I told him about your story, but the only thing he saw was that you don't have a bank account. For them this is more than important," she explained to me, confirming my ideas.

"Will you let us talk to him, please?"

"No, he doesn't receive anyone, and once he says no, the answer is no. I'm sorry."

We leave defeated, feeling completely denigrated, rejected and discriminated against, as if we were sick cattle. We open the passport and we see an enormous "DENIED" stamp on it. Cande starts to cry, not because she can't get into Canada, but for the stamp and the powerlessness to do anything. The feeling is horrible.

"Because we don't have a bank account, they will not let us enter. In my home, many many more come in who don't have one. And they are just as special as those who do," she comments through her tears.

They have excluded. We never imagined we would be denied, not only because of what we're doing, but also because we also believe that we are good people acting sincerely. Now we cry with rage, a lot of rage for the helplessness. One person who hasn't even looked in our faces, who didn't come out to meet us who wouldn't even come out when we asked, discriminated against us. This is what caused the helplessness: we couldn't even talk to him...explain ourselves. We want to rip the page out of the passport; which I am that close to doing it.

"Cande, Alaska is our destiny, whatever it takes, we will get there. We didn't manage to get this far for only one person to stand in our way."

"It's just one stupid man who doesn't know anything about dreams. For sure he hates his work, he hates being in Mexico. How is it possible that only one person could decide my fate? How could he deprive his fellow countrymen from participating in this dream and all the good energy that our story spreads?"

We think about what we could do to reverse this stamp and this feeling. It occurs to us to send letters to the Canadians we've met on the road, those who have written to us without knowing us, and the members of the antique car clubs in Canada, who have all offered us their homes... We'll write and tell them what happened. However, we'll do it in a few days when we've calmed down, with less anger and more room for productive ideas.

Don Quixote, Rocinante and...

We return to Puebla to spend Christmas, as we promised our half Uruguayan-half Mexican family where we were staying during our first stay at that city. We also go to collect our calendars, of which there aren't 4,000 as the owner of the newspaper had told us, but 7,000!! We have no idea how to fit them all in the car, let alone sell them.

"Who's going to want to buy a calendar with our picture? Who's going to want to hang a calendar on their kitchen wall with our faces for a whole year??" we ask.

The first city where we try our luck is Querétaro. We go to a hotel that we had been invited to stay in during the Autoexpo. Across from it is the newspaper office where they are at the point of finalizing tomorrow's edition. They hold the presses, literally, to write a story about us for the front page.

The next day, we go to the central plaza, situated among incredibly beautiful stone buildings. We park where there is a sign stating it's prohibited, we hang up our map of the trip, and the pictures. Additionally, on each side of the Graham, we arrange some calendars. Right away, the people start to gather around us: they are attracted by the car, or because of the newspaper article, or they come just to figure out what all the commotion is about.

A man buys a calendar...then another and another one asks us to sign it for him. When we look up, we see a line forming, consisting of folks waiting to buy our calendars with coins in their hands. We could hear them questioning one another, "What are they giving away?"

"No, they're not giving away anything, they are selling their calendars," is the response.

"And, who are they?"

"We don't know, but they must be famous, because they are autographing them."

That night, we go to eat dinner with the president of the University of Mexico, although we don't know who he is until well into the dinner.

"You know, I am not a car lover. I don't know why I went to the expo, but I met you there and I bought your book. I liked it so much that a few days later, when I had to write my end of year speech, I based it mostly on your book. For many, graduating is their own dream or the dream of their parents, no matter what it takes. For the majority it's the biggest step in their lives. There are thousands of people who graduate as lawyers, doctors, and architects, but how many graduate as dream chasers?"

We remain in silence, thinking about his words, until one of his friends breaks it commenting: "This car of yours is like the horse in Don Quixote, Rocinante; the pure bread, with style, for gentlemen…and you, you really look like Don Quixote, tall, thin, a little bit crazy, " he indicates me and then in Cande's direction. "On the other hand you, you look like…" the pause makes us think that he's going to say "Sancho Panza", his short, fat sidekick, so collectively we smile mischievously, "…Dulcinea." He continues seriously making us understand we have misinterpreted him. "This car, this lady and this character," he points, indicating me again, "you are the second part of 'Don Quixote de la Mancha', the long awaited end to such a beautiful story…"

As You Look, I Looked myself too

Before going from Querétaro, we write a letter. We send it by e-mail and through the post to everyone we know in Canada, telling them about our situation with the visa. Awaiting their responses, we go to beautiful San Miguel de Allende, from where we travel to the mysterious Guanajuato. It doesn't seem like we are in America, because its style is reminiscent of a feudal European city.

In Guanajuato we visit the Museum of the Mummies. They exhibit corpses retrieved from the cemeteries that no one claimed and because this is a very arid zone they don't decompose, instead they turn into mummies. We pass through halls surrounded by hundreds of mummies; they range from completely dressed, including their boots to completely nude. Some are women who died in childbirth along with their babies, others, children. They all have the face of suffering, and their bodies are emaciated. Just before the end, there is one holding a plaque. Some as they read it laugh, others leave here pensive. "As you look now, I looked too. As I look now, so will you." Cande and I leave in deep thought. We are thinking that every one with life runs a race with death. Death always wins. However the triumph is during the race, not at the end; a race we are running and enjoying.

Among the places we have been invited we find the Hacienda Ciénaga de Mata, near the city of Aguascalientes. It's to there we're headed. The road is deserted, we see almost no one, the sun is scorching and our clothes are sticking to us. At midday the high temperature compels us to stop. But, where? The asphalt is almost bubbling and there is no shade to invite us. We keep going. Better the hot breeze than the smell of melted tar.

On the straight road we see a truck coming toward us, some movement in the scorching desert. Before it passes us, something dark and spherical flies out from between its back wheels and at a tremendous speed bounces off the ground and rebounds straight at us. We hear a noisy metallic bang and smashing glass. Reflexively, I duck at the same time that I hear another bang, a scream from Cande, and glass shattering all around, then silence. I look at my wife, she has a cut on her forehead, but it's not deep. She looks at me and she's very frightened. My hand is full of blood and in the mirror's reflection, I see my face covered with tiny cuts. I'm bleeding, but nothing hurts. Cande is still nervous, trembling.

"What-was-that?" she asks me.

"I think it was a rock, I saw it coming. Where is it? Where did it end up?"

We look in the back seat, we don't find it. We lift our gaze and in the canvas roof we see a big tear. I put in my hand and feel that one of the wooden ribs is broken; a bit farther back, the rock, bigger than a big grapefruit.

"It could have killed you…"says Cande when she sees it, now even more nervous, "What would I do if something happened to you?" Alone, with only her thoughts, she becomes with each question even more tense, "Here, in the middle of the desert, where could I have taken you?"

She helps pick the glass off me. With each one she takes off, she repeats what could have happened if the rock had hit me in the face. She looks at the hole in the windshield, and in the roof, making a straight line with her arm: yes, if I hadn't reacted, if I hadn't ducked, I would be in very bad shape.

I get out and look at the front of the car. The headlight was destroyed in the first bang, the one that served as a warning for me to bend down. Then the rock hit the windshield and ultimately the roof. The stone has rubber marks, for sure, it was trapped between the two rear wheels of the truck and it cleared them exactly when we were passing. I help Cande to finish cleaning the seats a bit and we continue.

Poncho Charro

Only sixty yards from the accident we find the entrance to the hacienda. This has belonged to the same family, Rincon Gallardo, since 1650. At that time, the ranch was like a kingdom covering a total of 889,000 acres and had 1850 inhabitants. It still has its own church, one that any city would envy; its own village, and its own dam.

"Poncho" Rincon Gallardo, whom we had to wait for because he was out rounding up the cattle, receives us. A senior gentleman who doesn't look his age. For this man, old age will have to wait. Poncho is a total *charro*, that is to say, a true Mexican cowboy, an honor to meet.

Charmed by the house and by the history of the place, we ask him to tell us more about it. First, he shows us the facade of the church and the house. We observe in them various broken statues and many bullet holes.

"Pancho Villa," comments the *charro*. Later he shows us the interior of the house and invites us to eat on the inside patio, around an enormous table, together with his son. During dinner, they tell us the hacienda isn't as grand as it once was. Revolutions, agrarian reforms, family divisions and sales of various parts have caused some of it to be lost. Still, the antique house, the stables, and other constructions bring memories of that golden era.

"How's the pregnancy going?"

"In León we had a check-up in a hospital. The owner's daughter was our hostess there. I had an ultrasound there and the baby looks marvelous," Cande reports, very happily.

"So? Could you tell if it's a boy or a girl?"

"The doctor wanted to tell us, three times! We didn't want to know, but even so she still insisted on telling us. We had to stop her. We love surprises."

"Speaking of expecting, I have to go and check the pregnant cattle," comments the charro's son.

"You mean to say I look like a cow?" grumbles Cande.

"Oh, you're not too far from it with your four-month belly," the youth laughs and to smooth out the situation, he invites us to come along with him.

At my request I get dressed in the clothes of a charro and an enormous Mexican hat. We go, together with six other *charros*, to round up the cattle. Once we're in the corral, my wife and the vet palpate each one of the animals. She looks very happy, in her element, because this is what she's studied. She celebrates each pregnancy with the veterinarian, and the rest of us catch her happiness.

In the house of the foreman, next to the corral, a young man is waiting to talk to the ranch owner. He has brought his saddle to sell. He is selling what little he has because he's crossing the Río Grande to enter the United States illegally. He can't take anything, except his documents and a little money. In any case, this must be very little because if someone manages to catch you, they might take it.

"And what if they pick you up?"

"They bring me back and I will try again to get back in. I have nothing to lose and I want to go, I have as much of a right to live there as them. They formed their country with immigrant people from all over the world who were looking for somewhere to live, work, and accomplish their dreams. Now their own sons and grandsons are rejecting the immigrants. They call themselves Americans, but none of them have my color nor my race. My father was born here, just as the father of my father, and so on for a hundred generations, but now we have to enter, live and work in hiding. We're branded 'the undocumented', when we can document with our race, with our blood, that we are 'Americans'."

We understand what he is saying very well, because we are experiencing the same thing since the rejection of the visa to enter Canada. Rejection stamped by only one person, whose father or grandfathers at some time requested permission and which was granted.

"Do many go to the US?" I ask Poncho when we're alone.

"Yes, many, they are usually the best ones that go, the most determined, the most capable of us all. They are truly those who have the greatest desire to work, to progress, to grow. There they are unwanted and here we lose them. They talk down about them there, they are disapproved of, and they are accused of crimes and other things. It could be that some are criminal, but the majority risk themselves just for work."

With a Little Earth

We depart along the same road on which we had our accident. I remember how close we were to living something terrible and I experience a strange sensation that becomes more acute when we pass by a cemetery. At the entrance we read: "Passerby, I wait for you." "You're just going to have to wait, because I still

have a long way to go," I reply in my sincere thoughts.

We stop in Aguascalientes, to repair the car. We take advantage of our state to check messages on the Internet. To our surprise, the responses of the Canadians don't take long and all reveal shame for their consul that denied the entrance to a dream.

Not only did we receive very beautiful invitations,

but they also asked their friends and relatives to write, we even receive letters from churches. Two messages ask for photos and material about the trip for articles in the newspapers. The correspondence we have received is so heartwarming that we jump out of joy. The only one who denied us entrance is the man at the embassy, not Canada itself.

With the car back in shape, for many miles, we inch our way up on a hand-built cobblestone road leading to the mouth of a mine in the mountain.

We drive into the tunnel that connects to another mine coming out at its mouth on the other side of the mountain. Surprisingly, a village appears right in front of us, as we come out. This is the way we enter Real de Catorce, connected to the rest of the world through a mine. A small village of less than 800 inhabitants at 8400 ft. above sea level, situated in a narrow valley.

Because of its silver mine, it grew to be very rich having a population of 40,000 souls. All its buildings, constructed of stone and mud, are mostly in ruins. We drive past bridges, cemeteries, theaters, ancient churches and even a bull fighting ring. Everything is built on a slope upward or downward, because we are on the side of a mountain. We stay in an ancient building, in a huge room crowded with noises and spirits. Later, walking, we visit abandoned mines and small ghost towns. During dinner, we meet a tourist enthralled with the place desiring to find a cactus plant called peyote. This is a hallucinogen used by the indigenous during their rituals:

"If you want to, tomorrow we can go out together. I hired someone who knows the area and where we can find some. They say it's fabulous, that you see the stars," he invites us.

"No, thanks. We're not here looking for peyote," I answer.

"But, peyote is unique to this area, you can't leave without trying some…"

"Others have offered us drugs during our trip, but we didn't accept any. We don't need anything to make us feel good temporarily, only things that make us feel better forever. We want to feel good by doing something, not for taking something that afterward we will need to take again," explains Cande.

"It's not that we're afraid of being addicts, we already are…" the tourist is amazed to hear this, "…We're addicted to love, to dreams, and to life. The more love we have, the more we want, the more dreams we accomplish, the more we want to go for. We are hooked on life."

"If I don't like how the world is, I don't want to see it differently because of a drug. I want to see it transformed because of something I changed, something I did or at least I am trying to do," concluded my wife.

The next day, we take off again to walk following a footpath that leads to the abandoned mines whose pitch blackness frightens us. Later we wander around some tiny abandoned villages.

Inside of a church in ruins, we find a shepard tending his sheep. The day, the place, the mountain, and this shepard bring forth a beautiful sensation of peace. We speak a long while with him in a healthy envy because in his small world, with his small flock, he has it all.

He tells us about his sheep, the personalities of each one. He explains that some are better than others and that all of them have a name. He also speaks very well of his dogs.

"My sheep aren't my sheep, they are my dog's sheep. They are not my dogs, I am also theirs. This is why they take such good care of me, just as they do of the sheep.

When we tell him we are travelers, he tells us, "Work to live, good; live to work, bad. Eat to live, good; live to eat, bad. Travel to live, good; live to travel, very good! How are you doing in your trip?"

"Up to now it's been marvelous, but we are a bit worried about what's coming next." I respond alluding to our inconvenience with the visa for Canada.

"Do you have faith?" he asks me.

"Have faith in what?"

"In yourself, in that some way you will be able, in that you'll know how to find some solution for this thing or that other. If you don't have faith in yourself is impossible for anyone else to."

Content with what our shepherd said, and realizing how much sense he made, we return to Real de Catorce. On the way, we see a man making mud bricks by hand, for his house. This image makes us think that with a little earth you can make a brick. With a few bricks, you can make a house; with a few houses, you can make a town. With a few towns, you can make a nation. With a few nations, you can make a continent. With a few continents, you can make the earth. And with a little earth, you can make a brick...everything goes back full circle.

We get to Monterrey. This is a perfect site for us to relax. However, during the night, I wake up, doubled over with a terrible pain near my stomach. The anguish let up for a few minutes, but very shortly returns with greater intensity. It hurts so much I see stars. Cande wakes up frightened by my groans, and watches me as I walk around the room, bent over from pain. The pain makes me throw up. Neither of us knows what it could be. At the break of day, we look for a clinic. When we find one, the pain had already subsided.

"Kidney stones!" affirmed the doctor, "Drink a lot of water, from what you've told me it seems that you've already passed it in your urine."

Hasta la Vista Latin America

As if it were magic, as if it were a rule of the trip, before we leave Mexico, in Nuevo Laredo, we are given a marvelous send off. It is in the form of a procession of antique cars, whose route ends in the central plaza. It's been organized by Oscar Chavarria, who happily gives us the last hug of the thousands we have received in Mexico.

This much affection helps calm our nerves of being at the door of a gigantic nation, where the differences in language, laws and culture are enormous. We feel we are in the presence of a new stage of the trip, as if we're beginning all over again. Those same fears from the beginning resurface and the same questions return. "How will it be?" "What's waiting for us?"

"I want to know the United States, but I don't want to leave Latin America. I am sad, my love." Cande hugs me to hide the tears flowing down her cheeks.

"The Latin American people were fabulous, they made us feel at home and not miss our own so much. Now, I am afraid for the rest of my pregnancy, and the birth in a country with another culture, another way of living… I don't have anything near me except for you and this baby. I feel that I'm leaving my family once again, my friends…"

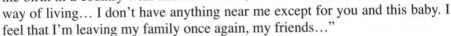

"What happens if they don't let you in?" a man asks us, throwing a bucket of cold water on our warm farewell.

"Why would they refuse us?"

"If they see her in her condition or if they ask you to prove how much money you have. Or for no good reason…"

"Look, it could be that what he's saying is justified. Up until this point you've been crossing brother countries, Latin American countries, but the gringos… well, if they want to, they will deny your entrance. They don't have to give you a reason nor motive: if they want to, they will send you packing…" agreed another.

We know they are right. Still the words of the shepard give me confidence and now I have to spread it.

"Don't worry, nothing bad will happen. Trust in us. Nothing is opposed to a dream."

United States & Canada

TILL HERE:
20094 miles
in 2 years and 1 mo.

White Horse

Hyder

Pince George

Parksville · Vancouver

Seattle

Portland

Denver

Yosemite N.P.

ancisco

Grand Canyon N.P.

Los Angeles

San Antonio

Laredo

Houston

Fort Worth

Jackson

Kansas

Saint Louis

Chicago

Detroit

Cleveland

Hershey

Greensboro

Toronto

Ottawa

Montreal

Quebec

Buffalo

Halfmoon

Boston

New York

Washington D. C.

Halifax

P.E.I.

N

United States & Canada

Starting All Over Again

Godspeed

From the fence that keeps people from getting to the Río Grande River, hang planks of wood. There are many, each one marked with the names of those who have perished in search of a new life. We are waiting, in a long line of cars, to enter the United States. We feel anxious, nervous and afraid. What will they require for entry? What questions will they ask us when get there? Will they be able to deny our entry? Are we not entering into the country of the "American Dream"? Will we find people who will take us in and help us or will we have to do it all on our own? Will we be able to continue to earn money to go on with the journey? There is only one way to find out, and that's by going there!

The official directing the traffic that crosses the river asks us in English, "Are you really traveling from Argentina to Alaska on this?"

"Yes."

"Couldn't you have found another car?" he asks us with a note of amusement in his voice.

"It was this one, or the old one," I respond. He gives me a smile as he points out which way we should go.

We are attended by a man inside the booth on the edge of the bridge who doesn't respond to our greeting, nor show any reaction to the Graham or the trip. He gives us a paper on which he has checked the box, "Complete Inspection" and indicates which way we should go.

We park the car and while we are waiting for it to be inspected, a man tells us that first we have to finish the immigration papers. We go into a large office where yet again, there is a long thread of people waiting. Upon reaching the counter, we hand over our passports at the same time as we see the couple next to us being denied entry. They ask why but the official dealing with them doesn't

294

answer. He merely automatically calls the next person in line. Since September 11, they are much more cautious and pressured "from higher up". Now they deny entrance to applicants when they have any reservation whatsoever. "You were born in San Francisco, California?" questions the agent.

"Yes," I reply.

"And you don't speak English?"

"Almost none. I have lived in Argentina since I was a year old." He studies my face, then the passport, checking to make sure it's authentic. When he gives it back he says, "Welcome home, guy." He doesn't ask us anything else. Cande filled out the forms asking for six months' permission to stay in the United States, but they only authorize her for three.

"Can this be renewed?" she asks, "because of the car we are traveling in, we are going to need more than three months to get to Alaska."

"Yes, sure, when it's about to expire just ask for an extension."

When we return to the Graham, we see many uniformed men surrounding it. There are five men who are auto inspectors; three armed soldiers and several others whom we can see work here.

"What's the problem?" I whisper to Cande with a great knot in my stomach. She shrugs her shoulders. We go closer.

"Are you the owners of this car?" inquired one of the soldiers.

"Yes," I respond nervously.

"Have you really traveled in this car all the way from Argentina?" Everyone is silent.

"Yes, we have already driven nearly 20,000 miles during this two-year trip, and our goal is Alaska."

"Wow, man, you are really nuts!" he declares as we hear the rest of them exclaim: "That's Great!" "Incredible!" More questions follow and Cande, and I look at each other and begin to relax.

They don't inspect the car at all. They prefer to fire questions at us and listen to our stories. They tell us farewell with hearty handshakes and point out the road that will take us to Alaska. They shout after us, "Godspeed!" I never heard this before, and it really touches me.

After leaving the border and getting into the United States we give each other a congratulatory kiss, pleased to begin this new leg and relieved that the border crossing turned out to be so easy. To celebrate, we stop to eat. Faithful to our custom of trying something typical of each new country, we head straight to McDonald's!

Wetbacks

We continue traveling up to San Antonio, Texas. We stay in the house of some *chilangos* whom we met in Nuevo Laredo. By the time we get there, they have already made us famous. Several people come to meet us at the family's auto repair shop and we are interviewed on television. Usually, the reports are in Spanish, and we answer all the questions easily. But, when we are interviewed for the English channels, it is very difficult for us to respond.

At the shop, several of us very enthusiastically work on repainting much of the car. Because of the poor quality of the previous paint job, the black paint is cracking and peeling. Citlatli, the one-year-old daughter of our hosts hugs Cande once and then again. "It's going to be a boy," her mother states with assurance.

A boy? We don't have a name for a boy. Our intuition tells us it's going to be a girl and we have thought of the perfect name for her, "America". We don't have any preference for one over the other, boy or girl, it's just a feeling.

The Graham bids farewell to San Antonio with a new paint job, a new battery and an alternator. Since people in this country aren't used to fixing old parts but instead replace them with new ones, we went to a giant auto salvage yard to find an alternator from a Chevrolet to put in our car. If many of the cars in the junkyard were taken into Latin America, they would be back on the streets, fixed up as good as new.

A Hunch

We come to a crossroad while we are in Texas. We have to choose between two ways: one goes west and directly to Alaska. If we go this way, we will without a doubt reach Alaska in four months, ahead of the birth of the baby, and before winter sets in.

The other option is to set out east, participate in the Graham Owners Club meet and visit New York, Washington, Toronto and Ottawa, the capital of Canada, and Detroit, the birthplace of our car. It follows then that this direction means countless more miles, months more time and a great deal more money. The distance doesn't frighten us since we would like to see and learn more.

On the other hand, the time does trouble us because this option entails traveling with a baby on board and being obliged to wait until the following year, for the Alaskan summer. Additionally, the money...money we don't have to pay for the birth of our child, nor for the many miles in a nation where everything is expensive. While we still have some books that we can continue selling, they are in Spanish and farther north it will be more difficult to find readers who'll buy them. We do have some crafts but those won't get us very far. Cande continues to paint, although if we expect to live off of the paintings, it would be necessary to paint one every day, which is impossible.

"So, what should we do?" I ask Cande who is sitting next to me staring at the turning point in the road ahead of us.

"If I think about it, I say west..." she pauses silently, wishing to say something more, "if I go by what the heart says, I say east."

I put the car in first gear, let out the clutch, and turn the steering wheel pointing the grill of the car east. I remember the words of the Spaniard when we were climbing up to the ruins of Machu Picchu, "If you let your heart lead, you will never go the wrong way."

Having left the decision of which direction we continue until the last instant has made us able to choose more rapidly. If we had put any thought into it, we would have traveled west. Instead, it's toward the magic we go. Our hearts carry us east. We don't take the great highways that are all over the place, but far from the real life. We follow the lesser roads that pass through towns. This way we get a closer look at the houses and a more intimate view into at life in the United States.

We are passing through the aridness of a desert. We pull over in a small town, in front of a bar, to ask for directions to a gas station. Out front, there are enormous pickups, two of which have large cow horns mounted on their hoods. I push the door open and cross the threshold into a Wild West movie. There are wooden floors, a bartender with a moustache and white shirt, and only two tables occupied by various cowboys who even though they're indoors are wearing their 10-gallon hats. Barely two steps in the bar, everyone turns to look over me. What an impression I make on them! I have messy hair because I have been driving with the windshield open, a bright yellow T-shirt with the logo of the Colombian beer Aguila, shorts and sandals…all that's missing is for me to ask for a glass of milk.

Fairies and Angels

Houston is waiting for us, and with open arms. A couple of Argentineans whom we met in Costa Rica put us up. They live in a grand house located in a beautiful district, with their son, daughter-in-law and grandson. As they show us to our lodgings, a game room with a television, they assure us that the two-year-old will surely wake us up before 6:00 A.M. to play in here. Nevertheless, the following day we wake up after nine o'clock and the whole house is in silence.

We go to the kitchen and see things out of place, slightly disordered. What we notice the most is that there is no one in the house. We don't know what to do. We don't understand and can only speculate about the facts. We wait for half an hour until the grandparents show up.

"Excuse us for having left you and waking you up like this."

"We woke up ourselves, about half an hour ago," Cande tells them.

"What? You mean you didn't hear anything? My son's wife had an epileptic attack in the bathroom; she hit her head and it bled a lot. We called an ambulance. It arrived along with police, waking up the whole neighborhood. They were here for a long time. In the middle of everything, our grandson woke up crying and we couldn't calm him down. Finally we all went to the hospital, and you didn't hear anything?"

"No, nothing."

"Well…never mind. Right now you have to get ready to go to a meeting with the Argentina Club of Houston. It's an important get-together and they are expecting you."

Before going to the meeting we check our e-mail. We want to continue selling books to advance; not only to finance us but also, because it's part of the trip, to share our message. But we have run into the barrier of language; translating the manuscript, correcting it, designing and printing costs too much money, way beyond our means. However, today we encounter a miracle. At exactly the right moment, a friend in Guatemala sends us the English translation via e-mail. Charmed by the book, Richard Skaggs offered to translate it. At that time, we had replied yes that we would love that, but we thought that it might not happen because it is such a big job. Even so, here it is in our hands, translated and at no charge.

We go to the meeting and are warmly welcomed by the colony of Argentineans, which is much larger than we had imagined. Everybody celebrates our success for having gotten so far. They are so enthusiastic that they try to persuade us, competing among themselves about who gets to invite us to their house or to go fishing or to eat, or whatever. In addition, a doctor shows up and offers lab work for Cande as well as the name of an obstetrician.

Our fairy godmothers also appear. Juanita is an American married to an Argentinean. She is enthusiastic about everything Latino and offers to correct the translation of our book and since this will take a while, she invites us to hang around at her house.

Hearing about what we hope to achieve, another Argentine woman, a graphic designer, offers her and her husband's service to design the book. This means

that now all we're missing is the printing. With all that is happening we wonder how it's possible and we remember the shepherd we found in the church on that mountain in Mexico. "Everything is possible, everything comes to you. If you have faith in yourself, it is contagious to others." So here we are, surrounded by people who caught the bug of our hope. Before we leave the meeting, we receive the icing of the cake, they introduce us to a Colombian who offers to print the book in his small print shop. He will do everything that he can for us and will charge us only what it costs him.

Once we get to Juanita and Eduardo's house, we begin working. We had planned to be in Houston for only a couple of days but we have been here now for more than a month focusing on the book and receiving or visiting all kinds of people. We receive numerous invitations. We go to dinner at the home of a couple that toured Europe in a Model T Ford. This surprises us, but not as much as another wonderful thing they have done during their lives. They have adopted many children, most of whom were no longer infants. It appears that they are a couple with infinite love for their fellow human being and for dreams.

Since this man, Peter Reinthaler, has a lot of knowledge about old cars, we ask him about insurance, which is mandatory here in the States but we haven't gotten any yet. Insurance for antique cars is very economical if you have a local driver's license, but this isn't our case. When we ask about prices we are always quoted incredibly high rates because of the type of adventure trip we are undertaking. He understands what we're saying and at the end of my explanation he tells me, "Your car insurance is on me. That's my business." Peter's answer amazes us. "I own an insurance company for antique cars."

Cande and I stare at each other, speechless. How is it that we always fall into the right place? During the whole trip so far, there has not been one coincidental encounter; every one is causal. Before we leave, the couple buys some artwork and suggests that we take our things with us to sell when we attend the meeting of the Antique Automobile Club of America (AACA) next week.

At that meeting we are treated to a fabulous welcome. We are invited to give a speech about the trip. Thanks to our desire to share and the audience's wish to hear about the trip, we manage to make them understand in our English, which, little by little, is getting better.

During the gathering we meet up with the Hardeman family who has gone twice from Texas to Alaska in a Model T Ford. We spend a couple of hours chatting about trips and dreams. At the end of the chat, I ask them if they know where we can find new tires for the Graham since our tractor tires can't go any further. Immediately, from his briefcase the man produces a catalogue published by a company that sells tires for antique cars. When we see our tires we are petrified by the price, $125 for each one.

"We'd better wait to see about them after the baby is born," I say.

The next day while we are putting books together, the phone rings.

"I took the liberty of talking about your one-of-a-kind-story and your dream to my friends who live all over the United States," a highly excited Ben Hardeman reveals to me. "I also told them about your shabby tires. Everybody pitched in and we already bought you a set of four new tires! There are donations from Kentucky, Montana, Tennessee, Texas and Alaska. Some of them gave enough to purchase a quarter of a wheel, others a half and others the whole tire. Additionally, when I told the Coker Tire Company what we were up to, they donated the spare."

I ask Ben "Why are all these people from states we're not even going to visit willing to help us?"

"Because there is a dream to fulfill."

We go to Bryan, Texas, to get the tires. Ben and his friends meet us, greet us and help us mount the new tires on the car as well as repair some mechanical troubles. In the evening, the car club of the region has organized a barbeque potluck for us.

This is the first time since arriving in the United States where we are surrounded by only English-speaking Americans. All the same, our hosts call the television station to set up interviews, and their friends show us around. Because of the way that they treat us, their hospitality and their willingness to help us, we feel as if we are still in Latin America. The only difference is the language.

In the end, not only do we leave with new wheels, but also a new kitchen to break in. Ben configured a rectangular pot whose bottom comes into contact with part of the motor and absorbs its heat. This gadget is perfect for this part of the trip, where the food is much more expensive.

As soon as we leave, like children with a new toy, we try it out. We put on some chicken soup to heat and after a few miles we begin to smell something yummy inside the car. We stop under the meager shade of some trees and enjoy delicious steaming soup in the sizzling Texas afternoon.

The car looks cool with its new sneakers. Besides that, now it goes much faster. We have increased our cruising speed by twenty percent. Before we traveled at 25 miles an hour but now we manage 30! So, get out of our way, here we come!

The Border: Hot zone

On the recommendation of the Argentine Consul and others, only one month and a half after arriving, we request an extension of the visa at the office of immigration. To do this we go at 4:00 A.M. in order to stand in line, but when we arrive, it's already quite long. There are people from all over the world. Many of them are here for the twentieth time; others, like ourselves, for the first. The majority of them want their residency. When we get into the building, they give us a number that looks like infinity because we wait and wait and wait. When they finally get to our number, we are attended for less than a minute, horribly.

"You can not renew this, it's no good. You must leave the country," an unyielding man with a rigid face discourages us.

"But we were told that it could be extended," Cande manages to say.

"You didn't read the back. It states very clearly: 'NON renewable.' You'll have to leave."

"But she is my wife. I was born here and I want my child to be born here too."

"She is the pregnant one, not you. She has to leave. Take a plane to Argentina, do the paperwork and then come back."

"But don't I have any rights?" The man turns his back on me, leaving my words hanging in the air. I cannot believe it. We ask at the next window if there isn't anything they can do. They say no for an answer, but if we want to, we can consult a lawyer. We go to see three of them who all give us the same information. I could apply for a green card for Cande, but the process in Texas could take from two to three years and costs two thousand dollars. In any case, since we don't have any income, somebody has to sponsor us and we would have to acquire a permanent address. Additionally, during this time, Cande may not leave the country.

"We don't want to settle down, we are traveling to Alaska," I explain to the third lawyer.

Looking for a solution to our problem, we go to the Argentine Consulate. There is nothing they can do either. "Why don't you hurry up and go on to Alaska in the month and a half remaining on your visa?"

"I don't think we would make it. Because of the car and also because of the pregnancy. At least 15 or 20 days before the baby is due, we will have to stop. Anyway, the trip is not about hurrying to Alaska. The best part is along the way, not at the finish line. We have learned a lot and we know that, on this last leg, there is much more to learn."

We see no other way out than to leave the country and come back. Cande needs to renew her visa but her big seven-month belly is not in her favor. Besides, the land border with Mexico is not the best place to cross in this condition.

This problem becomes common knowledge in the Argentine community of Houston. A compatriot who owns a travel agency offers us a Caribbean cruise. Since people take cruises for pleasure, the immigration officials are more flexible with them. We like the idea of a cruise, a "get-away" together for the last time as a couple before we become a family of three. Sadly, the next day the Argentinean woman calls to warn us that no plane or cruise ship will take a passenger who is more than seven months pregnant.

We decide to return to Mexico by land against the advice of everyone. Many people say goodbye as if they'll never see us again. During those two days returning to the border, one after another they call. How peculiar, a 1928 automobile with a cell phone!

They tell us about a woman who has often come to Houston for cancer treatment, who previously received three months stay is now granted only 10 days. Another who wanted to enter with her maid who no longer received permission and a great many other negative stories that provoke us into wanting to throw the phone out the window. We take the road back to Laredo. We are nervous, but we are both intent on calming down one another. We know that what we are doing is right, we are pursuing a dream and nothing bad will happen. On the way, we're frightened when we see immigration officers open a trunk of a car and find two men hiding under blankets and clothes.

As soon as we get to the city on the border, we look up the Chilean writer whom we met on the first time through. He tells us he has a solution to our problem. He is helping a female lawyer with her campaign for mayor of the city. Cases similar to ours are her specialty, so perhaps she can help. She may even get a political boost from it. We wait in his house while he goes to check it out. Time passes and there are no new developments, not even a phone call. After dark, the Chilean appears, but without a solution.

"Cande, you stay here. I'm going to go to the border to ask on my own." I manage to park the car in front of the office windows. I go inside and wait in the same line as the first time we were here. As soon as I get to the counter, I show him all the U.S. newspaper clippings and articles where we appear. I tell the official what we are trying to accomplish and point outside, showing him the car. The man, accustomed to only seeing passports, doesn't understand and asks me what the problem is.

"I want to know the following: If my wife and I leave and come back with this visa will there be any problem? Do we have to meet any other requirement?"

The man takes the passport and shows it to his boss as he explains our situation. After his superior makes him verify the visa is valid, the officer returns to me. "Go into Mexico, have a cup of coffee and come back."

I leave almost running to go get Candelaria. When I get in the car, I see that it is almost eight o'clock. I'm afraid the shift change will be soon. As never before, I step on it, speeding to the Chilean's house. When Cande gets in the car, I tell her the good news. She celebrates shouting with joy and relief.

We cross into Mexico but we don't drink any coffee. As soon as we cross the bridge, we turn right around and cross back over. Once again, we leave the car in the inspection area and quickly go into the immigration office. Cande is wearing loose, black clothes in order to hide the big curve of her tummy. With the same intention, she carries a large folder containing our documents under one arm, and under the other, she carries the same newspapers clippings I brought before. Once in line, I look at the personnel behind the counter, which produces an intense pain in my soul.

"The one that told me to go to Mexico and come back…"

"Which one is he?" whispers Cande, anxious to know.

"He's not here anymore. The whole crew has changed." She shrinks; I can feel her defeat.

"Herman, what are we going to do?"

"Well, we're here, we've already dived into the pool. Now let's find out if there is any water in it."

When they signal us to advance, Cande hides behind me. As we get to the counter, she rushes up, squashing her belly against it.

"Hello, we are Candelaria and Herman Zapp. We are traveling from Argentina to Alaska in this car," I explain to the new official as I show him the newspapers. He is not sure if this is allowed or not, but I press on, not letting him speak. "Because of the nature of our trip, we would like to be allowed as much time as is possible." The man stares at us and then curiously fingers the newspapers, but he doesn't say anything.

Cande fills out the form but makes a mistake because she is so nervous. She completes it for a second time and the man, looking through the newspapers without looking up tells us, "I can't possibly give you more than six months."

Although inside we are jumping for joy, we coolly say,

"O.K., I guess we'll have to do the trip in six months."

"Oh no, you can always renew it if you need to," he gives us back the newspapers and takes the passport looking for a space to stamp it. While he's doing this, a line of new agents file out of an office. One steps up behind the officer who is attending us. He immediately stands up, dropping everything and leaves without stamping our six months permission. We cannot believe it; the situation just keeps going from bad to worse.

"Where were you?" questions the new agent.

Cande takes out the newspapers and shows him. The man puts on the same face of not understanding as the last one "He was about to stamp my passport with six months' permission because..." Cande begins to explain, when the boss comes out of the office. He's the same one who was here when I came by myself.

"Give the Argentines what they ask for," he orders.

"What is it you are asking for?" asks the agent

"Six months' permission," we say in unison.

Bam! We hear the stamp.

We cheerfully leave the office and once again find the car surrounded by people. This time without nervousness, we answer all the questions.

The Eagle Inside of Me

Searching for new roads, we return to Houston, to give the good news, which surprised many. Now, our new destination is Greensboro, North Carolina, where there will be the annual meeting of the Graham Owners Club.

First, we go close to Dallas to meet the president of the club and to attend an auto show where we sell books and art, and talk to people from all over the country. Many, with accents of their region that we barely understand, offer us places to stay when we pass through their area. Those I can maintain a long conversation with and who we truly understand the best are two deaf mutes, through signs and gestures.

Next, we go to Louisiana where we stay with a man who possesses more than 40 antique cars. Not a single one of them runs. Although all of them, according to the owner, are in some stage of repair. For anyone in the trade, they would be scrap. The house is crammed to the rafters with spare parts; including those under the bed we're offered. The life of this man is his two sons, his plans for the cars and to be a Rebel. His family is native to the South, and fought in the war against the Yankees. He is convinced that he would fight if there were another war today. While we are taking pictures of him dressed like a confederate with a cannon and weapons from that era, next to the car, he says, "Here in the South you'll be received very well, we are famous here for our Southern hospitality. That will change in the North…the Yankees, no; they're not like us."

It's always the same story. The people from here are the good guys; the bad guys are farther over there. Before we got to the "The South" here in the States, they warned us that this region was the worst. They don't like foreigners, they're racist, and Latinos aren't welcome.

In a restaurant along our route in Mississippi, the Ford Model A Club is expecting us. After dinner, we go out to take a group photo with the car but we find it tipping to one side. For the first time in the trip, we have a flat tire. A tire I can't change, because none of the chivalrous men from a previous era would allow this youngster hamper their work.

We follow two members of the club, John and Jane, to their house. It's very beautiful, tucked back in the woods in front of a shimmering pond. The next day, while we are patching the inner tube, a young neighbor couple brings us a welcome basket full of delicious things. When he sees the state of the seats, the husband offers to reupholster them.

In this house as in many others, Cande is lavishly pampered. Her pregnancy moves people to tenderness, ever since Mexico. Previously, it was I who created the impression when I got out of the car. For the people, I was the hero of the adventure accompanied by my beautiful damsel. Now it is Cande who has become the incredible globetrotter, crossing the continent in an antique car and pregnant, nonetheless, accompanied by her husband, so as not to say her chauffeur. Suddenly first is Cande, then her pregnancy, after that, the car and finally, me a distant last. Moreover, everybody tells me to take good care of her, but who is going to take care of me? I think I am a little jealous. Not so much because of the treatment the people are giving Cande, but because of the baby that's coming. I'm afraid she's going to toss me over.

As it is our custom on the trip, we attend church with the family with whom we are staying without asking what religion they practice. Not only do we go and celebrate with the people, but also we pay close attention to the sermons. Now usually they give us a message that nearly always is associated with what we are doing. On this occasion we are accompanied by Jane and John and the pastor relates the following story:

"A baby eagle falls from its nest. A farmer finds it, picks it up and takes it to the farm. He puts it in his hen house where it mixes with the chickens. The eagle grows eating, sleeping, doing everything like them. One day when the eagle was grown, a man walks by and sees it eating corn in the hen house.

'Sir, why is that eagle in there with the chickens?' He asks.

'What eagle, sir?' responds the farmer.

'That one there in the middle of all those hens.'

'There are only chickens in my henhouse, sir.'

'Look', indicates the stranger, 'this one there, is an eagle, one of the most aggressive in the world.'

'As I told you, I only have chickens,' insists the farmer.

'If you permit me, I'll prove this is an eagle, I will take it to the barn roof and make it fly like an eagle does.' proposes the passerby.

'If you take that hen and throw it up there you'll see that it flies like a chicken,' responds the farmer.

The stranger puts a ladder up to the roof, takes the eagle, climbs up and throws it off the highest point. The eagle flaps and flaps but ends up on the ground like a chicken.'

'If you permit me another chance, I'll demonstrate this is an eagle,' he insists.

'If you want to make this chicken fly then it will take you longer than you think,' the farmer warns him, but the stranger goes up to the roof and throws the eagle again, and once again it flaps its wings but ends up on the ground, just like a chicken.'

'Can't you see? It's a chicken.'

'Tell me, farmer' says the stranger, 'will you sell me your eagle?'

'Yes, I sell my chickens,' he responds.

He pays the price, and takes it, heading up the road to a high mountain. When he gets to the edge of a steep cliff, he stops, takes out his eagle, carries it to the edge of the abyss and drops it. It starts flapping like a chicken, but out of fear of crashing into the cliff and dying, he begins flapping his wings vigorously. They begin to fill with air and he takes off in flight. He flies higher and higher until he is lost on the horizon. The eagle inside the chicken woke up," explains the pastor. "Why is it although we are all eagles, we act like chickens? We have been raised among chickens and think we have to be like those around us. Even though it is comfortable to be a chicken, we are eagles and that is exactly how we should act. Never mind the fact that they tell us, repeatedly, and even swear to us that we are chickens. No, we're not, we are eagles."

By the time the sermon ends, the eagle inside me is flapping its wings more strongly. Cande leans over to me and whispers, "We have to write a book after the trip is over to push the chickens off the cliff and incite the eagles to fly."

The Best Reward

We continue through Alabama where the members of the AACA are waiting for us in the home of a big Cadillac collector. Many people see us get out of the Graham.

"We thought you would be older, with that kind of car," they comment, surprised.

They entertain us splendidly and give us an enormous flag of the United States with a certificate noting it has flown over the capitol building for one day in Washington, D.C.

We continue on a beautiful highway, through the Great Smoky Mountains National Park until we get to the city of Greensboro, in North Carolina. Mike and Mariann have been expecting us for quite some time.

Since the baby is due in only two weeks, we don't want to be an inconvenience, surely the day of the birth as well as the next few days will be complicated. Nonetheless, Mike and Mariann sincerely want us to stay with them and offer us everything; home, friendship and love, which at a time like this, far away from home and family, we need so much. Additionally, a neighboring couple, Bob and Jeneil who are also members of the Graham Club, offer anything we might need. Enthusiastically, she even has prepared for us a bassinette she saved from her own children, in which will sleep our own.

The first weekend, we go with Mike and Mariann, each in our own Graham, to a small town where there is a car show. What attracted my attention to this car show is that the participants are the ones to decide who goes home with the "Best of Show" award. While we are looking for a place to park, we pass in front of incredible cars in mint condition. Some are very expensive makes that are nearly blindingly shiny. We don't see much chance of winning anything among these one hundred and fifty fabulous automobiles. Our intention is to sell books.

We receive a card with our number on it that says: "Please don't touch." We scratch out "don't", and attach it to the car: "Please touch", it reads now. For us, every caress and pat that the car collects or each time a child takes a seat inside, is a blessing. During the course of the afternoon, our visitors include local newspaper reporters and the mayor, who like many others, carry away our book. It is a marvelous sensation to see people who take the book, sit down to read near their cars and afterwards return to share their comments.

Among all the visits, the best one of the day is a ten-year-old boy who spends almost all day with us. His grandfather, who brought him here, has a Studebaker in mint condition. When the time comes to vote, the man is about to choose an incredible Franklin, but his grandson stops him.

"Oh no, Grandpa, you won't vote for that one, you have to vote for this one," he says pointing at us.

We also overhear two men talking. They already listened to our talk in front of a map and now one says to the other,

"Sorry, but I'm not voting for your car, I'm going to vote for that one" he excuses himself while crossing out the number of his friend's car and marking ours instead. We begin to have some hope that of the fifteen prizes, maybe we could win one. The awards ceremony commences and they announce the 15th place first and slowly proceed to first place.

"And in first place…" says the master of ceremonies, as he raises an enormous trophy and a bag of gold coins, "The first prize is for a car, a dream and an incredible couple, it's for a 1928 Graham Paige!"

I jump up and shout. Many people celebrate along with us and hug us. We are so very happy, not so much because we won the award but because we are impressed that the people have voted with their hearts, for a dream that is embodied in a car that obviously is not in condition for this level of exhibition.

With an Open Heart

We are seduced by the idea of a natural childbirth in a birthing center. It is much more affordable than a hospital: despite the fact that we have been saving money since we found out we were going to be parents, we are still far from the seven or ten thousand dollars that a hospital asks for a normal birth without complications

Therefore, we visit a birthing center where they do natural childbirth with midwives, the only one in Greensboro. They tell us they can't help us because Cande is too far along, a reason we don't quite understand. Later, we visit the Medicare office, a government agency that provides medical care for people with low income. After asking us the routine questions, the lady states firmly and tersely that even though I was born in this country and expecting a child, there is nothing they can do to help us because I am not a North Carolina resident. We aren't residents of any state.

After this negative reply, we go back to the street in complete silence. We hold each other feeling alone and discriminated against. Feeling like this, we get into the car and head over to The Women's Hospital. There neither a nurse nor doctor attends us but a business manager with whom we share our situation, how much we have saved and our suggestion to work off the rest in a barter agreement by painting pictures, doing electrical work for the hospital or publicity. The woman, in silence, listens to our whole account.

"This is a private hospital, which operates for profit. We do not do charity work, we have a responsibility to our investors who expect their earnings," she answers.

"But madam, we need help, my wife is ready to give birth," I say being unable to hold back the tears in my eyes.

The manager is unmovable and nothing will change her position. Something that I notice greatly is that despite her attitude she wears a large shiny crucifix hanging around her neck as if to show the world her grand love of religion. The cross inspires me, and with tears I say to her, "Ma'am, what would you do if instead of us Mary and Joseph were here to ask you for help? Would you send them back to the stable again?"

The woman sits there frozen. Never could she have even imagined this situation. She remains silent for a few seconds. Then she answers, but badly. Like Pontius Pilate, she washes her hands of the situation saying, "I only work here."

She is religious, but evidently just not during business hours, "Ma'am," I continue painfully, "when you get to heaven's gate and Saint Peter tells you 'No', and you ask him 'Why?' do you know what he will say? 'Lady, I only work here'. We leave her office completely destroyed; we cannot believe such coldness toward fellow humans and toward health. Now, more than ever, we wish we were at home where when you go to a hospital, they take care of you without asking anything. It was also like this in Ecuador, Belize and Mexico, all undeveloped countries. In contrast, here, in the country where I was born, they shut the door in our faces.

We head back to the house in total silence. We don't want fill our heads with fury, neither do we have time for it. We have to consider what we are going to do. At a stop light, Cande takes my hand and places it on her tummy, I feel a small kick, I feel my baby who freely can be assured of our love, the love of our friends and surely many others, if only they knew that he or she were coming soon.

"Cande, let's call the newspapers and tell them! They can write an article." it occurs to me.

"Mike and Mariann have already called them, both before we got here and afterward too, but it doesn't seem any reporters are interested," she interrupts me.

"Let's call them again, send them an e-mail. Somebody in the newspaper has to realize that this is a story that will interest the public."

In the afternoon, I buy the newspaper and send e-mails to those who cover events of a social or human nature. After a few hours, I start to call them on the telephone:

"Hello, my name is Herman and I sent you an e mail about our trip and what we are doing in Greensboro."

"Oh yes, I read it. I don't think I can do any article but thanks for calling."

"Hello, I am Herman and I sent you an e mail..."

"When did you say you sent it? Let's see, here it is. Interesting trip but it's not my type of story."

"Hello, this is Herman..."

"How long are you staying? Maybe we can do something, call me in a few weeks and we'll see."

I insist but receive responses either negative or evasive. In the very city where we most need to be in the news is where it's most difficult to achieve it. Now I am down to the two last possible calls.

"Hi, I sent you an e mail, my name is Herman."

"Hello, yes, I read your story with great interest," responds a female voice sounding somewhat insecure. "I have to ask the editor if I can cover it. Give me your phone number and I'll call you back." I don't really think she will because I have already sent a message to her editor too. Shortly, the phone rings and Cande answers.

"Good afternoon, I spoke with your husband about the possibility of writing a story. Can you tell me where you are?"

We wait very anxiously for the reporter to arrive. There's a knock on the door and we see a very young woman who introduces herself as Fia. She states clearly that we shouldn't have any illusions about the story being published because she is a short-term, voluntary intern. In addition, there is almost no room left for her story in the newspaper. Apparently, she isn't exaggerating because they didn't even send a photographer with her.

Just the same, we put all of our energy into telling her enthusiastically and joyfully about our trip, our dream. Little by little, she becomes enamored of the story and we win her over completely when we show her the car.

"Okay, I'm going back to the newspaper, and I am going present the story to the editor and try to convince him to send a photographer, but I can't promise anything. Your story seems like a movie, with what you've told me. I could write not only an article, but a whole movie script...and for the crowning touch...you're pregnant?" comments the young woman, giving us the chance to talk about the problem we are having with finding a place for the birth of the baby.

We watch her leave, convinced she has a good story and we hope she'll send a photographer, a photo would help us a lot.

"Are you going to be there? They've confirmed the photographer," she announces by phone half an hour later.

The next morning we run out to buy the newspaper. We search through it page by page in great hopes of finding our story, but we get to the last page and there's nothing. We are crushed. Getting back to the house, we can hear the phone ringing from outside.

"I have been trying to call you," says the reporter, "I have more questions to ask you, I need more details. Can I come over?"

Face to face, she tells us, "The editor is very enthusiastic about the article. He enjoyed the photos, and I dared to ask him for the cover of the Life Section in the Sunday paper. No one else has asked for it yet and let's hope they don't, because if any other reporter puts a bid on it, I'm sure to lose it.

I'm thrilled with the story; it's exactly the kind of story that I would love to write more of in the future. And guys, I have to confess, this is my first story with photos and the cover."

Mariann and Mike, wanting to help us any way they can, and feeling dreadful about the way we have been treated, offer to let us have the baby at home, their home. However, for this, we need to find a midwife. Mike discovers someone who could help us: a mechanic across the street from where he works who assisted in the birth of his own daughter. The perfect solution…as long as he doesn't forget his tools! We laugh so much with them, perhaps more out of nervousness than anything else.

On Sunday very, very early, before we are awake, the telephone rings.

"Pardon me for calling so early, but I just finished reading your article and I couldn't wait any longer. I would love to be part of your dream. Do you have any paintings? May I come over to buy one."

This catches us totally by surprise. As soon as we hang up, the phone rings again, then again, and continues like this successively for four consecutive days. They call us wanting to buy our paintings, copies of our book, our crafts. They call us with gifts of clothes and things for the baby. Very importantly, we receive calls from doctors, midwives, anesthesiologists, nurses and pediatricians from the hospital offering their services free of charge.

Additionally, church groups call us and without asking what religion we profess, organize baby showers, money trees and other events for us. Likewise, antique car clubs invite us to a meeting and take up a collection. In all, among many, many other items, we receive offers for 14 strollers and 7 car seats. We just had to say, no thank you, we are only going to have one kid!

The house is a beehive of people coming and going, anxious to be part of our story and to become future uncles, aunts and grandparents. Deserving a separate chapter are Mike and Mariann, who receive everyone with an open heart.

To Be a Child Again

I watch Cande painting a pair of Carolina Wrens. I gaze at her belly. I put my arms around her and feel the baby move, which inspires me as much as the reaction of all these beautiful people. I want to describe what I feel, share this moment in which even a gray, rainy day would look sunny to me, even the most insignificant thing is important to me.

There are still a number of days before I earn the title of "father" but I haven't studied the lessons yet. I ask for books, there aren't any; when I ask what I need to do, people tell me, "You'll know." The moment is approaching. Will it be a boy or a girl? I only hope she will be a dreamer. What will I do? How will I hold him? How will I feel? How will it be hugging someone that I made by love and with love? What will it be like to look at her? Will she make me see things with other eyes? Will he make me feel things in a new way?

A new feeling is starting to come to me: a certainty of love at first sight and for always. For ever? Even if I have to punish him? Even if she breaks things that belonged to my grandmother? How about when he becomes a rebellious teenager? Oh! What will I do? How will I be? Son, I only ask you to be patient, I have never been a father and with you I have to learn. Oh, dear God, You only gave me nine months to get ready. Doesn't that sound like such a short amount of time?

On the other hand, I want to have her here with me right now. Why? To play with, to sing "Old McDonald" and all these childhood songs again. To make castles in the sand without people saying "He's too old for that," but instead "how nice, that daddy is playing with his child." To go fishing for minnows, to catch tadpoles, to play in the mud making pies, to play houses and all these games.

Dear God, I only want to teach my son that if he learns to love, to dream, and to have faith in You, he will have it all, but please, God, don't leave me alone in this, help me! Remember that I don't have any instructions.

I want to thank You for Cande. Today, I love her more than I did when you presented her to me. I have so many more reasons to love her today, she is more beautiful every day. But, yes, there is another 'but' it looks like I am no longer her hero. For example, she doesn't knit anything for me anymore, it's the baby who will get to wear all the little sweaters and the caps and the booties she has made. While I…"Me?" "Fine, thanks." When our child is born, will Cande have any time for me? Will she still give me those lingering embraces for no reason, or will the baby be always saying, 'Mommy is mine'? Yes, I'm happy with the idea of being a daddy but once in a while I get a touch of jealousy and don't have any idea how to cure it. God, you tell her don't forget about the Daddy. OK?

"What are you thinking about, Herman?" Cande asks, interrupting my thoughts. "Do you like the nuthatches? They are ready to be framed."

A Unique Dawn

Today, June 4, I wake up with an unexpected jolt. Cande leaps out of bed at seven something when she feels a gush of water. I thought I was dreaming. But no, the dream just begins when she exclaims, "My waters broke!"

Nervous through and through! The long awaited day has arrived. What should I do? Cande is calm; divine, in contrast to me. I am anxious, standing here frozen to the spot. How can this be? It's still 4 days before the due date… I need those days more than ever. I clean this sacred water that announces the new arrival. Cande serenely takes a bath, Mariann is helping her. Mike doesn't know what to do. White as a sheet, he paces in and out of the house.

I get the car ready and we get in for our last trip as a pair. Mike will follow us in his car. The Graham, as if enthusiastic, starts right up. I drive hoping that… praying for…even begging that this baby is not born right here. Cande starts labor. Oh, Man!! This makes the road seem even longer than the one to Alaska.

The hospital is waiting for us and receives us. The midwife examines the future mom. We are overwhelmed with bliss. But the lady's expression changes and she orders an ultrasound as she explains, "The baby is upside down"

While she calls the doctor we are completely crushed. We see on the screen that the baby is resistant to do it in the usual way; why is he so gutsy? Then the doctor arrives.

"What are we going to do?" he asks us, "if you don't want to, we won't operate. We can try for a natural birth, the dilation is good." The ghost of a caesarian doesn't alarm us much, it seems it isn't the only way for this new life to join us.

"However, you must know you are running some risks."

"Like what?"

"Well, he because he will come out feet first, with the head emerging last, it could get stuck and he won't be able to get out or to breathe. And…this is something you have to decide, but you have to do it now, this baby is coming!"

The doctor leaves us for three short minutes. What a situation! Cande and I feel that this is a test of faith and we rely on it. We take the medal of the Virgin of Guadalupe and flip it in the air. If it's Virgin's head, we go with the natural birth, if it's tails, to the operating room. When the medal comes down it lands on Cande's huge tummy and the Virgin is looking at us!

"At least let me give you some anesthetic just in case," pleads the doctor to my wife, when we tell him about our decision. Cande consents.

On her stretcher, on the way to the delivery room, Cande prays, "May Your will be done, Amen." To me it seems that everyone around us has wings. Things continue to progress; Cande, amazing, dilates rapidly, so quickly there is no time for anesthetic.

The doctor requesting life of her, "Push, push!" he insists.

"Cande push!" I am thinking. "Come on, my love." Absolutely everything goes through my mind in this instant.

"Don't scream. Just push! He is coming," declares the doctor.

In an act of rebellion, the baby shows his bottom first. He is born as he is supposed to be born, strong and healthy. Not only a child is born, but also a mom and a dad and a new whole heart love.

"It's a boy, darling!" We cry, we embrace each other and we cry a little more, accompanying the baby in his first cry.

The nurse hands me a tiny boy, so small that in my two open hands, I can cradle him. I feel his smooth skin and his featherlike weight; I feel heaven in my hands. I lift him to my heart for the first time hugging my son. I melt in love for him. He is so unbelievably exquisite and longing to start a wonderful new life, desiring to dream and to learn what life is all about. These are the first seconds that I have you, my first as a father and the most amazing moment in my life.

Mom also wants to hold you and to her I bring you. She has tears that shine,

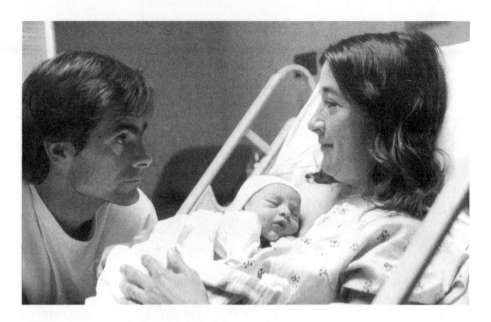

the sort that leaves tracks of love and only appear in very special moments. With effort, her voice trembling, Cande tells me that she is very happy. So happy that she open her arms, inviting us to join her in the first embrace of a new family.

Son, we feel that between the two of us you are very well. You stop crying and close your eyes in peace, but your little hand doesn't stop moving. Searching for something, you catch my finger, catching my life, capturing me forever. Pampa, our son, we love you infinitely, immeasurable gratitude for this blessing.

"Congratulations, you made the right decision," says the doctor.

"We didn't decide, we only trust our faith."

"What is the name of the new traveler?"

"Nahuel Pampa."

In the hospital, we receive many visitors who bring flowers and gifts. Even the television reporters come and there is another article in the newspaper announcing Pampa's arrival.

We get into our home, our "home on wheels", itself very small but with the biggest yard in the world, I mean the world itself!

"Macondo, another new generation for you to carry. And all the way to Alaska, no less." I tell the Graham as the three of us get in. Our car becomes our son's cradle and lets him sleep on its lap. To see Pampa in the backseat living and sleeping brings me peace.

We arrive at Mike and Mariann's house where they are waiting for us. The house is decorated with colorful streamers and two posters on the door saying "Welcome Home!" and "It's a Boy!" As our own parents would have received us, they do, with all the love in the world. In the afternoon we get the three

Grahams together, this means, Mike's, Bob's and ours, which we decorate with balloons and streamers. We all celebrate, taking Pampa on his first day, for a ride in each of the three cars. During the following days we participate in many gatherings and parties introducing everyone to their new nephew and grandson. There are people from auto clubs, churches, and other groups. Pampa continually receives gifts; some of them are very sentimental such as hand knitted clothing or blankets with his name embroidered.

We are just learning how to be parents. For this reason, we will stay here for a month as Dr. Lukas, the pediatrician, recommended. Together with Pampa we begin a new stage in the journey, one of a family that travels together in a dream toward Alaska. How will it be? The constant question is: What will the trip be like now?

"You Are Our Guest"

It's time for the Graham meet, organized by Mike, Bob and their wives. It lasts five days and in attendance there are people from all over the United States and Canada and even from Europe, many of who bringing their cars. In all, there are over twenty different cars of various models.

One day, we park all the cars in front of a country house where we have arrived in a procession. We sit around on the lawn chatting. The Graham Club members know about our trip through the club's web site where we have been telling some of our experiences. Otherwise, none of them would know anything about what has happened to us in the United States because we haven't written anything about it yet.

"How has the trip been since getting here?" inquires a man, quieting the group, as everyone present is interested in the answer.

"Truly, much better than we had ever imagined. We have lived some incredible experiences; with the insurance, the tires, the extension of the visa and now with Pampa's birth. All of these events have been resolved in the best possible way. What we find even more curious is that before coming here we were told we wouldn't be received into families' homes; nevertheless, we have been here four months and have only slept on our own one night."

"I'll give you an example. We were at a gas station in the Great Smoky Mountains and a man came up to us. After the usual questions, he asked us if we would like to stay in a cabin that he has in the mountains. He takes us there in his pickup and presents us with an incredible place. Not only that, the next day, he took us scuba diving in a river, and then yesterday he appeared here to meet Pampa. Another person we met in Guatemala, traveled here from Florida to congratulate us and to hook up with us again. There have been other surprises as well, like the time we slept in a very modest house trailer."

Bill Conley and his wife, along with a few other Canadians, take advantage of the walk through the gardens to pull us aside. With that small group, we discuss the problem we have with the Canadian visa. This group of fellow countrymen is ashamed of what happened and sincerely want to lend a hand in resolving the problem.

"Have you received many invitations to visit people in Canada?" Bill inquires of me.

"Yes, hundreds of invitations have come from families, clubs and organizations."

"This means that the newspaper article has had an effect. I brought a copy so you can read the piece that recounts all your marvelous adventures on the trip and the people you've run across. The final paragraph is about Canada, reporting this is the only country impeding your entry, thus putting an end to your trip. With these invitations, your position has improved, now we want you to come to Canada. They can turn down the request of a non-citizen but they can't deny an invitation. Not only do you have these invitations in your favor but also many have called their representatives in Parliament to tell them about your situation. The person who decides agenda items for the Parliament collects antique cars and is a member of the Vintage Car Club of Canada. He is angry about what happened with you."

"Also, other Canadians told us that they have called the Canadian Embassy in Washington telling them that we will be there to apply for another visa," adds Cande.

"We have even received an offer from a person to take us illegally into Canada in his boat as a last resort," I put in.

"I don't think that will be necessary. The fact that a single person in the embassy in Mexico City did something foolish doesn't mean that we are all going to act the same way," concludes Bill.

On the last day of the meet, during the closing ceremony, prizes are awarded. Pampa wins the honor of being the youngest member at the meet. This award is presented by descendents of the Graham family who founded the company.

Regarding us, we take the longest distance driven award, hands down. We also experience five marvelous days during which we get to meet people face to face that we have only previously known through e-mail, who now offer us their homes and support.

Parade

After a month, the pediatrician, Dr.Lukas, gives us the okay to go on. It is July 4, and we decide that the best way for us to show our appreciation for everything the people of this city have done for us is to participate in the Fourth of July parade. On the front fenders are the children of the anesthesiologist, Mike and Mariann are inside the car with us, and many familiar faces take turns riding on the running boards. As the parade moves along, we hear applause and people saying encouraging things to us, but above all, they want to see the baby and call out to him. Cande shows him to the people, from one window to the other one.

Exhausted from too much partying, we go back home. Cande is very pensive as she packs and gets everything ready for the trip. She confesses to me, "I feel like the closer we get to the moment of saying good-bye, the less I want to do it. A part of me will remain here just as in every other place we have already left. I keep moving ahead with new lessons and new faces that will be difficult to erase from my memory. This encounter, as all the others has changed me. I've learned and grown. I'm trying to avoid thinking about tomorrow when I leave, and I cry saying good-bye. The thing is that neither they nor I know when the next encounter will be, because in the majority of the cases, it will never be. The intensity of the experiences we share is what moves me. One day or a month doesn't matter, what's important is what was lived.

"I can see myself trembling, saying standard phrases like, "we'll see each other again some day". I don't want to get to that part, but I know it will happen because the road continues, more surprises and more people to know are waiting for us." Just as Cande has predicted, we leave Greensboro desperately crying our eyes out. Mike and Mariann comfort us and promise to see us again before the trip is over and also in a few years in Argentina. With that hope, we drive away.

Just As We Came

On the road, two different people call us saying that they have found a sponsor for us. This news takes us completely by surprise and we have to decide what to do. On one hand, to have sponsors means that we won't have to continuously be searching for ways to generate income to continue traveling. This would leave us significant amounts of time to dedicate to other things. In other words, a comfortable security.

On the other hand, if we put some company's decal on the car it would seem like the whole journey was possible due to them, and not to the people who have received us, supported us and helped us out of the love of their hearts asking for nothing in exchange. In the beginning, especially in Peru and Ecuador we searched for advertisers but all of them said no. What is more, our intention is to demonstrate to the world that anything is possible without people discrediting us by saying, "Oh sure, with sponsors…that makes it easy."

Furthermore, we enjoy selling books, it is our way to be in contact with people, to inspire them to be eagles, and this is gratifying to us. We almost don't need to discuss it; Cande and I want to continue on our own. The best part of the trip began when we ran out of money, so why screw it up now? They call us back. We thank them and let them know our decision is to keep going just as we came.

Recipe for Love

As if the car is part of the landscape with which it harmonizes, we travel by small, undulating roads with little traffic. We cruise over covered wood bridges, surrounded by small villages of Amish in Virginia and Pennsylvania, to get to the town of Macungie. We come to this small town almost without wanting to, but the family hosting us last night knew there was to be a big classic car show here. Seeing an opportunity to sell books, we headed that way. The event doesn't open until tomorrow morning, but there are already so many cars, things for sale, tents and people moving.

"Everything is occupied, there aren't even any spaces available for next year. You have to make reservations two years in advance, and without a pass you can't get your car in," various people comment. In any case, we stay to see if by introducing ourselves tomorrow we can arrange a way in.

We get ready to sleep in the car for the second time since entering the United States and for the first time with Pampa. A family approaches us and invites us to stay in their home and we accept, but only to bathe and eat. Tomorrow we want to be here very early to ask if we can enter the show.

When we get to the house, we find a home where there's not just enough love, there's and abundance. They have adopted seven children, not infants. For many, adopting older children creates a problem. However, not for this couple who, with a recipe for love, solves all the problems.

"Give them love, it is what they look for. If they do things to attract attention, it is because they need it, they want us to give them our time, our attention and love," the woman advises us.

In the morning, while trying to talk to the person running the show, we meet Bill, an important man in the AACA.

"They are sticklers about the rules here, very difficult, there isn't anything I can do. I invite you to Hershey in October, to the largest antique auto show in the world."

Later, when we get to talk to the man in charge, he happily positions us smack dab in the center of the show under the flagpole. A generous space that immediately fills with people. During the three days of the show, we receive all kinds of affectionate attention. The woman in charge of the park gives us passes to use the showers and pool; the organizers of the show give us breakfast and many people who pass by come back with something for us to drink or a sandwich to eat. There is no stopping them. We sell many books but better than that is the number of invitations we receive to stay both in this area and in many other states.

A New Attempt

Entering the city of Washington, D.C. with our car turns out to be a lot easier than we thought. We used a parkway along the river where you can't drive very fast. Isn't it funny that here, you can park in the driveways and drive on the parkways? Once we're in the city, it's not difficult either to find the house of Paulita, a great friend and classmate of Cande's, whom she hasn't seen in many years. It is touching to watch them hug and recount many events from their childhood.

There is so much to go around and see in this city. Just to see the museums we would need several days, but we don't have anything like that on our minds for now. What we want to do first is resolve the issue of the Canadian visa. We present ourselves at the Embassy of Argentina, where they receive us as if it were a club without even knowing anything about us. The minister, Jorge Osella gets into our car and dream, wanting to be a part of it all. He organizes a press conference and is able to arrange appearances for us on various international television channels. He takes us to the headquarters of the Organization of American States where we are named Ambassadors of the American Continent, and to top off the day, he hosts us at an Argentine style barbeque with many of his friends at his home.

Along with Jorge, we dedicate the next day to putting together a folder in which we place our letters of invitation to Canada, an explanation of the reason for the trip, newspaper clippings, a copy of the book, a letter from the Argentine Embassy and one from the Organization of American States.

"We can't forget anything!" says the minister as he sends his personal assistant to write letters, photocopy, and translate.

Together with the Minister of Argentina, we arrive early at the Canadian Embassy to request a visa. We are already well aware that getting one isn't easy; now we'll find if it's possible to reverse a previously denied one. We pay the fee for the second time and begin to fill out the form. At the end there are three questions with boxes to check yes or no. The first is, "Have you participated in terrorist acts or other crimes?" The second is, "Have you been arrested for drug trafficking or other crimes?" and the third, as if it were a serious crime, "Have you ever applied for a visa and been denied it?"

We wait in a long line, surrounded by people from all over the world. At that time, some ugly memories come to mind, difficult to erase. When our turn comes, the minister introduces himself to introduce us, but the woman behind the thick glass window interrupts him before he can finish.

"Who is the person applying for the visa?"

"She is, but I want you to know the gov..."

"Then she has to request it by herself, the woman interrupts curtly.

Cande presents the application and the minister gives the folder to her. Preempting the woman from saying anything, Cande begins by saying, "I would like to show you, if you would allow me, why we want to go into Canada," while the first thing the woman sees is an enormous newspaper photograph of the car and us. "We are invited by many Canadians...."

"Are you the ones traveling from Argentina to Alaska?" she asks, surprising us with her knowledge of us, then adds, "We have been waiting for you."

After this point, everything is much easier. They simply ask us what it is that we want to which the minister replies,"The maximum time limit and with multiple entries." Our wish is granted.

Happily, as soon as we get back to the Embassy, we call our friends in Canada and they tell us, "We are waiting for you, don't be too long."

We hang up the phone and hug each other, thrilled about our triumph. The victory is sweeter when you have tasted defeat.

The End is Written

The car has begun to idle too fast and I can't figure out what the problem is. Sticking my hands into the motor and with assistance from the doorman of the Embassy, we adjust the idle by loosening a screw. Meanwhile, Cande is inside the embassy selling books and crafts at a fair they have organized especially for us. On the return to the house the car begins to conk out, getting worse the closer we get. It finally gives out about three blocks before we get to Paulita's, in front of the home of an adventure photographer who comes out immediately and begins snapping photos at the same time he offers his help. I ask to use the phone and call Pino, a Paraguayan, around seventy something who quickly comes to our rescue. We met him on the Tango radio program. He had heard an interview with us on the air and called the station to give us a copy of his book. A freshly printed manuscript recounting the story of his trip from Paraguay to NY in 1951 with another couple in a Model T Ford.

I read the book in just one night. It tells how, after only a short time since beginning the trip, they ran out of money. Then the wife became pregnant and the baby was born in Colombia. In Costa Rica, they built a raft to cross a jungle river, which sunk, leaving the car under 5 ft. of water. Since they couldn't find anybody to help them to get it out, they began taking it apart to rebuild it back on the other side. Later, in the United States, when they were almost at their destination, a car hit them from behind, causing them to crash into the car in front of them, breaking all four of the wooden spoke wheels. The police towed the Ford to a junkyard but they didn't give up. Pino found some pieces of wood and began making the spokes. When the owner of the salvage yard saw his determination, he gave them a Model T Ford that wasn't running from which they are able to get all necessary parts. They finally arrived in New York and finished their dream. Pino began a new life there since he met the love of his life.

Now, on a street in very picturesque neighborhood of Georgetown, under his supervision, we are trying to figure out what is wrong with the car. I have already removed the hood, the radiator, the cooling fan, and the cover of the chain case. Pino thinks that when the car accelerated, the timing chain slipped a few teeth, causing the motor to be out of tune. Many people come to poke around, give opinions and to ask questions. Meanwhile, the photographer, Robert Hyman, entertains folks by telling them about adventures that he has read in our book as we had parked in front of his door. From all the publicity that he is giving us, he is selling a book to each curious person who comes around.

In the afternoon while Pino and I continue working, some of those in attendance sit in the grass or on the Graham's running boards to philosophize about life and dreams while the photographer serves everyone refreshments.

"How does it feel to have everybody on the road passing you?"

"I'm used to it," I answer.

"They may be going slowly on their road, but you know clearly where you are going," adds another.

"What does a successful man of business have that others don't? What is the difference between one who prospers and one who doesn't?" an elderly gentleman questions everyone.

"Perseverance? Hard work?" risks someone.

"No, there are many who work hard and persevere, but they keep running against the wall and don't succeed."

"So, what is it?" I ask without shifting my eyes from the nut.

"It's imagination; it's the use of imagination put into practice. Where some people see everything crashing down, others imagine what they can do and take action. They act without being influenced by what is going on, by unsuccessful attempts of others, without crying for what's been lost and without regard for collective negativism. They adapt to the situation and try to discover a way to thrive."

He explains to us, "Whenever a person develops a new practical and simple product, that earns him millions, we tend to ask ourselves 'Why didn't I think of that?' It is simply because we don't want to use our imagination. We think that everything has already been invented, that there is nothing new under the sun, but even in the simplest things in a family house, there is a world of products to be developed. Let your imagination and your logic team up and you'll make a million."

"Sorry, but why did this comment come up?" the photographer asks him.

"You've told me," he says to me, "that when you ran out of money, you didn't go home but kept going, and for each new country you entered, you would start over again, imagining new things, changing the products you sell, adapting yourself to the economic situation in each area, and modifying your sales strategy. You arrived in each country with your car and the clothes on your back. In countries where there are millions having a hard time, making a living day to day, you get around, work and leave it having had a great time."

"Yes, sure, but always with a lot of help from the people."

"People don't help those who don't deserve to be helped, but instead help the ones who are taking action; they help the guy who is trying, who is fighting for something. Wherever you are, you demonstrate that you are pursuing a goal, a dream, that you'll do everything within your power to achieve it. Seeing this, people can't resist helping you."

I never imagined that people help us because they can't resist... It sounds very nice, as if we were doing them a favor. However, I feel like it reduces the value of the help we receive.

"Do you know how a company grows, becoming stronger and profitable?" posing a new question is the same man.

"No, I don't think I know."

"By making every employee in the company feel the company belongs to him, that he owns it. By making him see that every movement he makes is influential and if he has an idea to improve the company, he shares it. If there is a way to save in photocopies, telephone calls, cleaning supplies, material, electricity or whatever, he does it because it's his company. It's that simple." He pauses and looks at me squarely, "...I made this comment because that's what you are doing, you make every one of the people who has helped you feel like this dream belongs to them too, that they are a fundamental part. This is why your dream is functioning like a completely successful company. Even though you don't know it, you are using tools that lead people to the road of success. Your dream or company, whatever you want to call it, has an outcome already written: success."

He makes me think. I don't know what to say. I don't like calling my dream a company and even less that the end is written. Of course, we have faith that we are going to get there but we live every mile we advance as an achievement without planning nor knowing where or how it will end up.

Although Pino is doing everything he can to help us, his heart is not doing well and the hot afternoon is making him feel poorly. The men from the Tango radio station have another solution for us. A tow truck takes the car to the Champion Garage, owned by an Argentine. Guillermo, one of the Latino mechanics that works in the shop, is in charge of our repair, which turns out to be a problem with the carburetor. I spend that night at the mechanic's house, in a neighborhood full of immigrants, mostly Latinos. He, his son and I all go to play soccer. It seems like I'm not far from home. We get to the field, intent on pulling together a team from those who are sitting out and ask to play against the winners of the game in progress.

Guillermo and his son are geniuses with the ball and assume that since I am from Argentina, I am like them too. So, they send me to the highest position, but before too long, little by little, I am moved back until I am almost off the field on account of my bad game.

If You Give, Forget it, If You Receive, Remember It

Getting into New York City truly, is very complicated; there are so many bridges, tunnels, detours, cars, freeways that we keep missing our intended exits and taking the incorrect ones. In the end, in order to get to Fifth Avenue we must go on an obligatory tour of most of the city. Our first destination is the Argentine Consulate, where they know about our arrival and have arranged a place for us to stay.

Following their instructions, we go to the Bronx; the farther we venture into this borough, the more it looks like the set of an action movie. We arrive at the door of the church specified by the consulate. We knock and a woman who introduces herself as Mariana opens the door. Excitedly she tells us, "Now, I'll call Father Carlos" Shortly, she returns with him. He gives us an enormous smile as he asks Cande if he could hold the baby. After welcoming us, he tells us that Mariana will be receiving us in her home, two blocks away. She is delighted to be helping us and she comments that it makes her so happy to host us.

"Mariana, please come here," someone calls to her and she leaves.

"She is the secretary of the church," he tells us as we go out to see the car. "How marvelous, so incredible, excellent!"

"You like the car that much?"

"No, what you're doing. Sure, the car is nice, but what you are doing is glorious!"

"Father! A gang jumped the fence of the parking lot and they're still there. Should I call the police?" interrupts Mariana.

"No, what for? They are only kids up to some mischief. We are going to go over there right now to park Herman and Candelaria's car."

His answer leaves us petrified. Here we are in the Bronx, famous worldwide for its terrible dangers. It looks as if we were going to leave the Graham parked all night in a place where gangs can jump over the fence while we are supposed to be asleep, if we could possibly sleep a wink, 600 feet from here. The father instructs us to drive around the block and he will wait for us at the parking lot.

"Did you hear that Cande? A gang in the parking lot. What are we going to do?"

"I don't know; I'm terrified; let's go to check it out..."

Making matters even worse, as we turn the corner, we see that the parking lot is across the street from the church. The father has already opened the gate and is signaling to us to go in.

"Father, do you think the car will be safe here?" I ask as I look at the gateposts, which have already taken a beating.

"Sure, have faith," the father tells me sounding very confident.

What's wrong with me? How could I have forgotten about my guardian angels? How could my fear make me forget my faith that nothing bad is going to happen to me? How could I let myself get carried away like this? Since we arrived at New York, I have been a bundle of nerves. Before arriving, I was wondering how we could get here with so many freeways and where could we possibly find a place to sleep? In addition, here we are. In the city, after driving through most of it, from Manhattan to the Bronx, having been able to find a place to sleep and a place to park the car. My nervousness wasn't letting me see how everything had been arranged for us before we even got here. I breathe deeply, relax and I feel my faith renewed again.

"Yes father, you are right, I won't abandon my faith."

The father invites us into the kitchen of the church and on the table there is a plate of food, a set of silverware and a glass of water. He finds another plate, divides the food into two, fills another glass and gets out another set of silverware.

"Go ahead and eat kids, this is absolutely delicious."

"Have you already eaten Father?"

"No, but don't worry…"

"No Father, we can go out and get something else."

"Look, you don't know how much satisfaction I get from sharing my food with you. Please don't take away this moment of joy from me." After his words, we eat everything on the plate. It is delicious enhanced by the special ingredient of someone fasting on our behalf.

A Sparkle of Light

Mariana's house is big and even though she is paying a mortgage, she gives us a room that she usually rents out. Her husband, Marceliano, invites us to stay for as long as we want.

We go out to see the city. We take the ferry to go to admire the Statue of Liberty that represents so much. So many people saw it as a welcome to a world full of new possibilities, of new horizons. Millions of people saw glimpses of it before they even distinguished firm ground. I remember Cuba and those who taught me much about the value of freedom. The statue is much bigger and more beautiful than I had imagined. It looks as strong and eternal as my own freedom.

We go back to the ferry, and to our surprise, we find out that the tour still hasn't ended. Off we go to an island that for all immigrants was the place they first set foot on this continent upon leaving the ship. There they mixed and shared tables, elbow to elbow, with people from all over the world. Waiting in huge rooms, they heard the echo of hundreds of different languages and they slept in barracks full of strangers. Nevertheless, they all had one thing in common, dreams. On the walls of what is now a museum, there are hundreds of photographs that illustrate, by the clothes, just how different they were from

Driving from Argentina to

one another. There were gypsies, Turks, Greeks, Russians, Spanish…. All of the faces show exhaustion from the long journeys and nervousness from uncertainty. However when you look closer, deep into their eyes, they have a light that sparkles. It is the light of hope, a hope to a dream, that never goes out and now shines brighter than ever.

Silence We Don't Want to Break

Except for a place to park, New York City has it all. It has the richest people in the world riding in the longest limousines passing by the same corner where homeless people look through the garbage for food. In this city, you can taste food from every country in the world and visit neighborhoods of communities which no one has ever heard of before. We get to the place where the Twin Towers stood. Here, the silence is painful and palpable. Not even the cars passing in the street dare to honk their horns; there are many people around us and everyone is in complete silence. Some take photos, but nobody asks for a smile. There is no reason to smile in this place where so many people died. They were people who were full of life, who had nothing to do with this, who could have been us if we had gotten here sooner… We depart, we remain in a silence we don't want to break.

Once recovered from so much intensity, we go to Queens. At the union of four corners, we feel like we're at home. It's an Argentine neighborhood with a barbeque restaurant, a butcher, a bakery, a glassware store, a bar, a social club, a barber shop and the love with which this neighborhood receives us makes us, after two and a half years far from ours, forget for a moment the distance. We park the car and immediately people start crawling out of the woodwork. They just can't believe that we've come all the way from Argentina in "this", as they call our vehicle.

"This is my dream…to drive from here to the doorstep of my house in Argentina," says a young man. To them we offer our books and almost everyone buys one.

Up to the Altar

Sunday arrives and we can't refuse an invitation from Father Carlos to attend his Mass. He conducts it in Spanish, since thousands of Latinos live here in the Bronx. The father asks us to park the car right in front of the church, although it's prohibited. "This will pass as a wedding car and the police won't bother you," he assures us. After this, he sits us in the first pew and starts the service. The lovely church is full; it's been a long time since we've heard Mass in Spanish. Toward the end of the service, the father begins saying something that makes us a little nervous.

"Here with us today is a couple of beautiful people who are chasing their dream. As you came in, you may have noticed a handsome, old car. In it, they have traveled from far away, for almost three years on the road, and have received the blessing of another member that has turned them into family," He gestures to us. "Please, Candelaria, Herman and Pampa come up to the altar. Tell us something about your trip and your dream." This takes us totally by surprise.

"The father is right when he says that God has blessed us by turning us into a family. We don't say this only because of Pampa but also because of the magnificent family of the whole American Continent that we now have. More than ever we feel that we have many brothers, because when we went through your countries we were received in their homes, they shared their food, and they gave us their time. You should be very happy and proud of your countrymen who opened their homes to us as they opened their hearts, making us feel that we were in a special place and very loved."

After saying this, the father doesn't let us go back to our seats. He ends the Mass, and takes us with him to the doors of the church where we find three people with buckets in their hands who shout, "Let's contribute to the travelers so they can continue with their dream! To the travelers!"

We want to die! I'm not sure whether from the happiness of the support everyone is offering or of the embarrassment of being the recipients of the collection. In any case, they don't give us time to think about it because they immediately begin buying books and telling us where they are from, something that we can quite easily guess by listening to the typical accents of each one. By the end of the day, they give us an offering of more than \$300, a gesture for which we are very grateful.

Heart to Heart

What would a trip to New York be without visiting Times Square? This place is almost impossible to imagine. In the space of only two hundred yards, there are millions of lights, thousands of signs and gigantic billboards and moving image screens, an incredible flow of automotive traffic and an unstoppable current of people. In the center of all this, the television studio of Good Morning America has its windows facing the street. We have come up with idea of sharing our dream with the whole country by coming out on the TV program "Good Morning America", which is broadcast every day.

So, off we go very early to the square in the car. What better place is there to park than in front of these windows? This way maybe somebody will notice us and interview us on TV. The only problem is that in New York, a parking space isn't open for more than twenty seconds.

From the red light on the corner, we can see that there are no empty spaces and it's not possible to double park because the street is only one lane wide. The light changes to green and we crawl forward slowly searching for a parking space but the traffic behind us pushes us to go faster. Suddenly in front of us, a car cuts in, forcing us to hit the brakes hard, but this doesn't annoy us; on the contrary we are grateful because he has now vacated a parking spot, leaving it wide open just for us, right in front of the plate glass window of the studio.

There are many people in line waiting to get into the studio; many carry posters they hope to show on camera. One poster announces a couple's wedding anniversary among others. Since we don't have a poster, Cande looks for our gigantic map, the one we stick photographs onto that says "Driving for a Dream." She stands up on a chair in the back and stays there displaying our "make shift" poster. Looking for something interesting, the commentator of the program notices it and asks, "What is that poster in the back?"

"It is our dream! It is the trip that my husband, baby and I are taking from Argentina to Alaska, in this car," shouts Cande, pointing to the car.

"Wow! That is a story." After this, the commentator calls us forward, telling the others that he will be closing the next segment of the program with us.

The man is as enthusiastic as we are and conducts a very nice interview. As soon as we leave the studio, calls start to pour in from people we know who saw us on the program.

Since we're already strategically parked in Times Square, we decide to take the opportunity to sell some books and we get into a smooth rhythm. A policewoman comes toward us and my intuition tells me that she is going to make me move the car and that our party is over. She stands there, watching us, absorbed, until somebody asks her to take him a picture with us. To my surprise, she does so and then she asks, "What are you selling?" I am scared stiff. I show her my book and she buys one, asking for a signature, relieving all my worries.

A very well-dressed man, of about forty, stopped by the traffic light, stands on the corner, watching even though he can now cross. He comes up to us and says, "You are doing something that millions dream of, but no one has done."

A thousand times, I have heard this comment, but I'm not doing this to be different from the millions; I'm doing it for myself.

"What is the book about?" the man questions.

"I'll sum up what the book says in a few words. The secret to accomplishing a dream is to start."

"Good, I'll take one."

This is probably one of the quickest sales I ever made, surprising me so much that it's important for me to ask him, "May I ask you what you are doing for your dream?"

"Yesterday, just yesterday, I reevaluated my life. I don't know what I'm doing nor for what reason I'm doing it. Have you ever asked yourself why and for what? Or why you came into this world and what are you doing for it? Sometimes I ask myself, 'What am I doing here?' I should be fishing with my son at the lake or walking with my wife on the beach, or in the woods or wherever, but with her. How is it that everything got so complicated? How is it possible that I don't have time for the simplest things, for my friends or loved ones? I earn an excellent salary, but I don't have time to enjoy it. Between my job and the commute, going to and from it, I am away from home eleven hours a day. My wife works too and we get home at different hours and our vacations aren't even at the same time. And my son…I spend so little time with him!"

The man needs to be heard and I need to listen. "In this country there are statistics for everything but there are no studies made about how many people are happy, in love or living the dream they have," he tells me as he gives me the book to sign.

"If you ask anyone what he would rescue from his house if it were on fire, he would say first his family and second, his photo albums. This means that the most important things in our lives are our families and our special moments. It's a pity that we only remember them during a fire!"

I don't know what to say to him. He knows the truth about what to do and that he's not doing it. He wants to be taken by love, dreams, faith and hope. He desires to be won over by happiness but he is trapped or rather said, he feels trapped. The greatest enemy to accomplishing a dream is oneself. And the best hope is also oneself. As a farewell, he says, "Take care."

"Everybody tells me to take care, but of what?" I inquire of him.

"Be careful with your life, so that nothing bad happens to you."

"But, I do what ever I do, still I end up dead."

"Okay then, while you're living, take care of your life."

"That's exactly what I'm doing; I'm making sure that my life has life, and to have it I have to risk it a little bit."

He extends his hand to me in parting; I give him a hug.

"You hug because you are Latino."

"No, because I need it. A hug puts us heart to heart. Listen, you're in a crossroads in your life. You may feel like you're in a crisis, but this is the moment you can begin a completely new life. If you let this moment pass you by, you may not have another crisis. It is your heart screaming, pleading for you to change. Don't silence it, listen, and follow it.

To Live One Day at a Time

One of the stops that we make on our way to Canada is on the banks of the Hudson River, to visit a couple we met in Macungie, Lou and Peg. The first thing that you notice about them is that they have a very clear picture of what they want out of life: to live it day to day. Their house is not showy and doesn't

contain valuable things. They don't own the land, so they built their house provisionally knowing that someday they will have to leave it. However, they have constructed a beach volleyball court where their friends come to play, a Jacuzzi overlooking the river and they dine every night with champagne even if they're only eating hot dogs. She is an environmentalist and he is a mortgage analyst for a bank but he doesn't answer his telephone, the answering machine does that. He knows that working only two days per week provides him enough to live on and that is the amount of time he dedicates to it. We see them happy, full of life, with everything they expect out of life.

They give us their room to sleep in. Although it is so small that the only thing that fits in is the bed, it feels enormous. An entire wall is made of glass overlooking the Hudson River. Another wall has a large window with a view of the forest. Moreover, the ceiling, which is also made of glass, offers the "starriest view" I have ever seen. For our after-dinner coffee, they invite us to sit on benches near the river, from which you can see an enormous mansion with a huge lawn on the bank on the other side. "The owner of that house you see over there is one of the richest men; he has millions of millions, anything he wants, he can buy it. However, the real fortune of the person cannot be measured in coins, but by his happiness. Millions of coins can impoverish one while another is enriched with few.

In this house, we relax completely, not only because of the personality of the couple but also because of the dip Cande and I take alone in the Jacuzzi, observing the excellent view of the river while Pampa dreams.

Canada

Harmony

Autumn Colors

The roads that take us to Canada are beautiful. They are all small; some of them are dirt roads. For many of the little villages we pass through the road we're on is the only one. We eat in small, mom and pop diners tended by their owners and fill up with gas at stations that haven't been modernized in decades. There are plenty of surprises. Once, after having something to eat, we asked for the check only to be told that it has been taken care of by the folks who had already left from the table next to ours. That gesture is repeated in another restaurant too, and occasionally the owner doesn't want hear anything about paying from us.

The border with Canada seems like a simple traffic control point, in front of the small booth, we stop. We remain inside the car and present our documents including the very hard-to-get and expensive visa. Without any questions or checking, we pass through. While we are covering the first few miles Cande comments, "Herman, have you realized that Canada is the first country of our trip that no one has warned us about?"

The change after the border is enormous, because of the architecture, but mainly because we are in the French part of Canada and we have a hard time understanding the language. Gilles comes to our rescue! He's a person who is eager to give us his best attention and treatment and escorts us to his home in Montreal.

With him and his friends, we tour around this very beautiful city in a procession of antique cars until we arrive at a picturesque cobblestone square with a fountain in the center, situated in front of a tiny church. As we listen to

the sweet music of a harp, they tell us that Montreal was founded in this historic area. All the buildings surrounding us are very old, built of stone and bricks. Vehicles are prohibited from entering this zone. However, according to our guides, this doesn't apply to them. They don't consider their cars as "vehicles," they are jewels, and all the tourists seem to share this opinion. Gilles and his friends strategically position us in front of the door of the church. We share our story and sell our books to many groups of visitors entering and exiting the church. There are so many that we don't have time to enjoy this place. So, the first moment we have free, we escape to wander the cobblestone streets of the area. We know that we can sell books at any time, in any place, but to enjoy being here we have only today. Everything is embellished all the more by the melody of a harp. Gradually, we get closer to the music. In the past, I never paid attention to the artists, even less to those in the streets playing for coins, but my view has changed so much that now I admire them. Now I know what art is and what it is to be in the street. Francisco, the painter from Colombia, the artisans we met on the road, the writer in Laredo, and many musicians have proven to me their work is marvelous, it expands humanity, and enhances it. For many, the man with the harp will be merely someone trying to collect a few coins, but for a few, like Cande and me, he is a humane flower in a civilized desert. We are paused 3 feet from the musician and instead of a coin, I place a book in his hat. When he completes his melody, he thanks us for the gift and asks us if we have a copy in Spanish.

"Are you from Chile?" we guess from his accent.

"I was born and raised there, but I grew up and matured in the world. From every place I passed, I carried something with me, something that molded me into a citizen of the world." He takes out a CD and begins to autograph it. "Are you Argentines?"

"Argentines, Latinos, Americans, earthlings," I answer, inducing an accomplice's smile. "Live or survive?" he asks me rhetorically, as he hands us his CD. "Enjoy, or endure? Grateful or conformist? Hopeful or hopeless? Planning or improvising? With a routine, or spontaneous? In love or living with? Do you dream or what?" is his last question.

He then declares, "Don't just survive, because you'll die just the same, live because you are going to die. Don't just endure, because everything changes and you can change for the better. Be grateful for all your achievements and what you have, but never let yourself become a conformist. Do it all with faith because without it there is no hope even for you. Plan and while you're carrying it out, improvise. Break out of the routines, they destroy you, they lock you up and close you in. Dare to change and never stop loving. Cultivate love day by day, without thinking why you live with her or him. Dream or else! If you are not going for your dream, why are you doing what you are doing? Live because you are alive, for this, for dreams.

Moments

Notified by Gilles and now waiting for us in the beautiful city of Québec, are the antique car club, the television, and a fabulous couple who host us in their home. She is Mexican, from Puebla.

"Puebla is a marvelous memory," Cande comments to her.

"My brother lives there; he is a journalist."

"With which media?"

"For the newspaper Síntesis."

"Síntesis? There was an article about us in that paper."

"Could it have been my brother? His name is Mariano Morales."

Cande checks her folder and it is! Thousands and thousands of miles from there and without any plan, we run into his sister! The world is small, you must be on your best behavior all the time…

We take part in a meeting of antique car owners that is attended by many people from the city. One person speaks to me in French and another translates.

"I collect coins from all over the world. Do you have any from Argentina?"

While I am searching for the last few coins that I have, he asks, "What do you collect?"

"Moments in life."

"You mean you don't collect old cars?"

"No, the car came with us because he collects miles and knew that with us, he would accumulate quite a few."

"What moments have you collected?" he questions curiously.

"I have many, and none of them are repeated. They weren't purchased nor can I sell them. Whereas, some of them I sought out and others found me. I have moments both precious and tough."

"For example?"

"Precious, for example, when my mommy patched up my knee, blowing on it and putting on a band-aid. My first kiss. I also have some moments shared with films such as: Dead Poets Society or Il Postino and with books like The Little Prince. Others are moments with my friends, with nature, and conversations. There are moments of love like one afternoon in the park with my arm around Cande. Another marvelous one I remember is when the church door opened and the most beautiful, amazing woman in the world enters to join me in marriage. A more recent one is the first smile of my son, as we looked at each other while I was holding him."

"And tough ones?"

"When my mother was in that cold coffin, knowing it would be the last time I ever saw her."

"Why do you keep the bad ones?"

"To enjoy the beautiful ones even more."

The Walker

After a few days of enjoying Québec, we hit the road again. The road that many think is the wrong one because we're headed to the Atlantic when Alaska is toward the Pacific. However for us it's still the road to Alaska, it's just that this is the extended route, and lets us enjoy more places, new worlds and personalities.

Going through the province of New Brunswick, we pass through a valley surrounded by green fields and behind them, mountains carpeted with trees of colors, full of leaves in reds, burgundies and yellows. The stiff wind that whistles as it barges in through the gaps in the car plays in our favor. In the distance on the lonely road, we perceive a spot where the same current plays in opposition. We slow down and focus all of our attention into it. It is a man who is walking with a big stick as his only companion. His cape inflated with wind renders the big bigger, his puckered face and beard frightening. The man comes closer, smiles and presents himself as Moesch, a Canadian who is walking from his home in Toronto, to Newfoundland, a round trip of some 3700 miles. I ask him for the reason of his feat while Cande pours him some apple juice.

"Because I'm more alive than ever. One day, I woke up after dreaming of walking. I called my mother to tell her about it and she said, 'Son, start walking and walk to the east. Walk all the way to the sea.' Why should I be walking? To find something? Like what? A girlfriend, perhaps? Truly, I had no idea, but, just the same, I packed my bag with my guitar and a couple of dollars. I didn't understand what I was doing, but I set out, heading east as advised. Initially, I searched for a motive in each person and place I saw different things than I had never seen, but it didn't feel like this was the reason for my pilgrimage. When I got to the ocean, I sat in front of it and I asked, 'Why did I walk all the way from Toronto to you?' The only answer I got was the rhythmic sound of the waves so I got quiet and remained sitting on the sand, waiting for an answer. One wave brought me a stick, I stood, picked it up and imagined from where it came. Surely, from very far, as there were no trees in the vicinity. I found that we had something in common. We were brother travelers; and our point of contact a solitary beach. I lifted my gaze, observing the area and the only noticeable thing was my own footprints that came from a long way west. In them I realized at the end of the road, what I had been searching out since the beginning. On seeing these tracks, my own footprints that I retraced with my eyes from as far as I could see until I was looking at my own feet, and I saw myself.

I looked at my self, and all I had done and everything I was capable of since I had accomplished this. I saw someone very important, and this very important person was me who I never knew I always was, I am and always will be. I knew others could be, but me?"

The wind gusts even stronger but it's not capable of distracting our attention or stopping him from continuing. "I set out to lose myself along the way, but it was the road that made me find myself. Now I know who I am and what I can achieve. I know I am capable of attaining incredible heights. I am returning, and I still have a long way home, but at least now, I don't feel like a stranger in this world nor in this body. And you? Why are you traveling?" he asks this as he finishes his remarkable narrative.

"To get to know people on the road...like you."

Tiny Love

That night, we stop in a small village at the Four Seasons hotel, which is next to a beautiful lake. This is the first hotel in a long time. We inquire about prices, asking for the most economical room. We go out to the car to get our things and when we come back inside, we see the owners of the place talking to their children.

"Are you the ones traveling from Argentina to Alaska, the ones who were on television?" they ask us.

They treat us like celebrities. They give us the best room free of charge and while dinner is being prepared, they call the mayor and other personalities from the small town who bring us welcome gifts. The daughter of the owner cuts my hair so that I will be ready to receive the press and the son promises to take us tomorrow to see the lake and the mountain.

While getting ready to sleep like kings, I create a crib for Pampa out of a dresser drawer and watch Cande nurse him while she writes. Hmmm...wonder she's writing...I drift to sleep peacefully.

"Pampa my tiny love,

Today we sit together in front of the mirror and I look at you carefully, observing how you fall asleep in my arms ever so slowly. I look at every inch of your soft skin. How much you've grown in only three months! Your hand on my breast and my heart takes it. The sweet harp music plays behind us and, as if understanding the delight we are sharing, continues its sweetness. You have finished nursing, in my arms I continue holding you, although you are sleeping; I adore just looking at you. Tiny love, who every day surprises me, how much I love you, how much I adore you, only I know. Tiny love, companion of my dreams, I follow you and you follow me. We live life following roads of surprise. We fill our souls with kisses and happiness. Now, someone who completes our love also falls asleep, in peace, while observing us. The harp continues to dance, my two loves are asleep and watching them, I will close my eyes. Sweet dreams, I will have, waiting anxiously for you to wake up. A smile I will dedicate to you, with my arms I will surround you. Pampa, my tiny love."

"I love you."

"Your mom."

A Story of Brothers

We wanted to get to Prince Edward Island before dark but rust in the gas tank plugged the fuel filters, forcing me to stop and clean them. It's very hard to drive ourselves on. Night has fallen; it's cold and raining too.

We go by a country home. The light in the barn is burning and the door is open. We back up and pull in to ask. I encounter a man of about sixty who is sitting there fixing his fishing trap. I tell him about my problem with the car and even though I point in its direction, all he can see are its lights in the night. I ask him if he can take us in for the night.

"Of course I can, son," he answers as he puts the traps aside. I loved the way he said it. He takes us into the house and on entering, he requests to the lady of the house, "Sweetheart, add two more plates to the table; we have company."

The lady, without appearing to be surprised, extends her hand in greeting. The man is a lobster fisherman and they quickly fix us some exquisite, tiny lobster tails. While we are eating, the man tells his story.

"I was born in England during the crisis of the thirties, very difficult times in which there wasn't much to eat. The English government divided us involuntarily, my brother and me from my parents just like many other children from their families. They deported us, putting us on ships to Canada. Here they placed us with families who needed help in the fields or in domestic work. The luckiest ones were received as adopted children but many only as extra hands. My big brother and I went to separate families, far from one another. And, even though he received a punishment afterward, he would always figure out a way to come see me. When he was older, he left that family and moved to a place much closer to me. He helped me with everything and acted like a very good big brother. The day I was married, I chose him as my best man and during the party he told me something I would never have imagined hearing from him. 'Now you have somebody to take care of and somebody to take care of you.' He said good-bye and I never saw him again. Some people said that he went to England, others that he had enlisted in the army."

After dinner, the woman tells us something that happened more recently.

"Not long ago, a man called the county clerk's office where I work. He asked me about a certain man. I told him that man had died two years before and I questioned him why he wanted to know about this man in particular. He answered that the man had been his father, but he had never known him. And now, according to what I was telling him, he never would. I asked the caller how he knew that man was his father and he told me, 'During the Second World War, my mother's husband left for Europe. My mother missed her husband a lot. She found comfort in the touch in another man. When her parents found out that she was pregnant, they sent her to Prince Edward Island. She was there for six months until I was born, after which my mother gave me up for adoption. She then returned to the mainland as if she had only been gone to study. Nobody ever found out that she had been pregnant...about me. When I learned I was adopted, I wanted to know the details and went to Prince Edward Hospital where my name was recorded next to those of my biological mother and father'."

"He then asked me if I knew the man in question. I answered him that yes, I knew the man well. I told the caller that if he was talking about a man who was his father then he was talking to his sister. That man was my father. Within a week, he came to meet me. We had both lost a father but had found each other."

Back to the United States

A Rock in the Road

After being on Prince Edward Island two days, we take a ferry to the Province of Nova Scotia and from there we return to the United States on a cruise we immensely enjoy. As the miles advance, we continue receiving invitations from Bill, whom we met in Macungie, to participate in Hershey, the largest antique auto exhibit in the world. He has sent us a book with all the members of the ACAA with their addresses and phone numbers, in case we need anything, and an emblem of the club to put on the front of our car amongst those of the other clubs.

Accepting his invitation to participate in this show means that we'll have to retrace much of the ground we've already covered, almost as far as Washington, D.C., which would cost us much time, that in this moment, so close to winter, has the value of gold. However, it's not only Bill who insists, but also some friends we have met along the way, who will attend Hershey and want to see us and meet Pampa.

The people who finally convince us are Dave and Agnes Wiltsey, who welcomed us into their home in Halfmoon before we went to Canada. For nearly thirty years, they have been going to Hershey, and haven't missed it once. They always rent three spaces in which they sell used Chevrolet parts. They tell us that if we go to the show, this year they won't sell anything, but will take a motor home, rent a bathroom, set up a big pavilion and hang a big sign announcing "Driving from Argentina to Alaska." All for us, how can we possibly say no? Additionally, how could we refuse given that since our departure from their home, they and their friends have assembled more books? Yes, they have gotten together nearly every night to do this; page-by-page they have compiled the new edition of our book. Therefore, without changing our plans to get to Alaska, we take a huge detour and go to Hershey, Pennsylvania to participate in the car show that lasts for almost a week.

Between thousands and thousands of parts and accessory booths, and cars for sale we park the Graham under the awning with our recently made books. Just like a very good grandma, Agnes has found everything a baby needs including a playpen. She takes care of Pampa while Dave talks to many interested folks and helps us sell the books. Alone, with the vast number of people here, we are not able to attend to them all.

In addition to successfully selling books, with delight we reencounter many of the people we have met on the road. In the evenings, along with them, their friends, those of Dave and Agnes and whoever comes back after reading the book we hang out near the motor home, until very late. Doing this every night, we become a sort of club. One night, while everybody is fast asleep in the motor home, I wake up really needing to pee. To do this I would have to get up, move stuff around, create a racket and besides it's very cold outside. In other words, to go to the port-a-potty means I would have to wake somebody up. Nevertheless, I really have to pee, so there's no other choice. As I begin to move, I find the plastic bottle where I carried drinking water. I empty it by drinking all the water and slyly fill it back up. Hee, hee, hee. Tomorrow, before anyone sees it, I'll throw it away.

When I get up, I go out for my mug of coffee that Agnes has already made. Although it's still not daylight, actually, it's not even seven in the morning, there are already people out and about, asking about the trip so I begin to chat with them. While I am answering questions Cande calls to me from bed.

"What is this?" she asks me, showing me the bottle that I forgot to throw out.

"It's…I…really needed…"

"Tell me this isn't pee or I'll kill you!"

"Well, I just couldn't wait..."

"I'm going to kill you!!! I woke up thirsty and took a big gulp!!! I thought it was juice because of the color. It tasted strange but I couldn't spit it out! That's disgusting, I think I'm gonna throw up! Don't tell me that I drank your pee!!"

I got out of there as fast as I could before she threw the bottle at my head.

It's Friday so I accompany Dave to a meeting. He is like our manager, and makes sure that everything is okay for us. Dave has requested a conversation with Bill to arrange our presentation tomorrow beside all the marvelous cars that will arrive from all over the country.

"What do we need to get in?" we ask Bill.

"You just go and they'll let you in," he assures us.

"Where do we park the car?"

"They'll find a place for you."

The next day we go with the car to the presentation area. Dave advises those at the entrance that we are Bill's guests and they let us pass. Immediately they place us a short distance from the rest of the cars. There is an abundance of space, since it has been raining since the first day of the show and even though today is a beautiful day, they have predicted showers and many didn't come. The cars are in mint condition and competing for the car of the year award. For the judges it will be very difficult to decide a winner.

Many of the car owners and a sizeable quantity of the general public ask us questions and when they find out that we have a book about the trip they begin buying them like hot cakes. The energy and enthusiasm that surround us are intense. People are so happy that they hug us, pat us on the back and cheer us on because we are doing something that they would all love to do.

"Whose car is this?" unexpectedly asks a woman in an imperative tone. She, along with the man next to her, is in charge of the organization of this part of the show.

"Ours."

"You MUST remove this car from here immediately," while she raises her hand pointing to the exit.

"What!? Why?!" we question in unison with the visitors.

"You don't have permission, so get-it-out-of-here!"

"We were invited by Bill."

"Bill? What? Bill? I can't believe it! He has nothing to do with this field. Move this car NOW!" she tells us in a tone of voice that no one likes to hear.

"They are the best part of Hershey and the most impressive participants we've had in years. They don't deserve this treatment," says one of the onlookers.

"When I get home, I'm suspending my membership. You should be ashamed of doing this," states another moving in close to her face. Before too long, we can hear booing.

"We are going to move them from here to put them in a better spot," intervenes the man with her to save the situation.

I feel like I don't have to leave, I am invited and everyone is happy with us being here but in order to avoid problems we follow them with the car and they really do take us to a better location. We're now situated behind some food and souvenir booths on a platform beside the stadium, far from the rest of the cars. They retreat and leave us with all the people who have followed us to this new location to get their books.

Cande, hearing Pampa call, gets inside the car to nurse him. Since I don't want to disturb her, I sell the books outside. I put them on the running boards, from where I pass them out to the super enthusiastic mini-multitude.

Suddenly six uniformed men in security garb arrive. The one out in front gets in my face and tells me to leave; to which I answer, "I have permission to be here." He grabs my books and throws them into the car without being cautious that Cande is in there nursing our baby.

He says to her, "My orders are to get you out of here!"

The other guards try to disperse the people, moving them out. I keep telling them that we are here with permission, while other witnesses try to clarify the situation.

"The same ones who brought you here gave me the order to remove you," confesses the guard, feeling surrounded.

I cannot believe it. First, a high director invites us, but it seems he doesn't have the right. Then, the organizers change our place, and disappear only to send in security later, as if we were "bandidos".

"If you don't move this car, I'll call the police and a tow truck. You are on private property," insists the man, shouting as he pushes me even though many shout at him to leave me alone.

I glance at Cande and at the people, I feel terrible. We were all doing something good but two people, only two who know nothing about dreams, even when if they are right under their nose, sent these six men to throw us out, apparently ready to use force. I can either leave or remain to demonstrate who the bad guys are. I hear a page for Bill on the loudspeakers, so I decide to stay. If he were here, everything would be fine, but we wait in vain.

All the while, the vigilante continues to bellow. So much, it moves me into exercising my right to go on strike. I take a board that Cande uses for painting and write, "We are chasing a dream, only this. And from here, they're kicking us out." Visitors who don't know what is happening read my sign and ask what is going on. Our supporters and I tell them while the guard calls the police and more security personnel. He even tries to grab it and take my sign away from me so I climb up onto the roof of the car from where I show my sign.

"Don't kick them out!" "Stay! We're behind you!" shout the bystanders. Some go up to Cande to tell her they are so ashamed about what they are doing to us.

"I'm just doing my job," says the guard as if this were an excuse, as if this justified his awful treatment.

One of the guards, a young woman, looks like she is very sorry for what she is doing. She looks into my eyes begging for pardon. We have already spent a half hour in this horrible standoff, the worst thirty minutes of the trip. Why should we keep this up? I get in the car, start it up, and we leave, defeated, destroyed... Never have we ever been so mistreated. We leave the area for cars and go three feet beyond the fence into the one devoted to used parts sales, where many have left because of the bad weather. This permits us, quite comfortably, to choose a spot very close to the auto show.

The people, who can see us from where we are, come to us and some who know what happened, ask us to forgive them. We don't know what to say, we have knots in our stomachs and much anger to the point of exploding that we prefer not to make any comment until we know why this happened.

This is the last night of the event. Next to the motor home, an impromptu farewell party takes shape. Many people support us and explain she only wanted to demonstrate her power. It's true, it was only one woman and one man...not, the members of the club or Hershey. This ignorant woman knows nothing of dreams, but she did her best to crush one.

The next morning, we leave Hershey having been mistreated by two people but with invitations to hundreds of family homes, so many that it would be impossible to accept every one. We also have a new family and friends. Dave and Agnes. It makes us so sad to say goodbye to them, but before leaving, Dave with his arm around his wife makes us feel good with his wonderful words of warning.

"You can't get rid of us that easily, we'll see you again."

With this image, I accelerate, rushing north. We want to get back to Canada, visit the capital and the city of Toronto. Later visit Niagara Falls, reenter the States and, to escape winter, take route 66 south to California, and then follow the Pacific coast all the way up to Alaska.

What We Do, Who We Are

Before leaving Halfmoon, NY, we stop by a newspaper office where we have an appointment with a journalist who will write an article. The reporter finds herself with a story that is out of the context of her typical articles. Surely, she would know the questions to ask if she's covering an accident, a robbery or interviewing a political figure. But how do you cover a dream? She starts the interview like this, "What is a day like for you?"

"We don't know how to tell you, because we don't have the routine life any more in which the day is pre established and differs from the one before only by the date. Now, a day is totally unpredictable."

"Typically, there is no typical day," adds Cande with a smile.

"Do you sometimes sleep in the car?"

"Yes, we do. Sometimes, the canvas cover for the car absorbs the sun in the morning, like a thermal blanket, this means it raises the temperature in the car, in effect converting it into an oven. It also depends on where we park the car. It might be a busy street, a service station, or a field."

"What do you have for breakfast?"

"Bread with a piece of cheese, maybe some fruit, mate tea or coffee with milk. When we are staying in a house, we have a typical breakfast of the region that can range from something very simple to an elaborate breakfast prepared by the couple who gets up early to fix it. It is very common to hear the husband say, 'Why don't you come more often, it's been a long time since we've had such a good breakfast'."

After a chuckle the reporter continues, "What time of day do you start out?"

"This depends more on our hosts than us. Sometimes they organize so many plans for us. They can include touring the area where they live, a visit to a museum, meeting the relatives, trying typical foods or a stop at some other place we 'just can't leave without seeing.' Some folks organize enough events to keep us busy for a week!"

"But when you leave, what do you do?"

"Despite our hosts even wanting to tell us which way to go, we always decide the precise road the day we leave.

"What do you do while you are on the road?"

"This is our time; unique, marvelous and mysterious. Those who feel the freedom of the road understand this. It's our time to have a conversation. It is when we are alone and remember what we have done, what we feel, the magic and incredibleness of the people who receive us and the surprises of each day. It is time of ideas about what we can do and places we can go. Herman drives and I write down the names of the people we photograph, the number of miles we covered the previous day, update the journal and make note of the people we meet. We drink mate tea and take movies. We stop all the time to take pictures and to fill up with gas...the tank is small. Or sometimes we stop just because people signal to us," says Cande

"Why do people stop you?"

"To know what we're doing, and why, where we're going and where we've been already and many more questions that turn into conversations during an unexpected stop. They also tell us their stories.

"When and where do you stay?"

"Again, this doesn't depend on us. Opportunities just turn up, magically. Many times the same people who stop us ask where we usually sleep. When we tell them, they look one to the other as if to say 'Should we invite them?' An angel always appears."

"What do you mean 'an angel'?"

"It's true, they are in abundance. They are everywhere," replies Candelaria. "Once we were in Pennsylvania, very near New York State. It was getting kind of late, and at night we don't like to drive. Although there were people waiting for us at their home further up the road, we couldn't get there in time. So, we stopped at a crossroad, an intersection where there was an abandoned barn and a few houses, to think what to do. We first looked for the name of someone recommended to us to call, but there was no one close by. 'Look in the Graham Club member roster and see if any of them could house us', Herman told me. I looked until I found someone who lived about 20 miles from where we were. After a short debate, it was Herman who made the call while I listened attentively. After introducing himself, he asked the member if we could stay with him for the night. The man didn't know what to say, he asked us where we were, and while not saying no, he didn't say yes either. While I was envisioning the answer, a car stopped next to ours. It was a two-door jalopy; the car was a mess. Out of it climbs a young guy in his early thirties who looks like he's skipped a few days of shaving. He approached me and said 'I read the sign on your car and I just had to stop. Did you really come from Argentina? I love Latin America so much. What are you doing here? Are you lost?' Very enthusiastic about our trip, he couldn't resist telling me that he is also a traveler, he's been to Argentina, Asia, and Europe and he even had a girlfriend from Argentina. While I was listening, I thought, 'This is our angel of the day', and I gave Herman's arm a squeeze so he wouldn't worry any more. Then this young man asked me where we thought we were going to sleep. I answered that we didn't know and he told me, 'I have a log cabin in the mountains and I would love you to come with me, I have a horse, a cow, two goats, a dog and there is a creek, I have some trout that we can cook...'

'Yes, yes, we'll go!' we interrupted him."

"We followed him and with every mile we advanced, the view became more rural and picturesque, we were surrounded by small mountains in a valley full of trees. I think that our faces gave away our surprise when we saw the marvelous cabin he had built by himself and the stable with the promised animals. It was a fantasy place. While we cooked, he told us about his travels and we realized that he was a special person who adapted to each place he traveled. Herman asked him how he made himself understood with people who spoke other languages to which the young John Longmore responded 'Every human can make himself understood, and for me it is easier to communicate with those people than the people who speak my own language. These, I assure you, don't understand my trips and the type of life I live. I work six months a year to make enough money to travel, the other semester I dedicate to living in the simplest manner, so my money lasts longer and I can continue traveling for more time. I hardly understand 'them' either; simply working and working to pay the bank for things they buy and don't need. 'They' give their lives to the bank and the companies they work for, more than to their families and themselves. They don't have time for their kids, but for their bosses, yes. They only take fifteen days of vacation and use those to fix the house, instead of repairing their lives. When I travel, I am with families who may speak differently, but I don't need much to understand them, I know with a smile that I am welcome. I know their family is their greatest treasure and when I watch them, I perceive they know that the best thing for the family is to be together. I don't understand those who speak my same language, because I show them the photos of these families and they say 'Poor people, look where they live, they don't have anything.' The ones that say this are divorced, or their child is far away and they don't see him and can't enjoy time with the new wife because they're both working extra hours...'"

"That night we go to sleep remembering the many families with whom our first communication was a smile. This guy is right, the smile is the international language, and it means many beautiful things. With our own son, a smile was our first communication, and filled us with happiness. Solely and simply with a smile we can be understood." says Cande, summing it up.

"Isn't he an angel?" I ask the journalist, who doesn't respond. She waits in silence hoping to learn more. I insist, "Isn't he an angel?"

"Is it like this every day?" she reacts.

"With a thousand variations, yes, this occurs every day."

"What was your worst moment?"

"Hershey."

We both tell her in detail what happened to us. The reporter, who is very saddened that this has happened in her country, asks us "Did you call Bill to ask what happened?"

"Yes, we called him, but since he didn't answer our calls, we had to ask a friend to call and then pass his phone to us to speak to him."

"And, what did he say?"

"That we should forget about it, it was just a mistake, that it's too late to do anything about it."

"Sad that an important director didn't want to straighten things out or to say he's sorry..." comments the reporter. "Was that the most difficult moment?"

"No, the most difficult was to begin, leaving everything: the family, the house, our work, and our friends, to go directly into the unknown, unpredictable, the strange."

"Wasn't it more difficult to go down the Amazon, cross the deserts, the mountains, the birth, or running out of money?"

"No, none of that. It was much more difficult to start."

Return to Canada

Fisherman of Gulls

Back into Canada, the first thing we do is go to Cardinal where Karen and Ray, a couple we met at the Graham meet in Greensboro, are expecting us. In their home, in front of the St. Lawrence River enjoying watching the gulls flying, Karen asks us, "What's your opinion of Canada?"

"Many see Canada as a country in the first world, while for us it's the last," surprising her with my comment.

"What? Last?"

"Yes, it's the last country in our journey."

"Oh!" she sighs with relief.

"Karen, it's of no importance how your country is viewed. It is how it is. The same goes for your family, your home and yourself. Who cares about someone else's opinion? "

We sit in silence. During our previous meeting, Karen had told us that one day she went to pickup her niece from preschool. When the youngster saw her, the girl ran to meet her and hugged her, but Karen didn't recognize her and asked a teacher who is this little one? That same day they took her to the hospital. They diagnosed a cerebral tumor and told her the next day they would perform an emergency operation. Her world crashed in seconds and without warning. The operation had no guarantees; it was possible she could come out of it with severe mental impairments, or a loss of function, or she might not even come out of it al all, but she must have the surgery. Incredibly, she came out of it perfectly.

"Never have I faced death so closely, never have I been one step from losing everything." She comments to us. Today, on one of the walls in her house, hangs a Chinese symbol that signifies longevity. This is what Karen desires now, to live many, many years. After discussing this, I question her.

"Which would you like more, five gallons of ice cream with no flavor, or a very tiny cup of your favorite flavor?"

"A small cup of ice cream with my favorite flavor," she responds without any hesitation.

"The same goes for life. It doesn't matter how much we live, only how we live. Don't look to live eternally, look to live something that you can carry eternally. There are those looking to kill time and others who live preoccupied with how to live longer. The reality is that we have to live it. Imagine the following: the results of your routine medical exams are confused with those of another person and the doctor tells you that you only have three months to live. What would you do?"

Karen thinks about it. When she is about to respond, I interrupt her.

"Then why don't you do it? Imagine that you only have three more months to live. Each additional day you will appreciate with all your heart and you will live each day as if it were your last. Even if a doctor doesn't tell you, I'm telling you. Every day you live is a gift, live it as if it were your last, because some day it will be. Life only gives you life, everything else you have to work for. Don't wait to be given love, happiness, unforgettable moments, dreams…it's you that has to go for them. All these things won't come to you merely because you ask for a long life. A thirty-year old man could have lived much more than one of ninety. It's like a movie. Which do you prefer, an excellent film of thirty minutes or a boring one of ninety?

"The thirty-minute one."

"Okay, then that's how you have to live. An excellent life, which if it's lengthened, what a welcomed gift! God has blessed you with another chance to continue living. Have your favorite ice cream, savor your life.

In total, we remain in Cardinal three days in which we only go out for walks and check our mail on the Internet. Among the messages, I read one from a couple who had received us in Texas. They told us they lost their only son, who was about 30, however, despite all the pain that accompanied burying their son, they thank God for the blessing to have lived all those years with him. The message astounds me. I have always been incensed that God took my mother but this couple taught me to be grateful. I was permitted to enjoy her for those twenty one years. It could have been less, it could have been...none.

Formula of Love

Upon entering the capital city of Ottawa we head straight to the market, where among fruits and veggies, meats and foods, coffees and other teas, we park the car to do our shopping. We are amazed by the quantity of Canadians who speak Spanish and surprised by the number who have traveled the world but mostly by the way they do it; nearly everyone with a backpack, regardless the age. Close to there, the Antique Auto Club of Ottawa entertains us splendidly during a breakfast in our honor, complete with newspaper interviews.

In the city, the married couple Moore receives us. They are an older couple that isn't the least bit interested in cars. We have contacted them through mutual friends in Mississippi. They succeed at being the type of couple we all would like to be at that age, or better, for life. They act like newlyweds, constantly pampering and declaring sweet sentiments. For this, we ask them to tell us the secret to their way of marriage.

"Never fail to respect the other, not even during an argument, and neither in jest. Never make jokes for others to laugh at your partner," enumerates Mr. Moore.

"Never go to sleep without a good night kiss, nor get up without one in the morning, even if you're mad. It's not important that it's short...you must give a kiss. Never sleep separated, even if you feel like you want to after an argument. Know that when a dispute is finished, it's finished for good, don't bring it up again. When you forgive, you forgive for eternity. Don't get elegantly dressed for work and put on the comfy old sweat suits, robe and rollers when you're at home. Always dress properly and neatly as if you were going out on a date. Always to the conquest. Another very important and difficult thing to understand is that children are not the result of marriage; they are the fruit of it. The couple must continue to feel as important as it was before the birth of the child. Happy parents, happy kids. And lastly, put a lot of attention into the details; bring a surprise, send flowers, write a note, make time for the two of you, for talking, to go out or just to be alone," culminates Mr. Moore, confident in what he's saying.

"Love isn't a sentiment that you continue feeling eternally just because," adds his wife as she rocks Pampa in her arms. "You have to cultivate it, water it, take care of it every day. Love has to grow and get bigger than when it was new, if not, on the contrary, it will die, little by little. One falls in love with the other person because of his or her dreams. If he or she forgets them, you forget what made you fall in love with him or her. Dreams that are worth fighting for fortify love and it grows if you're trying to complete them.

"The greatest treasure that one may encounter in life is love, to love someone and to feel loved. Without it, we're no one, nothing has any value. One has to look for it, because there is one for everyone, out there somewhere, there is a love you've always hoped for," he concludes.

Yonge Street

After a few days of traveling, we enter the city of Toronto, on a huge highway to go to the house of Carolina and Gonzalo, some Argentinean friends who with their children moved a short while ago here to Canada. They miss the country intensely, but the things there were getting complicated so the company that he works for offered him a transfer to Toronto. In this beautiful city, Gonzalo has an attractive house, a nice car and a great job, However, he and Carolina are longing for so much of what makes them happy; their families, their friends, their home that little by little they were building themselves, their culture, their foods... They left so much that they miss in excess.

The land where you grow up is like one's first love, you'll never forget it and it is always remembered as the best. The love of one's land is not diluted by anything, because one loves his place and wants to live in it without caring about how it is nor what it can give one. We marry the one we love, not the convenient one. The same occurs with the land. That's why the majority of those that leave their own do so for strongly compelling reasons, with great pain and feeling like they are betraying their own land. Many immigrants are perceived negatively, regardless of whether they're illegal or not, however after having lived with many, let me assure you they deserve our admiration. They must give up so much, few would have the courage to do it.

It is Sunday and we tour around the city of Toronto, we are enchanted. We drive along the most important thoroughfare in the city, Yonge Street, making our way to sell books in the zone where there are many pedestrians.

The red light stops us; when it turns green and I put it in gear to move, we hear a "something's broken" noise and instantly we look at each other with "what was that?" faces. The car doesn't move even though I am stepping on the gas. We get out to push it closer to the curb. A man shows up to help me, but when we try to move it, part of the car collapses to the ground, the rear driver's side wheel has fallen off.

"Your axel is broken. What bad luck!" exclaims the man.

"You think so?" I reply. "It could have broken on the highway we just left. If that had happened, I would have lost control, crashing into other cars and the tire could have rolled away, causing other accidents...instead, here we only broke the axel. I think we're very lucky."

"If you look at it this way, you can say yes, you are very lucky."

"Can I help you at all?" offers another person.

Soon, more people approach and with everyone's help, we lift the car. Little by little, we get closer to the sidewalk, trying to alleviate the disaster we have created with the traffic. All the time, increasing numbers of people come up to us asking if they can do something for us. Someone comes with hot chocolate to ease the cold, another calls the Canadian Auto Club, and a Colombian woman who had knitted a blanket for her grandson, happily gives it to Pampa instead who immediately use it.

The police come.

"Excuse us, Officer, for the mess we are causing with your traffic."

"Did you do it on purpose?" he asks.

"No, of course not."

"So, why are you worrying?"

While we wait for the Auto Club tow truck, I call two members of the Graham Club, one in the States, and the other here in Canada, to ask them help us find a replacement part. Some folks invite us to their homes; others take away an autographed book, which Cande has begun to offer.

The police see that my wife is selling something nonstop and they want to know what she's promoting. We get a little nervous; maybe we're not permitted to sell in the streets. However, when Cande shows them the books, they buy two copies.

The television reporter Peter Gross comes and makes a very funny report, which makes us laugh at the situation, he implies we simply want more time in Toronto. The camera films the tow truck coming, pulling away the car and us saying good-bye to the people who although it's freezing have waited to see if there's anything else they can do to help us.

For being members of the Argentina Auto Club, we have the benefit of 3 miles free towing, the 15 miles remaining to the house where we're staying we'll have to pay for, and it won't be cheap. The chauffer of the tow truck calls the club headquarters.

"Boss, I wish you were here to see this. For sure, you'd tell me they shouldn't pay anything. Please don't ask me to charge them. These guys are actually doing something that everyone dreams about doing. Let's give them our support."

"For you to ask me, it must be good. I trust your judgment," answers his boss. That's how we get home.

The next day, we call the Argentine Consulate. Immediately, they give us the address of a mechanic. When we call him, he treats us as if he already knew us, and asks us the

address of where to send the tow truck. When the truck from there arrives, the driver gets out with his mouth wide open, he can't believe what he's seeing.

"Oscar sent me here assuring me I would find something amusing that I would love, but I never imagined this! Much less a car from the twenties with Argentinean plates that arrived here being driven!"

The man turns out to be from Argentina and is thrilled beyond words. When the time comes to pay him, he tells us he only accepts Argentine pesos or nothing. Obviously, we don't have any.

The shop where he leaves us seems like a typical one of Argentina; posters of soccer teams, pictures of race cars, and others with the image of a woman promoting a product that no one pays any attention to…the product. The son and the wife of the mechanic also work here and from the speakers that animate the shop we can hear an Argentine radio station, which is being transmitted via Internet.

"I knew you'd show up here when I saw you on TV last night, I told my wife 'Watch and see, tomorrow, they'll be in our shop'," the owner of the shop tells us.

He is welding the axel when I receive a call telling me that two new axels are headed our way. While we wait, we put the repaired one back on the car. When all is said and done, we leave from Toronto with new friends, many books sold and two spare axels, all thanks to a broken wheel.

What's the Plan?

Right after we leave the city, we receive a call from Dave and Agnes who are on the hunt for us. They would like to accompany us to Niagara Falls, so we communicate frequently just to have an idea of one another's whereabouts.

"Where are you?" Agnes asks.

"We're driving on a little road surrounded by colorful trees. We'll be at the falls in about three hours, we'll meet you there," Cande tells her.

Simultaneously as she hangs up there is a horribly ugly metallic noise coming from the motor and it's beginning to smoke. I put it in neutral and slowly roll to a stop on the shoulder. At the same time, a pickup passes us and immediately pulls over. I open the hood, the fan blades are bent. In addition, since the piece that holds it on also broke it collided with the radiator causing some damage. From it, water is leaking, drenching the exhaust pipe producing the steam that we thought was smoke.

The man in the pickup is standing looking at my engine without saying anything. I notice that his hands are work hands and I ask him his name.

"Stewart," he answers without looking up.

"So, Stewart, what's the plan?"

"I know a machine shop where they can repair your fan mount, and I also have a friend who repairs radiators and while everything's being put right, you have my house where you can stay," he tells me without hesitating.

"So, what we are waiting for?"

We get there being towed by his truck. He introduces us to his family; he lives with his wife, children and grandchildren in a cozy country home. Cande stays inside with the granddaughter who plays a lot with Pampa. Stewart shrugs into his overalls and I help him disassemble the car. In the meantime, Dave and Agnes arrive and they are received as life long friends. At dinner time, we all sit together to enjoy a wonderful stew.

Our actual farewell to this part of Canada has to wait three more days, in which besides fixing the car, we enjoy ourselves with the family of benefactors who take us to their favorite places. Not only does the machine shop not allow us to pay, because they had read about us in the newspaper, but neither the radiator man, who says to us, "Any friend of Stewart's is a friend of mine and I don't charge my friends."

United States Anew

First Snow

Right after visiting Niagara Falls, we once again reenter the United States together with Dave and Agnes. The idea is to go to Detroit, where the car was born, and from there advance as far south as possible, meaning, California, to escape this winter which we can already feel as a result of the first snow fall.

We have an invitation to a house near Buffalo, and since it's already dark, our friends prefer to accompany us then return to their own home. Suddenly, on a bridge that crosses a highway, the back end of the car takes a hard hit to the ground. The same wheel that fell off in Toronto again flies off the car, only this time, while in motion. Sparks are flying! Metal is dragging on the pavement. I pray the wheel doesn't fall off the bridge, or land in oncoming traffic at the same time I try to keep the car straight until it comes to a stop on its own.

When I get out, I find the rear fender severed completely in half. The drum is worn from the scraping, but not broken, and the wheel, as if it were lassoed, landed six feet behind the car with a piece of axel still attached. The same axel we welded broke again.

We call the house in Buffalo; Sharline and Vernon, our hopeful hosts, invite Dave and Agnes to stay over as well. Thanks to the AAA (American Automobile Association) tow truck we get there.

The next day, everything wakes up covered in white. Over night, there has been about 3 inches of snow. We dedicate this day to taking off the broken axel and replace it with one sent to us in Canada.

That night, during dinner, Dave and Agnes invite us to spend the winter with them. They don't want us to continue in this cold and to convince us, they offer a change of piston rings and other repairs. There is nothing to compare with the pleasure created by simply being with this beautiful family and their friends. The motor really does need new piston rings; it's burning so much oil and is loosing power. On the other hand, it's also true that from the day we left, it's burns oil and we really could continue until he final says "enough!" But, why all this; first, the axel in Toronto, then the cooling fan, then the axel here again? Aren't these signals telling us to stop for the winter? Cande and I discuss the proposition together, and that night we decide to go home, the home of Dave and Agnes.

We set out for Halfmoon once again after a high-carb breakfast as winter really has set in. In this region, it snows a lot, even more than in Alaska and we are getting a demonstration. In deference to the weather, we march on, yet again following Dave's truck. Around noon, the snow yields to sleet, changing from ice to snow and back to ice again. During one part of the trip, I can only see through the place my manual windshield wiper swipes because everywhere else is completely snow covered. In the afternoon, the temperature drops, getting colder yet, a freezing rain falls which freezes and sticks to the car, creating a thick coating of ice everywhere except the hood. The windshield is now completely iced up except for the small section my wiper is still cleaning. Dave, in his modern truck, with heater and defrost, has to stop driving more than once to remove the ice from the windshield. He correlates the fact that I don't have to do this in my car to some kind of divine intervention. The road rolls over many hills and valleys all covered with snow and ice; all I see are the lights of the truck in position in front of me, on which I focus all my energy, striving not to loose sight of them.

We arrive at daybreak the following morning, having accomplished the longest day's driving of the whole trip, 340 miles in one day. Although it was difficult and we're exhausted, we feel victorious.

Discovering New Friends

Taking apart the car, we discover that a change of rings won't be sufficient. We have removed some of them and they are in pieces, also two pistons are cracked and one of the connecting rods is nearly destroyed.

"It's incredible that in this condition, you ever made it here. I believe there couldn't be a better time to rebuild this engine," declares Dave before turning himself and his friends into a temporary official Graham Paige shop.

The Graham Club sends us an extra axel, but there's no way they can help with the pistons and the rings. Those we can't get a hold of, though we search high and low so we decide to have them made.

The first estimate we get is $3375 and it will take three months. Dave talks with his friends Doug, Vernon, and others; between them, they are willing to pay for it, but we don't want them to. It's too much help to receive; it would be excessive along with everything else to spend so much on the pistons. Friends like Doug have taken the vacation days they have earned at work to repair our car; some have given parts, Ray has come from Canada to collaborate and so have other people from areas surrounding Halfmoon, for example the turner and Dave's business partner as well.

Dave has an idea. He organizes a sale in his repair shop, next to where he sells chain saws. We invite all his friends to participate and the results are a success: many bought our books and handicrafts that Cande, Agnes, her daughter and Doug's wife are selling.

Additionally, our friend helps spread the word about what we need and someone gives us information about a company in California that makes pistons for racecars. We call, explaining why we need these pistons, and succeed

in getting the company to agree to make them for $800 and in only one month.

During this time, I am present for all the work in the shop, and despite the cold, Cande goes for walks out side with Pampa, who is growing and is much more attentive, enjoying being able to sit up by himself. She is also becoming great friends with Diane, Agnes, Pam, Jane and their friends who take a class together, learning how to create beautiful quilts.

All the movements of the mechanics are very precise. Dave and Co. have many years of practice working on their antique cars, but not on Grahams. Not a problem, Bob, from Greensboro, city of Pampa's birth, clears up any questions, directs the work and precisely instructs us over the phone. Everyone has his own job, except me. When the motor is disassembled and it's impossible to go anywhere with it, the shop jokes commence. I know they're kindly teases directed at me, but I can't retort because my trip is in their hands.

"How can I help?" I ask them.

"See that corner? See it? Go over there and stay there! That would help us a lot!"

Another day, I ask where I could go and buy some brake fluid, and they take me to the fruit stand to buy some grapefruit! My pronunciation still isn't perfect, but it's good enough for them to kid me. Dave is a Chevy fanatic and one afternoon he commented:

"If you'd made this trip in a Chevrolet, we wouldn't be fixing this motor here." he tells me mockingly.

"Yes, it's true, I'd still be in Chile fixing it," I comment beginning to return their jokes, but without quieting my friend.

350

"Herman, what's your favorite car make?"

"Ford," I respond just to be contrary even though I'm not.

"Oh, Ford, did you know that half of the Fords ever made are still on the roads?" He states, a rare optimistic comment, "… the other half made it home!"

In Dad's Arms

While we're in Halfmoon, I receive a call from California. It's from my father, who lives in San Francisco. When I was a year old, my mom separated from him and she and I went to Argentina. He stayed on and we never had any communication after that, we lost all contact. When I wanted to get to know him, I didn't know how to get in touch with him. I started looking for him when I was 16 and asked every person who traveled to the States to look hoping someday to find him.

When I was 19, a friend of Cande's brought me a telephone number. I called and answering the phone in English was a guy who sounded happy to talk to me but whom I couldn't understand because of the language. I passed the phone to my mom, who talked to him and got another number. "That was your brother, he has the same name as your father," she told me. That's how I found out I have a brother in the States.

After that, I called the other number and my father answered the phone. No one had given him any kind of warning: here calling him was a son he knew only as a baby, whom he had never seen or heard since. At moments, some full of delight and others in a state of shock, he tells me a few things and asks for my phone number saying he would call me back in a few minutes. He did and then, more relaxed, we talked for hours. I remember he asked me how tall I was, what I liked to do, what my hobbies were and about my friends. He wanted to know everything about me. He invited me to visit him, he asked me what I looked like, and I responded, "You'll see."

I went to San Francisco three months later. No one, him nor the rest of the family, could believe how much I looked like him. One of his neighbors asked how come Peter looked so young. She thought I was him after some operation. I lived three months with my dad and together we discovered that besides looking alike, we have many things in common, habits, preferences, and even gestures. The time spent together was spectacular; I got to know my dad, two brothers and a sister, what a thrill.

But getting back to this call, he wants us to spend Christmas together as a family. Happily, we accept his invitation. It will be the first time with him. We travel there on a plane thanks to the tickets he has sent us. Being with the "old man" again is great, especially because it's Christmas time, my first one with my dad. With Pampa in his arms, he can't stop repeating that he has never had such a wonderful gift. Our son is already crawling and my dad carries him to the park on his shoulders, feeds him and all the other things that grandpas like to do.

However, we're not completely happy. While we were at Dave's we had received another family call, in addition to the one from my dad. It was to tell us that Cande's mom is not doing too well at this moment. From Argentina, they contacted us to say that she had surgery to extract the tumor from her liver and it was unsuccessful. She has to begin treatments again. Throughout our whole trip, we have thought much about her mom, and now Cande really wants to go and be with her and actually me too, I would like to accompany her.

With this objective, we call a travel agency of an Argentinean that is in New York to ask for prices to Buenos Aires. He offers us the tickets at his cost. The barber from the shop where we sold books in Queens and another man who went from Argentina to NY on a bicycle helped us pay for passage but there were no tickets available until after Christmas.

The Chosen Star

Just the thought of going back to Argentina feels very strange. How will it be to back at home? We never supposed that we would be going back before we finished the trip, but there's things you can't plan, things the heart asks that one just can't refuse. Because of this, we are in an airplane for Buenos Aires, anxious to get there and spend a whole month with Gramma.

We get out of the plane and in the lobby, we see everyone in our family. Our first reaction is to laugh until we almost wet ourselves because everyone is in weird costume jumping and screaming. Then come the hugs, we feel wonderful, we're all crying from emotion. Three years have passed without seeing one another, but it feels like many more. Cande squeezes her mother in her arms. She is overcome and doesn't want to let go.

"I have missed you so much, my daughter."

"I have missed you too, mama."

That night Cande and her mom point out in the sky which star they have chosen to communicate with one another. They indicate one then another, laughing happy to be once more together. Later we speak with my father-in-law who is a doctor.

"The prognosis isn't good. However, there are no illnesses but only ill individuals and your mama is special. She has the strength to want to fight and this grandson will be a magic potion that may make her very well," he says while we watch Pampa enjoying being seated on Gramma's lap.

We spend a super "family month" together; hosting many barbeques at home, which after three years alone, is in need of few repairs. Being in Argentina, we realize how much we miss it, but even so our desire to return and continue the trip to Alaska remains firm. Another thing we notice is the enormous change in ourselves. Simply talking with our families and friends demonstrates this to us. For many, the fact that the house is in bad shape due to these years is something terrible, a complete disgrace, whereas we think it's only a material thing that can be repaired.

During one of the barbeques:

"Let's see if you leave all this traveling and get a job!" is the comment of one.

"After all this wandering through the world it will be quite hard to get back to work," says another.

"You work to what end?" I asked them.

"For the well-being of me and my family."

"And to what end do you think we work at this trip day by day? Surely, it seems to you that we're only enjoying ourselves and yes, we are. We enjoy putting our books together, autographing them for those who take them home. We like painting and framing the pictures, creating handicrafts, driving to new horizons, meeting many people and once in a while servicing the car. For now, this is our work and it is for our well-being. As Mother Teresa says: 'our best distraction.'"

"You know what? Everyone is used to relating work with a sacrifice, but you're right, you are doing the right job."

The month passes very quickly, in the same way as the last three years, as all time passes when you're enjoying yourself. We leave Cande's mom in much better shape than we found her: a tiny grandson has worked wonders on her, filling her with happiness and energy.

It is a bit difficult to leave the house and the family again, but not as hard as three years ago: now we're jumping back into our dream with much more faith than when we left the first time.

New Motor

Dave and Agnes, ready as always to share their affection, are waiting for us at the airport in New York. The change is brusque: we leave Argentina on a beautiful summer day and now, at Dave's I am shoveling snow again. To our surprise, our car is not only almost ready, but seems to have received various extra repairs as well. For example, the fender has been

repaired at a technical high school where Dave taught classes before retiring and where we go to give a speech as a thank you to the guys for their excellent workmanship.

Although it's still cold and snowy, spring is approaching so we return to the road, leaving Halfmoon with a mix of happiness and sadness: Many people have helped us so much, and we have reaped many new friends. Nevertheless, now is the time to set off. By far, the best part of this journey is the people; the worst is saying good-bye to them.

A Meticulous Genius

We have easily received twenty-five calls from Jim in Cleveland, Ohio. We met him in Hershey. During the car meet, he invited us to come to his shop on the way to Detroit. At that time, he looked crazy, his clothes and hat gave him a strange look and his interest in the details of the mechanics of the car was over the top. Our first impression was that he was a crazy car fanatic and if we accepted his invitation it would mean we'd be in Cleveland a long time, because Jim could become obsessed in repairing every detail and Macondo has thousands.

During successive calls he promised, as a way of convincing us, that if we came he'd arrange something with the local TV stations and newspapers. He implored us not to fail him, to please come and see him. Could it be he who wants a bit of fame? And what if he is a phony? In spite of our doubts, he is insistent; we just can't turn him down. After all, he told us something in Hershey that unites us. Jim intended to complete his own dream, which was organizing and reinitiating the 1908 New York-Peking race, complete with antique cars. It never came to be for want of a few dollars more in addition to the many he had already raised. In some way, we feel Jim sees in us the possibility of completing his own project, although the points of departure and arrival are not the same.

He receives us with a friend at the entrance to the city of Cleveland and we go directly to his shop, which is full of incredibly valuable cars. We can see Jim is enthusiastic; it's late, but he doesn't care. Along with his engineer friend and other mechanics, they begin going over the car, looking for things to do. Jim only restores Rolls Royce and Bentleys plus in his office is a plaque alerting clients, "If you have something to tell me, I'll listen, but know that my time costs $150 an hour and the clock is ticking." But for the Graham, he is ready to dedicate all the time in the world to adjust items large and small that only he sees need it.

"Here we're leaking a little brake fluid, here there's a little play…"

"Jim, please," I interrupt him, "we don't want to be here a week fixing things, we really need to get back on the road. I beg you only repair the things which are absolutely necessary," I request of him firmly.

Beside, he has organized many other things; in the bar he frequents he wants introduce us to everyone, he has located a newspaper reporter and another for TV, arranged for us to meet the mayor of Berea as well as the inventor of a new spark plug that we will use in our car. If we combine all these plans with the ones he has in mind for the car, we will need a whole month. There is nothing for it; I have to gather all my courage and tell him.

"Jim, I'm serious, please do only the work that is absolutely necessary, we have to get to Alaska this summer. I mean it!"

The following days we receive visits from numerous people who read about us in the newspaper. Some are looking for our book, others Cande's paintings, and many offer themselves what ever we need. Here are those who simply stop by, wanting to watch, not interrupting our work. All of them radiate a lot of energy and it spills on to us. They bring many gifts that often become a problem because we have no idea where to put them. It doesn't matter, every time we see them, beautiful memories flood back to us. They stick their heads in the windows, looking at everything, even smelling the scent of the adventure, of the dream…they walk around the car, running their hands affectionately over it. We observe them, seeing them fill with energy, taking it, and returning it to us with their best wishes for a happy trip, a happy return and a happy life. We often hear "God bless you" from the people. What touches us deeply is when anyone tells us they will pray for us, making us wonder just how many different faiths are part of this dream.

If we need a nut or something that Jim doesn't have, a volunteer surfaces to go and look for it. Folks offer to take Cande somewhere more comfortable or to buy diapers or anything else we need. Plus, for Pampa there are many arms that want to hold him, play with him, make him laugh. This is how the whole trip has gone, we arrive and are splendidly received, very warmly even though outside is all snow and cold.

With a Big Heart, a Big Family

One of the families that come to visit us offers to host us at their home. We happily accept. This home is in front of a lake full of swans and a forest full of deer. While we're having dinner, the couple tells us how it was possible for them to buy this place:

"We were living in a small apartment with our two boys and were looking to move into a house. Given the money we had saved and our possibilities for credit, it couldn't be too big. We told our real estate agent this and she, heaven knows why, brought us to see this house first. It had only been on the market for two days. Of course, when we saw it, we fell in love with it; it was perfect for us but also completely out of our price range. Nevertheless, the next day we came back without the agent and introduced ourselves to the owner and told him sincerely, "Please excuse us, sir, we had to come back, we just can't buy it, but we feel something really special about this place but we don't want to bother you…' The owner asked us to come in and over coffee he said to us:

"I have a promise to fulfill, a pact that I made with the person who sold the house to me. I can sell you this house, we'll all sign a paper for the receipt of a large down payment of money that you don't actually make, and instead you just pay me the money you have saved. All this is in exchange for giving me a promise: you must do the same that I have done for you with who ever wants to buy this house in the future whenever you put it on sale, given that it's the house of their dreams. That's how I bought it and that's how I now sell it to you, and that's how it has to be sold any time in the future."

However, it is not only this story that turns out to be surprising, but the whole life of our hosts as well. She is from the States, and when she was an adolescent she was sure she swore never to marry, let alone have children, because she believed that it would tie her down to one person, one place, and too many possessions. Nevertheless, she got married. The first child came as a surprise; the second was looked for to give the other a companion, and when she finally said that's enough, the third one arrived unexpected.

The surprises didn't stop there. They found out that a distant relative of her husband's, who lived in Argentina, was putting his three children up for adoption. The man's wife had died because of alcohol abuse and the man, who suffered from the same condition, was not able to, nor did he want to take care of the kids. That's not all: two of the children have been handicapped their whole lives because of the mother's drinking during her pregnancy.

Our host had never thought of adopting, they already had three kids. Plus, the Argentinean kids not only have these dysfunctions; they're also older than the couple's own children. Moreover, because of their disabilities, they could barely speak, how could they possibly learn English? How would they adapt? How would they influence their own children? What traumas do they carry from their upbringing in adverse conditions like this? How could they economically support such a large family? The whole night they keep awake thinking of what to do, until the light of a new day brought the answer. "The longer we think about it, these boys will be without a home, without a family", and with these words they decided to enlarge their family.

Here is this wife with her six sons in a perfect harmony. Together with all of them, we are eating in an enormous house around a big table, surrounded by dogs and their pups and feeling once again like we are at home, in a happy sweet home. We stay and spend a few marvelous days with them. The house, the family, and the place all overflow with energy where many visitors come here in search of it.

It All Converges

As regards to Jim, we soon realize that we were mistaken; our first impression of him was completely inaccurate, as first impressions often are. They don't count, because they're false, anyone can give a first impression entirely different from the reality. We made a mistake in forgetting this. We have already learned this lesson during this trip, and now we've made that mistake again. Everything we thought about him is misguided. He only wants us to accomplish our dream, that way he completes his too.

Now, ready to leave Cleveland, I see how this meticulous genius disassembles the steering mechanism, steering wheel included. I see his astonished face when in the steering wheel, there is something completely beyond reason. He finds a piece cracked on one side and fissured on the other on the verge of splitting completely in two.

"You've made it this far and nothing has happened, but this piece only needs one slight jolt to break in half. You could have ended up holding the steering wheel in your hands and only God knows what would have happened after that."

Jim is with a machinist and his engineer friend and a man who fabricates parts all trying to figure out how to make a new piece. It is has a complicated shape, and is cast of soft metal. Meanwhile, I call the Graham Club, but no one has what we are looking for. Now everyone thinks we'll need to stay here for quite a while until the new part is made.

"I have one of these cars…" comments a man who enters the shop, but no one pays any attention because it's common to confuse a Graham with a Ford or Chevrolet. "…It's a 610!" he continues succeeding now to capture our interest: only someone who has a Graham knows that this is a model 610.

"How is your car?" Jim asks very excitedly.

"It's complete, but it's been about 30 years since it was running, it needs restoring."

"Could we take this part out of your steering column?" Jim inquires showing him the piece, "Afterwards we can make a new one for you."

"Yes, sure, let's go."

What could have taken days is resolved in a matter of hours. When we needed a spring for the starter, it appeared, when we needed an axel, it appeared, now when we needed another very difficult part, it also appeared.

I remember the Uro Indian in Peru who told me that on the road I will come across everything I need. I remember the words of many that assured me that God would provide, I remember that if you have faith, you can do anything. Everything converges into the same current for the dream to be accomplished.

Could It Be That We Are the Problem?

The day before we leave Cleveland, we go to have lunch, as if we were settled down members of the neighborhood, with all of Jim's friends. The chat begins to revolve around the excellent state of the car now, but soon the topic changes to the rumblings of the imminent beginning of the war. They all believe in their government, and as it has implanted fear in them, they see the necessity of going to war. How good it would be for them to go to Machu Picchu and mix with people from all over the world. I remember the worlds of my friend Dave, who told me, "If there was life on other planets, we would already be at war with them."

"Herman," a voice interrupts my thoughts, "what's your opinion?"

"What opinion could I have after visiting twenty countries and meeting people of every class who made me feel loved? What opinion could I have after visiting countries that were at war not so long ago, causing only death and destruction? What opinion could I have when I feel every place as my home and every person as my friend? Although I only know the American continent, I'm sure that the people there are as marvelous as they are here and that among them there are hundreds of friends to meet. A war that is very well handled by few will carry for much death and destruction. War, which we continuously repeat without learning that nothing is achieved by violence except to generate more hatred; wars waged on false pretenses that will end up in destroyed communities. How many children have to die? Do you want my opinion? I think there doesn't have to be a war."

"But how come? They hate us! Those terrorists are capable of anything…"

"So, you might find out the reasons they do and work on it. It's like with your friends, they don't love you or hate you for no reason, you make them love you. And people don't just hate you, you make them hate you. War is not the way to peace; peace is the way. If you go to war, you will see that many more will come to hate you…"

One of those present at the table put down his soupspoon. During all those days that we have sat together at the table, he always was the one who participated the least in the conversations, but now he has something to say:

"When we came to this continent, our enemies were the Indians, after that, the English. When we got our independence we looked for enemies amongst ourselves and we fought with those in the south. Later, there was another war with the Indians in the west, and then one against Mexico. Later still, our enemies were the Germans and the Japanese. When those grand wars finished, it became the Communists, Korea, Vietnam… Now we have these new enemies… could it be that we're the problem?"

No one has anything to add: perhaps no one had thought of it like this or, perhaps, they just don't want to discuss it in front of me.

The Inheritance

We enter "Motor City," Detroit, where the car first saw the light of day. People from the area accompany us to see the factory that is still standing and almost the same as it was in 1928. The only difference is that now the commercial offices are a huge bakery, the technical offices a big hardware store and the factory buildings have been converted into storage units.

We take photos that simulate the car rolling out of the factory once again, rejuvenated to begin its life anew. How strange that a car that came out of here, and went to Argentina in a boat, returned to the place of it's birth by land 75 years later! We four, plus the people who accompany us, celebrate this memorable moment for the Graham and for us with a toast of champagne.

The next day, someone comments that if our car were a Ford or Chevy, Detroit would have celebrated our return with a really big party. But we don't believe so. Today the war has started and there is nothing to celebrate, quite the opposite. The people in the streets are protesting holding posters that say "NO WAR."

We met our local hostess, Donna, who we met in Canada. She is wonderful and takes us all over the city. Including, among other places, the fabulous Henry Ford Museum, where they treat us very well, inviting us to go through the whole place with a guide who, more than inform us about the exhibits, wants us to narrate to him everything we've done up to now.

Among the cars on display, we come across a beautiful surprise. We have to use our imagination to recognize it. It has gone through thousands of changes, it looks almost destroyed and poor among all the luxurious autos, but none shines as brightly in my eyes as the one in front of me. A very run-down and dilapidated '28 Model A Ford, that father and son drove all the way from Chile to Detroit.

The Windy City

In the windy city of Chicago, people recommended time and time again not to stop in a certain part of the city that is considered very dangerous. However just as in Peru, as if it happened on purpose, we run out of gas exactly in this frightening place. Taking the gas can, I enter a bar and ask where the closest service station is, and they tell me there is one about three blocks away. I walk through a very poor neighborhood in a very rich country. This is a marginal zone and I feel it, just as surely as the people who live here do. On one corner, there is a gang of teenage boys, and as I pass, they yell at me shouting that I smell like a pig. I don't answer.

I walk on until I get to the gas station, which is more heavily armored than a bank. The cashier stands behind bulletproof glass and I have to put the money in a box that then is opened from the other side. As I return to the Graham, I again pass closely to the group of kids. This time no one asks me if I am a police officer, but swear at me instead as if I am one. I stop and explain to them that I am here only as a tourist, getting to know their city.

"Oh, OK," they say without quite understanding. Astounded, one adds "Do you like it?" None of them ever imagined a tourist in their neighborhood.

When I get back to the car I encounter the same scene as in Peru. Cande is surrounded by the "dangerous" people who are asking her for details about the trip and doting on our baby.

Route 66

Route 66 starts in Chicago; it's where we begin our crossing to the west, heading so far south, which at the end we will be almost in Mexico again. The mythical route takes us through small towns and cities; spring is on its way and this stretch of the trip is extremely pleasing for us. We really get our kicks on Route 66!

After departing from St. Louis, we detour away from Route 66, entering Kansas and "tornado alley". The road is perfectly straight and flat. A truck that is following us signals us to pull over. The man driving, cowboy hat riding high, gets out and comments to us, "If what it says here is what you're doing, I would love to receive you in my home."

We happily accept the invitation. Later in his home, a local newspaper reporter interviews us, and with him we coordinate a "meet and greet" the following day in the central square. Many people come and we receive many types of invitations and affection. Almost everybody takes home an autographed book, and everyone tells us that we're in the wrong place at the right time; this is tornado territory during tornado season.

"In this car of yours you could never get away from a tornado," comments one.

"If you see a bank of clouds, gray sky and a strong wind, try to escape. Always have the radio turned on so you can hear the weather bulletins," others tell us.

"We don't have a radio."

At the end of the day in town, we go to sleep in the home of an odd couple. According to what they tell us, they used to be very similar when they lived in California, where they met and married. At that time, he was a photographer and she created art from discarded found objects. They moved to Kansas because he was offered a job as an artistic director of a big television company with a big salary. Here, she continued with her art, but because she was a long way from California she began selling to her clients over the Internet and through this media continuously accumulated more customers, also increasing the value of her work. This way, in a short time, she began to match her husband's salary, but with the significant difference that while she has continued doing what she always liked to do, her husband works more all the time and doesn't have time to take any pictures anymore. Nevertheless, the man doesn't complain: with what he makes he was able to buy another house which he moved into and in the garage are a couple of antique Jaguars and a spectacular motorcycle, which has yet to hit the streets.

We are staying in her house. We are sitting in the living room singing songs along with the guitar accompanied by Pampa on the maracas. Later we make some art from "trash." After an raw vegetarian dinner, the couple leaves us alone to go sleep in the other house, his house. We say our good-byes to him tonight because he will go to work in the morning and not be able to come see us off, however she'll come over in the morning. She has promised us a vegetarian breakfast.

When we wake up, a surprise is waiting for us. He has decided to go into the office late for once, he wants to buy autographed books for many of his friends.

"You know what? You've made me remember my dreams. I have always wanted to be a photographer. My dream has always been to travel around my country in a motor home, taking photos of the personalities of the road and assemble a mosaic of the faces and the places of the United States."

A short time after leaving their home, we receive a card from them. He has quit his job, they have sold both houses, bought a motor home and he has begun his photographic journey. The pair is beginning to become two-of-a-kind once again.

A Rushing Wind

On the way to Colorado, in the plains of Kansas, a wind in a hurry passes us. We look behind us and see gray clouds. The current is in our favor and pushes us, it's strange: When I put my hand out the window the wind pushes it forward when usually it's pushed back. This means, the wind is moving faster than the velocity of the car and my presumption is proven when it hits us from the side. It tips the car from side to side making it hard to control. It is tense driving, looking behind us every 5 seconds. This keeps up, for two hours, when finally the calm returns suddenly. Since it's getting dark, we stop in a farmhouse close to the road and ask if we can stay there. An old man, who doesn't even open the door, tells us no.

The second homestead we come across is back off the road and much simpler than the last one. Out of a big barn, a man emerges dressed in overalls. He walks over, wiping his greasy hand and extends one to me in greeting. As soon as we introduce ourselves, we tell him we are looking for a place to sleep. He doesn't say anything; he just looks up over the field to the end of the drive where his wife has just turned in.

"I don't believe that would be a problem, but I better ask my wife."

She gets out of the car with her grandchildren. "These kids are from South America and are on their way to Alaska. They're looking for somewhere to sleep," explains the husband.

"Fine, kids, in some way or another we'll fix everybody up, come on in," she replies.

When night falls, the house fills up with the grandparents, the children, their four grandchildren, who play with Pampa until midnight, and us. The whole family is happy for our visit. They enjoy hearing stories of far away places and the personalities of the world. The youngest daughter shares the pictures of her graduation trip to Alaska, describing what a wonderful time she had. When they see this, her nephews and nieces get out their own photo albums for us to look through, then it's the grandparents wedding photos and also a video of a trip

they took. Grateful for their warm hospitality, we go to a rural school where the grandma teaches. We give a talk surrounded by hundreds of kids.

Fiesta Latina!

We happen to arrive in Denver just in time for the big Latina festival of "Cinco de Mayo" which is celebrated right in the heart of the city. The only problem is that the booth spaces are for sale but they are completely sold out. We see this event as a possibility to get together sufficient money to cross the Rockies, and the deserts of Utah and Nevada so we look for another way to get in.

We ask every Latino, of which there are thousands in Denver, until we find one who is helping a woman in her campaign for city council. He takes us to the woman who quickly makes a call. "I have with me a couple that is an example of what Latinos are capable of. This is something to be celebrated and where better than at a Latin fiesta?" When she hangs up, everything is set. We have a space and free of charge.

We park the car on an excellent corner, where we hang our enormous sign: "Driving from Argentina to Alaska" and we spend a marvelous four days during the festival. We never thought we'd ever find so many Latinos on this side.

This place makes us feel like we're in Latin America again. It is full of food booths selling burritos, corn on the cob, street venders selling clothes and household goods, which reminds us of the markets we have visited so often. In the aisles between the booths that are chock-full of things we hear people debating the prices, in another the seller swearing that these clothes won't shrink or fade, and in this one the lady is selling herbs, telling me that she even has one to make me fall in love. But me…Lady, I couldn't be any more in love. Commotion surrounds us; shouts of things on sale, people partying and yelling they call out to one another. We hear typical phrases from every country we've passed through on this trip and we are delighted. We haven't heard these expressions in quite a while.

Living all this brings back so many incredible memories that we want to live out again. Most of all, this fiesta reminds me of every lesson I ever learned from our Latin American brothers, which I carry inside of me.

Among Hippies and In Tune

We head into the mountains again, which we like so much. The Graham goes slowly, but surely. We pass through ghost towns, abandoned, exactly like the ones in the Wild West movies. We drive over dry dirt roads, occasionally loose soil, sometimes sandy, and all of a sudden around a curve we hit a "wash board" surface, and the car begins to jump. I try to turn, but loose control. The precipice starts right at the edge of the road and there is no guardrail. Because of the bumping and the rear wheel drive the back end of the car fishtails toward the side, the abyss. If I break, I could completely loose control. If I maintain my speed, we will certainly drop off the edge. I accelerate like never before, and the car shoots forward straight toward the mountain. Thank God, no one was coming the other way at this minute. Cande, who has screamed as much as me, although mine were silent, asks me to stop. We do it just to breathe deeply and exhale. On his part, Pampa just smiles.

After this big shock, we keep following the road. As we drive on we fall in love with beautiful places like Mesa Verde National Park and in Utah, the national parks of Bridges, Bryce Canyon and Zion.

A family we meet during our drive invites us to pass by their house which is in Boulder, Utah, a very charming little town. They are 100% hippies. Their house is a white tent in the shape of an igloo called a Yurt, it is one room with a wooden stove that is also used for cooking. The two girls of the family are dressed in clothes made from deer skin that they tanned. All of them wear loose clothes, long hair and sandals but only when they go out. The family cultivates the land, cans their own vegetables and everything we eat is bred, made or raised by them. They search for simplicity, tranquility and peace. Working with the land is very important for them, because they need to be in contact with it, feel it in their fingers.

"We are part of nature, we're not separated from it, but in it. We don't need to try to surpass it, but to develop with it in total harmony. The dependence of our bodies on the earth is complete and it absolutely influences our health, for good or for bad. Everything we do to it we also do to ourselves," he teaches us.

We can see their daughters are happy. Proudly they show us what they have planted, their rabbits, and everything for which they are responsible. Without any timidity, they hold our hands, and hug us. They take  Pampa outside to play with homemade wooden blocks. At one point, I see Pampa pick up some dirt and raise it to his mouth. My first reaction is to stop him.

"Don't worry, if he does that, it's because he needs it. There are no chemicals on this soil, so he will be fine. He'll only take one or two handfuls," the man tells me and he's right. After the second handful, Pampa stops doing it.

In the same town, a larger hippie community lives in mobile homes. When we enter one of them we get a huge surprise. In the middle of the United States, thousands and thousands of miles from South America and hundreds from any Latino, they are drinking yerba mate tea with all the right equipment: gourd, silver straw and even a thermos.

"A couple of Argentineans who came here to do a survival course asked us to try it and since we saw how good it is for the body we really grew to enjoy it," they explain to us.

While we drink mate, we talk with them some more. They tell us they are dedicated to the earth and give classes in survival. We converse about our trip and the many experiences they have also acquired while traveling. They understand miracles and they are not surprised about the incredible things that have happened to us, of our anecdotes about the marvelous people we meet and the excellent way we're treated and assisted. For these people, this is how it should be; they receive people all the time and when they travel, others receive them. They love the earth, but they are not stuck to any one part of it, they want to traverse it.

"Living in these times, at the speed of a demanding society, is getting harder and harder. First appeared the radio, the car, the television, household appliances, the telephone, the computer, the cell phone, and when we have all those things the newer, more modern models appear because society demands to have. More effort is demanded of us, in a race that never ends, in a race where, you have to go more and more quickly all the time," comments a young blond with hair past his shoulders.

"We have gotten off this highway and we are taking the road a little more slowly, we're not opposed, just more calm, in tune with nature and in concordance with the new times," agrees the woman who knows exactly how to serve mate properly, bubbles and all.

The Bad Guys

We follow the road until in front of us appears a colossus of nature: the Grand Canyon. Here, seated on an overhang, one can spend hours looking at the immense scenery replete with a diversity of forms and colors. I greet the canyon like a king and admiring it for it its beauty, I repeat a small ritual I have performed at each place that affects me greatly. I wet my index finger, and put it in the red earth and bring it back to my mouth along with some of the soil. Now this place is part of me and I am part of it.

We return to the famous Route 66, after having traversed the Nevada desert and visiting the ostentatious city of Las Vegas, which dazzles us. We enter California on the same route that many immigrants chose with hopes of beginning life anew in a land of good weather, beaches, movies and dreams.

Right here, on the road through the desert, we are nearly out of gas. Even though we thought that around here there would be an abundance of gas stations, we haven't seen a single one. We decide to go to the small towns marked on the map to see if we could find any. We get there to discover them almost abandoned, their gas stations closed long ago.

Night is quickly approaching and we stop in the first house to ask for this precious liquid. Two men appear who, in any movie, would have been the bad guys: both of them are dressed in striped overalls, one has a big belly, wears an unkempt beard and uncombed hair sticks out here and there from under his cap. The other is thin, has also gone a few days with out shaving and with a toothless grin agrees with everything his cohort says to us.

"There aint no stations 'round here for miles," he tells me while I inspect the amount still in the tank. "What cha got l' getcha out inta this dangerous night 'n y"ll find yerself stuck in the middle of th' scary desert. If ya want, I could sell ya 'bout six gallons which is wha' cha gonna need te get cha te th' nex' station," offers the fat one, while the skinny one nods.

We leave feeling robbed, what we have paid for the gas was three times the market price. Plus, we realize indeed, we have been duped, too, when only three miles down the road, we find a gas station.

If You Can Dream It, You Can Do It

Entering the city of Los Angeles means traversing many cities joined together. It is gigantic. Right away, someone shows up to invite us to sleep at his house, but we have people already waiting for us in Hollywood. The house we stay in is among the houses of actors, writers and movie directors. The man hosting us is a director of commercials: during the 70's he, along with some friends, traveled around much of South America on bicycles.

Among the places we visit is an Argentine restaurant where we can sell our book in Spanish. People from all over converge at this place: Americans, descendents of Arabs, Asians, Italians, Spaniards and many Latinos of every race and place. It's not important to anyone what our religion nor nationality are, nor even our ideals, only that we are completing a dream, and they want to do something, because all humans have them.

While signing a book, I ask an elderly man to write down his address for me so we can let him know when we get to Alaska. While he is writing, I see a tattoo with a number on his lower arm. I ask him if it's from the Second World War:

"Yes, it's what they did to us in the concentration camps," the man who speaks in perfect Spanish, tells me without hatred. "It was an error that a few made against many, we have to remember so it never happens again."

"Hey! I hope you never get to Alaska!" yells someone so everyone can hear him. "I hope you never get there!"

"Why not?" asks someone else, provoked at the other's wish.

"Because I completed my dream: traveling from Patagonia to New York, and the saddest part is when it ends. The best part of a dream is when you're achieving it."

He has a point. We have been feeling something strange since we got to California. We are in the final stretch, there are no more detours to make and something is different when you know that you've only got a short way more to go. A man who bought our book yesterday comes back at the right time to join the conversation and advise us, "Don't stop, please, don't you do it. I did eighteen years ago when I got to L.A. with a friend; we were trying to accomplish our dream of getting to Alaska. We got this far hitchhiking and we stopped here to make some money. Don't you do it! You can't imagine all the memories that came back reading your book. Today when I reminisce, those days were the best of my life, and they stopped when we did to gather a little money to continue, and here we are still putting it together without knowing what for and having lost about two decades. The best things I've gathered in my life are memories of that trip, so please, keep going, do it for me."

Thanks to Pampa, before leaving L.A. we have a wonderful time at Disneyland, after being invited by a man who works there. When we get to the monument of Walt Disney we read this message: "If you can dream it, you can achieve it."

"Mr. Disney, you are completely right!" I say aloud to the statue. I see the few people standing around looking at me, and I tell them, "This guy knows what he's talking about."

First Steps

After our very respectful salute to the Pacific Ocean, which we happily go to see, I wet my finger, taste a few drops, and leave it heading toward San Luis Obispo.

We climb back into the mountains, making this assent to touch, feel and embrace the sequoias. As soon as we begin to see the first trees, we stop and run to see who will be the first to touch them, Pampa doesn't understand us at all.

They are precious, incredibly gigantic. In one part of the forest we go up to walk among many of them, they make us feel like tiny ants. We sit, resting our backs against these trees that radiate so much energy, just as much as they have to tell. Like the mountains they are silent witnesses to the last three thousand years of humanity. Since the beginning of the pyramids, before the prophets walked the earth, they witnessed Columbus setting foot on America and witnessed men walking on the moon. They have witnessed events for thousands of years. As we think aloud, Pampa being supported by the tree walks with his tiny steps around the whole circumference of the trunk until he stops and surprises us with his first three steps. Suddenly and without knowing what he did, he looks at us giving us a beautiful smile of happiness. Cande holds out her arms and he comes to her with other steps, more sure. The sequoias witness these first tiny steps as well...something else to relate from humanity.

I feel so well with everything that's happened and all that's surrounding us. I say to Cande: "I know where I want to live."

"Where?" my statement startles her a lot.

"Close to you."

After we share a hug, she stands up and following the shade of these gigantic trees, looks for her journal and pen. I see how, with much affection, she writes, "From here I can see you and I want to tell you what I feel having you by my side. It's so much that I must commit it to paper to release in some way all the love I have inside. So you'll know that since you were born I've done nothing else but love you.

"You love to play. When you think we are going to start a game, you pretend to be shy and look the other way to hide your anxiety. Your daddy and I always dedicate some time every day just to play with you. The game you like the best is when we hop around pretending 'I'm gonna get you!' and you getting me, too. Every time I 'get you', you just can't wait to play it again and again. We both chase you around on the floor. It's incredible how we're transformed into children, just like you. We crawl around, answering you in your own language; we play with your toys. We all enjoy it so much! You love to swing, and just laugh and laugh when we push you, making funny faces at you. We are captivated by your laughter; it fills my soul, making everything three times more delightful; for your daddy, for you and for me, too.

"This trip with you is amazing. All day, your daddy and I are by your side, not missing one minute of your progress. I want you to grow up, but at the same time, I don't. Who can understand me? You are an excellent traveler. You enjoy riding in the car as much as you like to show up every night in a new place. In each home, the first thing you deliver is a smile while looking all around, as if to ask:

'So now, where am I?' But, you're not worried, you're just curious. You're 'a winner', as daddy says. You adapt yourself, for example, you can sleep anywhere. You're accustomed to improvised beds of folded blankets on the floor, sometimes a play pen, a child's bed and even a doll's cradle. The only thing that is always the same is that your favorite, soft giraffe accompanies you to sleep.

"We travel during the hours you're napping and we stop much more just so you can play and walk around. Also, since you have been with us, I only do my trip work while you sleep. When you're not, daddy and I sing songs with you, or I play with you, tell you stories, and entertain you the most cheerful way we can.

"We had to give away so many or our own things to make room for you. We reorganized things and put your car seat between the two seats. From there, you can see the scenery. The car is stuffed to overflowing but he doesn't complain because he's happy to know you. He even carries your stroller on his roof. The whole rear part of the car is your room. In each corner, there is a teddy hanging and all your toys are on the deck behind your seat."

"You are already one year old, a big little person. You crawl all over; almost nothing is inaccessible to you. You pull yourself up by holding to what ever you can reach. Sometimes we are stopped for many hours in a place to sell books. Since you can't be in our arms all the time, one of us stays with the visitors while the other takes you for a walk. You also like to stand up holding onto the running boards but only for a minute then you're off again, crawling somewhere else.

"When I'm holding you and I need to autograph a book, I'll ask the person to hold you for a little while. It's amusing to see their faces, some seem like experts, but others make expressions that say they're not sure what to do with you. You? You are always a saint, always happy just to look at them. They don't know that you love this, sometimes they get nervous and hand you right back.

"I don't know how or when you started to be the star of this dream, the people ask more questions about you than about us or the car. With the TV and the newspapers, it's the same. Everyone wants to know about you. Before we had you, we wondered what our trip would be like with you for company, what would change: 'would people still receive us?', 'Will our child like to travel?', 'Will he get sick?' were just a few of the questions we had. However, when you were born, what we never imagined happened: your presence made everything better. You have grandparents, aunts and uncles, siblings and cousins everywhere who request that some day, when you're all grown up, to come and visit them. Who knows? Perhaps you will be able to do it, giving them all a huge thrill."

"I have something to ask you, special and simple: don't forget them. Never forget the people that receive you and help us in this dream. Open your door and your heart for any person that needs you and is chasing a dream. You will learn much from them. It's not important how much you have to give a little or a lot, just give it. It will be one way to repay all those who made a bed for you. Son, no one ever shut their door to you and when they open it, they do so with great pleasure.

"Today, Pampa, you took your first steps. I couldn't count how many times you've fallen trying to take them, but you kept trying. God willing you will always be like this, that everything you do, what ever you do and you fall, always get back up to continue on your way. The one who gets there is not the one who falls, but the one who gets back up again. From here, I continue watching you, son, and I adore you. To this dream, Pampa, I welcome you.

"I love you so very much, your mom."

A Rag Ball

After a week visiting the marvelous Yosemite National Park we return to the Pacific coast searching for a road that isn't a freeway. Returning to San Francisco and knocking on my father's door feels quite peculiar. I remember when I told him about my idea to go to Alaska by car and he said: "Please, take a cruise, don't do anything weird," he begged me.

We're received by Susan, his wife, who already loves us like we're her own children and takes us to where my father is working. He renovates Victorian homes which this city seems to be full of. In the city, with my dad, we spend a number of days. I like to see him transformed into a grandfather: taking Pampa to the beach, or Golden Gate Park, or the zoo... On one of their outings I accompany them to the park. To watch them is to enjoy them. My father is sitting there in the sand with my son playing. How I would have delighted having him as a dad to push my swing, to wait for me when I came out of school, to answer my 'whys', to be my refuge during my scary nights, and to ask him to help me fly that kite. How much I lost – we lost. I observe my old man and I enjoy him as much as he does his grandson.

To Be Remembered

We cross the Golden Gate Bridge to go to Sausalito, a beautiful little town. After an invitation, we celebrate Independence Day as part of a parade that ends up in a park where there is a huge picnic that feels like a family reunion. We eat and talk. We are more relaxed than usual. There has been so much publicity about us that we haven't had to try to sell our book because people ask for it as soon as they see us.

On our way back to San Francisco we stop at a gas station. A homeless guy approaches me asking me for some "grass". Although he's holding a can of beer it seems he's not yet intoxicated enough. I tell him that I don't even smoke tobacco. When he hears my accent he asks me where I'm from. I tell him about the trip but he doesn't believe me. To verify it I show him one of our books.

"Can I buy it?"

"You don't need to, let me give it to you," I answer.

"No, seriously, I want to buy it."

He hands the can of beer to me to hold, and sits down on the ground, takes off his shoe, then his sock and hands me some damp, crumpled bills. He presents me almost all of them and I try to give them back telling him that ten dollars is enough. He continues insisting, pressing the money on me again.

"I have done very little with my life but I want it remembered that Jamie Thompson contributed to the completion of a dream!" he shouts happily as he searches his pockets for more money. Cande and I give him a hug. Saying farewell, we get into the car. Looking like he wants to say something more, he makes signs for Cande to roll down the window.

When she does, he throws the rest of the money that he found into the car saying, "Enjoy it; nobody is going give more meaning to these bills than you."

"Many miles of this trip belong to you Jamie, they're yours!"

We left him with his arms open, lifting the beer, toasting and cheering us.

It is difficult for us to leave San Francisco, but we do feeling happy to have spent this time with my family and also because Cande has spoken to her mom who feels very well following her treatment. Ever since we've been there with Pampa she has improved day by day and as my father-in-law says: "There are no illnesses only ill people." Also, my mother-in-law is content and anxious because she knows that we are nearing Alaska and that means that soon we will soon be heading back home. She just can't wait to see her daughter and grandson.

Hugging the Pacific Coast

Even though we are still more than 3100 miles from Alaska, we see it being very close. We feel that now the days and the miles are countable. We travel along beautiful coastal roads, passing through little towns and cities. In almost every place, folks are acquainted with our journey and are waiting to offer us a place to stay and receive us with parades. There are even people who stand by the road waiting just to see us go by. The number of invitations we receive is so great, that we regrettably have to decline many of them. Otherwise, we would arrive at our destination in the middle of the winter.

Before getting to Eureka, surrounded by giant Redwood trees, we are escorted by many Model A Fords that travel with us for many miles. We go through Trinidad, Gold Beach, Reedsport and Beaver, and arrive in Portland, Oregon where Scott and Carrie Hass are waiting for us.

We met them in a national park where they made us promise we would visit their home. While we are eating together, Scott tells us he has always had this idea to travel solely on public bus all the way from the city of Vancouver, Canada to San Diego, California. With time, this thought turned into his dream, so he found out the details of every bus line along the route. Luckily, very few gaps have to be walked between the busses.

"But it was only a dream that I thought about in my free moments," he confesses, "I was searching for data, looking at maps and other things simply to pass the time. However, I never really became determined to do it and I put it aside. We used the money that I had saved for that trip to go to the national park where we met you…and your book. You cannot imagine how important it was for me to meet you there. It was the best thing about the park: I read in your book that dreams can be accomplished and as an example, here you are, happy. Now my dream is very close to becoming a reality. It truly is."

A short time after we left, he sends us an e-mail telling us that he is in Vancouver, on his way.

The Traveling Baby

Being in Seattle is very special. First because a long time ago, we were on the front page of both of the two main newspapers and because of this, we have many invitations. Second, because when we arrive the newspapers run another article inviting people to come to meet us in the Pike Place Market by the port, a very picturesque place crowded with people. Everybody is as happy as we are at how close we are to achieving our goal.

A young lady passing by the place sees us and freezes. Despite being distracted by questions, I notice the shock on her face who remains there petrified.

"Hello, my name is Herman," I introduce myself.

"Yes, I know who you are!" she says with a little tremble in her voice. "My mother who lives in St. Louis…" while talking she searches for something in her purse "…sent me this letter at a very difficult moment in my life. I don't know how, but she just knew that there was something seriously wrong with me," she takes the letter out of her purse and continues.

"That's why she cut this story out of the St. Louis newspaper," she shows us the article about us, "I read it and it cheered me up. You cannot imagine how much better it made me feel! It filled me with hope and happiness for you. What impressed me the most was to see wherever you go how many people help you chase this dream. I felt alone, but since then, I know that there are thousands of people out there ready to help me with whatever I need. It gave me a tremendous push to live my life and now I feel like a new person," she pauses to look at Cande, Pampa and the car.

"I never imagined that I would meet you and have the opportunity to talk with you. I didn't even know that you were here and I don't usually come to the market. I only came out to take a walk."

"Surely there has to be a special reason for this encounter." I interrupt her while I pass Pampa to her to hold.

"My mother will really be happy when she hears that I met you!"

"Why don't you call her now?" I propose, and with excitement, she starts to call her from the cell phone.

"Mom, I'll bet you can't guess who I have in my arms, you'll never guess! Pampa!" she pauses, "Yes, the traveling baby, he's very sweet and I'm so very happy to have met them," she tells her mother.

There Is Love in and for Everyone

During our stay in Seattle, the Willie family who also own a Graham-Paige hosts us. They are wonderful folks who do everything for us. For example, they organize an enormous pitch-in barbeque to get together all the people from this city who wrote us. Among them is a woman in her nineties. She brings with her many newspaper clippings and photos of a trip made by her and her now deceased husband. They went from the United States to Argentina, the opposite direction to our trip and she recounts how well people received them along the way.

Later, a young traveling couple arrives. They were married in a small village in Argentina because after having chased their dream of traveling, they felt more united than ever. Another young guy from Los Angeles heard us on the radio and flew from there to Seattle simply to meet us. Also Jim and Roberta Heath are here, members of the Graham Club, who sent us the axel when we needed it.

The day after the barbeque our host, Rod Willie, asks me what kind of shape the car is in.

"Well, there is kind of a weird noise coming out of the gear box…" Without even letting me finish explaining, he puts on his coveralls, and jacks up the car. He doesn't come out from under the car until he manages to remove the gearbox. Once he's out, he proceeds to dismantle it until he discovers that the most important piece is almost completely worn out. He owns a car like ours, except it's a convertible. Rod sacrifices the piece out of his own gearbox and puts it in ours. As if this isn't enough, he and I are late for his grandson's birthday party.

When we get there, Cande, Pampa and Rod's wife, who are waiting for us, introduce us to a child that speaks almost no English.

"He's from Chernobyl, Russia. He comes every year for fifteen days to receive medical treatments. The nuclear power plant in his city exploded and like many others, he got sick from the radiation," explains the lady.

Later, we find out that her daughter is the person who pays the travel and medical expenses for the boy. What is remarkable is that she is not wealthy, she toils all year round in order to have enough money for this and her children don't protest. Even more, they collaborate with their parents so that it is possible to help this youngster.

"Many times we would like to change the world for a better one but we don't have the solution in our hands. That's why we put our hands to work doing this which fulfills us so much," comments this fairy godmother of the little Russian.

On behalf of many, we say: "Thank you, thank you so very much!"

After three days in the market and living with friends, we say goodbye to Seattle. As, usual, we wish we could stay much longer but we have already accepted an invitation to be on Vancouver Island, in Canada, to participate in a huge car show.

Return to Canada

Hearty Applause

We take the ferry to Vancouver Island. The reception organized by Roy is beyond our imagination. Before we even reach the port, we can see the bay is crowded with ships and boats arriving from all over. There is also a squadron of Army acrobatic planes maneuvering overhead completing difficult drills, giving a great show. To complete the picture, when we get off the ferry a large crowd of people is there to receive us with applause and Roy presents us with a large bouquet of flowers.

"Did you like the planes?" he asks. "You can't imagine how much I spent, but who cares?" he adds, laughing happily at the coincidence.

"Roy, who are all these people?"

"Oh, they are just people waiting for the ferry. I convinced them that as soon as they saw you appear to give you an ovation. You will also notice that the day is perfect, just like I ordered," he adds chuckling.

Our friend has been writing to us ever since we encountered the inconvenience with the Canadian visa. Now, in his territory, he has everything set for us. First, he leads us to a house he has arranged for us, where we will be by ourselves since the owners are on vacation. Upon entering, we find it full of products that he sought out for and stocked up from Argentina: wines, lunchmeats, cheeses, books and even music from our homeland.

For the two days following, Roy goes with us to a couple of terrific car meets where they are fully aware who we are and what we do thanks to everything he has already told them. At one of these meetings we receive a welcome certificate from the mayor; first prize for the best car, selected by the president of the club, and many gifts that the public brings us.

Even though everything is marvelous, the people are quite worried because we will arrive at end of the season; cold weather is approaching fast and all of the tourists that we meet, which are many, are already leaving.

One of them tells us, "Look at the sky, see the birds, they are telling you it's getting late." We look and see they're flying a direction contrary to ours.

"Alaska only has two seasons, this winter and last winter," adds another.

"There is no car heater that's adequate. You will need an electric device to keep the water, oil and gasoline from freezing. In addition to this, in case of a blizzard, each car has to have a box with emergency items such as extra food, a shovel, warm clothing, and a candle for heat, among other things."

Sealed words

In the Ferry that takes us back to the continent and the city of Vancouver, Cande is writing. She is doing this a lot more recently; we are both feeling things that we want to put down in words, to remember them after we've accomplished the dream. I see how she lets her tears drop on her words; she writes with a pen and seals it with her soul. When she finishes, I ask her to let me read it.

"We are close, so close. How do I feel? I don't know, but my eyes are filled with tears. Vancouver, a city I wait for, a city very far from home and at the same time close to my destination. But what is my destination? Alaska? I think I have quite a few. Now, it is to accomplish my dream.

"I am nervous. I want to relax but I can't. When have I felt nervous during this trip? One week before leaving, the minute before starting the car and taking leave of my house, family and friends. I still remember that first day as if it were today. I laughed at every little thing, feeling anxiety. It felt like I was forgetting everything: documents, medicines, clothes, the camera. My mind was operating at a thousand revolutions per hour while everything else around me was barely moving at 25 miles an hour. I had so many worries and now I understand that they were unnecessary. Many fears. Only now can I see and explain what I felt at that moment.

"When will I be able to explain how I feel now? In Alaska? I don't know. I'm nervous but this time it's different; I want to arrive and at the same time I don't want to. Physically, I'm making my way toward the unknown, where the surprise is waiting for me; sentimentally, I am going to the past where I have already been surprised.

"Yesterday, a lady approached me greeting me saying, 'I've come with the sole aim to shake hands with a woman who possesses the courage to pursue her dreams.'

"We shook hands firmly and I couldn't keep the tears from falling, feeling my legs trembling. That woman really admired me. I could feel it not only in her words, but also strongly when I touched her hand. Many times people show admiration but why did I tremble this time? I believe it's because we are so close. In this firm grasp of hands, I saw my miles traversed: I saw myself as a girl already dreaming of traveling and immediately, I saw myself on Vancouver Island. This is why I tremble, because I feel admiration for myself.

"The woman left, I turned around and here was 'the car of dreams,' as they call the Graham. When I look at him I perceive him much larger, stronger and with so much personality. He didn't seem like that to me at the beginning of the journey. At that moment, I had my doubts: will he be able to carry us to the other side of the map? I saw him weak, fragile with old age, small. The time, experiences and the distance have fortified him. Exactly the same thing happened with us: we got stronger every mile.

"Every minute that passed, passed, but they continue living inside me. Each mile I traversed, I felt it and walked it firmly. Now I look at myself and see myself differently. I grew without being aware of it and it was the people that showed me the world in a different light. But how do I feel now? I don't know. What can I do to feel more serene I have been looking for this answer lately, listening to the comments of the people to find it and comfort myself, but no. Many, looking forward have said: 'You're nearly there' 'And then what?' 'How will you adapt to not traveling?' Phrases that make me feel even more nervous. It is incredible how intensely I have lived these years. However, not only days gone by appease me, the future too. Herman said something very true: 'I don't see Alaska as the end of the dream but instead as the beginning of another one.' The past is concrete and the future uncertain. Although I dread the uncertainty, I know that some day the future will be concrete. Now since we are so close to Alaska, I know that nothing is impossible."

I finish reading what Cande has written. Now it is me who seals her words with a tear.

Be a Part of It Again

Jack is waiting for us on the way to Prince George. An elderly man of about eighty whom, in order for us to recognize him, has written a sign that says: "Argentina". Arriving at his home, he gives us a lovely surprise. He shows us pictures of two Argentines whom he had received previously. They are the guys who were traveling to Alaska in a Model T Ford and whom had escorted in their car to their wedding the couple we had met on their anniversary in Manta, Ecuador.

Jack's voice quivers when he tells us about all the repairs they did on that Ford, it is significant the pleasure he feels for being part of that dream that he considers his own. Actually, it seems as if these guys made the whole trip, to end up in this exact location in Canada just to complete Jack's dream. The next day, at breakfast, Jack is already wearing his overalls. As if it is his custom to receive travelers from Argentina bound for Alaska just to repair their cars, immediately he discovers something on the car that needs fixing and tracks down a welder to help him. Once he completes the work, touched by the coincidences, we bid Jack farewell after having delivered to him our dream too.

Bonnie & Clyde at Bear Creek

We continue the march driving many more miles than we are accustomed to. We stop in beautiful log cabins near creeks in which, coupled with the hospitality of our hosts, we would like to stay several days. While looking at the sky, watching the geese leave, we are reminded that we haven't even arrived yet. We travel by dirt roads, occasionally asphalt, surrounded by forests and sometimes by enormous mountains with glaciers descending them. We see a moose and black bears crossing our path; we even encounter a bear with her two cubs. Wishing to see more of these, we go to Hyder, a small town with no more than 100 inhabitants. To get there, we have to leave Canada, when we do, there is no border control.

The road into Hyder is only 2 miles long and even though it is part of Alaska, we don't feel like we're there yet. Thousands of salmon come to this town to

spawn in small streams, salmon that are easy picking for the bears of the area. The bears have no fear of humans and we can get very close to observe them. There are so many salmon, they choose the one they fancy and eat only the part they like the best. We stand there totally amazed by their immense size, their claws are the size of my pinky finger and in a couple of bites they can devour a whole salmon.

"We aren't on the bears' diet and there many fish to eat that taste better than us, so don't be afraid," says a man dressed in hunting clothes. "Every year, there are bear attacks but the majority of these occur because the bear feels surprised. I recommend that if you want to go into the woods, make a lot of noise and take along some pepper spray. I've used it twice and it really works. If not, I wouldn't be here to tell you this," explains the man who is into studying and photographing the bears.

We leave Hyder to return to Canada, where there is a border control station. A uniformed woman gives a signal for us to stop the car, and then says something that sounded to me like "pull forward". So, I begin to move the car.

"Get out of the car!" she bellows while she assumes the position and prepares to stop us by force.

We stop and get out and with another shout, slightly less loud, she indicates for us to get in front of the car. She puts on latex gloves and calls another woman to help her. They check everything. They wipe the steering wheel with chemical cloths to see if I smoke marijuana, then they continue looking for reactions in specific places as well as inside our bags. I try to tell them that we were only in Hyder for three hours and that we got there from Canada.

"Back off! Stay where I told you! Answer only what I ask you!" she gruffly orders me with a voice of authority. I start thinking that in this remote location it's possible that still hanging in the office is the poster offering a reward for Bonnie and Clyde, and this thought causes me to laugh, which the woman hears.

"What are you laughing at?" she asks me angrily.

"I can't believe this. We've made twenty-five border crossings through countries famous for drugs, or arms or contraband and we have never been searched. And here, where we have only been maybe 3 hours in a town that is only famous for bears you search everything. Excuse me, but I find it funny."

"I'm just doing my job," justifying herself as she gives us back our documents and signals us to keep going.

Before Returning, You Have to Get There

We spend the evening with a German couple that has a truck from the 60's converted into a motor home in which they have been traveling around the world for the last 6 years. Two days before they started their trip, they realized that she was pregnant. Even so, they still didn't give up on their dream. Today their daughter is almost six years old.

"Initially, we imagined it would be impossible to travel with her. Instead, now we can't imagine how we could have done it without her. In countries like

Thailand and Vietnam it was she who learned the language of the place by playing with the children. Naturally, that helped us tremendously with basic things like shopping in the markets," explains the father of the girl who very confidently comes and goes, playing with Pampa.

We are beside a lake, in a site we come across by following a dirt path. The place entices me to walk and I enter the forest that enfolds me, very silent, only an eagle alerts my presence. I walk whistling softly. I raise myself and I can see myself walking through this immense woodland whistling for fear of bears. I have never imagined myself doing this, much less in a place like this!

I set off to fulfill a dream and never did I imagine myself assisting an autopsy and a delivery, constructing a canoe, going down the Amazon River, running out of money, watching Cande become a painter and both of us becoming writers, or having a child and countless friends. We just set out to travel a continent and ended up living it. We knew our departure and God our destiny and return…a return that we still have no idea how it will turn out.

Everybody asks us what we're going to do once we reach Alaska, as if we've planned it! It's taken us so long to reach this destination that now I don't want to even think how we'll depart from it. First, I want to get to Alaska, live it, enjoy it. I don't know how we are going to return. The only thing that I am pretty sure of is that taking the car back home is totally out of our reach because of what it would cost. But in order to start coming back, first we have to get there.

I see how life is like a puzzle that is assembled with moments: there are pleasant ones and annoying ones, some parts are difficult and others come together easily. It is so fragile that at any moment, everything could break down. However, what's so beautiful is that you can always begin again. In some way or another, we will begin our return.

Beginning Another Dream

It's possible that we arrive in 4 or 5 days. Everything is as beautiful around us as it is inside us and we enjoy it in silence. We only break the silence in order to point something out or to share a memory about a certain place or person and then we return to silence, taking pleasure in it. The majority of the businesses along the road are now closed, as it is the end of the season. We look at the sky and now there are few birds flying south. We carry on north.

Cande takes her journal and writes: "August 11, 2003, Cassiar Highway, British Columbia, Canada: Alaska is right there, coming very quickly. At this moment, looking at the road ahead of me is when my mind navigates with my feelings. I can imagine people's faces when we give them the news. I can hear their enthusiastic comments, their shouts, their laughter, but I can't imagine myself. I just can't wait to tell everyone "We did it!"

We are close to Alaska and the mountains I see in front of us remind me of the

Andes Mountains from the outset. I am living mixed feelings, similar to the ones I felt at the beginning, which now encounter the same desolation of the landscape.

Not today

Today is August 15, 2003 and we are very few miles from the border with Alaska. Cande starts to cry, I ask her what happens, even though I know what she is going through.

"My love, I don't want to get to Alaska, I don't want to end this dream. Something is telling me that I'm still not prepared," Cande comments to me.

When I hear her I think that neither of us wishes to get there today. It's odd but that's the way it is, the best part of a dream is to be in the dream, not to finish it.

"Where will we write the final book?" she asks me, thinking more about the future than the present.

"Cande, forgive me, but this is a moment I need to live," I respond to her.

She remains silent, her gaze lost in the mountains, on the road, undoubtedly thinking about today. Suddenly she gives me a kiss, another to Pampa, another to the car, and finally she blows a kiss into the air. This startles me until she says to us, "Thank you my love, for accompanying me; thank you Pampa for your excellent company; thank you Graham, for carrying me with great effort up to this point; and thank you everyone for helping me in my dream. I didn't do it alone. You know, I am so grateful for having begun the dream that day. I feel my soul complete, full of satisfaction. I am happy."

We keep driving and silence returns. Neither of us asks where he is flying in his mind. We are each in our own world. I sing in a soft voice: Manso y Tranquilo (Easy and Tranquil) by Piero – the ideal song for this moment. It is getting late, but we could still cross the border today. We stop at a gas pump at a campground. I don't really know why because we don't need any gas. From the shop comes a man in his mid-fifties. He poses a question:

"Do you remember me? I'm Bill, and we met on Vancouver Island. I just can't believe I am bumping into you here. I live there but I come to the Yukon in the summer to work and pass the time with my friend Bob."

Bob is painting some giant moose antlers to decorate his salmon and fishing tackle shop. Bill introduces us.

"Welcome to my campground. I'd love to invite you to stay for dinner and I can also offer you one of my cabins, sleep in and breakfast together tomorrow before you head off for Alaska." When he makes this proposal, we look at one another and know the decision is made: we'll go no further today. The big day will be tomorrow.

After an excellent dinner, all three of us are in the cabin illuminated by a single lamp. Pampa, who is still so small, sleeps placidly not knowing how significant tomorrow will be for us. I fall to sleep beside him while Cande writes in her journal. I don't know why but later on I wake up and see her still writing. She doesn't realize that I am awake. Silently, I continue watching her concentrate on her paper. The soft lamp light shines on a single tear that is rolling down her cheek. She must be writing with all her emotions. She looks beautiful; much more beautiful than when we started dating, much more than when we got married. She looks radiant, full of life, happy. She looks like a mother, like a dreamer; in her you can see what any man would wish to have. I would exchange an entire life in heaven for just one more day with her.

"Cande, what were your wishes when we released the balloon in Ecuador?"

"You're awake? How long?" she questions, surprised.

"No, only a few minutes. What were they?"

"If you want them come true, you're not supposed to tell."

"I've already accomplished two of them," I tell her, revealing my happiness.

"Which ones?"

"If you won't tell me yours…"

"Fine, I have accomplished one," she says.

"To have a baby! That was also one of my wishes."

"And the other?"

"If you don't tell me yours…"

The Goal is Close

We wake up very early. Yes, today we feel prepared and ready to get there. The day is marvelous; it seems like the warm sun doesn't want to miss our arrival and it feels more radiant than ever. The day that we have wished for years has arrived!

The breakfast with Bob and Bill is stupendous. After that, we take off, very grateful for the opportunity to have kept another tradition of the trip: to say good-bye splendidly from every country we visit.

At the last gas station in Canada we fill our tank but an Italian tourist doesn't let us pay. Like him, there are others who are sharing in the happiness of the realization of our dream. The pats on our backs and the hearty handshakes are some of the prizes we receive. We are very anxious; we both seize the hand of the other, we share a kiss, another, and we bring Pampa into the front with us.

He doesn't understand why all the emotion. We make a game of who will see first something to tell us that we've arrived. We look around every curve. Its absence makes us want it, why hasn't any sign appeared? Could we have passed it already?

Alaska!!!

The Last Frontier

A wine Toast!

"There! It's there! We're here! We made it!" we shout together while we hug each other, squeezing Pampa, who is between us. We keep shouting while the car weaves back and forth over the center of the road. We see the sign from 500 yards away; they take forever. Cande starts wiggling her legs in anticipation of actually standing on Alaskan soil. We jump out of the car, run and shout. Pampa in my arms laughs, celebrates.

The few people here first look at us without understanding why so much celebration. Then one of them sees the sign on the Graham and points it out to the others. We approach them as they break into applause. We hug everybody; we just need to. We have to share our joy.

I take the camera and begin filming Cande who starts singing a stadium victory song. "Ole, ole, ola! From Argentina, we got to Alaska! We couldn't stop! Ole, ole, ola!" As I tape her, I am seeing the same little girl that I saw in her during the carnival in Bolivia and also the eight year-old child that I met and fell in love with and with whom I fall in love over and over again today. I feel happiness and the formula is a mix of love with dreams.

We park the car closer to the sign. There is nothing around us except the forest and this sign that says: "Welcome to Alaska." We are accompanied only by the six tourists who are watching us, as if we were an unexpected sideshow. We uncork a bottle of Argentinean red wine that we had put away saving it for this occasion and we drink a toast after serving his deserved part in the car's radiator.

It took us so long and so much to get to here that we really don't want to leave. While we heat water and drink maté, many more tourists show up and every one of them takes a picture of us.

"Congratulations, you've done it!" a Mennonite couple cheers us happily. They tell us that they are on their honeymoon trip. They have two signs on their station wagon: "Just Married," and "Alaska or Bust." I think that these posters could just as easily be in our car; I still feel newly-married and I think things should be done "or bust."

Welcome!

Once in Alaska territory, checking at the map, we realize the state is enormous and has very few roads crossing the huge distance. There are more than 550 miles just to get to Anchorage and from there, more than 900 to the Arctic Ocean. We spend our first night in Tok with a family that has sled dogs and rents room.

They surprise us by saying, "A man from Argentina came all the way from Patagonia on a horse and stayed here. We didn't charge him so we won't charge you either." We're moved, once again, to know that another dream has been completed.

On our way to Anchorage, a white truck passes us. The couple inside signals for us to stop and pulls over ahead of us. When we do, the man gets out and without even saying hello, points to one of the wheels and says, "That tire is mine."

"I hope you don't want it back right now!" I answer.

Bruce and his wife give us a big hug, happy to see us in Alaska. They are partly responsible for us being here. They were one of the couples that helped us by contributing a tire when we needed new ones in Texas. We are meeting them in person for the first time. They leave us saying they will spread the word that we are coming.

Anchorage, How Near You Are

Before we even get into Anchorage, people are waiting for us. Dennis and his wife are standing next to their red 1936 Ford waving at us. Right away, they direct us to a parking lot where a group of people is waiting. They all greet us with applause and hugs. Representatives from radio and newspapers are there too.

It comes as a total surprise to find my brother and my father here too. I never imagined they'd be here. If there is something we don't have in common, it's a desire to travel. The last time we had talked they were very interested in knowing the exact date we would be getting to Anchorage and now I understand why.

When we get close to the red Ford we see many signs painted on it. One of them that stands out: "Ushuaia – Alaska." Dennis explains that he bought the car from some Argentineans when they finished their trip in it and had promised them he would keep it just as it was. We are happy to sit inside just to discover what it must have felt like to travel in it.

Dennis and his wife, special and generous people, host us while we are in Anchorage. We got to know them by mail. They also received an e-mail with a request for our wheels and they signed up for one. Tonight they prepare a dinner in our honor at their house for all of the members of the Antique Auto Club. The next few days they take us to see other clubs that are anxious to help us get the car ready for the last stretch to the Arctic.

While we stay in Anchorage, the Governor of Alaska receives us and gives a beautiful letter of welcome and the organizers of the State Fair invite us to participate. We happily accept and before we can figure out where we are going to stay during the fair, Dennis offers us his motor home, with a fully stocked fridge and pantry.

The End of the Dream?

The Alaska State Fair is a really big one and with all the publicity that we have received we have the possibility of selling all the books and crafts that we have left. Besides this, it will give us a chance to meet more people. Maybe for the last time, we hang our "Driving from Argentina to Alaska" sign on the car. We display the map of the Americas. It is 3 feet wide and almost five feet long. It is marked with our route and is covered with photos we took along the way.

Nearly everyone at the fair is a resident of Alaska. There are almost no tourists this far north this late in the year. A local man points to a mountain we can see from where we are standing and calls our attention to the snow on its crest, saying, "With the first dusting of snow comes winter."

People come effusively to congratulate us on completing our dream. Those days are like one big party! But for us, to really complete the dream, we have to get to Alaska's end, the extreme northern tip of the American continent.

"You can go as far as Deadhorse, but you won't be able to get to the Arctic Ocean. The last few miles belong to an oil company and no one can get there," comments a visitor.

This is hard for us to believe but it seems to be true because many more people confirm this. Everybody repeats the same thing, "You can't get to the Arctic." Not only is it not permitted, but also it's so late in the year.

"The Arctic is 875 miles from here, 375 of these are asphalt, but beyond Fairbanks, only semis and 4x4 pickup trucks travel the remaining five hundred miles of dirt road." A man in his 50's who works in Deadhorse explains almost without pausing for a breath. "There aren't even any shoulders. Trucks go by at high speeds, throwing up rocks that will break your car windows. Besides, at this time of year, the road is covered with ice and unless you have tires with steel studs, you can't control the car. As if this weren't enough, you have to cross over the mountains by a pass full of ice and if it snows you have to wait until they dynamite it in order to avoid avalanches. Then you have to wait for them to clear the road. This means that if a snow storm hits, you'll have to wait days until you can keep going and there is no place to take shelter. After this you get to the Arctic tundra. This is a flat expanse of earth without anything. There are no trees; there is absolutely nothing except the freezing wind."

"You should consider your trip complete." This is the opinion offered by those who hear this conversation as if there is nothing that can be done. They don't know our thoughts and feelings. We have our hearts set on seeing ourselves touching the cold water of the Arctic Ocean.

"We haven't come all this way and gone through all this just to stop here," is our reply. "We are going to finish for sure and we'll do it where we always said," I exclaim pointing to the map, "where America ends, not one mile before."

They all hold their comments. They don't show any enthusiasm or hope. They know for a fact that it is private property and no one is ever allowed in.

"I hope I don't have to be the one to deny your entrance," a man says. "I work security at the entrance gate of the company that owns the final stretch; British Petroleum (BP). I don't want to be the one who turns you away. Many people have come as far as the gate and they don't know how terrible it is for me to have to tell them that I am absolutely not allowed to let them pass."

Memories

Many of the fair visitors have read anecdotes and details about our trip in the newspapers. But, they still want to know more and to hear stories about the trip first hand. We tell our story time and again to groups of fifteen or twenty people. We take turns doing this. While one of us answers questions and signs books, the other one takes care of Pampa and begins the story with another group of people. The narration is never the same twice. We invite people to ask questions as we are telling the story and this makes it different each time.

"Are you the ones who drove from South America and had a baby on the way?"

"Yes ma'am, would you like to hear about our trip?" I ask slightly raising my voice, attracting more people who form a group.

"Come on over here, honey, come to listen to their story," a man tells his daughter.

"Good afternoon, thank you so much for being here. We would like to share the story of our trip that little by little became the trip of many people. I'm going to start from the beginning and go pretty quickly but if you have any questions, please ask me. I'm a little shy and giving speeches scares me so it's easier for me to think of this as a chat."

"The trip began on January 25, 2000. We planned to get to Alaska in six months. Since we are now almost in 2004, you can see that we didn't get here exactly on time." Everybody smiles. "We started out from Buenos Aires, Argentina, saying good-by to our friends and families. The majority of our friends thought we were crazy; some thought we would get pretty far but nobody thought we would get here."

"How did you get the idea of going to Alaska?"

"A dream. As soon as we met, we started thinking about taking an adventure trip and it grew until it became this. While we were dating, we decided we would do it after two years of marriage. But…you know, work, the house, some fears, all the "buts," and many excuses contributed to us postponing the trip time after time. When we had been married for six years, we seriously began wanting to have a child, but we ask to ourselves 'What about the dream?' So, we decided to do the trip first and then have a child. As you can see," I point to Pampa, "we ended up chasing two dreams at the same time." The people smile again but this time touched. "The reason for this trip is so simple and essential…just a dream."

"What was the hardest part?"

"To start; the day we began, when we had to take all the fears that are always with us and put them on the side so we could advance. By doing this, we didn't get rid of them; they're still with us, but they are not in front of us anymore, blocking us from moving forward like they once had. You have no idea how difficult it was to leave the house, our work, our families, our friends and even our beloved dog Lucy, who isn't there waiting to greet us anymore."

"But we HAD to take those first steps. Life doesn't give you anything if you don't go for it. So we set out to breathe some life into our lives. We left with only one map, the one of Argentina, with enough money for six months, without a plan nor route and with a car…a car we didn't know and that we barely tested the day before we left by taking it on a practice run of only 90 miles. As soon as we left we started having problems with the wooden spoke wheels."

"They may tell you this isn't the way to do it, you must be prepared, you must know what you are doing. But, in truth, when are you prepared? How could you know everything? We started out and crossed the Andes Mountains into Chile. Then we crossed the Atacama Desert, the driest one on earth, to get to Bolivia. In Bolivia, at an altitude of almost 16,000 feet, we celebrated an authentic and colorful carnival, having as much fun as when we were children."

"In Peru, we visited Machu Picchu and Lake Titicaca, crossing the Andes another time. The car had no problems because of the altitude. We were the ones suffering from height sickness. Then in Ecuador, the best thing of the whole journey happened to us: we ran out of money."

"That was the best thing?" asks an incredulous woman.

"Yes, just like a bird that learns how to fly when its parents stop feeding it, we left our nest and began to see everything from a different perspective. Starting in Ecuador, we stopped being tourists that only see things from outside as they pass through. We began to live each place. It was magic. The people began to open their doors much more and we entered into a new world where we lived and cohabited with new customs and traditions."

I look at the map and continue my story. "In Ecuador, with a lot of help, we built a big canoe and took the car on it for 2500 miles down the Amazon River into Brazil. For a month, we lived with aborigines whom in addition to steering the boat, also found food for us. We also met people from various indigenous communities. In many of them, this was the first car they had ever seen and surely they must imagine that all cars look like the Graham."

"Once we landed, we traveled overland through the jungle to Venezuela. We visited one of the largest national parks in the world and saw the Caribbean for the first time. Putting our fears aside again, we went into Colombia. Thanks to doing this we met some truly beautiful people, ready to help any way they could. In the Port of Barranquilla, Colombia, we asked for help in shipping our car from Panama and found not only one company willing to help us, but three. We had to decide which of them would be the lucky one to take our car free of charge. The owner of one of the companies we didn't choose asked us to at least give him the pleasure of paying for our air fare."

The people, as they listen now appear more impressed and this attracts other people to listen to the story.

"From there we went through Central America visiting many islands and beaches on the Caribbean. In Costa Rica, we were an ambulance for a woman who was in labor and ..."

"So, how did you finance the trip after you ran out of money?"

"Well that's when we had to put our brains to work. Because, what would work in one country didn't work in another and we had to figure it out all over again. Cande began to paint birds in watercolor, something she had never done, and I framed them and sold them, something I had never done either. Then we produced hand made crafts and post cards. And in Costa Rica we printed our first book that was presented in the International Book Fair of Costa Rica, which turned out to be a best-selling book. From there we went to Nicaragua, Honduras, El Salvador..."

"Weren't you afraid to go into countries with so many wars, and what about the people?"

"In countries such as Nicaragua, El Salvador and Colombia, where people have endured a lot because of war, guerrillas, or earthquakes is where we found the people most willing to help and ready to give. They know what it is like to be in a difficult situation because of what they have lost, and they are still losing, including loved ones. In many cases, they need others help to be able to go on. People that have everything they need don't have to depend on other people and may not understand this. But, those people did, and when were passing through their places, they gave us everything they had."

"We continued north. In Guatemala...we had a romantic moment," the people laugh as I point to it on the map, "well, among others, this one was particularly important. And, when we got to Belize, we discovered that somebody else wanted to join this dream. In Mexico, with all the tacos and tortillas, Cande's belly began to grow and in North Carolina, with the help of many wonderful people, Pampa was born. From the very beginning, he was surrounded by lots of folks who like aunts, uncles and grandparents gave us so much love and kindness at a time when we needed it most. When he was a month old, the pediatrician gave us the okay to continue with the trip. We hit the road again, this time going up the Atlantic coast to Canada. Later we headed to Detroit where the car was born. We visited the factory, but we got there late, 60 years late! We got our kicks on Route 66 all the way to LA. From there we went up the Pacific coast all the way to here with a son who is already walking."

"Why did you come in such an old, used car?"

" 'Any car in the street is used'. We read this once on a sign in a used car dealership. I can only justify some of the 'whys'. First, because I fell in love with the car when

I saw it; secondly, because of its simplicity; and third, because it has style. Somebody once told me, 'If you're going to do something, do it with style'."

"Did the car ever break down?"

"Yes, thank God it did, and also, thank God, it never happened in a place where we couldn't get it fixed. Every time it broke was for a reason. In Puebla, Mexico we broke a spring in the starter motor four blocks from an antique car museum. They disassembled one of the display cars to get the replacement part. Then they organized a party with a Mariachi band. They also helped us to print the book and gave us 7,000 calendars with our photographs to sell along the way. All this happened thanks to a spring that broke! This also occurred in Toronto, where we broke an axle and because of this so many wonderful things came about."

"How did you get parts?"

"That is a question we have heard a thousand and one times. Don't worry so much about replacement parts, worry about your life; it is the one that has no replacement. A replacement for this car can be made. What we can't do is to make time go in reverse and recover a wasted life."

"All of you have marvelous memories and I would bet that the three most important memories you treasure involve you and a loved one. Surely, if you think about it, it would be that first kiss, the first time you held your child, or a day you went fishing with your dad. Do you realize that none of these moments has anything to do with material things? Then why do we spend so much time and effort trying to acquire and take care of material things instead of trying to accumulate more cherished memories?"

"When we set out, we were searching for these kinds of moments without caring about spare car parts! If we had worried about this, we should have brought another car along just in case. If we had carried all of the things that we might have needed, we would have sunk, because the more you have, the deeper you sink. You have to live light, because everything you need in life you will find along the way."

"During the trip, we were assisted by many antique auto clubs and mechanics that little by little left the car almost like new. Parts were made for us, bumpers and other parts were chrome plated. Our engine was rebuilt, and we were given new tires. We had to turn down new upholstery twice and a new paint job once. If we had accepted, we still wouldn't be in Alaska. The car is now in much better condition than when it departed from Buenos Aires. The same thing happened with us. We started out one way and we arrived totally different, also a much better couple. In the car, we are separated by only eight inches. We had two choices, either we were going to kill each other in the first month," I look at Cande, "or we were going to realize that there is nothing better than love, which can only get deeper if both of us are pursuing a dream together. If you have those two things you've got it all. We don't need anything more than what can fit into the car, or even less. The less you possess the more freedom you have." The best years of our lives have happened to be during these four years, when we didn't have a lot and we were out of money.

"We set out to see a marvelous continent and we did. We have memories of all these beautiful places in our minds. However, above all, we found something we never imagined we would discover, the greatest creation of God: the people. We will always keep their memories in our hearts. The individuals who make up genuine humanity, without caring from which side of the border we come and neither to which God we pray, welcomed us. They helped us, they shared their food, they gave us their beds, and they even asked our forgiveness for not having more to give us. We have been welcomed in more than 800 homes. In all of them, we were treated like family, like best friends. We left each one of them with the same feeling as saying good-bye to a loved one. We can assure you that, based on our experience, when God created humans, He didn't make a mistake, He made the most magnificent creation."

"What religion are you?" asks a woman hearing us thanking God so much.

" Let me tell you first that the same families who invited us into their homes, also invited us to their places of worship. We discovered that the message was always the same as our religion. There are no bad religions, only bad religious people. There are no bad countries either, only bad citizens. Never let a tree hide the forest from you. God is everywhere, and in every heart although in different forms and different interpretations. Everybody feels Him differently but God and His message are always the same. I call my father 'Papa'," and I point him out to them. He smiles with his grandchild in his arms. "On the other hand, one of my brothers calls him daddy, one of my sisters calls him dad and another calls him by his name, Pedro. We all use different names for him, but he's the father of all of us. I now feel like I am part of every religion."

"Gandhi once said: 'I am a Christian, a Hindu, and a Muslim'," cites someone, greatly deepening the conversation.

"You had an easy time of it in those countries because you are Latinos," says another voice looking for what we call excuses.

"Don't look at the color of my skin. If God had asked me what color I wanted to be I would have asked him to mix them all together and paint me that color. Just look into my eyes and you'll see that my heart is the same color as yours. When we were in Latin America, many U.S. citizens we met along the way told us that we wouldn't be treated as well here in the States as we were there. And let me tell you, for the last 15 months, we have been in the United States and Canada. During that whole time we've had to spend the night on our own fewer than 20 times. All of the other nights we were guests in families' homes. I can assure you, it has nothing to do with borders. When God made the world He didn't draw borders. It was a few men who did it to divide us just like others divide us with religion. A nationalist and a religious fanatic are the most harmful tool for a country or a religion, just as jealousy is for love. Don't look for excuses, look for reasons to live and among them you'll find your dreams. Inside of each of you there is a dreamer. Inside of each of you is something divine. Don't deny that part of you, give it a chance. We haven't done anything that can't be done by anyone. We just went after our dream. Your heart will never dream something that you can't handle." I wait for a minute and then continue by pointing to the map again.

"Now, here we are in Anchorage after traveling more than 43,000 miles. This is a lot more than the 12,000 that we were planning when we left home. Having come this far, we still have to keep going to our final destination: the Arctic Ocean."

"But there is no way you can reach the Arctic Ocean." The more I hear this, the more I want to get there.

People begin asking for autographed books while Cande forms a new group and starts another talk right away. I can hear the questions starting again, which she answers spontaneously with a calm, firm voice.

"Did you have many problems?"

"Before, we found a problem in every solution. Now we know that there is a solution for every problem."

"How was it having a baby on the trip?" asks a woman with a baby in her arms. "I wouldn't have been able to handle it. I would have needed my doctor and to know where I was going to have the baby, have a bag packed, ready to take to the hospital, decorate the baby's room and anyway, what if he was to get sick?"

"I thought of everything that you are saying. Ever since I was a girl, I had imagined it like that. But you don't know how wonderful it is to realize one dream within another. The happiness is doubled. When our son was born, he found us so happy because of what we were doing with our lives. He has always had both of us with him, and what better gift is there than to see your parents pursuing their dream and living a life? Happy parents mean happy kids."

"What was the biggest obstacle?"

"Fear: to leave everything behind, fear of starting, of the unknown, of what's going to happen, of dangers."

"How did you get over it?"

"We never did, but we never let it overcome us either."

"Did you carry weapons?"

"Weapons are made to kill and whoever has them has felt a desire to use them, even if only in self defense. When you don't have weapons you don't have that kind of desire."

"Now that you've finished, what are you going to do?"

"We are going to try to travel more, take more risks, to live more for the present, to have more children, to cross some ocean, to climb a mountain, to get to know more people. In fact, we are going to collect moments of life. Some will happen spontaneously and others we will have to go out to look for. We are going to chase more dreams."

"What other dreams do you have?"

"We want to live in the country, in the mountains and to raise our children there. We want to build cabins and receive people from all over the world to learn from them and to hear stories from each place, stories that fill the soul."

"You've made a big bridge between Argentina and Alaska."

"No, really, it's just a path; a bridge would pass above too many places. We feel like we have merely left a trail. It would be great if everybody were to go out and blaze their own!"

"Four years to get to Alaska?" asks a young man with a surprised look on his face.

"What surprises me are not the four years it took us to get to Alaska but the thirty years it took us to get started on those four marvelous years. When we left home and living the first days of the trip, I realized how much time I wasted with excuses and fears."

"Are you going to write another book?"

"Yes, it is going to be a book about life to inspire others to go after their dreams."

Listening to Cande's answers inspires in me a great deal of respect for her. The changes I can see in each of us are enormous. One of the biggest changes for me is that before the trip I felt like the world was coming down on me while now I feel on top of the world.

"Will you sell the car when the trip is finished? It could be worth a lot of money. It could help you realize your..." a man interrupts my thoughts as I interrupts his comment.

"You are a man of business and I am a man of dreams. I don't possess a lot. I have a wife and we have a family that is worth more to me than all the gold in the world. And now I have a huge fortune of a dream completed and nobody can take this away from me. The car is not for sale. Maybe someday Pampa will return to Alaska in it, or maybe he'll go to another corner of the world."

"I know what to do with the car, but I have no idea what I would do with the money. When I had money, the money had me. Now that I don't have any, I have myself."

A Wise Echo

"Hello, my name is Dave and I am about to take a trip to Patagonia with a Brazilian friend. We found out about your trip and I wonder if you could help us with some information."

"Whatever you want," I reply to these young men who show up at our booth.

"We are thinking of taking the trip in a Jeep 4X4."

"Any vehicle is fine. It isn't an issue of how prepared the vehicle is, but how well you are prepared. The only advice I would give you about the vehicle is the same that would be true of everything: that whatever you take with you, make it simple, nothing complicated. Simplicity ensures success."

"What about mechanical troubles and health problems?"

"I won't wish you a problem-free trip, but the strength and faith necessary to overcome the problems. Nothing bad is going to happen to you arbitrarily;

everything has a reason and you will see that all difficulties will end up turning out well. Don't focus on the problem; look for the solution, there will be one.

"Can you think of anything we ought to know?"

"Never forget that whatever you do, you will be representing the people from your homeland. You will be an ambassador. Take a lot faith, have faith above all. Listen to your self. You know what you are capable of. Have confidence in what you do and people will help you." I continue telling him our lessons at the same time I remember how we learned them. "Don't look for excuses. Don't begin to think that dreams are simply dreams. Be free. If you fail, you can begin again. Appreciate the value in people. Let your inner child grow and soar." I take a deep breath to continue.

"Don't be afraid. Miracles happen, and you're not alone. Ask for help, you can't do everything on your own and there are thousands of people who would be happy to help you. Accept and offer help to realize dreams. Remember that in this world there is nobody more important than you and there is absolutely no one who is less important than you either." Dave remains silent as if he were expecting more.

I continue, "During a journey, many things occur that usually take a lifetime to experience. Because of what you are exposed to, events transpire at a much faster rate. Life is a journey and what we learn on the journey serves us our whole life. Nothing that happens is casual, but causal. Nothing takes place on accident, but is joined synchronically in such a way to help you be able to reach the goals of your dream. There is nothing against you, it's just a test. Be watchful for the signs, there could be a grander purpose for you and I to be here together today; and pay attention to everything that happens to you because there will be some lesson you can learn from it. Be like clay and be molded by whatever happens so you can enjoy it, never compare…"

"It seems like you have learned a lot. You sound like a philosopher."

"I don't consider it's me talking. I feel that what you are hearing are the echoes of my feelings and the echo of hundreds of others who all along the way have taught me everything I am sharing with you. Open yourself to people, to the world. The best masters, those who taught me the most about life, surely have no idea how much I learned from them."

"When do you think will be the best time to begin?"

"Right now! If not now, when? You are ready, so don't waste any time."

"Is there anything we shouldn't forget?"

"To get started; the secret to fulfilling a dream is taking the first step."

"That's it?"

"Yes, because all the riches you've accumulated in your life could be gone in an instant. The dreams that you have accomplished, you will never lose."

We exchange e-mail addresses and give him a book. We say goodbye after a powerful hug promising to meet again in Argentina.

"Hey," I call out to him as he's walking away. He turns around and I ask him, "Do you have faith in yourself?

"Sure."

"Then you're destined to succeed."

This Is Not the Moment to Falter

When night comes, we are exhausted. We put all we had into each narration of our story and answering every question. Only the marvelous energy we receive from the public permits us to continue standing for so many hours and be so enthusiastic for so many days.

During the fair, we are invited to participate in a parade. After proceeding all over town, we pass in front of the grand stand. About 900 feet past the grand stand, the car simply stops running, as if to say, "Enough! I've brought you all the way to Alaska, no more!"

"Hey Macondo, this is not the time to give up, not now when we are so close to finishing, we still need to get to the Arctic," I say, challenging his laziness.

After failed attempts at getting the car to start, Dennis and Scott tow it back to the fair grounds. The next day Scott, who is a member of the Antique Car Club of Alaska, removes the distributor and the carburetor to see what he can do. Two days later, he comes back with two pieces that look brand new; he and a friend have repaired them.

During the fair, we meet people who are interested in helping us to obtain permission to access the restricted area owned by BP so that we can get to the Arctic Ocean. However, we never get any response from BP, and the rumors we hear about them are all negative.

Inversely, some truckers, who are supposedly "the bad guys of the road", tell us that they all have radios and as soon as they see us heading north, they will all be at our service. There are also people giving us contacts to start figuring out how to get the car back to Argentina and, of course, so many invitations for all of Alaska and offers of all kinds; to go horseback riding, on a sleigh ride, or ride in an airplane. As if this weren't enough, they give us gifts such as coats, fresh goat's milk, fresh home-made pasta prepared by an Italian lady every night and many more surprises.

After the fair, we say goodbye to my father. Dennis and I prepare the car, protecting the headlights and the windshield against flying gravel and repairing a leak in the exhaust pipe. Cande tries to find everything we will need and empties out the car so we take only what is essential.

As for access to our destination, we depart without any positive response from BP and nothing indicates this is likely to change.

However, we don't head out alone. A guy from Texas who is in Alaska on vacation sees us and decides to accompany us in his small pick-up, which is not a 4X4, nor prepared for this kind of trip. Happily, we accept the company of Nicolas Hernández. The cold and the snow have arrived to various parts of Alaska, mostly in the north, which is exactly where we're headed.

Animal Intelligence

Cande and I feel a little strange, we really don't have very much farther to go and neither of us wants our journey to end. Many ask us if we aren't a little tired and wishing to finish and get back home again, and the truth is no. We would love to be back with our families and friends but we are not tired of traveling. This would be the same as being tired of living.

On our way to Fairbanks, we stop to contemplate Denali, a mountain that looks marvelous and impressive under the sun that illuminates its snow covered surface. At the beginning of our trip, still nervous about starting out, we passed close to the face of Aconcagua. Now, at the end of the trip, with the nervousness of being almost finished, we pass by Denali. The two colossi of America: we salute you!

We arrive in Fairbanks after two days of travel. Waiting for us before we enter the city are about twenty antique cars full of happy and hospitable people who applaud our arrival. They have organized a welcome party for us. A delicious barbeque at the house of Willy and Wilma, where Pampa has a great time playing with the granddaughter of the couple.

Willy is aware of our problem about getting permission to go to the Arctic Ocean and calls the owner of the Lynden Trucking, a company that hauls petroleum products for BP. Somebody at Lynden has the idea of putting our car on one of these trucks and hauling us to the Arctic Ocean. This seems perfect for us; any way we can get there. Lynden asks permission to do this, but BP refuses.

Although this is Sunday, Willy opens up his garage. In his shop they only work on trucks and charge $100 per hour for work done by an employee. I don't even want to imagine how much it's going to cost me to have the owner of the shop work on my car during a weekend! It's not that anything is broken; Willy simply wants to be sure that everything is safe for us to continue. He finds bolts to adjust and places that need to be lubricated. As well as other problems we can do nothing about right now, such as replacing the drive shaft. This mechanism transmits rotation from the engine to the wheels of the Graham. According to our new friend, it has too much play, and is even dangerous.

At lunchtime, we meet up with his wife and Cande in a restaurant. Wilma tells us they came here to visit from Montana and fell in love with the place.

"Was it difficult to get to Alaska?" asks Wilma.

"Yes, a little hard."

"Well, it is going to be even more so for you to leave. When you get to know it you will hate to leave it too."

What she sees as part of her place, for me is part of my world. Many people have asked me if I am looking for a place to put down roots. But, why do I have to do that? Plants are prisoners of their lives and always see the same landscape, they have roots. I have feet and now that I have seen other lands, I don't want to have roots. There is nothing wrong with having roots, but there is much to be said for having wings. My roots show me where I come from and my wings where I'm going.

"Did you see any animals on the road?"

"Yes, a lot of bears, even with cubs, but we only saw one moose and it was a female. I would like to see more of them. I don't know why, but it was my mother's favorite animal and I've always wanted to see it. Do you know where I can see some meese around here?"

"Meese?!?"

"Yeah, one moose, two meese, right? Oh, don't tell me I'm wrong again…one mouse, two mice, one goose, two geese, it's not one moose, two meese?"

"Oh no, no, no, they are moose." He says shaking his head and laughing heartily. He goes on to explain, "The moose is an intelligent animal and now that we are in hunting season, they hide where the hunters can't find them easily. It is against the law to hunt females and they seem to know it. They don't hide like the males. Forget about seeing male moose on the road at this time of year." His words sadden me because I have been hoping to see them, I look for them around every curve and in every lake we pass. "Nevertheless, if you can't see them from a car we can see them from the air no matter where they are hiding. Let's go."

We climb into his pick-up. Once at the airport, we get into his plane and, as if this is something he does every day, starts the engine and takes off with us in search of moose. The view of Alaska from the air is extraordinary. We fly over a swampy area where no man has ever set foot. Nature amazes us. Yes, we find moose, many, many of them, in a place where getting there over-land would be nearly impossible. As Willy said, moose are intelligent animals and know right where they have to stay until hunting season is over.

We Are Millions

On Monday, we get back on the road so we don't lose any more time. Always steadfast and not far behind, Nicolas follows. We are now wearing the heavy coats and sweaters given us to be protected from the cold, which proportional to our advance up north, we feel much more.

For our safety, Willy has installed on Nicola's truck a "slow moving vehicle" sign, a revolving yellow light on the roof, and a CB radio to be able to communicate with the trucks or who ever is in the area since every vehicle this far north has one.

The pavement yields to a dirt road and into the desolation, we do not see cars. We do not see anybody. According to what we have been told, for the 500 miles remaining we will only find one gas station, a couple of houses and a few miles after that, Wiseman, a small town that has been almost abandoned since the end of the gold rush with only five or six inhabited cabins. That's it until we get to Deadhorse, where the public road ends, less than five miles from the Arctic Ocean.

While dodging rocks and potholes, I think about the comments everyone made in Fairbanks and Anchorage about our problem of not being able to reach our destination.

"You made it to Alaska."

"Consider your dream accomplished, you've gotten a lot further than most."

"Now that you're about to cross the Arctic Circle, you have to be really grateful if you get as far as Deadhorse." Another comment that invites us to give up. At moments, I feel like I want to surrender and to convince myself that they are right; we really have done enough.

However, my heart tells me to fight on, to not give up, but to keep going. If not, I will always regret that we missed it only by five miles. Only five!! The words of Alexis Montilla of Venezuela begin coursing through my head, again and again as if my heart found them to make me hear them one more time. "There is one more, another difficulty that will spring up in your way at the very end. Don't look at it as a difficulty but as the final trial. Do not give up. Don't make the mistake of the majority, who give up at the last moment. Do not give up on your dream. When you pass that final test, then you can say, 'Dream fulfilled'". I don't know exactly how we'll do it, but there has to be a way.

On the way, we stop to take pictures and to film. We take a break at a monument that indicates we are entering the Arctic Circle. The road, although not paved and rather rocky, is not a problem. The truckers aren't a problem either, they all slow down as they go by, as much out of courtesy as out of curiosity.

Nicolas tells us what he hears truckers saying about us on his radio and this makes us laugh. "Does anybody know what is doing a car from the beginning of the century around here?" "They're Bonnie and Clyde. On their way to rob the bank in Deadhorse!" These are some of comments that make the trip more pleasant for our companion.

After 260 miles, which takes us all day, we arrive in Wiseman. Jim is awaiting us. He is a member of the auto club in Fairbanks and owner of one of the cabins where we'll stay. He has a husky build, somewhat overweight, and has an enormous white beard that covers half of his face and all of his neck. In this handsome log cabin he offers us so much that he gives the impression of Santa Claus at the North Pole, all he's missing is a red outfit. Jim is the grandson of a man who came here looking for gold a long time ago. He follows in the family tradition, but in order to make ends meet, he works maintaining the roads.

Well-informed of our wish to get to the Arctic Ocean, Jim tries to comfort us but his words are useless. He tells us that he has talked to Willy, in Fairbanks, but that there is no news for us. Soon he departs to spend the night at the road maintenance department, leaving us alone in this beautiful setting.

The night is terribly cold. Even so, after dinner I go out for a walk. I am searching for a way to truly complete our dream. I don't know why I'm not tired; I drove all day, concentrating my five senses on the road and thinking exactly what I am thinking right now: "How the hell can we get to the Arctic?" How is it possible that a single company can own the end of an entire continent and controls everything: the road, the ocean and even my dream? To relieve the tension I start skipping stones in the river beside me, in a place where its water is still and calm.

Suddenly I see something strange in it, as if it were changing color, from green to blue and then slightly red. Besides, it's moving. It is like a reflection. I gaze into the sky and marvel to see something amazing: colored lights floating like clouds that don't want to stand still. I run to the cabin to tell Cande and she is so sleepy but still come outside with me. We stand there, arms around one another, in awe of what we are watching: It's the Aurora Borealis that we have heard so much about.

Cande goes back in to the warmth of the sheets and since I can't fall to sleep, I lie down on the cold ground, which I ask to fill me with energy. The northern

lights continue their dance, enjoying the freedom of the heavens as I return to my thoughts. To start was difficult but it seems that after three years and seven months, the hardest part is going to be to finish.

Since we are nobodies, just dreamers, we won't be able to pass. They don't merely deny access to us but also to the thousands and thousands of people who have climbed in our car since the onset and are waiting to reach the ocean. And the millions more that are following us in the media and are now waiting for the final report. It's true: we are not alone, we are not just a family chasing a dream, we are millions… Millions to whom they are saying no, millions whose dreams will not be fulfilled. I will have to call the media and tell them that they can't have their final interview because there's not going to be an end. I have to call them and tell them: "BP doesn't want the dream of millions to be completed; ask them 'Why not?'"

I wake up Cande and Nicolas again: "I think I have the solution! I think I've got it! We are going to get to the ocean; I assure you that we're going to do it! We represent millions of people who want to get there and we have the tools to obtain it. Tomorrow I am going to call the Associated Press, (AP) and National Public Radio (NPR). They are waiting for our call as soon as we finish the trip. After telling them my plan, it's them who can't settle down. Since I am more relaxed and convinced that this will work, I stretch out and sleep.

Call for Your Life

I wake up early and search out the only public telephone; the one that I pray is working. And yes, it is. First, I call BP. I want to try to speak with the person who always refuses to take my calls and the only one with the authority to give me permission to pass. Once again, the answering machine receives my request. So then I call New York where with the time difference, it is now mid morning. I speak with AP and tell them about our problem. Looking for news, they ask me for the telephone number of BP and the names of the responsible parties there. I hang up to call NPR. They request the same information in order to put together a program. I end the call knowing the wheels are in motion. How will all this end up? I don't know…I guess I will have to wait a few hours to find out.

Another call. This time with Dennis, to advise him that I've given his telephone number to AP and NPR as a local contact and that I'll be calling him every two hours to find out what is going on. Finally, I call Fairbanks.

"Hello, hello," the call is disconnected.

"You have no more credit on your calling card, please deposit coins or enter a new card number to begin your call." I don't know what to do. There is no coin slot and there is no place to buy a card. What do I do? I start stamping my feet, pulling out my hair in frustration. I run to tell Cande and Nicolas about my calls.

"I've stirred it up and now we don't know what's going on," I tell them anxious and sad.

"Use my card," Nicolas offers making me immensely pleased but then frustrated when I see that it is a credit card.

"It's a phone, not an ATM."

"Yes, but this card can also be used to recharge telephone cards," he explains as if this were elementary.

"Well, let's go try it out."

Each walk to the telephone takes more than half an hour. We have to go over a wooden bridge, on a path between mountains, then a stretch of woods along a rushing river whose sound relaxes me a bit. The majority of cabins that we pass are empty, used only during the summer. The two or three families that spend the winter here have gone hunting, which is the only way to obtain enough to eat until the following summer. Nicolas tries to enter the numbers of his card but he makes a mistake.

"Oops, I entered my code wrongly," he says after his second attempt and then tries another time and runs into another snag. "I don't know what I did wrong this time but they tell me to try again."

Before I blow my top, I leave the phone booth. I am a bundle of nerves, I want to know what is happening, how everything is going, if they need anything from me in New York, or Anchorage or Fairbanks. I want to know what questions they have, but I don't want to go back into this phone booth. My nervousness could be contagious and his fingers fail to work again.

"What number do you want to call?" Nicolas asks me peeking his head out of the cabin with a "happy birthday" face after been able to recharge the phone-card.

I call Dennis.

"Herman, this is a revolution. I'm getting calls from everywhere, everybody is asking me questions but nothing has been resolved yet. Call me back in two hours."

"Two hours?" Two hours in this booth are an eternity. I hang up and call Fairbanks.

"Herman, BP called me asking for a description of the car. There may be good news coming," comments Willy.

I go to find Cande to tell her the news. Together with her, our companion and Pampa I walk along the riverbank. Why is it always like this? Why is one always walking along the edge of something, a river, an ocean, a cliff, a situation...why is it?

I know that we will not be able to travel today. With the phone calls and all the waiting we will have to hold off until tomorrow. I want to know what is going on so I go back to the phone booth. I call Dennis but he doesn't answer. Maybe he went out to get his mail, so I wait ten minutes and call again. Again, I get the answering machine. I call Fairbanks but Willy hasn't received any call nor any news. I try to call New York, I ask for the reporter, but she is not in her desk. I call NPR, however, the journalist who received my call is already gone for the day. I look at the time. Yes, in New York, it is already late.

Please, would someone just tell me what did it happen! How did this day end up?!? Even if the news is bad for us, I just want to know. I call BP, I don't know why but I do. Anyway, I am going to reach an answering machine.

"You have reached the desk of…" always the same tape.

"Hello, good afternoon," I speak to the machine so the director can see that I'm still around, "my name is Herman Zapp. I am the traveler who…"

"Who do you think you are? What do you think Prudhoe Bay is? A camping ground where you can go to have a picnic?" reprimands the man I have been searching for who is none too happy. "Do you think that we can permit everyone who passes by to enter just like that? I have received calls from the AP and NPR and now this matter has been made public, putting me in a situation that I do not like. Prudhoe Bay is considered an area at high risk for terrorist attacks; we are two days away from the anniversary of September 11, and the whole country is on orange alert."

"Sir, good afternoon, I can assure you that if you knew my wife, my son, our car and me that you would realize that we are not terrorists. Neither are we responsible for the wars of the world, but we are responsible for a dream, just as you are. When we left Argentina, it was the dream of two people, but if you say no now, you will be denying the fulfillment of millions. We are willing to do something for BP in exchange."

"BP doesn't need anything from you, it's only you who need something from BP."

"Yes I know, but you don't need to exhibit your supremacy to me. Demonstrate your power to everybody by allowing us enter."

"What is the car like?" he asks, more distended.

"It's a 1928…"

"Does it have seat belts?"

"No."

"Can it go at least 45 miles per hour?"

"Not all the time."

"The car does not comply with the minimum safety requirements and anyway to enter you'd have to pass a driving test. Could you go without the car?"

"Yes, we could."

"Fine, that will help a little. Let me see what can be done."

An hour later, we call Dennis again and he gives us the excellent news that everything is set for our arrival at the Arctic! They are waiting for us at Prudhoe Bay, and he has already paid for two nights in the hotel at Deadhorse.

The Last Tree

The next day we start out at the first light on the final stretch. We feel like it's the home stretch of a race. On the road, Jim signals us from his road grader for us to stop.

"I watched CNN this morning, I saw that BP has authorized your access!" We cannot believe what we are hearing: our permission is already on the news.

We continue north so happy, stopping to look at every bear beside the road. So far, we've counted five. We travel parallel to an enormous oil pipeline that carries crude oil beyond Anchorage for shipping to California to feed millions and millions of cars daily. Right now, we are only concerned that the gallons we have in our own tank and the reserve that we are carrying is enough for us to get there.

We pass a sign telling us that this is the last tree. The falling snow covers the surface of the road. The car begins to drop in temperature, so we cover part of the radiator with a custom made apron created by Pam, our friend in Albany. We are so wrapped up that there is no more room between Cande and me. Pampa is a bundle of clothing and hats. We can only see his face and it looks happy. With every hole we hit or with every ridge the car goes up and down he celebrates. His happiness is contagious, increasing the happiness we already feel.

On the windshield appears another trial, a very difficult one: the great Atigun Pass that very steeply crosses the face of the Brook Mountains. It's an obstacle in our path, as people have warned us.

We pull over to put chains on the tires. With gloves, it is impossible for me to do this, without them, my fingers cannot endure much time without freezing. Therefore, I hook on one piece, hastily put on my gloves, warm up my fingers a bit, take off the gloves again and put on another section. Slowly, I finish attaching them.

We are facing a test and very nervous about it. Even with the chains on our wheels, we continue sliding over the ice. The ice combined with the incline makes it very difficult even to walk. The car slides from one side to the other. The chains are a little too big, but slowly we advance. I ask the range for permission and help to allow us to climb it.

"Let's go Graham, come on! Don't give up now!" Cande encourages him at the same time she presses her hands against the dashboard as if wanting to push.

The sky, the mountain, the road and our front window are white from the flakes that fall. We look behind us and can barely see the revolving yellow light on the pickup. I shoot for the center of the road in order not to fall off into a ravine on the side. More than ever, I ask again that a truck won't meet us head on because we'd have no time to do anything. The pass zigzags taking us up switchbacks, from the right and then to the left then back to the right and so on.

We finally reach the highest point and before we begin going down, we stop for a breath of air and to refresh our senses. We put water on to heat in the car's pot so we can stop further on to have hot coffee.

We must confront another big test: the descent. We get back into the car and devote all our attention on searching for a track in the road that will take us to the bottom of the mountain. We came up in first gear and now we start down in second.

Slowly we descend to the flatness of the tundra. We recover our speed a little and run into less snow as we continue north. Cande, more relaxed, brings Pampa up front in her lap. In the back seat it's much too cold, here in the front, it's warmer thanks to the small heater installed in Mexico.

We stop to watch an enormous herd of caribou cross in front of us and to fix coffee but the water still isn't warm enough.

As we begin to relax after the pass over the mountain we develop long contagious yawns. We are still nervous, the whole area around the road is completely desolate; we can't see anything except the flat tundra. Just in case, whenever we stop the car and get out, we don't turn off the engine, just to make sure it doesn't freeze.

Later, we make another long stop to observe a vast herd of musk oxen that go by close to the road. We are surprised to see so much animal life in such an inhospitable place.

The next rest stop is to appreciate a huge brown bear. What is he eating in a place like this? It is beautiful. Its thick fur is lavishly decorated with sticking flakes of snow.

Deadhorse

After a whole day of driving, we celebrate with honks when we see the first buildings in Deadhorse, which as we get there, we realize are the only ones. As they say: if you blink, you miss it. No one is in the street; no one lives here. People come here only to work a few days at a time and almost always under cover.

We pass between industrial buildings while driving the frozen roads in search of our hotel. We approach it and I try to select the perfect place to park. There is a spot very close to the main entrance. I stop, I place for the last time my hand on the gearshift lever and slowly, enjoying it, I take it out of gear for the last time. It feels as strong, as the very first day, when for the first time we put it into first gear and began our journey.

Cande and I put our arms around each other once again squeezing Pampa in the middle. It is very cold and everything appears frozen but not us. We stand there together for a moment, relishing the joy of this moment. There is so little left to go. Only one more day to fulfill our dream.

Two people come out of the hotel and when they see us, they shout: "They're here, the travelers are here!"

One goes back into the hotel to inform the others and comes back with more people who bring today's newspaper for us to sign. We see the article from AP. A title in large print announces that we have authorization from BP to go to the Arctic Ocean to finish our dream. We are so happy for those people who will read and find out that tomorrow will be the big day in which everyone accomplishes the dream.

We enter the hotel, which isn't for tourists, but for petroleum workers. They all stand up at their tables to toast us. At once, we sit down to eat a huge steak with fries then go to our room where we collapse, totally exhausted.

During the silent night, I wake up. I don't remember when we fell asleep, it seems that the nerves of these last days have consumed us.

"I can't go back to sleep," Cande tells me, who has also woken up. I understand her and we hug each other.

"What are you thinking?"

"Much the same that you're thinking. Should we pray together?"

"Lord, we pray not to ask You for something, instead to thank you. I think we've only done this a few times but we feel more than ever the need to express our gratitude; for this day, for this journey, for this child, and for this dream that together we are fulfilling."

Colorful Medals

Our last breakfast, in our last hotel, on our last day, in the last location of our journey, we feel everything. I go out to see how the car is.

Yesterday we arrived in Deadhorse with the first snow of winter and it seems that nature has been holding off for us to arrive, to celebrate and for us to take our pictures. Today sunrise is dressed in enormous flakes of snow that drift from the heavens, little by little covering up our travel partner.

Cande and I see these snowflakes as a tickertape parade celebrating a triumph, bits of confetti celebrating the joy of the arrival at the finish line. We can see Macondo from the lobby window. It is very cold outside and the rest of the cars have an electrical device to keep their motors warm, but not him, because in the first place, he doesn't have any place to plug into and he doesn't need it either. Our old fellow traveler is still warm, his engine pulses, he's so happy. Like us, he couldn't sleep last night remembering the traveled road.

Snow covers him everywhere, but it can't conceal his flags, symbols of each one of the countries he has passed through, which because of the colors seem like his medals. In four years, we have fused two extremes that don't look like that anymore. Now it seems united and we never want it separated.

A man comes up behind me while we are looking at the car through the window and says, "Only you could have done what you've accomplished."

"No, not even we could have done it alone. We were able to do it because others joined us and helped us. Whoever is open to people can count on human support and can go anywhere or accomplish anything that seems impossible. We aren't the first to do something like this and thank God we won't be the last."

Caressing the Sea

The date is September 11, 2003. It is 3:00 in the afternoon, the wind blows cold and the sun illuminates the flat land of the tundra. Today is the big day. The odometer reads a little over 43,000 miles completed, the calendar marks three years, seven months and seventeen days of travel: quite a difference between the 15,000 miles and six months we had initially planned.

But there is no plan when you learn that living each day with its surprises is life. Life endures as long as the heart beats but to live is a myriad of marvelous moments.

The same guy who, at the state fair, said he wouldn't want to be the one to tell us we couldn't access BP is waiting for us at the entrance to Prudhoe Bay. He offered himself voluntarily to pick us up and to take us to the ocean. We get into his truck.

We make out the ocean a few yards before we reach it. We gleefully get out of the truck. We jump and sing, we shed tears, wave our arms in the air and squeeze Pampa intensely. We cannot believe it; we have achieved the dream, the greatest dream of our lives.

"How do you feel now that your trip has come to an end?" the security man asks. How strict that question sounds! How ugly the word "end" sounds. No, no we don't want it to end; we don't want to conclude such an amazing journey. We don't want to stop meeting new friends in new places. We don't want to stop starting anew each day, waking up in a new place and figuring out how we can continue: begin a new road, make a little money, learn something new, something different, speak with the personality of the day, find a place to sleep, to wake up in another spot and begin again. No, we do not want it to end...

Nevertheless, the man has a point. The end of the road is here, right in front of us, from where we can see only the ocean. The horizon is no longer the road that continuously took shape through our windshield like a suspense movie: not knowing what will happen, not knowing what the next surprise will be. No, this is the end of the road.

The only one we can see from here is behind us, overflowing with wonderful memories of incredible individuals who are suddenly here, they all accompany us in this place. Why? Because since the moment we met them they opened the door, climbed aboard the car and came with us. This is why they are here. We see them delighted, ecstatic, celebrating and leaping around.

Here is Carlitos, the barber who left his customer half way through a hair cut when he saw us park in front of his business. Here is Julio, the mechanic with a coal black skin and a pure white smile who fixed the car as if he was repairing the most important car in the world. Here is Eduardo, the artist who wanted to teach us all the secrets of his trade. Here is Agnes, who pampered us as if we were her own. Here are Francisco, Hortensia, Mario, Alonso, Juanita, David, Doug, Mike, and him and her and you...everyone is here.

"And how does it feel to finish?" comes the question from the man who still hasn't received an answer.

"To end feels like starting over again. It feels like we finished one dream but here, another one begins. We feel our souls full of life and full of stories. We feel the joy of a dream attained. Of a dream that once seemed impossible, but today it is not. We feel that the best thing we did on this trip was to begin and we feel like we are going home."

How strange it sounds, "To go home". It could be because we never felt like a stranger and people always made us feel like we were at home.

We feel someone seizing our hands. It's Pampa. He is fifteen months old and is gathering rocks like someone who is collecting a treasure. He presents them to us to look at, to enjoy them as he does, and we put them in our pockets, as a precious souvenir of the trip.

Words begin to pour out of my heart and I recite, "Pampa, son, throughout the years, throughout my life, I have filled my pockets with treasures and fortunes. Now I want to give them all to you. In the right pocket, I saved sand, still wet from the ocean, with foam and shells. In the left one, I've saved silences from mountains and deserts where I could hear peace. In the back one, I saved water, earth and air, and didn't mix them to feel freshness, warmth and perfumes. In the other, I saved rays of the sun, stars and clouds, because they gave me heat, love, and company. I couldn't save coins; they were heavy and noisy and didn't bring me any memories. I do have another pocket, a secret one. There I saved a letter, a kiss and a flower, but I'm not going to give you these. They are from my love, from Cande, and they are in my heart."

We wet our hands in the cold Arctic waters, we sit down on the pebbles and remain silent, silence that says it all. I wet my finger in the ocean again and enjoy drinking a few drops. Cande, who just discovered my ritual, wets her finger and one of Pampa's too and both raise them to their lips. We are part of this place. We feel part of all America.

"Cande, do you know which my favorite place was during the entire trip?"
'Which one was?"
"My favorite spot was and it is to be close to you.

TILL THE ARTIC OCEAN:
43612 miles
in 3 years and
7½ months

Let's go Home

'How to Get Back Home'
This is Everyone's Question, Including Ours.

Just to start, from Prudhoe Bay to Anchorage, the Carlile Trucking Company will take the Graham free of charge in one of their otherwise empty trucks since the first snows have rendered the roads impassible for the Graham. We on the other hand will go first to Fairbanks and then to Anchorage in the pickup, with Nicolas.

For a month and a half, we continue to travel all the roads of Alaska. We visit schools, where we give talks about dreams with the intention of demonstrating that they can be achieved. We also give speeches to other people, such as a family that races dog sleds. When we go to visit them, they rig up the dogs to the car and they haul us around, as if they were pulling a sled. The Graham is a nine-dog power car!

During all this, the offers to get the car back to Argentina start to roll in: the TOTE Company wants to take us all in their ferry to Seattle, another company offers to ship the car from Houston, Texas to Argentina, and another offers a flight from Miami to Colombia.

However, it is Lynden the one who gives us a huge surprise.

"Lynden wants to take the car from Alaska all the way to Argentina!" Willy shocks us from Fairbanks by phone.

We don't miss a minute and take the car over to them. As soon as we get out of the car, we are very well received.

"Thank you, thank you so much," they tell us.

"We are the ones who want to thank you," we said without understanding their gratitude.

"No, thanks to you for letting us take part."

We can not believe it. Nothing that they are doing is for any commercial end, they are not interested in any press or publicity, they don't even want us to put a sticker on the car with the company's name; they simply want to be part of the dream. We say good bye to the Graham not knowing how we'll get back to Buenos Aires ourselves or how much time it will take for the car to get there, but we are happy because little by little we will all end up back at home together.

And it happens like this: Scott, sacrificing the free air-miles which he was saving one by one to go with his wife to England, gives us two tickets to San Francisco. Touched because of the heartfelt way we have been received in Alaska, with tears we bid farewell.

In San Francisco we stay for a month enjoying a little bit more my father and he enjoys his grandson, because nobody knows when we'll see one another again. We depart in an airplane to Argentina, retracing in only twelve hours the whole distance that took us more than three years to cover. We land in Argentina and we are once again received marvelously by our families. The hugs and joy goes on and on, we have only told our families of our return: we want to celebrate with everyone else when the car arrives, just like when we left.

"Impossible" doesn't Exist

For taking the car out of the country for so long, the fines and reentry costs amount to about $9,000!! Why is it that in one's own country, everything is harder to do? Since we don't have this kind of money, we look around for help. We meet many people in the political arena, a former director of Customs, and others but they can't help us.

Additionally, we go personally to Customs and leave a folder with our petition with the director, who enters it as an official file without creating any expectations. The car is on its way and if it gets here without having any results to these bureaucratic issues, it will have to wait in the port and we will have to pay in addition to the fines and the reentry fees, the rent and storage of the container.

A month after filing our petition, we return to Customs to ask where it stands, but the manager's office can't remember where they sent it. We go from office to office and in each one, they search through enormous register books to see if our petition had passed there, but they find nothing.

"You'll pay what you have to pay," says one. "We'll have to see if the car has an impound order from customs after you take it out…" comments another.

"It might be that some of the fines are waived, but the taxes and the other things…" informs the third.

We finally arrive in another office where in which, through a tiny window, we ask about petition file 1800-03.

"Let's see…" the administrator begins to search in the huge book of actions. He doesn't say anything to us and leaves. Upon returning, he says, "Please come in, the manager wishes to talk with you both."

"I am charmed to meet you, guys," the boss says to us in a way we like very much. "Your case was just resolved this past week."

"How was it resolved?" we ask anxiously.

"Let's see…file 1800-03…entered December 3, 2003…Buenos Aires, December 23, 2003…Better if you read it yourselves, it will have more meaning for you." We take the document and read: "Taking into account that the temporary exportation in addition to the tourist aim that necessitated the utilization of a 1928 model auto with the objective of reaching Alaska for the duration of the whole excursion, it corresponds to consider the special situation that the accessory (the vehicle) should follow the luck of the principle (the person). For this reason we therefore extend permission to the accessory for reentry into the country for 20 days after date of notification. Signed: Pedro Girondin"

"I think I understand what this says, but could you explain it to us?"

"What this says is that you have twenty days to bring in the car without any charges, or fines, or taxes, and the twenty days start after we notify you. So when the car is about to get here, let us know and we'll notify you."

We look at one another astonished; he is offering everything we need so we don't have any problems nor cost.

Before we leave Customs, we search out the office of the signer of the resolution to offer our thanks. We knock on the door.

"Come in," we hear.

"Pedro Girondin?"

"Yes, what can I do for you?"

"We are the travelers with the antique car and we want to thank you for all the support you've given in the solution of our problem."

"There's nothing to thank me for, I am just doing my job, I did what I had to do and everything the law allowed."

His words surprise us, he could easily have told us he did it himself, that thanks to him we can bring in the car or not to forget him if some day we write a book… but nothing, he was merely doing his job knowing which law applies.

"Thank you, Pedro," I tell him while I look into his eyes with a great affection and respect.

Back to the Beginning

Today is February 18, 2004 and we go to the port where we once again meet our wonderful companion: the Graham. It was strange not being with him, not seeing that which we have been with every day for the last four years.

The company owning the port, Exolgan, not only charges us nothing but additionally receives us marvelously and allows the entrance of TV cameras and photographers. We go the container; we know that our friend is in there.

Pampa, in Cande's arms, comes with us to open it. And here, here he is, steady as he always has been, once again back on the land where he grew up. We kiss him and give him little pats while all the people around applaud our reunion.

We reconnect the battery, put some gas in the tank, a little more in the carburetor, we make contact, we turn the starter and the Graham fires up on the first try, in front of surprised journalists and other people who've gathered around.

We're not surprised though, we know that he is always ready to start and that he wouldn't fail now when a caravan of antique cars and many other people are waiting to accompany us to the Obelisk, in the center of the city. Waiting to accompany us to end our dream where it began.

After the celebration, we all go home. Four years ago, three of us departed, and today, four of us have returned. We park the car in its spot and exhausted due to the tiring day, we get ready for bed.

"Cande…"

"What?"

"And what if we go in the car? I ask her. It is night, we are lying down, with the lights out. We've already shared our good night kiss and we just need to fall asleep, but now, who can sleep after this question?

Cande and Herman are now in Argentina hoping to complete more dreams. One is to have a farm near the mountains with cabins to receive people like you.
Cande paints more pictures, Pampa plays with his new brother, Lucas, and Herman writes. Meanwhile, a new call of the road grows in them. Asia: their next destination?

Please communicate with the travelers:
three_americas@ argentinaalaska.com

Many, Many Thanks!!

We got to Alaska with every one of these persons who in one way or another contributed to thi dream. To all of them, we are sincerely grateful.

AAAP, AACA, AACA Furnitureland Chapter, NC, Chris Aandewiel, Jorge Abarcia Arnes, James Abarza, Alyssa Abbey, Bob & Denise Abbey, Dawn & Ray Abbey, David Abbott, David Abbott, To
Abbott, Lorenzo Abbruzzes, Jose Abelar, Ana Abella, Ana Abella, Tom Abert, Michelle Hyde Abilal, Patrick Abood, Jose Abraham, Anna Abrams, Arnaldo Abruciati, Norman & Mary Abston, Ma
Acargo, Elaine & Paul Accampo, Adrian Acebedo, Jose Antonio Acevedo, Pablo Aceves, Marsha Ackerlund, Rosemary Ackerman, Gary Ackley, S & L Acomb, Daniel y Gaby Acosta, Eva Acosta, Jo
Acosta, Julio Angel Y Miguel Angel, Acosta, Moises Acosta, Omar Acosta, Ricardo Acosta, Rigoberto Acosta, Omar Acosta Duarte, Mario Acosta Gonzalez, Petronilo Acosta Mendez, Bimba Acri, Gusta
(Guto) Actis Piazza, Kim Acuna, Ignacio Acuña, Jorge Acuña, Sandra Acuña, Nora Acuña de Quesada, Dessiree Madeleyne Salas Acurio, Gale y Bob Adair, Steve and Diana Adam, Ed Adamitz, Barba
Adams, Dwayne & Sandy Adams, Emmitt Adams, Fred Adams, Fred Adams, George Adams, Gord Adams, Larry & Una Adams, Lawerence & Maye Adams, Mary & Tom Adams, Peggy and Gord Adar
Ronald Adams, Steven Adams, Virgil and Betty Adcock, Robert Addis, Flake Adkins, Keith Adkins, Mary & Cal Adkins, David Adler, Adrian Flores Acosta, Felipe Adriana, A'Lucro Adrigal, Adruan
Manuelle, Bruke Agenter, Harry Russell Agnes McIntyre, Telmo Agnese, Esteban Agodstan, Rick & Melanie Agosto, Gabriela Aguero, Roberto Aguero, Rocío Aguero, Pedro Agüero, Jose y Ca
Aguerrido, Antonino Aguiar, Alfredo Marta y Humberto Aguilar, David Aguilar, Eduardo Aguilar, Eduardo Aguilar, Esteban Aguilar, Juan Gonzalez Aguilar, Leysi Aguilar, Moises Aguilar, Raul Agui
Yolanda y Anselmo Aguilar, Lidiette Aguilar Almaña, Hugo Aguilar Cruz, Familia Aguilar Fuentes, Angel Aguilar Victorino, Leon Aguilera, Claudina Aguirre, Jose Manuel Aguirre, Luis Aguirre, Man
Aguirre, Ramon Aguirre, Ricardo Aguirre Ayala, Angel Aguirre Tenorio, Jane Ahbott, Lance Ahern, Horst Ahlers, Harpreet Ahluwalia, Steve & Robin Ahmands, Alejandro Ahn, Ana Ahn, George & Ma
Ahrens, J.R. Aiello, Guido Akerman, Jim & Diane Akers, Stephanie Dyer Al Miller, Wyne Alambaugh, Dave Alan, Alan and Lista, Juan Alaniz, Marcelo Alaniz, Federico Alarcon, Manolo Alarcon, Ma
Alarcon, Gerardo Alarcon ZT, Baraquiel Alatriste, Rafael Alazraki, Eduardo Alba, Pablo y Camila Alba Vasa, Nathalie Rodas Alban, Horacio y Nicolas Albarracin, Nicolas y Maria Albarracin, Rodo
Albergati, Bob & Marg Albert, Cathy Albert, Ana Maria Albertelli, Barbara Albright, Dave & Anne Albright, Ellen Albright, Gene & Linda Albright, Tom Albright, Tom Albritton, Woody Albro, Ser
Alcala Sanzalez, Mercedes Alcantara, Miguel Alcantara, Freddy Aldana, Aurelio Aldaz, Mark & Cherryl Alder, Rafael y Sandra Alderete, John Aldous, Nancy Aldrich, Ralph & Nancy Aldrich Wander
Jim and Gary Aldridge, Grey Aldrings, Alan Alducin, Niqueta Alem, Judy Moroz Alex Thrower, Bill Alexander, Don Alexander, Jamie Alexander, Rick & Merrilee Alexander, Roy Alexander, David Va
Alexandra, Carol Aley, Anabelle ALfaro, Antonio Alfaro, Carlos Alfaro, Daniel Alfaro, Hector y Silvia Alfaro, Veronica Alfaro C., Alonso Alfaro Ureña, Luis Alfaroli, Damian Alfaron, Susana Alfons
Roberto Alfonso, Debra Alford, Kim Algood, Ruben Alhadeff, Martin Aliandri, Larry Alkire, Andrea and Daniel Alleman, Alice Allen, Dennis and Diane Allen, Gary Allen, Glen & Jan Allen, Mark All
Mark Allen, Mark Allen, Vernon Allen, Andres Allik, Robert Allred, Nancy y Ralph Allrich, Katarine y Cristino Almeida, Alejandro Alonso, Ma Lourdes y Jose Antonio Alonso, Alonso Noriega Posad
Jorge Navarro, Ral Alphy, Flora Alpizar, Mayela Alpizar, Ann Altaffer, Beto Altamirano, Fabiana y Jorge Altamirano, Harow Altice, Florencia Aluero, Jose Antonio Alva Meriso, Adriana Alvarado, Darv
Alvarado, Guido y Xevia Alvarado, Juan Alvarado, Tess Alvarado, Marlene Alvarado Camacho, Jorge Alvarenga, Ana Victoria & Paul Alvarez, Andres Alvarez, Antonio Alvarez, Eduardo Alvar
Elizabeth Alvarez, Gustavo y Carlos Alvarez, Ignacio Alvarez, Israel Alvarez, Jose Alvarez, Lorena y Armando Alvarez, Marco Alvarez, Margarita y Ubaldo Alvarez, Mariola Alvarez, Raul Alvarez, Sil
y Eduardo Alvarez, Teresa Alvarez, Ignacio Alvarez R., Oscar y Martha Alvarez Tou, Fernando Alvariza & Marcelo Maero, Jorge Alzerreca, Victor Amado, Jhossianne Amaya, Manuel Amaya, Zo
Amaya, Anita & Frank Ambrogno, Pete Ambrose, Alejandro Amed, Joe Amendolia, Manuel Ameneiros, Bob y Carol Amento, Victor Ameri, Jose Amesalida, Luis & Linda Amesanta, Alberto Amezc
Reed Amgwert, Paul Amieux, Jorge Amieva, Manuel Amigo, Brigitte Ammon, Nate Amos, Flia. Amsel, Patricia y German Amunches, Sheri Amundser, Tom Amyx, Mario Anaya, Ismene Gome
Anchondo, Rich and Mina, Eric & Cleo Andersan, Ken Andersen, Marcia Andersen, Bertha Anderson, Bestsy and Frank Anderson, Bobbie Anderson, Ed Anderson, Jerry and Carolyn Anderson, Kathy a
Ed Anderson, Lynn Anderson, Monica Anderson, Patricia Anderson, Peder & Jessica Anderson, Roy Anderson, Steve & Beulah Anderson, Ted Anderson, Val & Ron Anderson, Vonnie Anderson, Ale Anc
Gil, Eugennia Andraca, Rafael Andrada Villalobos, Daniel Andradde, Alejandro Andrade, Edgar y Diego Andrade, J Andrade, Rodrigo Andrade Carranza, Gladys y Javier Andrade Loranca, Andre Merc
& Daniel Desjardins, Fabio Andrea, Milos Andrejic, JosË Andres, Ferry Palanga Andres Serrutt, Billy Andrew, Andrew Cleek & Barbara, Silvina Valenza Andrew Timmis, Ed Andrews, George & Ka
Andrews, Pamela Andrews, Robin Andrews, Trieste Andrews, Ana Anella, Aneta, Charles Angel, German Angel, Juan Angel, Angela Harp, Carlos Rivera y Angelina Castilla, Mike Angell, Tom and Na
Angellotti, Victorino Angelvaguilar, Dina Angress, Jose Angulo Smith, Ronald Ankney, Anne Middleton, Susana Ansaldi-Anderson, Williams Anthony, Jose Anton, Ror Antonio, Antonio Olvera Range
Moria de la Luz, Lorne Antonsen, Carole & Don Anttila, Vickki & Victor Anzalone, Axel Aogspach, Celeste Aorley, John Apen, Orlando Aport, Sigi Appelt, Steve Apperson Katley, Howard Apple, De
Applegate, Carlos Apraiz, Carlos Arabolaza, Raul Aragon, R. Paul Aragon JD, Yonder Arama S., Oddi Arambula, Roberto Arambula, Carlos Aramburu Tudela, Luis Aranda, Walter Aranda, Rafael Arand
Villalobos, Marco A. Aranibar, Javier Aranov, Roberto Araona Diaz, Alberto Araujo, Manuel Araujo, Paula Aravena, Shirley Araya, Eduardo Araya Fallas, Hector Arboleas, Eduardo Arcas, Adriana Ar
Jorge Arce, Peter Arce, Michael Arce Sancho, Monica & Chris Archambo, Carlos Jose Archbold, Michael Susan, Katie, Archer, Ben Bundick & Ardis, Victoria Arechaga, Robert Areham Baux, Dani
Arellano Leiva, Pedro Arellano Leiva, Guadalupe Arellano Romero, Vince Arenchir, John Aresta, Javier Arevalo, Rosa Isela Arévalo Gonzalez, Fernanda Arez, Diana Argeres, Alejandro Arguelles Py
Antonio Arguelles R., Yesenia Argueta, Andrea y Adela Arias, Lucio Arias, Raul Arias, Javier y Nidia Arias Montero, Gohlke Ariel, Alice Arielly, Rachel Arington, Orlando Aristrabal, Carlos Ariza, Fred
Armandi, Angelica y Mario Armani, Gil y Juanita Armas, Oscar Armav, Alan Armbruster, Bruce Armer, Clyde Armitstead, Elizabeth Armstrong, Maria Armstrong, H. Arnarson, Bonnie Arndt, Benjar
Arnold, Bonnie & Henry Arnold, Danny Arnold, Duare Arnold, Ronge & Mykg Arnold, Teri Arnold, Tobbie & Ben Arnold, Michael Arnone, Victoria Aronosky, Natalia Arraigada, Rigoberto Arraya, J
G. y Maria Arredondo, Antonio Arriaga, Ma. Isabel Arriaga, Claudia Arrua, Margarita y Carlos Arrutti, Bob Arsenault, Jorge Artavia Alvarez, Gerardo Artavia y Janette, Roberto Arte, Maria Luisa Ar
Osvaldo Arvizo leiva, Sam Asaris, Jerry & Judy Asbuck, Valerie Asbury, Max Asch, Ted Aschman, Blake Ashley, Wendy Ashley, Katie Ashmore, Asoc de Autos San Luis Potosi, Asoc. Arg. de Aut. Sp
Asoc. de autos antiguos de Ojo Caliente, Asoc. de Autos Antiguos Rio Cuarto, Asociacion de Autos Antiguos de Cali, Asociacion de Autos de Aguascaliente, Asociacion Mexicana del Automovil Antig
Asociacion Salvadoreña de Carros Antiguos, Asociación Cordobesa de Coleccionistas de Autos Antiguos, Patricia Asorey, Dave Aspelund, Arne Asphjell, Arne Asphjell, Ellen Ast, Rod Astl, Allan y Elc
Astorga, Gustavo Astorga, Monica Astrid F., ATAACO, Dena Atkinson, Newell Atwood, Auburn-Cord-Duesenberg Museum, David & Brenda Aubury, Virginia Augustine, Bill & Marilou Aulwes, Rob
Auman, Bob Aumphrey, John Auriana, Hans y Elena Austerhuhle, David Perri y Eduard, Austin, Kim Authense, Jim Auto, Automovil Club Boliviano, Automovil Club del Ecuador, Automovil Club
Ecuador, AutomovilSport, Carlos Autos Clasicos Ecuador, Gary Lanin Pte, Autos Coleccionables de Guatemala, Autos Coleccionables de Guatemala, Bob Auvil, AVAAC, Hector Alejandro Avalos, Hu
Avalos, Joaquin Avalos, Belly & Myra Avant, Millon Avant, Lelia Avaria, Raul Avellaneda, Rodrigo Rafael Avellano Garcia, Matias Avenali, Ma. Auxiliadora Averruz López, John Avery, Ron Avey, Ca
Avila, David Avila, Michell Avila, Rodelaida Avila, Oscar Avila M., J. Alberto Avila Toledo, Carlos & Pat Avilas, Tim Avritt, Byron Ayala, Carlos Ayala, Roberto Ayala, KT Ayers, Karina Aymerich & Jus
Gustavo Aynie, Pablo Aynie, Alex Azar, Mauricio Azucena, Baudilio Azuero, Carol & John Azzaro, Phillips B., John & Margi B. F. Smith, Jasmine Baba, Cheryl Babbe, Kaytee & Boby Babcock, E
Bablock, Cello Baca, Gilles Bachand, Ray Bachand, Albert & Mary Bachman, Howard & Brenda Bachman Jr., Mabel Bachy, Everett Bacon, Mark & Jan Bacon, Jorge Auge Bacque, Marguerite Bada
Patricio Badaracco, Annie Hugo y Alex, Badell, Jill Badger, Waynp Badger, Edgar Badillo, Howard & Kathy Baer, Emilio Baeza, Clifford Bafter, David Bagatoli, Sabrina Baggio, Ed Bagley, Leslie Bag
Andy Baher, Robert Bahr, Alejandro Bailey, Bill Bailey, Cathryn Bailey, Gene Bailey, Ken & Cindy Bailey, Richard Bailey, Sam Bailey, Wiley Bailey, Alejandro Bailey H., Jan & Russ Baily, Jackie Ba
George Bairey, Ingrid Bairstow, Bill Bajeczuk, Isidoro Bajo, Gary Bakeman, Gorge Baken, Andy Baker, Bob Baker, Craige & Kathy Baker, Cris & Rod Baker, Dennis & Joan Baker, Gerald Baker, Har
Baker, Jackie Baker, Jackie Baker, Jane Baker, John Baker, Mike & Cindy Baker, Paul and Holly Baker, Erla Oscar Balarezo, Lucia Balbi, Manuel Balbontin, Sally Balchin, Enrique Balderas, Jan &
Baldwin, John & Sue Baldwin, Kurt Baldwin, Michelle Baldwin, Phil & Eunice Baldwin, Ron Baldwin, Rosanna Balestrini, Steve & Irma Balko, Harold Baller, Gloria Ballestero Montoya, Blanca Ba
Loera, Ann Ballow, Laura Mariela Castillo Balmaceda., Edgardo Baltodano, José Baltran, Bob & Bernita Balzer, Ruben & Marta Ban Gert, Riushi Banderas, Armand Bandiera, Walter Bandt, Kevin Bar
John Banhman, John y Henry Banman, Hector Banon, Francisco Banosa, Steve Banter, Franco Bañato, Emmanuel Baptist, Keith & Sue Bara, Albrecht Barajas, Adil Barakat, Ezequiel Barakat, Ser
Barake, Roberto Barba, Pablo Barbara, Anthony Barber, Eduardo Barberena, Eduardo Barbiero, Javier Barbosa, Rita Barboza Cisneros, Roberto Barcena, Familia Barco, Karen Barela, Emily Barevic
Ann Barker, Jerry Barker, Mike & Karen Barker, Doug Barkham, Omar Barletta, Garza Barlon, Milton Barndt, Billie Barner, Brian Barnes, Cecil Barnes, George Barnes, Gerry Barnes, James Barnes, J
Barnes, Jay & Ronnie Barnes, Steve & Barnett, Sherron Barnhill, Charlie and Connie Barnow, Gustavo Baron, Jules Baron, Claudia Ibañez de Barón, Patricio Barona, Jose y Bea Barone, Ferna
Barquero, Julio Barquero, Luis Barquero, Bob Barr, Fedra Barracosa, Alfredo Barragan, Rodolfo Barranca J., Denise Barrand, Carolina Barrantes, Francisco Barrantes, Haisel Barrantes, Jose Barrar
Rojas, Lisa Barré, Laurence Barreas, Joe and Jo Barrell, Enrique y Angel Barrera, Mauricio Barrera Pineda, Rodolfo Barretero, Rodolfo Barretero, Alberto Barreto, Aaron Barrett, Omar Barretta, Ma
Barretti, Abel Antonio Barrias Nieto, Jose Antonio Barrias Nieto, Marcela Barrie, Henk & Betty Barriel, Mario Barriga, Eddie Barrington, Ana Elizabeth Barrios, Carlos Barrios, Rubelina Barrios, Fau
Barro Viejo, Angel Barron, Barry Elementary School, Ian Barry, Patricia Barry, Esteban Barta, Luciana & Pedro Bartes, Catherine Barth, Ken Barthe H., Jane Bartlett, Ronnie Bartley, Maureen Bar
Leonor Bartons, Cecilia Barvino, Patsy Bascom, Harold Bashford, Osco Basinger, Ralph & Diana Basner, Roberta Basquin, Tania Basrton, William Bass, Fred & Kathy Basset, Kathlryn Bassett, Will
Bassett, Rick Basta Eichbrg, Ed Bastecki, Bin Bastien, Bing & Theresia Moeltner Bastlen, Raul Basurto, Bill & Teddie Batalis, Clare Batchelor, Caryl Bates, Dave Bathke, Deira Batista, Charles Ba
Stebe Battershall, Atilio Batti, Paul Bauchand, Joe Bauer, Carrie & Mark Baulard, John Baumgarten, Ivan Bauret, Agustin Bautista, Fernando Bautista, Lucia & Juan Bautista, Sara Bautista, Miguel Bava
Valeria Baviera, Jayme Bawden, Monica Bawden, Marsha Bawton, Perry . Baxter, Carole Bayard, Christian Bayas, Bill Bayer, Mary Bays, Daniel Bea, Joe Beach, William/Karen Beach, Doug Beach
Jim and Judy Beagle, Mike Beam, Carla Bean, Ed & Debbie Bean, Steven Bean, Terry & Kathy Bean, Antonio Bear, Francisco Bear, Luis Antonio Bear Morales, Jeff Beard, John Beasley, Maureen Bea
Bob & Caulene Beatty, Charlotte Beatty, Angelina Beaty, Lorenzo and Noella Beaulieu, Irene Beaupre, Marilyn Beaven, Amy & Vic Beaver, Darrel & Stephanie Beaver, Cecilia Bebby, Hector Bece
Adriana Becerra, Cristina y Salvador Becerril, Fernando Becerril Castaneda, Avis Beck, David Beck, George Beck, Jorge Peter Beck, Keith Beck, Mike Beck, William Beck, Bob Becker, Karl Bec
Kristine Becker, Jennifer Beckman, Lavern Beckner, Mark Beckstedt, Bruce Beddulsh, David & Donna Bedell, Luis Bedilla, Paul Bednar, Armrel Beecham, Victoria Beecham, Gregory Beemer, Ed & Su
Beeson, Marilyn Behle, Melissa Behnke, Sue Beidelman, Steve Bein, Dietmar Beinhauer, Maria Bel Campo, Loretta Belac, Gene Belanger, Jean Beliveau, Dr. Luciano Belizan, Belize Ports, Anne & Cha
Bell, Hlenn Bell, Kim Bell, Les Bell, Mona Bell, Dan & Kim Bellinger, Francesco Bellini, Christina Bellis, Jorge Bello Dominguez, Tom Belovich, Silvia Benavidez, Adriana Benci, Mario Benci, Ca
Benedetti, Javier Benedetti, Bill Benedict, Roger Benedict, Ann & Rory Benfield, Sue Benfield, Robert Benge, Marion Benham, Squeaki & Marion Benham, Sandy Benites, Ana Benitez, Jose Beni
Ramon Benitos, David Benitz, Seth Benkowitz, Barry & Joan Bennett, Brian Bennett, Connie Bennett, Newsp Dartmouth NS, Greg, Bennett, Wayne Bennett, Guy Bennett Jr., Rart & Haron Bensh
Ilham Bensmail, Elizabeth Benson, Kitty Benson, Lorri Benson, Em Bensussen, Ethel Bent, Bobby Benton, Bree Benton, Robin Benzle, Linden Ber Jr., Jose Berardinelli Alvarez, Roger & Mary Bercht
Aida Bereo, Marcelo Berestovoy, Ken Y Louise Berg, Randy Berg, Cacho Bergantiños, Danon Berge, Evi Berge, Bob Berger, Laurie Berger, Guy Bergeron, Richard & Joan Berghorn, Tom Berkem
Robert Berkey, Antonio Bermudez, Otto Bermudez, Enrique Bernain, Bruno Bernard, Olivia Bernard, Fernando Bernat, Jim Berning Family, Josh Bernstein, Luis M. Berras, Mary Ellen & Art Be
Kathryn Berta, Martin Bertie, Jorge Bertochi, Roberto Bertolina, Sebastian Bertoncini, Floria Bertsch, Jaime y Aida Beruman, Dot Besch, Adolfo Besga, Carole Besner, Radio Sol Bet or Clay, Arn
Betancourt Rodriguez, Maribel Betanor, Steve & Amy Bethnne, Earl Betts, Janet Betts, John Renati Betty, Julio Bevegni, Sara Bevgquist, Andrea Bevilacqua, Joshua Bewig, Tom Beyd, Luis Beza, Joh
Julie Bhend, Naj Bhora, Natalie Biadlecome, Sara Biancardi, Gino Bianchi, Horacio Bianchi, Mirtha Bianchi, Errol Bickford, Betty & George Bickley, Belén Bidart, Key Biddle, Rhonda Biddlecome,
Bidonde, Hugo Bidondo, Don & Ann Bieberich, Moraima Biederman, Sule- Peter Biedermann, Dick Bievens, Paul & Therese Bigalow, Joe Bigelli, Diane Bigelow, Mark Biggin, Katherine Bigler, Jac
Mickey Biickert, Pedro Bilbao, Bill Jennings GOCI, Suzanne Billips, Sophie Binder, Jim Binegar, Linda Bingham, Marge Binner (mayor), Lew Bird, Sena Biruchenko, Marcel Bischof, MShirley Bis
Kevin Bishop, Paul Bishop, Peter Bishop, Dennesse, Carlos y Teresa Bisogni, Gerry Bisson, Clara Bitman, Immo Bitschkus, Belind Bittaer, Esther Bittel, Jorge y Jimena Bittleston, David Bitton, Ama
y Milton Biurrun, Donald Bixler, Gary Black, Jim & Sharon Black, Black River Valley Region AACA Club, Doug Blackburn, Ted Blackington, Robert Blackledge, Connie Blackman, Kevin Blackm

n Bladen, Bim Blair, Dorie Blair, Scott Blair, Rayna Blakesley, Ben Blakewood, Sarina Blandeau, Chuck & Karen Blaney, Chamaco Blank, Rodney Blankenship, Steve Blanusa, Mike Blaser, Geri
ton, George Blau, George & Raquel Blaw, Andy Blaydon, Mike Blaylock, Andres Blazquez, Pablo Blazquezy Jacqueline Wallcer, Case Blazyk, Oswin Blease, Deidre BLEDSOE, Michael Bleicher MD,
ph Blessing, Pete Blevins, Jack Blickert, Roger Bliss, Stewart Blocher, Bill Blockcolsky, Charles Blodgett, Carina Bloj, Bob y Marianne Bloom, Jack & Flora Blue, Todd Blum, Barryl & Shirley
menthal, Barbara Blundell, Barbara Boagey, Rusty Dornin Bob Cranston, Felipe y Ana Bobbia, Jack Bobruk, Bibiana Noemi Boccolini, Marion Bochenek, Jr., Marcus Bochler, Lloyd Bock, Jerry &
n Bodden, Jerry & Joan Boddle, Catherine Bodry, Tom Boergert, Elisa Bogado, Kathy Bogart, Loren & Teresa Bogart, Carlos Y Nancy Bogley, Esteban Bohaarczuk, Sean Bohanan, Sven y Tanja
anert, Bernardo Boken Fohr, Moraima y Eva Bolaños, Shirley & James Bold, Rich Bolden, Max & Mary Bolin, Fernando Escalante Bolio, Hugo Bolivar, Marcela Bolivar, Magdalena Bolland, Susan
le, Richard Bollenbocher, Daniel E. Bollo, Savah Bolovjack, Diane Bolte, Ray Bomberger, Richard Bonchers, Ryan Bond, Will & Bond, Ivan Bondoletti, Marion & Peter Boniface, Jennifer Bonila S.,
erto Bonilla, Eugenia Bonilla, Jenifer Bonilla, Julio Bonilla, Luis Bonilla, Rosalbina Bonilla, Rosaura Bonilla, Mario Bonilla Cortes, Fernando Bonilla G., Frank & Ber Bonin, Jim & Mary Bonini,
ana y Manuel Bonites, Juan Carlos Bono, Jorge Bonomo, Esther Bonveki, Cecilia Bonvino, Marcela Bonzi, English Book, Maribeth & John Bookter Gilbert, Dave Boon, David Boon, Eryn Boone, John
th, Paul Boozan & Vicki Williamson, John Borchers, Bill & Brenda Borden, Reeve Borden, Elaine Border, Ginette Borduas, Sandra Borel, Matias Borelli, Fabian Borensztein, Emily Borevics, Manuel
ge, Donna Boris, Marisol y Miguel Angel Borja, Benjamin Borjas, Don & Amanda Borland, Jim Born Sr, Roy Bornmann, Polly & Bill Borntraeger, William & Polly Borntraeger, Randall y Maria Laura
querso Rodriguez, Mar Borrego, Clyde Borton, Adela & Vicente Bortone, Luciana y Pedro Bosio, Rodine & Gary Boss, John Boswell, Mike Boteler, Jorge Botello, Brian Bothomley, Teresa Bottcher,
lerico Bottero, Sandra Bouchikhi, Jaca un Bougher, André Bouillon, Ray Bouman, T.J. Bourdon, Ed Bourget, Sid & Pat Bouschor, Regina Bouvia, Stephen Bove, Holga Bowden, Mickey Bowen, Neal
wes, Dene Bowman, E.W. Bowman, Geoff & Marilyn Bowman, Kaseu Bowman, Jim Boyd, Chana Boyko, Karen Boylan, Greg Boyle, William Boyles, Ricardo Bozzo, Inabeth Braatfish, Exequiel
cco, Adam Brace, Tom & Cyndi Brace, Florencia Braceras, Miriam Bracho Ojeda, Jim y Kim Brackett, Bob Bradburey, Bill Bradburn, Lisa Bradem, Chris Bradey, Jim Bradford, Betty & Ron Bradley,
Bradley Bennett, Tom Shehla & Saira, Bradner, George Brady, Louise Brady, Ralph Brady, Sean Brady, Frank y Norma Brainard, Kim Brame, Jorge Brana, Matt Branam, Patricia Brancafu, Armando
ndo, Heath & Amy Brandon, Ray & Yolanda Brandon, Paul Brandsema, Brian & Cathy Brandt, Matthias Frances, Julia, Nathaniel, Evangeline, Brandt, Betsy & Rick Brandt-Kreutz, Oscar Brardo, Walt
tton, Walter Bratton, Pablo Braude, Ben Braun, Lynn & Greg Braun, Alejandro Bravo, Jaime Bravo, MS Roxana Bravo, Roxana Bravo, Tito Bravo, Veronica Bravo, Ernie Brawley, Don & Amy Bray,
nald Bray, Richard Bray, Kathy Brazeau, Robert Brealey, Fabricio Brebion, Tim Brenda, Sergio Manuel Brenda Varela, Dana Breneman, Mervin Breneman, Miguel Brenes, Yender Brenes, Patricia
nes Ullos, Nic Brenkall, Jeffrey Brenman, Yechier Bresier, Lauren & Dylaan Breslin, Mike Breslin, Carlos Breton, Denise Breton, Jeff Breton, Kevin Breveleri, Nancy Brew, Jeff and Mary Brewer, Jhon
wer, Rex Brewer, Yvonne Brewer, Sara Bribraun, Y. Briceño, Babs Bridge, Rose Brigmon, Rose Brigmon, Phyll B & Ken Briles, Byron Brill, Margaret Brilly, Clinton Brinkley, Fran Brinkman, Shelby
nser, Romulo e Iris Brito, Dennis Brittingham, Sue and Mike Broadbent, Norman Brocard, Rosa Brochado, Beverly & Fred Brockschmidt, B. W. Brockway, Wayne Brockwell, Cetilia Brodziak, Ted
mage, Max Bromberg, Glen & Barb Brong, Richard Bronkall, Cool Brook, Grg Brooker, Dave & Bonnie Brooks, David Brooks, Jeff Brooks, Mike & Jackie Brooks, Ned Brooks, Carolina Broomand,
b Brosowsky, Bill & Mary Beth Brouch, Jack Broughton, Jane Broughton, Theresa & Rod Broughton, Theresa & Rod Broughton, David & Carol Broun, Pam Browen, Herman & Sue Brower, Timothy
wer, Androw Brown, Andy Brown, Barbie y Peanut Brown, Brenda Brown, Brian Brown, Carolina Brown, Emmett Brown, Franzi Brown, Jorge Brown, Jorge & Nancy Brown, Joseph Brown, Judee
wn, Keith & Jenn Brown, Kent Brown, Kim & Scott Brown, Lester & Padie Brown, Maia Brown, Mark Brown, Michael Brown, Paul Brown, Sam Brown, Sam & Harry Brown, Tim Brown, Virginia
wn, Richard Browne, Joe Browning, Todd Browning, Jack Browser, Art Broyles, Philip & Kara Broyles, Jerry & Kim Brubaker, Jill & Mike Brubnker, Mark Bruce, Bruce Davis & Anariba Greay, Ray
ammy Bruening, Celia Brugman, Ron Brumley, Herchell Brummitt, Pamela & Henry Bruneau, Gabriela Bruni, Donald Bruno, Patrick & Juliet Bruno, Steve and Cisly Bruntlett, Peter Brutolino, Todd
an, Bill Bryant, Kevin Pat & Alex, Bryant, George Bryson, Gwendolyn Bryson, Caro BS, Pat Bubb, Dante Buchanan, Hans Buchel, Dick Buchel Van Steengber, Salvador Bucio, John & Betty Buck,
na Buckley, Bob Buckley B., Carole & Bryan Buckridge, Olav Budde Utne, Roberto Bude, Luik Budillo, Justin Buehner, Steve & Airlean Buehner, Adela Buelvas, Eduardo Buenfil Perez, Alex Bueno,
gar Bueno, Carol Buetens, Eric Buetens, Marcelo Buezas, María Eugenia Buezas, Barbara Buie Keeler, Dolores Bulit, Jack Bull, Derek & Jean Bullard, Mike & Jan Bultemeier, Pam Bumeister, Robin
ngardner, John Bundy, Charlie Bunker, Monica Bunner, Mark Bunten, Me Burciago, Gene & Dorothy Burdo, Gilbert Bureau, Andy y Loretta Burgess, Richard Burggraf, Sheila Burgh, Karina Burghard,
y Burian, Mike Burin, Christian Burjogc, Gerald Burke, Jeffrey Burke, Robah Burke, John & Mary Burkett, Maomin Burkgart, Florine & Lill Burkholder, Michael & Mariann Burkholder, Alvim Burks,
enan Burn, Lee Burner, Bev Burnett, Denny Barb and Dennielle Burnett, Ed Burnett, Linda Burnett, Susi Burnette, Jim Burney, Sue & Bill Burnham, Caryn Y Jim Burns, Mike Burns, Rex Burns, Roy
Vendy Burns, Denis & Pat Burr, Janice Burrough, Bill Burrow, Lane Burrow, Andrew W. Burrowes, John Burrowf, Dianne Burrows, John T & Jane Burrows, Matt Burrows, Cecilia Bursa, Buff & Sandra
tis, Paul Burtlett, Bob & Linn Burtness, Mike & Lynn Burton, Bill Burungame, Judy Busack, Anita Busches, Horacio y Luz Maria Buschiazzo, Padre Buscuttil, Dale & Marge Bush, Kathryn Bush,
thew Bushue, Vedran Busija, Edward Buss, Tour Buss, Daniel Bussolotti, German Bustamante, Jonathan Bustamante, S. Bustamante, Diego Bustamentes, Alejandro Bustos, Cesar y Diana Bustos, Diana
Bustos, Juan Bustos, P. Busuttil, Charlie Buszuk, Blancha Butcher, Connie Butler, Mark Butler, Grisel y Jose Luis Butron Pereda, Marilo Butrone Spanglee, Andrew Butt, Barb Butt, Bob Butter, Susan
at Buttle, Chris Button, Derek & Martha Button, Rick Buzga, Joe Buzzetto, Simon Bwn, Blaine Byecly, Patrick Bygott, John Byingotn, Chad Byrd, John P Byrne, Vickie Byrnes, Jeff C., Juan C.Pari,
AAC, Martin Caballero, Carlos y Elsa Cabello, Cecilia Cabezas, Abel Cabral, Jorge Cabral, Adriana Cabrera, Ana Cabrera, Emilio Cabrera, Gabriel Cabrera, Omar Cabrera, Alberto Caceres, Miguel
heux E., Ma. Eugenia Cacho, CADEAA, Patricia Cadena, Bill Caetenholz, Fara Cahn, Flavio Cahrera, Fernando Caicedo, Allen & Cindy Cain, Juan Caino, Isamel Cala, Nevina & Paul Caldarazzo,
stavo Caldarelli, Mark Calder, Carlos Caldera, Humberto Caldera y Flia., Liz Calderon, Salvador Calderón, Wagner Calderon Rizzo, Jim & Pat Caldwell, Richaro Calhoun, Brian Call, Chris Callafhan,
ce Callahan, Arthur Callan, Juan Calle, E. Leonardo Callegari, Gene y Lois Calman, Hugo y Fernanda Calo, Paul Calo, Gabriela y Javier Calviño Pazos, Luis Calvo, Calvo Autos Arica, Nancy Calvo
z, David Calwell, Astrid y Sergio Camacho, Hector & Amanda Camacho, Samune Camacho, Roberto Camacho Jauanillo, Roberto Camahvali, Christian Camargo, Israel Camargo, Sandra Camargo,
acio Cambeiro, Lenora Cambs, Karm Camden, Carrie Cameron, Creig Cameron, Marlene Cameron, Wayne Cameron, Araceli Camillo, Pablo Victor Camiolo, Valentina Camp, Edgar Campa, Telva y
no Campaniolo, Bill Campbell, Bruce Campbell, Claire & Al Campbell, Donna Campbell, Doug & Joan Campbell, Julie Campbell, June Campbell, Layard Campbell, Luey & Donna Campbell, Robert
npbell, Tobias Campbell, Paul Campisi, Alejandra Campos, Carlos Campos, Edgar Campos, Gustavo Campos, Henry Campos, Raul Campos, Silvano Campos, Juan Campos Galindez, Tony Campo,
drigo Campos Lozano, Martin Campoy, Angeles y Alejandro Canales, Sherrie Canavos, Sonia Canda, Manuel y Sandra Cando, Chuck & Diane Cane, Aurora Canha, Zach Canizales, Mary Cannell, John
nizzaro, Randy Cannon, Carlos Cano, Kelvin Canon, Enrique Canseco Luna, Heidi Cantin, Roberto Canto, Santiago Canton, Chuck Cantwell, Lelio and Sylvia Capitani, Leticia Capitania Puerto, Greg
shaw, Capt Jack, Dario Carabajal Torres, Francisco Carabes Antonio, Monica Caramazana, Jesus Carapa, Jesus Carapia, Jesus Carapia, Jesus Carapia G., Manuel Caras García, eduardo Caravajal
aña, Hernan Carazo, Hernan Carazo, Jerry Carbajal, Lito y Norma Carbajal, Bill & Syloce Carberry, Atilio Carbone, Ovidio y Jose Carbs Beauregard Gimenez, Marie Cardenas, Miguel Cardenas, B.
dinal, Jackson & Olivia Cardinal, El Nene Jose Cardo, Jose y Esther Cardo, Griselda y Luis Cardona, Louis Cardona, Orlando Cardozo, Pablo Cardozo, Wendy Cardwell, Carmen Cardy, Denise Carey,
chael Carey, John Cargile, Yvonne Carhegre, Jose Luis y Jimena Caride, Ricardo Maria Teresa y Walter, Carino, Carina Caritango, Ann & Steve Carkeek, Belva Carley, Gustavo Carlino, Habiague Carlos,
neron Carlos Sanchez, Bob Carlson, Lou Carlson, Randy Carlson, Mauricio Carman Tack, Héctor Peloche carmen, Earl Carmichael, Javier Jorge y Victor, Carmona, Jose Carmona, Arleen Carner, Dave
en Carnevale, Pepe Caro, Dave and Carol, Carol Rockwell, Agustin Caroma Garcia, Carlos Caroo, Nora Carothers, William Carothers, Gaston Carozzi Pizarro, Harold Carpenter, HD Carpenter, Kennet
Carpenter, Roger Carpenter, Sylvia & Regzey Carpenter, Jamie Carr, Alberto Carranza, Isabel & Antonio Carranza, Juan Carranza, Brianne Carras, D. Andrew Carrasco, Paul Carreiro, Blanca Carreon,
rgarita Carrere, Oscar Carrescia, Ana Carretero, Marcelo y Sonia Carrica, Marcelo Carrica & Sonia Lopez, Julie Carrier, Edy Carrillo, Joe Carrillo, Yaneth Carrillo & Alex Rico, Orly Carrion, Fernando
rizo, Ixchel Carroll, Marin Carroll, Pat Carroll, Zac Carroll, Carros Antiguos en Merida, Lori Carson, Pedro L. Mogollon Cartagena, Daun Carter, John Harvey Carter, Mary Carter, Myra Carter, Nadine
ter, Richard Carter, Tony Carter, Manuel Cartin, Jim and Carol Cartmill, Jim & Carol Cartonwell, Connie Caruso, Miguel & Lisa Carvallo, Vic Carvell, Claudia Carville, Jorge Casabella, Jorge Casabella,
nardo Casadiego, Cipriano Casado, Rosa Casali, Abel Casarrubias, Octavia Casas, Viviana Casas, Cheryl Casaus, Silvio Cascino, Silvio Cascino, David Case, Greg Casey, Kevin Casey, Ernie Cash, Val
hman, Miguel Casino, Walter Casorla, Martin Cassidy, Daniela Castañeda, Hector Castañeda, Juan Castaneda, Rene Càstano A., Guadalupe Castañeda, Rodrigo Castañeda Maselli, Gloria Castaño,
ar Gomez Castañon, Pedro Gomez Conde, Miguel Castelino, Karen Castellanos, Bill Castenholz, John Castenholz, Maria Castilla, Dana Castillo, Eduardo Castillo, Enrique Castillo, Ernesto e Imelda
stillo, Itzel Castillo, Manuel Castillo, Oscar Castillo, Silvestre y Nora Castillo, Julia Castillo de Lozano, Carlos Castillo Fregoso, Ernesto Castillo Guilbert, Suzette Castillo Rivera, Rafael Castillo Solana,
nando Castillon, Kathy Castor, Teodoro Y Maria Castrillo, Alfredo Castro, Anabell Castro, Andres Castro, Aurora Castro, Dyal Castro, Edgar Castro, Fernando Castro, Gabriel Castro, Gabriel y Gabriela
tro, Jame Castro, Jessica Castro, Jorge Castro, Karina Castro, Marcelo Castro, Miguel Castro, Mireya Castro, Natalia Castro, Tania Castro, Primo Lourdes y Gabriel, Castro A, Sonia Castro Garcia, Luz
ria Castro Luna, Corina Castro Parra, Rodrigo Castro Z., Dawn Caswell, Humberto y Josefina Catalan, Ron Cataldo, Fernando Catalinas, Catalinas Super Market, Christine Catania, Tom Catania, Margie
oes Cate, Phillipe Catherine, Ron Catterall, Dave Cauble, Jose Caudillo Sanchez, Sergio CausecoLaisaquilla, Brian Donna, Daniel & Whitney, Causey, Nancy Cavalie, Gerardo Cavero, Jose Cavero, K.
iziel, Donna Phil, Bailee, Cavos, Linda Cayabyab, Bill Cazzola, Miguel y Luis Fernando Cchs, Elsa y Emiliano Ceballos, Rafael Cecchini, Heidi Cece, Vera Celada R., Helene Cenedese, Daniel
nteno, Juan Centeno, Ralph Centoni, Dulce Cepula, Elva Cerda, Elva Cerda, Hugo y Marisol Cernantes, Julio e Isabella Cerritos, Alberto Certain, Daniel Certain, Maria Ceruantes, Valeria y Carlos Ceruti,
gel Cervantes, Anna & Gerardo Cervantes, Maria del Pilar Perez Cervantes, Araceli Cervantes Medina, Ana Cervantes Rojas, Franko Cerviño, Rodolfo A. Cerviño, Ivan Cespedes Vargas, Arturo Chable,
Chabot, Bill & Joyce Chace, William Chace, William L. Bill & Joyce Chace, Marcia Chacon, Phaedra Chacona, Marco Chalico, Bill Chalmers, Donald Chambers, Donald & Rosario Chambers, L.
mbers, Rich and Bertha Chambers, Ronda & Louie Chambers, Carol Chamdlee, Gerald Chamey, Rudy y Facundo Champion Auto Repair, Tim & Ann Chance, Lewis & Sherry Chandler, Sarah
ndler, Vivian Chaney, David Chanuel, Marco Chaparro Piña, Ana Lucrecia Chapeton, Guadalupe Chaplin, Frances Chapman, James Chapman, Elizabeth Chappel, Charles Knaster, Richard Chartrand,
k Chase, Nelson Chassavoimaister, Jerome Chate, Dennis Chausser, Ana Chavarria, Kevin Chavarria, Leonard Chavarria, Oscar Chavarria, Walter Chavarria, Oscar Chavarria Contreras, Gaby y Oscar
varria Trejo, Carmen Chaves, Ignacio Gonzales Chaves, Nora Chaves, Tatiana Chaves, Adrian Chavez, Angel Chavez, Christiane Chavez, Rudy Chavez, Veronica Chavez, Yeseuia Chavez, Luis Chavez
, Rene Chavez Ruiz, Rene Alfonso Chavez Ruiz, Rene Alfonso Chavez Valdepeña, David Cheezem, Jordan Cheng, Dan Cheron, Gustavo Cherquis, Scott Cherry, Kyle Banks Cherryl, Cheryl, Cheryl
mpson, Pat Chesnut, Charles Cheung, Paola Chevarria, Art Cheverton, Carlos Chialastri, Jose María Chiavassa, Idair Chies, Hensi Chile, Jerry Chilipko, Jesos Chillon, Chad Chilstason, Don Chilton,
e Chilton, Jose Chimbay, Noshir Chinwalla, Pat Choffy, Vale Chovet, Estela y Jorge Chovet, Keep-Saint Chow, Parvine Chowfla, Barbara Chrappelli, Mike Moad Christene Comstook, Charles
istensen, Del Christensen, Del and Mary Christensen, Henry Christensen, Grant Christenson, Russ & Yvonne Christenson, Vern Christhieb, Bill Christman, Nicholas Christoffersen, Mark Christopherson,
n Chrystal, Ellen Chrystal, Sebastian Chua, Brenda Church, Lidia Chyla, Juliette & Cia Sponsel, Thomas Cibik, Larry Cicardo, Daniel Ciccolini, Cristina y Antonio Cicero, Alicia Cidade, Alberto
ron, Rodrigo Cienfuegos, Vincent Ciesielski, Hugo Eduardo y Hilda Cifuentes, Daniel Cillis, Michel Cinquin, Michel Cinquin, Andre Ciostek, Don Cirasuolo, Pilar Cisnero, Maria Cisneros, Claudia
neros Gomez, Julio Ciudas, Kurt Claksen, Liz & John Clapp, Daniel Clara, Joe Clare, Alejandro y Garry Clark, Andrea Clark, Bill Clark, Dave and Kathy Clark, Lisa & Kevin Clark, Marian Clark, Rob
Toni Clark, Sue Clark, Susan Clark, William Clark, Gerry Clarke, Len Clarke, Monette Clarke, Jim Clarkson, Club de Autos Clasicos, John Di Rizio Claudia Bravo, Claudia Lora y Armando Mendoza,
onio Silva Claudia Pattan, Sara Clawson, Estim Clay, David Clayton, Ken Clayton, Tammy Clayton, Jim Clement, Kathryn Clements, C.H.I. Cliff, Graham Clifford, Wanda Clift, Gene Cline, Barbara
Charles Clinton, Travis Clontz, Kelley Clouser, Andre Cloutier, Jeanne Cloutier, Rosso Clover, Dianne Clower, Doug Clowers, Club Autom. Historicos de Rosario, Club CADEAA, Club Colombiano de
omoviles Antiguos y Clasicos, Club Amigos del Ford A, Club de V8, Club de Autos Antiguos de Escobar, Club de Autos Antiguos de Luján, Club de Autom. Clasicos de San Isidro, Club de Automovil
rt, Club de Autos Clasicos del Ecuador, Club de Autos Clasicos del Ecuador, Club de Autos de Leon, Club del Automovil Antiguo Nvo. Laredo, Club MG Argentino, Lee & Druce Cluff, Lorna Clutch,
ne Clutier, Clyde Castle, Sam Coakley, Mary & Tim Coalwell, Ed Cobbler, Dave Cochran, Steve & Mary Cochran, Thomas Sheela & Teresita, Cochran, Peter Cochrane, Francisco Cocuzza, Dalia
ena, Joseph Coe, Siobhan Coen, Pam & Rick Coffex, Rick & Pam Coffey, Daryl Coffman, John & Marlene Coffman, Ann Cohen, Domont & Jessica Cohen, Victor Cohen, Toni Cohn, Bill Cohoon,
netrios Coidakis, Kevin Coker, Coker Tire Company, Fernando Adrian Colaci, Aldo Colantonio, Carlos Colautti, Leroy and Cora Cole, Pete Cole, Robert Cole, Walter & Frances Cole, Cliff Colee, Bobie
eman, John & Virginia Coleman, Lee Coleman, Neila Coles, Ray Colesworthy, Enrique Coll, Al Collen, Bob Collette, Brian Collins, Charles Collins, Chris Collins, Debbie Collins, Eric Collins, Joyce
lins, Laurie Collins, Mike & Deb Collins, Nick Collins, Pierre Collins, Christian Colon, Gerardo Colon, Rafael Colon, Chris Colt, Carol & Roy Comer, Jack Comer, Lisa Comer, Ben Compton, Edward
nway, Allin Conant, Janelle Conaway, Lou Concepcion, Peter Concepcion, Javier Concha, Cora Condiluz, Alberto Conducci, Brian Cone, Conejo Valley Mafca, Bill and Mary Conley, Denise Connee,
& Irene Connnery, Fred Connolly, Celia Conrad, Ted from Constructor, Consul de Arg. en El Salvador, Steve Cont, Alexander Conteras, Steve and Holly Conti, Carlos Contreras, Marcos Contreras,
enia Contreras, Fernando & Kaya Cooaci, Dave Cook, Gretchen Cook, Mary Cook, Richard & Judy Cook, Sean Cook, Sherwood & Linda Cook, Thomas B. Cook, Nick Cookman, Vinny & Dave

Cookson Tara, Herbert Cools, Terry & Jim Coomes, Alyssa Cooper, Beth & Billy Cooper, Jacinta Cooper, Jen Cooper, John Cooper, John H. & Sandy Cooper, Loorne Cooper, Ralph Cooper, Scott &
Cooper, Steve Cooper, Trent and Dee Cooper, B. Trent Cooper & Dee, Al & Carl Coose, Juan Copado, Anne Cope, Autumn Copeland, Harold Copeland, Steven Copeland, Jane Copenhagen, Sharon Co
Judy Coptn, Denny Corathers, Wade Corbett, David Corbin, Louise Corcoran, Esteban Cordero, Maria Cordero, Willie Cordes, Johanna Cordeso Campos, Fabian Cordoba, Dana Cordova, Eduar
katiuska Cordova, Eric Coreao, Mary Coreland, Cora Corella, Coremar, Diane Corey, Ken Corey, Chuck Corgiat, Steve Corgiat, Mike Cormany, Israel Cornejo, Javier Cornejo, Maribel Cornejo, Osv
Cornejo, Luis Cornejo Sanchez, Dave & Jon Cornevale, Judy Cornevale, Fernando Corona, Jorge Corona, Soni y Alez Coronado, Arturo Coronel, Ernesta Coronel, Mecieran Bertie Coronel Chapr
Meredith Corp, Blanca Corrales, Maria Corrales, Felix Correa, Guillermo y Angelica Correa Servin, Manuel Correia, Edward Corriher, James & Billy Corry, Gregorio Corso, Alejandro Cortes, Franc
Cortes, Roberto Cortes & Jeronimo Ramos, Cristina Cortes Cossio, Francisco Cortez, Israle Cortez Israeta, Familia Cortez Villegas, Henry Corvera, Olga Corzantes, Kevin Cose, Dennis Cossio C
Gaston Costa, Jerry Costa, Jorge Costa, Anibal Costanso, Wilu Costello, Kevin Coston, Maxine & Joe Cotler, Bill & Julia Cotnea, Jorge Cotoz, Pia Cottini, Newell Cotton, Peggy Coughin, Sheila Coug
Eric Coulsono, Tim Coulter, Winfield Courrier, Paul Cousand, Charles Cousins, Joan Couts, Raymond Coutu, Greg Covalchuc, Jorge Covarrubias, Malvin Coventon, John & Kayli Cover, John Covey, A
Coviña, Ken Cowan, Dale Cower, Frank Cox, Lee Cox, Meline Cox, Virginia Cox, Mary & Dick Crabtree, Tommy Crabtree, Danny y Chris Craft, P. Craig, Sandecp Craig, Vernie Craig, Sebastian Cram
Chris Crandall, Adrian Crane, Chuck Crane, Laura Cranmer, Cranswicks, Terry Crassley, Larry & Louise Crawford, Marilyn Crawford, Sarah Crepeau, Diego Crescenzi, Judith Crespo, Julio Crespo, Ar
& Joan Cress, Gloria Crest, Alicia Creste, Barry Crews, Brace Crews, Anne Cridler, Colleen & Sam Cripe, Cheri Crippen, Luciana Sosa Cristian Lento, Carlos y Dolores Cristofalo, Charles Critch, Ma
Critelli, Carolyn and Lewis Cromer, Antonio Cromos Ant., Programa Cronica TV, Jeanne Cronon, Gerry Cronquist, Bill Crook, William Crook B.A., Mary Crosby, Peter Crosby, Peter & Bonnie Cro
Robert & Patricia Crosby, Suzi Crosby, Roy Crosier, Andrea y Kevin Cross, Tom & Martha Cross, Dave Cross Grove, Paul Crossman, Jamie Crosson, Karl Croswhite III, Doug Crouch, Desiree Cro
Sarah Crowe, Tony & Robin Crowe, Pat & Dick Crowell, Mary & Colleen Crowley, Rob Crtojenett, Charles & Cristie Crump, Scott & Susan Cruse, Alex Cruz, Carla Cruz, Carla M. Cruz, Catalino C
Cristian Cruz, Edith Cruz, Jose Cruz, Pablo Cruz, Patrick y Malma Cruz, Rodrigo de Santa Cruz, Tomas Cruz, Tommy Cruz, Wendy Cruz, Juanjo Cruz Ruesca, Mr. Bill Crye, Ma. Eugenia y Alvaro Cub
Rodrigo Cubero, Nelson Miguel Cuella, Fausto Cuellar, Juan Cuentacuentos, Leonardo A. Cuesta Mejías, Jose Cuevas, Lourdes Cuevas, Gabriel Cuevas Ramirez, Maria Cuevillas, Catherine Cullen,
& Maroe Culler, Pauida Culver, Shelley Culver, Anne Cummings, Pete & Barb Cummings, William Cunningham, Keith Cuomo, Julie Cupernall, Lorane & Mark Cupples, John Cuprisiw, Gordon C
John Curley, Cindy Curpis, Juan manuel y Jennith Currea Herrera, Rigdon Currie, Stradton Curry, Viviana Curutchet, David Curylo, Fillipo Cusimano, Hector Cusinato, Norberto Cusinato, Lorr
Cuthbertson, Jay Cuthrie, Zup & Jill Czaplieki, Stephanie D, Paquito D' Rivera, Marco D¥Amore, Ines D¥Hoghiam, Susan Dabelsteen, John Dacey, Andres Dacosta, Babetta Daddine, Don & Virg
Daetweiler, Victor Dagnest, Jess Daiger, Cindy Daigle, Andy Dale, Jennifer & Carl Dales, Richard D'Alessandro, Hilde D'Alessio, Marta D'Alessio, Scott & Cheryl Daley, Marie Dalia, Rob Dalin, D
Dalla Libera, Monica Dally, Cami Dalton, Rerid Dalton, Tim & Gail Dalton, Enrique Dalzaso, Dan & Kerry Kubicki, Sharon Duray Dan Wilkerson, Robin Danae Mari, Bob Dance, Shirley & Bob Da
Robert Dandrea, Dennis D'Angelo, Wayne & Mia Danghtridge, Kevin & Yoly Dangle, Boggio Daniel, Bruce Daniel, Scott Swaney Daniel Stone, Mitchell Danielson, Dante y Elizabeth N.C., Edu
Darakchian, Pat Darcey, Bob & Connie Darga, Hector y Welly Darmich, Rick Darr, Kenneth Datts, Scott Daub, Leora Riley Dave, Lou & Sue Dave, Jen Dehoyers Dave Carmevale, Jose David, Mir
David, Ana Ramirez David Hiller, Florence Petock David Orion, Guillermo Esparza David Uribe, David y Vivian, Bethany Davidson, Paul Davidson, Don y Sarah Davidson y Stanley, Scott Davies, Ed
Davila, Luis Davila, Luis y Ayda Davila, Iganacia Davila Bazon, Javier Davila Medina, Bill Davis, Bob Davis, Brandy Davis, Brent Davis, Connie Davis, Dakota Davis, Dakotah Davis, Doug Davis,
Davis, Jamie Davis, Jim Davis, John & Susan Davis, Kellie Oren Davis, Ken Davis, Keneth S. Davis, Lee Davis, Lieroy B. Davis, Normy Davis, Pam and Doug Davis, Priscilla & Ron Davis, Ruth Da
Sinclair Davis, Terry & Marsha Davis, Toni & Kirby Davis, Wendy Davis, Kathy Davis-Urbas, Peggy & Jay Daw, Peter Dawidcit, Rose Dawson, Sonia Day, Tony Day, Antonino y Julieta De Aguiar, K
y Carlos De Anda, James R. De Angelo, Ana De Anzorena, Ma. Luisa de Bruin, Maria Mercedes de Corro, Sandra De Esquina, Alejandro de -Evars, Mike De Felice, Pablo De Francesco, Eduardo Fra
de Franco, Susana de Gonzales, Marlene de Grasse, Jose De Jesus, Harold De Jona, Harry De Jong- NC, Angelica y Francisco de la Barrera, Ricardo De la Fuente, Jorge de la Garza, Juan De La Hoz, K
De la Mora, Santiago de la Peña, Carlos De la Plata, Felipe de la Tejera, Alejandro de la Torre, Olga De la Torre, Ruben De la Torre, Ciro de la Victoria, Manuel de Leon, Nelson De Leon, Raul De L
Walfredo De los Reyes, Juan De los Rios, Gabriela de Luna, Lloyd De Manville, Jose Angel Martinez De Martinez, Nuria de Masis, Kathy & Sal De Mercurio, Jose Carlos De Mier, Jose de Mier Mo
Lorena Ofelia de Monterrey, Galdys De Monteso, Eduardo Monte de Oca Gutierrez, Angel y Enrica De Pedro, Miguel y Carolina De Pedro, Hugo De Port Hope, Bill y Carmen de Puerto Rico, Virgini
Ramos, Regina de Riquer, Gloria y Walter de Rojas, Marcelo De Roy, Daniela Igabela, Graciela, Marisol y Antonio, De Sainz, Peter De Salay, Rodrigo de Santa Cruz, Mary De Santos, Luisa Garci
Serrano, Maria Lourdes De Shippritt, Carlo De Simine, Crisitina De Simone, Guisela Nanne y Richard de Skaggs, John De Sousa, Maria De Sousa/ Pete, Jill de St Jeor, Jon De St. Paer, Tristan y Cor
villa Allende, George de Walder, Marcel Deag, Clyde Deague, Di & Ian Deakin, Anthony Dean, Bill and Lenny Dean, Mike & Helen Dean, Jyce Deas, Ed & Bev DeBacker, Barbara DeBeaord, Ti
Wayne DeBlock, Steve DeBoer, Glenn Debrosky, Osca Decal, Kenneth DeCerce, Frank Decker, Paul Decker, Ruth Decker, Ed Deentino, Mike DeFelice, Juan Deffis, Mary Ann Degonia, Bar
Dehonchamp, Dick Deibert, Mick Deines, Tracy DeJuan, Gerardo del Bosque, Zayda Del Caprio, Angel Del Castillo, Francisco del Carril, Rey Del Corral, M. Del Corro, Miguel del Grosso, Pocho
Mercado Bs as, Isaac e Ismael Del Moral, Manuel Del Moral, Mauricio Del Rio Calderon, Alex Del Risco, Jaime Del Valle, Virginia Del Valle Carazo, Armando Del Vecchio, Francisco Del Vecchio, D
Martha(col), Don y Cristina(col), Hilda(vzla) yAna(arg) y Paul, Juan Dela Ot, Dave Delabar, Patricia and Robert Delabar, Emile & Lise Delage, John Delaney, Art Delaund, Robert & Patricia Delbar, De
Russi, Miguel Delgadillo, Alberto Delgado, Cubano Delgado, Eliu Delgado, Ing. Rafael Delgado, Jairo Delgado, Javier Delgado, Mario y Carla Delgado, Miguel Delgado, Natalia Delgado, Familia Delg
Parker, Frieda Delgado Parker, Andy Delgado Yani, Bob Delgatty, Dante Della Libera, Daniel y Emi Dellaporta, Matt Dellinger, George Delmeh, Paoli Delso y Vanessa, Jerry Delson, Jeanne Delu
Rodrigo DeLuna, Oswaldo Delvalle, George Dely, German Demarchi, Chris Deming, Michael Demyan, Ed Deniko, John Dennis, Matthew Dennison, Terry Denomme, Carlton Densmore, Ed Dentino,
Dentler, J. Depietro, Nestor Deppeler, Margaretha Derasary, Francois y Sandra Deroeux, Blaine Derstine, Don & Donna Deschaine, Diane Deschanel, Eric Desfachelles, Francis Desimone, Ernesto De
Jane Desnoyers, Kevin & Lynn DesRosiers, Don Devilbiss, Bill Devine, David Devine, Miguel Devoto, Colin Dewey, Dick Dewey, Richard Dewey, Bert Deyaert, Jackie & Marcelo Dhers, Pino Di B
Javier Di Carlo, Dianne Di Fabio, Anselmo Di Matteo, Marcelo y Daniela Di Rauso, Donna Di Sante, Richard Diamante, Diario de los Andes, Mendoza, Ma. Eugenia Vargas Diario El Merc
Antofagasta, Antonio Diaz, Cristian Diaz, Ivan Diaz, Jaime Diaz, Jorge Diaz, Julio Diaz, Laura Diaz, Lilia Diaz, Mireya Diaz, Pablo Diaz, Patricio y Luana Diaz, Pedro Diaz, Rodrigo Diaz, Rodrigo y C
Diaz, Sergio Diaz, Victor Diaz, Esteban Díaz, Luis Orna Díaz, María Díaz, Roberto Diaz Anguiano, Rodolfo Diaz Granados, Alfonso & Diaz Infante, Amalia Diaz Roman, Jaime Diaz Torre Llamas,
Diaz Torre Macias, Jan Dich, John Dick, Wayne Dick, John Dickenson, Jack Dickerson, John Dickerson, Bobby & Stacy Dickinson, Janet Dickinson, Rick & Colleen Dickinson, Herve Dickner, H
Dickner, Don & Joyce Dickson, Jose Dico, Connie Diebcove, Arellano Sanchez Diego, Sharon Diehl, John & Pat Diehm, Alfredo Diez, Roberto Diez, Stephen & Mathew Difietro, Hilda Difrieri, Blad
Dig, Paulette Digesare, Don Dignah, Ruben Digrazia, Neol & Ron Dike, Nestor Dileo, Elsbeth Dillon, Margo Dillon Leardim, Michele Dilow, Kevin Dimitroff, Earle & Jean Dimmick, Russ & Joyce
Miguel Dinamarca, Donald Dinnie, Tomas Dionisio, Tim Dionne, Joe Dipietro, Louise Dirats, Maria Dirce Silva, Angela Disante, Donna Disante, Diolien Disenhaus, Donna Disnate, Jim & Pat Dix, Ro
Dixon, Fernando Dizitti, Don Dniggers, Derwin Dobles Castillo, Jerry Docair, Mary Dodson, Murray & Donelda Doepker Annaheim, Sask & Brady, Robert Doering, Steve Doggan, Dennis Doian, To
Amye Dome, Ron Domen, Ed Domery, Manny Domingos, Adrian Dominguez, Claudia Dominguez, Jimena Dominguez, Trini Dominguez, Victor Dominguez, Sonia Domínguez, Lourdes Doming
Campos, Francisco Dominguez G., Angel Dominguez, Joe Domme, Wendy and Don, Peter Donaghub, Eileen Donahoe, Kathleen Donahue, Max Donaldson, Kathy & Ralph Donato, Kangwond Dong M
Hilton & Barbara Donin, Mark & Teresa Donnell, Jim Donnelly, Judy Donnelly, Phil Y Sue Donohne, Clo Donopetry, Herman Donoso, Carl Dooley, Carl Dave Dooley, Laurian Door, Fabian Dora
Victorio Santos Doris, Roger Dorn, Rick Doroeke, Andrew Dorris, Norberto Dos Santos, Estela Y Roberto Dosil, Charles Doss, Jim Doss, Ed Dotson, Priscilla & Jim Dougherty, Dylan Doughty, Dou
Ashlyn Douglas, Don Douglas, Hugh & Maxine Douglas, Jeff Douglas, Joe & Ana Douglas, Paula and Ron Douglas, Greg Douglass, Lew Dove, Joe Dovidio, J. Dow, Peter Dow, Jim Dowgin,
Dowling, Rick & Janet Downey, Jim Dowss, Meaghan Doyle, Dr Grandis, Oscar Dr Mangini, Liliana Drab, Paul Dragavon, Jeremiah Drage, Ernesto Draghi, Elizabeth Draper, Gary Draper, Rick Dra
Gary Drasky, Jimm & Kasey Drath, Drath, Orville Dreashen, Irene Dreher, Nancy Drew, Ed Drexler, Stephen Driver, Ralph Drover y Sharon King, Michael & Laura Drowns, Ron & Beth Droz
Gretchen Drukes, Richard & Charlotte Dryman, Giselle Duarte, Rob Duarte, Beverly Dubie, Lee Dubin, John Dubone, Bob Due, Cornelius Dueck, William Dueck, Chris & Kelly Duepner, Kelly & De
Duffy, Eddy Duggan, Lee Duggan, Slawik & Darla Duggan, Lou y Peg Duke, George & Estrella Dulleck, Starley Dullien, Don Duncan, Howard Duncan, Jerry Duncan, Bob & Nancy Dunfee, Herb Dun
Jack Dunifon, Larry Dunlevy, John & Martha Dunn, Mary Dunn, Royce y Frances Dunn, Susan Dunn, Aj Dunnink Wellandport on, Ken & Stephanie Dunsire, Emily Dunsmore, Gary & Elaine DuPen,
Dupuy, Roberto Dupuy, Jorge Duque Gardoño, Frank Duran, Julian Duran, Juan Durante, Carolina y Nano Duranti, Marcello Duranti, Steve Durham, Chase t Clayton Durttam, Byron Dutcher, Evang
Dutchover, Glyn Dutton, Pia y Guillermo Duval, Jeff Duyek, Gabriela Dveksler, Brian Dwiggins, Donn Dwyer, Aneta Dybel, Bob Dyer, Donald Dyer, To Claude & Dykstra, Bill Dymond, Marlynda D
Jan Dzick, Louise Dzimian, Karrie Eads, John Earl, Cecile Earle, Gordon Earle, John & Joanna East, Anita & Curtis Easter, Anthony Easterwood, Matt Eastling, D. Easton, Steven Eayers, Patricio E
Sally & Billy Eberhart, Jim Eberly, Norma & Roy Eblen, Bob- Mandee- Bobby Eby, Daniel Echegaray, Mariano Echegoyen, Luís Echeverría, Devon Eckert, Cristina Perez Ed Yates, Debra & Jamie E
Paige Kayleigh Tolin, Elizabeth Caetano Eddy Pay, Kevin Edens, Edgar Diaz Q., Michael Edgelow, Nicado Ediciar, Edith Gonzales y Guillermo R.Navarro, Paul Edmond, Chris Edmunds, Dale Edmu
Eduardo y Carlos Ortega, Alexandra Eduardsen, Mr. & Mrs. Edward B. Allen, Carol Edwards, Christina Edwards, Libby Edwards, Patty & Wayne Edwards, Pete Edwards, Joe Edword, Roy Effler,
Efremov, Familia Trujillo Efren y Aydee, Dan Egan, Dennis Egan, Alejandro Egea, Fernando Egea, Mike Egge, George Ehinger, Bob & Kelly Ehlers, Freddy Ehlers, Rick Ehrhart, Pilar Eibeck, D
Eisenhart, Bob & Cherry Ekoos, Alejandro el Chileno, Programa El Garage, Roxana y Jim El Patio, Alvaro El Pibe, Hansy Elena, Carlos & Maria Elena Zubieta, Luis Esteban Torres Elespuru, Kev
Elfrink, Freddy Elhers, Jim Patty Eli Fraley, Rodolfo Eliando, Rosalinda Elias Rincon, Adolfo Elizalde, Gabriel Elizondo, Mayela Alpizar Elizondo, Flora Elizondo Solís, Rodrigo y Nedi Elka, Ray Ell
Diane Elliot, Bette & John Elliott, David Elliott, Diane Elliott, George & Helen Elliott, Harden Elliott, Ken & Chase Elliott, Shirley Elliott, Curtin & Jean Ellis, Gordon Ellis, Jean Ellis, Steve Ellis, T
Ellis, John Ellison, Deb Elsey, Donald E. Elson, Mary Elton, Robert (R.) Elton, Chris Elugel, Dunia Elvir, Tuline ElZorkany, William Embree, Mauris Emeka, Emerson Caetano, Gail Emgblom,
Emhoff, John Emmi, Dan Empey, Dick Emrich, Jorge Endara, Shelden Endes, Alan Endries, Jeanne Enesloge, C. John & Lynn Eng, Mark & Andrea Engbretsen, Jodie Engel, Melissa & Harold Engel, L
Engelgau, Karl Engelk, Fred Engelman, Ken & Janet Engelman, Fred Englert, Dail English, Damien English, Peter English, Alejandro Engstron, Bill Eninger, Enrique Macias y Laura Lavana, Mart
Carlos Enriquez, Edgardo Enriquez Vazquez, Julia Ensley, Connie & Dick Enslie, John Ensslil, Henrietta & Clay Enzminger, Carlos Epp, Donald Erb, Cathy Erickson, Jon Erickson, Shane Erick
Brandon Erikson, George Erikson Pastor, Dan Erisman, Mike y Rita Erland, Alex Ernst, Gene Erricson, Dick y Norma Ertl, Richard Ertl, Stacy y Bernard Ertl, Bruce Erts, Richard Erwin, Richard & C
Erwin, Adriana Escalante, Fernando Escalante Bollo, Roberto Escalarte, Adolfo Escalona, Enrique Escalona, Gerado y Dorca Escalona, Giuseppe Escalona, Kaki Escalona, Nellys Pinto de Escalona,
P. Escamilla, Leonardo Escamilla, Pastor Escamilla, Adolfo Escobar, Alejandra Escobar, David Escobar, Hugo Escobar, Isabela y Francisco Escobar, Israel Escobar, Rodrigo Escobar Perez, Ann Escob
Raul Escolar, Carlos y Vivian Escrig, Boris Eserski, Perry Eshelman, Jun Eslong, Diego España, Julian Español, Agustin & Daniel Esparza, Marlon Rubi Fuentes Esperanza, Horacio Espindola, Edu
Espinosa, Juan Espinosa, Roberto Espinosa, Sur Espinosa, Juan Jose Espinosa Perez, Capitan Fabian Espinosa Rio Frío, Mindy Espinoza, Orlando Espinoza, Ives Esposito, Alvaro esquivel, David Esqu
Felipe Esquivel, Jonatan Esquivel, Mario Esquivel, Allan Esquivel Quiros, David Essex, Marc & Kim Esslinger, Xavier Esteinov, Bryan Estes, Yolanda Esteves, Francisco Estevez, Emilio Estevez Espin
Alex y Maribel Estrada, Luis Estrada, Marcos Estrada, Joel Estrada Zuñiga, Luis Estudillo, Gordon y Addie Etherredge, Micael T. Etling, Ana & Paul & Tomas Etrene, Barbara Eudy, Maria Eugenia, M
Eulin, Marta Euredjian, Michael Evangelista, Deb Evans, Diana Evans, Kent & Rhea Evans, Mary Lou Evans, Pam Evans, Randy Evans, Rochelle Evans, Tim Evans, Bill Evant, Ivan Oscar Vargas Eve
Evergreen, Dl Everhart, Katie Evett, Exolgan, Expomavis, Ermosa Exporrencca, George Eyerman, Guillermo Eyherachar, Edie John y Catherine, Eyler, Guevara Fabian, Araceli Fabila, Carlos Fa
Manuel Fabregas, Marta Fabris, Ruben Fabris, Hernan Facal, Bill Facenda, Kyril Faenov, Bobby Fagge, Ronald & Frances Fagge, Rodrigo Fagundes, Mike Fahey, Mel Falck, Gisele Falcon, Rod Fa
Karen Falkasi, Laura Fallas, Russ & Shane Fallkenberry, Walter Fallos M., Familia Carlino, Horacito Gonzalez Familia Pharr, Familia Valverde Rodriguez, Adam Family, Carlos Maure Family, C
Family, Mufson Family, Rafalski Family, The Condy Family, The Mann Family, Sayer & Karen Fancher, Carmen Fanelli, Jack Fanning, Lou Fargo, Ruth Ann Farhsworth, Mark Farley, Phil Farley,
Farling, Roxanne & Alem Farmer, Roberto Farquharson, Angel Farray, Doug and Barbara Farrington, Doug Crystal & Barb, Farrington, Cathrine Faught, James Faulk, Claudia Faulkner, Ed & Gl
Faulkner, edwin faulkner, Liliana Faure, Stephenia Fauther, Sonia Fawa, James Fawuk, Dan Fay, Don & Carol Fay Petersen, Bill Fayle, Claudio Fazio, Janet Feagin, Leon & Janet Feagin, Aleida F
Edgar Fears, Tito Febo, Joe Federmann, Rachel Fedewa, Hernan Fedorowicz, kevin Fehr, Kurt Fehr, Walter Fehrmann, Kurt Fehz, Eric Feige, Bob & Jeneil Feldes, Curtis Feldmann, Sylvia & Luis Felic
Don Feller, Frank Feller, Don Felts, Larry Felvarg, Lisa Fendley, Ken Fendrick, Alan Lili, Esteban, Sofia y Irene, Fenseca Villalogos, Ulber Ferati, Lynn & Evans Feredinos, Chuck Ferguson, Glenn & L
Ferguson, John Diana & Sara, Ferguson, Katie Ferguson, Yvonne Ferguson, Patty Ferguson Bohnee, Angel Ferioli, Jose Luis y Alejandra Fernadez, Gimenez, Alfredo Fernandez, Annie Fernandez, C
y Mirta Fernandez, Carmen Fernandez, Daniel Fernandez, Donald Fernandez, Francisco Fernandez, Gabriel Fernandez, German Fernandez, Joaquin Fernandez, Johanna Fernandez, Jose Fernandez, Jo

s Fernandez, Maria Ines Fernandez, Mario Fernandez, Mercedes y Gabriel Fernandez, Raimundo Fernandez, Ramiro Fernandez, Raul Fernandez, Reynaldo Fernandez, Roberto Fernandez Alejandro
ıandez Chavarría, Oscar Fernandez Gomez, Arturo Fernandez Hernandez, Emilia y Elisa Fernandez Leon, Carolina y Florencia Fernandez Madero, Familia Fernandez Mena, Juan B. Fernandez
uera, Ricardo Fernandez Schutt, Paola Fernandez y Miguel Hernandez, Alex y Maria Ferrari, Antonio Ferrari, Carlos Ferrari, Louise Ferraro, Nancy Ferraro, Delia Ferrato, Jose Ferreira, Larry & Guay
eira, Bud Ferrell, Jackie Ferrenburg, Rodrigo Ferrer Diana, Horacio Y Gladys Ferreras Dalegre, Nestor Ferrero, Sue Ferrlb, Peggy Ferrin, Mario Ferriz, Mario Antonio Ferriz, Michael Ferro, Roberto
o, Juan Feu, Andrew Feudner, Ray & Linda Fich Miorn, Christi Fieder, Ed Fields, Vicky Fields, Adalberto y Dorian Figueroa, Enrique Figueroa, Vanesa Figueroa, Martin Figura, Sebastian Filho, Trevor
ay, Billy & Janet Finch, Trevor and Jennifer Finch, Liv Fincken- Stan, Robert Finey, George & Dorothy Finkas, Dale Finky, Dave & Freda Finlay, Kelly Finley, John Finn, Don & Krista Finney, Rokana
avanti, Frank & Franca Fiore, Silvia Fiorilo Gomez, John Firth, Bob Fischer, Luciano Fischer, Paul Fischer, Kathy and George Fischer Jr., Bill Fisher, Derrick Fisher, Don Fisher, Tim Fisher, Larry
e, Gary Fitterman, Claire Fitygandel, Kim Fitzgerald, David & Peggy Fitzpatrick, Libby & Dave Fitzpatuir, Stephanie Fjeld, Loren Flagg, Lori & Kandon Flaherty, John Flannery, Ray Flasherty,
hael Flatterty, Jose Fleitas, John Fleming, Ryan Fleming, Conrad Fletcher, Flia Tapia Delgado, Jack Flora, Rosario y Alejandra Flore, Alcides Flores, Antonia Flores, Cesar Flores, Eduardo & Irma
es, Freddler Flores, Guillermo y Ana Flores, Heather Flores, Jose Flores, Juan Flores, Juaquin Flores, Rolando Flores, Luis Flores Dulce, Adrian FLores Gonzalez, Lorena Flores H., Asoc. de Autos
guos de Nuevo Laredo Flores Medina, Miguel y Aracelli Flores Medina, Antonio Flores Ortiz, Papo Florez, Catarino Floriano, Charles Floyd, Darrel Floyd, Nick Flynn, Patti Flynn, John Flynt, Steve
ıeringham, Daniel Foden, Tom Foden, Lerland & Mary Fogwell, Gerardo Caruso Foia, Foia, Alvin H. Foleen, E. Foley, Jimmie Folsom, Vic & Donna Fondy, Katharine Fong, Nani Fonkatz, Ricardo
seca, Minor Fonseca Sepulveda, Jose Fontes, Manuel Fontes, Javier e Irma Fonticoba, Louis Foo, Barbara Foote, Ben Forbes, Chris Forbes, Gart Forbes, Gordon Forbes, Sheila Ford, Patricia Foreman,
n Forest, Jason Forgit, Mark Forgnone, Dan Forney, Liz Forrer, Alan Forrest, Roy Forrest, Steve Forrest, Lloyd Forry, Erin Forsell, Mike Forster, Ed & Gina Forstner, Richard and Debbie Forsyth, Anahi
e, Fabian Forte, Andar Fortin, Luis Fortte, Familia Fosado, Ross & Jill Fosberg, Gary & Shawnae Fossum, Bill Foster, J. Foster, Keith & Marlene Foster, Kevin Foster, Mike Foster, Riley Foster, Rodney
onna Foster, Susan & Kevin Foster, Wayne Foster, Jared Fotsch, Rusty Fotsch, John & Susan Fouse, Andy Fowan, Curtis & Joyce Fowler, Dave & Joanie Fowler, Lynn Fowler, Milton Fowler, Scott
ler, Lisa Fox, Mary & Jane Fox, Marcelo Frabolini, Pablo y Lucas Fraire, Suzanne France, Ronald Frances, Pablo de Francesco, Jeff Francis, Chuck Franco, Max & Lynette Franco, Hughlene & Bill
k, Pun & Susan Frank, Ron Frank, Thomas Frank, Annette Jackques Frank Weingartner, Lisa & Robbie Frankel, Wally Franklin, Bonnie Franko, Alberto Fraschini, Conie Fraser, Robert Fraser, Jane &
ert Fraser PTE deblumbdt, Lexia Frasher, Laurence & Suzy Frauman, Frazer Farm Equipment Co., Blake Frazier, Christa Frazier, Colin Frederikson, Emily Fredrix, Jeanne Freed, Barbara Freeman,
ie & Carol Freeman, Fred & Suzanne Freeman, Hannah Freeman, Josepph Freeman, Tojj Freeman, Richard Fregonese, Erich Freimuth Jr., Maria del Carmen Freire, Dick Freisinger, Harold E. French,
renchy, Patricia y Alejandro Fretes, Monserrat Freyre, Louis & Joan Fricke, Barry Fricks, Judy Fridley, Fran & Ken Friesen, Jay Friesen, Mary Friesen, Carole Henmi & Frigstad, John & Gail Frisbie,
ela Frisella, Alastair Frizzell, Mike Froatus, Frog, Regis Frola, Dave Frost, Amelia Fuentes, Angelica Fuentes, Edgardo y Gaby Fuentes, Lorena Fuentes, Luis San Martin Fuentes, Jose Fuentes Salinas,
& Lynn Fuerst, Sergio Fufnifs, Daniel Fuhr, Matt Fuhrmann, Susan Fulcher, Bruce Fulton, Doug Fultz, Tim Fultz, Fundador de Asoc. de Autos Antiguos de San Luis de Potosi, Eric Funes, Freddy
es, Jose Funes, Roberto Funes, Ricardo Funes Aguero, Mike & Christy Funk, Clem Furlong, Rudy G., Tom & Betty Gabele, Jose Gablo Farias, Rick Dana & Payton, Gaches, Rodrigo Gaete-Chile, Chris
z, Marvin Gage, Bernard Gagne, Kelly Gagne, Penney Gagne, Phil Gagnon, Dick Gailagher, Edixa Gaitan, Wandolin Gaiten, Rose Galacz Weir, Isabel & Jaime Galarraga, Denise Galbraith, Jill
raith, Victor Galdames, Gale & Clyde, Dave Galeone, Hector E. Castillo Galera, Rafael Galeth, Jose Galicia, Victor Galicia Gonzalez, Ruben Galicia Martinez, Edgardo Galimberti, Agustin Galina,
ch Gall, Rene Galland, Doris Gallano, Willy Galli, Arnold Gallimore, Rick Gallimore, Rick Gallion, Daniel Gallo, Ethan Gallo, Frank & Bobbie Gallo, Carolyn Galloway, Dale- Mary & Senz Galloway,
ert Galloway, Kathy Gallup, Jon Galt, Kennya Galvez, Rafael Galvez, Roberto Galvez, Jann Gam, Jimmy Gerardo Gambea, James Gamber, Kat & Rob Gambill, Mike & Cindy Gamble, Luis Gamboa,
Gambs, Gary Gamel, Diana Gamiño, Ofelia y Wilson Gammido, Phil & Polly Gammons, Tarz Gamule, Isidoro Bajo Gancedo, Mike & Diane Gandy, Sharon Ganger, Conrad Gann, Mary Lou Ganop,
r Gantt, Ningjing Gao, Dustin Gape, Claudio Garach, Dana Garber, Jorge Garces, Alejandra Garcia, Alfredo Garcia, Arnold Garcia, Benjamin Garcia, Elsa y Javier Garcia, Francisco Garcia, Frank
cia, Guillermo Garcia, Gustavo Garcia, Hector Garcia, Horacio y Berta Garcia, J. Garcia, Joe Garcia, Jorge y Mirta Garcia, Jose A. Garcia, Julio y Lucy Garcia, Kristin & Raul Garcia, Luis Garcia, Maria
cia, Mario Garcia, Martin y Patricia Garcia, Mel Garcia, Robert Garcia, Ruben Garcia, Rudy Garcia, Samuel Garcia, Sharon Garcia, Guillermo García, Isabel Garcia (peruana), Miguel Garcia Gonzalez,
na Garcia Hernandez, Javier Garcia Lascurain, Santiago Garcia Lascurain, Fernando Garcia Limon, Manuel Garcia M., Edsel Garcia Martinez, Rodrigo Garcia Navarro, Vanesa y Sergio Garcia
nelas, Eduardo Garcia Silva, Mirian Garcia Perez, Miguel Garcia Torres, Alfredo Garcia Valdez, Luis Garcia Villaseñor, Santiago y Ma. Teresa Garcia-Lascurain Leon, Laura Garcia-Lopez, Graciel de
ez, Bob Gardinier, Bill Gardner, Cassandra Gardner, Leonard Gardner, Marshall Gardner, Steve & Roger gardner, Ernesto Gardon, David Garduño Valdes, Carlos Garegnani, Francisco Garela, Mirta
baldi, Rolando y Ana Garita, Pauline & Ted Garland, Paul Garley, Don Garlson, Eduardo Garmendia, Sue Garner, Bruce Garrett, Bruce Garrett, Jack & Nancy Garrett, Armando y Sofia Garricho, Ofelia
ilson Garrido, Santiago Garrido Valdeon, Xavier Garrion, Shannon Garris, Mark Garrison, Douglas Garthwaite, Fay Garvey & Linda Baxter, Bob Garvin, Jose Garza, Luis Garza, Mario Garza, Miguel
cilia Garza, Miriam Garza, Raul H. Garza, Tonatiuh Garza Delgado, Miguel Garza Hoth, Ezequiel Garzon, Charly Gascich, Scott & Mary Gast, Barbara Ines Gastell, Diego Gatabria, Alvaro Gatgens,
cedes Gatica-Canton, John & Thea Gaudette, Paulita Gaudino, Carmen Gaugler, Janice Gauldin, Nelly Gauna, Dany Gauthier, Wanda Gautier, Dana Gavie, Vesna Gavrilovic, Ray Gay, Ernesto Gaytan,
rio Gaytan, Sarita Geddes, Sarita y Henry Geddes, Wim Geerts, Bill Geierman, Barbara Geisler, Neva Geisler, George & Ann Geist, Larry Geist, Mariela Gelves, Alyssa Gendron, Rick Gentilo, Gordon
try, Howard & Marilyn Gentry, Georgia Geoblis, Greg & Amy George, Kelly George, Maria Hicks George, Mary George, Frances M. Gipps Gerard Fyap-Gipps, Carlos Gerbaudo, Bob German, Cristina
nosen, Dan Gernatt Jr., Steve Gerst, Jose Gerstl, Richard Gervais, Victor Gerwin, Bob & Ron Gestler, Monica Getta, Ruby Gette, Silvia Gette de Ceballos, Blaine A. Ghan, Lina Ghbeish, Gary Gi
nes, Daniel Giacometo, Carlos Giangrasso, Rodolfo Giangrasso, Guillermo Giannattasio, Marcos Giannoth, Bob & Dory Gibbs, Bruce Gibby, Don & Virginia Gibson, Mystic Gifts, Gilles Giguere,
es GiguÈre, gih gih, Amado Gil, Amalia Gil, Carlos Gil, Jose Gil, Lorenzo Gil, Mauricio Gil, Veronica y Carlos Gil, Pedrito y Carlitos Gil Davila, Gustavo y Marta Gil de Sagastizabal, Alejandro Gil
dez, Larry & Linda Gilberston, Lois & Terry Gilbert, Paul & Jackie Gilbert, Marilou Gilbert Roffi, Nicole Giles, Doug Gill, Jack Gill, Roger O. Gill, Jeff & Nancy Gillentines, Tim Giller, Steve Gilles,
ilia Gillespie, Graham Gillespie, Wayne Gilley, Sam Gillie, Shaun Gillies, Erica Gilligan, Bob Gillihan, Barry Gillispie, Jim Gilmartin, Deborah Gilmer, Cristine Gilmore, Joaquin Gilmuys Medina,
othy Gilroy, Adrian Gimenez, Alejandra Gimenez, Hugo Gimenez, Idalia Gimenez, María Gimenez, Mario Gimenez, Susana Gimenez, Sergio Gindel, Mark Ginnard, Phil Ginsber, Lucas Giolrent, Peter
mousis, Tony Giorno, Erick Giovanny Pimentel Portillo, Paul Girard, Giovanni y Giovanna Girardi, The Ewert Girls, Oscar Giron, Dan Katz Giselle Foss, David Gish, Myrtle Gislason, Austin Gittens,
e Giuliano, Gene & Jo Giuliano, Florencia Giusti, Satn y Steven Gjurich, Georgina Glad, Michael Gladfskor, Colleen Glastetter, Ellen Glauert, Bob Gleason, Edie Gleason, Mike Gleeson, Paul &
my Glendinning, Cliff Glenn, Ricardo Glez, Fernando Glickman, Victor Glidden jr., Debbie Glosays, Brad Glover, Debbie Glover, Daniel Gochi, George Goci, Clark Godfrey, Dana Godfrey, Martin
inez, Fabiana Godoy, Guillermo Godoy, Jenny & John Godprey, Allan & Mary Goellner, Harvey Goho, Juan Goin, Alejandra y Arturo Golato, Hernan Goldaracena, Judy & Ralph Goldbang, Art
dbery, Mark Golden, Daniel Goldenberg, Ed Wertz & Nancy Goldfinch, Fernando Goldschmidt, Tomas Goldsmith, Zoe Goldstein, Sergio Golfo, Barbara Gollert & Joel, Rachel Abrahams, Mel
nzalves- Delaney, Alex Golubovich, Horacio Gomenzaro, Alejandro Gomez, Alfonso Gomez, Alfredo Gomez, Antonio Gomez, Camilo Gomez, Darwin Gomez, Edgar Gomez, Eduardo y Polly Gomez,
Gomez, Fernando Gomez, Florentino Gomez, Gustavo Gomez, Humberto Gomez, Jesse Gomez, Jesus Gomez, Juan Gomez, Juan & Elia Gomez, Kelly & David Gomez, Luis Gomez, Luis F. Gomez,
Gomez, Manolo Gomez, Margarita Gomez, Maria Gomez, Marisa Gomez, Miguel Gomez, Rocio Gomez, Alicia Gomez, Raúl Gomez, Camilo Gomez (colombiano), Gustavo Gomez D., Daniel Gomez
Vegga, Juan Carlos Gomez Durañona, Adrian Gomez G., Ricardo Gomez Jaime, Jeseria Gomez Jerez, Monica Gomez Nava, Javier Gonazalez Diaz, Martha Gondra, Ruben Gongora, Felipe Gonzales,
nel Gonzales, Oscar Gonzales, Robin Gonzales, Wendy & Drew Gonzales, Milagros Gonzáles, David Gonzáles H., Marco Gonzales Vargas, Aaron Gonzalez, Adriana Gonzalez, Alberto y Cesar
zalez, Amalie Gonzalez, Arnovia Gonzalez, Barbara y Pablo Gonzalez, Cacho y Ana Maria Gonzalez, Carlos Gonzalez, Cesar y Margarita Gonzalez, Cinthia Karim, Ana Maria y Cacho, Gonzalez,
a Gonzalez, Danny Gonzalez, David Gonzalez, Dem Lucio Gonzalez, Dolores y Raul Gonzalez, Edgar Gonzalez, Erick Gonzalez, Ernesto Gonzalez, Gabriela y Jose de Jesus Gonzalez, German
zalez, Harold & Helena Gonzalez, Hipolito Gonzalez, Javier Gonzalez, Jesus Gonzalez, Jose Luis Fuentes Gonzalez, Lucky y Oscar Gonzalez, Luis Gonzalez, Luis F. Gonzalez, Manuel Gonzalez, Mari
zalez, Max Gonzalez, Miguel Gonzalez, Ony Gonzalez, Pablo Gonzalez, Pedro Gonzalez, Rebeca Gonzalez, Ricardo Gonzalez, Roberto Gonzalez, Rodolfo Gonzalez, Ruben Gonzalez, Ruth Gonzalez,
iago Gonzalez, Victor Gonzalez, Amber Gonzalez & Elisa Roybal, Federico Gonzalez Alvarez, Alejandro Gonzalez Amaya, Ricardo Aaron Gonzalez Carreon, Veronica Gonzalez Chavez, Jose Antonio
zalez Dias, Antonio y Andres Gonzalez Gross, Guicha Gonzalez Hernandez, Margarita Gonzalez Icaza, Alfredo & Anita Gonzalez Luna, Pedro Gonzalez Mejia, German Gonzalez Mena, Astolfo
zalez Murffeta, Edwin Gonzalez Pacheco, Alejandro Gonzalez Padilla, Nidia Gonzalez R., Carlos Gonzalez Vera, Felix Gonzalos, Hugo Goñi, Jessica Good, Paul & Mary Ann Good, Josephine Goodin,
iam Goodin, Betty & Carl Goodman, Craig & Suzanne Goodrich, Steve Goodwin, Brian & Verra Goral, Hector Gordils, Lalo y Luis Javier Gordoa Lopez, Clifton Gordon, Dan Gordon, Don Gordon,
Gordon, Ernest Gordon, Pedro Gordon, Ron Gordon, William A. Gordon, Carolyn Gorin, Vince Gorman, John Gorosh, Carlos Gorosito, Phyllis Gosnell, Larry & Su Gosney, Dave Goss, Waynne
sett & Jerry, Harry Gould, J.Eric Gould, Jon Gould, June Gould, Anita & Hank Gowdy, William & Roberta Gowl, George Goy, Carlo y Estela Goyano, Nicolas Goycoolea Calezon, Familia Goyenechea,
Graaf, Judith Grabel, Guadalupe Graciela, Mark Graczyk, Tim Grady, Evelyn Graetz, Ana Graf, Barbara Graff, Jerry Grag, Andy Graham, Barbara Graham, Betsy & Jim Graham, Bill and Waldie
ham, Carol Lehm Kuhl Graham, David B. Graham, Farrell Graham, John y Linda Graham, Nicole Graham, Paige Graham, Terry y judi Graham, Z. Daniel Graham, Marcelo Gramier, Roberto Grana,
n Grana, Elias Granadeño Mejia, Rodrigo Granados, Jorge Granados Zúñiga, Roberto Granda, Susana Grane, Jacobo Granizo, Conrad Grann, Hugh Grant, James Grant, Roberto Graña, Karen Grass,
Sceone Grasse, Stephen Grassi, Mike Grasso, Leonard Grau, Maurice & Marie Graves, Carol Gray, Debbie & Scott Gray, Frank Gray, Geoff Gray, Jim Gray, John & Cathy Gray, Marty & Kent Gray,
e Gray, Mike & Krystle Gray, John Grayam, Gino Graziani, Tina Greaser, Susan y Carlos Grecco, Anita Greco, Penni Greco, John & Linda Gredier, Alison Green, David Green, John R. Green, Larry
en, Oliver Green, Sam Green, Tom & Edna Green, Allan J. Greenberg, Susan Greenberg, Terry Y Sue Greene, Harry & Mary Greenhough, Barry Greenstein, David Greenwald, Buz Greenwood, Dave
llen Greenwood, Doug and Elaine Greer, Marty Greer, Luis Fernando Grefa Tanguila, Julie Gregoric, Jim & Carol Gregory, Ruhlin Gregory, Viviane Gregory, Viviane & Eric Gregory, Paul Gregson,
Grein, Ron & Tona Greisen, Roberto Gremler, Ricardo Grempel, Sal Grenet, Aurelia Gresillon, Ravi Gretchen Gurujal, Al Gretzinger, Alimin Greva, Charles Grewe, Larry Gribble, Jim & Jill Griebel,
seppe Grieco, Charles C. Grier, Stephanie Griffin, Lori Griffith, Greg & Adrienne Grigorian, Fernando Grillo, Decio Grilo, Andrew Y Yolanda Grimm, Bernui Grinastaff, Miguel Grippa, James y Ruth
zell, Jim Grizzell, Harvey Grodjesk, Riki Grohmann, Nathan & Kelly Gromen, Roger Grondin, Sharon Groomer, Jim & Marilyn Groover, Dorle Gross, Peter Gross, Bernd Grote, Karyn Avam &
alina, Grove, Jill & Gaylen Grover, Cliff Grube, Richard & Andrey Gruhl, Emma Grundler, Mecanico Guadalupe, Luis Moreno y Guadalupe Aguayo, Tello Arellano Sanbaña Guadalupe Arias Salazar,
rado Guajardo, Daniel Guajardo, Daniel Gualtiai, Jimena Guardia, Ra´l Guastawino, Mario Guazzelli, Jaime y Mauricio Guell, Lawroncey Guerin, Eduardo Guerra, Elsa y Angel Guerra, Maria Guerra,
io Chiriqui Guerra, Ramon Guerra, Elsa Elia, Carmen, Angel, Guerra Leon, Luis Guerramo, Edgar y Rafael Guerrero, Isaura Guerrero, Jose Guerrero, Luis Guerrero, Miguel Guerrero, Dayanira
rrero Briceño, Eduardo Guerrero C., Edwins Guerrica, Joyce Guest, German Guevara, Jose Guevara, Juan Guevara, Carlos Guevara Jr., Ariel Guido, Irene y Hector Guijarro, Sergio Guillen, Claudia
ller, Mario Guillermo, Hector y Jackeline Guiral, Jaime Guiraldo, Jess Guislain, Serge & Jessamine Guislain, Adrian y Karina Gula, Wes Guldemond, Gulf Coast AACA, Tom Gullickson, Choi Gum,
Gun, John Gunnill, Wayne Gunst, Victor Gunther, Joe Gunyan, Joseph Gunyan, Joe Gurewsky, Larry Gurkan, Frank Guseman, Scott & Lisa Gussett, Karolin Gustavsson, Andrea Gutauskas, Dawn &
ica Guthrie, Ran Guthrie, Katherine Guthys, Angel Gutierrez, Armando Gutierrez, Claudio Gutierrez, Eivar Gutierrez, Gisella Gutierrez, Gustavo Gutierrez, Jose Gutierrez, Juan Gutierrez, Juan Carlos
errez, Luis & Marlene Gutierrez, Mario Gutierrez, Rodrigo Gutierrez, Tito Gutierrez, Violeta Gutierrez, Alejandro Gutierrez Cervantes, Marisol Gutierrez Cruz, Luis Gutierrez Viloria, Marla Guttmano,
Guy, Sean Guy, Carlos Guzman, Daniel Cordobes Guzman, Hector Guzman, Jesus Guzman, Mauricio German, Juan Alberto, Guzman, Rita Guzman, Haiza Guzman Banilla, Ronald Guzman Chavez,
German Guzman Franco, Enrique Guzman Garcia, Enrique Guzman Garcia, Sylvia Guzman Hidalgo, Agustin Guzman Reyes, Diane Gwin, Brian & Della Haas, Jeff Haas, Scott & Carrie Haas, Steve
ay, Walter & Ann Haberski, Dorothy Habert, Phil Habowski, Keith Hacker, Cecil Hackney, Gary & Mary Haff, Christiane Haffner, Shirley Hage, Dick Hagen, Rick Hagen, Jean Hager, R. W. Hager,
& Gina Hagger, joseph Hagman, Jerry & Mary Ann Hagnie, Kenneth S. Hahn, Georgia Haiberger, Joan Haid, Gottfried Haider, Beth Haidle, John Haigler, Bob & Sandy Hains, TTomas Hakansson,
e & Terry Halbleib, Don Haldane, Peggy & Jim Halderman, Jim Haley, Martina & Alan Halfenger, Aaron Hall, Brian Hall, C.J. Hall, Charles & Frances Hall, Daniel & Beth Ann Hall, Frank Hall, Norm
, Ren Hallenbeek Alive, Elie Haller, Stu Halll, Bryon & Marylou Hallman, Wil Hallman, Jim Hallmark, Jan Hallock, Mark Halpern, Lloyd Halsey, Lloyds Halsey, Silvian Halter, Andrea Hambach,
aldine Hamilton, Gerardo Hamilton, Jim Hamilton, Nancy Hamilton, Scott Hamilton, Jack Hamlett, Stan Jo & Ann, Hamm, Andy & Abby Hammond, Chris Hammond, Frederick Hammond, Jody
nmond, Jake Hammons, Larry Hammov, Mel Hamp, Bill Hampton, Jana Hampton, Norman Hampton, Vincent Hamrick, Arden Hander (Ann), Bob & Leah Handley, Herb Handley, Jeff & Tammy
ey, Ralph Haney, Stacy Hangemanle, The Hankinson's, Graciela y Peter Hanley, Mike Hanley, Frederick P. Hanmond, Bernie & Helen Hann, Victor Hanna, Mary Hannigan, Lynann Hanover, Bob
sberger, Larry Hanse, Cary Hansel, Frederick Hansen, Howard & Barb Hansen, Joe & Susan Hansen, J. Hanson, Toia Hanson, Scott Hansson, Rich & Heidi Harbaugh, Ben and Nancy Hardeman, Ginger

Hardeman, Dennis Hardie, Larry Hardiman, Charlie Hardin, Kelly Harding, Debbie Hardwick, Calvin Hardy, Cathy Hare, Peter Hare (Mary Ann), Fred Harford, Judith Hargreaves, Sandy Hargy, I
Hariffman, Sunshine Harion, Sarah y Tim Harless, Barbara Harlslein, Don Harmon, Glen Harmon (Beverly), Willie Harms, Sandy Harne, Jim Harnett, Paul Harpe, Kevin Harper, Wayne Harper, Dave H
John y Karea Harrill, John & Mary Harrington, Les & Connie Harrington, Harry Harrinrton, Bill Harris, Fred and Peg Harris, Lynn & Darlene Harris, Robert Harris, Verry Harris, Clynn Harrisc,
Harrison, Gerry Harrison, Hank Harrison, Steve Harrison, Peggy Harsch, Peggy Harsch, Judy Harshberger, Marco Harster, Lusi hart, Richard Hartel, Jim Harth, Susan & Joe Hartless, Paul & Sue Hartm
Rich Hartman, Steve HartSell, Mark Hash, Tom Haskins, Jeremy Hass, Marisol & Cristian, Hassen, Silvina Hassoun, Ruth Hastlnes, Ann Hatch, John Haubecker, Marian & Kent Haug, Dave Haug
Cyndy Ryck, Michel, Haugh, John Hauler, Jerry Haulett, Bill Haupert, John Hauselet, C.J. Hauser, John Alexander Hauser II, Ro Hauus, Haward and Jannet, David Hawick, Camerino & Kathleen Hawi
Nm. L. Hawken, Del Hawkins, Gordon Hawkins, Jerry Hawkins, Lee Hawkins, John & Joann Hawks, Bill Hay, Clifford C. Hay, Kelly Hay, Terry Hayden, Jonathan Hayder, James & Dorothy Hayes, Jo
Hayes, Nancy Hayes, Jeff & Joanna Haynes, Ray Haynes, Donna & Russ Haytx, Lisa Hayward, Allen Haywood, Walton Haywood, Jan Hazen, Ahmed Hazim, Richard Hazzard, Adriana Hdez, Header
Ben, Charles Headrick, Susan Healey, John Healy, Maurice Healy, David Heap, Ray Hearn, Bill Heath, James Heath, Jenny & Martin Heath, Roberta and Jim Heath, Jim Heazlett, CLaudio Hectorqu
Caleb Hedberg, Dan Heddon, Dennis & Carol Hedler, James Hedlund, Glenn Hege, Dave Hegeberg, Don Heiberg, Laurie Heifetz, John Heilig, Steve Heimel, Joe Hein, Sandy & Dennis Hein, James Hei
Sebastian y Mariana Helbig, Vicky & Harry Helfand, Terry & Stephanie Hellickson, Bob Hellstrom, Warren Helm, Wilbar Helm, Arthur Helmuth, Edna Helyer, Charles M. Helzberg, Christine Helzer, P
Hemken, Godfrey Hemmerde Castaños, Murray and Jean Hems, Micky Henderson, R. J. (Jim) Henderson, Rex & Diane Henderson, Bear Hendricks, Rudy Hendricks, Roy Hendrickson, Marie
Hendriks, Melissa Hendriscks, R. Allen Hendrix, George Henke, Catherine Henkels, Richard Henmi, John Hennerich Denver, Don Hennesey, Terry Hennessey, Michael Henning, Jim Y Pat Henrie, N
Topeka KS, Alicia, Henrikson, John & Kristina Henry, Ken Henry, Paul & Carol Henry, Grandson- Kasey Hensley, Chuck Hentz, Lorne Hepting, Mike Hercog, Orlando Hercules, Michael Herd
Fernando Heredia, Layla Heredia Mendoza, Ralph Herendeen, Ed Herman, Francisco Herman, Gaylord Herman, Jeremy & Nichole Hermann, Rev. Motor Sport Hernan Carazo, Agustin Hernan
Gutierrez Hernandez, Alba Hernandez, Alfredo Hernandez, Allan Hernandez, Anabella Hernandez, Analucia Hernandez, Donaciano Hernandez, Edemir Hernandez, Ericelda Hernandez, Euge
Hernandez, Fernando Hernandez, Gabriela Hernandez, Joel Hernandez, Jose Hernandez, Luis Hernandez, Manuel Hernandez, Mauricio Hernandez, Maximo Hernandez, Miguel Hernandez, Nic
Hernandez, Olinda y David Hernandez, Romulo Hernandez, Saul Hernandez, Victor Julian y Barbarita Hernandez, Yolani Hernandez, Zore Hernandez, Agustin Hernandez Gutierrez, Rafael Hernan
Juarez, Pepe Hernandez Montes, Liz Hernandez Ochoa, Javier Hernandez Pliego, Mariela Hernandez Ramirez, Carlos Hernandez Ramos, Rodrigo Hernandez Teran, Martin Hernandez Torres, Je
Hernandez. B, Alejandra Herren, Alersey Herrera, Carlos y Parisina Herrera, Hugo Herrera, Juan Herrera, Mario Herrera, Mario Herrera, Rick & Evie Herrera, Roger Herrera, Stella Herrera, Victor y N
Herrera, Ximena Herrera, Alberto Herrera Moreno, Oscar Herrera Novoa, Luis Herrerias, Patty Herrick, Jackie Herring, Dirk Herrmann, Xenon Herrmann, Darlene Hershberger, Wayne & Marcy Hersh
Ralph & Janice Herstine, Elizabeth Hess, Ken & Nancy Hess, Peter Hess, George Hesser, Karen and Ray Heuvel, Ray and Karen Heuvel, Georgina Hewes, Brenda Hewitt, Loren Hewitt, Jack Hiatt, T
Hickman, Bob Hicks, Maria Hicks, Peggy & David Hicks, Carmen Hidalgo Rivero, Todd Hiester, Rafael Higareda, Anastasia Higgins, Loretta Higgins, Tebra Higgins, Kay & Bill Higgs, Wordrow Hi
Felipe y Andres Higuera, Mary Hildenbrand, Karen & David Hilder, Mel Hilgenberg, Brett & Emily Hill, C. Larry Hill, Daniel Hill, Donnie Hill, Doug Hill, Duncan Hill, Jeff Hill, Johnny & Kathy H
Ken Hill, Larry Hill, Linda Hill, Nancy & John Hill, Nate Hill, Stephanie Hill, Wes Hill, Zack Hill, Clif & Deborah Hilliamson, Stan Hillis, David & Charlotte Hillman, Alex Hills, Bill Hills, Jimmy H
Mary Hilowitc, Xaxva Hindl, Al & Vicki Hinds, Don Hines, Jerry Hines, Ray Hinnant, Sherry Hinnant, Santiago Hinojosa, Rogelio Hinojosoda, Jim Hinson, Margaret Hintz, John & Janie Hipps, Rich
Hipwood, Jose & Elisa Hirales, Henry & Alice Hiraza, Paul Hirschler, Jody Hite, Kevin Hitzges, Lorin Hixssen, Wendy & Owen Hnatiuk, David Hochhalter, Fred Hodgeh, Mary Hodger, Craig & Del
Hodges, Donna & Bob Hodgman, Fred & Sandy Hodgow, Cinda Hodson (hija de Dick), Rick Hoehn, Stan Hoekstra, Heike Hoendgesberg, Ray & Ella Hoerning, Fram Hofer, Carl & Laureen Hoffm
Chuck Hoffman, Amy & Spencer Hoffmann, Kenneth Hogan, Michelle & Sean Hogan, Patrick & Dorothy Hogan, Jessi and Linda Hoggard, Lane Hoggson, Gary Holbrook, Joann Holcomb, Scott & I
Holcomb, Jud Holcombe, Ken Holden, Teresa Holem, Roger Holgnin, Hans & Lidia Holl, Bill Holland, Greg & Jody Holland, Ky Holland, Laura Holland, Ralph Holland Jr., Jerry Hollenbaugh, Je
Holler, Charlie Holliday, Merydie Hollingworth, Michael Holloran, Sleepy Hollow, Doyle Holloway, Larry Holmberg, Alvaro Holmes, Carl Holmes, E. Thomas & Nancy J. Holmes, Sean Holmes, Anth
Holowsko, Ken Holroyd, Bev & Becky Holst, Rob & Karen Holt, Wayne & Beverly Holt, Don Holton, The Holts, Brian Holtzhafer, Ted & Linda Holz, Ted & Linda Holz, Mark y Sharon Holzband, Ke
Honeycutt, George Honke, Robin Hood, Steve & Kathleen Hoogland, Lyn & Becky Hook, Diann & Robert Hoops, Tom Hoosier, Coryd Hoover, Bob & Barb Hope Spishak, Ann & Bill Hopkins, Chri
Hopkins, David Hopkins, Debra Frank, Tyler / Ashley, Hopkins, David Hoppe, Norb Hoppe, Tedd Hoppin, Donald Hopson, Stephanie Horine, Clara Hormaeche, Gary Van Horn, Lee Horn, Don Ho
Kyle & Toby Horne, Tom Horner, Warren Horowitz, David Horsford, Robert & Yoko Horsting, Denna Horton, Mario Horvilleur, Cleen Hoselton, Grant Hosfore, Clay Hoskins, Mauhion Hostetlen, El
& Esta Hostetter, George Hotton, Kyle Houghton, Martha Houle, Rich Houle Funstyx, Bob & Lenore Houston, Cliff Howard, Dan Howard, George & Mary Howard, Ron-Linda Howard, Sonny How
Beverly and Dick Howe, Dick Howe, Richard A. Howe, Ashley Howell, Dick y Linda Howell, Earle Y Carlo Howell, Glenn Howell, Joann & Doug Howell, Joanne y Doug Howell, Linda and Dick How
Richard & Linda Howell, George & Helen Howells, F. Howes, Linda Howes, Katie Howlay, Zoiro Hoyos, Owen Hoyt, Joanne Hoyward, Juan Hoz, Bill Hozheimer, Len Hrechka, Lewis Hrivmak, Wa
Hrper, Dannis Hruska, Chen Lien-,Hsing, Antonio HuaiQuivil, Dave & Christine Hubany, Stephen Hubbard, Steve Hubbard, Sharon Huber, Fred Hubler, Stephen Huckstep, Cliff Hudgins, Karl Hudin, C
Hudson, Erin Hudson, Ivette & Juan Manuel Huerta, Roberto Huerta, Leonor Desi y Roberto, Huespe, Tamuny Huffer, Sam & Pat Huffine, Gordon Hugg, Marguereite T. Huggins, Ron & Mary Hugh
Jennifer Hughes, Lori & Alex Hughes, O.D. Hughes, Richard Hughes, Sherrie & James Hughes, Tisha & Jeff Hughes, Tom Hughes, Javier Huizav, David Hulier, Jane Hull, Pat Hullenbeck, John Hullow
Scott Hulse, Traay Hulse, Patricia Trueba Humberto Jauregui, David Hume, Lisa Humphriers, Brenda Humphries, Ian Hunneybell, Robert Hunsicker Sr., Dane & Judy Hunt, Jimmy Hunt, John Hunt, Ja
Hunter, Trun Hunter, Tom Huntington, Sam Hurley, Steve Hurley, Luke & Wendy Hurlimann, Juan Cruz Hurtado, Naomi Hurtado, Gino Hurtado Castellanos, Jorgen Hurtig, Celine y William Husc
Maresa & Marvin Huske, Husson, Fred Huston, Mari Huston, Sharon Huston, Jacqueline Hutchins, Sam Hutchinsen, Hutch and Trudy Hutchison, John Hutchison, John Hutnick, Ed Hutter, Leo &
Hyche, Jack Hylton, David Hyman, Robert Hyman, Jacques Hymans, Richard Hymns, Matt Hyrnick, Michael Hytoponlos, Jorge Iacovina, Wilfrido Ibañez, Isidro Ibañez, Rosa Ibañez Martin, Jose Iba
Raul Ibarra, Andrea Ickes-Dunbar, Lob Ida, Sebastian Ide, Jane Ideen, Peggy & Jim Iderman, Jorge Igartua, Maria Elena Iglesias, Mariana Iglesias, Walter Iglesias, Ing. Luis Iglesias Alvaro, Douglas Ike
John & Julie Ilitt, Jerry Ilkenhons, Ramon Illarramendi, Kenneth Imanuka, Tiks & Ruby Imperial, Imprenta Instant Copy, Imprenta Roger Printing, Tammie In fanger, Jessica Inarez, Mel's Inc., Ru
Incirillo, Daniel y Ricardo Inda, Rodolfo Indras Varilla, Barry C. Ingalls, Nathalie & Duke Ingles, Dave & Sharon Ingraham, H. D & Charlotte Ingram, Mercedes Iriarte, Jorge Iriberri, Juan Regalado e I
Arenas, Walter Irrutia, Kirt Irvine, Mike Irwin, Jeffrey Irza, Omar Isaak, Capitan Manuel Isaguirre Belardes, Valessa & Valerie Isbaell, Orrin & Sharon Iseminger, Ali Ishailow, Hirofumi Ishihara, Iba
Isidro, Angel Iorio, Bill Israel, Yael Israel, Gordon Istenes, Jose Guillermo Ituarta Reynava, Gabriel Iturbe, Diego Iturralde, Lucas y Maru Iturriza, Roseliano Valenzuela Ivan EdilioVivas GAri, Glady
Bill Ivansco, Emeka Ive, Michele Ivory, Jay Iyer, Mayri Izaguirre, Melania Izaguirre & CArlos Hernandez, Luis Izquierdo, J. Prado Rivas, karl Jack, Glenn Jacks, Irma Jacks, Andy & Celia Jackson, C
Jackson, Gene & Mary Jackson, Howard & Frosine Jackson, Jan & Mara Jackson, Judy Jackson, Kyle Jackson, Steve & Christi Jackson, Jose B. Jacobi, John Jacobin, Edward y Marlis Jacobowitz, Ma
Jacobs, Stu Jacobs, Carl Jacobson, Matt Jacobson, Kevin Jacoby, Bob & Cathy Jacques, Deborah Jacques, Gilbert Jacques, Enrique Jadad, Andy Jaeger, Lisa Jaeger, Dennis & Marsha Jaehnig, Alvaro Ja
Fritz Jaggi, Bud Jahn, Veronica Jaime M, Alejandro Jaimes, Camilo Jaimes, Navin & Helene Jaitly, Sarguis Jalil, John James, Chris Jameson, Jamkam, Bill Jammings, Emilie Jan van der Woerd, Sar
Janer, Beatriz Janet, Roberto Janett, Michel Janicka, Suzie Janke, Tom Janosz, Janice Jansen, George & Kathy Janssen, Eugenix y Juan Pablo Jantii, Ed & Jan Janzen, Edgar Jara, Fernando Jaramillo, Mo
y Alfonso Jaredo, Magdalena Jarrys, Denise Tim & Sam, Jarvis, Darin y Dawn Jaske, Mary Matt, Mueller, Jasmine, David & Sharon Jasper, Juan Jasso, Felipe Jauregui, Francisco Jauregui, Automovil C
Boliviano Jauregui ACB, Maritza Jaureguiu, Soheil Javid, Nayade Fragoso Javier Arevalo, James Jaworski, Marilyn Jaycox, David Jefferson, Rester Jeffries, Mary Jeffris, Steve Jelf, Chris Jenkins, P
Jenkins, Bill Jennings, C. Jennings, Doug Jennings, Mary Ann Jennings, Carl & Marjie Jensen, Ivan Jensen, Jaime Jensen, Mort & Lois Jensen, Robert Jensen, Willard Jeral, Aida Jeris, John P. Jero
David Jeron, Luis Jesscca, Jeff Jessen, Leonardo Benz Jessica Arnold, Archard Jessup, Jon & John Jessup, Rex Jessup, Alvaro Ledesma Jesus Neira, Larry Jett, Richard Jevons, Nancy & Roger Jewell,
Jewett, Thomas Jhaddeus, Dorian Smith Jim Van Gorder, ALberto Jimenez, Alejandro e Hilda Jimenez, Ana Jimenez, Andrea Jimenez, Angel F. Jimenez, Carlos Jimenez, David Jimenez, Gabriel Jime
Jenny y Ricardo Jimenez, Jose Jimenez, Marcelo Jimenez, Marisol Jimenez, Olman Jimenez, Rodrigo Castillon & Jimenez, Tony Jimenez, Valeria Ernesto y Leonardo, Jimenez, Yuri Jimenez, Levi Jime
Andrade, Ricardo Jimenez Vazquez, Steven Jimesik, Rich & Marianne Jlusser, Kippy Jo, Barbara Jo Birt, Eduardo Canabal Joaquin Sosa, Charles Jodrey, Jean Campbell Joe Bobrowski, Liliana Jofre Na
Bob Johannesen, Gertie and Ed Johanson, Candy John, David John, John & Dot, Belle K. Oropeza John Bolez, Nancy Polkinghorne John Hines, Johnny C. Dowdy, Jaime Johns, Aldie Johnson,
Johnson, Bonnie Johnson, Brian Johnson, Bruce & Mary Lou Johnson, C.R. Johnson, Camie Johnson, Carol & Douglas Johnson, Charley & Lanee Johnson, Dorothy Johnson, Doyle y Dottie Johnson,
Johnson, Gail Johnson, George Johnson, Helen Johnson, Irma Johnson, Jo Johnson, Keith & Nancy Johnson, Ken & Judy Johnson, Larry y Eva Johnson, LeRoy & Rhonda Johnson, Marjorie Johns
Marylou Johnson, Mel Johnson, Mike Johnson, Mrs. Helen Johnson, Peter Johnson, Rev. Guy Johnson, Robbie Johnson, Robyn Johnson, Ruby Johnson, Scott Johnson, Skip & Susie Johnson, Steph
Lindy Johnson, Steve Johnson, Susan Johnson, Terry Johnson, Travis Johnson, Wade Johnson, Wayne Johnson, Jack Johnston, Jennifer Johnston, Jim Johnston, Robert & Kathy Johnston, Tom Johns
Wilma Johnston, Natalia Jojart, Alison Jones, Berton Jones, Bob Jones, Bobby Jones, Christie Jones, Gene Jones, Helen Jones, Jacquelyn Jones, Jean & Bob Jones, Jennifer Jones, Jim Jones, K.C. Jo
Karen Jones, Kim Jones, Linda Jones, Mark Jones, Mark & Pamela Jones, Mike & Ruth Jones, Peggy Jones, Robert Jones, Jesse Jordan, Marian Jordan, Peter Jordan, Donaldo Jordan Luna, Arq.Franci
Jorge, Inocencia y Ruben Jorge, Jorge Luis Godoy Cabrera Jorge Luis Alberto, Rick Jorgensen, Jacques Jorin, Dehran & Lisa Jory, Andres Josa, Annette Joseph, Suzanne Joseph, Jessie & Jorge Joshua,
Joslin, Carlos Josue, Herman Joubert, Jacquelyn y Ulises Joves, Sharon Joy, David Joyner, Norman Joyner, Sellers Jr William J., Jose Jr. Hernandez Olesinski, Bob JRuggiero, Joel Juan, Carlos Juarez, C
Juarez, Luis Juarez, Roberto Juarez, Terri Juarez, Oscar Juarez Hdez, Jim Jucker, Chester Judah, Dick Juelson, Angie Juenemann, Louise Julien, Janis Jung, Jeus- Peter Jungolaussen, Juan Juri, Ted &
Justen, John Justice, Michael Justice, Justo Guevara, Karen Kable, Diane Kaczmarcyk, Kaden & Crawford, Frank & Hazel Kaiser, Barbara Kajawn, Urmas Kaldvezk, George Kale, Alan Kallam, J
Kalush, Gray Kamaryn, Karina Kamenetzky, Frank Kamermans, Karla Kaminski, James Kamp, Julie Kamp, Richard Kamp, Trish Kanafany, Roman Kancepolski, Lynda Kaner, Rick & Christy Ka
Joanne Kankler, Demitrios Karabinis, Alfred J. Karcheski, Antonio Karg, Doug karlsam, Leo Karlyn, Iain Karroll, John & Donna Karsten, Maximo y Gerardo Kaser, David & Judy Kashoff, D
Kaspariani, David Kast, Joe & Diana Kastner, Erickson/Foster Kathie, Kathy Hall & Eddie Sloan, Hajo Katinszky, Roger Katula, Gabriel Katz, Dan y Suzana Kauffman, Dr. Rick Kaufman, Lisa Kaufm
Jorge Kaufmann, Denis Kavanagh, Helen Kaye, Jud Keah, Bob Kean, Nancy Kearney, Micael Keating, Patricia & Dale Keefe, Thomas Keehan, Wayne Keele, Barbara Keeler, David Keeley, Gregg Keel
Stu Keen, James Keene, Jan & Dick Keene, James Keeneu, Jeff Keeter, Allan & Pat Kehrley, Jim Keiling, Ray Keinert, Amy Keiter, Karon Keith, Mickey Keith, Mark Kell, Anahy Keller, Ed & Carol Ke
Maynard Keller, Michael Keller, Jim Kellet, Graham Kelley, Mike & Terry Kelley, Warron Kells, Brian Kelly, Chris Kelly, Frank Kelly, Gart Kelly, Heather Kelly, James & Judy Kelly, Lisa Kelly, Ric
Terry Kelly, Scott Kelly, Jeff & Kate Kelsen, Jim & Lesley Kemnitz, Carol Kemp, Bill L. Kemp, Beth Corey & Maya, Kemp, Bill Kemper, Ken Kemper, Kempton, Ken Gordon, Stephen Kendall, B
Kendrick, Dawn Kendrick, Bruce Kennedy, Cindy Kennedy, Colin Kennedy, Gary Kennedy, John Kennedy, Tom & Sandra Kennington, William Kent, E & G Kenyon, Mike & Lois Keossnik, C. Will
Kephart, Gladys & Ralph Kepner, Raept Kepner, Pet Kern, Peter Kern, Colleen Kerr, Randy & Rike Kerr, Christine Kerschbaum, David Kersten, Dan Kessinger, Alicia Kessler, Don Kessler, Jim Ketchar
Margarita & Keith Ketchum, Kevin & Michelle, Arshiya & Yahya Khan, Joseph Kichler, Alice Kidd, Nicole Kidder, Sue Kieburtz, Ralph Kilbourne, Kevin Kilduff, Carrie Kile, Marian Kile, Ken Kill
Scott Kim, Gordon & Joan Kimball, Robin Andrews Kimmel, Danny Kimsey, Ed & Julie Kimsey, David Kincaid, Don & Judi Kincaid, Morris Kindig, Al King, Alice & Stew King, Chris King, Karen K
Mary & Robert King, Michael King, Rhonda King, Roger King, Vern Kingsford, Vorn & Lura Kingsford, Phil & Susan Kinney, Jack & Margaret Kinsey, Margaret & Jack Kinsey, Jim & Lou Kirk, Caro
Kirkland, Inge O. Kirkland, Justin Kirkland, Mark Kirkland, Sharon and Bill Kirkland, Bill & Low Kirkman, Janine Kirkpatrick, Megan Kirkpatrick, Mark & Lisa Kirmse, ken & Cindie Kisller, G
Kissee, Ken Kisselman, Victor y Rosa Kitamoto, Carol Kitchen, Philip Kitchin, Dick Kivsalas (Est), Lynn Klassert, Mari & Lynn Klassert, Scott & Cheryl Klatt, Lois Klayman, Kleeberg's, Bar
Klehfoth, Jay Klehfoth, Harry & Karen Kleinman, Matt Klenke, Gary & Sara Kling, Howard Klinger, Ed & Louise Klinkenberg, Ken Klooze, Gary Klopt, Juan Klue, Herb Kluttz, Lynndeen Knapp, L
M. Knaus, James Knauss, Allison Knight, Edwin John Knight, Heather Marie Jim, Roberta Health, Knight, Heather y Andrew Knight, Neal Knight, Rick & Lahne Knight, Carl Knissel, Kendra Knoe
Karen Knolauch, Bill Knopy, Dan Knorr, Victor & Chrityna Knott, Anna Knowlson, C.L. Knoxviles, Patsy Knudbon, Alf Koch, Chris & Kathleen Koch, Daryl Koch, Jerry Koch, Krista Koch, Philli
Margret Koch, Karen Kochekian, Al Kock, Marie Koecher, Mil Koehler, Daniel G. Koenig, Barbara Koenig Bob, Rachel & Abigail, Nik Koesis, Sid & Helen Koffski, Richard Kofler, Dr. Gregory Kofn
John Kohlhas, Dennis Koi, Lanin Kokinda, Paul Kokkinides, Marilee Kolb, Taylor Koldyke, Margaret Kollekowski, John Attanasio & Kollin, Hanni & Walter Kolouch, Jacquie Kolter, Darcy Koma
Ingrid & Dr. Hans Konig, George Koows, Steve Kopacz, Mary Kopcho, Jim Kopp, Peter Kopperud, Karen & CJ Kord, Sam Korsmo, John Kosak, Violet Kosc, Merrick Kosken, Anthony and Judy Kostu
Peter Kovacs, Sallyann Kovacs, Pat Kowaleski, Bernice Kozak, George Kozak, Avallon Kraft, James Kraft, Joe Kraftt, Ken Krall, Rich & Estelle Kramer, Brian Kraner, Theo Kranz, Brenda Krauss, K
Krauss, Len Krautheim, Arnie Kravath, Tom Krave, Jack Kreeger, Jake Kreeger, Tinw Kreetz Tyler, Larry & Connie Kreh, Vanesa y Marcelo Kreindel, Greg Krell, Peter Kremer, Jenice Krenmayr, D

ızelok, Mario Krinsky, Verena Kristof, Larry Kristoff, Robert Krizanee, Donna Krol, Philip Krone, Annette y Giesbert Krug, Bob & Nancy Krug, Giesbert Krug, Nancy Krug, Paul Kruger, Scott Kruger,
ter y Carolina Kruger, Al Kruha, Tom Kruse, Vickie Kruse, Sherwood Kubone, Ron Kubord, Bret Kucharski, Jack Kugler, Helga K¸hlmann, Greg Kuijpur, Eddie Kula, Jim Kulling SR, Alex Kumpan,
vsp Cleveland OH, John, Kuntz, Richard Kunz, Alexander Kurbato, Marisol y Cesar Kuri, Judie Kurpgeweit, Roger Kuyatt, George Kynman, Dave & Dee La Combe, Mary & Dick La Fever, Robert y
dra La Francois, Gustavo La Fuente, Luis La Grama, Roberto La Guardia, Anthony La Mantia, La Marca Asador Argentino, Charles La Porte, Craig La Roque, Nancy La Schaefer, Marcelo Dario
orde, Roberto y Ana Laboureau, Thiago Lacerda, Jim & Camila Lackey, Dean Lacoe, Dick & Mary LaFever, Jeffy Laffon, Juan Lago, Enzo Lagos, Julio Lagos, Rene Lagos, Usiel Lagunas, Donald
lig, Kenneth Lail, Jr., Kristy Laine, Ken Laing, Andrew Laird, Kevin Laird, Dean & Judy Lak, Shelagh Lalonde, Ignacio Lama Rojas, Diego Lamacchia, Robin Lamar, Ana Maria Lamas, Ignacio Lamas
ıs, Charity Lambert, Lance Lambert, Julius Lambeth, Tom Lamera, Nestor Lamilla, Alton Lamm, Kurt & Larac Lamoreaux, Petra Lamoureux, Bruce Lancaster, Tyo Lancaster, Darwin Lance, Dennis
'armen Lanci, Nestor & Nanette Landeira, Abe Landes, Bill & Cathy Landles, Calos Lando, Fernando Landoo, Jerome Landry, Paul & Janet Landry, Alberto Landucci, Bill & Susan Lane, Gary Lane,
ıua Lane, Larry & Patricia Lang, Bob & Sandy Langager, Mark Lange, Bill & Ruth LangMeyer, Charles Langrell, Teresa Lanier, Denise & Ken Lanik, Harold Lankenal, Johny & Kay Lankford, Heidi
tin, Nancy Lanzolla, Peter Lanzt, Debora Lapidus, Eleanore and Gaston Laquerre, Estella Lara, Jaime Lara, Einar Lara Sosa, Luis Lara Sosa, Natalia y Agustin Larco, Jose Larin, Andrea & Michelle
ıec, Craig LaRocgue, Alfredo Larrea, Luis Larrea, Horacio y Gabriela Larreguy, Francis Larrera, Andres Y Cristina Larrivey, Frances Douglas Larry Rowe, Grant Larson, Jan Larsson, Yadira Lascarez
ıno, Javier Lascurain, John Lasesecre, Ann & Kevin Lash, Bill Lasher, Chris Lassen, Stewart Y Alejandra Lasseter, Rick Lassiten, Artur Latko, Juan Latorre, Gerardo Latour, Vernie & Robert Latto, Jon
iretchen Laubach, Chuck Lauby, Sanchez Laura, Craig & Sheri Laurie, Lisa Dordal Laurie Samuels, Larry & Pat Lauth, L G & Sandy Lauxman, Carlos Lavalle, David Lavalley, Jose Lavicount,
ıando Lavin, J. Law, Skip Law, Ankota & Gapi Lawrence, Bill Lawrence, Christopher Lawrence, Indra & Sakhi Lawrence, Martha Lawrence, Al & Marily Lawrie, Mike Laws, Rick & Pat Laws,
ıany Lawson, Brandt Lawson, Hal & Donna Lawson, Heather Lawson, Joree Lawson, Joe Lawton, Jane & Sonny Lawyer, Bruce Layman, Kelly & Lisa Layman, Tyler Layman, Ann Layton, Patricia
aravich, Horacio Lazarri Mathieu, Horacio Lazzari Mathieu, Vic & Joan Le Cause, Robert Lea, Miguel Leal, Dave & Katty Leary, John Leath, Ronnie Leatham, Michel Lebas, Marc Leberger, Louise
ılanc, Richard Leblanc, Matthew Lebrato, Cal Lebsack, Jean y Hinette Leclerc, Idoia Ledercq, Antonio Ledesma, Miguel Ledesma, Rodrigo y Laura Ledesma, Andrew Lee, Brigitte Lee, Georgia Lee,
Lee, Maria Lee, Mike Lee, Carol And Ross Leef, Larry Leek, Axe Leer, Jim & Katie Lefebure, Barbara Graff LeFurgey, Andrea & Brice Legare, Huquette Leger, Wayner Leger, Amanda Legernes,
re & Steve Legler, Dave Lehman, Eddie Lehman, Leigh Tomfohk, Bill & Barbara Leighton, Barbara Leiker, Bill Leinonen, Frank Leipe, Yoiman Leiton Castro, Eduardo Leiva, Paula y Carlos Leiva,
gio y Ana Cristina Leiva, Rick Lemley, Martin y Loretta Lemmo, Bill & Sharon Lemmons, Enrique Lemol, Kelli Lemon, Raul Lemosoff, Juan Lemus, Mary Elizabeth Lenahan, Fernanda Lencina, Jerry
dreth, Willie Leng, Scot Lengel, John Lent and Mary Ann Castimore, Richard Lentinello, Silvio Di Leo, Adriana y Jesus Leon, Dan Leon, David Leon, Don Juan Leon, Ernesto Leon, Gera Leon, Juan
n, Oscar Leon, Alfonso León, Paulo León, Arturo y Ernesto Leon Coronel, Adrian Martha, Benjamin y Adriancito, Leon Sanchez, Dan y Christine Leon Stilphen, Jose Leon Vargas, Benny & Sharon
ıard, Boby Leonard, Dan Leonard, Steve Leonard, Rick Leonardi, Sam Leone, Puebla Leonel, Ramiro Leonel, Julie Leovard, Ramon Lepage, Ronald Lerch, Paul Lerd, Abel Lerena, James Lerie, J.
ıer, Jacques Leroy, Hershey Les Wohlgemuth, Bill Leschensky, David Lesley, Robert Leslie, Anne Lesser, C. Lett, Curt Leuenberger, Larry Leuttinear, Harriet Levaine, Pablo Levano, Vanesa Levi, Anita
ı, Chad Levis, Gabriel Levman, Harold & Judith Levy, Joyce Levy, Moses Levy, Alan & Sylvia Lewis, Aram Lewis, Bonnie Lewis, Elizabeth Lewis, Frank Lewis, Hillary Lewis, Rachael Lewis,
ıard Lewis, Robert & Dianna Lewis, Marshall Lewis MAFCA, Jonathan Ley, Libby Leyrer, Ariana Liakos, Shep Liams, Juana Libedinsky, Carlos Liberti, Frank & Grella Lichorobiec, Ed & Carol
ıtenberger, Jack Lictzke, JosËe Liessard- Hanza, Don Lietzan, Janet Liftin, Randall Light, Jack Lightcop, Anne Lightwine Dustin, Norma Lilian, K Lim, Arnoldo Lima, Joe Lima, William Lima,
ıandra Limmer, Antonio Limon, Howard Lin, Leobardo Lincoln, Judy Lind, Suzanne lind, Ma. Linda, Aleta Darlene & Linda Slack, Philip Lindau, Tomas Linde, Mike Karen, Tanya & Mosoa, Lindeen,
g Linden, Linderberg JR., Dick and Dolores Lindley, Richard Lindley, Russ Lindsay, Erskine Lindsey, Doug Lindstrand, Britt Lineberger, Paula Lineberry, Darin Link, Ray Linkous, Edward Linnebur,
e & Shirley Linnebur, Nancy Linvill, Mike & Renee linville, Michael Lione, Andy Lipeti, Rodney & Tina Lipman, Rod Lipp, Ann Lippincott, Guillermo Lira, Salvador Lira, Susan Lisa's Roder Mom,
ıne Lisenbardt, Reutter Lissa, Rickey Liston, Ray Litschauer, Roger & Debbie Little, Larry Litvak, Dick Livant, Carlos Lizano, Edgar Lizano, Henry y Ingrid Lizano, Javier Lizano, Krissia Lizano
ıno, Jorge Lizaw Stos, Marcel Llaca, Jorge Llera, Coul Llewellyn, Romina LLomovatte, Juanita y Eduardo Llorет, Leda Lloret, John & Jane Lloyd, Jim & Sue Lloyed, John & Rita Locascio, Gerald
es, Jim & Blythe Locke, Steve Locke, Winona Locke, Silvia y Thomas Locks, Bob Lockwood, Ellen Lockyer, Frank & Camille Locy, Jose Juan Rodriguez Loera, Martin y Ana Loera, Kathy Lofton,
y and Margo Logan, Irv Logan, Richard & Marla Logman, John Logmore, Kenneth Lohorn, Edgar Lojan, Carlo Lombardo, Jed & Gloria Lonax, Andres Londoño, John Lones, Doug Long, Frank Long,
y Long, Johny Long, Roger Long, Willie Long, John Longmore, Warren Longwell, Bill & Mary Lonley, Margaret Lonsdale, Bruce Loose, Darío Lopera, Gabriela Lopetegui, Carlos Lopez, Constantino
ula Lopez, Eduardo Lopez, Estela Lopez, Fabiola Lopez, Gricel Lopez, Jorge Enrique Lopez, Josuel y Adilia Lopez, Juan Lopez, Julio Lopez, Keyla Lopez, Lillian Lopez, Lorena Lopez, Omar Lopez,
ar Lopez, Oscar & Lily Lopez, Patricia Lopez, Patricio Lopez, Rodolfo Adrian Valdez Lopez, Sergio Lopez, Shindy Lopez, Virgilio Lopez, Maydileinee López, Lucinda Lopez Ascorteve, Luis Lopez
gos, Alberto Lopez Esquiver, Andrea Lopez Estrada, Jorge Lopez Flores, Victor Lopez J., Guillermo y Juan Carlos Lopez Lopez, Victor Lopez Lopez, Gustavo M. Lopez Ramos, Alan Lopez Rivas,
ias Lopez Vega, Lic. German Lopez Veraztegui, Juan Lopezz, Lisa Loprinzo, Roland Lord, Lord Fairlane, Soren Loree, George Lorenz, Michael Lorenz, Familia Lorenzana, Silvia Lorenzana, Christian
egina Lorenzen, Rodrigo Lorenzini, Silvana Lorenzo, Kathy Loretta, Carlos Loria, Daniel Losada, Carina Losano, Dan Loseo, Lydia Lott, Louis Julien & Fritz Jaggi, Jim Lounsbury, David Garcia
rdes Aleman, Harold Loutzenheiser, Eric & Karen Love, Phillir Love, Rick Love, William Love, John Lovejay, Mark & Alicia Lovejoy, Walt & Margaret Lovejoy, James Loven, Marcela Lovera, M
imen, Sharon Lowe, Vincent Lowe, Eric Lowell, Vic Loyer, Ana Maria Loyola, Ignacio Loyola, Lielro y Valentina Loza, Alfredo Lozano Amparo, Cia. Hyman Ltded, Leslie Luai, Aduiro Lucas, Bud
erry Lucas, Dr. Kathleen Lucas, Nick y Caro Lucas, Adam Lucchesi, Maria Rosa Lucchini, Rosa Lucchini, Roderito Lucena, Sergio Lucero, Sofia Lucero, Quality&develop Luciano, Cesar Montes
ila Lopez, Juan Lucio, Juan Reinaldo Lucio, Gabriela Lucke Guzman, Thomas Lucus, Bob Ludwig, Santiago y Mateo Lueje Ruiz, Fernando Lugo Bustillo, Jacobo Luis, Luis Duvoy, Luis Lopez, Luis
EncisoTorres, Pam Luka, Rhodie Lumanog, Carmelita Lumbau, Baba Lumomba, Eduardo Luna, Liliana Luna, Maria Luna, Jessica Luna Cardenas, Cindy Lund, Barbara Lundgren, Laura & David
din, Dennis y Tina Lunsford, Tony & Kristi Lupercio, David Lupke, Luis Luque, Mike Lury, Enzo Lusso, George Luster, Fred Lutes, Ed Luther, Gretchen Luttmann, Bob Lutz, Larry & Jeannie Lutz,
e Luzza, Lilia Luzza, Stan Lydell, Thomas Lyford, M.L. Lyke, Mary Lynn Lyke, Katie Lyles, Pat & Lori Lymak, Angie Lynch, Dudley Lynch, Ian Lynch, Scott Lynch, Lynden, Daniel Lyom, Donna
n, Barry Lyons, Margarita & Richard Lyons, Dick Lytle, Ricardo M., Weimar M., Chris Mac, I. Mac Bride, Erin Mac Call, Alon Mac Carthy, Aaron Mac Donald, Kelly Mac Donald, Jerry & Willy Mac
and, Cheryl & Darren Mac Isaac, Patricio & Bettina Mac Loughlin, Andrew Mac Millen, Robert Mac Znnis, Eaith Macaluso, Maria Macarmout, Jeannette MaCarone, Ruben Macaya, David MacDonald,
& Yvonne MacDonald, Paul MacDonald, Phil Mace, Familia Terrazas Macedo, Brandon Macer, John & Lydia MacFadden, Luis Machado, Maruy Machlovel, Dinorah Macias, Genaro Macias, Jaime
ias, Jose Macias Garcia, Trish Mack, Bruce & Tammy MacKay, Bob Mackenzie, Dan MacKenzie, Malcom Mackenzie, Suzi Mackenzie, Norm & Kathryn MacLeod, David Macondo, Neil Macready,
ert MacZnnis, Rhonda Madden, Juan Madeira, Bruce Friedberg Madelyn Baran, Jayce Mader, Florencia Madero, Rafael Madero, Alvaro Madgrial, Paul & Becky Madison, silena madison, Ramiro
drid, Ramiro y Misa Madrid, Gian Madrigal, Marta Laura Madrigal, Rodrigo Madrigal, Gerardo Madrigal Maxegor, MAFCA, Michael Magadley, Noe Bernardo Magallanes, Elizabeth Magana, Vanessa
ian Magana, Emma Magania, Gerardo Magaña, Luis Magaña, Helga Magdzik, Mike & Kathy Magdzik, Annita Magee, R. A. Magelssen, Norman Mages, David & Marcia Magill, David Mahakfey,
k Mahoney, Dan & Wanda Mahony, Ray & Lui Mai Kirkman, Jorene Maier, Marmi Mairs, George & Colleen Makovic, Bill Makovsky, Rodrigo Malagan Cienfuegos, Frank Malatesta, Malcom, Karen,
, Rowan, Angel Maldonado, Azucena & Luciano Maldonado, Christina Maldonado, Daniel Maldonado, Javier Maldonado, Leonor Maldonado, Wilmer y Nancy Maldonado, Marty Schnitzer Malkin,
ian Malla, Richard Mallett, Jane Malnoske, Mike & Steph Malome, Miryam Maltinskis Davis, Bohdan Malyczewsky, Norene , MAmani, Creed Mamikunian, Eddie & Angelines Manangon, Bruce
ıce, Maggie Manchester, Georgina Mancinelli, Patricia Mandatori, Susan Manelli, Gabriel Manera, Oscar Mangini, John Manhu, Horacio Manjon, George y Evelyn Mankel, Sigfrid Manl, Tim Manley,
nie Mann, Jennifer & Jason Mann, Murdock Mann, Noel Mannion, Shannon Mannion, Osvaldo Mansilla, Regina Mantenfel, Ana & Yair Manzano, Mercedes Manzi, Horacio Marafioti, Marcos Marani,
Maravilla, Mario Marcel, Carlos Marchen, T.C. Hatter Marcianne, Paul Marck, Jeff Marcom, Ron Marek, Gustavo Margarita, Margie & joe Talaugon, Ketch & Marguerite, Robin Mari, Gilbert Maria,
Romay Maria de Romay, Max Romano Maria Schmidt, Joe Marian, Mariana, Kim & Inkook, Humberto Marin, Liliana Marin, Margarita Marin, Mario Marin, Rafael Marín, Marin¥s A Chapter of
FCA, Marcello Marini, Roberto Marino, Tiffany Nesson Mario Vera, Maritima Providencia, Oscar Solares Maritza, Ruben & Donna Markgraf, Mike Markinen, Freda & Philip Markley, Cheryl Marks,
Marksheid, Pearl Markstein, Ken Marler, Duke & Sara Marley, Robert Marlow, Ricardo Marnaghi, Cesar Maroquin, Elizabeth y Rafael Marquez, Emily y Juan Jose Marquez, Juan Marquez, Raquel
rquez, María Luisa Carrión Márquez, Juan Carlos Marquez Hernandez, Rafael Marrero, Antonio E. Marrocco, Hector Marroqui, Andres Marroquint, Bob Marsh, Debra Marsh, Randy Marsh, Brandon
shall, James Marshall, John Marshall, Ronny Marshall, Sheila Marshall, Suzy Marshall, Eric Marshall Onderdonk, Buck Marsters, John Marten, Miks Marti, Leonel Y Reina Martieneau, Alfie Martin,
son Martin, Andrea Martin, Bill Martin, Brian Martin, Damian Martin, Doug & Gladys Martin, Gary Martin, Jeanette Martin, Kavin & Renate Martin, Pheilm Martin, Reid Martin, Reid and Ana Martin,
ard & Dorothy Martin, Silvia Martin, Tetta Martin, Tom Martin, Carlos Martín, Noemi Martinelli, Abelardo Martinez, Alejandro Martinez, Ali Martinez, Ariel Martinez, Bernardo Martinez, Bolivar
tinez, Carlos Martinez, Carmen Martinez, Cornelio Martinez, Fabian Martinez, Francisco Martinez, Freddy Martinez, Hector Martinez, Hermany Martinez, Hugo Martinez, Irvin Martinez, Ivonne
tinez, Jose Martinez, Jose y Theresa Martinez, Laura Citlatli y Abelardo, Martinez, Marcelo y Maria Martinez, Marisel Martinez, Mitch Martinez, Patty Martinez, Ramiro Martinez, Steve y Lucinda
tinez, Sofía Martínez, Daniel Martinez Benitez, Alex Martinez Castañeda, Pablo Martinez Labat, Margarita Martinez Lopez, Santiago Martinez O., Roberto Martinez P., Jorge Martinez Ramos, Mauricio
tinez Sanchez, Juan Martinez Sierra, Yolanda Martinez von Wernich, Zaira Martinez von Wernich, Luis Martinez-Poema, Alejandra Martins, Victor Martins, Angel Ranger Maru Zuñiga, Michael Marus,
Mary, Paul Lowithein Mary Wilson, Daniel Maschel, Jan Masek, Alison Masemann, Mary Mashburn, Ben & Lou Mashu, Carlos E. Masia Vieweg, James Mason, Jim Mason, Leann Mason, Steve
son & Glen Fudge, John Massengale, Vera Master, Gerard Mastropaolo, Deanne Masur, Amado Mata Gil, Familia Mata-Martinez, Carlos Matamoros, Jose Matamoros, Raul y Lupe Matamoros, Debby
en Mate, Pajntar Matej, Jaroslav Matejovsky, Carina Mateo, Hugo Mathey, Craig Mathues, D.L. Matias, Jose Maticorena, Geo & Linda Mattes, Andrea Matthews, Roland Matthews, Peter Matthiesson,
ph Mattina, Ernie & Marilyn Mattison, Dan & Marsha Mattson, Mark Mattson, Ray Matz, Billy Maude Streett, Earl Maudlin, Jean Mauger, Scott Maulain, Lee Mauldin, Dave Maunsell, Joel Mauny,
h Maurer, Horacio Mauri, Mauricio Zapiain y Hugo Leon, Jenna Mauser, Janet Mautner, Duke Mauzy, Irian Mavard, Fanny Max, Martin Urdangaray Maximiliano Rathjen-Lori, Rosa y Jorge Maxit,
Maxlofill, Cori Maxwell, Tom & Donna May Bewley, Debbie Mayes, Scott Maynard, Jose Mayorga Garcia, Michael & Coree Maysonet, Eduardo Maytorena, David Mazurek, Steve Mazzarella, Mario
zaro, Sherry Mc Adam, Jennifer Y Marcus Mc Adar, Brian Mc Auliffe, Jerry Mc Bride, Bill & Polly Mc Call, Vincent & Jullie Mc Call, Ed & Betty Mc Callister, Connie Mc Cann, MIke Mc Cardell,
Mc Careley, Jade Mc Carthy, Cathy Mc Carty, Patrick Mc Clanahan, Kevin Mc Closkey, Dan & Dorothy Mc Clure, Paul Mc Cold, Doyle Mc Comb, Rosa y Roger Mc Condie, Maureen Mc Cormick,
cio Mc Cormick, Don Mc Cuaig, Misty Mc Dermitt, John Danila & Jaidyn, Mc Donald, Sharon Mc Evoy, Randy Mc Feeters, Sebra Mc Ghan, Jim Mc Goldrick, Paul & Erin Mc Larnon, Darcey Mc
ghlin, Robin & Charles Mc Lead, Marie Mc Manus, Stan Mc Meekin, Tim Mc Mulden, Elizabeth Mc Mullan, Kathy Mc Mullen, Jerry Mc Namara, Barb & Ron Mc Nawghton, Jeff Mc Ney, Pat &
s Mc Pherson, Ernie Mc Reynolds, Ford Mc Williams, Edson and Anne Mc. Cord, Patricio Mc. Cormick, Shannon & Colin Mc. Grath, Kathy Mc. Mullen, Roger Mc.Kinney, Eric Mcacham, Eric &
Mcachan, Travis McBee, Rhonda McBride, Andrea McCabe, Mary McCabe, Henry McCalelo, John Mccall, Bruce McCalley, Connie & Kevin McCann, Frank McCarthy, Jade McCarthy, John & Judy
Carthy, John & Mary McCarthy, Stacy McCaskill & Ronda Devold, Suzanne McCausland, Heather McCausled, Bill McClain, Jolin McCleskey, Robert McCluse, Duncan Mccolley, Robin McCollo,
a & Brenda Mccomber, Doug McCord, Edson McCord, Terrel McCormack, Philip & Betty McCormick, Kevin McCormik, Rickey & Elizabeth McCoy, Linda McCraw, Fred & Tina McCurtcheon,
l McDaniel, Donna & Lee McDaniel, Burl McDonald, Eric McDonald, Judy McDonald, Walt McElroy, Bert McEwen, Amy McFarlane, Betty Mcferrer, Jack McGahey, Alyssa McGill, Patrick
Ginnis, Terry McGrath, Susan McGreeny, Patrick McGreevy, Adolfo McGregor, Dr. Adolfo Mcgregor, Jim McGuire, Mike McGuire, Dianne McIntosh, Darlene McInturff, Raymond Mcintyre, Robert
Kay, Carol McKee, David & Cecy McKee, Laura McKenday, Daniel McKesson, Slim Mckillican, Howard & Debbie McKinney, Sue Mckinney, Greg McKinnon, Ted McKown, Paul & Erin McLannon,
ert & Christy McLaughlin, Ernest McLean, Rich & Mint McLean, Jennifer Mclellan, Garry & Suzanne McLeod, Roy & Gail McLeod, Carrie & Jeff Mcmahon, Mike McMamara, Anna McManus,
h & Shane McManus, Jim McNabrey, Brian McNair, Andy McNeil, Glen McNeil, Bernice & Len McNeilly, John Mcnicholl, Steve Mcnitt, Dorothey McPherson, Steve McPherson, Mike McQuaid,
id McRae, Les McRae, McWalters, Jay & Vicki Meacham, Jim Mead, Melissa Mead, Andrew D. Meadors, Edward Meadow croft, Ed Meadowcroft, Don and Mary Helen Meadows, Randy & Joellyn
dows, Mike Mealham, Robert Craig Mechner, Claudio Mecina, Jose Medel, Carlos Medel Ramirez, Andres Medellin, Vickie Medick, Edgar Medieta Victoria, Beatriz Medina, John Medina, Lolly
ina, Nefertiti Medina, Nestor Medina, Sandra Medina, Araceli y Miguel Angel Medina Lara, Jose de Jesus Medina Loguano, Claudia y Luxi Medina Macias, Lauren Medley, Luis y Claudia Medona
ia, Hildon Smith Megan Healey, Familia Megra Ayela, David Mehakfey, David Meinhard, Dick Meinhold, Juana & Julian Mejia, Maria Mejia, Guadalupe Mejia Diaz, Carlos Mejia Trejos, Anayeli
orada, Richard Melain, Belem Melchor Ocampo, Guillermo Melindez, Kelly Hay , Melissa Wanamaker & Tribal Bellydance, Karl & Marsha Mellert, Jim Melo, Nestor Melo, Shera & John Melson,

Bob Melton, Louis Melton, Len Meltor, Jorge Mena Toribio, Hector Menacho, Tom & Carmel Menasco, Carlos y Lidia Mendez, Eduardo Mendez, Fernando Mendez, Jaime Mendez, Jorge y An
Mendez, Jose Mendez, JosÊ y Yamilis Mendez, Josefa Mendez, Lidia y Carlos Mendez, Luis Mendez, Michael Mendez, Rodrigo Mendez, Rocío Mendez Araya, Eluis Mendez castro, Jose Mendez Sanc
Roberto Mendez Vargas, Pablo Mendivil, Carlos Mendoza, Dany Mendoza, Francisco Mendoza, Ismael Mendoza, Juan Mendoza, Juan y Maria Mendoza, Lilian y Ramon Mendoza, Lorena Menc
Lucho Mendoza, Tello Mendoza, Jose Mendoza Garcia, Jaime Mendra, Rebeca Meneses, Susana Meneses Jimenez, René Mengivar, Ronald Menlema, Edgard Mentado, Agueda y Emilio Menvielle, C
Mercado, Gracie Mercado, Luis Mercado, Mercado Buenos Aires L.A., Carlos Mercado H. y Nury Molina H., Simon Duffy Meri Hoffster, Ruth Merica, Everth Merida, George & Janet Merkel, M
Merlos, Harold Mermel, Creig Merrick, Lili Merritt, Mariano y Micaela Merzario, Diego Mesa, Alejandro Mesch Arias, Luisana Mesen, Abebe Mesfin, Mike Ashe Kay, Meshawn, Kindley Ashe, F
Messaer, Bob y Karen Messercola, Ivonne Messier, Julie Messier, Dean Messmer, Dean & Sharon Messmer, Jerry Metscher, Erik Metzelar, John & Maggie Metzler, Roger D. Meunier, Peter Meusi
Richard Mevke, A. Meyer, Ann Meyer, Ingrid Meyer, Jeff Meyer, William A. Meyer, Greg & Jody Meyers, Jo- Ann Meyers, Harry Meyerson, Mindy Meyn, Curt Michael, George & Betty Michael, R
Michael, Craig Somers Michael keating, Bill & Karen Michel, Richard H. Michelhaugh, Alan Michelson, Mario Micheo, Louis Mickler, Maria Micks, Eric Mieczynski, Diane & Steve Mierz, Jeff S
Jeff and Kate Kelsen, Mierz, Rick & Paula Miesowitz, Sergio Migliavacca, Jorge Miguez, Mihnea y Mendy, Eduardo Mihura, Sergio Mijangos, Susan & Stan Mikelsavage, Christine Milakovic, Hora
Marcela Milano Conti, Saverio Milervini, Iva Miles, Henry Milette, Nancy & Robert Milgrim, Judi & Marvin Milich, Michael Militello, Mike Militello, Andres Milla, Rigoberto Milla, Betty & Roy M
Chuck Miller, Danny Miller, Dave Miller, David Miller, Deant Miller, Emmett & Julie Miller, Frank & Katharine Miller, Gabriel Miller, Greg Miller, Jay Miller, Jim Miller, Jim & Linda Miller, Jimn
Elisa Miller, John & Virginia Miller, Julio Miller, Kitty Miller, Lewis Miller, Maggie Miller, Matt y Kim Miller, Peter Miller, Randy & Mary Miller, Rendall Miller, Robert Miller, Ronald Miller, S
Miller, Stacey Miller, Steve Miller, Will Miller, Frank E. Miller III, Blair Milligan, Diane Milligan, Locomax Milligan, Michael Milligan, Al & Margy Mills, Alane Mills, Edgar Martin Milo Bastida, Ric
Miltenberger, Paul Milton, Henry Minassian, Larry Mindel, Andrew Miner, Gail Miner, Roger Miner, Armida Mineros, Tony & Sylvia Mines, Liz Mingo, Larry Minguet, Carlos Mino, Carlos M
Fernando Norma y Elisabeth, Minor, Paul & Jessica Minor, Larisa Minsky, Carlos & Mabel MIño, Gregoria y Julio Cesar Miño, Victor Miramontes M., Antonio Miranda, Fernando Miranda, Franc
Miranda, Jorge Miranda, Matias Miranda, Ramon & Patricia Miranda, Ricardo Miranda, Familia Miranda Luton, Ray Miras, Francisco Miraval, Jason Mireau, Zarco Miriam, Alessia Rojo Mirko Pra
Mirror Lake Middle School, Muriel Mirvois, Hilbert Misenheimer, Karam Mishalani, Dave Mitchell, Dennis Mitchell, Eo Mitchell, Erin & Shane Mitchell, Janet Mitchell, C. Mitchley, Radio M
argentina, Yoshi & Connie Miyagi, Kelly Mize, Peter Mjos, Luois & Bonnie Modler, Jesse Moege, Theresia Moeltner, Andrew Moffat, Guiseppe Moga, Ian Moggach, Alan Mogol, Pedro Luis Mogo
Allison Mohrman, Kayla & Bill Moilanen, Dick Moir, David Moise- Seattle, Nelson Mojica, Nelly Moldenaers, Alina Moldovan, Virgil Moldovan, Teresa Molen, DG & J Molenkamp, Adriana Mo
Aidee Molina, Cesar y Rosa Molina, Gustavo y Angelica Molina, Jose Molina, Juan Molina, Raquel Molina, Rodolfo Molina, Rolando Molina, Roxana Molina, Saul Molina, Cnel Hugo Molinari, Ilea
Hans Molle, Robin Mollenhauer, Pascal Molliere, Don Monaco, Dan Monaghan, Fernando Mondezuma e Irma, Mike Mondo, Berhta Mondragon, Elizabeth y Leonardo Mondragon, Maximo Mondra
Daniel Monestes, Luis Monge, Ronald Monge, Jorge Monge Agüero, Zenon Monge Hernandez, Hector Moni, Ron Monica, Christian Monnier, Tony Monopoli, Laurie Monroe, Pat & Janet Mo
Mauricio Monsalve Monsalve, Florencio Monsalvo, Mike Monsef, Bob Monsen, Robert M. Monsen, Patsy Monser, Mel Monset, Richard Monson, Bernardo Montaño, Roberto Montaño, Nick Montalb
Francisco Montalvo, Osvaldo Montano, Jose Montealegre, Rosita Monten, Josemaría Monterey, Andree Montero, Ivonne y Fernando Montero, Marco Montero, Carlos Montero Ayala, Jessica Montero
Jose Maria Monterrey, Antonio Montes, Javier Montes, Jenibeth Montes, Gary Montes de Oca, Jesus Montes de Oca, Velky Montes de Oca, Eduadro Montes de Oca Gtez, Joel Montgomery, Lor
Montgomery, Walter Montidoro, Dulce Montiel, Tre Montigue, Jorge Montilla, Sergio Montivero, Gilberto Montoga, S. Montoya, Jose Montoya Orosco, Barry & Bert Moore, Chris Cindy & Brian, M
David Moore, Frank Moore, Jack Moore, Jim Moore, Karyn & Dale Moore, Laura Moore, Marian and Stewart Moore, Martin & Jacqueline Moore, Matt Moore, Myra Kay & David Moore, Randy M
Robin Moore, Ronald J. Moore, Scott & Deb Moore, Sharon Moore, Steve Moore, Lisa Moorhead, Antonio Mora, Luis Mora, Manuel Mora, Maria Mora, Norma Mora, Pablo Mora, Ing. Jose Mora Ac
Hector Mora Inda, Mark & Julie Moraes, Jose Moragrega, Barbara y Pablo Morales, Byron Morales, Carola Morales, Carolina y Felicia Morales, Cynthya Morales, David Morales, Fabian Mor
Francisco Morales, Jaime Morales, Lorna Morales, Mariano Morales, Jorge Morales Alduein, Andrew Moran, Evelyn Moran, Robert Moran, Stella Moran, Francisco Moranda K, Wilbert Morata, Cl
Moratoya, Ron Moreau, Yves Moreau, Robert & Nelda Moree, Sylvie & Rodrigo Moreira, Ross & David Morelli, Ezequiel & Josie Moreno, Jorge Moreno, Luis Moreno, Miguel Moreno, Rafael Mo
Raimundo Moreno, Salvador Moreno, Luis Moreno R., Luigi Moresca G., Alessandra Moreta, Mariana y Marceliano Moreyra, George Morfitt, Peggy & George Morfitt, Bob and Morgan, Care &
Morgan, Daniel Morgan, Greg & Penny Morgan, Jesse Morgan, Jesse Morgan, Jim Morgan, Liz Morgan, Mary Anaruk Morgan, Robin Morgan, Rya & Madolyn Morgan, Ryan Morgan, Anne Mor
Mark Moriarty, Susan Moriarty, Ariel Moriconi Iara y Daniela Sosa, Steve & Silvia Moriel, Andres Morin, Vince Morin, Alejandro Morleone, Marcelo Morocho, Sara Morrehead, Bill Morrill, Be
Morris, Joe Morris, Joyce Morris, Laura Morris, Mark Morris, Doyle Morrish, Doyle & Bob Morrish, Misti Morrison, Paul & Sharon Morrison, Sue Morrison, William Morrow, Blanca Morse, David M
Claudio Morsucci, Diego Morsuci, Mark Ramona & Aaron, Mortier, Don Morton, Bruce & Joan Mosby, Pedro Moscoso, Miguel Moscozo, Don Moseman, Larry Moses, Mike Moskowitz, John Mo
Jose Mosre, Hushel & Bobby Moss, Oscar Motta Adalid, Andres Mounetou, Tom Mountford, Nestor Mourelo, John A. Mowat, Diego Moya, Francisco Moyano, Paola Moyano, Niko Moyar, Dave M
Lori Moyer, Steve & Joan Mraz, Jose Mtz, Aurora Muñoz, Carlos Muñoz, David Muñoz, Francisco Muñoz, Hail Muñoz, Noe Muñoz, Octavio Muñoz, Rafael Muñoz, Julio Muñoz del Bosque, A
Muñoz Toro, Darwin Muchow, Carolyn Muegge-vaughan, Betty Mueller, Richard Mueller, Stephan & Rebeka Mueller, Lani Mujer, Kinnete & Erik Muki, John Mular, Hugo Mule, Ken & W
Mulhollanel, Kelly Mullican, Bill Mullimites, Cary & Leigh Mullinnix, Bill & June Mullins, Brenda Mullins, Glenn Mullins, Padre Carlos Mullins, Scott Mulse, Jackie & John Munchel, Bill Mundorf
Mungay, Daniel Mungay, Wilson Muñiz, Alfredo Muñoz, Jorge Muñoz, Jorge Luis Muñoz, Noemi Muñoz, Donald & Julie Munro, Nick Munson, Carlos Muñoz, Eppie Muñoz, Franco Muñoz, Guill
Muñoz, Linda Muñoz, Tatiana Muñoz Brene, Eimy Muñoz Sanabra, Bob & Cindy Muratti, Lloyd Murdock, Fernando Murga, Edith Murillo, Kattya Murillo, Luis Murillo, Manuel Murillo, Eleonora M
Castro, Don Murk, Jorge Muro, Howard Murph, Jewel Murphy, Mark & Karen Murphy, Pat & Pam Murphy, Ron & Maria Murphy, Tim & Peggy Murphy, Donna y Stewart Murray, James Murray, S
Murray, John Murrell, Robert-Stephen Muschamp, Museo del Automovil (Argentina), Alexander Musillo, Carol Mussel, Curtis Musselman, Ed y Carol Musselman, Fotog Dean Musser, Dean Muss
Alejandra Mussi, Luisa y Carlos Muszak, David Mutchler, Prasanna Muthireddy, Alan Myers, James Myers, Kim Myers, Tom Myers, James Myriam Marin, Samira Naba, Joe & Andrey Nachilo, R
Nader, Charles & Shelley Nagel, Venkata Nagireddi, Bill Nagy, Paul Nagy, Ariel H. Gonzalez Nahum, Tasnim Najaf, Abel Najera Campos, Bruno Nancy, Fabian Nanni, Mary Naples, Samoel Nap
Hernandez, Hannia Naranjo, David Narantom, Jacob Narayon, Hernaldo Narvaez, Dennis & Ann Marie Nash, Nathalie Vachon o Emilia, Mike Naughten, Cliff Naugle, Dennis Naugle Darlene, Ag
Navarrete, Ivan & Paty Navarrete, Francisco Navarrez, Ann Navarro, Family Navarro, Cesar Navarro Sevilla, Roberto Navas, Victor Navas, Eliana Navas Ecuador, Lesbia Navas Robleto, Patricia y H
Navas y Liriano, Mariel y Manolo Navascues, Craig Navey, Michael Nayadley, Norm Naylor, Paula Nazer, Marlene Nebel, Matt Nedom, David Needham, Cindy Steve & Jessica, Neff, Jessica & S
Neff, Oscar y Omar Negrete Rodriguez, Jose Negrette, Kathie Neil, William Neithercoat, Jack & Frances Nellist, Gary Nelson, Gerald & Bernadette Nelson, Jim Nelson, Kaynie Nelson, Lee & Ba
Nelson, Lee & Trevor Nelson, Rose Nelson, Tom Nelson, Van Nelson Sr, Ruben Nernezna, Omar Nervegna, Steve Neter, Evelyn & John Nettleton, Dan Netzley, Dan & Carol Netzley, Hardy Neubert,
Neurohr, Graham Neve, Luty Neveleff, Brad New Harm, Allan Newberry, Steve Newberry, Sam Newcomb, Steve Newell, Jack & Carol Newhouse, Thomas y Teresa Newins, Teresa & Tom Newis, Ri
Newman, Hemmings News, Donald & Ruth Newton, Minh Nguyen, Roger Nice, Nancy y Milton Nichaes, Bernum Nicholas, Bill & Mimi Nichols, Bobby & Eliza Nichols, Marian Nichols, Milton & N
Nichols, Slaunalee Nichols, Murd Nicholson, Ted Nick, David & Karla Nicol, Carlos y Juan Pablo Nicoleau, Hugo Nicolini, Jorge Nicolini, Dulio Nicolini Ayerza, Cathy Nicoll, Mark & Barb N
(Brandon & Trevor sons), Brad Niemcek, Eduardo Nievas, Louis Nigro, Vicky Nikhols, Liliana Niko, Kevin Niles, Terry Ninger, Alex & Theresa Nino, Jose Nino Pineda, Amy Nisbett, Nattan Nisin
Steve Niskep, Carol Nisna & Ravi Anand, Steven Nissley, Hart Nittel, Al Noble, Alexander Noble Villareal, Claudio Nocciolino Argaiti, Bobby noell, Dave Nofsincyer, Laura Noggle, Bob Nog
Gonzalo Nolasco, Bob Nolin, Betty Nomba, Claudio Nonchenti, Irma Norberto, Joe & C.C. Norbury, Norm Norby, Perry Norby, Curt Nordgren, Linda Nordin, Thea Nordling, Virgil Norg Roue,
Norgoard, Steve Norman, Jay Norris, Marilyn and Merv norsky, Bob & Linda Nortes, Cherie Norton, Tor Norway, Matt Nosky, Nick Notarangelo, John Nothacker, Lance Nothstein, Jerry Novak, G
Novella, Luciano Novellino, Jaime y Gloria Novello, Marco Novelo, Carlos Novotny, Rev. Imagen NY, Carlos, Novotny, Jim Nowell, Peter Noyes, Alex Nuñez, Ana Nuñez, carlos Nuñez, Rodolfo N
Alejandro Nuñez Carbajal, Aida Nuñez Nuñez, Jorge Nuñez Perez, Dick Nullen, Betty Nunez, Candido Nunez, German Nunez, Martha Nunez, Lindsay Nunnelee, Aida Nuñez, Betty Nuñez, Guayo Ed
Nuñez, Luchis y Guayo Nuñez, P. Nuskey, David Nussbaum, Dick Nymar, O.D. Hughes, Kelly O¥Dette, Marilyn O¥Dowd, Fran Oakes, Bill & Louise Oatway, Enrique Obando, Julieta Obedman
Obeirne, Tom OBerg, Bert & Pam Obert, Charles A. Obreiter, Ronnie Obriant, Bill O'Brien, Dennis O'Brien, Jack O'Brien, Timothy O'Brien, Jose Ocampo, Claudia Ocaña, Gustavo Ocariz, Fer
Ocejo Robaina, Marco Ochoa, Natalia Ochoa, Antonio Ochoa Jr., Deborah OConnor, Leslie O'Connor, Mike & Jane O'Connor, Nick O'Connor, Steve O'Connor, Tim Octavio, Luis Odbal, Alberto
Merilu O'dell, Michael Odleo, Janelle O'Donnell, Michael Oesch, Model T of America, David Ogalde, Michael Ogando, Patricia Oiontane, Regina O'Keefe, Gloria Okeson, Linda Okland, Howard &
Okumura, Gordon Okyley, Eduardo De Luna Olague, Kris Oldenburg, Brian & Janet O'Leary, Jerry Olexson, Familia Olguin, Raquel Olguin, Claudio Olid, Sergio Oliva y Carina y Brandon, Dan
Jesus Olivares, Familia Olivares, Mauricio Andrea, Adrian y Rodolfo, Olivares, Bradley & Angela Oliver, Dave & Yvonne Oliver, Linda Oliver, Daniel Olivera, Sonia Olivera, Agustina Olivera Ch
Dora Olivera Quesada, Enrique Olivo Servin, Alejandro Olivos, Julieta Olle, Alberto Olmedo, Jose Olmedo, Oscar Olmedo, Santos Olmos, Sergio Olmos, Gene Olofson, Brad Olsen, Dan Olsen, D
Olson, Eric Olson, Roy Olson, Ed & Dan Olszewski, Ricardo Olszewski, Derek Oltman, Luis Olvera Correa, Tim & Lori O'Malia, Michael O'Malley, Jerry Omalleyed, Doug Oman, Lee & Mary O
Daniel Gallo , Omar Barletta, Erk Onderdonk, Georga & Susie Ondola, Jim & Suzane O'Neale, Jack O'Neil, Cathy O'Neill, Joe & Cheryl Onesto, Laureen Ong, B. Onixon, German Ontiveros Ra
Opercar Ltda, Edeline Opheen, Danial Orange, Danial Orange, Mike Orange Collahan, Juanita Oras-aman, Jose Ordaz, Jorge Ordonez, Alonso Ordoñez, Mercedes Ordoñez, Angel Ordotana, R
Oreamura Chaves, Silvio Orellana, Victor Orellana, Eugene Ori, Nathan Abels Orianna, Norma & Mike Origer, Jose Ignacio Orma, Andrei Ornelas, Sandra y Tito Ornelas, Joe Ornie, Maria & Ro
Orofina, Roberto Orofina, Nestor Oropeza, Arturo Orosco Hernande, Virginia O'Rourke, Maria & Alfonso Orozco, Rosa Orta, Juan Orta Rodriguez, Juan manuel Orta Rodriguez, Andrea Ortega, Ca
Vicentica Ortega, Eduardo Ortega, Enrique Ortega, Carlos y Eduardo Ortega del Rio, Ernesto Ortega Hegg, Raul Ortega Sr, Silvia Ortelli, Alexis Ortiz, Cataline Ortiz, Cecilia Ortiz, Gerardo
Humbelina Ortiz, Humbelina Ortiz, Javier y Javier Jr. Ortiz, Maricel Murillo Ortiz, Rodrigo Ortiz, Tom Ortiz, Maurice & Judy Ortiz Jr., Elizabeth Ortiz Tapia, John Osborne, Mitchel Osborne,
Osborne, Ron & Ellen Osborne, Tom Osborne, Yudi Oscar, Oscar Manuel López, Jay Oschrin, Lauren Oschrin, Jorge y Graciela Osella, J. Osendorf, Ed Osgood, W. D. Osgood, Bryan O'Shaughnessy,
Osio, Sarah & Dean Osmar, Gustavo A. Osorio, Rogelio Osorio, Luis Osorio Rodriguez, Mark & Limbania Osredker, Bill Oster holt, Stephan & Anke Osterburg, Bill Osterholt, Chris Ostermann,
Ostrovsky, Fernanda Otalora, Silvia y Thomas Otaola, Allan Otarola, Carla Otero Norta, Bert & Kurt Otten, Irene & Bill Otten, Bert Otto, Victoria Otto, David Outten, Oscar Ovalles, Fausto Ovando,
& Barbara Overman, Sofia Oviedo, Jose Oviedo Garcia, Bob Owens, Hunter Owens, Hunter & Orion Owens, Janel Owens, Lynn Owens, George y TV Oyle, Connie Ozer, Alfredo Pañart, Richy G
Pablo Uriegas, Claudia Pace, Lance & Shally Pace, Pablo Pachalian, Alvaro Pacheco, Claudio Pacheco, Eduardo Pacheco, Luz Ma y Eduardo Pacheco, Ruben Pacheco Redes, Keith Padden, Stanley P
Stanley Paden, Angel Padia, Martin Padia, Alejandra y Fausto Padilla, Jose Padilla, Oscar Padilla, Wanda Padilla, Ayrton Padilla Rivera, Gonzalo Padron, Hilda Padron, Jay Page, Jim Page, Paul & Da
Page, Sean Page, Stacy Pagel, Tony Paget, George Paggelto, Francis Pagnotta, Vanessa Paimann, Michelle Painter, Shauna Pajak, Ana Pajuelo, Charles Pakmoran, Ed Pakulak, Daniel Palacios, Flore
Adolfo Palacios, Marielena y Guillermo Palacios, Rafael Palacios, Raul Palacios, Yosi Sideral 90 1 FM, Palacios, Rosa Palacios Lopez, Marcelo Palafox, Bill Palisin, Nieves y Carlos Paliza, M
Pallevro, Adrian Pallotto, Francisco Pineda Palma, Ramon Palma, Vilma Palma, Maximo Palmbaum, Alan Palmer, Allison Palmer, Brenda Palmer, Bruce Palmer, Martin Palmer, Brenda Palmer-Per
Gabriel y Cata Palomar, Alejandro Palomares, Rita Palomba, Natalia Palomino, Brawonie Palton, Ron Palyu, Oscar y Veronica Pamio, Erik Pampa Mauricio, Phil Panciera, Mauro Pando, Peter P
Eduardo y Mariela Pani, Victor Paniagua, Alejandra Pantas (Mendoza), Justin Panter & Laurie Almouist, Norma Panza, Carlitos Papirri, Wendy Papulias, Georges & Liliane Paradis, Jorge Paraje, Yv
Sebastian Paratte, Paula Pardeiro, Ricardo Pardo, Sergio Paredes, Jorge Pareedes, Paul C. Pareneau, Bob Parent, Dick & Nancy Parent, Steve Pargeter, Jerry Park, Louise & Michael Park, Maiyon
Sunny Park de Ahn, Ricardo Park Venezuela, Ann Parker, Don Parker, Robert Parker, John Parker III, Joanne Parkin, Gene Parkins, Bill Parmott, Leonardo y David Parra, Rafael Parra, Debbie
Parsons, Joan Parsons, Linla Parsons, Larry Parter, Mike Parts, Julio Pasantez, Norberto Pasarino Vigadmier-Attara, Judith Pascal, Jim Pascale, Chuck & Betty Pasceri, Miriam Pasetti, Carlos Pasqu
& Gert Passalaqua, Paul Passidomo, Andrew Passmore, Pat & Andy Passmore, Silvia Pastor, Pilar Pastoriza, Humberto Patargo, Steve & Sue Pate Sr., Kirtie Patel, Ketan Patol, Fred & Karen Patrick,
Patrick, Leland W Patscheck, Diana & Bob Patten, Angela Patterson, Barbara & Neil Patterson, Becky Patterson, Chris y Ada Patterson, Goerge & Ganna Patterson, Robert Patterson, Robert Patt
Stephan & Ceci Patterson, Vicki Patterson, Joe Patton, Terry Patton, Manuel Pucar, Joel Paul, Maria Paula Paul Rendir, James W. & Sarah Paulson, John & Eleine Pauly, Joseito Pava Toscano, José
Caballero, Steve Pavlick, Pawelo, Joseph Payan, Silvina Paykovzki, Glen Payment, Bill & Denise Payne, Jack & Jean Payne, Sarah Payne, Eugene Payne Sr., Dan Paynich, Lorraine Paynter, Nick P
Christopher Paz, MIguel Paz, Gladys Paz, Miguel Paz B., Ernesto Paz Tuvi, Juan Pazos, Victor Pazos, Tom Peacey, Clyde Pearce, Edward Pearcy, Anne Pearlman, Adele Pearlstein, Dave & Deana Pe
Maria Pearse, Amy Pearson, Cheri Pearson, Allison y Steve Pease, Hector Pecerrill, Ctibor Pechlat, Bernie Peck, Velma Peck, Anthony Pedercini, Carlos Pedra, Andrea Pedraza, Sergio Pedraza, Yola

er Pedraza, Laura Marcela Pedraza Florencia, Loures Pedraza Llamas, Luis Pedrotiela, Burton Peebles, Raymond Peek, Russ and Peg, Max & Joan Pehlke, Jerry & Jordana Peil, Arturo y Alejandra ano, Ramiro Pelaez, Camilo Pelliccione, Carmen y Hector Peloche, Hector y Carmen Peloche, Mary C. Peloche, Matthew Peltic, Adolfo Penas, Buzz & Nancy Pendry, Edwin Pens, Juan Pens, Juan y nen Peña, Priscilla Peña, Walter Peña, Javier Peña Valle, Sandra y Julio Peñaloza, David Pepper, Raul Peralta, Natalia Peraltaa, Javier y Daniela Peralya Chanpenel, Anais Peraza, Mary Percak-hinnett, & Mary Perdios, Alfonso Perdomo, Jorge y Lila Pereira, Luciane Pereira, Juan Pereira Jimenez, Jose Pereyra, Alex Hop y Liu, Perez, Brian Perez, Claudia y Heriberto Perez, Fabian Perez, Felipe & a Perez, Fernando y Mishel Perez, Guillermo Perez, Hector y Lucia Perez, Ignacio & Emilia Perez, Jose Perez, José Perez, Juan Jose Espinoza Perez, Luis Perez, Marcelo Perez, Maria Gabriela orell Perez, Miguel Perez, Mirtha Perez, Nelson Perez, Pedro Perez, Rafael Perez, Rolando Perez, Sherri y Hugo Perez, Solange Perez, Tte Eric Perez, Victor Perez, Juan Perez Camarillo, Jose Perez eroa, Jesus Perez Gonzalez, Mayela Perez Hernandez, Valentine Perez Luisa, Jose Perez Martinez, Miguel Perez Piña Leon, Pedro Perez Soto, Jose Perez Villarreal, Peter Perf, Kevin Perin, John Perine, el Perioli, Clarence Perisho, Christian Perizzolo, Andrea & Jeff Perkins, Jerry Perkins, Ken & Shirley Perkins, Martha Perkins, Mary Perko, Phillip y Betty Perley, Aldo Perlini, Norali Permalete, Leroy ian, Juan Pernisco, Roxana Perrault, Isabel y Philip Perrier, Veronique Perrier, Elizabeth Perrins, Bill Perry, Roy Perry, Shirley Perry, Tracey Perry, Dennis Perry Jr., Carlos Peru Squia, Marco Pesaresi, Lori, Jack, Pesta, Sven Peter, Helen Peters, Mike Peters, Ronnica Peters, Brian Petersen, Carol & Dennis Petersen, Christina Petersen, Don & Carol Petersen, Jack M.Irene Petersen, John & Gayle sen, Mariann Petersen, Anna Peterson, Ashlee Peterson, Cynthia Peterson, Jean Peterson, Neil Peterson, Susan Peterson, Vernon y Sharline Peterson, June Peterson Crane, Don Petrice, Bob & Barbara ch, Patrick Petrillo, William Petro, Renai Petter, Maru Pettit, Eduardo Pezzimenti, Ernesto Pfirter, Patrick Pfleger, John & Kim Phelan, DKK Phelps, Gail Philiips, Bua Philipp, Barbara Phillips, Bill ips, Brad & Sue Phillips, Erik Phillips, Gertrude Phillips, Jacquetta Phillips, Jeff Phillips, Jerry & Lue Phillips, Jon & Susan Phillips, Keith Phillips, Mark Phillips, Tim Phillips, Ken Briles Phillis re, Gayle Phipps, María Eugenia Piaggio, John Piasta, Gustavo Piazza, Eddie & Judy Piazze, Rafael Picada, Aldo Pichado Madriz, Jim Pickel, Alan Pickersgill, Alan Pickersgill, R.H. Pickett, Scott e, Ruben Pidal, Piedmont Mopars Unlimited, John Piedrahit, Harry Pierce, Layne Pierce, Ray Pierce, Jean Pierre, Alfred & Barbara Pietroforte, Suzi & Dani Pignataro, Winslow Pillsbury, Melody Y dio Pinacoli, Carla Pineda, David Pineda, Ema Pineda, Karla Pineda, Sheree Pineda, Francisco Pinedo Palma, Peggy Pings, Robert Pinkey, Taylor Pinkley, Lydia Pinkston, Frank Pinkus, Martina os, Claudio, Pinnau, Albino e Irene Pino, Alejandro Pino, Bill Pino, Josef Pino Guimera, Antonio Pinta, Maria Rosa y Manuel Pinto, Melissa Pinto, Roberto Pinto, Guillermo PinzÚn, Larry Pippin, r Dragolovich piriz, Liliana Pitra, Dana Pittman, Monica Pivaral, Noemi Pizarro, Pablo Pizarro, Sammy Planchart, Francoise Plante, Rene Plata, Alejandro Plata Tapia, Shirley Platt, Alfonso Plaza nez, Phill Pletcher, Monica Plevoets, Derek Plummer, Danyla Plungis, Gary Plusam, Isidoro Población, Jose Luis Poggi, Paul Pogue, Luz A. Polanco Diaz, Steve Polasko, Natalia Poli, Julie Pollard, cio Pollo, Denise Pollock, Doug Pollock, Irmgard- Rose Polsterer, Barbara Jean Pompei, Aaron Ponce, Francisco y Erika Ponce, Jose Ponce, Leonardo y Mabel Ponce, Erika Ponce de Leon, Javier e Guzman, Carlos Pons, Guillermo Pons, Juan Carlos Pons, Diana Ponzielli, Bill Pooler, Joe Poore, Oscar Poplawski, Dale Pormeleau, Chacon Porras, Hazel Porras, Chris & Sandra Porter, Fred Porter, as J. Porter, Wendy Porter, Mary Y Cliff Porterfield, Carlos Portillo, Gil & Carol Portillo, Lili y Victor Portillo Rosete, Lalo Porto, Margarita Posada, Teddy Posana, Gustavo Posse, Caittin Post, Cindy Gary Postlethwait, Dean Potter, Jon Potter, Tommy Potter, Anne Powell, Art Powell, Brad Powell, Cliff Powell, Don Powell, Harry Powell, James Powell, John Powell, Karon Powell, Sarah Powell, el Pozas, Walter Pozo, Jerry Pr2byla, Miguel Doblas Prades, Angela Prado, Arturo Prado, Javier Prado, Jose Prado, Asoc.Salvadoreña de Carros Antiguos Prado Rivas, Rich Pramuk, Mark & Debbie r, Janeen Pratt, Jonathan Pratt, Jonathan Pratt, Steve & Kate Pratt, Mitchell Praver, Linda Preciado Chavez, Jose Luis Prendas, Dick Prentice, Sheryl Prentice, Benny Presley, Orris Presley, Georgia ell, Marissa Preston, William Preston, Pablo Prezioso, Benjamin & Andreza Price, Roger Price, Armando Prida, Anita Priest, Barry Priest, Steve & Anita Priest, Sebastian Prieto, Ana Prima de Cristina, es Primera, Edward Prince, Nick Prince, Regina Prinz, Alan Prior, Kerth Privett, Dra Monica Prochnuk, Dave Proehl, Cristina y Stephen Prokop, George Pruitt, Marcia Prunty, Alan Pryor, Vince iev, Dave Pucci, Samuel Puccio, Alisa Pucher, Randy Pucher, Julian Puente, Adrian Puentes, Osvaldo Puentes, Laurian Puerta, Arturo Pugach, Miguel Pugliese, Adriana Puig, James & Tracie Puiker, Pulido, Rogelio Pulido, Andy Pulizzi, Samantha Pullman, damel puma, Luciana Puntillo, Daniel Pupko, Joni Purcell, Don Purdey, Kin Purdye, Mark Purneil, Howard Purvis, Phil Pusateri, Denis Pust, ard Pye, Jim Quackenbush, John & Beverly Quackenbush, Donna Quaker Bush, Mike & Aprile Quales, Mercedes Quant, Alexandra Quesada, Maria Quesada, Tzetzangari Quesada, Lucia Quesafa a, Harry & Eva Quest, Eduardo Quevedo, Fernando Quezada, Lupe Quezada, Carlos Quiñonez, Silvana & Stephen Quigley, Stephen Quigley, Ximena Quijano, Jeff Quilici, Mike Quinlan, John ley, Richard Quinn, Kim Connie, Quinn Widrick, Luis Quintana, Marco Quintana, Fernando Quintero, Jorge Quintero, Nuria Quios Mendez, Juan Quiroa, Camila Quiroga, Jorge y Norma Quiroga, a Quiroga, Pedro Quiroga, Fabian Quiroga y Flia, Jose y Andres Quiros, Ernesto Quiros Rellca- Costa Riza, Fernando Quirva, Jesus Rabadan, Victor Rabbone, Federico Rabe, Arlene Rabin, Janella al, Richard Radcliffe, Lisa Rader, Maxine Rader, Robin & Tynan Radford, Jim Rae, Phyles Raemheld, Carla Martinez Rafael, Ignacio Rafael, Sergio & Rene Chavira Rafael Garcia, Pato Rafel, Joseph zzo, Alba Raidel, Kathryn Railing, Pat Railing, Rudger Raino, Don Raker, Jeff Rakes, Bill Raleigh, Trish Ralph, Wunona Ralph, Michael & Heather Ralston, Echo Ralton, Francisco Ramales, Luis & a Ramallo, Adriana Ramat, Carlos Rames, Silvio Ramin, Adolfo Ramirez, Alejandra Ramirez, Ana Ramirez, Angel Ramirez, Christian Ramirez, Enrique Ramirez, Esteban Ramirez, Gabriel Ramirez, or y Josefina Ramirez, John Ramirez, Leonardo Ramirez, Luis Ramirez, Maricela Ramirez, Oscar Ramirez, Rafael Ramirez, Victor Ramirez, Zaire Ramirez, Lucila Ramirez Arreguin, Erosto Ramirez ngel Ramos, Antonio Ramos, Carmen Ramos, Daniel Ramos, Jose Ramos, Marcelo Ramos, Melvin Ramos, Valmique Ramos Grandez De Araujo, Pablo y Alida Ramos R., Vicente Ramos Segundo, de Autos Antiguos de Nuevo Laredo Ramos Segundo y Tercero, Vicente Ramos Segundo y V.R.Tescano, Scott Ramsay, José Ranchos, Leticio Ranco, Jake Rand, Joseph & Cindy Randall, Darlene olph, Peyton Randolph, Jaime Rangel, Monica Rangel, Francisco Rangel Perez, Justin Ranney, Floyd Ransom, Scott Ranson, Alejandro Ortega del Risco, Arnold Rapaport, Dan Rappleye, Dan leye, Scott Rariek, Kirk Rashka, Steve Kailin, Erika, Rasmusser, Pat Rasor, Alex & Elena Raspa, Patricia Rassuli, Lauren Terri & Riley Ratkoviak, Frank & Barbara Rauch, Raphel Rauen, Roxanne r, Charles & Nadine Raugh, Yoland Arreola Davila Raul Garces Medina, Jeff Raunt, Harald Rauser, Diego Ravera, Sandra Ravine, David Rawley, Kelly & Larae Ray, Laura Raymond, Garth Rayne, n Rayon Napoleon, Regina Raz, Josue Razo, Eduardo Real, Phyllis Ream, Barbara Reasor, John Rebecek, Gustavo y Lorena Recalde, Emily Recalma, Pepe Recio, Jen Reckley, Nevin Recter, Steve or, Riequel Red horse, Mario Reda, Juan Reda El Gaucho, Dick & Marilyn Redd, Gaby Reddin, Juan Redo, Javier Redondo, Dave Reece, Gene Reece, Kenny Reece, Peter Reece, Jim Reed, John Reed, Reed, Scott Reed, Phil Reedbluecrown, Regina & Chris Reeder, Mike Rees, Alfred & Ann Reeves, Rogelio Refaccionana, Refaccionaria Rolcar, Judy Reff, Nicetta Regalado, Pepe Regens, Michael rs, Cecil Regier, Rafael Regina Moreno, Paul Reich, Susie Reich, Erich Reichen Bach, Larry & Jan Reichenbaugh, Richardo Reichert, Bruce y Gloria Reid, Kathie Reid, Sue Reif, Vladimir Reil, Flor Hard, Martha Reinares, Audi Reinthaler, Pete Reinthaler, Geoffrey & Corine Reis, Russ Relyea, Kristin Remus, Ronny Manuel y Alicia, Ren, Marco Rendon, Jaime Rendon Esteva, Sherry And Rene, & Nellie Rene Gar, Ninel Rengel, Lenny Rengifo, Donald Rennett, Bills Rentals, Andres Repetto, Susan & Norm Repplinger, Jorge y Paloma Resa, Alberto Resendiy, Abel Elizabeth, Eric & Sheyla, ndiz, Clemente Resendiz, Familia Resendiz Andrade, Tomas Resendiz O., Jose Resendiz Olivera, Beth & Rudy Reshetar, Patrick & Chrystal Ressse, Restaurant Cambalache, Restaurant El che porteño, urant Garufa, Jose Retamales, Laura Retta, Lindsay Reusch, Rachel Revett, Revista CADEAA Argentina, Univ de Monterrey Revista vision FC, Jenny Rex, Benjamin Reyes, Carmen Reyes, Juan s, Julio Reyes, Marco Reyes, Salvador Reyes, Javier Reyes Cedilh, Manuel Reyes Jr., Alicia Juan Antonio, Marcos y Marisol, Reyes Ortiz, Chris Reymann, Daniel Reyna, Victor Reyna, Olliver Reyna ero, Ituarta Reynava, Art Reynolds, Steve & Becky Reynolds, Tom Reynolds, Alfonso Reynoso, Alfonso Reynoso, Ruben Reynoso, Antonio Reynoso Calderon, Richard & Nancy Rheingold, Veradiz esmith, James Rhoads, Jo Rhode, Ron Rhodelhamel, Dusty Rhodes, Jason Rhodes, Nancy & Richard Rhungold, Guillermo Riascos, Roberto Ribeiro, Angel Ribulotta, Narciso Nayeli Salas, Ricardo a, Prisciliano Ricardo Sosa, Jorge Ricatti, Teresa Riccobuono, Carol Rich, Kerry Rich, Lucy Rich, Marvin Rich, Rich From Berea, Christopher Richard, Pauline Richard, Mr. & Mrs Richard Carlson, & Irene Richards, Milt Richards, Darren & Roberta Richardson, Steve Richardson, To the Richardson's, Joanne Richcreek, Cristobal Richer, Debbie Richey, Jerry y Faye Richmond, Claris Richter, her Richter, Marc Ricii, Deborah Ricker, Linda Ricks & Andreu V. Brannon, Flores Rico, Ken Ridden & Daniel Pau, Paul Riedel, Veronica Riedel, Mike Rieser, María Jose y Patricio Rifo, Kin Riggs, fer Righetti, Dick Riley, Russell Rinckey, Isabel Rincon, Alfonso Rincon Gallardo, Eduardo Rincon Gallardo, Diana Rindom, Ron Riodelle & Jill Nelson, Jose Riojas Molinas, Aurora Rios, Cecilio Elio Rios, Juan Rios, Luis & Tona Rios, Santiago y Rocinda Rios, Sergio Rios, Ricardo Ríos Abarca, Elisabeth y Moises Rios Juarez, Eugenia Ripari, Arnaldo Riquelme, Rita G. Riquelme, Giuseppe Tom Rissler, Pat Boothe Rita Shaw, Don and Lillian Ritchey, Marcel Ritchot, Larry Ritter, Sarah Mike & Daniel, Ritthaler, Stephen Lizette, Michaela, Ritz, Guy Rivard, Arturo Rivas, Gonzalo Rivas, Basilio Rivas, Angelo Rivera, Carlos Rivera, Charles Rivera, Dania Rivera, Jesus Rivera, Mayeli Rivera, Miguel & Victoria Rivera, Sixto Rivera, Dr. Julio Rivera Alvarez, Alan Rivera Martinez, ia Riveras, Raul Riveros A., Erma Rivotta, Anthony Rizk, Roberto Armando Rizzi, Ivano Rizzieri & Family, Robin Rizzo, María Alejandra Roa, Joe & Marilyn Roach, Nan Wigington Rob Scene, lfo & Carmen Robaina, Dale y Maggie Robbins, Maggie and Dale Robbins, Sandra Roberge (Denis), Antonio Robert, Curtis Robert, Harrasser Robert, Robert Lowrey, Glenn Roberts, J.D.v & Harriet rts, Joann & John Roberts, June & Tom Roberts, Lola y Leslie Roberts, Valerie Roberts, Will Roberts, Corry & Andrew Robertson, Darrell & Barbara Robertson, David Robertson, Sigrun Robertson, l & Nathan Robinette, Patsy Robins, April Robinson, Arthur Robinson, B. Robinson, Charles Robinson, Karen Robinson, Keith & Sarah Robinson, Linda & Jim Robinson, Mike Robinson, Mouret son, Sasha Robinson, Terry Robinson, Matias Robles, Rudy & Pat Robles, Analia Robles Guerrero, Terri Robson, Alfredo Roca, Dr. Gustavo Rocatagliatta, Peter Roccanova, Fernando y Leticia a, Sergio Rocha Muñoz, Eustache Roche, Jonathan Rochon, Maurice Rochon, Brett Schmoll Rocio Garcia, Ben & Dan Rock, David Rock, Vaughn Rockafellow, Serena Rocks, Carol & Leo Rockwell, Rodas, Nathalie y Kerly Rodas Alban, Dale Rodebaugh, Lisa Roder, Susan Roder, Susan & Lee Rodgers, Patricia Rodino, Mary Pepa Rodolfo Loyola, Sebastien Rodrigue, Agustin Rodriguez, ndro Rodriguez, Alexander Rodriguez, Alfredo Rodriguez, Allan Rodriguez, Antonieta Rodriguez, Antonio & Juanita Rodriguez, Barry Rodriguez, Carlos y Claudia Rodriguez, Clelia Rodriguez, obal Rodriguez, Daniel G. Rodriguez, Darin Rodriguez, David y Pablo Rodriguez, Delfin Rodriguez, Ferraro Valades Rodriguez, Francisco Rodriguez, George & Dora Rodriguez, Gustavo Rodriguez, y Rodriguez, Hiram Rodriguez, Hugo Rodriguez, Jadith Rodriguez, Jose Rodriguez, Juan Rodriguez, Juan Carlos Rodriguez, Lililan Rodriguez, Luis Rodriguez, Marcelo Rodriguez, Maria Rodriguez, icio Rodriguez, Nicholas Rodriguez, Norma Rodriguez, Omar Rodriguez, Osvlado y Chichita Rodriguez, Paola Rodriguez, Patricia Rodriguez, Rafain Rodriguez, Sergio Rodriguez, Silvana Rodriguez, Rodriguez, Wendy Rodriguez, Franz Rodriguez, Luisa Rodríguez, Moisés Ramos Rodríguez, Ximena y Guillermo Rodriguez Cavallazzi, Paola Rodriguez Cospinera, Roberto Rodriguez Haydee, an Rodriguez Hernandez, Eduardo Rodriguez Islas, Erika Rodriguez Lara, Cachan Rodriguez Loera, Jose Rodriguez Loera, Jesus Rodriguez Mexico, Gustavo Rodriguez Panyagua, Jose David guez Vallejo, Jaime Rodriguez Zamudio, Glen Roebuck, Karl Roenick & Joan, John & Judy Roettgen, Bob & Jean Rogers, Craig Rogers, Gene & Annette Rogers, J. D. Rogers, Jay Rogers, Krista s, Michael Rogers, R Mike Rogers, Linda Roggensack, Alex Rogovin, Jorge Roimiser, Dario Roitbourd, Luis Rojano Campillo, Alejandro Rojas, Carolina Rojas, Fernando Rojas, Gaby Rojas, Ignacio , Jesse Rojas, Juan Rojas, Kattia Rojas, Manuel y Sandra Rojas, Maria Rojas, Mariano Rojas, Mauricio Rojas, Ra'l y Carmelo Rojas, Rogelio Rojas, Vicror Rojas, Macielos Rojas de Alajuda, Karla Montero, Alejandro Rojas Morales, Victor Rojas Ramirez, Jose Rojas V, Peg Rojen, Adan Rojo, Roberto Rojo, Fabian Roldan, Maria Roldan, Marie Roldan, Manuel Roldan Roboz, Helen Rolls, to Roman, Cesar Roman, Diego Roman, Luis Roman, Paco y Crisitna Roman, Bruce Romann, Miriam Romano, Terry Rombeck, David Romero, Enrique Romero, Jaime Romero, Juan Romero, Marta ero, Raul Romero, Victor Romero, Wilmer Romero, Monica y Moises Romero Peloche, Olivia Romero Ramos, Rodrigo Romero Saldivar, Sarai Romero Sanchez, Camilo Romerp, Carlos y Ofelia llo, Dick Romm, Geovanny & Erica Romo, Pepe Romo Madrigal, Dr. Hector Romo R., Liz Franklin Ron Spittka, Brian Rongo, Donna Ronnan, Luis Angel Barbero Rosa Alvarez de Barbero, Julio es, Kenneth Rosales, Moises Rosales, Zonia Rosales, Karina Rosas, Jose Rosas Caro y Daniel Ramos, Alejandro Rosas Robles, Marco Rosas Velazquez, Alma y Jeannie Rosas y Kever, Romano spina, Joe Rose, Kandy Rose, Susan Rose & Jose R. Lopez, Elaine Roseborough, Miguel Rosemberg, Diana Rosen, Al & Margy Rosenbaum, Barbara Rosenberg, Daniel Rosenblatt, Rosie Rosenblitt, Rosenski, Peggy Rosenthal, Fausto & Luis Rosero, Frank Rosin, Brian Rosner, Bob Ross, Brandon Ross, Doug Ross, Joan Ross, John Ross, Steve Ross, Amy Rossetti, Francisco Rossetto, Giovanni , Peter Rotelle, Gerald Roth, Pam Roth, Laura Soledad Rotta, Maria Rougel, Mercedes Rouges, James Rough, Ricardo Roura, David Rouse, Mike Routt, Gustavo Rovaretto, Andy Rowe, Ray & Allene and, Kathy Rowly, Art & Mary Roy, Takalek Roy and Sandra, Jeff Royce, Owen Royce, Kate & Owen Royce & Mary Elizabeth, Gary Royer, Maria Rozada, Ross Rozsees, Collado Ruben y Jorge , Jose Rubio, Milagro Rubio, Judy Rubright Belac, Ricardo Ruchman, Sam & Anita Rudd, Robert Ruddy, Gene Rudolph, Rodolfo Rudy, Diego Tax Rudy Zepeda, Alfredo Rueda Mendoza, Frank , Gary Rugaber, Cunthia Ruggeiro, Anteo Ruiz, Arnaldo y Betty Ruiz, Daniel Ruiz, Familia Ruiz, Francisco Ruiz, Guillermo Ruiz, Jorese Ruiz, Lucila Ruiz, Pablo Roberto Ruiz, Sergio Ruiz, Ulises Fco. Ruiz Charape, Federico Ruiz Diaz, Omar Ruiz Diaz, Adrian Ruiz Garcia, Jorge Ruiz Peña, John & Jan Rulka, Kevin & Lisa Rumeas, Eva Rummel, Mike Rumpf, Marlene Runkle, Horacio Rur, rey Rus, Edgardo Rusca, Art Ruschev, Ross Russel, Grathe Russell, Hugh & Pat Russell, Sonja Russell, Harry and Agnes Russell and Mc Intyre, Delerio Russi, John Russo, Joy Russolillo, Bette Rutan, vo Rutilo, Laverne y Harriet Rutschman, George Ryan, Jerry & Kathy Ryan, Margery Ryan, Mike & Carrie Ryan, Tom Ryan, Ron Ryder, Barbara S., Jose S. Romo Madrigal, Ghanem Nahla y Suso, Wolf and lani Saar, Adrian Sabanero, Anibal y Graciela Sabate, Donna & Jerry Saber, Hernando Sabogal, Angela Sacchetto, Arnaldo y Carmen Sacchetto, Damon Sacco, David Sadowski, Norma , Brian Sagar, Dori Sage, Corky & Madeline Sager, Alvaro Sagot, Marcela Sahade, Rita Sahai, Sal & Joy Saimieri, Steve Sais, Marie Salanitre, Steve Salankey, Damais Salas, Elizabeth Salas, erto Salas, Ricardo Salas, Victor Salas, Desiree Salas Acurio, Raul Salas Gonzalez, Jorge Salas Sánchez, Carmen Salazar, Cristina Salazar, Gustavo y Nora Salazar, Irene Salazar, karina Salazar, Juan ar B., Eduardo Salceda Andrade, Jose Saldaña Cortes, Julio Saldana, Carlos Saldaña, Dave Salem, Mouner & Rebecca Salem, Ralph Salerno, Marcelo Salgado, Hanni Salik, Latifah Salim, Delfina as, Jose Salinas, Jun Salinas, Raul Salinas, Santiago Aragon y Salinas, Raul Salinas Sosa, B. Salinger, Grant Salisbury, Steve & Salisbury, Gonzalo Sallaberry, Joe Sallmen, Cristina Salmon, Micheal

Salmon, Ron Salmon, Eduardo Salseda Andrade, Luke & Heather Saltzman, Diario La Prensa Grafica Salvador Reyes, Diego Salvadori, John & Julianne Salverson, Renee Salvucci, Richard Salyor, Cris
Sam, Rigby Sam, Francisco Sama, Nelson Samaniego, Peter Samaroo, Nicholas Sammond, Rathie & Jamie Samoa Cookhouse, Lucia Sampayo Zarate, Joel Sample, Harold Samuels, Laurie and
Samuels and Dordal, Luis San Martin Fuentes, Gilbert San Miguel, Norma y Daniel San Pedro, Freddy y Valentina Sanabria, Danyela Sanches, Agustin & Sonia Sanchez, Antonio & Melissa Sanchez, Be
Sanchez, Diego Sanchez, Emilio Sanchez, Evangelia Sanchez, Familia Sanchez, Francisco Sanchez, Gilberto Sanchez, Heuton Sanchez, Hortensia Sanchez, Idalia y Crystal Sanchez, Javier Sanchez, J
Carlos Sanchez, Julian Sanchez, Mayra Sanchez, Miguel Sanchez, Miguel A. Sanchez, Milagros Sanchez, Octavio Sanchez, Oscar Sanchez, Pablo Sanchez, Ray & Ciria Sanchez, Roberto Sanchez, Rod
Sanchez, Ruben Sanchez, Salvador Sanchez, Tom Sanchez, Vicent Sanchez, Gerardo Sanchez A., Federico y Mercedes Sanchez Gomez, Laura Sanchez H., Mariela Sanchez Iglesias, Gabriela Sanc
Lopez, Francisco Sanchez M., Familia Sanchez Nuñez, Ana Sanchez Otero, Alda Sanchez Peña, Marco Sanchez Quiroz, Marco Ignacio Sanchez Quiroz, Marco Antonio Sanchez Rodriguez, Jose Sanc
Torres, Hector Sanchez Ugarte, Leticia Sanchez Zavala, Arsenio Sancho, Sandra Sancho, Veronica Sancho, Alexander Sancho Bunett, Lori & Dacy Sanda, Dave Sandberg, Dave Sandberg, Dirk Sar
Mongel, Alyce Sanders, John Sanders, John Mark & Kein Sanders, Paul Sanderson, Cynthia Sandi Bazo, Edwin Sandoval, Familia Sandoval, Felipe Sandoval, Linda Sandoval, Maria Luisa y Ar
Sandoval, Rosa Sandoval, Jorge Sandoval Leon, Jorge Michelle Sandra Brito, Alisy Sandu, Jose Sandval Osorino, Bill & Gerry Sandy, Charlie & Jane Sanerwein, Maria Sanfilipo, Teresa Sanga, Cata
Sanint, Pat Sanker, Exequiel Sans, Juan Carlos Sanseviero, Vicente Sanseviero M., Frank & Louise Sanson, Laura y Jorge Santa Ana, Eduardo y Andrea Santagati, Juan Santana, Peggy Santana, Salva
y Mao Santana, Ada & Jorge Santangelo, Anthony Santasien, Luisa Santesteban, Alejandro Santi, Guillermo y Cristina Santiago, Larry & Vicky Santiago, Sonia Santiago, Martin Santipolio, Pat
Santisteuan, Ignacio Santo, P.J. Santoro, Daniel Santos, Eduardo Santos, Fco. Santos, Horacio Santos, Luz y Francisco Santos, Ricardo Santos, Richard & Nely Santos, Pete Santrock, Scott Santulli, An
Sapone, Ernest Sapp, Hector Sarabia, Tricia Saraceno, Tatiana Sarasty, Matias Saravia, Eduardo J. Sardi, David Sarfati, Henry Stenson Sarita Geddes, Leonard Sarja, Padre Sarleedo, Roberto Sarlo, Grac
Sarmiento, Miguel Saronia, Alejandro Sarria, Carlos Sarullo, Juan Carlos Saseviero, Irene Sassaman, Orkid Sassohim, Gustavo Satarain, Carlos Sato, Tita Saucedo, Mike & Norma Sauer, Pablo y Mela
Sauma, John Saunders, Wermer Sauter, Bill & Midori Savage, Nancy & Rudy Savage, Phil & Betsey Savage, Robert Savant, Donna and Jerry Saver, Beto Savina, Chuck Savitske, Dario & Mar
Savoretti, Marga Savorin, Benjamin Sawyer, Liesa Sawyer, Willlard Sawyer, Peter & Oris Sayer, Dick & Marilyn Sayers, Andrea Sayfy, John Saylor, Helen Sayre, Jay Sayre, Terry Sayther, Jose Scal
Evangelina Scalpelli, Sheila Scaney, SCCA, David Schaeffer, Sheldon Schafer, Juan Schaffer, Shirley Schaffer, Ed Schafield, Art Schagfer, Peter Schaible, Donna & Ryan Schanlane, Margie & D
Schantz, Jill & Rich Schanzlin, Nestor Schatzky, Peer Schauwecker, Brad Scheafmocker, Jim & Emilie Scheidel, Don Schellenberg, Todd & Corrie Schelling, Amy Schenck, Ray Schenk, Katie & Gun
Schennach, Andres Schert, Mark Schertzer, Shelby Schetstream, Cheryl Schey, Miriam Schifer Castro, Randy Rorin & Evan, Schiller, Ron Schilling, Ronnie Schilling, George Schimmel, Barry Schinma
Rodrigo Schippers, Fred Schirk, Dortje Schirok, Cindy Schisler, Dave & Cyndie Schlie, David Schlosser, Steve Schmauch, Alfredo Schmidt, Doris Schmidt, Hank Schmidt, John & Diana Schmidt, Lo
and Becky Schmidt, Maggie Schmidt, Milton Schmidt, Richard Schmidt, Rolf Schmidt, Sandra Schmidt, Hugo Schmitt, Klaus Schmitt, Vernon y Sharline Schmitt, Brett Schmoll, Walter Schmucker, H
Schnam, Annemarie Schnedler, Bodile & Ouane Schneider, Paul & Beth Schneider, Rob Schneider, Carl Schneidor, Nancy Schnell, Kraig Schnitzmeier, Maria Schoch, June Schoeff, Robert &
Schoemaker, Barry Schoenly, Joan Gary & Jared, Schoenly, Mrs. Eva Schoettle, Peter Schofield, George Scholl, Adam Schoolsky, Inger Schou, Alex & Olivia Schrimp, Fred y Ina Schubert, John & Ma
Schuhle, Peter Schuler, Ana Schultz, Mike Schulz, Mickel Schulze, Linda Schutt, Ken Schwall, Doug Schwandt, Miguel Schwarcz, April Schwartz, Robert & Arlene Schwartz, Tim Schwartz,
Schwartzman, Clara Schweitzer, John Schwieds, Peter y John Scoiriduk, The Robert Scoon, David Ryan, Tom, Scott, Evil Scott, Kathie Scott, Leslie Scott, Mike Scott, Andrea Scribano, Ron Scrivner,
Scroggins, Brooke Scruggs, Rett Scudder, Joseph Scuderi, Robbyne Seagert, Daniel Seagnolari, Lee Seagondollar, Scott & Lynn Seals, David Sealza, Donna Searer, Bob Sears, Esther SEatle, Dan Sea
Frances Seay, Tatjana Semina Sebastien Ide, Roy & Mary Sebring, Ariel y Silvia Seco, Anne Sedola, Judy See, Gonzalo y Caro Seeber, Lela Seefeldt, Larry Seeman, Debra & Tom Seery, Sharly Seese,
Segal, Enrique Segarra, Mike Seggie, Oscar Segovia, Carlos Segovia Silva, Jorge Segoviano, Carlos Segura, Nejtali y Silvia Segura, Paola Segura, Patricia Segura Alvarez, Mary Ann Seher, Rene & Le
Sehug, Ben- Willie Seibold, Daniel & Mapy Seidel, Rikki Seidlitz, Brandon Seidman, Lisa Seifert, Carol Seitz, Martini Selay, Raquel Selinger, Marianne & Chuck Selkirk, John Sell, Leo & Dorotea Se
Bill & Steven Sellers, Marty Sellers, David Semmel, Hugo y Silvia Semperena, Carla Roxana Cruz Sempértegui, Michael Senta, Sandra Senteiro, Eduardo Sepulveda, Rodrigo Sepulveda, Carlos Seque
Ra´l de J. Ramos Sequeyro, Nury y Oscar Serafini, Yolanda Beltran Sergio Mansilla, Sergio¥s Towing, Guillermo y Ma. Emilia Series, Carlos y Vivian Serig, Guillermo Serpa Ratti, F. Serralde, Amar
Serrano, Carmen Serrano, Juan H. Serrano, Manolo Serrano, Maria Serrano, Nick Serrano, Miguel Serrano y Familia, Orlando Serrato, Andres Serrutt, Customer Service, International Service, M &
Service, Delia Settecase, Don Setters, Donna Setzer, Mike Seuffert, Alfredo Sevilla, Mary Sexton, Tori Sexton, Jack Seymour, Brian & Linda Shaefer, Billie Shains, Brock & Janice Shamberg, Ma
Shamdasani, Jim Shane, Sharon Shangi, Bob Shanks, Claudia & Robert Shannon, Luke Shannon, Ron & Judy Shannon, Family Shapiro, Lou & Debi Sharick, Milan & Pat Sharik Jr., Dona Sharket,
Sharp, Rick Sharpe, Rickie Sharpe, Tina Sharpe, Erika & Ryan Shaugnessy, Helen Shaw, Kevin Shaw, Toni Shaw, Brian Shawbads, Acoli shcks, Mathew Shea, Ron Sheardown, Janet Shearer, Te
Sheehan, Paul Sheehy, Paul Sheehy, Raymond Sheets, Jim & Ronni Sheflo, Joe & Jackie Shekman, Melissa Shelby, Shell de Belize, Shell de Guatemala, Charles Shelley Nagel, Kevin Shellhamer,
Shelton, Ben & Christine Shennum, Debbie Shepack, Steve Shepard, Carlos y Bill Shepheerd, Rajendra Shepherd, Rob Shepherd, Alberto Sherard C., Bill Sherk, Angela Sherman, Joe & Jackie Sherr
Joe and Jackie Sherman, Johnny Sherman, Kerry Sherman, Larry Sherman, Miranda Sherman, Ruth and Larry Sherman, T. David Sherman, Terry and Charlotte Sherman, Janet Sherrill, Harry Sherwe
Steven & Debra Shie, Ray Shields, Jim Shilman, Lynn Shine, Doug & Phyliss Shipman, David Shirley, James Shirley, Marget & Jim Shively, John Shoemaker, Shopping Plaza Dorada en Merida, Kath
Shore, Bill Shorklox, Don & June Short, Rich Short, Ken & Heather Showers, S. Shroff, Vera Shugak, Steve & Sally Shugart, Jim Shulman, Catherine Cecil, Hannah & Heidi, Shuman, Shelly & Joe Shw
Randall Shymko, Joao A. Siciliano, Athelene Sickler, Vanesa Sicolo, Jean & Keith Siebarth, Danielle & Mike Sieberer, Manuela Siegfried, Michael Sienkowski, Randy Sierk, Fernando Sierna, Angel Sie
Juan Sierra, Keith Sierra, Marjorie Sierra, Oscar & Liliana Sierra, Oscar A. & Liliana N. Sierra, Allen Patrice &Lauren, Sigmon, Paavo Siitam, Elizabeth Sikora, David Silberman, Luis Silbert, David S
Ronald y Mary Silesky, Jack Sill, Betty & Elvio Silva, Cesar Silva, Marcos Antonio Silva, Oseias Silva, Tomas Silva, Cesar Silva Castro, Josiel y Norma Silva Matos, Kamila Silveira, Eugene Silve
Andrew Silvoy, Nancy Simcax, Enoch Simerly, Carlo De Simine, Thomas Simmonds, Harold & Cora Simmons, Jim Simmons, Mike Simmons, Tom Simmons, Geneva Simms, Dewwis Simon, Al Simo
Phil & Karen Simons, Phillip Simons, Jim Simpson, Lee Simpson, Pat Simpson, Sue Simpson, Robert Sims, Vice Pte Jersy Sinclair, Jerry Sinclaire, Cathy Singer, Ed Debbie & Katherine, Singer, S
Singer, Tim Singer, Sean & Lizz Singh, Jack Sink, James Sinn, Michael Sinn, Janet Siomiat, Michael Sipes, Mauricio Sisterna, John Sivanich, John Sivanich, Zoia Siz Goric, Pentti Sjoman, Guisela Ska
Richard Skaggs, Sean Skibec, Aaron Skinner, Gary Skinner, Robert Skinner, Sarah Skinner, Frannie Skomurski, Bob Skudera, David Skutca, Richard Slater, Karen Slattery, R. Slepine, Eddie and Ka
Sloan, Mike Slone, Dic & Lynne Slunaker, Vernon & Snipes Slurley, Carlos Slythe, Clyde & Betty Small, Gary Small, Greg & Sue Smallwood, Bob & Bonnie Smetts, Randy Smiley, Karl Smily, Bi
Smirololo, Andy Smith, Angel Smith, Bob & Irene Smith, C.T. Smith, Charles Smith, Charlie Smith, Cindy & Steve Smith, Cristina Smith, David Smith, Debbie & Tommy Smith, Don & Cristina Sm
Donna Smith, Earl Smith, Editor Charlie Smith, Federico Smith, Floyd Smith, Grant & Holly Smith, Harold Smith, Hartley Smith, Hawley Smith, Hugh Smith, Ian Oliver & Robin, Smith, Irene Smith,
Smith, James Smith, Jennifer Smith, Joann Smith, Lawrence & Mary Smith, Len Smith, Linda Smith, Martin Smith, Mary Smith, Micah Smith, Oliver Smith, P. Smith, P. Clifford Smith, Phil Smith, Ph
Smith, Rick Smith, Robert Smith, Russell Smith, T. Smith, Tammy Smith, Terry Smith, Tom Smith, Tracy Smith, Tyler Smith, Virginia Smith, William Smith, William H. Smith, Yvonne Smith, Richar
Jo Smithen, Kimberley Smithers, Chris Smithey, Danielle Smithey, Danny Smithey, George Smolenyak, Tony Smoot, Ruth Smoyer, Gary Smullin, David Snead, Dale Snelson, Grace Snider, Laurie Sni
Ken Sniper, Harvey Snitzer, David Snow, Bill Snyder, Jim Snyder, Kerry Snyder, Kris Snyder, Pat Snyder, Robert Snyder, Alex Sobol, Mikce & Lou Sobotka, Marina Sobrino, Mario Soch, Socie
Portuaria de Barranquilla, Ray Soderlund, Ryan Soderlund, Joanna & Bill Sodrel, Mike Soehnleins, Daniel Sojo, Scott Sokol, Andrea Solano, Laura Solano Carranza, Dennis Solares, Denny Solberg, I
Solecki, Ana Maria Soler, Damian Solis, Luz Solis, Martin Solis, Mercedes Solis, Milagros Solis, José Solís, Mara Solla, Jasper Solomon, Jorge y Patricia Solorzano, German Solveira, Catherine Soly
Craig Somers, Joanne Somers, Deg Somerville, Dennis Somerville, Steve Sommerhalter, Bill Sommers, Jon Sonen, Tim & Denise Sonnentag, Edmar Sonza, Revista Sophia, Lynne Sorber, Jack and Ar
Sorensen, Thomas Sorensen, Ignacio Soria, Juana Soriano de Leon, David Sorokurs, Daniel Sosa, Marcolina Sosa, Vicent Sosa, Carlos Sosa Estrada, Bill & Linda Sosnowsk, Linda & Bill Sosnowski
Soss, Adam Sotelo, Jess Sotelo, Jose A. Sotelo, Eduardo Soteras, Jose Soto, Jose Soto, Carlos Soto Alfaro, Jose Soto Cruz, Norma Soto y Martin Campos, Selene & Greg Soucy, Jim& Debbie Sou
Anthony South, Craig Southern, Joan Southon, Helena Sowinsky, Luis Spadafora, C. Spady, Sylvia Spady, Tim Spangler, Steve Spann, Willie Spann, Bill Sparrow, Bob & Martha Spence, Kippy Sper
Esteban Spera, Edgardo Spik, Philip Spinella, Maria Eugenia Spinelli, Tony Spirer, Ian Spiridigliozzi, Fernando Spirito, Robert and Hope Spishak, Alberto Spognardi, Stanley Spohr, Paula Spoila,
Spoto, James Spottiswoode, James Constance, Spottiswoode, Rw Spraggins, Frank Springer, Philips St John, David & Paula St. Clair, Tom St. George, Donald Stacker, Julia Stadler, Jim Staehli,
Stafford, Angel Stamatis Lopez, Jeffry Stambor, Bill Stame, Daniel Stamm, Joe Stancil, Tom Standing, Denns Stanffed, Fred Stanffer, Debra Jim and P.J.,Stanford, Amy Stanley, Bill Stanley, Jean Stan
Kathleen Stanley, Loretta Stanley, Martha Stanley, Tom Stanton, Judith Stapleton, Gale & Louise Starman, Bobby & Rose Stearns, Carl Stecker, Mary Kay Steele, Shirley Steele, Bruce Steely, Mic
Steely, Lynn & Mark Steen, Embaj. Arg. en Trinidad Stefanelli, Juanvla Stefani, Mica Stefani, Milagros Stefani, Vladimiro Stefani, Alfredo Stefanini, Rob & Yumi Stehle, Steve Stein, Howard Steinb
Isaac Steiner, John Steiner, Megan Steiner, Todd & Jana Steiner, Mark Steinhardt, Andrew Steinhover, Mariel Steinman, Susan Steinnerd, Mariela Steller, Ron Stellhorn, Nancy Stener, Stephen y Li
Bonna Stephens, Brad Stephenson, Dorin & Fred Steputes, Guillermo Steta, Barbara Bein Steve, Steve & Grace OR, John Steven, Berry Stevens, Dennis Stevens, Gary & Sandee Stevens, Ken Stevens,
& Jane Stevens, Mark & Eliza Stevens, Nicole Stevenson, Roger Stevenson, Clates Steward, Caroline Stewart, Fred Stewart, Jim Stewart, Ken Stewart, Marjorie David, Harold y Tina, Stewart,
Stewart, Ralph Stewart, Tina Stewart, Wayne & Judy Stewart, Peter Stienstra, Tim Stigen, Mike & Diane Stiles, David & Hazel Stimpson, Ricardo Stinga, Henry Stinson, Holly & Wayne Stinson, Ca
Stipanicic, Mary & Mike Stobe, Jill Stockwell, Jerry Stoeppler, Jacob Stofko, Hank Stokbroekx, Jim Stoker, Phillip Stokes, Thomas Stoll, Kathryn Stoltzfus, Harry Stombaugh, Brewer Stone, Jen & Ju
Stone, Tony Stone, Bob Stoner, Dick Stones, Carl Stormer, Tom Stott, Tom & Jeanne Stott, Gene Stout, Patrick Stowell, Glynn & Ed Strable, Matt Strack, Al Stragier, L. Straka, Robin Stramb, Stefan St
James Strank, Heidi Strant, Violeta Strash, Robert Straub, Carol & Rudy Streng, Sandra Strength, Abelardo Stringel Laguna, David Strobert, Paul Strobl, David Strunk, Julie Strunk, Jim & Janet St
Richard Strybe, Kelly & Bill Strycharz, Debbie Stuart, Jesse & Mary Stuart, shari and Stuart, Mr. C. Stuart Small, Stacy Stubbs, Connie Stucky, Paul & Erin Stucky, John Studebaker, David Stugart,
Stuhr, Chuck Stuller, Kenneth & Bonnie Stuller, Leon Stuller, Mark Stumm, Jim Stump, Dave Sturges, Jorge Sturich, Jose Victor y Angela Suares, Beatriz Suarez, Guillermo Suarez, Hugo Suarez, Joha
Suarez, John Michelle & Ethan, Suarez, Jorge Suarez, Jose Suarez, Juan Diego e Isabel Suarez, Mauricio Suarez, Rodrigo Suarez, Vladimir Suarez, Jolanda Y Marcos Suaréz, Juan Suarez Ledesma, O
Suaste Blanco, Keith & Joan Subarth, Alejandro Subia, Raul Subia, Deepak Sudam, Jane Suehck & Harry Cuwe, George Suggs, Mark Suggs, Eun Suh, Patrick Suh, Gerri Suhadick, Gerri Suhadolink, S
y Julia Sulivan, Bob Sullivan, Joe Summerour, Wendy Summers, Cal Sumrall, Cookie Sun Peele, Jeff Sundin, David Suppes, James Supple, Lucas Surddo, Bill Surry, Kerry Wilbur Susan Crowder,
& Vicki Sutcliffe, Derry & Ann Suther, Yrene Suttle, Matt Suttle & Kathie, Meg n Suz, Michael Swaidner, Ron Swails, Ken & Joyce Swan, Gary Swaney, Betty and Joe Swann, Bob Swanson, Britt Swan
Mel Swanson, Scott Swanson, Richard Swartzman, Pat Sweat, Francis Sweeney, Loreine & Frank Sweeney, Jason Sweet, Brad Sweetest, Patrick Swett, Tom & Janice Swiderski, Peter & John Swiri
Don & Lynn Swofford, William Sydney, John & Paula Syle, Sylvia Stoner, Donnie Syphrett, Dave Syren, Barbara Szatmary, Joe & Caroline Szeremet, Jessica & Paul Sziebert, Chip Szlivko, Berta Sz
Berta Sztern, Merchu Szucs, Patricia T. De Romero, Catia Taboraa Mora, Hugo Tafel, Bud Taft, Rusty Taft, Roberto Tagua, Jorge Tami, Gina Tamlolni, Julio Tampan Velasquez, Cindy & Morgan T
Peter Tanid Jr., Bob & Ben Tannenwald, Mike Tanner, Gilberto Tapia, Miguel Tapia, Gerardo Tapia Vargas, Jaime Tapia (Jr), Jose Tapia Fernandez, Sue Tappe, Jane & Dave Tappy, Domingo Tarango, Ca
Tarazona Codina, Edgar Tardio Miranda, Diego Tarquini, Mario Tarud, Pat Tarwell, Facundo Tassara, Jimmy Tate, Gary Tatro, Esteban y Silvia Taussig, Gail & Rick Tavares, Cindy & Jeamme Taves, M
Tavitas Rodriguez, Alec & Nancy Taylor, Bill & Betty Taylor, Deborah Taylor, Dennis Taylor, Duncan Taylor, Forest & Lori Taylor, Gene Taylor, Janell Taylor, Karen & Mike Taylor, Pauline & Dave Ta
Ray Taylor, Reed Taylor, Natalia Tcledon, Omar Tecuapacho, Fred & Linda Teela, Bob & Marian Teeling, Melt Agnes Teeter, Reinholt Teichgraber, Nestor Telarmendariz, Eber y Lorena Telecher, D
Tello, Marta Tello, Jacob Temares, Carl Temple, Dave Templeton, Norm Tennekoss, Chuck Tenney, Alexander Tepax, Anneloes Terbeek, Maria teresa y Santiago, Tom Terko, Carla Termes, Freddy Terra
Robert Terretz, Courtney Terry, Sharon & Ralph Terry, Terry Saythee &Debbie Stuart, Alan Tervil, George & Debbie Tester, Roberto Testi, Faye Teter, Gabriella y Justin Tetrault, Ingrid Teufel, Ar
Franke Tewari, Jennifer and Trevor Thacher, Linda & Shannon Thaggard, Jean Thampson, Chris Thary, The Bee Family, The Big Print, The Cavells, The Graham Owners Club, The Handleman, The IA
Classic Car News, Montvale, NJ, The Jarl Family, The McGilveryts, The Pollocks, The Porter Family, The Quinn's, The Selk Family, The Snyders, Ann & Bert Theis, Steven Thelem, Zach Thenhaus,
&Karen Theoret, Diana Small Theresa Arthur, Yves Therien, Ron Theriot, Clara Thiesen, Samantha Thoeschechtey, Doug: Roberta Thomas, Efird Thomas, Frank Thomas, George Thomas, Henry Tho
Ian Thomas, Janet Thomas, Laurie Thomas, Miriam Thomas, Fred Porter & Thomas Ngruyen, Elisa Thomases, Lisa Thomason, Robert Thomason, Marvin Thomasson, Ahe & Goanne Thompson, A
Thompson, Bill & Marlene Thompson, Caryl Thompson, Cathy Thompson, Dave & Linda Thompson, Deryk W. Thompson, Dow Thompson, Eg & Tracey Thompson, Jaime Thomson, Jason Thomp
Jim & Pat Thompson, Ken Thompson, Liowel Thompson, Ross Thompson, Russ & Ellie Thompson, Wren Thompson, Jim Thornton, Mary Thornton, Bill & Johanne Thorpe, Bill Thrash, Gerha
Durothee Thullner, John Thurman, Lois & Fred Tibben, Julie Tilburt, Rick & Kathy Tiller, Dog Lee Tilley, Barry & Ruth Tillson, B.H. Tilton, Mary Tilton, Pat Tilton, Jason Tim, Tim Hillman, Sylvia &

ninskis, Clifford Timm, Robert Timm, Tom & Evelyn Timmins, Silvina Andrew y Victoria, Timmis, Kathryn and tim Timpany, Jaime Tincher, Tim & Alexia Tinda, Stacie Tindle, Antonio De La Cruz,
ai y Alfredo De La Cruz, Ben and Julie Tinkey, Robert Tinkey, Ron & Laurie Tinkey, Bob Tinkey & Gris, Ben and Julie Tinkey Ben, Paul Tip, Helga and Horts Tipp, Will Tipton, Adolfo Obando Tirsa
stillo, José Tissera, J Judi Tisserand, Julie Tizraus, Chan & Tam To, Carlos Tobar, Cesar Tobar, Elizabeth Baker Toby Pugh, Mai Toda, Lori Todd, Lorin & Tom Toedter, Marian Toews, Kolija
oni,,Tokyo, Juan Toledano, Carmen Alvarez de Toledo, Jane Tolhurst, Jim Tolisano, Mimi Tolva, Adolfo Tom, Mike Tomainc, Marcelo Antonio y Pia Tomassini, Michael Tomasson, Jennifer Tomeny, Jim
mer, Libby Tomicki, David Tomlinson, David Tomlinson, Ann Tompkins, Toribio Tones, Manuel y Ricardo Tones Vaca, Rita Toney, Omar Tonini, Mauro Tonon, April Silverman Tony, Don Coltranc
aya Cecil, Gary & Dori Topp, Alejandra Toribio, Bob Torling, Kristina Tornquist, Rich Torok, Gustavo y Lima Torrado Casadiego, Juvenal Villegas Torrealba, Ana Torregrosa, Bernardo Torres, Deborah
rres, Diego Torres, Hector Torres, Irac Torres, Juan Torres, Luis y Fernando Torres, Maria Torres, Mario Torres, Marisa Torres, Martin Torres, Martina Torres, Miguel & Sonia Torres, Nerissa Torres, Raul
rres Arias, Dolores y Bili Torres Astigueta, Alejandro Torres B., Manuel Torres Baca, Carlos Torres de la Torre, Aldo Torres Gonzales, Sofia Torres Madrigal, Antonio Torres Villareal, Miguel Torroella,
nald Tortoriello, Daniel Toscano, Laurie & Michael Toth, Sergio Toti, Enrique Totola, Miles Totten, Touring y Automovil Club del Perú, Sergio Tovar, Hugh Towe, Mike Towle, Bob Townes, Dan
wnsend, Keith Townsend, Rosana & Omar Trabado, Pat & Brian Tracy, Mike & Josi Trainor, Jenny Trammell, Oscar Tramontana, Bocha Trancoso, Atlexpress Transport, Lynden Transport, Tote
ansport, Rodney Trask, Marco Traslosheros, Dean Travis, Meadwell Treadwell, Neal Treadwell, Rick & Jenny Trees, John Treeter, Alejandro Trejo, Edgar Trejo, David Alejandro Trejo Espinosa, Monica
ejo Montoya, Alejandro Trelo, Jean Tremblay, Jean-Claude Tremblay, Pierre Tremblay, Ron Treviño, Gerald Trew, Triad Austin Healy Club, Dawn Trice, Joan Triggs, Elsa Trillo, Frank Trimboli, Connie
Mike Tripp, Triumph Club of the Carolinas, Triumph Club of The Carolinas, Servio Tribaldos, Miguel Trivi, Eulises Bocha Troncoso, Al Trowbridge, Franz Troyer, Teresa Truang Waitress, Guy Truex,
na Trujillo, Alejandro Trulla, Arlie Tucker, Kathy Tucker, Larry Tucker, Richard & Paul Tucker, Sylvia & Larry Tucker, Tim Tucker, Tom Tucker, Marco Tulio Amores, Michael Tullins, David Tulloch,
ck and Kirsten Tullock, Mauro Tunon, Gunay Turgut, Angela Turletti, Joanne Turnbull, Ben Turner, Zelma Turner, Zelma & Jerry Turner, Dale & Nora Turpin, Mark & Barbara Turpin, Benny Turrano,
briel Turriago, Monica Turrin, Edna & Luke Tursi, Edna and Luke Tursi, Lajos Turtsanyi, Paula Tuttle, James Tyler, Melanie Tyler, Slattery Tyler, Annette & Mike Tyndorf, Penny Uadle, Luis Ubalde,
is Alejandro y Yolanda Ubalde, Muhammad Ubayy, Ofelia Uceta, Uchi Mariela Wendy Paola, Aracelly Ugalde, Pedro Ugalde Solis Ugalde Rodriguez, Kara Ulasewicz, Marcelo Uliarte, Warren Ulrich,
milia Umaña Alvarez, Al Umaske, Uncle Paulc., Ronald Underwood, Dirane & Paul Unland, Sillon Uno, Louis Unterberger, Del & Martha Urban, Max Urbano, Oscar Urbina, Manuel Urbroca, Dinia
eña Retana, Claudio Uriarte, Daniel Uriarte, Guillermo Uriarte, Crisanto Uribe, Gary Uribe, Cindi Urick, David y Daniel Uriegas, Jorge Urquidi, Christian Urricariet, Andres Urrutia, Galina Urrutia,
tonio Urrutia Morales, Juan Ursic, John Uru, David James Usavage, Bert Uthe, Fabian Vaca, Familia Vaca Arrona, Fernando Valdes, Amelia Valdez, Kristine Valdez, Silvia Valdez, Alberto Valdez
tierrez, Gerardo Valdez Hdez, Maria Elena Valdivia, Alejandro Vale, Judy & Mark Valen, Victor Valencia, Jorge Valencia Diez, Jorge Valentin, Cindy Valentine, Sarah Valentine, Claudio Valentino, Juan
lenzuela, Marta Valiente, Ivan Valladares, Naftali Valladares, Jaime Vallbona, Axel Vallebueno, Julio Vallejo, Miriam y Wilfredo Valles, Jessica Vallieres, Valmik, Lorena Valotto, Wes Valpey, German
tierra, Juan Valtierra, Jesus Valtierra Gomez, Arnaldo Valtorta, Antonio Valverde, Jose Valverde, Marjorie Gabriela Valverde, Virginia Valverdeloghi, Chi Van, Cheryl Van Andel, Wayne Van Bauel, Hilda
Bert Van Bovenkamp, Susan Van Camp, Gerry Van de Hel, Meredith & Judy Van Deerwerken, Hendrik-Jan and Emilie van der Woerd-de Jonge, Linda Van Deren, Jan Van derhande, Chris Van Duin,
yle Van Dyke, John & Mary Van Dyke, Joe Van Haverbeke, Graham Van Hegan, Gary Van Horn, Glen & Pam Van Horne, John Van Luyk, Jerry Van Ooteghem, Mariann & Jeff Van Ryen, Rob Van Slyko,
e Van Stee, Daryl Van Steenburg, Tom Van Tamelen, M. Van Veen, Pat & Paul Van Volkinburg, Rick Van W, Job y Jessica Van Wely, Kim Vanada, Rich & Carol Vande Water, Rosa Maria Vanden
ngaert, Patrick & Sandra Vandendriessche, Sid Vander Meer, Herman & Maureen Vanderbyl, John Vandercooh, Skip Vanderhoof, James Vandersea, Ben Vanderweele, Carol y Rich Vandewater, Daniel
Rosa Vanegas, Vanessa Katz, Jim Varas, Tammy Vardnadore, Monica Varea, Dolores y Florencio Varela, Pedro Varela, Arturo Vargas, Ivan Vargas, Maria y Gregorio Vargas, Mayra Vargas, Miguel Vargas,
mar E Ileana Vargas, Orlando Vargas, Roberto Vargas, María Vargas Arias, Matilde Vargas Moya, Maria Eugenia Vargas Pasten, Elizabeth Vargas Salas, Salvador y Aurora Varilla, Tammy Varnadore,
rman Vasquez, Maruvia Vasquez, Roberto Vasquez, Raul H. Vasquez S., Deb Vastine, Don Vaughn, Arturo Vayda, Elios Vazquez, Federico Vazquez, Fermin Vazquez, Fernando Vazquez, Francisco
zquez, Mateo Vazquez, Raul Vazquez, Sebastian Vazquez, Nora Vázquez, Angel Vazquez Lelis, Raul Vazquez Salgoso, Dan Veach, Manuy Veal, Claudio Vecchi, Denis Vega, Elizabeth Vega, Familia
ga, Maiza Vega, Oscar Vega Antonini, Olga Vega Arce, Sonia & Edgardo Vega Raleigh, Oscar Vega Ruiz, Ma. Teresa Vegas Jimenez, Hector Vejariel, Juan Pablo Vela G., Carmenza Velasco, James R.
lasco Sr, Juan Velaso, Alejandro Velasquez, Familia Velasquez, Luis y Geika Velasquez, Alejandro Velazquez, Arturo Velazquez, Carla y Miguel Velazquez, Gabriela Velazquez, Jorge Velazquez, Lea
lazquez, Pedro y Esperanza Velazquez Davila, Jorge A. y Damian Velazquez Garcia, Rodrigo Velazquez Gomez, Isabel y Philip Velazquez perrier, Sandy Velde, Eduardo Veleff, Alberto Velez, Ana Velez,
bi Velez, Miguel Velez, Yessenea Velez, Mario Velez Palatox, Raul Velez Sonera, Cecilia & Mario Veliz, Juan Vella, Beverly Velsko, Ron & Jan Veltkamp, Jorge Venegas, Flia. Ventura, Victoria Ventura,
uardo Vera, Delta Gensen Vera Barrett, Angel Bernardo Verbareal Medina, Joseph Verdad, Alberto Verdaguer, Nancy Verde, Dante Verdejo, Ramon Veregas, Ricardo Vergara, Rita Vermilione, Vernon
sh AAC, Dick and Els Verschuur en Schaap, Vivian & George Vest, Chuck & Laura Via, Roberto Viales, Reed Vickerman, Rolanda Ward Victor Mikulin, Micah Bennett Victoria Oppenheimer, Vidal
interos, Patricio Videla, Carlos Videly, Javier Vieira, Alex Viera, Norberto Viera, Matew Vigil, Ricardo Vigil, Juan Carlos Viglione, Daniel y Norma Vigluori, Jose Vigueras, Fer Vilardebo, John Vilas,
n & Julie Vilas, Adrian Vilchis, Armando Villa, Marta Villa, Margret Villain, Pedro Villagra Delgado, Jorge & Andrea Villalba, Jorge & Lorena Villalba, Pablo Villalobos, Guadalupe y Jaime Villalon,
me Villalon, Jose Villalpando, Alejandra Villalta, Familia Villaman, Rebeca Villanueva, Alvaro Villapando O , Nayali Villar y Ernesto Laureiro, Mayela Villareal, Alfredo Villarruel, Daniel Villarruel,
ario Villasenor, Max Villegas Deschamps, Carolina Villegas Terraza, Juan Villicaña, R. Vines, Willy y Wilma Vinton, Violeta Gonzalez, Delmer Visser, Familia Vital, Alejandro Liliana, Mauro y Rodrigo,
tullo, Pedro y Anna Vivas- Camacaro, Jorge Gonzalez Vivian Cachin, Daniel Natenzon Viviane Schack, Adrien Vlach, Yiannoula Vlachos, Croat Vlatko, Kathy Vogel, Janine Vogt, Jeary Vogt, Don Voigt,
ari Vois, Christine Volk, Leo Volkering, Laura Brodax Volkstorf, Francisco Voltaire Sanchez, Juan German Voltierra, Rebeca Volverde Altamirano, Kurth Von Burg, Leo & Patti Von Keitz, Mary & Bernie
n Keitz, Jewel & Bill Von Loenen, Boris Von Schwedler, Berta von Wernich, Carmen von Wernich, Caro von Wernich, Carolina von Wernich, David Antonio von Wernich, Elsa von Wernich, Elsa von
ernich, Estela y Herman von Wernich, Graciela y Facundo von Wernich, Guillermo von Wernich, Jose von Wernich, Jose Erick von Wernich, Max von Wernich, Yolanda von Wernich, Zaira von wernich,
cio Von Wernich Madrigal, Ron Vorst, Kay Vosika, Don Voss, Karl Voss, Ana Voytek, Tamara Vrooman, Kassie & Todd Vuckvich, Sony W, Jason y Vanessa Wa, Gerard Waaentz, Miguel Wabi, Alyssa
Dave Wachob, Anne Wade, David Wade, John y Karen Wade, Luke Wade, Clint Waggoner, Paul & Carol Waghorw, Tam Wagnek, Bob Wagner, James Wagner, Joan Wagner, Kyra Wagner, Lisa Wagner,
il & Melanie Wagster, Alfred Wahabby, Harold Waig, Albert Waisueen, John Wake, Bruce Wakeman, The Chithi Wala's, Fred Walatka, Horace & Jane Walco W, Charlie & Peggy Walczak, Thomas
lder, La Donna Waldo, David & Vicki Walher, brent walker, Danielle Walker, Dwayne & Lisa Walker, Frank Walker, Jack Walker, Joel Walker, John Walker, Murphy & Darla Walker, Ronda Walker,
rman Walker, Steve Walker, Scotty Walkins, Audrey Wall, Carolyn & Charles Wallace, Crystal & Brian Wallace, Dennis Wallace, Dianne Wallace, Russell Wallace, Sandy Wallace, Peter Wallen, Sharman
llen, Bill Waller, Craig & Sandra Walles, Denny Wallette, Robert & Nancy Walling, Jeremy Walmscgy, Magnet Walrer, Barb Walsh, Brit Walsh, Jerry Walsh, Oisin Walsh, Todd & Debbie Walsh, Carl
lston, Sebastian Walt, Brian Y Ann Walter, Carina Edward Walter, D B Walter, John Walter, Brenda Ross & Addy, Walther, Joseph Walton, Mary Walton, Nicholas Walton, Horacio Wamba, Bill Wambold,
elissa Wanamaker, Elson Wandscheer, Dewayne Ward, Rand y Caroline Ward, Nancy Warden, Jose & Viviana Warik, Lorraine Warner, Mike Warner, Robert Warner, Care Warrell, Elizabeth Warren, Ken
arren, Kyle Wasielewski, Gary & Maribeth Wasmund, Guy Wassertzug, Javier Wasserzug, Lois Watanabe, Ed Waterman, Killi & Robert Waters, Bill Watkins, Bill Watkins, Sallyann Watsjold, Bobby &
a Watson, Eric Watson, Eric Watson, Otto & Mary Watson, Shari Watson, Stuart Watson, Wendell Watson, Stuart Watson & Shari, Web & Edena Watt, Anthony Watts, Riley Watts, Muriel Wattum, Muriel
Ben Wattum, Col Wayne A. Ross, Trail Ways, Elizabeth Weakley, Jim Weakley, Jerry Weaver, Monte Weaver, John Webber, Kay Weber, Ron Weber, John Webster, Richard Webster, Dale Webston, David
edeking, John Wedin, Steve Wedlock, Peer Wedvick Jr., Larry Wehr, Susan y Carlos Weidemann, Santiago Weigandt, Thomas Weil, Martin Weimann, Bill Weimer, Dora & Bob Weinley, Leo Weinsten,
ne Weir, Paul & Jan Weisenberger, Tommy Weiser, Carol Weishampel, Cliff Weisman, Jim Weiss, Carleton Weker, Andy Weland, Bill & Kathy Welborn, Diane Welborn, Cher & Brian Welch, Thomas
lch, Diane Welker, Paul Welker, Amy Wellard, Earl Weller, Dave & Andi Welles, Lynn & Lonnie Wellman, Harry Wellons, Bill & Kathy Wellosn, Dick Wells, Larry Wells, Tom Wells, Dave Wellwood,
ndell & Gale, Eileen Wendorf, Dennis Wentz, Walter Wes Olaski, Joseph Wessel, Celia Wesselman, John West, Dave Westenberger, Win Westervelt, Cyril & Joan Westhaver, J & C Westhaver, Don
stly, Kenneth & Sandra Weston, Dewey & Josie Wetherby, Carol Ann Wetzel, Chris Wetzel, George Weyand, Latty & Linda Weyand, Rod Whedbee, Bruce & Diane Wheeler, Charlie Wheeler, Gary M.
heeler, Gaye Wheeler, Mary Wherrett, Whidbey Islans, Karen & Charlie Whinney, Cecil Whipple, Jim Whisenand, Bill Whitakier, Danny White, Gary White, Jacque White, Mike White, Todd White,
ny White, Vera White, Mike Whitford, John Whiticar, Charlene Whiting, Chuck Whiting, Jay Whitney, Tom Whitstine, Jim Whitters, Whitties of Mafca, E. Whitty, Paul Wichterman, Care Wicker, Jim
ckett, Val Wickins, Owen Widin, John Widmen, Kim Connie y Quinn, Widrick, Janine Wiederkehr, Mike & Gwyn Wiedmer, Judyth Wien, Pat & Glorig Wiessert, Steph Wiffler, Melba Wifon, Randal
ginton, Joanne & Joe Wigle, Arthur Wigntow, Ed Wiitala, Brett & Kris Wilcox, Dennis and Joan Wilder, Robert Wildt, Jack Wiles, Andrew Wilk, Bob Wilkins, Geri & Pete Wilkins, Patty Wilkinson,
A Will Miller, David Willard, James Willard, Tom Willardson, Ken Willhauck, May Willhite, Roger & Marlene Willhite, Ann-Marie Williams, Braxton Williams, Courtenay Williams, Deb Williams,
ine & Peter Williams, Fulton Williams, Gar Williams, George Williams, Gladys Williams, Jeff & Helen Williams, Jeff &patricia Williams, John Williams, Kay Williams, Kelly Williams, Lee & Dorothy
lliams, Leonard Williams, Phyllis Williams, Ray Williams, Ray Williams, Richard & Carol Williams, Robert & Chris Williams, Vicki Williams, Woody Williams, Mike y darcy Williamson, Ray
lliamson, Scott Williamson, Vivian Williamson, Calgari Williard, Rod Willie, Jerry Williford, Taylor Willing, Barry Willins, Avery Willis, Jeremy Willis, Rus Willis, Zeke & Linda Willis, Leonard
illiams, Tamis Willmar, Dave Wilmarth, Larry Wilmarth, Ben Wilson, Bob Wilson, Chris & Verna Wilson, Cynthia Wilson, Denver & Barbara Wilson, Don Wilson, Eddie Wilson, Harold Wilson, Joan
William Wilson, John Wilson, Juanita Wilson, Karen Wilson, Kristi Wilson, Lom Wilson, Mark Wilson, Nate Wilson, Paul & Andrea Wilson, Robin Wilson, Robin Wilson, Sherrie & Rem Wilson, Ward
lson, Karen Wilson & Mark Werner, Dale Wiltsee, David y Agnes Wiltsey, Pat Wiltshire, Bob Wimmer, George Wimmer, Paula Carroll Win Wdge, Bruce Winchell, Tyler Wind, Marcelo Windler, Jim &
e Windram, Beny Winebareer, Earl Wineck, Jim Wineman, Georgine Winn, David Winnet, Brian & Jill Winsor, Patrick Winsor, Art & Ana Winston, Gary Winston, Patty & Greg Winters, Jeremy Wire,
Wirken, Ben Wirtz, Ben Wirtz, Judy & Jenniss Wise, John Wiskus, John A. Wiskus, Denton Wisler, Neil Wisler, Jim & Diane Wiswall, Duane Wit, George Withers, Wendy Withrow, Kenneth Witmer,
cia Witt, Mike Wittmann, Mischellean Wittrockk, Michael & Yvonne Woddington, Jens Wohlers, Philip Wohlstetter, Clayton & Annette Wohlwend, Chester Wojcik, Sandy & Don Wojtalewicz, Dan &
rie Wolch, Cecilia y Fernando Wolf, Cecilia y Fernando Wolf, Brenda Wolfe, David Wolfe, Karen Wolfe, Leonard & Sherby Wolfe, Melissa Wolfe, Monique & Roy Wolff, Beverly & Norman Wolfson,
ggy Wolker, Joseph Wolkow, Shalel & Allan Wolpe, Nancy & Bill Womack, Wally Women, Jennifer Wong, Juan Carlos y Marisol Wong, Al Wood, Brad & Vicki Wood, Chris & Zachary Wood, Ernesto
tierrez Wood, Garth Wood, Gordon & Karen Wood, Irma y Javier Wood, Jerry Wood, Nick Wood, Penny Wood, Vreeland & Linda Wood, Warren Wood, Wyatt Wood, Agnes & Bob Woodin, Larry
odriff, Charles Woodruff, Art Woods, John Woods, Tomas Woodward, Jullie & Steve Woofler, Jack Woolf, Tom & Jean Woolley, Kevin Worrell, Bill Worsham, Sarah Worthington, Steven Worthy, Don
ay, Dave & Jayfree Wrench, Butch & Edie Wright, Chad Wright, Charlie Wright, Christian & Michelle Wright, David and Julie Wright, David y Julie Wright, Eark Wright, Jack Wright, Kathrine & Lee
ight, Patricia Wright, Rick and Lisa Wright, Robert & Mini Wright, Skip Wright, Tim Wright, Tom & Dove Wright, Vern Wright, Wayne Wright, Wendell Wright, Robbie Wuitschide, Michelle WW, Jean
lie, Howie Wyman, Jack Wymore, John Wynkoop, Clay Wyrick, John Wyrick, Frank X. Zeimetz, Gabriela Y Carlos, Rodolfo Sazo , y Maite Marroquin, Miguel Yabur, Ivan Yacub y Sonia Plaza, Eli
lico, Diana Yang, Dave Yanoshek, Santiago Yanzi, Charlie Yapp, Gerorge yarbrough, Bill Yates, Chris Yates, Jeff and Cathie Yeagle, Rosa Yebra, Luis Cambron Alvarez y Eduardo Cambron Rivera,
via Yelin, Diane & James Yeo, Rosa Yerba, Michael R. Yergovich, Mike & Mayanne Yergovich, Rob Yergovich, Kent & Josette Yetter, Ramiro Yih, Carlos Yoc, Chuch & Beaulah Yockey, Richard Yoder,
hard Yodis, Mario YOivelli, Daniel Yomayra, Durmus Yoruk, John Yosaitis, William Youne, Barry Young, Chris Young, Doug y Glenys Young, Geri Young, Jason Young, Jim Young, Kenneth & Joanne
ung, Kit Young, Mark Young, Stephanie Young, John Youngbroder, Jennifer Youngdahl & Joseph Mitola, David & Dorothy Yount, Robert Yourt, Martin Yoverson, Bill y Waldie Yraham, Dogan Yuksel,
an Yunes, Laverne Zachary, Peter Zacks, Louis Zadra, Gustavo Zaffaroni, Mark Zagger, Peter Zaklukiewiez, Mario Zakowilz, Zamar Viajes, Mark Zammuto, Diego Zamora, Juan Zamora, Lisa Zamora,
naldo Zamora Ramirez, Christian Zander, Eva Zander, Mister Z Ron Zandman, Ron Zandman-Zeman, Oscar Zapata, Patricia Zapata, Tte Jaime Zapata, Ivar Zapp, Jackie Zapp, Mario Zapp, Peter Jr
p, Susan y Peter Zapp, Nestor y Maria Zappeli, Cleo Zarceno, Mario Zatocki, Carol & Norm Zatzar, Hector Zavala, Hugo Zavala, Norberto Zavala, Ruben Zaya, Masha Zazlengo, Yelena Zege, Frank
Zeimetz, Stephanie Zelada, Pablo Zelikowicz, Rich Zell, Alejandro F. Zelter, Martha Zeman, Linda Zemotel, Roberto Zendejas, Douglas Zeno, Earl Zentzis, Terey Zepeda, Larry Zepp, Leticia y Federico
menio, Jose Zermento, Alejandro Zetter P., Dave Ziebart, Stan Ziegler, Mark Zienan, Jim Zimmer, Luke Zimmerman, Mike Zimmerman, David Zink, Mirna Zinlay, Dianne & Alan Zitnik, Justin Zmk,
ge Zmud, Danny Zoeller, Family Zoltzman, Dodie Zonakis, Juan Zorrilla, Jose Zorron, Steven & Jennifer Zregler, Mauricio Zuñiga, Cliff Zubrycki, Bill Zucca, Ricardo y Olga Zucca, Pablo Zulquelti,
onica Zumbado, Flor Zuñiga, Guisselle Zuñiga, Juan Zurita, Nichiolas Zuvic, Los Pinguos.

/e know there are some omissions. Our Apologies.

Dreams
to spark

This is the perfect spark gift for your friend, relative
or any beloved one WHO needs to spark THEIR dream.

*This book is my way to be part
of your Dream.*

I Stand by you.

...I watch Cande, I gaze at her belly. I put my arms around her and feel the baby move. I want to describe what I feel. There are still a number of days before I earn the title of "father" but I haven't studied the lessons yet: Will it be a boy or a girl? I only hope she will be a dreamer. What will I do? How will I feel? How will it be hugging someone that I made by love and with love?...

...Every one with life runs a race with death. Death always wins. However the triumph is during the race, not at the end...